ESSAYS ON
THE HISTORY OF
AMERICAN
FOREIGN
RELATIONS

HRW Essays in American History Series
Paul Goodman, Editor

John Braeman	*Essays on the Progressive Era*
John Braeman	*Essays on the Recent American History: The 1920s and 1930s*
John Braeman	*Essays on Contemporary America since 1945*
David Brody	*Essays on the Emergence of Modern America: 1870–1900*
Frank Otto Gatell	*Essays on Jacksonian America*
Lawrence E. Gelfand	*Essays on the History of American Foreign Relations*
Paul Goodman	*Essays on American Colonial History, 2nd ed.*
David L. Jacobson	*Essays on the American Revolution*
James Kindregen	*Essays on the History of the South*
John Lankford and David Reimers	*Essays on American Social History*
Leonard Levy	*Essays on the Early Republic: 1789–1820*
Stephen Salsbury	*Essays on the History of the American West*
Wilson Smith	*Essays on American Intellectual History*
Irwin Unger	*Essays on the Civil War and Reconstruction*

ESSAYS ON THE HISTORY OF AMERICAN FOREIGN RELATIONS

EDITED BY

LAWRENCE E. GELFAND
The University of Iowa
Iowa City, Iowa

HOLT, RINEHART AND WINSTON, INC.

New York · Chicago · San Francisco · Atlanta
Dallas · Montreal · Toronto · London · Sydney

Cover: "Battle of New Orleans." Courtesy
of the I. N. Phelps Stokes Collection of
American Historical Prints, Prints Division,
New York Public Library.

For my mother, Rachel S. Gelfand
and
my mother-in-law, Elizabeth Ifland
with affection and appreciation.

Preface

The preparation of an anthology can be a creative enterprise for its editor. In any field of scholarship, much significant research is published first in the form of journal articles. Such literature for the history of American foreign relations is scattered through a broad range of serial publications in the United States and abroad. There are, in addition, other channels for the publication of article-length treatises, including collected papers of individual scholars and *festschriften*. From the several hundred published essays and articles extant, the editor must make his ultimate selections, by no means an easy or mechanical chore.

In the preparation of this collection of essays several criteria were employed. Through approximately thirty articles I wanted to cover the broad field of American foreign relations from the eighteenth century to the 1960s. I sought those papers which treated significant themes and at the same time would do justice to the literature by reflecting the variety of methods, approaches, and interpretations which historians concerned with American foreign relations have employed in their scholarship. Moreover, if the collection was to have maximum value for the present generation of students, it seemed wise to place an emphasis on that body of research published within the present generation, defined to be the most recent thirty years. Today's students, it seemed to me, should have an opportunity to read articles prepared by the masters of the field as well as younger men whose careers have only recently been launched. It also seemed appropriate to emphasize certain historical periods notable for their significant, often complex, and controversial activities. Four periods were chosen for such concentration:

> 1) The era of the 1840s and 1850s, when the United States went to war with Mexico; entered into formal diplomatic and commercial intercourse with China and Japan; acquired California and settled the Oregon issue with Great Britain.
>
> 2) Diplomacy during the 1890s and its consequences—the crisis with Great Britain over the Venezuelan Boundary dispute; the Spanish-American War, and the acquisition of Hawaii, Puerto Rico, Guam, and the Philippines; the national debate over imperialism; and America's resurgence of interest in Europe and Asia, a period from which some historians date America's rise to the status of a great world power.

3) The period of the First World War and the 1920s when the United States broke with precedent by participating in decisions that would affect the entire world community only to be followed by a revival of nationalist reaction.

4) The era of the 1930s and the Second World War, when the United States responded to the threats of totalitarianism, a Second World War, and the Cold War which followed in its wake.

I also endeavored to take into account the literary quality as well as the scholarly value of articles selected for this volume. It seems to me that today's students should become aware that historians can and do write with clarity and verve. Undergraduate readers may possibly develop an appreciation for both the intellectual and literary skills of professional historians. The volume does not have a single doctrinaire point of view. Although representative selections range the political spectrum from right to left, from orthodox scholarship to revisionism, no attempt has been made to balance one writer's interpretation with some contrasting interpretation on the same subject. Teachers and students should bear in mind that significant historical literature is often controversial, and that no two historians will necessarily interpret the same evidence in exactly the same manner.

During the past ten years I have conversed with a great many of my students, undergraduate and graduate, who have conveyed their candid impressions of various reading assignments amongst the journal articles. From these students at the University of Wyoming and the University of Iowa, I have learned much that has been useful in the preparation of this volume. I want to express special appreciation to the several research assistants at the University of Iowa whose enthusiasm in, and services for, this anthology were especially valuable to me: Charles Blank; Marshall Getscher; Michael Hogan; Jonathan Kolb; Nina Noring; Joseph Rosenberg; and John Schacht. I am deeply grateful to Professor Paul Goodman, Editor-in-Chief of this series, for his encouragement and constructive comments. Lastly, I want to thank Mrs. Mary Strottman and Mrs. Carolyn Quarles who typed portions of the manuscript.

Lawrence E. Gelfand

August, 1971
Iowa City, Iowa

Contents

ESSAYS ON THE HISTORY OF AMERICAN FOREIGN RELATIONS

Part I

AN EMERGING NATION

1 / The International Approach
to Early Angloamerican History 1492-1763

Max Savelle[1]

America's involvement in international relations does not date merely from the creation of the United States as a sovereign, independent republic in 1776. America had already been an important element in European diplomacy from the Age of Discovery beginning in the late 15th and early 16th centuries when Spain and Portugal, later England and France, established claims to territories in the New World. As Max Savelle indicates in the following article, it was during the colonial era that various principles of statecraft were adopted both by the imperial-commercial powers in Europe and also by their colonies in America which sharply modified the traditional practices of international diplomacy by the mid-18th century. Thus, at the time of the American Revolution, American leaders were able to draw on a considerable body of diplomatic precedents, policies, and procedures which had evolved over the earlier centuries. Even the press in the American colonies reflected the importance with which international diplomacy was regarded by the colonists through its consistent publication of international news. Americans were much aware that their very status, politically and economically, could be decided by events and decisions occurring in Europe and by statesmen whose knowledge about America was often limited to their readings of government dispatches. Clearly, no very deep appreciation of American foreign relations after 1776 is possible without an understanding of at least the importance which the Americas occupied in the totality of European diplomacy and commerce during the formative, colonial era.

For further reading: Frances G. Davenport, *European Treaties Bearing on the History of the United States and its Dependencies*, 4 vols (Washing-

Max Savelle is Professor Emeritus of History at the University of Washington. This article is reprinted with the permission of the author and the Henry E. Huntington Library and Art Gallery. From *The Reinterpretation of Early American History: Essays in Honor of John Edwin Pomfret.* Copyright © 1966 by the Henry E. Huntington Library and Art Gallery.

[1] It is a pleasure to acknowledge my great indebtedness to Miss Margaret Anne Fisher, who contributed much to the research and the thought upon which this essay is based—Max Savelle.

ton: 1917–37); *Felix Gilbert, *To the Farewell Address: Ideas of Early American Foreign Policy* (Princeton: 1961); Max Savelle, *The Origins of American Diplomacy: the International History of Anglo-America, 1492–1763* (New York: 1967).

The involvement of America in the web of international relations among the Atlantic community of states has been important and constant from the very beginning of this continent's history.[2] It began at the moment when Columbus, driven by a storm into the Tagus River on his return to Europe from his first voyage, was haled into the presence of King John of Portugal and accused by the King of having trespassed upon Portugal's exclusive colonial sphere as recognized by the Castilian-Portuguese Treaty of Alcaçovas of 1479. One result of this interview, as is well known, was King Ferdinand II's appeal to Pope Alexander VI for a confirmation of Castilian ownership of the lands Columbus had discovered, an appeal that induced the Pope to issue, in 1493, four bulls recognizing Spain's claim and dividing the "New World" between the two kingdoms by a line drawn from the north pole to the south pole one hundred leagues west of the Azores Islands.

From that moment on, throughout the colonial period, America occupied an increasingly important place in the international history of the western world. It is, indeed, difficult to understand the history of colonial Angloamerica without a constant reference to this context.

In the international history of Angloamerica in the colonial period there are to be seen two parallel but generally interlocking streams of events, developments, and ideas. One of these was the course of European diplomatic exchanges with regard to America; the other was the intercolonial contacts and quasi-diplomatic exchanges that took place among the various sets of European colonies in America itself.

In the course of European international exchanges relative to America many subjects were discussed, such as rival territorial claims, European commerce with colonial empires, questions having to do with the freedom of the seas, and so on, and certain principles of international law and custom were formulated, always in the interest of the citizens of the European countries involved. Along the "great frontier" in America intercolonial, quasi-diplomatic exchanges were concerned with such local matters as boundaries and the national ownership of territories, fisheries, missionaries, Indian trade and alliances, and intercolonial commerce, licit and illicit. These exchanges, especially after the Peace of Utrecht of 1713, exposed the specific local issues that provided the factual groundwork for the demands of the mother countries upon each other in Europe. In general, the claims made by English colonies against non-English colonies, or the reverse, were claims made in the interest of the colonies themselves. Nearly always, the local intercolonial objectives of the colonies became

---

* Books which are currently available in paperback editions.

[2] It is an arresting fact that since the publication of Frances Gardiner Davenport's magnificently edited *European Treaties Bearing upon the History of the United States and Its Dependencies* (3 vols., Washington. The Carnegie Institution of Washington, 1917–1931), the second and third volumes of which were brought to publication posthumously by J. Franklin Jameson, no significant study of the international history of the English colonies in America has been undertaken or published.

parts of the diplomatic objectives of the mother countries. In only one major area of intercolonial relations, that of commerce, did the international objectives of the colonies run counter to the diplomatic objectives as well as to the laws of the mother countries, and that was because the commercial needs and ambitions of the colonies stood in positions essentially of economic rivalry with those of the mother countries. Thus it was that whereas, in most areas other than that of commerce, the international objectives and policies of the colonies coincided with those of the mother countries, they were not always identical, since the American objectives were formulated to serve American, rather than European interests. Indeed, a colony might differ from the mother country, and often did, in its policy with regard to any particular local or colonial issue. It was out of this circumstance that there appeared in the colonies certain diplomatic inclinations, or policies, that may properly be called American, as distinguished from English or European policies.

I

European diplomacy with regard to America in the sixteenth, seventeenth, and eighteenth centuries was a diplomacy of rival colonial empires.

The first of these imperial rivalries was between Portugal and Spain over their respective domains in Africa, the Far East, and America. It began in conflicting claims to the coast of Africa explored by Prince Henry the Navigator's captains and to the Canary Islands, earlier granted to a Spanish nobleman, Luis de Cerda, by Pope Clement VI. The "new world," as it came to be explored, was divided between Spain and Portugal by a series of papal bulls, beginning in 1455 and running well into the sixteenth century, and by the Hispano-Portuguese treaties of Alcaçovas (1479), which awarded the Canaries to Spain and the African coast to Portugal, of Tordesillas (1494), which drew a line through the Atlantic, from pole to pole three hundred seventy degrees west of the Cape Verde Islands, the lands west of which were assigned to Spain and the lands east of which to Portugal; and of Saragossa (1529), by which a similar line was drawn in the Pacific seventeen degrees east of the Moluccas, a line of longitude that was supposed to pass through the islands of Santo Tomé de las Velas.

In the course of this imperial rivalry, the first to be concerned with non-European lands lying about the Atlantic basin, there were formulated certain principles of international relations and custom, relative to colonies, that were to underlie European diplomacy relative to America for centuries.

Out of the disputes over the ownership of territories there emerged the basic and generally accepted proposition that prior discovery of hitherto unknown territory gave prior title of national ownership of that territory. Not only that, the ownership of overseas territory was understood to convey with it national title to the natives of those territories and to the oceans over which the sea routes to the colonies lay. Thus, for example, after the Treaty of Tordesillas Portugal understood—and Spain agreed—that the oceans east of the "Line" over which Portuguese ships must pass in going to the Portuguese colonies in Africa and India belonged exclusively to Portugal, and that oceans west of the Line, over which Spanish ships must pass en route to and from Spanish colonies west of the Line, belonged exclusively to Spain.

Once a territory was effectively occupied by a colonizing power and its ownership of that territory recognized, tacitly or explicitly, by the other imperial powers, the state owning the territory or colony customarily sealed it off from penetration, for trade or any other purpose, by citizens of other empires. It was generally recognized that the trade of the colony was the exclusive, monopolistic property of the mother country, and it was one of the international tenets of mercantilism that the colonies and their economies existed chiefly for the profit of the mother countries. The commerce of colonies was expected to enrich the mother countries; presently the colonial commerce of any European state came to be thought of as the most important determinant of its national wealth and, therefore, of the mother country's position in the scales of the international balance of power in Europe. Colonial commerce, therefore, was of prime national interest in the diplomatic exchanges among European powers, and the stringent closing of the doors of the commerce of their colonies to all foreigners was undertaken in the interest of the mercantile doctrine that such commerce should be a national monopoly.

Similarly, it was generally agreed, in these early stages of the evolution of European diplomacy with regard to the new world, that the religion of the colonies should be the religion of the mother country. In the case of the Iberian powers, although both were Roman Catholic, the principle of national monopoly still held: the religious conversion and development of an acquired colonial area was generally entrusted to religious orders of national character and connections. Thus the imperial rivalries of the maritime powers was religious and cultural as well as political and economic.

The Iberian paper monopoly of the entire new world "discovered and to be discovered," could not be expected long to stand unchallenged. In the realm of diplomacy the challenge came in the repudiation of the monopoly by French, English, and Dutch governments, their diplomatic representatives, and their theorists. Such, for example, was Francis I's sarcastic quip at the preposterous claims of the Iberian powers: "The sun shines for me as well as for others; I should like to see the clause in Adam's will that excludes me from the division of the world."[3]

Similarly, when the Duke of Mendoza, the Spanish ambassador, protested to Queen Elizabeth Francis Drake's violation of Spain's *mare nostrum* in the eastern Pacific, Elizabeth replied bluntly that

> For that their [the Spaniards] having touched only here and there upon a coast, and given names to a few rivers or capes, were such insignificant things as could in no ways entitle them to a propriety further than in the parts where they actually settled and continued to inhabit.[4]

In thus stating the doctrine of effective occupation, subsequently to be accepted by all of the colonizing powers, Queen Elizabeth was also informing the Iberian monopolists that England would not recognize, any more than France, their self-awarded monopoly of the new world. It was precisely upon the basis of this doctrine, indeed, that King James I was to justify to Philip III of Spain the occupation of the lands upon which was founded the colony of Virginia.

Out of the conflicts over the new world, and particularly out of the French,

[3] Quoted in Charles de la Roncière, *Histoire de la Marine Française* (6 vols., Paris: 1899–1931), III, 300.

[4] *Camden's Annals,* year 1580, quoted in J. Holland Rose, *et al.,* eds., *The Cambridge History of the British Empire* (8 vols., New York, 1929–1959), I, 185.

English, Dutch and other challenges to the Hispano-Portuguese monopoly, there also appeared the proposition that Europe was one sphere of international institutions, law, and custom and that the new world of the colonies, beyond European waters, was another. This was the so-called "doctrine of the two spheres," under the terms of which, for example, treaties between two European states did not necessarily apply to the colonies or special treaties relative to America might be made between two such powers which did not apply to Europe. More informally, under this doctrine, it was understood that seizures of ships, violent disputes over territory or trade, or other conflicts in the new world "beyond the lines of amity" were not necessarily to be taken as causes for war in Europe.

This doctrine was made explicit, for example, at the time of the Franco-Spanish Treaty of Cateau-Cambrésis (1559), where it was orally agreed that

> They [the French] would not go to the lands possessed by your Majesty [Philip II of Spain] and by the King of Portugal, or that one would abide by the terms of past treaties, according to which the Indies are not mentioned; and if they [the French] were found doing anything there that they should not be doing, they would be punished. . . . We [the Spanish negotiators] declared to them [the French] that if they went there in time of peace, one [the Spaniards] would throw them into the sea, with the understanding that this action would not be thought a contravention of the treaties of friendship between us. . . .[5]

The "doctrine of the two spheres" continued for centuries to be one of the basic principles of European diplomacy relative to America. It was explicitly written into the Anglo-Spanish Treaty of Madrid of 1670, the Anglo-French Treaty of Whitehall of 1686, and the Hispano-Portuguese Treaty of Madrid of 1750. But it was also invoked by the colonies themselves in such treaties as that of Sandy Point, St. Christopher (1678), by which the English and French colonists agreed to remain neutral in case of war between their mother countries in Europe. It was this doctrine, and the experiences that substantiated it on both sides of the Atlantic, that provided a host of precedents in the colonial period for the basic principle contained in the famous pronouncement of President James Monroe in 1823.

It was not, however, until the other maritime states of western Europe achieved colonial empires of their own that they became deadly rivals both of the Iberian empires and each other. This situation became a condition of fact in the seventeenth century, in the course of which England, France, Holland, Denmark, and Sweden established colonies in territories formerly claimed by Spain or Portugal. Much of European diplomacy with regard to America in that century, therefore, was concerned with the settlement of these new colonies and their relations with the colonies of other countries. Such, for example, was the diplomatic duel between England and Spain over the settlement of Virginia, or that between England and France on the one side and Spain on the other over the occupation of the islands in the West Indies, or that between Holland and Sweden over their respective colonies around Delaware Bay.

Actually, it was only under duress, and very slowly, that Spain and Portugal were led even to admit that other countries had a right to send ships to the new world. The first breach in the monopoly was made in 1609, in the Twelve Years Truce between Spain and Holland, in which, in carefully veiled language in which the

---

[5] Quoted in Frances G. Davenport, ed., *European Treaties*, I, 220–221, fn. 9.

Indies were not mentioned, Spain finally admitted the right of the Dutch to sail, for the purposes of trade, to the "lands of all other princes, potentates, and peoples who are willing to permit them to do so," which really meant the countries in the East and West Indies not actually under the domination of Spain.

The breach was widened in the Dutch-Spanish Treaty of Münster (1648), by which Spain agreed specifically that

> The Navigation and trade in the East and West Indies shall be maintained as under present arrangements [that is, the charters of the Dutch East India Company and the Dutch West India Company] or under contracts to be made later, . . . and the King [of Spain] and the Estates-General, respectively, shall remain in the possession and enjoyment of the . . . commerce and the countries in the East and West Indies, as also in Brazil and on the coasts of Asia, Africa, and America respectively that the said King and Estates-General [now] have and possess.[6]

This surrender by Spain marked the beginning of the final end of the Hispano-Portuguese claim to a monopoly of the new world. The end did not come all at once, however, for it was not until the Anglo-Spanish "American" Treaty of Madrid of 1670 that Spain made the same concession to England. Even so, Spain was still not ready to admit the right of England, France, or Holland to seize unoccupied lands in America that were claimed by Spain, and continued to protest the occupation of islands in the West Indies, as well as of Georgia, well into the eighteenth century.

All of the non-Iberian challengers of the Hispano-Portuguese colonial monopoly were heavily involved in overseas commerce, and all, following the precedent set by the Iberians, closed their colonies, with varying degrees of tightness and rigidity, to commercial contact with foreigners. Such a mechanism of exclusion or semi-exclusion, for example, was the English system of laws of navigation and trade. Spain, France, Holland, Sweden, and Denmark all had similar systems of national regulation and control, although they varied in specific application and in the rigidity with which they were enforced.

It thus fell out that a significant portion of the diplomatic correspondence of western European states relative to their American colonies in the seventeenth century was concerned with commercial relations with or between colonies. Such a correspondence was that between England and the Netherlands in the middle of the seventeenth century, in which the Dutch sought to procure some sort of relaxation of the English navigation laws that might enable them to continue their lucrative trade with the English colonies in North America.

Many European treaties were made, in the seventeenth century, providing for and regulating commerce between the subjects of the signatory nations. Most of these commercial treaties were understood not to apply to America. They did, however, as in the case of the Anglo-Dutch marine treaty of 1674, define "contraband" and "non-contraband" goods, among which generally appeared such American products as tobacco, sugar, and dye-woods. They also contained the principle that "free ships make free goods," which was calculated to establish in international law the right of a neutral nation to trade with belligerents in time of war.

It was out of the activities of colonial commerce, also, that there emerged the classic expression of the doctrine of the freedom of the seas, formulated by Hugo

---

[6] *Ibid.,* I, 363.

Grotius in 1609. This principle, even before Grotius, was one of the chief bases of the English claim to the right of going to America in the first place, and, later, to the exemption of English and colonial ships upon the high seas from search and seizure by Spanish *guarda costas* in the bitter years of controversy that preceded the War of Jenkins' Ear.

Although the interest of all the European states with colonies in America was focused chiefly upon the contributions to the national wealth that the colonies could make, whether derived from commerce, from the production of raw material not produced in the mother country, or from the mining of gold and silver, European diplomatic interest in America was not solely economic or purely mercantilistic. For there were strong elements of imperialism for its own sake, of political or dynastic interest, of nationalism, and of religion present in the thinking of most European statesmen relative to America, thoughout the colonial period.

Thus, it was by reason of a combination of motives that the European colonial empires became world-wide rivals, and European diplomacy with regard to them was a diplomacy of nationalistic and imperialistic rivalries. In the course of such rivalries England came almost to eliminate the Dutch from the colonial world in America and to dominate the American colonial commerce of Portugal. The Dutch had already absorbed the Swedish holdings on the Delaware when England seized New Netherland; the Danish colonies in America (the Virgin Islands) were claimed by both Spain and England, but they were never very significant in the total panorama of European imperial rivalries in America. As the eighteenth century dawned, only the French and British American empires were active and aggressively expansive. The Spanish Empire, while not exactly moribund, was somewhat less than a rival of the other two. Indeed, France and England were both seeking to expand in America at Spain's expense, or, at the very least, to reap the greatest possible profit from Spanish colonial commerce.

But no colonial empire was to be allowed to become so large as, by contributing an overwhelming national wealth to any single state, to give that state an inordinately preponderant weight in the balance of power in Europe. As François de Salignac de la Mothe Fénélon, Archbishop of Cambrai, wrote, about the end of the seventeenth century, "Anything that upsets the balance [of power among the nations]', and which gives any nation a decisive power to establish a universal monarchy, cannot be just, even though it be founded on the written laws of a particular country." The careful maintenance of this sort of equality and balance among the nations, he wrote, assured the common security.[7]

The greatest and most tempting American plum to appear in the second half of the seventeenth century had been the American segment of the Spanish inheritance, which began to dangle before the eyes of European imperialists from the moment of the accession of the childless and ailing Carlos II to the throne of Spain. The American possessions of Spain had been promised to one after another of a number of aspiring monarchs between 1668 and 1698, but Carlos had reversed the field by making a will, prior to his death in 1700, which left all his kingdoms and territories, *in toto* and including Spanish America, to Philip of Anjou, the grandson of Louis XIV. Since Philip was potentially an heir to the throne of France, in the fear that he might one day rule over both France and Spain and all their dominions and, thereby,

---

[7] François de Salignac de la Mothe Fénélon, Archbishop of Cambrai, *Oeuvres Choisis de Fénélon* (4 vols., Paris, 1872), IV, 361.

upset the balance of power both in Europe and America, the other aspirants to parts of the Spanish inheritance organized themselves into the Grand Alliance of 1701 to prevent Philip from ascending the throne of Spain.

The maintenance of the balance of power, then, both in Europe and in America, was the chief reason for the so-called War of the Spanish Succession. As the allies stated it in the treaty of the Grand Alliance, since

> the Kingdoms of France and Spain are so closely united [by the naming of Philip, Duke of Anjou, as Carlos II's heir] that . . . the French and Spaniards being thus joined will in a short time become so formidable to all that they may easily arrogate to themselves empires all over Europe, . . . and since France and Spain are taking advantage of this state of affairs to unite more and more closely for suppressing the liberty of Europe and destroying trade, . . .

the signatories have been forced to take military action and to form a close alliance to prevent any such upset of the balance of power, whether in Europe or in the new world.

The war that followed, the War of the Spanish Succession, was, on final balance, a victory for the allies. By the Peace of Utrecht (1713) Philip was admitted to the Spanish throne, but he was forced to forswear any future claim he might have to the throne of France. As for America, Philip was required to promise in the Anglo-Spanish treaty of peace never to alienate any part of the Spanish American empire, to France or any other nation. England, on its side, undertook to guarantee the territorial integrity of Spain's American colonies.

At the same time, in the Anglo-French treaty of Utrecht Louis XIV was required to make a similar disclaimer, to the effect that he renounced any

> intention to try to obtain or even in the future to accept for the benefit of his subjects that anything be changed or that innovations be made, either in Spain or in Spanish America, whether in matters of commerce or in matters of navigation, from the usages practiced in those countries under the reign of the late King of Spain Charles Second. . . .[8]

Thus England, in the name of the balance of European power, forced upon Spain and France its own eighteenth-century analogue of the Monroe Doctrine for the preservation of the territorial *status quo* in Spanish-America.

More specifically, by the Anglo-French Treaty of Utrecht England was ceded vast territories in America by France—Hudson Bay, Newfoundland, Acadia, and St. Christopher, along with a vague recognition of Britain's suzerainty over the Iroquois Indians, while Spain granted to the English South Sea Company the *Asiento*, or contract for supplying slaves to the Spanish colonies, along with certain very promising commercial privileges in Spanish America. Thus, while the Peace of Utrecht, by preventing the union of the crowns of France and Spain, ostensibly preserved the balance of power in Europe, its provisions, with regard to America rather sharply tilted the balance in England's favor in the western hemisphere. The theory of the European balance, however, along with its corollary, the idea that the balance of power in Europe depended upon the balance of colonial and commercial power in America, continued to be one of the major principles in the conduct of eighteenth-century European diplomacy dealing with colonial matters. As the Duke of New-

---

[8] Davenport, ed., *European Treaties*, III, 210–211.

castle put it, speaking to the House of Lords on May 2, 1738, if no nation had a monopoly of the Spanish colonies or their trade, all European states benefit from it equally,

> Whereas, should too large a share of them [the Spanish colonies] come into the hands of any other nation in Europe . . . they might be employed to purposes inconsistent with the peace of Europe, and which might one day prove fatal to the balance of power, that ought to subsist amongst her several princes.

A combination of other states would inevitably be formed against the strong one.[9]

In the three decades following the Peace of Utrecht the "Concert of Europe" gave attention to many of the conflicts among the European nations over their possessions in the colonial world.

Actually, Europe did not achieve a full pacification until some seven years after Utrecht, because Spain and Austria were still in armed disagreement over their respective claims in Italy. But France and England drew together in 1716 in an alliance for the maintenance of the balance of power, and this alliance presently grew into the Quadruple Alliance by the accession of the Netherlands and Austria. The Alliance invited Spain to make peace, but Spain refused. On the contrary, it attempted to seize by force certain territories it claimed in Italy, and the Alliance resorted to war in 1718 and 1719 to force Spain to accept its peace terms. Spain finally acceded to the Alliance in 1720.

By the terms of the general treaty, the details of peace were left to be settled at a Congress to be held at Cambrai, in France. The treaty did, however, embody a general agreement to the mutual suppression of the activities of corsairs against the commerce of the signatories; the signatories also agreed to protect each other's territories. The colonies were not specifically mentioned, but it would appear from the wording of the treaty and its annexes that these provisions were expected to apply to the commerce and the territories in America and in other parts of the world.

With the accession of Spain to the Quadruple Alliance and its acceptance of the terms of peace, France, England, and Spain drew together, and there ensued a series of complicated negotiations in 1721 relative to the colonies of the three powers in America. By the Franco-Spanish treaty, after much dickering with regard to American possessions, Pensacola, seized by France during the short war, was returned to Spain. Similarly, after much haggling over England's proposal to give Gibraltar back to Spain in return for some American territory, the Anglo-Spanish treaty of friendship provided only for a renewal of the *Asiento*, although the British guarantee of the territorial integrity of the Spanish colonies in America contained in the Peace of Utrecht was repeated. Other disputes, either between Spain and France or between Spain and England, were referred to the Congress of Cambrai.

The Congress of Cambrai was eventually held in 1724, and representatives of France, Spain, and England went prepared to debate their American disputes. But the Congress bogged down in matters of protocol, and the attention of England and the Netherlands was diverted to the business of getting the Emperor of Austria to abolish the Ostend Company, a company founded in the Austrian Netherlands to procure for Austria a share of the rich profits of the colonial trade. Because of certain vicissitudes of European international politics, the Congress of Cambrai presently

---

[9] William Cobbett, ed., *Parliamentary History of England from the Norman Conquest in 1066, to the Year 1803* (36 vols., London, 1806–1820), X, 772.

dissolved in confusion, and Spain made an alliance with Austria for mutual defense of the commerce and territories of the two signatories, "whether on this or the other side of the Line," with special privileges and encouragements provided for the Ostend Company.

The Austro-Spanish Alliance of 1725 presented the threat of a new general European war, and led to the formation of a new alliance, called the Alliance of Hanover. Hostility, never entirely ended, flared up between England and Spain in the Caribbean area, and Europe stood once more on the brink of war. Thanks, however, to the efforts of Cardinal Fleury, now the ruling minister in France, the members of the "Concert of Europe" were once more brought to the conference table, this time at Soissons, near Paris. Again, after endless wrangling over European and American questions, this Congress, also, arrived at a stalemate, chiefly because of the obstinacy of Spain. But the stalemate was broken by the collapse of the Austro-Spanish alliance of 1725, and Spain finally acceded to the terms proposed by the Congress in the Treaty of Seville, signed by France, England, and Spain on November 9, 1729.

By the terms of this treaty, Spain and England promised to make mutual restitution for damages done each other in America; other claims and counter-claims were to be adjudicated by a joint commission; the *Asiento* granted to England in 1713 was specifically reviewed. But Spain had acceded to the Treaty of Seville chiefly as a concession to France and England in return for their support of Spain's effort to seat Don Carlos, eldest son of Queen Elizabeth Farnese, upon the ducal thrones of Parma, Placentia, and Tuscany. The settlement of colonial disputes in America was thus linked to the dynastic disputes of Spain and Austria in Italy.

When England and France procrastinated in effectuating the terms of the Treaty of Seville relative to Italy, Spain threatened to denounce that treaty. But England saved the day by making a treaty of friendship with Austria by which Austria agreed to a final dissolution of the Ostend Company and an acquiescence in the occupation of the ducal thrones by Don Carlos, in return for England's acceptance of the Emperor's Pragmatic Sanction assuring the Crown of Austria to his daughter, Maria Theresa, after Charles VI's death. Once this was achieved, Don Carlos proceeded to Italy and the Anglo-Spanish commission for the adjudication of American disputes could proceed—which it did, without success.

With the outbreak of the War of the Polish Succession, France, isolated by the Anglo-Austrian Treaty of 1731, fearing England might side with Austria, and needing the aid of Spain, turned to that country for aid, and signed with it the so-called Bourbon Family Compact. This treaty was ostensibly an alliance between France and Spain against Austria; but here, again, the American interests of the two signatories were tied to the dynastic ambitions of the European powers. For the compact was aimed, so far as Spain was concerned, chiefly at England, and it provided that France would assist Spain, both in Europe and in America, should England attack Spain. Should Spain, because of English abuse of its commercial privileges in Spanish America, see fit to suspend those privileges, and should England therefore begin hostilities against Spain or its colonies, France would make common cause with Spain against England. At the same time, France was granted most-favored-nation treatment in the commerce of Spanish America conducted through Cadiz, and Spain agreed to ameliorate French complaints, whether pertaining to ships seized, commerce at Cadiz, or territorial conflicts in America.

England did not join in the War of the Polish Succession. But France and Spain remained allies, with France generally supporting Spain's complaints relative to America against England and assuming a role of benevolent neutrality in the Anglo-Spanish War of Jenkins' Ear that broke out in 1739.

Meanwhile, after the Peace of Utrecht, the French and British empires had emerged as the two great contestants for the domination of North America. They faced each other along the entire continent, from Canada to the Gulf of Mexico and across the Caribbean to the coast of South America. Despite the Anglo-French entente in Europe that lasted, roughly, from 1716 to 1731, in all the areas in America where French colonies confronted English colonies—Acadia, the Lakes area, the Ohio Valley, the lower Mississippi Valley, and the West Indies—conditions of conflict at times approximating actual warfare existed throughout the third and fourth decades of the eighteenth century. Neither the Anglo-French joint commission of 1719 nor the joint commission of 1750, both created for the purpose, was able to settle these disputes; that settlement had to await the final adjudication of war in the Peace of Paris of 1763. It was this peace that, once and for all, ended the Anglo-French diplomatic contest for domination of America by the almost total elimination of France from possession of any significant parts of the hemisphere. It was this peace, also, that marked the end of the European phase of the international history of Angloamerica during the colonial period. From this date onward, the international history of Angloamerica centers about the history of the independent United States of America.

If the imperial rivalry of France and England was a rivalry for the domination of territory, the commercial aspects of the relations of the two empires in America amounted almost to a conflict between the two mother countries on one side and the English and French colonies on the other.

It is true that, from the point of view of the mother countries, the imperial policies of each of the metropoli were identified with the expansion of the interests of the national commerce. Indeed, it is difficult to distinguish between the direct profit motives of merchants, such as those who composed the English Hudson's Bay Company and the South Sea Company, and the high policy of government. Both these commercial companies participated directly in the diplomatic negotiations of their government relative to the areas of America in which they were interested. Their interest, of course, was in profits, and hardly anything more. But the statesmen who planned and conducted national diplomatic policies were mercantilists who reasoned that the expansion of the national commerce in America would redound to the benefit of the whole nation. Thus the English diplomats fought at Utrecht for the whole of Hudson Bay, with its fur trade, and at Madrid for the *Asiento*, with the rich anticipated profits to be derived from the trades that would be conducted under it. Thereafter, throughout the eighteenth century, English international policy with regard to America was focused upon the promotion of the expansion of imperial commerce. France, on the other hand, excluded from the *Asiento* by the Peace of Utrecht, directed its diplomacy with Spain relative to American commerce toward controlling a major share of the commerce of the Spanish empire that flowed through Cadiz, while it constantly reminded the Spanish rulers of the extent and the unscrupulousness of the English contraband trade with the Spanish colonies, conducted by Englishmen and Angloamericans, both under cover of the *Asiento* and apart from it.

But English international colonial policy directed at expanding the commerce of the Empire involved the effective enforcement of the English laws of trade and navigation, just as France's international policy with regard to its own colonies was thought to involve the rigid enforcement of prohibitions upon the foreign trade of the French colonies. When it came to enforcing their systems of commercial control in the colonies, however, both France and England had to face the open violation of their systems by their own colonists. If France and England failed to achieve the great colonial commercial monopolies they sought, that was less because of their rivalry with each other than because of the nullification of their restrictive laws by the colonists in America.

It is to be noted that all of the diplomatic policies and practices of the European colonizing powers having to do with colonies derived from the interest of the mother countries, and had little or no regard for the interests of the colonists or of the natives in the colonies. The rights of the aborigines, however, were not without their defenders, for there appeared in Spain an extraordinary group of legal theorists—Francisco de Vittoria, Francisco Suarez, Luis de Molina, Domingo da Soto and others—who raised embarrassing questions of international law relative to title to new countries by conquest, the rights of the aborigines, and limitations upon forced religious conversion. The theories of these great jurists, although of great significance in the history of international law, had little or no practical effect upon the conduct of international relations.

In other areas, however, the formulation of a body of international law and custom was a direct outgrowth of the experiences of the European states in their rivalries and conflicts with each other in the colonial world. Out of the Hispano-Portuguese monopoly, for example, came the principle of the "closed door" in colonial empires. Out of the French, English, and Dutch challenges to that monopoly came the principle of the freedom of the seas and the doctrine of effective occupation. Out of the disputes over participation in colonial commerce came, in part, at least, the doctrines of the rights of neutrals, "free ships make free goods," definitions of "contraband" and "non-contraband," the British "Rule of the War of 1756" and "doctrine of continuous voyage." Out of the many efforts to solve colonial disputes by joint commission or by arbitration there came a general acceptance of the idea that colonial disputes might be settled by peaceful methods, although there is no record of any international dispute with regard to America that was actually resolved in that way.

II

In contrast to the history of European diplomacy relative to America, the history of the international relations of Angloamerica itself was a history of the direct contacts between the Angloamerican colonies and the French, Dutch, Swedish, Portuguese, Spanish, and Danish colonies in the hemisphere and the correspondence, the agreements and disagreements, and the intercolonial treaties that were produced by them.

These international contacts among the European colonies during the seventeenth century arose out of local situations, and the agreements and correspondences that grew out of them were made or conducted by Americans on the spot, often entirely without or with a minimum of instruction from Europe. They sprang from the needs of the Americans themselves and were calculated to promote American interests. Not only that, in the course of the history of the contacts of the Angloamerican colonies with their neighbors there were formulated certain generalized principles or policies that represented the long-term interests of the Americans, although those principles of colonial self-interest did not always coincide exactly with the principles governing the international relations of the mother country. Thus, in the Treaty of Boston between Massachusetts and Acadia (1644) and in the negotiations surrounding it there were clearly enunciated the principles of freedom of trade and of the freedom of the seas; in the Treaty of Hartford between the New England Confederation and New Netherland (1650) is to be seen the importance of territorial expansion of the colonies; into the Virginia-New Netherland Treaty of 1660 there was written a principle of freedom of commerce that ran directly counter to the British Navigation Act of the same year and the English position in the Anglo-Dutch negotiations going on in Europe at the same time.

In the eighteenth century, and especially after the Peace of Utrecht, there were fewer directly negotiated agreements between colonies. But there was a vast amount of correspondence between English governors and French, Spanish, Dutch, and Danish governors, a correspondence that constituted a corpus of international negotiation, as it were, on the frontiers of empires.[10] The colonial governor became, in reality, a diplomatic agent of his mother country, operating semi-independently in the field. In the eighteenth century the governor was more closely bound by his instructions than had been the case earlier, but, more often than not, his instructions relative to his correspondence with the governors of neighboring foreign colonies were based upon reports of the local situations that he, himself, had made to his home government and recommendations that he had suggested as to the international policies to be followed, locally or in Europe. The colonial governor was thus no mere agent in the field executing the wishes of his home government, based purely upon the interests of his mother country; he was, in fact, and in a number of ways, the instrument of American intercolonial contacts and a formulator of international policies to be followed with regard to them. The situations he reported were local, and often had no direct connection with diplomatic negotiations in Europe. The self-interests he served in the recommendations he made, while usually integrated, in his mind, with those of his empire as a whole, were local, American self-interests, and the mother country was expected by the Americans to use its European diplomatic machinery to promote their interests—as it usually, but not always, did. The American colonial frontiers, then, whether the frontiers of commerce, of fishing, of territorial expansion, or of relations of the colonies with the Indians, were, in this sense, the matrix in which the origin and the gestation both of European diplomatic policies with regard to America and of later international policies of the United States took place.

The governor-to-governor relations between the governors of the Angloamerican colonies and those of the neighboring foreign colonies were concerned with many issues. Rival imperial claims to territory and the boundaries between empires loomed large in this corpus of colony-to-colony correspondence, and the territorial rivalry

---

[10] This correspondence reposes chiefly in the colonial archives of England, France, Holland, and Spain. The greatest single collection of printed examples of it, often in the form of "calendars" or digests, is in the *Calendar of State Papers, Colonial Series*, published by the British Public Record Office.

on the continent of North America had its Caribbean counterpart in rival claims to
the ownership of hitherto unoccupied islands. But much of this intercolonial correspondence, especially in the West Indies, also had to do with commerce, licit and
illicit; much was concerned with relations with the Indians, piracy, the seizure of
ships thought to be violating territorial waters, freedom of the seas, and so on. It was
often concerned with military matters, such as fortifications, Indian alliances, and the
exchange of prisoners. But it was often concerned, also, with the legal or religious
rights of national or cultural minorities in ceded territories, the sending of missionaries to the Indians, and the transfer of populations.

The intercolonial disputes over territory in America began immediately after
settlement. Governor Thomas Dale sent Captain Argall to destroy the French settlements in Acadia in 1613, in time of peace, because, as he claimed, the French on
Mt. Desert Island and at Port Royal were trespassing in English territory. The area
was seized again by the English in 1628, in the course of the Huguenot War, but it
was returned to France by the Treaty of St. Germain-en-Laye in 1632. From that
time on the ownership and extent of Acadia and the lands lying along the Bay of
Fundy constituted an area of constant and -bitter dispute between the English governors of the New England colonies and the French governors of Canada until the
final cession of Canada itself to England by the Treaty of Paris in 1763. Similarly,
the Dutch governors of New Netherland challenged the English title to Connecticut
on the east and the Swedish title to Delaware on the south. After the English seized
New York the English governors of that colony disputed for a century with the
governors of French Canada the boundaries between New York and Canada. Out
of those disputes there came the French claim to the watershed as a boundary, as
against the English claim to the highly flexible boundaries marked only by the limits
of lands owned by the Iroquois Indians, whom the English claimed as subjects of
the British King under Article XV of the Anglo-French Treaty of Utrecht. As the
population of the English seaboard colonies began to trickle over the Alleghenies
into the valley of the Ohio, that valley became a base of intercolonial contention,
culminating in the mission of George Washington from the colony of Virginia to the
French commandant at Fort Le Boeuf in 1753. Farther south, the governors of
Carolina and, later, Georgia, corresponded with the Spanish governors of Florida
and Havana over the boundaries between English colonies and Florida and with the
French governors of Louisiana and "Mississippi" over the Anglo-French boundary in
that region. In the West Indies, governor corresponded and disputed with governor,
especially after the Peace of Utrecht (1713), over the ownership of the Virgin Islands, St. Lucia, Dominica, St. Vincent's, Tobago, and others.

The territorial claims of the governors on both sides were invariably expansionist,
while the protagonists on each side professed to believe that the other was consciously
and diabolically determined to drive their people out of the hemisphere. This imperialistic rivalry reached a climax about the middle of the eighteenth century, when
the English, beginning to flow over the Alleghenies, aroused in the French the dread
of English domination. The most eloquent of the French Cassandras was the Marquis
de la Galissonière, one-time governor of Canada. "Motives of honor, glory and
religion," he wrote in 1750, "forbid the abandonment of an established colony. . . ."
Canada had always been a burden to France, and must be expected to continue
such for a long time into the future, but it constituted "the strongest barrier that can

be opposed to the ambition of the English." Canada alone was in a position to wage war against the English possessions, "possessions which are as dear to them as they are precious in fact, whose power is daily increasing, and which, if means be not found to prevent it, will soon absorb not only all the colonies located in the neighboring islands of the Tropic, but even all those of the continent of America."[11]

But the English felt almost exactly the same way about the French. The Albany Congress expressed its conviction in 1754,

> That it is the Evident Design of the French to Surround the British Colonies, to fortifie themselves on the Back thereof, to take and keep Possession, of the heads of all the Important Rivers, to draw over the Indians to their Interest, and with the help of such Indians added to such Forces as are already arrived and may hereafter be sent from Europe to be in a Capacity of making a General Attack on the Several Governments, and if at the same time a Strong Naval Force be sent from France, there is the utmost danger that the whole Continent will be subjected to that Crown and that the Danger of such a Naval Force is not merely Imaginery. . . .[12]

The Angloamericans were not only conscious of the continentwide nature of the life-and-death territorial struggle of the two empires for the control of the continent of North America; their most aggressive leaders were out-and-out imperialists, determined to drive the French out of America; they urged the mother country to undertake the task; and they took pride in being associated with the mother country in that enterprise. And always, it was the colonial governor who was, as it were, the aggressive activist leading the forces of the empire westward.

From the very beginning of their existence the American colonies of the European powers traded with each other. This commerce, wherever found, ran counter to the mercantilistic policies growing out of the doctrine of the monopolistic, "closed door" commercial and colonial policies of the mother countries, as illustrated by the English navigation laws or the rigid Spanish or French prohibitions of foreign trade in Spanish and French colonies. These "closed door" policies were mutually accepted by the European states, and were written into such treaties as the Anglo-Spanish Treaty of Madrid of 1670 and the Anglo-French Treaty of Whitehall of 1686. Even the Dutch were compelled by the British, in a series of treaties beginning with the Anglo-Dutch Treaty of Westminster of 1654, to recognize the "closed door" in the English colonies represented by the British Navigation Acts.

Despite the near unanimity of the European powers in their formal agreements, the "free" or "illicit" trade of English, French, Dutch, and Spanish colonies with each other flourished, especially after the Peace of Utrecht. For the Spanish and French colonies the trade with foreigners was clearly and entirely prohibited by law. For the English colonies, trade with French, Spanish, Dutch, or Danish colonies was not illicit except insofar as it might directly or indirectly violate the Staple Act of 1663, or the Treaty of Whitehall (1686), which never was implemented by Eng-

---

[11] The Marquis de la Galissonière, "Memoir on the French Colonies in North America," December, 1750, in E. B. O'Callaghan and Berthold Fernow, eds., *Documents Relative to the Colonial History of the State of New York* (15 vols., Albany, 1857–1887), X, 220–232.

[12] Albany Congress: "Representation of the Present State of the Colonies," July 9, 1751, *The Papers of Benjamin Franklin*, ed. by Leonard Labaree, *et al.* (8 vols. to date. New Haven, 1959–   ), V, 366–374.

lish municipal law. The English government made various attempts to stop it, nevertheless.[13]

This trade with foreign colonies, while shared by merchants in the mother country, as in the case of the South Sea Company, was of prime importance to the continental colonies and, on the face of it, ran counter to the mercantilistic interests of the mother country. However, as many a colonial governor was to point out to the British ministry and the Board of Trade, this trade was also of great value, not only to the British colonies, but to the mother country itself, since with the profits of foreign trade the continental colonies could import a vast quantity of goods from England that they would not have been able to afford, otherwise, to buy.

For the British colonies in the West Indies, however, the sugar and molasses trade of the northern colonies with the Dutch, Danish, French, and Spanish colonies in the Caribbean area actually brought the foreign colonies into a direct competition with the British West Indies for the trade of the English colonies on the continent, even though many merchants in the British Islands were partners in it. It was against this competition that the British West Indies protested and agitated until they brought about the passage of the Molasses Act of 1733, which was just as futile as a mechanism for restraining the foreign trade as all other efforts had been.

Because of this divergence of economic interest between the continental colonies and the British West Indies, on the one side, and between the continental colonies and the mother country, on the other, the governors of the continental colonies were often torn between the Charybdis of obedience to their instructions to suppress the trade and Scylla of their realization, immersed, as they were, in the commercial interests of the colonies they governed, that to stop the foreign trade must have disastrous effects upon the economic life of those colonies.

In their correspondence with the governors of the French colonies in the Caribbean area, therefore, the British West Indian governors were generally disposed to collaborate with their French colleagues for the suppression of the trade, even though the French governors often actually winked at it because they, too, as their English colleagues on the continent, realized that this commerce was essential to the economic welfare of the colonies they governed. The Spanish governors were much

[13] In 1728 the Board of Trade asked the Attorney-General and the Solicitor-General of England for an opinion as to the legality of Angloamerican trade with the foreign colonies in the West Indies. It explained that the colonial governors were customarily instructed to prevent Angloamerican trade with foreign colonies in accord with Articles Nos. 5 and 6 of the Treaty of Whitehall of 1686, but that there was some doubt as to whether such instructions were proper. The Attorney-General and the Solicitor-General, in their opinion, ruled that the Treaty of Whitehall, being a Treaty between the kings of France and England, simply gave either king the right to seize the ships of subjects of the other if caught trading in his dominions. It was not intended by the treaty, they said, to lay down a law prohibiting Englishmen from trading with the French colonies if they wished to run the risk involved in doing so, nor was it intended to authorize the king of either signatory to seize and condemn the ships of his own subjects in such a case. The trade, therefore, they ruled, was entirely legal for Englishmen, since there was no English law prohibiting it. This ruling was of importance among the considerations underlying the steps that led eventually, in 1733, to the passage of the so-called Molasses Act of that year (Secretary Popple to Mr. Attorney and Mr. Solicitor-General, May 13, 1728, Great Britain, Public Record Office, *Calendar of State Papers, Colonial: America and West Indies, 1728–1729*, No. 195, pp. 92–93; Mr. Attorney and Mr. Solicitor-General of the Council of Trade and Plantations, June 3, 1728, *ibid.*, 1728–1729, No. 230, pp. 107–108). See, also Ira W. Taylor, "Massachusetts Trade With the French West Indies 1686–1733," unpublished Master of Arts Thesis (1959), University of Washington Library.

more sincerely disposed to enforce their laws prohibiting foreign trade than their French colleagues, and they issued commissions to the Spanish *guarda costas* for the enforcement of those laws. Where the French governor might quietly share in the profits of the trade with the English northern colonies, despite the activities of his own *garde-côtes,* the Spanish governor was likely to share in the profits of the *guarda costas.*

It thus came about that whereas the correspondence of the British West Indian governors with the French governors was aimed at suppressing the northern trade, their correspondence with the Spanish governors was weighted with complaints against the activities of the *guarda costas* in suppressing trade with the Spanish colonies, since the *guarda costas* seized many North American, English, and British West Indian ships, innocent as well as guilty, far out on the high seas as well as in waters that the English would recognize as territorial.

On the other hand, the Dutch and Danish colonies were heavily committed to trade with all their neighbors, English, French, and Spanish, and in great measure they lived by it, especially the trade with the English continental colonies. They also profited by their role as middle-men in trade among all of them and between them, on the one side, and continental Europe, on the other. The little governor-to-governor correspondence between the English governors and their Dutch and Danish colleagues relative to trade, therefore, was likely to be confined chiefly to matters pertaining to the control of piracy, with little or no correspondence relative to trade itself.

But there was a lively and acrimonious correspondence between the British governors and French and Spanish governors, especially the latter, over the seizure of British (English and North American) ships by French and Spanish cutters and retaliation by the British. Since the British were the most numerous "interlopers" in Spanish colonial trade, more British ships were seized, probably, than of any other nation. Needless to say, the seizures and reprisals became the subject-matter of a vast correspondence of claim and counter-claim in the diplomatic relations of Spain and England in Europe.

If the governors of the British West Indies shared the opposition of most of their constituents to the North American trade with foreign colonies, the governors of the North American colonies shared, as extensively as they could, in view of their position, the sentiment of their constituents in favor of it. Thus, for example, Jeremiah Dummer, brother of Lt. Governor William Dummer of Massachusetts and agent for Massachusetts and Connecticut in England, wrote, in his famous *Defence of the New-England Charters* (1721) a defence, also, of the intercolonial trade:

> Why then should not Great-Britain form the same Judgment, and proceed by the like Measures [in encouraging foreign trade] in regard to her American Dominions, from whence she receives the greatest Advantages? It were no difficult Task to prove that London has risen out of the Plantations, and not out of England. 'Tis to them we [England] owe our vast Fleets of Merchant Ships, and consequently the Increase of our Seamen, and Improvement of our Navigation. 'Tis their Tobacco, Sugar, Fish, Oil, Logwood and other Commodities, which have enabled us to support our [English] Trade in Europe, which would otherwise be against us, and to make the Figure we do at present, and have done for near a Century past, in all Parts of the Commercial World. . . .
>
> As this is evident, so is it that whatever injures the Trade of the Plantations, must in Proportion affect Great-Britain, the Source and Center of their Com-

merce; from whence they have their Manufactures, whither they make their Returns, and where all their Superlucration is lodg'd. The Blow then may strike the Colonies first, but it comes Home at last, and falls heaviest on our selves.[14]

The great climax in the history of intercolonial commerce came during the Seven Years' War, during which the northern colonies furnished vast supplies of provisions to the French colonies, both directly and indirectly by way of neutral Dutch, Danish, and Spanish ports in the West Indies. So great was the injury thought to be done by this trade to the British cause in the war that Parliament passed the so-called Flour Act of 1757, which placed provisions on the list of enumerated articles, and William Pitt issued his famous circular letter of August 23, 1760, to the colonial governors requiring them to suppress the trade with the enemy, in all its forms and by every means. A number of colonial legislatures passed laws intended to stop the direct "flag-of-truce" trade, or the indirect trade with the enemy by way of neutral Spanish, Dutch, or Danish ports. Despite all the efforts to suppress it, however, this international commerce continued.

The fact of the matter was that the international trade of the continental colonies with the foreign colonies in America lay so close to the natural economic growth of the English colonies, and was so nearly essential to their economic existence, that it was next to impossible to suppress it. To have suppressed it, whether in peace or in war, as several of the colonial governors recognized, would have been a disastrous blow to the colonial economy. Besides which, as these governors pointed out, such a suppression would have been a serious blow at the economic prosperity of England itself, since it was with the profits from this foreign trade that the colonies paid the unfavorable balance of their trade with the mother country. As Cadwallader Colden, Lt. Governor of New York, for example, wrote William Pitt in 1760,

> The Northern Colonies cannot pay for their consumption of the British manufactures by their own produce, exported only to the British Colonies. . . . The result of the whole trade of North America, taking it in every shape, as [is] barely sufficient to pay the ballance due to Great Britain. The consumption of British manufactures in the Northern colonies increases in proportion to their ability to purchase them, and nothing can make the Northern colonies interfere with the British manufactures, but their poverty or inability to purchase. . . .
> I have informed you Sir of these things, in hopes that my doing of it may be of use, not as an excuse for any remissness on my part. However as to presemtious or penal laws, I must beg leave to observe, that it is difficult to prosecute with success against the bent of the people, while they are under the prejudice to think that the Sugar Islands have gained a preference inconsistent with the true interest of their Mother Country, and whence prosecution fails of success it is of prejudice to the service it was designed to promote.[15]

Thus, from the role of negotiator for his colony with the governor of a foreign colony the English governor turned, as it were, to that of negotiator for his colony with his own home government in the interest of promoting his colony's trade with that same foreign colony. In demanding a greater, if not a complete freedom of foreign trade, these governors, as agents of their colonies, were expressing an inter-

---

[14] Jeremiah Dummer, *A Defence of the New-England Charters* (London, 1721), pp. 38–40.

[15] Cadwallader Colden to William Pitt, December 27, 1760. New York Public Library, Manuscripts Division: "Colden Papers." Printed, *Colden Letter Books*, I, (*N.Y.H.S., Colls.*, 1876), 52.

national outlook that was to become one of the cornerstones of the international policies of the later United States.

If the Angloamericans were ardent imperialists, rejoicing in a close collaboration with the mother country in the territorial expansion of the Empire in America, they were the reverse of that, they were isolationists, in everything that might draw them into purely European conflicts. And if the English guarantee of the territorial integrity of the Spanish dominions in America contained in the Anglo-Spanish Treaty of Utrecht of 1713 was an European analogue of the Monroe Doctrine calculated to block French colonial and commercial expansion at Spain's and England's expense, that doctrine was also anticipated in the strong feeling among Americans of the reality of the "two spheres" and of the desirability of American isolation from European affairs—a mood that found expression in the writings of many Americans.

This sense of the desirability of isolation and abstention from European involvements was expressed by the Massachusetts General Court as early as 1651, when it reminded Oliver Cromwell that it was to escape the conditions of Europe that the original settlers of Massachusetts had emigrated in the first place. They had found peace in America, they said: "We know not any country more peaceable and free from Warre [than Massachusetts]."[16] And Francis Daniel Pastorius, in Pennsylvania, expressed the same mood when he wrote back to his friends in Germany that "after I had sufficiently seen the European provinces and countries, and the threatening movements of war. . . . I was impelled through a special guidance of the Almighty, to go to Pennsylvania."[17]

But the American feeling of isolation was not limited to sentiment. Governor Peter Stuyvesant, for example, when the first Anglo-Dutch war broke out in 1652, proposed to the New England Confederation that the English and Dutch colonies maintain a policy of neutrality in the war then beginning between their "Nations in Europe." Connecticut welcomed the prospect of war in the hope of territorial gain, but the Massachusetts General Court voted for neutrality, because, as it said, "it was most agreeable to the gospel of peace which we profess, and the safest for these colonies at this season, to forbeare the use of the sword."[18]

The same mood of isolation from European wars was also written into the Treaty of Sandy Point, made between the French and English colonists on the island of St. Christopher in 1678, a treaty which provided that the two groups would remain neutral in any war that might break out between France and England in Europe. Similarly, the French merchants of Montreal, when Queen Anne's War was approaching in 1701, proposed that New York and Canada remain neutral for the sake of their trade, the trade with the Indians, and the stability of the frontiers, and the New York merchants and Assembly agreed. New York thus remained neutral until 1709, when the British government inaugurated plans for a massive land and sea attack upon Canada, and neutrality could no longer be maintained by either the French or the English colony.

In general, then, the Angloamericans had formulated, by the middle of the eighteenth century, a strong aversion to inclusion in purely European conflicts. On the

[16] Hutchinson, *History of Massachusetts,* I, Appendix IX, 450–452.

[17] Quoted in J. Fred Rippy and Angie Debo, *The Historical Background of the American Policy of Isolation* (*Smith College Studies in History,* IX, Nos. 3 and 4, April-July, 1924), 71.

[18] Hutchinson, *History of Massachusetts,* I, Appendix X, 452–453.

other hand, they were almost eager for conflict in America whenever such a conflict might promote either their territorial expansion, their control of the Indians, or their international commerce. Essentially, the policy of most Americans was still one that might be called the mood of the two spheres: isolation from Europe, to be sure, but conflict in America.

By the middle of the eighteenth century, literate Angloamericans were highly conscious of the international affairs of the world and their place in them. They were also conscious of the cultural differences that set them off from their non-English neighbors, especially the Spanish and the French. This consciousness of cultural differences was closely linked with the Angloamericans' thinking about the imperialistic competition for the continent, and was used to justify their demand that the French be driven out.

The most hysterical voice of this Angloamerican cultural nationalism and imperialism was probably that of the Reverend Jonathan Mayhew, of Boston. In his election sermon delivered before the governor and legislature on May 29, 1754, Mayhew preached a crusade of Angloamerican cultural nationalism and imperialism:

> And what horrid scene is this, which restless, roving fancy, or something of a higher nature, presents to me; and so chills my blood? Do I behold these territories of freedom, become the prey of arbitrary power? . . . Do I see Christianity banished for popery! the bible, for the mass-book! the oracles of truth, for fabulous legends! Do I see the sacred Edifices erected here to the honour of the true God, and his Son, on the ruins of pagan superstition and idolatry; erected here, where Satan's seat was; do I see these sacred Edifices laid in ruins themselves! and others rising in their places consecrated to the honour of saints and angels! Instead of a train of Christ's faithful, laborious ministers do I behold an heard of lazy Monks, and Jesuits, and Exorcists, and Inquisitors, and cowled, and uncowled Imposters! Do I see a Protestant, there, stealing a look at his bible, and being taken in the fact, punished like a felon! What indignity is yonder offered to the matrons, and here, to the Virgins! . . . Do I see all liberty, property, religion, happiness, changed, or rather transubstantiated, into slavery, poverty, superstition, wretchedness! . . . O dishonest! profane! execrable sight! O piercing sound! that *entereth into the ears of the Lord of Sabbath!* Where! in what region! in what world am I! Is this imagination? . . . Or is it something more divine? I will not, I cannot believe 'tis prophetic vision; or, that God has so far abandoned us![19]

And Mayhew urged his people to war:

> Shall the sword rust? . . . Shall our military garments be moth-eaten for want of use, when such things are doing! It is impossible, Gentlemen, you should be any ways backward, or parsimonius, in such a cause as this; a cause wherein the glory of God, the honour of your King, and the good of your country, are so deeply concerned; I might perhaps add, a cause, whereon the liberties of Europe depend. For of so great consequence is the empire of North America, . . . that it must turn the scale of power greatly in favour of the only Monarch, from whom those liberties are in danger; and against that Prince, who is the grand support and bulwark of them. . . . It is even uncertain, Gentlemen, how long you will have an House to sit in, unless a speedy and vigorous opposition is made to the present encroachments, and to the further designs, of our enemies![20]

[19] Jonathan Mayhew, *A Sermon Preach'd in the Audience of His Excellency William Shirley, Esq., . . . May 29th, 1754* (Boston, 1754), 32–47.
[20] *Ibid.*

These are Angloamerican voices which, among many, expressed a cultural and nationalistic self-consciousness which provided a deeper and broader emotional and ideological base for the hatreds and jealousies engendered by imperialistic rivalry. The "cold war" against the French was now a moral crusade; such preaching as this furnished the needed moral rationalization for driving the French out of the colonies they occupied on the continent.

III

The international history of Angloamerica in the colonial period is a double history. On the one side, the "thin red-line" of the international history of America runs unbrokenly and inseparably through the diplomatic history of the community of states of western Europe. In this sense, the history of colonial America is an integral part of European history. It is to be noted, however, that the American concerns of the European powers occupied only a part of the total context of their international relations. Their diplomatic policies relative to their European self-interest and objectives generally overshadowed their interests in America, although it may be said that for some states, such as England in the War of the Spanish Succession and in some wars, such as the Seven Years' War, the American interests of the maritime powers outweighed in importance their European interests. In all cases except the Seven Years' War, their diplomatic relations with each other were calculated to promote the interests of their citizens in Europe, first, and those of their colonists only incidentally. This meant that in many cases, as in that of the return of Louisbourg to France by England in 1748, and in many ways, as, most notably, in the mercantilistic restrictions upon colonial trade, the interests of the colonies were clearly and consciously sacrificed to those of the mother country. Because of their subservient position in the overall imperial perspective of British diplomatic history, the international history of the colonies was in significant measure moulded by the policies of the mother country. At the same time, the existence of the colonies and the deep involvement in them of many Englishmen, as well as of the British government itself, the colonies and their activities also had an increasingly significant influence upon the mother country itself.

On the other side of the ocean the international experiences of the European colonies centered in America itself. Whatever part they consciously played in international affairs was calculated to promote their own self-interests, first, and those of the mother country only secondarily.

But the international evolution of the colonies did not follow exactly the international ideologies and policies of their European metropoli. For the colonies soon discovered that they had international objectives of their own that often did not coincide with those of the mother countries. Thus, in America there emerged a body of international custom, such as the de facto practice of freedom of commerce, or the governor-to-governor diplomacy along the "great frontier," which often departed rather sharply from the desires and intentions of the home governments in their international dealings with each other. Furthermore, in the colonies there emerged a body of international concepts, or impulses, that diverged from the policies, customs and moods, of their metropoli. Such, for example, was the impulse toward freedom of international trade among the colonies; such was the American mood of isolation from Europe; such, indeed, was the rabid Angloamerican cultural imperialism that seems to have exceeded in fervor any comparable emotion in England or any other European country. Where the "enlightened self-interest" of the Angloamericans coincided with the policies of England, as in the matter of territorial expansion, the colonies enthusiastically allied themselves with the mother country. But, even here, the motivation was not the same. English motivation for defeating the French empire around the world was one thing; American ambitions to drive the French out of the West Indies and North America were something else. In any case, the general attitudes and the specific aims of Angloamerica in the world of international relations originated in and fed upon American experiences. They were not basically English or European, nor calculated primarily to serve English or European self-interests; they were American, and they evolved to serve the "enlightened self-interest" of the Americans in the new world. Representing what might be called the "natural" objectives of the Americans in international affairs, they clearly anticipated the basic diplomatic principles of the United States after independence.

2 / Foreign Affairs
and the Articles of Confederation

Paul Varg

In an important sense, the American Revolution was four quite different struggles, each related to the others but nevertheless distinct. It was a war for American independence; a civil struggle within the British Empire between loyalists and patriots in America and between their political counterparts who engaged mainly in rhetorical debates in England; it was a war for various social and political reforms; and it was also a world wide struggle in which most of the European continental nations lined up, formally or informally, in a coalition opposing British power. When the war ended and the peace settlement was concluded at Paris, the independent United States government realized that its foreign relations were beset by numerous problems which were legacies of the late war. In the paper that follows, Paul Varg describes several of the dilemmas that confronted the Confederation government in the 1780s, particularly commercial matters that proved especially troublesome to the new republic. The failure of the United States to effect a legal basis of trade with Great Britain should be coupled with the inability of the Confederation government to compel the British to evacuate their troops from American territory and compel the Spanish to permit Americans free navigation on the lower Mississippi River. Varg's central thesis that the weaknesses found in the national government operating under the Articles of Confederation hampered the conduct of the nation's foreign affairs more directly than other spheres of domestic public policy leads rather logically to the position that it was the inability of the Confederation government to resolve serious problems in foreign affairs that made necessary a constitutional convention in 1787 and the establishment of a stronger national government.

For further reading: *Samuel Flagg Bemis, *The Diplomacy of the American Revolution* (Bloomington: 1957) second edition; Merrill Jensen, *The New Nation: a History of the United States During the Confederation 1781*

Paul Varg is Professor of History at Michigan State University. This article is reprinted by permission of the Michigan State University Press. From *Foreign Policies of the Founding Fathers*. Copyright © 1963 by The Michigan State University Press.

–1789 (New York: 1950); Richard B. Morris, *The Peacemakers: the Great Powers and American Independence* (New York: 1965); Paul Varg, *The Foreign Policy of the Founding Fathers* (East Lansing: 1963); *Richard W. Van Alstyne, *Empire and Independence: the International History of the American Revolution* (New York: 1965).

Foreign affairs played a major role in undermining the Articles of Confederation and contributed in an important way to the movement that led to the Constitution of 1787. The most conspicuous failure of the Confederation was in meeting challenges from abroad. In the realm of domestic affairs Congress and the state governments performed reasonably well. The highly decentralized political structure of the Articles accorded with the combined preference for the retaining of control of the purse in local hands and the general distrust of political power. The major factors in overriding this preference were the dependence on profitable foreign commercial relations and the importance of security for the wave of settlers crossing the mountains into the lands that bordered on British and Spanish territory.

The sovereignty of the states under the Articles of Confederation accorded with lofty republican ideals, but the experiment rested on at least one fatal flaw. It assumed that even an impotent Congress could deal with foreign relations. Some leaders feared the worst even before the nominal union of thirteen sovereign republics faced the test of intense national rivalries. In February, 1783, Thomas Jefferson bemoaned the "pride of independence taking deep and dangerous hold on the hearts of individual states" and prophesied a civil war in which the contending parties would call on Great Britain and France to aid them.[1] John Adams, in London seeking to negotiate a trade treaty, criticized the individual states for not standing together and warned that they would become the "sport of transatlantic politicians of all denominations, who hate liberty in every shape, and every man who loves it, and every country that enjoys it."[2] As early as March, 1783, Alexander Hamilton confided to George Washington that only the establishment of a strong union could "prevent our being a ball in the hands of European powers, bandied against each other at their pleasure. . . ."[3] Less discerning eyes, more inclined to concentrate on the realization of republican ideals, tended to dismiss these warnings as the trumped up fears of conservatives who distrusted popular government and sought an excuse to tighten the reins at home.

The opponents of centralization held the upper hand until 1785. Four factors favored them. First, Americans gloried in republican principles, chief of which they held to be popular control of the purse. The purse strings must reside in the hands of the state legislators who, being closer at hand, could be subjected to closer control. As regulation of foreign commerce involved revenue this, too, must be reserved to the states. Secondly, state officeholders conditioned by long experience to defend-

[1] *The Papers of Thomas Jefferson,* ed. Julian P. Boyd (Princeton: Princeton University Press, 1954), Vol. VI, pp. 248–249.

[2] *The Works of John Adams, Second President of the United States; with a Life of the Author,* ed. Charles Francis Adams (Boston: Little, Brown and Company, 1853), Vol. VIII, p. 82.

[3] Gottfried Dietze, "Hamilton's Concept of Free Government," *New York History,* Vol. XXXVIII, October, 1957, p. 361.

ing the interests of their own states, provided the political leadership. As practical politicians they were not inclined to bold innovations. Only when more imaginative spirits among their constituency pushed them would they rise above their local orientation. Thirdly, the major factions distrusted each other. Land speculators and frontiersmen feared that under a strong central government the eastern states would exercise control and use it to profit themselves at the expense of the West. This western interest group did not forget that Congress, during the Revolution, yielded to French pressure on the question of free navigation of the Mississippi. Southern planters suspected northern merchants of being ready to establish a monopoly of shipping that would impose high freight rates on the export of southern commodities. Northerners, in turn, distrusted the avaricious land speculators who impatiently pressed for western interests and likewise believed the South generally hostile to commercial interests.

If a deep distrust among those who favored centralization had not existed, they might have been able to provide effective leadership earlier than 1785. The fourth factor was the ill will that had its roots in the crisis of 1779 and 1780. A rapid decline in the value of the continental currency, a desperate financial plight, and military disaster in the South led to a demand for a more efficient husbanding of resources. In this situation Robert Morris rose to a position where he controlled foreign loans, purchase of supplies, and made his influence felt in diplomacy.[4] Few questioned his ability, but his bold tactics and alliance with the merchants of Philadelphia left deep sores. The two representatives of Massachusetts, Stephen Higginson and Samuel Osgood, were among the many determined opponents of Morris. Higginson appeared before the Massachusetts legislature in 1783 "and gave them a general view of matters touching upon the Designs of the Aristocratic Junto in Congress."[5] The Massachusetts legislature, as a result, refused to approve the five per cent impost duty recommended by Congress. Samuel Osgood traced the intrigue of the French minister and Morris in acrid terms and warned of the insidious influence of Philadelphia where there were plans underway that would sacrifice the lower classes and give rise to an aristocracy.[6]

A later generation has looked back on the period of the Articles as one of both disaster and general dissatisfaction. Such was not the case. Professor Merrill Jensen has pushed back the shadow that John Fiske cast upon the constructive aspects of what was essentially a period of post-war reconstruction.

The southern states made strides toward developing their own merchant marine and increased the exports of major commodities. Locally owned ships soon carried one-fourth of South Carolina's exports, a sharp gain over prewar years.[7] Georgia greatly expanded its production and before long a third of her exports left her harbors in Georgia bottoms.[8] James Madison, in August, 1784, noted the recovery that had taken place in Virginia:

[4] E. James Ferguson, *The Power of the Purse: A History of American Public Finance, 1776–1790* (Williamsburg: Institute of Early American History, 1961), pp. 112–113, 119.

[5] Stephen Higginson to Theodorick Bland, October 6, 1783, *Letters of Members of the Continental Congress,* ed. Edmund C. Burnett (Washington, D.C.: Carnegie Institution, 1936), Vol. VII, p. 323.

[6] Samuel Osgood to John Adams, December 7, 1783, *ibid.,* pp. 378–380.

[7] Forrest McDonald, *We The People: The Economic Origins of the Constitution* (Chicago: University of Chicago Press, 1958), pp. 213–214.

[8] *Ibid.,* pp. 131–132.

Notwithstanding the languor of our direct trade with Europe, this Country has indirectly tasted some of the fruits of Independence. The price of our last crop of Tobacco has been on James River from 36/ to 42/6 per Ct. and has brought more specie into the Country than it ever before contained at one time.[9]

North Carolina, by 1789, had doubled its exports over the prewar figure.[10]

Signs of progress in the northern states were not lacking. There, too, some economic indices moved upward. New York City, virtually without a ship owned by one of its own citizens at the close of the war, had a merchant marine by 1789 that may have totalled 100,000 tons.[11] New Hampshire experienced some recovery as her shipowners engaged in a lively trade in livestock and lumber with the French West Indies.[12] The port of Salem witnessed a coming and going of ships that contrasts sharply with the traditional picture of stagnation.[13]

By 1790 American tonnage on the high seas reached impressive proportions. Of the ships entering from Great Britain 30,168 tons were American owned and 95,828 tons entering from the French West Indies belonged to Americans.[14] To these general observations must be added the fact that by 1787 the postwar depression had lifted and there were signs of recovery in all areas.

These signs of growth lend weight to the description of the critical period as one of postwar reconstruction. Some historians have gone beyond this point of reinterpretation to hold that the Articles satisfied the great majority of people and that it was only a minority group of conservatives, fearful of popular government, who brought about the Constitutional Convention and the replacement of the Articles with a more conservative plan of government. There is, of course, much truth in the statement of this school of historians that the Articles were not responsible for the spotty economic conditions but that the spotty economic conditions were certainly responsible for the demise of the Articles.

But the venture in historical revisionism appears to be weak at three major points. First, the movement for a stronger central government was by no means wholly the work of conservatives. Secondly, while the Articles were not the cause of economic difficulties, they did make it impossible for Congress to meet the major economic problem as understood by contemporaries. Finally, the thesis fails to give due weight

[9] James Madison to Thomas Jefferson, August 20, 1784, *The Papers of Thomas Jefferson,* ed. Boyd, Vol. VII, p. 402.

[10] John Richard Alden, "The South in the Revolution, 1763–1789," Vol. III of *A History of the South,* ed. Wendell Stephenson (Baton Rouge: Louisiana State University Press, 1957), p. 369.

[11] This figure is taken from an article by Samuel Duff McCoy, "The Port of New York (1783–1789): Lost Island of Sailing Ships," *New York History,* Vol. XVII, (January, 1936), p. 387. Whether the tonnage owned by New Yorkers was this great appears doubtful, but the growth during the 1780's was significant.

[12] McDonald, *We the People,* pp. 38–39.

[13] James Duncan Phillips, "Salem Ocean-Borne Commerce From the Close of the Revolution to the Establishment of the Constitution, 1783–1789," *The Essex Institute of Historical Collections,* Vol. LXXV (April, 1939), pp. 140–143.

[14] *American State Papers: Documents, Legislative and Executive, of the Congress of the United States, From the First Session of the First to the Third Session of the Thirteenth Congress, Inclusive: Commencing March 3, 1789 and Ending March 3, 1815. Selected and Edited, Under the Authority of Congress,* By Walter Lowrie, Secretary of the Senate, and Matthew St. Clair Clarke, Clerk of the House of Representatives (Washington: Gales and Seaton, 1832), Vol. I, p. 45. Hereafter cited as *American State Papers.*

to the problems of foreign relations both as regards foreign economic policy and the difficulties presented by the British and Spanish in the West.

First, it should be recognized that the fear of popular government did play an important part. There was a rather widespread apprehension that all authority was breaking down and that a reign of licentiousness was beginning. This feeling was shared by men of quite different points of view and was not limited to the conservatives who took their lead from Alexander Hamilton. In February, 1787, James Madison observed: "Indeed the Present System neither has nor deserves advocates; and if some very strong props are not applied will quickly tumble to the ground." He was appalled by the "late turbulent scenes in Mass'ts and infamous ones in Rhode Island" and thought that they had done "inexpressible injury to the republican character."[15] The existing order, he noted, had so lost the public confidence that some spoke of establishing a monarchy and others were now openly and seriously contemplating regional confederations. What Madison deplored was not popular government but the seeming inability of the states to become effective agents within their own boundaries and cooperative partners in the Confederation for achieving the public good. He was concerned with factions that irresponsibly pursued their own ends to the public detriment. Such fears were widespread, and they need not be interpreted as opposition to popular government.

Secondly, the history of the Critical Period centers around the widely held conviction that the existing system of commercial relations with the outside world, and particularly with Great Britain, deprived the country of the just fruits of its industry and natural wealth. A nationalistic spirit did underlay the struggle among local sovereignties. This nationalism gained its greatest strength from the common bond of republican principles which seemed to contemporaries to set the United States apart from the rest of the world. Next, it rested on the common dependence on foreign trade.

Virtually everyone had an interest in access to foreign manufactures and to foreign markets, in buying cheap and selling dear, in maintaining favorable trade balances that would increase the supply of specie and in lessening the weight of foreign debts that pressed heavily upon them. More important than the fact of a debtor class was the fact that the United States was a debtor nation. Herein lay the basis for the various states and the many interest groups in seeking a posture of strength that would enable them to counter the hostile measures of European mercantilism.

Americans in the postwar years labored under the conviction that the nations of Europe had contrived to lay down conditions for commercial relations that were inequitable. Great Britain played the role of the arch villain in this economic game. That nation had declined entering into a commercial treaty. Instead she laid down the rules of commercial relations in a series of orders from the Crown. These orders closed the West Indies to American ships and excluded American salt meat and fish from the islands. American ships were likewise excluded from the trade with the British provinces to the north. American built ships were no longer admitted to the British merchant marine; in fact, a ship that had been repaired by Americans thereby lost its right to sail under the British flag. American fish oil and whale products were likewise deprived of their former market in the British isles. These re-

[15] James Madison to Edmund Pendleton, Febrauary 24, 1787, Burnett, *Letters*, Vol. VIII, pp. 547–548.

strictions gained far more attention than did the fact that Great Britain permitted American ships to enter British ports in Europe on the same basis as British ships.

The British freedom to dictate terms withour any fear of retaliation by the Americans was especially galling, because the greater part of American trade continued to be with the former mother country. The hoped for trade with the nations on the continent of Europe increased but failed to attain the proportions expected. It at first appeared that the French government would pursue a less monopolistic policy. By an *arrêt* of August 30, 1784, the French government opened seven ports in the West Indies to foreign ships and admitted American meat and fish free of discriminatory duties. In the next few years the granting of special bounties to French competitors limited the effect of this order, but trade with the French West Indies did become of first rate importance and most of it was carried in American ships.[16] Trade with France itself was encouraged and American ships admitted, but the inability of French merchants to extend credit and the limited variety of French manufactures handicapped the trade. Prussia, the Netherlands, Sweden, Portugal, and Morocco entered into commercial treaties, and Russia and Spain admitted American ships, but none of these new commercial connections nor all of them together greatly changed the former close commercial relations with Great Britain.

The growth of an American merchant marine gave but slight comfort as long as American harbors were dominated by British bottoms. In January, 1785, Pierse Long, a Portsmouth shipowner, while visiting in New York, wrote: "It is amazing to see the quantity of Vessels in this City from all parts of England now in this Harbour carrying goods to market. . . ." "I hope very soon," he wrote, "there will be an end put to so diabolical a trade."[17] This was a constant complaint. In 1785 it dominated the discussions in Congress. Whether this British domination resulting from the monopolistic orders of the Crown in 1783 was the basic cause of the postwar depression is less important than the fact that most Americans thought it was. And there is no reason to question that the British did dominate the carrying trade. In the first year for which complete statistics are available, 1789–1790, more than 85,000 tons of British ships arrived from the British West Indies to none for the Americans, while in the direct trade with England the British tonnage was more than double that of the Americans.[18] Under these circumstances the growth of the American merchant fleet scarcely gave much consolation.

Depression stalked through the once prosperous state of Massachusetts where the former merchant fleet had dwindled to almost nothing by the close of the Revolution. During the last two years of the war the British tightened their blockade until insurance rates ran as high as forty per cent. A large part of the state's privateers fell into British hands.[19] The few ships still available at the close of the war were largely in disrepair. The new relationship between New England and old England required a readjustment of trade routes and the finding of new markets. True enough, Americans freely violated the prohibition against their ships entering the British West Indies, but the greater proportion of this trade was nevertheless carried

[16] Henri See, "Commerce between France and the United States, 1783–1784," *American Historical Review,* Vol. XXXI (July, 1926), pp. 735–36.

[17] Pierse Long to John Langdon, January 31, 1785, Burnett, *Letters,* Vol. VIII, p. 18.

[18] *American State Papers: Commerce,* Vol. I, p. 45.

[19] Samuel Eliot Morison, *Maritime History of Massachusetts 1783–1860* (Boston: Houghton Mifflin Co., 1921), p. 30.

in British bottoms.[20] In 1786 the exports of Massachusetts amounted to only one-fourth of the prewar total.[21] The fishing industry was particularly hard hit. At the close of hostilities only four or five boats survived of the prewar fishing fleet of more than two hundred. Recovery was slow in the face of the closing of the former markets in the British West Indies. The whaling industry suffered because the British market was closed to American whale oil. The shipbuilding industry, once of prime importance, recovered slowly as the former British demand no longer existed.

Stephen Higginson, a wealthy Boston merchant, in August, 1785, portrayed the far reaching effects of British measures closing both the northern maritime provinces and the West Indies to American ships. The difficulty centered about the problem of remittances. The Boston merchant deplored the disastrous effect on business at large. Many failures had already taken place and others would occur, for those indebted to England would, in many cases, never be able to meet their obligations.[22] Higginson thought the economy would recover, but he did not portray a bright picture. At the close of 1785 he observed that a good beginning had been made in the manufacture of nails, shoes, and clothing, that exports of pork, butter, and cheese had greatly increased, and that Massachusetts now enjoyed a favorable balance of trade with Pennsylvania, Virginia, and Carolina. These indices did not add up to prosperity. He could only take comfort in the fact that necessity would bring an end to the importation of British luxuries and a return to frugality and high morals.[23]

In each of the northern states one of the most compelling arguments for a stronger central government was that such a government would be able to negotiate a commercial treaty with Great Britain that would give greater advantages than the unilaterally imposed conditions set forth in the orders of the Crown. In New York trade and Federalism "appeared hand in hand." E. Wilder Spaulding, in his study of that state during the critical period, states:

> No other symptom of hard times had so marked an effect upon politics as had the depression of commerce. It was the stimulus most responsible for the organization of the Federalists by 1787 and their constant agitation for a Federal government strong enough to protect American commerce.[24]

The sharp commercial depression in New York in 1785 was due to broader causes than the impotence of Congress, but this does not negate the fact that merchants believed that a stronger Congress would be able to restore trade. In 1785 the New York Chamber of Commerce appealed to the state legislature to grant Congress the power to regulate commerce and attributed the decline of trade to the ineffectiveness of the central government.[25] The merchants of Boston had taken the initiative and appealed to the New York merchants to do so.[26] The fact that condi-

---

[20] This conclusion rests on the many observations recorded in the letters of members of Congress and also on the statistics for the first year under the new Federal Constitution.

[21] Morison, *op. cit.,* p. 31.

[22] "Letters of Stephen Higginson," *Annual Report of the American Historical Association for the Year 1896* (Washington: Government Printing Office, 1897), I, p. 719.

[23] *Ibid.*

[24] E. Wilder Spaulding, *New York in the Critical Period 1783–1789* (New York: Columbia University Press, 1923), p. 9.

[25] *Ibid.,* p. 137.

[26] *Ibid.*

tions of trade greatly improved before the Federal Convention met in Philadelphia did not prevent the merchants from continued use of the argument. In New Jersey, where geography and not the Articles was clearly responsible for the failure of efforts to promote foreign trade, the same argument was used. In October, 1787, Lambert Cadwallader wrote that one of the advantages offered by the Constitution was that it would give New Jersey "prodigious advantages from the Regulation of our Trade with foreign Powers who had taken the opportunity of our feeble State to turn everything to their own Benefit." He now looked forward to playing one nation against another and compelling them to show consideration to the United States.[27]

Rufus King, of Massachusetts, so long opposed to changing the Articles, noted the disadvantages imposed on American commerce by Great Britain and observed that these disadvantages now constituted the subject for general conversation. He thought the subject would again arouse the patriotic spirit, and

> if once more it becomes vigilant, and can be made active by the pride of inde-
> pendence, the idea of national honor and glory, the present embarrassments of
> trade and the vain sophisms of Europeans relative thereto, will not only direct but
> drive America into a system more advantageous than treaties and alliances with
> all the world—a system which shall cause her to rely on her own ships and her
> own marines, and to exclude those of all other nations.[28]

Joshua Wentworth, long active in New Hampshire politics, warned that the Union could only be supported by commerce, "it is the spring and life of the Most respectable Nations, and beside the honor & dignity of America depend on her asserting the right of sovereignty, and not suffer any Nation on earth to Ligislate [sic] for her,—at present Great Britain [sic] does."[29] Charles Pettit, of Pennsylvania, mourned over the fact that instead "of supporting the respectable Rank which we assumed among Nations, we have exposed our Follies to their View." He noted the result: "they treat us accordingly, they severally shut the Door of commercial Hospitality against us, while ours being open they enter and partake with us at their Pleasure."[30]

In the southern states the dominance of the British in the carrying trade was only part of the larger picture of the complete economic subordination of the planters to the British merchants. In all of these states the British merchants or their factors regained the complete domination they had enjoyed during the colonial period. The planters needed supplies at the end of the war and they brought these at high prices using the credit that the British merchant offered. As a result the prewar debts owed by Virginians to British merchants, amounting to an estimated £2 million soon rose

---

[27] It should be made clear that the strong support in New Jersey for the Constitution rested on the difficulty of raising revenue by impost duties in a state with virtually no foreign commerce. As as result New Jersey had to resort to direct taxes. New York served as the port of entry for most foreign imports to New Jersey and was able to raise adequate revenue by duties on imports. Nevertheless New Jersey did make some effort to promote foreign trade, and to some extent the British regulations were blamed for the failure. For a valuable discussion of the situation in that state see Richard P. McCormick, *Experiment in Independence: New Jersey in the Critical Period*, New Brunswick, N.J.: Rutgers University Press, 1950.

[28] Rufus King to John Adams, November 2, 1785, Burnett, *Letters*, Vol. VIII, pp. 247–248.

[29] *The State of New Hampshire Miscellaneous Provincial and State Papers*, Vol. XVIII, pp. 772–773.

[30] Charles Pettit to Jeremiah Wadsworth, May 27, 1786, Burnett, *Letters*, Vol. VIII, p. 370.

far above this figure.[31] Virginia had an essentially one crop economy, namely tobacco. While prices after the war were high for a period of years, the freight costs were also higher and sometimes amounted to as much as 14 per cent of the sales price.[32] British goods sold at premium prices but no others were available. This left the typical Virginia planter struggling to make up the balance between the income from his tobacco and the goods he purchased on credit. The merchants were constantly engaged in trying to collect. In this they met the opposition of the Virginia legislature which passed laws holding all pre-Revolutionary debts liquidated by the war. Scores of planters moved to the West leaving their debts unpaid. The net effect of this mercantile-agrarian relationship was great bitterness. When the prospect of a new federal government loomed, many planters opposed it on the ground that it would render the debts owed to British merchants payable. Ratification of the new Constitution by the state convention caused a prominent Virginian to write to his stepsons:

> You will have heard that the Constitution has been adopted in this State. That event, my dear children, affects your interest more nearly than that of many others. The recovery of British debts can no longer be postponed, and there now seems to be a moral certainty that your patrimony will all go to satisfy the unjust debt from your papa to the Hanburys. The consequence, my dear boys, must be obvious to you. Your sole dependence must be on your own personal abilities and exertions.[33]

Some Virginians might oppose the Constitution for this reason, but a majority saw the new government as offering the only escape from the British economic yoke.

The debtor relationship of planters throughout the southern states was much the same as in Virginia. The anonymous writer of a pamphlet in South Carolina, in 1786, stated that British ships filled the harbor at Charleston, and British merchants now ruled the state through their capital as effectively as before independence was achieved.[34] William Kilty, of Maryland, an astute and cautious observer, granted that there were many causes for the economic plight of Maryland, not least of them the effects of the war, but he concluded that it was the accumulation of these "with old British debts, now pressing on them with an interest nearly equal to the principal, and the addition of new ones which have been, through necessity, contracted, that has reduced them to their present state."[35]

Many believed that the answer to this economic problem lay in the encouragement of the American merchant marine so that their goods could be marketed more profitably not only in England but in the countries on the continent, which finally consumed a large proportion of them. Little attention was given to the fact that the merchants of other countries could not extend credit or that no other country

[31] W. A. Low, "Merchant and Planter Relations in Post-Revolutionary Virginia, 1783–1789," *The Virginia Magazine of History and Biography*, Vol. LXI (July, 1953), p. 314.

[32] W. A. Low states: "Whereas six percent of the total sale prices of tobacco went to pay freight expenses alone prior to the Revolution, the average after the war was higher—sometimes as high as fourteen percent. Duties on tobacco export also increased after the Revolution, consuming nearly four-fifths of the sale price." *Ibid.*, p. 313.

[33] *Ibid.*, p. 317.

[34] *A Few Salutary Hints, Pointing Out the Policy and Consequences of Admitting British Subjects to Engross Our Trade*, New York: Kollock, 1786.

[35] William Kilty, *A History of the Session of the General Assembly*, Annapolis, 1786.

could offer such a large variety of manufactured goods. The South bristled with a general resentment against the British who were made the scapegoat for all of the section's many problems. While proposals to grant Congress the power to regulate foreign trade invariably aroused fears in the southern states that the northern states would use such a power to achieve a monopoly of shipping, the opposition in the South gradually declined though it by no means disappeared.[36]

The assumption that a strong central government could quickly strike back with discriminatory legislation against those nations that continued to adhere to the monopolistic practices of mercantilism was an effective argument in favor of creating a stronger union. In the *Federalist Papers*, Hamilton, Madison and Jay gave great emphasis to the necessity of changing from a posture of "imbecility" before the outside world to one of strength. In view of the later conflict between Hamilton and Madison over the question of discriminatory trade laws, it should be noted that it was Hamilton who wrote:

> Suppose, for instance, we had a government in America, capable of excluding Great Britain (with whom we have at present no treaty of commerce) from all our ports; which would be the probable operation of this step upon her politics? Would it not enable us to negotiate, with the fairest prospect of success, for commercial privileges of the most valuable and extensive kind, in the dominions of that kingdom?[37]

He predicted that discriminatory laws would lead Great Britain to relax her present system and cause her to admit the Americans to the West Indies "from which our trade would derive the most substantial benefits." The argument was certainly not new nor invented by Hamilton; it had been at the core of the many complaints that found themselves expressed in scores of writings ever since 1783. In the first session of the new Congress, James Madison, in his sponsorship of discriminatory legislation against Great Britain, said that it had been generally understood that this was the first objective in establishing the new government.

[36] The question of regulating trade divided the northern commercial states and the southern staple states as did no other question. Richard Henry Lee freely predicted the avarice of the merchants would result in legislation ruinous to the South, a view he promoted with the greatest of vigor as President of Congress in 1786. But it is also interesting to note that when Nathan Dane went to Congress in 1786, he wrote to Governor Bowdoin of Massachusetts that "the disposition for vesting commercial powers in Congress appears to me to be more general particularly in the Southern States than I expected to find it." Burnett, *Letters,* Vol. VIII, p. 283.

The subject came up in the Constitutional Convention, and C. C. Pinckney proposed that a two-thirds majority be required for any law regulating trade between the states and with foreign powers. The response of several southerners is significant. Thomas Pinckney of South Carolina immediately arose to oppose the proposal. James Madison expressed a willingness to accept the temporary disadvantage of high freight rates because the "Southern states would derive an essential advantage in the general security afforded by the increase of maritime strength." John Rutledge of South Carolina likewise opposed the motion. He wished the convention to remember the necessity "of securing the West India trade to this country." "That was the great object," he said, "and a navigation Act was necessary for obtaining it." Forrest McDonald points out that the shipping interest in the Southern port cities had suffered due to the closing of the British West Indies. Southern ships usually made a trip to Europe at harvest time and engaged in the West Indies trade during the remainder of the year. The merchants found the trade with the French West Indies much less advantageous than their trade with the British islands prior to the war. See Forrest McDonald, *We the People,* p. 213.

[37] *The Federalist* (Washington, D.C.: National Home Library Foundation, 1937), Number 11, p. 63.

That the question of foreign economic policy became the focal point in political and economic thinking has long run significance. The aims formulated during these years deeply influenced future administrations. Other considerations were to enter into later Federalist foreign policy, but the South and West continued to hold these aims as primary. The suspicion of Great Britain in those sections and their sensitivity to British interference with their trade on the high seas is best understood against the background of the merchant-planter relationship that caused such deep frustration in the 1780's.

British occupation of the American Old Northwest furnished an equally delicate problem. The peace treaty gave the territory north of the Ohio river and south of the Great Lakes and the 45th parallel to the United States.

The British refused to evacuate the forts of the Old Northwest for reasons of economics and out of a regard for the Indians inhabiting the territory. The string of British forts began at Lake Champlain, stretched along the St. Lawrence river and the southern shore of Lake Erie, and anchored at highly strategic Detroit, with a final outpost at Michilimackinac, eight forts all together. During the peace negotiations the British peace commissioners felt no pressure to hold on to this area, little recognizing either the potential importance of the area or its immediate value as the source of furs. Only after the treaty had been signed did the British government in London awaken to the fact that it had made a settlement so generous that it would be difficult to convince those immediately affected, the fur traders and Indians, to accept it as a final settlement.

Announcement of the treaty provisions shocked the fur traders into making vigorous pleas for postponing the evacuation. The Canadian fur trade, largely a monopoly of the Northwest Company, amounted to £200,000 annually. Most of the furs came from the Indians living in what was now legally American territory.[38] If England yielded its military forts, from which the Indians drew their daily sustenance as well as protection from the oncoming land hungry Americans, that valuable trade would collapse.

The Indians, faithful allies of the British during the War for Independence, held the London government guilty of acting in bad faith, and British military officers sympathized with them. To admit the Americans would be to deliver the Indians into the hands of their worst enemies. Americans would inevitably push the Indians out and divide the area into farms. Most British officers felt like General Maclean, commander at Niagara: "I do from my soul pity these poor people and should they commit outrages at giving up the posts it would not surprise me."[39]

Faced with the dilemma of living up to the treaty, thereby surrendering their economic interests and deserting their loyal Indian allies, or having to face angry protests from the United States, the British chose to procrastinate. This policy, it was thought, would permit the goods already on their way to the Indians to bring their return in furs within the next two years. Secondly, some arrangements might be worked out with the Indians so as to avoid probable Indian attacks on British garrisons which would almost inevitably follow an immediate withdrawal.

During the early months following the treaty the British thought only of postponing the inevitable but circumstances soon led them into a much less justifiable position.

[38] Samuel Flagg Bemis, *Jay's Treaty: A Study in Commerce and Diplomacy* (New York: The Macmillan Company, 1924), pp. 5–6.
[39] *Ibid.*, p. 8, fn. 19.

As months passed into a year the British realized that the American government was incapable of action and nothing was to be feared from delay in observance of the treaty. In fact intelligence reports from the United States spoke of the impending breakup of the Republic. If this should take place, the British could take permanent possession. The failure of the various states to abide by the treaty provisions dealing with the payment of British creditors furnished the government with a good excuse. England, said the foreign office, could not be expected to fulfill its obligations when the individual states, in defiance of Congress, passed legislation making impossible the collection of debts by British creditors, as provided by the treaty. Gradually, British policy evolved into a positive program for nullifying the treaty as concerned the Northwest. They continued their occupation of the forts and after 1785 encouraged the Indians to resist efforts of the Americans to work out a peaceful settlement.

In the late summer and fall of 1785, John Adams despaired of making any progress in London on either a commercial treaty or British evacuation of the forts. Adams argued that as long as the British held the forts the Indians would feel free to attack Americans. Nothing would so arouse the emotions of his countrymen as the inevitable atrocities in warfare with the Indians. This could lead to a more general war with grievous consequences for the remaining parts of the British empire in North America.[40] His pleas met with silence.

Adams' frustration caused him to recommend a navigation act closing American ports to British ships. Should that fail, the next step would be commercial treaties with other powers so favorable as to give their goods a clear advantage over the British in the American market. As a last resort Adams recommended entry into alliances with the other powers.

Added to the controversies over trade and the Northwest were the disputes over such matters as British failure to pay for the great numbers of Negro slaves taken during the war and the British willingness to work with Ethan Allen and his brothers in a move to detach Vermont from the new republic. On their side the Americans violated the treaty by refusing to pay debts owed to British merchants and by discrimination against Loyalists who returned to the country. The treaty provided that Congress recommend to the states that the Loyalists be indemnified for their losses. No state government chose to compensate them for few measures would have been more unpopular.

Relations with Spain posed difficulties that for a time threatened more serious consequences.[41] These involved the interests and ambitions of a politically powerful group of Americans in a direct way. In this case the failure of the government to protect American interests threatened to lead to a breakup of the Union.

Spanish and American interests first came into conflict in the Trans-Appalachian Southwest during the Revolution when the Spanish retrieved the Floridas from the British. The peace treaty of 1783 between England and Spain recognized the Spanish conquest. The frontier posts seized by the Spanish in the course of the war now became the peacetime centers for the exercise of Spanish control. The Spanish success represented more than the acquisition of valuable territory. From the shores of

[40] *Works of John Adams,* Vol. VIII, p. 326.
[41] The author highly recommends Arthur P. Whitaker's *The Spanish-American Frontier: 1783–1795: The Westward Movement and the Spanish Retreat in the Mississippi Valley* (Boston: Houghton Mifflin Co., 1927). This excellent analysis and narrative account of relations with Spain provided the basis for the author's own treatment of the subject.

that territory British merchant ships had sailed into the ports of New Spain, undermining the whole Spanish colonial system. It would be easier now to insulate the empire against British competition.

The Spanish had long recognized that the Americans posed no less a threat to the empire than the British and they had no intention to compromise on their recently acquired territory. But compromise they must, for Spain lacked the resources for transforming the southwestern wilderness into a strong colony capable of withstanding American pressure.

The prize in the impending struggle was nothing less than the Mississippi Valley. To the Spanish it was something more, the maintenance of monopoly control over the trade of their empire. Control of the Mississippi and the gulf coast increased its chances of perpetuating its traditional system. So it seemed, but economic forces were arrayed against it. The Spanish government, recognizing that it could not compete with rival powers, would have preferred to exclude all foreigners, but it could not escape the fact that it could neither supply the newly acquired American territory with the goods it needed nor could it absorb the products of this vast territory in its own markets. So if it were to hold that territory it must of necessity compromise with tradition and admit foreigners to the trade.

On taking over the forts in East Florida in 1784, the Spanish official faced a crowd of Indians expecting supplies. Having none at hand, he turned to the British Panton, Leslie and company for the goods needed by the Indians and agreed in return that the company should be permitted to continue its operations in the area for another year. What was at first a temporary expedient became a permanent policy for the Spanish were not prepared economically or by training to run the Indian trade. Consequently the British company soon took over the fur trade in the entire area. To have refused this concession to a foreign concern would have thrown the trade into the hands of the Americans and given them an opportunity to win over the Indians to their side. The Spanish followed up this action with a series of conferences with the Chickasaws, Creeks and Choctaws and negotiated treaties in which the savages acknowledged Spanish sovereignty.

During the same period that Spain was taking over control of the Floridas and Louisiana, the Americans marched across the mountains into what is now Kentucky, Tennessee and western Georgia. Free from the restrictive policies of both the British and the colonial governments, the poorer elements along the coast could satisfy their yearning for land only by leaving the plantation area where economic opportunity was limited. By the close of the Revolution some 75,000 settlers had located in the trans-mountain area. Many of these frontiersmen saw in the war for independence nothing more than a fight for what they considered to be the inalienable right to emigrate. They had no intention of permitting Spain to deprive them of this "natural right."[42]

Leading the frontiersmen were the land speculators, many of them governors, members of Congress and in most cases leaders in their communities. John Sevier, governor of the State of Franklin, acquired title to 70,000 acres when North Carolina opened up its western tracts. James Robertson and William Blount, two more political leaders, secured sizable tracts and Patrick Henry, of Virginia, likewise

---

[42] Thomas Perkins Abernethy gives a very good account of land speculation in his *From Frontier to Plantation in Tennessee: A Study in Frontier Democracy* (Chapel Hill: University of North Carolina Press, 1932).

engaged in land speculation. Their fortunes depended upon the United States making good its claim to the territory north of the thirty-first parallel and compelling Spain to open the Mississippi.

The ambiguity of the treaties of 1783 invited both Spain and the United States to pursue their own conflicting interpretations. The Spanish could claim both Floridas. West Florida had no specific boundaries in the Anglo-Spanish treaties but the Spanish soon claimed the territory as far north as the mouth of the Tennessee River. The Anglo-American treaty set the boundary at the thirty-first parallel but a secret provision, unknown to the Spaniards, provided an alternative boundary at 32° 26′ if the territory should be returned to Great Britain. The American treaty provided that both the United States and Great Britain should have free access to the Mississippi; the Spanish treaty with Great Britain made no mention of navigation rights.

Spain's foreign minister, Floridablanca, responded to the American pressure by issuing orders for the closing of the Mississippi to foreign ships and by sending Diego de Gardoqui on a special diplomatic mission to the United States to negotiate a treaty. The United States was to be wooed with an offer of direct trade with Spain and the Canary Islands, some compromises on the line which Spain had drawn marking the boundary of West Florida, and an offer of a pact of military alliance and mutual guarantee of each other's territories. The instructions stipulated that there must be no concession to the United States on the question of navigation of the Mississippi River.

John Jay, Secretary for Foreign Affairs, made no headway on the issue of navigation of the Mississippi. A resolution passed by Congress in August, 1785 prevented Jay from agreeing to the closing of the river. Two considerations led him to venture a request from Congress for new instructions. As the American representative to Madrid during the war he had been instructed to agree to the closing of the river in return for a recognition of independence and a commercial treaty. The mercantile interests would be willing to make a similar agreement now. As yet the traffic on the Mississippi amounted to little. Jay reasoned that an agreement to close it would do little harm if the treaty provided that the question could be reopened after twenty-five years.

The Jay proposal became involved in internal politics at once. Virginia, North Carolina, and Georgia, the states with territory in the southwest, had long been of one mind on the question of the Mississippi. Even before Spain laid down any policy, James Madison, apprehensive that Spain would close the Mississippi, argued that such a course would be foolhardy and contrary to the laws of nature. In a letter to Lafayette he wrote:

> If the United States were to become parties to the occlusion of the Mississippi they would be guilty of treason against the very laws under which they obtained and hold their national existence.[43]

He had a firm ally in James Monroe who took the lead in opposing Jay in Congress. These Virginians held that Congress was under obligation not to sacrifice the vital interest of one section for some minor convenience to another section. Madison and

---

[43] *The Writings of James Madison Comprising His Public Papers and His Private Correspondence, Including Numerous Letters and Documents for the First Time,* ed. Gaillard Hunt (New York: G. P. Putnam's Sons, 1901), Vol. II, p. 122. Hereafter cited as *Writings of Madison.*

Monroe not only believed that the United States had a right to free navigation of the Mississippi, but they knew that a sacrifice of western interests at this time would do irreparable injury to the movement to increase the powers of Congress. In the early summer of 1786 they looked forward hopefully to the Annapolis convention. Approval of Jay's proposal by Congress would convince the south and west that they could not afford to entrust their interests to Congress.

Monroe's arguments before Congress failed to prevent the approval of Jay's proposal. Frustrated at the hands of Congress, Monroe joined with others in drafting a new proposal and sending it to Vergennes with a plea that he use his influence at the Spanish court. Monroe warned Vergennes that Spain was driving the westerners into the hands of Great Britain. That rival power, he added, would in all probability come to their aid, negotiate a trade of Gibraltar for West Florida, and then take over control of the interior of North America.[44]

Jay's victory in Congress was a hollow one for the seven to five vote showed that he could never get ratified a treaty closing the Mississippi. Open talk of disunion in the western settlements led him to drop the whole matter. From this time on Jay served as a symbol in the west of the unscrupulous and snobbish mercantile interests of the east.

In the spring of 1787 the convention for strengthening the Articles of Confederation was about to meet in Philadelphia. Jay had made no announcement of what course he would pursue in the Spanish negotiations but James Madison learned from Gardoqui that Jay had decided to surrender to the southerners. This was a victory but Madison feared that the consequences of what had taken place "are likely to be very serious. . . . Mr. [Patrick] Henry's disgust exceeds all measure, and I am not singular in ascribing his refusal to attend the Convention to the policy of keeping himself free to combat or espouse the result of it according to the result of the Mississippi business, among other circumstances."[45]

The new constitution was ratified by the people, but old habits of thought and sheer inertia manifested themselves in the relatively narrow margin by which the new structure won approval. The puzzling question is not so much why the opposition was so strong but, given the tradition in favor of local government and the deeply held view that any surrender over the power of the purse was tantamount to a sacrifice of sovereignty, that the change should have come so quickly. The change was undoubtedly hastened by such purely domestic factors as the financial problem, the fear inspired by the threatened breakdown of orderly government in Massachusetts and Rhode Island, the frustration of Connecticut and New Jersey in the face of the rise of New York, and the difficulties attending postwar reconstruction. However it is when we look at the close relation between domestic affairs and foreign relations that the abandoning of the Articles of Confederation after only six short years of experience appears less enigmatic. Economic interests with much at stake in the field of foreign affairs had solid reasons for supporting a change. And in advocating reform they could do so in the name of national honor. American nationalism was still in the nascent stage, but the most ardent of the states rights advocates was quick to resent injury at the hands of foreign powers.

[44] *The Papers of Thomas Jefferson*, ed. Julian P. Boyd (Princeton: Princeton University Press, 1954), Vol. X. The editor presents a careful and detailed account of Monroe's maneuver on pages 277–279.

[45] *Writings of Madison*, II, p. 329.

3 / Washington's Farewell Address:
A Foreign Policy of Independence

Samuel Flagg Bemis

An historical event or idea should be understood in terms of its immediate context, and the circumstances which both preceded and precipitated it, and presumably affected it. President Washington's Farewell Address of 1796 took on meaning and significance not only because Washington intoned familiar generalizations that had developed out of American experience during the 17th and 18th centuries, but as Samuel Flagg Bemis makes abundantly clear in the following article, the events that occurred in the three years preceding the Address gave it a compelling immediacy. Washington counselled his countrymen to maintain friendly commercial relations with all countries but to steer clear of permanent foreign alliances. He harked back to the doctrine of the two spheres which had held that Europe had a different complex of interests from those of the Americas. In short, Bemis here places the Farewell Address within the sequence of events flowing from the Anglo-French War, the American struggle to assert neutral rights, Jay's Treaty and the continuing Franco-American Alliance.

For further reading: *Samuel Flagg Bemis, *Jay's Treaty: A Study in Commerce and Diplomacy* (New Haven: 1923) and *Pinckney's Treaty* (New Haven: 1926); *Julian P. Boyd, *Number 7: Alexander Hamilton's Secret Attempts to Control American Foreign Policy* (Princeton: 1964); *Joseph Charles, *The Origins of the American Party System* (Williamsburg: 1956); Alexander De Conde, *Entangling Alliance* (Durham: 1958) and *The Quasi War: The Politics and Diplomacy of the Undeclared War with France 1797–1800* (New York: 1967); Bradford Perkins, *The First Rapprochement: England and the United States 1795–1805* (Philadelphia: 1955); *Gerald Stourzh, *Benjamin Franklin and American Foreign Policy* (Chicago: 1954); Detlev F. Vagts, "The Logan Act: Paper Tiger or Sleeping Giant?" *American Journal of International Law*, LX (1966), 268–302; Albert K. Weinberg, "Washington's 'Great Rule' in its Historical Evolution," in *Historiography and Urbanization: Essays in American History in Honor of W. Stull Holt*, edited by Eric Goldman (Baltimore: 1941), pp. 109–138.

Samuel Flagg Bemis is Professor Emeritus of History, Yale University. This article is reprinted by permission of the author and of the editors of the *American Historical Review*. Copyright 1934 by the American Historical Association.

The Farewell Address is often thought of as an expression of abstract ideas of policy looking toward the future, but with little reference to the events of 1796. Its fundamental ideas were, on the contrary, suggested by experience, and very recent and painful experience. To comprehend Washington's point of view and feel the weight of his advice, it is necessary to consider the historical setting, and, for that, to go back to the outbreak of a general European war in February and March 1793.

In the desperate conflict with the allied monarchies of the First Coalition the French Republic expected to find a valuable counterweight in the independent United States, separated from Great Britain by French diplomacy and arms in the previous war. Thoroughly conscious of the naval impotence of the new American nation, France had preferred not to invoke the *casus fœderis* of the treaty of alliance of 1778—the defense of the French West India Islands. A neutral United States promised greater advantages: (1) as a possible transatlantic base of operations against enemy colonies and commerce, (2) as the largest remaining neutral supply of provisions and naval stores, commodities that perhaps might be passed through the British navy under cover of the neutral flag. To finance both of these objects there was the gradually maturing American debt.

President Washington's proclamation of neutrality and the refusal of his government to lend itself to Genêt's projects soon showed France that her ally did not intend to involve itself in the European war by becoming such a base of belligerent naval and military operations. France perforce acquiesced in that decision, being still unwilling to invoke the letter of the alliance. This was because the actual belligerency of the United States which had no navy was worth nothing in itself and had the really great disadvantage of making American shipping immediately liable to capture and confiscation as enemy property. The neutrality of the United States, even though it could not serve as a base for such projects as Genêt attempted, was far more serviceable than American military assistance. The principal object of France was to secure from neutral America provisions for her beleaguered homeland and colonies, imported in American ships under protection of the principles of the commercial treaty of 1778: free ships free goods; provisions and naval stores not contraband; neutral right to trade in noncontraband goods to and between unblockaded enemy ports.

This Franco-American treaty did not bind France's enemy, Great Britain, the principal maritime belligerent. The British had never admitted these "novel" principles. They considered them as exceptional articles in particular treaties binding only between the signatory parties. When hostilities commenced in 1793 Great Britain began seizing enemy property right and left wherever it could be found outside neutral territorial waters, whether in enemy or neutral bottoms. British prize courts under Orders-in-Council began to apply the Rule of 1756, itself an innovation as late as the Seven Years' War. Secretary of State Thomas Jefferson protested in the name of the United States against this practice, which was contrary to the articles written into the Franco-American treaty and all the other European treaties of the United States. But Great Britain was not bound by those treaties.[1] The United States was powerless to challenge the British navy. American credit, newly established, depended primarily on tariff revenue, and tariff revenue depended principally on imports from Great Britain. The collapse of credit at this time would have meant the collapse of the newly established nationality of the United States. Rather than go to war with

---

[1] Great Britain had accepted these principles in the treaty of commerce of 1786 with France, but of course that treaty had ceased to exist with the outbreak of war.

Great Britain, President Washington took Alexander Hamilton's advice and ratified Jay's Treaty with England which acquiesced in British naval practice for the next twelve years, in effect for the duration of the war.[2] That treaty did not violate the treaties of the United States with France. It recognized a condition which already existed, namely, that the United States could not compel Great Britain to observe the terms of the Franco-American treaty. In 1793 the other maritime powers, which in the War for American Independence had followed principles similar to those of the Franco-American treaty, made treaties with Great Britain agreeing to harass the commerce of France in every possible way. These powers included the old Armed Neutrals of 1780, except Sweden and Denmark. A group of ardent, hateful enemies ringed France about by land and sea to close her frontiers, to sweep her commerce from the seas, to take her colonies from her, and to deprive her of naval supplies and of foodstuffs. The neutral United States, the ally of yesteryear, which France herself had brought into the world, stood aloof and acquiesced in this British naval-diplomatic system of strangulation. Thus were frustrated the advantages of neutral carriage which France had relied on from the American treaty of amity and commerce of 1778.

This situation was aggravated in the eyes of French statesmen by Jay's Treaty. If in the face of that document and of British practice the French were still to adhere to the terms of the American treaty, they would have to stand quietly by and watch British cruisers take French property from neutral American ships, confiscate American-owned naval stores as contraband when en route in American vessels to France, and pre-empt (as was the British practice) foodstuffs under similar conditions. Deprived thus by belligerent action of naval stores, foodstuffs, and of the advantages of neutral carriage they would find themselves obliged to abstain from following the British practice; they would have to watch these same goods go unchallenged by French warships into British harbors to feed and strengthen the might of the enemy.

It is not difficult to understand that this seemed unfair to France, and that Jay's Treaty seemed an outrageous, even a treacherous, document, made by an ungrateful nation. But one would be more ready to sympathize with France if her own hands were clean. We must remember that when John Jay signed his famous treaty with Lord Grenville on November 19, 1794, France herself was pursuing and had been pursuing, off and on, since May 9, 1793, a maritime policy of retaliation in practice identical with that of Great Britain in the treatment of neutral shipping, and had been applying it to American ships and cargoes,[3] and that notwithstanding her

[2] I have dwelt in detail upon the significance of this in my *Jay's Treaty* (New York, 1923; rev. ed. New Haven, 1962).

[3] The various French laws and decrees affecting neutral commerce were:

May 9, 1793. Law of the National Convention decreeing orders to naval officers and commanders of privateers to bring in "neutral ships laden in whole or in part either with foodstuffs belonging to neutrals and destined to enemy ports, or with goods belonging to the enemy," the former to be purchased at the price they would have commanded at the port of their intended destination, the latter to be confiscated, and an allowance to be fixed by the prize court for freight and detention.

This act was professedly in retaliation for specified British spoliations on neutral ships, and was retroactive to all prizes brought in since the beginning of the war [which implies that some had been brought in before the occasion for "retaliation"]. Compare it with similar provisions of Article I of the British Order-in-Council of June 8, 1793. The law of May 9 was to cease to have effect when the enemy powers should declare free and nonseizable foodstuffs which were neutral property

obligations under her treaty with the United States. As in later European wars (1803–12, and 1914–17) the force of these belligerent retaliations fell heavily on the neutral United States and developed grave diplomatic problems. Unlike the later wars, in this case the United States was protected by the paper and ink of a treaty against such practice on the part of one belligerent. Nevertheless, French spoliations on American shipping rivaled those of Great Britain. French privateers and naval vessels also vied with the British in violence and outrages against neutral crews and passengers.[4]

The French diplomatic commission, headed by Joseph Fauchet, which in 1794 had succeeded the ruined Genêt in Philadelphia, did not even pretend to reconcile French maritime policy with the obligations of the treaty of commerce of 1778. Nevertheless it claimed for France all the articles of the treaty which were of advantage to her, and requested benevolent interpretations of them. The Committee of Public Safety, in drawing up instructions for these commissioners, anticipated that there would be objections in the United States to the retaliatory French decrees. Admitting deviations from the treaty it became the task of the commissioners to extenuate French policy on the ground of altered circumstances.[5]

---

and destined to the ports of the French Republic, as well as merchandise belonging to the French government or French citizens on board neutral ships. *Lois et actes du gouvernement* (Paris, Imprimerie Royale, 1834), 7, 51–52; the laws and decrees referred to here may also be found in J. B. Duvergier's convenient *Collection complète des lois, décrets, ordonnances, règlements, avis du conseil d'état, 1788–1830* (30 vols. 2d ed. Paris, 1834–38), under each date. A.S.P., F.R., 1, 377.

May 23, 1793. Law of the National Convention exempting American ships from the operation of the law of May 9, 1793, "conformably to Article XVI [sic] of the treaty of February 6, 1778." [Article XVI deals with the irrelevant matter of restoration of captures made by pirates. Presumably Article XXIII was meant.] *Lois et actes*, 8, 82; A.S.P., F.R., 1, 365.

May 28, 1793. Law of the National Convention repealing the law of May 23, 1793, which exempted American ships. *Lois et actes*, 7, 82–83.

July 1, 1793. Law restoring the exemption of American ships, in phraseology identical with that of May 23, 1793. Ibid., 7, 174.

July 27, 1793. Law decreeing the full execution of the law of May 9, 1793, relative to neutral ships loaded with foodstuffs owned by neutrals or with enemy property. Ibid., 7, 241–42.

March 24, 1794 (4 germinal an II). Law decreeing: "The treaties of navigation and of commerce existing between France and nations with whom she is at peace shall be executed according to their form and tenure." Ibid., 8, 414–15.

Nov. 18, 1794. Decree of the Committee of Public Safety enjoining French naval officers and commanders of privateers to enforce the law of nations and the stipulations of treaties, "conformably to the terms of the decree of the National Convention of July 27, 1793." A.S.P., F.R., 1, 689, 752. This decree does not appear in the *Recueil des actes du Comité de salut public*, edited by Alphonse A. Aulard. Jay's Treaty was signed on Nov. 19, 1794.

[4] In addition to an undetermined number of captures at sea, Fulwar Skipwith, American claims agent at Paris in October 1794, stated that there were nearly 300 vessels in the ports of France suffering from embargoes (a later list showed that the Bordeaux embargo accounted for 103 cases), spoliations, delays, breaches of contract, nonpayment of purchased cargoes, etc. The United States Court of Claims, which completed adjudication of the French Spoliation Claims for 1793–1800 (responsibility having been assumed by the convention with France of 1800) awarded a total of $7,149,306.10 for 1,853 authentic cases of spoliation. Each case did not, however, represent a particular ship. Congress has appropriated to date only $3,910,860.61, to pay part of these claims. To this may be added $5,000,000 for claims of a special character, assumed by the United States in 1803, in part payment for Louisiana—to wit: embargoes, detention and appropriation of goods in French harbors, money due from the French government for purchases, etc.

[5] *Correspondence of the French Ministers to the United States, 1791–1797*, Frederick J. Turner, ed., A.H.A., *Annual Report*, 1903, 2, 291.

Washington and his advisers had foreseen the possible further effect on France of the intended treaty between the United States and Great Britain when John Jay, the Federalist, pro-British diplomatist, departed on his famous mission to London. To mask this mission they sent to France the pro-French Republican senator from Virginia, James Monroe, an old opponent of Jay's diplomacy since 1786, who considered Jay's mission as mischievous and in the Senate voted against his confirmation. Monroe never saw Jay's instructions, possibly was not aware of their real scope.

Like an apostle of the rights of man, Monroe set to work to persuade the French government to observe the treaty of amity and commerce of 1778. The restrictions on private trade in French harbors, the embargoes, the delays in payment for purchased cargoes, had already so jeopardized the American provision supply that the Convention admitted the force of the American remonstrances on every point except free ships free goods.[6] The envoy now argued for the full and entire enforcement of the articles of the treaty. He appealed to old friendship and present interest. He contended that it would be good policy for France to repeal her obnoxious decrees before Great Britain should repeal hers. If she did so, it would combine all America in condemnation of the conduct of the British; if she did not, any later repeal would appear merely to be forced by her enemy. At just this time news arrived[7] of the setting aside, by an Order-in-Council of August 6, 1794, of the British provision order of June 8, 1793—this had been a means in London of easing the English negotiations with Jay. It re-enforced Monroe's argument in Paris. The French law of May 9, 1793, had made the duration of the "retaliatory" maritime measures contingent upon the repeal by the enemy of his illegal procedure. The Convention now (January 2, 1795) availed itself of this provision to yield to the importunities of the ingratiating James Monroe. "As a grand act of honesty and justice," it wiped out at one stroke all the offensive decrees and enjoined the strict observance of the provisions of the treaty of 1778.[8] Orders were immediately given for the adjudication of all claims arising out of violations of that treaty.

Monroe's triumph was short-lived. Before anything very effective could actually be done about the relief of the claimants the significance of Jay's Treaty[9] began to be suspected in Paris. In August 1795, the text arrived from Philadelphia. It completely undid Monroe's successes. In 1796 Washington recalled the unhappy minister for not having defended with sufficient vigor the new English treaty.[10] In truth Monroe had

---

[6] A.S.P., F.R., 1, 677.

[7] See report of Merlin de Douai, brumaire, an III, Arch. Aff. Etrang., Correspondance politique, États Unis, vol. 42, ff. 186–204.

[8] Law of 13 nivôse, an III, *Bulletin des lois de la République française*, 1ᵉ sér., 3 no. 107; decree of the Committee of Public Safety, 14 nivôse, an III (Jan. 3, 1795), A.S.P., F.R., 1, 642 [in English translation; not in Aulard].

[9] *Before* the repeal of the retaliatory decrees the committee had asked Monroe about the treaty; and he had conveyed to them information from Jay, to the effect that it contained nothing contrary to the existing treaties of the United States; and had promised that as soon as he might be informed of its contents he would inform the committee. This promise impelled Monroe to refuse to accept from Jay a *confidential* statement of the contents of the treaty. Monroe's *A View of the Conduct of the Executive in the Foreign Affairs of the United States, Connected with the Mission to the French Republic, during the Years 1794, 5, and 6* (Philadelphia, 1797), pp. xvii–xxvii.

[10] Monroe's instructions and dispatches are printed in A.S.P., F.R., 1, and in his exculpatory *View*. Washington's studied comments on the *View*, written at Mount Vernon on the margin of its pages, are printed in appendix II to Daniel C. Gilman's *James Monroe* (Boston, 1883,

repeated to the French government the arguments and defenses sent to him by Secretaries of State Randolph and Pickering. They read well, but one may doubt that his heart was in his words. He thought Jay's Treaty a shameful document.[11] There is evidence suggesting that he had confidential conversations with the French Revolutionary leaders about "the real dispositions of his countrymen," conversations which he did not reveal to his own government.[12] He kept up an intimate correspondence with Madison,[13] and other friends of Jefferson, who opposed Jay's Treaty and favored a pro-French policy. He certainly led the French government to believe that any treaty of amity between the United States and Great Britain would never be ratified.[14] When it was known that a treaty had been signed, Monroe repeated this assurance.[15] When Jay's Treaty went through Congress he tried rather lamely to explain its success, and still argued that it would be good policy for the French Republic to observe loyally the terms of its American treaties; the example of that loyalty and the contrasting attitude of the British government would win the good will of the American *people*, from whose eyes the scales of British deception must eventually fall.[16] He led them in Paris to believe that the people would overthrow the administration of President Washington as a result of the treaty, that better things might be expected after the election of 1796.[17] This supposition was re-enforced by advice from the French diplomatic representative in the United States, Fauchet, and his successor Adet, and by Americans in Paris like Monroe's friend, Tom Paine.

After Jay's departure from York Fauchet had become increasingly nervous about the object of the new mission. He sent one of his colleagues to Paris to warn the Com-

---

1898). Beverley W. Bond, Jr.'s "The Monroe Mission to France, 1794–1796," in The Johns Hopkins University *Studies in Historical and Political Science*, 25 (1907), 9–103, did not have available the valuable sources in the French Ministry of Foreign Affairs. The various deliberations of committees on Monroe's notes, and relevant reports, quite voluminous, are in Arch. Aff. Etrang., États Unis, vol. 42, particularly ff. 17, 141, 186–204.

[11] Monroe to Joseph Jones, Sept. 15, 1795. Calendar, in Division of MSS of the Library of Congress, of the Gouverneur Collection of Monroe Papers, now privately owned. Gilman, p. 62, printed a portion of this letter.

[12] Monroe wrote to the Committee of Public Safety a "non-official letter," Dec. 27, 1794, asking that a member of the committee be deputed to have frank conversations with him concerning any propositions about to be made to the American government "on this subject [i.e., possible propositions] or any other (if you desire) tending to acquaint you [the committees with the situation and the *real* dispositions of my *countrymen* [italics inserted]. Arch. Aff. Etrang., États Unis, vol. 42, f. 445.

[13] Stanislaus Murray Hamilton, ed., *Writings of James Monroe* (7 vols., New York, 1898–1903), 2, passim.

[14] Adet to the Committee of Public Safety, 14 thermidor, an III (Aug. 1, 1795), *Corr. Fr. Min.*, p. 762.

[15] "I assured them, generally, as I had done before, that I was satisfied the treaty contained in it nothing which could give them uneasiness; but if it did, and especially if it weakened our connexion with France, it would certainly be disapproved in America." Monroe to the Secretary of State, Apr. 14, 1795, *A.S.P., F.R., 1*, 702. He did convey to the Committee on Public Safety Jay's only statement to him about the treaty, that it contained nothing contrary to the treaty stipulations of the United States with other countries.

[16] "Exposé sommaire," etc., dated 1796, in the Monroe Collection of MSS, Library of Congress. Internal evidence proves Monroe to be the writer, and one presumes from the same evidence that it was directed to the French government, although I have not found it in the French archives.

[17] Monroe to the Minister of Foreign Affairs, Paris, Feb. 17, 1796 (28 pluviôse, an IV), Arch. Aff. Etrang., États Unis, vol. 45, f. 146.

mittee of Public Safety that something was in the air, and to say that the other two members of the commission, La Forest and Petry, could not be trusted because they hobnobbed with Alexander Hamilton and other Federalists.[18] When news of the signature of- the treaty and rumors of its contents began to leak out, the French minister became very much exasperated. His notes of protest against fancied violations of neutral obligations under the treaty of 1778 took on a more rasping tone, full of intimations of American disloyalty. Fauchet tried by fair means and foul, but in vain, to block the ratification of the treaty by the Senate. He hoped with Secretary Randolph that the President might not sign the ratification, even though the Senate had so advised and consented. His successor Adet, encouraged by the widespread popular protests, labored with the House of Representatives to refuse the appropriations necessary to carry it into effect. When the treaty passed unscathed through the House, Adet's last hope was that the people would overthrow the administration of President Washington in the forthcoming election of 1796.[19] Through the agency of organs of the Republican press which he manipulated and inspired to the extent of his limited financial resources, and by means of the democratic societies which had arisen at the wave of Genêt's wand to applaud the French Revolution, the French minister was working with might and main to that end.[20] He did not know, of course, of the President's determination, long since fixed and presently to be announced, to refuse a third term.

In Paris, American affairs had received less attention than they merited. Before the reorganization of the French government under the constitution of the Year III (1795) the rapidly changing administration of the Foreign Office failed to give methodical attention. French diplomatists at Philadelphia complained bitterly that their dispatches went unanswered. For months they waited without instructions. None of them had been told what to do about Jay's Treaty. Fauchet, and his successor Adet, had acted on their own responsibility in their protests against that instrument. The new Directory put the conduct of foreign affairs on a more businesslike basis, under a single minister, Charles Delacroix. He straightway brought in a report concerning the United States. Washington must go, he said. "A friend of France must succeed him in that eminent office." He continued:

> We must raise up the people and at the same time conceal the lever by which we do so . . . I propose to the Executive Directory to authorize me to send orders and instructions to our minister plenipotentiary at Philadelphia to use all the means in his power in the United States to bring about the right kind of revolution (l'heureuse Révolution) and Washington's replacement, which, assuring to the

[18] *Corr. Fr. Min.*, pp. 373, 389, 410, 419; Arch. Aff. Etrang., États Unis, vol. 41, ff. 291, 377, 408.

[19] *Corr. Fr. Min.*, p. 894. Neither Fauchet and the commissioners, nor their successor Adet, had any actual instructions concerning Jay's Treaty. Once they left Paris, they received scant attention from the Committee of Public Safety.

[20] Bernard Faÿ, *L'Esprit révolutionnaire en France et aux États-Unis à la fin du XVIIIᵉ siècle* (Paris, 1925), pp. 254–60. "All these intrigues are sad and displeasing to study when one remembers the sincere enthusiasm which the masses of the American people then testified for France." *Ibid.*, p. 255. John Bach McMaster, *History of the People of the United States* (New York, 1883–1913), 2, ch. 9, is in effect a digest of opposing press and pamphlet comment. The arguments of the Republican press against Jay's Treaty, against Washington, against the Farewell Address, and finally against the candidacy of John Adams, reflect the paragraphs of the political correspondence of the French Foreign Office with its American legation.

Americans their independence, will break off treaties [sic] made with England and maintain those which unite them to the French Republic.

As in the case of the Netherlands at that time, France and French agents regarded that political party in the United States which was most useful to their purposes as the "patriot" party. Jefferson, Madison, Monroe, Robert R. Livingston, Senator Tazewell of Virginia, Governor Clinton of New York, and Governor Mifflin of Pennsylvania were patriots. Washington, Hamilton, Jay, Rufus King, and John Adams were aristocrats unfriendly to real liberty. The French Foreign Office looked on the United States as "the Holland of the New World." It hoped for and expected a popular revolution there, on French models, such as did take place in Holland in 1795, to overturn the existing régime of ordered liberty, to cast off the formidable ascendency of President Washington and his Federalist advisers who themselves were esteemed to be beyond the reach of French influence and purpose.[21]

At first the Directory decided on a more positive step to offset Jay's Treaty: to send a special envoy extraordinary to Philadelphia to recall Adet and to announce the end of the Franco-American treaties and then himself to withdraw.[22] Monroe confidentially urged Delacroix against such action: it would please the enemies of both countries. "Left to ourselves," he hinted, "everything will I think be satisfactorily arranged and *perhaps in the course of the present year*: and it is always more grateful to make such arrangements ourselves than to be pressed to it."[23]

Delacroix[24] and the Directory took the advice of President Washington's minister to await the President's overthrow. They blamed Washington, Hamilton, and the Federalist Senate, in short the elected government of the people of the United States, against which, according to French agents and correspondents (including Americans in Paris), the people were now in an uproar, from Boston to Savannah. Well they knew that Monroe's hint referred to the approaching presidential election of 1796.[25] They decided to temporize, to protest, to argue (Monroe had advised them not to abandon their claims for redress), pending the new presidential election, to work up "patriot" sentiment against Washington's administration. To this effect they approved instructions to a new minister.[26] Later came news of the success of Jay's Treaty

[21] To this point there is a remarkable analysis of American politics in relation to French policy, by the undersecretary of the sixth division of the Foreign Office: Memoir on the United States, Florida, and Louisiana, 12 frimaire, an IV (Dec. 3, 1795), Arch. Aff. Etrang., États Unis, vol. 44, ff. 407–17.

[22] Report of the Minister of Foreign Affairs to the Executive Directory, 27 nivôse, an IV (Jan. 17, 1796), ibid., vol. 45, ff. 41–53.

[23] Monroe to the Minister of Foreign Affairs, Paris, Feb. 17, 1796 (28 pluviôse, an IV), ibid., vol. 45, f. 147 [italics inserted]. This highly significant note was not revealed to his own government and is enough to justify Washington's removal of Monroe. Monroe summarized the arguments he had made to Delacroix in a letter to the Secretary of State of Feb. 20, 1796, but made no reference to any written note of his and said nothing about the hint he had given.

[24] Delacroix to Monroe, Paris, 1 ventôse, an IV (Feb. 20, 1796), ibid., vol. 45, f. 160.

[25] Observations on Mr. Monroe's letter to the Minister of Foreign Affairs, not dated, ibid., vol. 45, f. 148.

[26] "Memoir of Political Instructions to the Citizen Vincent, to be sent as Minister Plenipotentiary of the Republic to the United States." *Recueil des actes du Directoire exécutif*, A. Debidour, ed. (Paris, 1910), 1, 748; 2, 621. Some charges against Vincent's integrity apparently stopped his departure. Later Monroe's protest against the appointment of Mangourit, the former French consul at Charleston during Genêt's obnoxious operations, was effective.

in the House of Representatives. They then decided not to send any new minister after all, but to keep Adet in Philadelphia for a short while at least, and to follow his advice and that of the returned Fauchet to hearten the pro-French "patriots" in America by an unmistakable denunciation of the policy of the executive of the United States, lest by French silence the election should go in Washington's favor.

The inveterate tendency of French policy to stir up the American people against their government had gradually steeled the sympathies of President Washington against the old ally. Though Washington could not know the inner counsels of the French Directory—least of all when he had a minister like Monroe in Paris—the policy of France had been made abundantly apparent by the French diplomatists in Philadelphia. Since Genêt's time they had been openly or covertly attempting to join forces with the anti-Federalist opposition. They had been able to promise themselves much from such strategy because of radical political affinities and because of the memory of French help in the American Revolution. But the French alliance, indispensable as it was to American independence, had always been a great embarrassment to American diplomatists. It was so even during the diplomacy of the Revolution itself, when Vergennes had wavered under the threats of a separate Spanish peace (though his wavering has become known only to scholars in our own day). It was so during the peace negotiations of 1782 in Paris. Experience with it showed the Fathers the danger to independence and sovereignty of any other alliance. Toward the close of the war Congress shrank from committing itself to the Dutch proposal to join the Armed Neutrality. In 1786 John Jay's initialed alliance with Spain (never revealed fully until the twentieth century) collapsed before the opposition of the Southern states who feared for the Mississippi. Soon after, the South united with New England (anxious about its fisheries)[27] and wrote into the Constitution that potent provision that no future treaty could be ratified except by the vote of two-thirds of the senators present in the upper chamber of the national legislature, that Senate in which there must always be exactly two senators from each state. To a certain degree this fixed a constitutional obstacle against European entanglements. More than one delegate supported it for that reason.[28]

The French alliance had become increasingly embarrassing after the French declaration of war on England, February 1, 1793. The proclamation of neutrality was a tangible expression of a sane American policy not of isolation but of diplomatic independence. Washington refused all new foreign alliances. As Hamilton so indiscreetly told the British minister, Hammond, in 1794, he rejected the Swedish invitation to join the second, abortive, Armed Neutrality of 1794. He also turned down Godoy's famous "propositions for the President," of that same year, for a Spanish alliance, as Pinckney too later repelled them in Madrid. In short, the very life-saving French alliance had long since cured the United States of any hankering for more allies.

The first twenty years of American independence had in fact made American statesmen shy of Europe, and they have remained so ever since. Their writings (with the possible exception of James Monroe, whose name after 1823 was to become so inseparably associated with abstention from European politics and wars!) are full of

[27] R. Earl McClendon published a useful note on the "Origin of the Two-Thirds Rule in Senate Action upon Treaties," *A.H.R.*, 36 (1931), 768–72.

[28] J. Fred Rippy and Angie Debo, "The Historical Background of the American Policy of Isolation," *Smith College Studies in History*, 9 (Apr.–July 1924), 140.

affirmations that it was the true policy of the United States to steer clear of European politics.[29]

Tom Paine had been the first to express this, in 1776: " 'Tis the true interest of America, to steer clear of European contentions, which she never can do, while by her dependance on Britain, she is made the makeweight in the scale of British politics."[30] "I do not love to be entangled in the politics of Europe," wrote John Adams in 1777.[31] In the Virginia ratifying convention in 1788, Madison, speaking for the adoption of the new Federal Constitution asked: "What is the situation of America?" and answered, "She is remote from Europe, and ought not to engage in her politics or wars."[32] Jefferson in France had written in 1787: "I know too that it is a maxim with us, and I think it a wise one, not to entangle ourselves with the affairs of Europe."[33] Again, in 1790: "At such a distance from Europe, and with such an ocean between us, we hope to meddle little in its quarrels or combinations. Its peace and its commerce are what we shall court. . . ."[34] Hamilton repeatedly had used words almost identical with essential portions of the text of Washington's Farewell Address of 1796.[35] So had the President, particularly in 1795.[36]

If George Washington had retired from the Presidency in the spring of 1793,[37] as he originally intended when he first consulted James Madison about the draft of a valedictory we may presume that he would never have said anything about foreign affairs. There would have been no Farewell Address of the kind that has become so familiar to us—though we cannot say that the policy itself would not soon have been formulated. Certainly Washington's suggestions, and Madison's draft, for a possible valedictory in 1792, did not touch foreign affairs. In the summer of 1796, however, foreign affairs were uppermost in the mind of the Father of His Country. Then unalterably resolved not to serve another term, he prepared to indite a final message to the American people at large.

[29] Rippy and Debo have collected numerous expressions of abstention from European politics.

[30] *Common Sense* (1st ed. Philadelphia, 1776), p. 38.

[31] Rippy and Debo, p. 90.

[32] *The Writings of James Madison*, Gaillard Hunt, ed. (New York, 1900–10), 5, 151.

[33] *Writings of Thomas Jefferson* (Ford ed.), 4, 483.

[34] To Monsieur de Pinto, New York, Aug. 7, 1790. *The Writings of Thomas Jefferson*, Memorial ed. (Washington, 1903–04), 8, 74.

[35] Over the signature of *Horatius*, arguing for the ratification of Jay's Treaty, Hamilton wrote in 1795: "If you consult your true interest your motto cannot fail to be: 'PEACE AND TRADE WITH ALL NATIONS; beyond our present engagements, POLITICAL CONNECTION WITH NONE.' You ought to spurn from you as the box of Pandora, the fatal heresy of a close alliance, or in the language of *Genet*, a true *family compact*, with France. This would at once make you a mere satellite of France, and entangle you in all the contests, broils, and wars of Europe." The text continues: " 'Tis evident that the controversies of Europe must often grow out of causes and interests foreign to this country. Why then should we, by a close political connection with any power of Europe, expose our peace and interest, as a matter of course, to all the shocks with which their mad rivalship and wicked ambition so frequently convulse the earth? 'T were insanity to embrace such a system." *The Works of Alexander Hamilton*, Henry Cabot Lodge, ed. (New York, 1885–86). 4, 366–67.

[36] To Patrick Henry, Oct. 9, 1795; to Gouverneur Morris, Dec. 22, 1795; *Writings of George Washington* (Ford ed.), 13, 119, 151. Washington refused to lend his official intercession to assist the release from Austrian and Prussian prisons of his dearest friend, Lafayette, for fear of involving the United States in Europe's wars. See Chap. 9 of this volume, pp. 209–39.

[37] I have profited from discussions of President Washington's policies with Frank Louraine of Washington, D.C., particularly on the significance of the Farewell Address in 1796, instead of 1792.

It was to remove foreign interference in our domestic affairs, to preserve the nation and the people from Europe's distresses, that the retiring first President, with a particular eye to relations with France, marked out for his now private adviser, Alexander Hamilton, the subjects which he would like to include in his final address. In characteristically familiar and felicitous phrases—many of which we may find already expressed in *The Federalist* and other products of his pen—Hamilton wrote out the President's ideas.[38] Of Washington were the trunk and branches of the sturdy tree. The shimmering foliage dancing and shining in the sunlight was Hamilton's. The President edited several drafts before the address was finished. He cast out at least one extraneous thought which Hamilton tried gratuitously to slip in. Despite Hamilton's principal part in the phrasing of the document, and his previous expression of some of the ideas, we may be sure that in the final text the two men were thinking together in absolute unison. The Address was as directly pointed to the diplomatic problems of the time of the French Revolution as were Woodrow Wilson's Fourteen Points to the intricate diplomacy of the World War. President Wilson and Colonel House worked no more intimately together on that document in 1918, drafting and redrafting its clauses, than did President Washington and Colonel Hamilton in 1796, composing and recomposing the paragraphs of the Farewell Address.

The immortal document, ever since a polestar of American foreign policy, represented the crystallization of the experience of remarkably clearheaded men with foreign affairs since the Declaration of Independence. It was given forthwith to the public in a newspaper.[39] It spoke directly to the great and simple audience of the American people. "The name of AMERICAN," it said to them, putting the word into bold type, "which belongs to you in your national capacity, must always exalt the just pride of Patriotism, more than any appelation derived from local discriminations."

We must keep in mind the involvement of the French alliance in American diplomacy and domestic politics as we read the Farewell Address, even as the authors of the document had that constantly before them.

It began thus with an appeal to support the *National Union*. The orthodox phrase Federal Union does not occur in the document, a very significant omission. It continued with a counsel against the practice of party politics, lest the new nation be undermined by internal dissension assisted by foreign intrigue. The first President and his adviser Alexander Hamilton believed that, with the system of checks and balances in the new government, party politics was unnecessary for the preservation of ordered liberty. The rise of an opposition they identified with a faction opposed not only to the policies of the administration but to the new national government itself. They connected this faction with the French government and its agents.

Turning to the subject of foreign affairs, the Address admonished his fellow citizens to steer clear of European alliances and wars. It justified American neutrality whilst the nation, assisted by the advantages of so peculiar a situation, might grow strong enough to command its own fortune. In these words and these counsels the authors of the Address had continually before them the apparition of the life-giving,

---

[38] Horace Binney in one of the first critical essays in American historiography analyzed the authorship of the document. *An Inquiry into the Formation of Washington's Farewell Address* (Philadelphia, 1859).

[39] *Claypoole's American Daily Advertiser* (Philadelphia), Sept. 19, 1796.

but the entangling French alliance, and the distant scene of the great wars engulfing Europe. They had behind them the problems solved by Jay's Treaty and by Pinckney's Treaty, thanks to the occupation of Britain and Spain with those troubles in Europe.

The immediate purpose of the Address was to strike a powerful blow against French intermeddling in American affairs.[40] After the victory of Jay's Treaty in the House of Representatives it had been Adet's advice, and this was also recommended by the returned Fauchet,[41] that some strong and positive action ought to be taken to make the American ally more amenable to French interests. The people, both of those agents had reported—and reported most voluminously—were in favor of France and opposed to their government, but if France did not call Washington's government to terms, and thus support the action of the "good" people to overthrow it, nothing could be hoped from them. Adet advocated[42] that the French Republic proceed to treat American ships precisely as the United States government allowed its flag to be treated by Great Britain, that is, according to the principles of Jay's Treaty. This was, indeed, what France had been doing up to January 3, 1795, when Monroe secured from the Convention the full and entire recognition of the treaty of 1778. But that "grand act of honesty and justice" had not been enforced since the nature of Jay's Treaty had become suspected in France. Nor was it ever to be. It was to be the United States government itself which was finally to pay—throughout a century of litigation—most of the damages to its citizens wrought by the French spoliations in this war.

Jay's Treaty at last having gone into effect, the French Directory prepared its denunciation of the treachery of Washington's government. As a warning to the American people of worse things to follow if President Washington were continued in office it decided to suspend Adet's functions, and with them formal diplomatic relations with the United States. Characterizing Jay's Treaty as equivalent to an alliance between France's principal enemy and her old, ungrateful ally, it proceeded to invoke against American shipping, as a reprisal for that perfidious treaty, the maritime principles of that document itself.[43] If Jefferson should be elected the plan was to restore relations on the old basis, hoping that a new treaty with France might undo Jay's.[44]

To his great satisfaction Adet was able to communicate to the United States government, on October 27, 1796, the text of a decree of the Directory announcing that "All neutral or allied Powers shall, without delay, be notified that the flag of the

---

[40] Enclosing the document, Adet reported: "It would be useless to speak to you about it. You will have noticed the lies it contains, the insolent tone that governs it, the immorality which characterizes it. You will have no difficulty in recognizing the author of a piece extolling ingratitude, showing it as a virtue necessary to the happiness of States, presenting interest as the only counsel which governments ought to follow in the course of their negotiations, putting aside honor and glory. You will have recognized immediately the doctrine of the former Secretary of the Treasury, Hamilton, and the principles of loyalty that have always directed the Philadelphia Government." *Corr. Fr. Min.*, p. 954.

[41] See Fauchet's long Memoir on the United States of America, 24 frimaire, an IV (Dec. 15, 1795), Arch. Aff. Etrang., États Unis, vol. 44, ff. 457–529.

[42] *Corr. Fr. Min.*, pp. 900–06.

[43] The Minister of Foreign Affairs to Adet, 7 fructidor, an IV (Aug. 24, 1796), Arch. Aff. Etrang., États Unis, vol. 46, ff. 144–45. See also drafts and reports associated with these instructions, ibid., ff. 133–40.

[44] Same to same, 12 brumaire, an V (Nov. 2, 1796), ibid., ff. 355–58.

French republic will treat neutral vessels, either as to confiscation, as to searches, or capture, in the same manner as they shall suffer the English to treat them."[45]

A few weeks later (November 15) he announced the definite suspension of his functions, not, indeed, to indicate a formal rupture between the United States and France, "but as a mark of just discontent, which is to last until the government of the United States returns to sentiments, and to measures, more conformable to the interests of the alliance, and the sworn friendship of the two nations."

It was now the eve of the presidential election of 1796. The several states were choosing their electors. They still had to meet and cast their votes. The precedent had not yet become set which allows the electors no canvas or deliberation among themselves. The French move was studiously calculated to influence the electors to choose Jefferson instead of John Adams.[46] With this in mind, according to his instructions, Adet accompanied his announcement of suspension of his functions with a long and *ex parte* review (with documents) of the whole quarrel between France and the United States over American neutrality. He included a passionate indictment of Jay's Treaty, all under cover of a fervid manifesto to the American people. A summary in English of the contents of this note appeared in the newspapers before the translation of the French original could be prepared in the Department of State. "Let your Government return to itself," wrote Adet, addressing the people rather than the government to which his note was delivered, "and you will still find in Frenchmen faithful friends and generous allies."[47]

To that uncompromising Federalist, Timothy Pickering, old soldier, negotiator of Indian treaties, professional and capable officeholder, and general utility man in Washington's Cabinet, now fell the task of defending the foreign policy laid down in the Farewell Address. Four others had declined the proffered appointment of Secretary of State, with its meager emolument, before he took it. Though Pickering had no special training for the office, he was a facile penman and a sharpminded debater. These were the qualifications principally in demand from 1795 to 1800.

Space only forbids us to describe and to analyze Pickering's defense of American neutrality, of Jay's Treaty with England, in short of the foreign policy of George Washington. We may be sure that it was inspired by Alexander Hamilton,[48] the man who inspired Jay's Treaty, and who phrased the Farewell Address. The remarkable public disputation took the form of instruction to Charles C. Pinckney, dated January 16, 1797, who had already sailed to France as successor to the recalled Monroe; but its real purpose, as shown by its immediate release to the press on January 19, 1797,[49] was to serve as a counter-manifesto to Adet's passionate attacks on the administration and his undercover efforts to secure the election of Thomas Jefferson rather than John Adams, the champion of Washington's policies. The historian today who is privileged to read the archives of France and of the United States

[45] Translation of an extract from the resolves of the Directory, of the 14th messidor, an IV (July 2, 1796). *A.S.P., F.R., 1,* 577. This extract is not printed in the proceedings for that date of the *Actes du Directoire exécutif.*

[46] *Corr. Fr. Min.,* p. 972.

[47] *A.S.P., F.R., 1,* 583.

[48] See Hamilton to Wolcott, Nov. 22, 1796, George Gibbs, *Memoirs of the Administrations of Washington and John Adams, edited from the papers of Oliver Wolcott* (New York, 1846), *1,* 398.

[49] It was transmitted to Congress on Jan. 19, 1797, and immediately ordered to be printed. It appeared in the *Aurora* in installments between Jan. 24 and Feb. 3, 1797.

can have no serious quarrel with Pickering's eloquent rebuttal of French charges of American ingratitude directed against Washington's government, or with his blunt conclusion after a long review that France owed fully as much to the United States as the United States to France in the way of service rendered. The day for finesse had passed. It was time that someone put the truth in this way to the American people, at a moment when foreign diplomacy was again trying to reach over the heads of their government to whip them into European complications. Even then in 1795 and 1796 while French diplomatists were accusing the United States of ingratitude and treachery, they themselves were plotting to re-establish control and tutelage over the American republic by getting Louisiana and West Florida back from Spain, allying France with the southwestern Indians, and tempting the allegiance to the Union of the new western states, to build up thereby a new colonial empire that would be the preponderant power in the New World.[50]

The instructions to C. C. Pinckney,[51] embodying these arguments, rank with Jefferson's rejoinder to Hammond of 1792, with John Quincy Adams's defense of General Jackson's execution of Arbuthnot and Ambrister in 1818, and with Lansing's reply to Austria in 1915 on the question of contraband, as one of the greatest defensive documents in the diplomatic history of the United States. Pickering's paper clinched the case for President Washington's foreign policy.

Before the document was printed the presidential electors had elected John Adams President by a majority of one vote and a margin of three votes over Thomas Jefferson, who became Vice President according to the original constitutional provision. Washington's successor fully recognized that the significance of his election lay in the question whether the American people were to govern themselves or be governed by foreign nations.[52] As President he took over Washington's policies, and, to his later vexation, his entire cabinet.

We cannot conclude that Pickering's instructions to Pinckney decided the election. It had been won already. The dispatch was published after the votes of the electors had been announced on the first Wednesday in January, but before they were formally counted on the first Wednesday in February. The document was rather an appeal to the people to support the foreign policy of Washington—and of Hamilton—and an argument to open the door to an escape from the French alliance, by proving, as Hamilton suggested, that the United States had maintained good faith with its engagements; that if the conduct of the other party released it, the release should not be refused, so far as possible without compromising peace. "This idea is very important," Hamilton wrote to Wolcott, of course for Pickering's benefit.[53]

Despite the high hopes which France had placed on Jefferson's election, both John Adams and his close contestant, the new Vice President, Thomas Jefferson, were equally good Americans (albeit of different political philosophy), and, incidentally, almost equally good friends of France. Nor were they unfriendly to each other. Jefferson had gone so far as to authorize his friend Madison to advise electors, in case

[50] Arch. Aff. Etrang., États Unis, vols. 39–42.

[51] A.S.P., F.R., 1, 559–76.

[52] In his Inaugural Address he said: "If the control of an election can be obtained by foreign nations by flattery or menaces, by fraud or violence, by terror, intrigue, or venality, the Government may not be the choice of the American people, but of foreign nations. It may be foreign nations who govern us, and not we, the people, who govern ourselves."

[53] Nov. 22, 1796, Gibbs, 1, 400.

of a tie, to vote for Adams as a statesman of senior claims to the Presidency.[54] Adet came to sense this relationship before he left. He wrote:[55]

> Mr. Jefferson likes us because he detests England; he seeks to draw near to us because he fears us less than England; but tomorrow he might change his opinion about us if England should cease to inspire his fear. Although Jefferson is the friend of liberty and of science, although he is an admirer of the efforts we have made to cast off our shackles and to clear away the cloud of ignorance which weighs down the human race, Jefferson, I say, is an American, and as such, he cannot sincerely be our friend. An American is the born enemy of all the peoples of Europe.

Such was the historical setting of the famous Farewell Address. Such were the reasons for its pronouncement in 1796, so different a pronouncement from what it would have been if given to the people in 1792. Such was its victory over foreign intrigue within our own country. It did not disown the French alliance, but it taught a patronizing ally that we were an independent and a sovereign nation, and that the French Republic could not use in America the tool that had been so successful with the border satellite states in Europe, the lever of a political opposition to overthrow any government that stood in the way of French policy, purpose, and interest. In Washington's time avoidance of foreign alliances and of foreign entanglement was a question of independence and national sovereignty. What we have generally construed as a policy of "isolation" we ought really to interpret as a policy of vigilant defense and maintenance of sovereign national independence against foreign meddling in our own intimate domestic concerns.

[54] Channing, *A History of the United States, 4,* 173.
[55] *Corr. Fr. Min.,* p. 983.

4 / 1812: Conservatives, War Hawks, and the Nation's Honor

Norman K. Risjord

American diplomatic and political historians have long been fascinated with the intriguing question of why the United States went to war against England in 1812. Until the 1920s, most historians were content to interpret the decision of President Madison and the Congress in terms of the long list of maritime grievances, including violations of American neutral rights on the high seas and the impressment of American seamen mainly at the hands of the British. Then in the 1920s, historians Louis Hacker and Julius Pratt seized on the apparent enthusiasm on the part of western frontiersmen for war and tried to explain the war hawks on the basis of traditional western land hunger, pacification of Indian tribes who had been under British control, and the alleged political alliance between westerners in the north who sought territory at the expense of England and westerners in the south who coveted lands held by England's ally, Spain. Since the early 1950s, there has been a new surge of research as many younger historians have endeavored to reassess the bases for military hostilities in 1812. With the writings of Bradford Perkins, Reginald Horsman, Roger Brown, Margaret Latimer and Norman Risjord, the relatively simplistic, uncomplicated theses of Hacker and Pratt which had seemed so plausible to the previous generation of historians could be superseded. Allowing some latitude for individual variations, the theme of most current historical interpretations explaining the War of 1812 emphasizes that American political leaders perceived but two alternatives: submission to the British commercial system or declaring war. Concern for preserving American national honor dictated the acceptance of the latter option.

For further reading: Irving Brant, *James Madison the President 1809–1812* (Indianapolis: 1956) and *James Madison Secretary of State 1800–1809* (Indianapolis: 1953); Roger Brown, *The Republic in Peril* (New York: 1964); Alfred L. Burt, *The United States, Great Britain and British North America from the Revolution to the Establishment of Peace after the War*

Norman K. Risjord is Professor of History at the University of Wisconsin, Madison. This article is reprinted by permission of the author and the editors of the *William and Mary Quarterly*. Copyright © 1961 by the *William and Mary Quarterly*.

of 1812 (New Haven: 1940); Reginald Horsman, *The Causes of the War of 1812* (Philadelphia: 1962); *Bradford Perkins, *Prologue to War* (Berkeley: 1961); Julius W. Pratt, *Expansionists of 1812* (New York: 1925); Lawrence Kaplan, "Jefferson, Napoleonic Wars and the Balance of Power," *William and Mary Quarterly*, Series 3, XIV (1957), 196–217.

The modern tendency to seek materialistic motives and economic factors in all human relations has greatly obscured one of the basic causes of the War of 1812. A generation of historians, brought up on the disillusionment that followed the failure of the attempt to "make the world safe for democracy" in 1919, has persistently searched for the hidden economic factors behind all wars. Yet a cursory glance at the statistics of American commerce in the first decade of the nineteenth century will show that the War of 1812 was the most uneconomic war the United States has ever fought. A casual search through the letters and speeches of contemporaries reveals that those who fought the war were primarily concerned with the honor and integrity of the nation.

Students of the period are familiar with the standard explanation for the war: the election of 1810, by providing 63 new faces in a House of 142, represented a popular disillusionment with the Jeffersonian system and supplied the new Twelfth Congress with a number of young war hawks, such as Henry Clay, John C. Calhoun, and Felix Grundy, who were determined to assert America's position in the world. Since the loudest demand for strong measures, as well as some of the ablest of the war hawks, came from the West, historians have been channeled into a search for reasons why the West should have demanded a war for "free trade and sailors' rights;" the historiography of the period has been almost exclusively concerned with "Western war aims." The desire for land, Canadian or Indian, fear of a British-backed Indian conspiracy, concern over the declining prices of agricultural products and the restriction of markets abroad—all at one time or another have been represented as basic causes of the war.[1]

The weakness in this interpretation is that it virtually ignores the vote on the declaration of war in June 1812. The West may have been influenced by economic as well as patriotic motives, but the West, after all, had only ten votes in the House of Representatives. The South Atlantic states from Maryland to Georgia cast thirty-nine, or nearly half, of the seventy-nine votes for war in 1812. Any explanation of the war must place primary emphasis on the Southern Congressmen, and neither feature of the standard interpretation—the concept of a "revolution" in popular sentiment in 1810 and the emphasis on economic factors—satisfactorily explains their votes for war.

[1] Warren H. Goodman, "The Origins of the War of 1812: A Survey of Changing Interpretations," *Mississippi Valley Historical Review*, XXVII (1941), 171–186, has a good discussion of the historiography of the causes of the war. The article was written before the latest interpretation in terms of neutral rights and impressments was published: Alfred L. Burt, *The United States, Great Britain, and British North America from the Revolution to the Establishment of Peace after the War of 1812* (New Haven, 1940). The most important recent contributions to the economic interpretation are Margaret Kinard Latimer, "South Carolina—A Protagonist of the War of 1812," *American Historical Review*, LXI (1955–56), 914–929, and Reginald Horsman, "Western War Aims, 1811–1812," *Indiana Magazine of History*, LII (1957), 1–16.

Most of these Southern Congressmen were "old Republicans," conservatives whose political Bible was the Republican platform of 1800 and who had sat in Congress for years. In the South there is no evidence of a sudden popular demand in the election of 1810 for a more energetic government and a more vigorous foreign policy. Maryland, which voted six to three for war in June 1812, had four new members in the Twelfth Congress, one a Federalist. The three new Republicans either won the election without opposition or they replaced men who had supported military preparations and a stronger foreign policy in the Eleventh Congress.[2]

Virginia, which held her elections for the Twelfth Congress in the spring of 1811, returned a virtually identical delegation of seventeen Republicans and five Federalists. The two Quids, John Randolph and Edwin Gray, were re-elected, as were most of the conservative Republicans of the Eleventh Congress. The Shenandoah Valley remained as solidly Federalist as it had been in 1800, and the tramontane region, the one part of the state that might have been concerned with Indians and Western lands, elected Thomas Wilson, its first Federalist since 1793.

Virginia's election as a whole produced five new Republican members; none apparently was elected on the issue of peace or war. John Wayles Eppes, the only strong leader Virginia had sent to the Eleventh Congress, moved to John Randolph's district in the Southside and was defeated by Randolph in the election. The contest was close even though Eppes never formally declared himself a candidate, but the objections to Randolph centered on his vigorous opposition to the Madison administration. No one maintained that the election of Eppes would ensure stronger measures toward Great Britain.[3] Eppes's seat in his former district was taken by James Pleasants, a war Republican who in the postwar period was to revert to the old Jeffersonian strict constructionist doctrines. In Thomas Jefferson's own district, which included Albemarle County, David S. Garland was replaced by Hugh Nelson, a close friend of James Monroe and member of the "minority" that had supported Monroe against James Madison's election in 1808 because it felt that Madison was too nationalistic. Nelson entered the Twelfth Congress with a decided preference for peace at any price. In the Fredericksburg area the administration regular, Walter Jones, declined to run again, and in the election Major John P. Hungerford defeated John Taliaferro by six votes. Hungerford was a former Quid and had sat on the Monroe electoral committee in 1808. Taliaferro contested the election, received the support of the war hawks in the House, and was awarded the seat. In the Fauquier-Culpeper district John Love, who had generally supported preparedness measures in the Eleventh Congress, declined re-election and was replaced by another war Republican, Dr. Aylet Hawes.[4]

Nearly half the Virginia Congressmen were elected without opposition, and even where there was a contest the election seldom turned on the issue of foreign policy. Typical of Virginia conservatives re-elected in 1811 was John Clopton, who had represented the Richmond district since 1801. If a letter to his constituents published

[2] *National Intelligencer* (Washington), Oct. 5, 8, 12, 1810. Maryland's three new Republicans were Joseph Kent of Bladensburg, Peter Little of Baltimore, and Stephenson Archer of the Eastern Shore. They replaced Nicholas R. Moore, member of the war party in the 11th Congress, Archibald Van Horne, who had generally supported stronger measures, and John Montgomery, who had resigned his seat after being re-elected to the 12th Congress.

[3] See "Corvus," *Virginia Argus* (Richmond), Jan. 29, 1811.

[4] *Enquirer* (Richmond), Apr. 26, 30, May 3, 10, 1811.

in the *Virginia Argus* is a fair summary of his campaign platform, Clopton was running in support of the nonintercourse law and against the Bank of the United States, giving no indication of any departure from the Jeffersonian system. Clopton had two opponents, one of whom withdrew before the election, while the other made public statements agreeing with Clopton on every issue.[5]

The election of 1810 in North Carolina similarly produced no great change in her representation. Of her twelve Congressmen eight were re-elected, two of them Federalists and one, Richard Stanford, a Randolph Quid. Two of the four newcomers had served in Congress during the Jefferson administration (William Blackledge from 1803 to 1808 and Thomas Blount from 1804 to 1808). The only new faces in the North Carolina group, Israel Pickens and William R. King, were war hawks, but neither defeated an incumbent.[6]

The political "revolution" in South Carolina in the election of 1810, which produced a unanimous vote for war in June 1812, was more apparent than real. The election of the three great war hawk leaders, John C. Calhoun, William Lowndes, and Langdon Cheves, was more an addition of talent than of numbers to the war party in Congress. In the campaign Calhoun had openly advocated war, but he was elected without opposition since the incumbent—his cousin Joseph Calhoun, a war hawk in the Eleventh Congress—declined re-election and supported him.[7] William Lowndes succeeded to the seat of John Taylor, one of the administration's floor leaders in the Eleventh Congress who had been elected to the Senate. Cheves was elected in 1810 to fill a vacant seat in the Eleventh Congress and was re-elected to the Twelfth.

The other prominent war hawk, David Rogerson Williams, took the seat of his brother-in-law Robert Witherspoon, who declined re-election and threw his support to Williams.[8] Williams, moreover, as a member of the Ninth Congress, had followed John Randolph in rebellion against the Jefferson administration in 1806 and thus fits more into the pattern of the converted conservative. Indeed, as late as May 1812 a Federalist member of the House observed that Williams was still trying to make up his mind between peace and war.[9] The only real contest in South Carolina was the defeat of Lemuel J. Alston by Elias Earle, but no current issue was involved for the two men had taken turns defeating each other for years.[10]

The election in South Carolina illustrates the real significance of the election of 1810. Without any fundamental change in public opinion, and partly by coincidence, South Carolina produced some of the outstanding leaders of the Twelfth Congress. But the change, as in the Western elections that produced Henry Clay and Felix

[5] *Virginia Argus,* Mar. 28, Apr. 4, 1811; *Enquirer,* Mar. 26, Apr. 2, 1811.

[6] *Star* (Raleigh), Aug. 16, 23, 1810; Delbert H. Gilpatrick, *Jeffersonian Democracy in North Carolina* (New York, 1931), 241–244.

[7] Charles Wiltse, *John C. Calhoun, Nationalist* (Indianapolis and New York, 1944), 51.

[8] Harvey T. Cook, *The Life and Legacy of David Rogerson Williams* (New York, 1916), 84.

[9] Samuel Taggart to Rev. John Taylor, May 9, 1812, "Letters of Samuel Taggart," American Antiquarian Society, *Proceedings,* New Ser., XXXIII (Worcester, 1923), 399.

[10] John Harold Wolfe, *Jeffersonian Democracy in South Carolina,* in *James Sprunt Studies in Historical and Political Science,* XXIV (Chapel Hill, 1940), 241, expresses a similar interpretation of the election in South Carolina; and Latimer, "South Carolina—A Protagonist of the War of 1812," 916, though she emphasizes the economic factors in South Carolina, does not contest this interpretation of the election.

Grundy, was primarily in ability rather than in numbers. Indeed, speaking strictly in terms of numbers, the actual war hawks elected in 1810 were outvoted by Federalists and antiwar Republicans in the Twelfth Congress. The young war hawks from the South and West were certainly able men, and largely by force of character alone they led an unwilling and apathetic country to war.

Yet was leadership alone enough? Several prominent war hawks—Clay, Richard M. Johnson, Ezekiel Bacon, Cheves, and Peter B. Porter—were members of the Eleventh Congress, but despite their ability they had been unable to lead that body in any consistent direction. At least as significant as the sudden appearance of a few talented war hawks in the Twelfth Congress was the gradual conversion of the average Republican from Jeffersonian pacifism to a vigorous defense of America's neutral rights. It was these men, most of them Southerners who had been in Congress for years, who provided the necessary votes for war, just as they had provided the main support for the embargo and nonintercourse laws. Their conversion seems to have stemmed primarily from a disillusionment with the old system of commercial retaliation and a growing realization that the only alternative to war was submission and national disgrace. Every expedient to avoid war honorably had been tried without success. Submission to the orders in council presaged a return to colonial status; war seemed the only alternative. The war, at least as far as the South was concerned, was brought on by men who had had a "bellyful" of England, not by men who were interested in Western lands, or Indians, or prices in the lower Mississippi Valley.

The major weakness in the various economic interpretations is their failure to explain the demand for war in the Middle Atlantic states and in the South. The "expansionist" school of historians, with internal variations, generally maintains that the war was the result of the Western desire for land, in Canada as well as in Indian-dominated Indiana, and that the conquest of Canada was demanded both for its own sake and because the British were backing the Tecumseh confederacy.[11] The difficulty is that the areas most concerned with these problems—Indiana, Illinois, and Michigan—were territories with no vote in Congress. Even Ohio, which presumably had a direct interest in the Wabash lands, was by no means unanimously in favor of war. Its one representative, Jeremiah Morrow, voted for war in 1812 just as he had voted for the embargo in 1807, but Ohio's two senators, Thomas Worthington and Alexander Campbell, opposed war in 1812 because the nation was unprepared and they feared an Indian attack on the defenseless frontier. Both preferred to retain the old system of commercial retaliation.[12] Some have suggested that Ohio's senators were out of touch with public sentiment, but a recent biographer of Worthington feels that a plebiscite held in the spring of 1812 would probably have shown a majority of the people of Ohio against war.[13] Kentucky and Tennessee, it is true, showed considerable interest in the Indian lands and in Canada, but even so their votes in Congress were hardly enough to carry the country to war.

[11] Louis M. Hacker, "Western Land Hunger and the War of 1812: A Conjecture," *Miss. Valley Hist. Rev.*, X (1923–24), 365–395; Julius W. Pratt, *Expansionists of 1812* (New York, 1925), 12–14; Pratt, "Western War Aims in the War of 1812," *Miss. Valley Hist. Rev.*, XII (1925–26), 36–50.

[12] Diary of Thomas Worthington, June 14, 17, 1812, Library of Congress, Washington, D. C.

[13] Alfred Byron Sears, *Thomas Worthington* (Columbus, 1958), 175. Nearly all reviewers have questioned this assertion, but Sears is certainly right in assuming that opinion was divided.

Julius W. Pratt, leading proponent of the "expansionist" thesis, circumvented this difficulty by conjecturing a "frontier crescent" of war hawks extending from New Hampshire (John A. Harper) to Kentucky (Clay and Johnson) and Tennessee (Felix Grundy) and ending in South Carolina (Calhoun, Lowndes, and Cheves) and Georgia (George M. Troup).[14] Yet this seems an arbitrary conjunction of dissimilar areas. Why should New Hampshire or Vermont have been interested enough in the Wabash lands to go to war? And how explain a Southern interest in the Wabash or in Canada? Pratt plugged this hole by surmising a bargain between Southern and Western war hawks in which Florida would be brought into the Union to balance the conquest of Canada. The only evidence he cites, however, is one editorial in a Tennessee newspaper.[15]

It is true that Southern war hawks talked much about the conquest of Canada, but they seem to have regarded it as primarily a method of conducting the war rather than as an ultimate objective. Secretary of State Monroe, for instance, felt that Canada might be invaded, "not as an object of the war but as a means to bring it to a satisfactory conclusion."[16] On the other hand there is evidence that some Southerners actually feared the annexation of Canada. John Randolph certainly considered the possibility that Canada might be acquired the best of reasons for not going to war, and a fellow Virginian elected in 1810 wrote home in December 1811: "The New Yorkers and Vermonters are very well inclined to have upper Canada united with them, by way of increasing their influence in the Union."[17] As to the other half of the bargain there is little evidence that outside of the border area the South was much interested in Florida, and recent scholars have tended to minimize the importance of Florida in the Southern demand for war.[18]

Somewhat more plausible is the economic interpretation of the war in terms of declining farm prices and the restriction of markets abroad. This point of view was first put forth in the early 1930's by George Rogers Taylor, who suggested that the declining price of agricultural products, particularly in the lower Mississippi Valley, may have been a factor in the Western demand for war. The gist of this argument is summed up in a letter of a Louisiana planter of July 25, 1811: "Upon the subject of cotton we are not such fools, but we know that . . . the British are giving us what they please for it. . . . But we happen to know that we should get a much greater price for it, for we have some idea of the extent of the Continent, and the demand there for it; . . . and, therefore, upon the score of lucre, as well as national honor, we are ready."[19] More recently, this argument has been adopted to explain the West-South

[14] Pratt, *Expansionists of 1812*, 126–127.

[15] *Ibid.*; Pratt, "Western War Aims in the War of 1812," 36–50.

[16] Monroe, *The Writings of James Monroe . . .* , ed. Stanislaus Murray Hamilton, V (New York, 1901), 207; see also, Marguerite B. Hamer, "John Rhea of Tennessee," East Tennessee Historical Society, *Publications,* No. 4 (Knoxville, 1932), 39.

[17] Hugh Nelson to Dr. Charles Everette, Dec. 22, 1811, Hugh Nelson Papers, Library of Congress, Washington, D. C.

[18] Burt, *United States, Great Britain, and British North America,* 306; Horsman, "Western War Aims, 1811–1812," 15; Weymouth T. Jordan, *George Washington Campbell of Tennessee,* in *Florida State University Studies,* No. 17 (Tallahassee, 1955), 94; Latimer, "South Carolina—A Protagonist of the War of 1812," 927.

[19] George R. Taylor, "Agrarian Discontent in the Mississippi Valley Preceding the War of 1812," *Journal of Political Economy,* XXXIX (1931), 499–500; see also, Taylor, "Prices in the Mississippi Valley Preceding the War of 1812," *Journal of Economic and Business History,* III (1930), 148–163.

alliance. Both sections were concerned with the declining prices of the great staple exports, cotton, tobacco, and hemp, and were inclined to blame the British orders in council for restricting their markets. The South and West, in this view, went to war primarily to defend the right to export their products without interference from Britain.[20]

That prices for these great staples declined gradually throughout the first decade of the century cannot be denied, but to what extent the British blockades were responsible is more difficult to determine. The direct trade in agricultural products was not generally affected by the orders in council; not till the winter of 1811–12 did the British interfere with cotton shipments, though their action at that time helped to justify war—at least in the mind of the North Carolina planter Nathaniel Macon.[21] It is interesting, however, that despite the British orders the market for cotton was rapidly increasing both in quantity exported and in geographical area. The declining price was a long-term phenomenon only temporarily interrupted by the postwar prosperity, rather than a result of British restrictions. Statistics on the export of tobacco similarly give no real indication that the British orders in council were responsible for the constriction in markets or the drop in prices.[22]

It is true, however, that the opinion that British restrictions were responsible for lower prices, even if unjustified, seems to have been widely held in the South. Margaret Kinard Latimer has recently brought to light evidence that this was a major factor in the demand for war at least in South Carolina. "Whether or not fighting a war with England," she concludes, "was the logical step to take as a remedy to the commercial and thus agricultural distress is not the question—the South Carolinians of 1812 were convinced that a war would help."[23] Yet this leaves unanswered the question of why South Carolinians preferred to ignore the probability that war would further disrupt their commerce, while others, notably the New Englanders, were so painfully aware of it. Is it possible that those South Carolina politicians who stressed the cotton depression as a cause for war were merely supplying additional reasons that might influence the wavering?

It must also be remembered that the decline in prices was not universal. Prices for beef, corn, and flour, the main exports of the Middle Atlantic states, actually increased over the decade, while the price of pork declined only slightly. In 1810–11 total exports in these products nearly doubled as American farms fed the Duke of Wellington's army in Spain.[24] Pennsylvania, which voted sixteen to two for war with England, can hardly have been following the dictates of economic interest.

The South and the Middle Atlantic states, whose Congressmen furnished the major support for war, had little to gain economically from the conflict. Their direct trade in agricultural products was scarcely affected by the orders in council, and England had long been the major foreign market for both sections. Indeed, it might even be

---

[20] Horsman, "Western War Aims, 1811–1812," 9; Latimer, "South Carolina—A Protagonist of the War of 1812," 924–929.

[21] U. S., Congress, *The Debates and Proceedings in the Congress of the United States* . . . , 12th Congress, 1st session, XXIII (Washington, 1853), 492–495; hereafter cited as *Annals of Congress.*

[22] Timothy Pitkin, *A Statistical View of the Commerce of the United States of America* (New Haven, 1935), 131–132, 134–137.

[23] Latimer, "South Carolina—A Protagonist of the War of 1812," 926.

[24] Pitkin, *Statistical View,* 96, 105, 119–120, 125–126, 128–129.

argued that these sections stood to lose as much by war as did New England. When, therefore, Nathaniel Macon spoke of going to war "to obtain the privilege of carrying the produce of our lands to a market"—an oft-quoted passage—he undoubtedly had in mind the "privilege" as much as the trade.[25] Southerners went to war primarily to defend their rights, not their purses.

This is not to deny that economic factors were present. The final synthesis of the causes of the war will have to take into account various material factors—the fear of an Indian conspiracy in the West, for instance, and the concern over declining prices in the South—but it will also have to recognize that none of these economic theses furnishes a satisfactory explanation for the general demand for war. The only unifying factor, present in all sections of the country, was the growing feeling of patriotism, the realization that something must be done to vindicate the national honor. In recent years historians have tended more and more to stress this factor, particularly in its influence on the West, where a feeling of national pride was an obvious concomitant of the youth and exuberance of that section.[26] Even Julius W. Pratt admitted that the war fever in the West "was doubtless due to various causes—perhaps most of all to sheer exasperation at the long continued dilatory fashion of handling the nation's foreign affairs."[27] This factor was probably even more important in the Middle Atlantic states and in the South where fewer material interests were at stake.

The system of commercial retaliation itself had not been defended on economic grounds. The first nonintercourse resolution had been introduced in the spring of 1806 by a Pennsylvanian, Andrew Gregg, as an instrument for gaining by peaceful means some recognition of America's neutral rights. The embargo and the later nonintercourse laws were intended to furnish the President with a lever of negotiation, to maintain the national dignity short of war. It was the growing disillusionment with this system, the growing feeling that war was the only means for maintaining the nation's integrity that eventually brought on the conflict. This mental conversion is aptly illustrated by the following letter of John Clopton of Virginia:

> Let us consider what our government has done—how long it has borne with the repeated injuries which have been touched on in this letter—how often negotiations have been resorted to for the purpose of avoiding war; and the aggressions, instead of having been in any measure relaxed have been pursued with aggravating violence without a single ray of expectation that there exists any sort of disposition in the B[ritish] Cabinet to relax, but the strongest disposition to persist in their career.
>
> . . . The outrages in impressing American seamen exceed all manner of description. Indeed the whole system of aggression now is such that the real question between G. Britain and the U. States has ceased to be a question merely relating to certain rights of commerce about which speculative politicians might differ in opinion—it is now clearly, positively, and directly *a question of independence,* that is to say, whether the U. States are really an independent nation.[28]

[25] *Annals of Congress,* 12th Cong., 1st sess., XXIII, 663.

[26] Bernard Mayo, *Henry Clay* (Boston, 1937), 326–334; Burt, *United States, Great Britain, and British North America,* 306ff.; Horsman, "Western War Aims, 1811–1812," 1–18 passim.

[27] Pratt, *Expansionists of 1812,* 42.

[28] To (?), Apr. 20, 1812, John Clopton Papers, Duke University Library, Durham, North Carolina.

Not all Republicans came to a similar conclusion at the same time. The process was a gradual one, beginning with the *Chesapeake* affair and the failure of the embargo to secure a recognition of American rights. The prominent Virginia Republican, Wilson Cary Nicholas, was one of the first to conclude that war was inevitable. Shortly after the Randolph schism in 1806, Nicholas had entered Congress at the behest of Jefferson, who needed an able floor leader in the House. The failure of the embargo convinced him that the whole policy of commercial retaliation was unsound, for it could not be enforced effectively enough to coerce the belligerents and it resulted only in the ruin of American agriculture. Since the Madison administration was unwilling to abandon the policy, Nicholas, rather than go into opposition, resigned his seat in the autumn of 1809.[29] "We have tried negotiation until it is disgraceful to think of renewing it," he wrote Jefferson. "Commercial restrictions have been so managed as to operate only to our own injury. War then or submission only remain. In deciding between them I cannot hesitate a moment."[30] George Washington Campbell of Tennessee reached a similar conclusion shortly after the *Chesapeake* affair, and he became one of the leading advocates for military preparations in the Tenth and Eleventh Congresses.[31]

The gradual realization of the need for a more militant foreign policy was also reflected in the prominent Republican newspapers. Thomas Ritchie of the Richmond *Enquirer* considered the embargo the only honorable alternative to war, and when it was repealed Ritchie and the *Enquirer* began openly advocating war with England.[32] William Duane, editor of the Philadelphia *Aurora*, generally supported the system of commercial retaliation, but the repudiation of David Erskine's agreement and the mission of Francis "Copenhagen" Jackson in the fall of 1809 convinced him that Britain did not intend to negotiate the question of neutral rights. By December 1809 he was advocating military preparations, the arming of American merchant ships, and, if those measures failed to intimidate Britain, "defensive war."[33]

The old Jeffersonian, Nathaniel Macon, struggled long and valiantly with his conscience in an effort to reconcile Republican dogma with the obvious need for a vigorous defense of American rights. Throughout the Eleventh Congress he had been one of the administration leaders in the House, yet his basic conservatism was frequently evident. In the spring of 1810 he co-operated with John Randolph's efforts to reduce the size of the army and navy, even advocating that they be abolished altogether.[34]

[29] *An Address from Wilson Cary Nicholas to His Constituents* (Richmond, 1809).

[30] Dec. 22, 1809, Carter-Smith Papers, University of Virginia Library, Charlottesville, Virginia.

[31] Jordon, *George Washington Campbell of Tennessee*, 66–67.

[32] Charles H. Ambler, *Thomas Ritchie* (Richmond, 1913), 45.

[33] *Aurora* (Philadelphia), Mar. 4, July 21, Dec. 14, 1809. Erskine, the British ambassador, had reached an agreement with President Madison in 1809, under which the orders in council would be withdrawn in exchange for suspension of the American nonintercourse acts. Erskine's instructions were to secure a suspension of the nonintercourse system as a prior condition to agreement, but he violated his instructions and Madison announced the suspension of the non-intercourse acts only as a consequence of the agreement. When word of the agreement reached London, George Canning repudiated it, recalled Erskine, and sent to the United States the notorious "Copenhagen" Jackson. Jackson arrived in Washington in August, refused to discuss either reparations for the *Chesapeake* or revision of the orders in council, and in November, Madison suspended all further communication with him.

[34] *Annals of Congress*, 11th Cong., 2d sess., XXI (Washington, 1853); see also, Macon to Nicholson, Apr. 3, 1810, Joseph H. Nicholson Papers, Library of Congress, Washington, D. C.

As chairman of the foreign relations committee, Macon reported the nonintercourse bill of April 1810, known as Macon's Bill Number Two, but he personally opposed it because he felt it too provocative.[35] Not until the beginning of the Twelfth Congress did he reach the conclusion that war was the only alternative. War was justified, he told the House in December 1811, because of the recent British seizures of ships carrying American agricultural products. This new aggression, he felt, showed that the British, instead of becoming more lenient, were actually tightening their system, and that further negotiation was useless.[36] Macon thereafter co-operated with the war hawks but with some reluctance and with an occasional lapse. He voted against every effort to increase the size of the navy, and he consistently opposed all efforts during the session to raise the taxes to finance the war.

A number of Republicans, though they co-operated with the preparedness measures of the war hawks, could not make up their minds on the basic issue of peace or war until the last minute. As late as May 1812 a Massachusetts Federalist reported, perhaps somewhat wishfully, that a majority of the Virginia delegation was still against war. Besides the Federalists and the Quids, Randolph and Gray, he listed Taliaferro, Nelson, William A. Burwell, John Smith, and Matthew Clay as opposed to war.[37] Representative of this group was Hugh Nelson. Nelson had been elected in 1811, but entered the Twelfth Congress with a lingering sympathy for the old Republican "minority" whose leader was John Randolph of Roanoke and whose prophet was John Taylor of Caroline. "I am a messmate of J[ohn] R[andolph]," he wrote to a friend in Charlottesville shortly after his arrival in Washington. "The more I see him the more I like him. He is as honest as the sun, with all his foibles, and as much traduced I believe as any man has ever been. . . . Do not be surprised if before the session closes I am classified with him as a minority man."[38] Nelson's maiden speech in the House came on the resolution to increase the size of the regular army. It was a rehash of all the old Republican antiwar arguments—war would centralize the government, strengthen the executive, burden the people with taxes, armies, and navies, undermine our "republican simplicity," and subvert the Constitution. "I care not for the prices of cotton and tobacco as compared with the Constitution," he averred. Moreover he felt it unlikely that the United States could ever gain recognition of her neutral rights, particularly since the only program the war hawks suggested was a territorial war begun by an invasion of Canada. Canada could not be conquered, but even if it could, would this enforce our rights? "Certainly not. The way to enforce these rights was by way of a great maritime force, which the nation were incompetent to raise and support." Nelson nevertheless felt the country should prepare for any eventuality because unless Britain relented there was no alternative to war. "I shall vote for the increase of the regular force," he concluded, "to go hand in hand with my friends, even in a war, if necessary and just."[39] The most important of these friends was Nelson's neighbor from Charlottesville, Secretary of State Monroe, who by the spring of 1812 was a vigorous advocate of strong measures. In June, John

[35] Macon to Nicholson, Apr. 3, 6, 10, 1810, Joseph H. Nicholson Papers.

[36] Annals of Congress, 12th Cong., 1st sess., XXIII, 492–495.

[37] Samuel Taggart to Rev. John Taylor, May 9, 1812, "Letters of Samuel Taggart," Amer. Antiq. Soc., Proc., XXXIII, 398.

[38] To Dr. Charles Everette, Dec. 4, 1811, Hugh Nelson Papers.

[39] Annals of Congress, 12th Cong., 1st sess., XXIII, 497–499.

Randolph wrote to John Taylor of Caroline that Monroe was "most furiously warlike & carries the real strength of the Southern representation with him."[40]

Even more important than the personal influence of Monroe was the stimulus provided by President Madison. Most of the conservatives considered themselves loyal Republicans and were accustomed to following Presidential leadership in dealing with Britain and France. The policy of commercial retaliation had been largely an administration measure, and when the Twelfth Congress assembled in November 1811 Congress naturally looked to the Executive for guidance. Madison not only encouraged the war fever but he co-operated with the war hawks to a degree that has only recently begun to be fully recognized. His Annual Message to Congress in November 1811 outlined a program of military and naval preparations that was adopted virtually intact by the war hawks.[41] His release of the correspondence of Captain John Henry in March 1812 and his request in April for a thirty-day embargo as a prelude to war have been interpreted by his most recent biographer, Irving Brant, as attempts to stimulate the war sentiment in Congress.[42]

The war hawks took full advantage of these moves by the President in their efforts to hold the conservatives in line. In the later stages of the session, when a number of Republicans began to get cold feet, the war hawks informed them that it was too late to back out. When in April the bill initiating a temporary embargo was reported for debate, Henry Clay warned the House that if it stopped now after all the war measures it had passed, it would cover itself "with shame and indelible disgrace."[43] That this argument was effective is indicated by John Smilie, who followed Clay on the floor. Smilie, whose western-Pennsylvania Republicanism dated back to the fight over the Constitution in 1787, admitted that from the beginning of the session he had only reluctantly voted for the various proposals of the war hawks. He actually preferred continuing commercial retaliation to a war and an army of 25,000. But he realized it was too late to back down now; the nation's honor was at stake: "If we now recede we shall be a reproach to all nations."[44]

Added to this internal stimulus was the pressure of continuing British intransigence. On May 22 dispatches arrived in Washington from British Foreign Secretary Lord Castlereagh that contained nothing but a restatement of the British position. President Madison himself concluded that this was the last formal notice intended by the British government and sent his war message to Congress on June 1. It is not difficult to conceive that many a reluctant Republican came to the same decision.

It was thus with mixed motives that a majority of Republicans followed the war hawks to war. It is nevertheless clear that a primary factor in the mind of each was the conclusion that the only alternative to war was submission to the British commercial system. The balance of power in the House was held by men who had been in Congress for years, who had tried every expedient short of war to secure a recogni-

[40] June 16, 1812, John Taylor Papers, Massachusetts Historical Society, Boston, Mass.

[41] Irving Brant, *James Madison, the President, 1809–1812* (Indianapolis and New York, 1956), 357–358, 363, 391.

[42] *Ibid.,* 415, 429. Capt. Henry was a British secret agent who had reported to Governor Craig of Canada on the discontent in New England during the time of the embargo. In February 1812 Henry, through the agency of a French nobleman, Count Crillon, sold his evidence of disaffection in New England to the American State Department for $50,000.

[43] *Annals of Congress,* 12th Cong., 1st sess., XXIV (Washington, 1853), 1588–89.

[44] *Ibid.,* 1593–94.

tion of American rights, and who at last had become surfeited with British commercial regulations. The war hawks, it is true, provided with their skill and energy the necessary impetus to war, but they could not have done so had not a majority of the Republican Party, particularly in the South, become gradually converted to the idea that war was the only alternative to national humiliation and disgrace. In this sense the war hawks acted as the intangible catalyst for a reaction whose basic elements were already present.

5 / The Monroe Doctrine—A Stopgap Measure

Gale W. McGee

The historical genesis of the Monroe Doctrine has provoked extensive research by scholars during the past half century. Dexter Perkins's painstaking investigations into American documentation and also numerous European governmental archives preparatory to the publication of his classic monograph, *The Monroe Doctrine 1823–1826* offers but a single example of the thoroughness and zeal displayed by scholars on this subject. The conventional or standard view has been that President Monroe and his Secretary of State, John Quincy Adams, prepared the unilateral American pronouncement of 1823 as a means of serving notice on France and Spain that the United States would not be favorably disposed toward any attempt to restore Spain's colonial empire in the New World. The United States would support the emerging republics which had only recently revolted against Spanish rule. Moreover, Monroe's pronouncement in 1823 gave notice to Imperial Russia that the United States would not acknowledge any extension of Russia's colonial holdings in America south of the Russian claimed territories in the Northwest. In the following article, Gale W. McGee suggests that the unilateral pronouncement by President Monroe may well have been intended to be a temporary pronouncement subject to further negotiations with Britain leading to some joint Anglo-American policy. McGee's article challenges the standard interpretation which has maintained that Monroe and Adams staunchly opposed a joint pronouncement with Britain because that would possibly limit any future American territorial designs on the continent and on Cuba.

For further reading: Samuel Flagg Bemis, *John Quincy Adams and the Foundations of American Foreign Policy* (New York: 1949); Bradford Perkins, *Castlereagh and Adams* (Berkeley: 1964); Dexter Perkins, *The Monroe Doctrine 1823–1826* (Cambridge: 1927); T. R. Schellenberg, "Jeffersonian Origins of the Monroe Doctrine," *Hispanic American Historical Review*, XIV (1934), 1–32; Edward H. Tatum, *The United States and*

Gale W. McGee served as Professor of History at the University of Wyoming. Since 1959, he has been a member of the United States Senate representing the State of Wyoming. This article is reprinted by permission of the editors of *The Journal of American History*. From the *Mississippi Valley Historical Review*. Copyright 1951 by *The Journal of American History*.

Europe 1815–1823 (Berkeley: 1936); *Arthur P. Whitaker, *The United States and the Independence of Latin America 1800–1830* (Baltimore: 1941).

The Monroe Doctrine has generally been looked upon as a unilateral policy, deliberately accepted by the United States in preference to an "entangling" British suggestion of a joint manifesto. The doctrine of the two spheres, moreover, has commonly been associated with the principles of isolationism. But both the determination of the Americans to "go it alone" and the attributes of isolation become apparent only when certain utterances of the principal statesmen involved are lifted from the context of the diplomatic conditions which produced them.

If those statements are left in their context it is possible to see that while the early spokesmen often voiced a desire to remain unfettered, they seldom permitted their ideals to blind them to realities. With a sagacity rarely equaled since then, they stood ever ready to compromise ideals with the exigencies of reality in order to obtain what was to them more fundamental than any theories of nonentanglement—the security of the nation. In the discussions which evoked the Monroe Doctrine this is clearly illustrated.

Long before George Canning became alarmed over the designs of the Holy Alliance in the New World, the Americans were concerning themselves with the threat. After turning down the repeated invitations of the Czar to accede to his European concert, the United States served notice that it would have nothing to do with any scheme for restoring Spanish control in South America.[1] As early as December, 1815, Secretary of State James Monroe instructed John Quincy Adams, then minister to Britain, to sound the London government on the question of recognizing the independence of the Latin-American nations.[2] Although nothing came of the gesture, Monroe as president made it the business of a cabinet session three years later, in May, 1818. From his official family he sought advice as to whether measures ought to be taken to ascertain Britain's attitude toward a concert of policies in which any project affecting the Latin Americans should receive no support unless the end result would be independence.[3] The upshot of the cabinet session was an instruction to Richard Rush, minister to London, which Secretary of State Adams drafted:

> It may be an interesting object of your attention to watch the moment when this idea [cooperation with Britain in recognizing the independence of Latin America] will become prevalent in the British councils, and to encourage any disposition which may consequently be manifested to a more perfect concert of measures between the United States and Great Britain towards that end—the total independence of the Spanish South American provinces.[4]

Nor was this informal proposal permitted to lapse. Two months later Monroe "very abruptly" asked Adams to propose to the British minister, Charles Bagot, joint action

[1] See John Q. Adams to Albert Gallatin, May 19, 1818, Worthington C. Ford (ed.), *Writings of John Quincy Adams*, 7 vols. (New York, 1913–1917), VI, 318. Note also Adams to Richard Rush, May 20, 1818, *ibid.*, 325–26.

[2] James Monroe to Adams, December 10, 1815, Instructions to Ministers, VII, Department of State Archives (Washington).

[3] Charles H. Sherrill, *Modernizing the Monroe Doctrine* (Boston, 1916), 81–82.

[4] Adams to Rush, May 20, 1818 Ford (ed.), *Writings of John Quincy Adams*, VI, 326.

to aid the ambitions of the Spanish colonies for independence. Although the Secretary thought the English were not yet ready to assume such an advanced position in American affairs, the proposal was not abandoned.[5] It was translated into a formal proposition and transmitted to the Court of London in August, 1818. As it read, the proposal was "for a concerted and contemporary recognition of the independence of Buenos Ayres." In refusing the offer, the British said only that it did not then suit their policy.[6]

The Americans, however, were not to be easily discouraged. In the following December joint action in recognizing Buenos Aires was suggested both to London and Paris.[7] Although neither overture evoked favorable sentiment, they were followed closely by the most definite offer to originate in Washington. In January, 1819, President Monroe, encouraged by the British refusal at the Congress of Aix-la-Chapelle to intervene in the Spanish colonies, brought the issue before his cabinet once again. On January 2, when Adams showed Monroe a dispatch prepared for Rush announcing the intention of the government to recognize the independence of Brazil, the President declared his opposition to a unilateral act, preferring to follow rather than oppose the current of European politics. In the cabinet, where Adams objected to any "deference to England," Secretary of War John C. Calhoun voiced the prevailing sentiment in expressing "the most earnestness to avoid acting unless in concert with England."[8] As a consequence, the Secretary of State's original dispatch was altered to say that in Washington it was hoped that the difference between the views of the two English-speaking nations was one of form rather than substance. The new instructions said in part, "If it should suit the views of Great Britain to adopt similar measures at the same time and in concert with us, it will be highly satisfactory to the President."[9] The offer, however, was accorded a cold reception by Lord Castlereagh.[10]

Further manifestations of a disposition in the United States to combine policies with the British appeared in 1821. Stratford Canning, His Majesty's minister in Washington, reported this to Castelereagh as the substance of an April conference with Adams. On that occasion the Secretary of State said that he personally "should view with pleasure anything which tended even to draw closer the amicable relations of the two countries." The mere tone of these opening remarks caught the British by surprise, since it was somewhat of a reversal of form on the part of Adams.[11]

"I inquired of Mr. Adams," reported Canning, "whether . . . the terms which he had

---

[5] This conference took place on July 23, 1818; its substance was recorded by Adams on July 25. Charles F. Adams (ed.), *Memoirs of John Quincy Adams*, 12 vols. (Philadelphia, 1874–1877), IV, 118.

[6] These exchanges were recounted for Richard C. Anderson, newly appointed envoy to Latin America, by Adams on May 27, 1823, Ford (ed.), *Writings of John Quincy Adams*, VII, 446–47. From Madrid George W. Erving reported that the French government expected "a dangerous concert of measures" between the Anglo-Americans in the event of a rupture with Spain. Erving to Adams (private), October 22, 1818, Despatches (the contemporary spelling has been retained), Spain, XVI, Department of State Archives.

[7] See entries for December 7, 12, 1818, Adams (ed.), *Memoirs of John Quincy Adams*, IV, 186 ff.

[8] *Ibid.*, 203–205.

[9] Ford (ed.), *Writings of John Quincy Adams*, VI, 525.

[10] Richard Rush, *Memoranda of a Residence at the Court of London . . . 1819–1825* (Philadelphia, 1845), 13–20.

[11] Stratford Canning to Lord Castlereagh, April 27, 1821, Public Record Office, Foreign Office, 5:158 (Library of Congress transcripts).

just used were directed to any particular object." He was told that nothing specific was contemplated. There was a new series of events just commencing in Europe, Adams explained, and "circumstances, affording ground for a closer connection might possibly arise in the course of their development." Coupled with the shift on the European political front was the added fact of new uprisings in Latin America. As a result of these conversations, Stratford Canning concluded that Adams was intimating "a readiness to *receive* any proposal from Great Britain."[12]

At approximately the same time, and coincident with Adams' startling gesture to the British minister, Richard Rush reported from London that English policy toward the Holy Alliance was preceptibly more frigid.[13] Mutual interest, it would appear, was driving the two English-speaking governments onto common ground.

By early 1823 the events of European politics were nudging the Anglo-Americans even closer together. The suddenness with which France in that year forcibly deposed the liberal government in Spain alarmed officials both in Washington and London. Even the suspicious Adams sensed the growing friendship. As Stratford Canning reported it to his cousin in the foreign office, George Canning, the apparent determination of Great Britain to oppose the South American ambitions of the Holy Alliance had made "the English almost popular in the United States," with Adams himself having "caught a something of the soft infection."[14]

The American Secretary of State in effect seemed to have executed a neat about-face in his attitude toward the British. Commenting on the "coincidence of principle" existing between the two governments, he went so far as to suggest to Stratford Canning that the two might compare their "ideas and purposes together, with a view to the accommodation of great interests upon which they had hitherto differed."[15] This was further indicated in the tone of the instructions prepared for Richard Rush in July, 1823. As Adams explained the substance of the new orders to His Majesty's minister in Washington, they had been drawn "with a view . . . of establishing a common understanding, on several points affecting the interests of the two Countries."[16] Rush was informed that in regard to the proposed negotiation, "the final result anxiously looked to from it . . . [was] a more permanent and harmonious concert of public policy and community of purpose between our two countries, than has ever yet existed since the period of our independence."[17]

It is apparent that by midsummer of 1823 Great Britain and the United States were close to a concert of policies. Both the time and the European setting were propitious for George Canning's overtures to Richard Rush; his "spectacular" proposals did not come out of a clear sky. They had a sound basis in the early efforts of the United States to team up with Britain on Latin America. They had an immediate

[12] *Ibid.*

[13] Rush to Adams, April 2, 1821, Despatches, Great Britain, XXVI, Department of State Archives.

[14] Stratford Canning to George Canning, Public Record Office, Foreign Office, 8:352, Stratford Canning Papers, cited by Dexter Perkins, *The Monroe Doctrine, 1823–1826* (Cambridge, 1927), 60.

[15] Adams (ed.), *Memoirs of John Quincy Adams,* VI, 152.

[16] Stratford Canning to George Canning, June 6, 1823, Public Record Office, Foreign Office, 5:176, Nos. 54, 56.

[17] Adams to Rush, July 29, 1823, No. 72, cited from the Richard Rush Papers, folder 1823, Arthur P. Whitaker, *The United States and the Independence of Latin America, 1800–1830* (Baltimore, 1941), 432–33.

source in the unusual American cordiality toward England manifesting itself in the spring and summer months of 1823. And finally, they were a logical consequence of the coincidental secession of Great Britain from the concert of Europe and the mounting American suspicion of the Holy Alliance.

The substance of Canning's conversations with Richard Rush during August and September of 1823 are too well known to need repeating. Let it be borne in mind, however, that by late September the distance separating the two men from some sort of joint commitment was surprisingly small. It could be measured by the distance between Canning's suggestion that Rush accept a British pledge for the *future* recognition of South American independence and Rush's insistence upon a British policy of *immediate*. recognition.

The crest of the tide of an Anglo-American diplomatic understanding was actually reached in the conference of September 26, destined to be the last exchange on the subject in London for nearly two months. The British foreign minister, in the meantime, would elicit from the French government, through Count Polignac, convincing assurances that France would not participate in an overseas expedition in behalf of the Spanish colonial interests. As a result Canning beat a hasty retreat from the position he had assumed in his talks with the American envoy.

In Washington, however, the tempo of official opinion on the question of an Anglo-American accommodation was on the increase, and continued so during October and November. The government there was not to learn until February of the following year that in London the project had been abandoned.[18]

When the British proposition was received by James Monroe, it touched off a series of spirited discussions among the President and his advisers. In the eyes of Thomas Jefferson it was the most "momentous" development since 1776,[19] and to John Quincy Adams it seemed to be "Of such magnitude, such paramount consequence, as involving the whole future policy of the United States."[20]

As a consequence of the official deliberations the American government manifested a disposition toward a policy of action which deviated substantially from the tenets usually associated with the Monroe Doctrine. That disposition constitutes a significant chapter in the origins of United States foreign policy. In order to keep in mind the contemporary setting from which the Monroe message evolved, it is well to recall the better known comments on the proposed policy of collaboration with Great Britain. President Monroe first of all sought the advice of two of the country's elder statesmen, his fellow Virginians and predecessors in office, Jefferson and Madison.

Thomas Jefferson stressed that while our true objective should be to make the western hemisphere the "domicile . . . of freedom," separate from Europe, yet, in

[18] Canning did not explain his change of mind to Rush until an interview of November 24, 1823, and followed it with another conference on December 12. Rush to Adams, November 26, December 27, 1823, William R. Manning (ed.), *Diplomatic Correspondence of the United States Concerning the Independence of the Latin-American Nations*, 3 vols. (New York, 1925), III, 1503–6, 1510–12. This particular dispatch from Rush was not received in Washington until February 2, 1824.

[19] Thomas Jefferson to Monroe, October 24, 1823, Andrew A. Lipscomb and Albert E. Bergh (eds.), *The Writings of Thomas Jefferson*, 20 vols. (Washington, 1903–1905), XV, 477.

[20] Adams revealed this to Henry U. Addington. Addington to George Canning, December 1, 1823, Public Record Office, Foreign Office, 5: 177, No. 25.

attaining that objective, "One nation, most of all, could disturb us . . .; she now offers to lead, aid, and accompany us in it." By acceding to the proposal, moreover, Britain would be detached from the European system. Even should a war result from the rapprochement, he added, such a war would not be "her war, but ours."[21] To James Madison, joining with the British would be a wise step "short of war." But for him this was not enough. He would have the two English-speaking peoples issue a similar declaration in behalf of the Greeks.[22]

Nor was James Monroe hesitant about what should be done. While no foreign entanglements was a sound policy, he said, the present seemed to justify a departure from it. "My own impression is," he observed, "that we ought to meet the proposal of the British govt. & to make it known, that we would view an interference on the part of the European powers . . . as an attack on ourselves, presuming that, if they succeeded with them, they would extend it to us."[23]

With the exception of John Quincy Adams, the cabinet members were pretty much agreed upon the threat and only slightly less so upon a course of action. The President favored giving Rush discretionary powers to effect a merging of policy with the British.[24] Secretary of War Calhoun believed sufficient powers should be sent to permit an accession to all of Canning's proposals, and if necessary, even to the point of relinquishing ambitions in Cuba and Texas.[25] The Attorney General, William Wirt, while fearful of the Holy Alliance, raised the practical question of the consequences of such a joint declaration. To be really effective, he pointed out, it would have to presuppose a war; and he doubted that the American people would support a war in behalf of Latin America.[26]

But around none of the cabinet members[27] has tradition spun a more romantic narrative than about the Secretary of State. Never one to hunt with the pack, it was natural that John Quincy Adams would hold divergent views. The conventional accounts of his courageous efforts to steer the administration along a course of true Americanism and independent action are well known. From his own accounts we learn that he alone opposed joining with Britain.[28] His reasons are significant. Strongly suspicious of Canning's motives, he felt that some ulterior objects were being entertained. These he thought to include an intention of blocking the further expansionist efforts of the United States to the southward.[29]

He regarded the threat from the Holy Alliance, moreover, as more fancied than real. Though willing to concede that the Allies "might make a temporary impression [in Latin America] for three, four, or five years," he thought it no more probable that

[21] Jefferson to Monroe, October 24, 1823, Lipscomb and Bergh (eds.), *Writings of Thomas Jefferson*, XV, 477–78.

[22] James Madison to Monroe, October 30, 1823, Gaillard Hunt (ed.), *The Writings of James Madison*, 9 vols. (New York, 1900–1910), IX, 158–59.

[23] Monroe to Jefferson, October 17, 1823, Stanislaus M. Hamilton (ed.), *The Writings of James Monroe*, 7 vols. (New York, 1893–1903), VI, 323–25.

[24] Adams (ed.), *Memoirs of John Quincy Adams*, VI, 192.

[25] *Ibid.*, 186.

[26] *Ibid.*, 202, 205.

[27] Secretary of the Treasury William H. Crawford did not participate in the sessions due to illness. Apparently there is no record of the views of Secretary of the Navy Samuel L. Southard and Postmaster General John McLean, whose position was not of cabinet rank.

[28] A diary note of November 7, 1823, Adams (ed.), *Memoirs of John Quincy Adams*, VI, 178–79.

[29] *Ibid.*, 188.

the Spanish dominions could be restored to the mother country, "than that the Chimborazo will sink beneath the ocean."[30] Believing that self-interest rather than adherence to idealistic principles would finally regulate the conduct of the courts of Europe, he could discern no practical basis upon which they could rest a policy of intervention in behalf of Spain.[31]

While inclined to minimize the threat from abroad, Adams, nevertheless, was ready to act on the question proposed by Canning. What concerned him most was that England was already disposed to act, in which case it would appear to the outside world that she had taken the lead; to her, thus, would fall the credit for preserving the interests of the western hemisphere. To England, as a result, would accrue commercial favors, probably at the expense of the United States. For this reason the Secretary of State observed that "It would be more candid, as well as more dignified, to avow our principles explicitly to Russia and France, than to come in as a cock-boat in the wake of a British man-of-war."[32]

Nowhere among his utterances at this point does Adams reveal a determination to reject the Canning overture on account of tradition or its entangling consequences. From his own phrases, in fact, one can arrive at the not unwarranted conclusion that collaboration was acceptable to him provided it neither barred America's future ambitions in Cuba nor relegated the United States to the position of an appendage to British policy.

Other indications that Adams was not as staunchly set against collaborating with the British as convention would have it are revealed in the dispatches of His Majesty's chargé in Washington, Henry U. Addington. While Canning had been sounding Rush in London, Addington was pushing essentially the same proposition in conversations with Adams.[33] These efforts had begun perhaps in late September when Canning perceived that he was getting nowhere with Rush. At any rate, by the first of November Addington and Adams held a conference at which the subject was a "joint manifesto on Spanish America." And shortly thereafter, at a dinner party, the British envoy received an account of the Rush-Canning exchanges from the American Secretary of State. With the proposition, reported Addington, "Mr. Adams seemed extremely gratified, and evidently contemplated his country as already placed by it on a much higher elevation than that on which she had hitherto stood."[34]

The following weeks brought no satisfactory agreement between the two. The diplomatic exchanges, however, fail to disclose any mounting hostility on the part of Adams. They reveal, on the contrary, a disposition on his part to accede to the proposal from London. This is apparent in the detailed account of the several conversations which Addington forwarded to his chief in Britain during December. On an occasion subsequent to the dinner party already alluded to, Adams again adverted to the Canning offer. "Mr. Adams was also evidently much pleased with the manner in which the proposition had been made, as well as the opening thus afforded for his Country to play so prominent a part in the affairs of the World," Addington re-

[30] Ibid., 186.

[31] Ibid., 207.

[32] Ibid., 179.

[33] An Englishman, William F. Reddaway, in an excellent, though brief, study of the Monroe Doctrine, was one of the earliest, if not the first, to disclose Addington's activities. The Monroe Doctrine (Cambridge, 1898), first published in the United States in New York, 1905.

[34] Ibid., 53.

corded. But when pressed for an immediate decision so that the compact might operate as a "preventive," the Secretary asked for more time, pleading the "paramount consequence" of the rapprochement.[35]

Calling again in a few days, Addington was once more put off. Adams advised him, however, that the terms laid down by Rush in London were those which the administration would insist upon. The critical issue, of course, was the matter of recognition. Without that acknowledgment "no durable concert and harmony of operations could be looked for," Adams declared, but "let one common basis be laid down, and there would be no longer any difficulty in concerting common measures." The Secretary of State extended a concession, moreover, as if to facilitate the conclusion of the pact. If Great Britain would only recognize one country, he told Addington, so as to lay down the principle, he would accede to Canning's proposition.[36]

Once again, on November 19, the British diplomat inquired whether the necessary instructions would be sent to Rush in the November 24 packet. Adams, who had received him "with unusual affability," replied that, "for himself, he was quite ready, but the President might possibly desire more time to reflect on a matter of such deep importance." He hastened to add, then, that "the United States were warmly and cordially disposed to make common cause with Great Britain," provided only that recognition came first.[37]

Finally, Addington made one last effort, this on December 1, only to discover that the decision was still pending. The subject, Adams explained, "was a more complicated one" than at first believed. But even without British recognition, he assured the visiting diplomat that "The United States would show by acts how cordially they concurred in the line of policy proposed to be pursued by Great Britain." On taking his leave the Britisher noted that the American Secretary "concluded by expressing in terms of warmth and apparent sincerity, his earnest hope that the relations which existed between our two governments would become daily of a closer and more confidential nature."[38]

It would appear that most students of the Monroe Doctrine have overlooked or ignored this Addington dispatch. That document suggests that the conventional accounts which have ascribed to Adams the airs of a knight-errant bent upon preserving independence of action for America perhaps should be modified. The Secretary of State possibly was not as much opposed to the British overture as is usually thought. How much of what he told Addington was personal conviction and how much was sheer diplomatic palaver cannot be precisely determined, of course. But Adams was not one to equivocate; if anything, his bluntness had on occasion plagued him.

It can be seen, therefore, that among government advisers there was a strong inclination in favor of a joint pronouncement with Great Britain. Disagreement existed principally on the specific conditions governing such a declaration. In the light of this disposition it becomes exceedingly difficult to account for Monroe's message of December 2 as one reflecting an American determination to "go it alone." Some other explanation is called for.

Although the American government had learned from Richard Rush that Canning

[35] Addington to Canning, December 1, 1823, Public Record Office, Foreign Office, 5:177, No. 25.
[36] *Ibid.*
[37] *Ibid.*
[38] *Ibid.*

had cooled toward his own proposal,[39] at no time before the Monroe message to Congress, did it regard the negotiations as having been broken off. There is interesting evidence, on the contrary, which indicates that the President's famous pronouncement was issued as a provisional measure—a stopgap, designed not only to secure for the United States a proper share of the responsibility and credit for looking after hemispheric interests, but also to fill the immediate requirements of world diplomacy —namely, holding the line against the Holy Alliance until the Canning-Rush conversations could be translated into a binding agreement.

It was not until November 29 that the new set of instructions which Rush had requested for guidance in dealing with Canning's overtures were ready to be sent to the American minister in London. Endorsing the envoy's own replies to the British diplomat, the directive stipulated that Britain must first recognize the independence of the new governments of South America. With the Anglo-Americans then occupying like ground, the United States would be willing "to move in concert with Great Britain for the purposes specified."[40]

For the time being, however, Rush was advised that the two nations should act separately, effecting a common policy through close consultations. But, "should an emergency occur, in which a *joint* manifestation of opinion . . . may tend to influence the Councils of the European Allies," he was to notify his own government immediately. In that event, the instructions concluded, "We shall according to the principles of our Government, and in the forms prescribed by our Constitution, cheerfully join in any act by which we may contribute to support the cause of human freedom, and the Independence of the South American Nations."[41]

The instructions bear upon American policy in two respects. First, they show that the Monroe government was wary of a sweeping commitment from which the British might retreat or fail to carry through. If Britain could be forced to recognize the Latin Americans the likelihood of their deserting the Yankees would be lessened since it would cost Britain her usual ally in Europe, Spain, and leave her to depend upon the Americans. That is why the statesmen in Washington demanded immediate recognition. In the face of the sudden coolness on the part of Canning as disclosed by Rush's dispatch of Ocotober 10, this action does not seem to have been unreasonable.

But perhaps an even more significant revelation in the instructions is the apparent belief that the negotiations on the question of joint action would continue. That the United States either expected, or hoped for, the resumption of the talks is clearly manifested in the endorsement of Rush's demand for prior recognition. This is illustrated further by the suggestion advanced in the orders which looked to the transfer of subsequent negotiations to Washington, where the projected entente was even then a topic of conversation between Adams and Addington.[42] The United States, it would appear, was carefully keeping the door open for a future arrangement.

[39] Rush to Adams, October 10, 1823, No. 336, Despatches, Great Britain, XXIX, Department of State Archives. In a private letter to Monroe, October 22, 1823, he noted: "The Spanish American topick has been dropped by Mr. Canning in a most extraordinary manner. Not another word has he said to me on it since the 26th of last month . . . and he has now gone out of town to spend the remainder of this, and part of the next month." Hamilton (ed.), *Writings of James Monroe*, VI, 390–91.

[40] Adams to Rush, November 29, 1823, Instructions to Ministers, X, 120–22, Department of State Archives.

[41] *Ibid.*

[42] *Ibid.*

It is, of course, impossible to say with certainty that the Monroe government was doing any more than probe for possible ulterior motives in British policy. But several hints and private opinions contained in the correspondence of individuals close to the administration indicate that the intent was something more than exploratory. From no quarter was this more apparent than in the White House itself.

Even after his message to Congress had been delivered, the President continued to worry over Canning's sudden coolness. On December 4 he wrote to Jefferson that in the face of the mounting threat from the Holy Alliance, "the most unpleasant circumstance . . . is that Mr. Canning's zeal has much abated of late." Just why, he was not sure, but he ascribed it either to the question of recognition being pressed so strongly by Rush, or to counteroffers made by the Allies to "seduce" the British.[43] Monroe, it should be noted, while regarding Canning's interest as having "abated," did not look upon it as having died. He suggested at least a hope that the negotiations with London might be continued.

This is borne out further by the tone of another set of instructions sent to Rush on December 8. Aroused by the rumor that Cadiz had fallen to France, a development which would release an Allied army of 12,500 to assault Spanish America, the President, Rush was told, was "anxiously desirous that the opening to a cordial harmony in the policy of the United States and Great Britain, offered on this occasion . . . [might be] extended to the general Relations between the two countries." The time required for the Allies to prepare the anticipated expedition, the orders concluded, "may yet be employed, if necessary, by Great Britain and the United States, in a further concert of operations, to counter-act that design, if really entertained."[44]

In a still later letter to Jefferson the President disclosed his belief that a rapprochement was still in the offing. After alluding to the continuing threat of the European concert, he reverted to an Anglo-American entente as the best means to guard against it. But to effect such a collaboration, he observed, it had best emanate from the United States in order to avoid the appearance that his government was only the instrument of England.[45]

Another letter to Jefferson, written nearly six weeks after the statement to Congress—January 12, 1824—discloses that Monroe was even at that late date still waiting for more news on Canning's proposal. "Since my last," wrote the President, "we have receiv'd no communication from Mr. Rush, on the subject of Mr. Cannings proposition."[46] Quite obviously he did not view the British project as having been dropped.

The thesis that the United States was still waiting for overtures from Britain after the Monroe Doctrine was announced is substantiated likewise in the letters of James Madison. Especially pertinent is his correspondence with James Barbour, chairman of the Senate Foreign Relations Committee. On the very day that the Doctrine was proclaimed, but in the morning before its delivery to the Congress, Barbour wrote to Madison on the subject of the message. As was reasonable to expect, the Senator had

---

[43] Monroe to Jefferson, December 4, 1823, Thomas Jefferson Papers (Division of Manuscripts, Library of Congress).

[44] Adams to Rush, December 8, 1823, cited from the Rush Papers, Whitaker, *United States and the Independence of Latin America*, 514–15.

[45] Monroe to Jefferson, December, 1823, Hamilton (ed.), *Writings of James Monroe*, VI, 344–45. This undated letter was written sometime after December 2.

[46] Monroe to Jefferson, January 12, 1824, *ibid.*, VII, 1–2.

apparently been permitted to examine the document in advance. Nor is it unlikely that the President at least outlined for his fellow Virginian the purport of his remarks. Barbour, at any rate, made reference to that portion of the forthcoming state paper which "will refer, but remotely, however, to the probable interference of the Allied Powers in the internal concerns of the Spanish provinces." Remote though that interference may be, wrote the Senator, "I have a serious thought of proposing a resolution advising the President to cooperate by treaty with Great Britain to prevent it. . . . I should be very much gratified with your views on this interesting subject."[47]

The significance of this note apparently has been overlooked by students of the Monroe Doctrine.[48] In regard to the shaping of American foreign policy, Barbour was the most influential member of the Senate. More than that, he was a Virginian close to the President. If there had been a disposition on the part of the administration to view the Canning overture as abandoned surely he would have been privy to it. Yet, probably with full knowledge of the Chief Executive's message, he was proposing Senate endorsement of an Anglo-American concert in *treaty* form to achieve ends identical with those sought by Canning. James Barbour, who was in a likely position to know, did not view the Monroe declaration as ending the negotiations with Britain.

James Madison, in his reply, placed essentially the same interpretation upon the December 2 statement. An Anglo-American joint policy, backed by military force, would be desirable, in his opinion. As he explained it to Barbour:

> It can hardly be doubted that Great Britain will readily cooperate with this Country, or, rather, that she wishes our cooperation with her, against a foreign interference for subverting the independence of Spanish America. If the attempt can be prevented by remonstrance, she will probably unite with us in a proper one. If she begins with that, she will not hesitate to proceed, if necessary, to the last resort, with us fighting by her side.[49]

That such a military combination would endure, he had no doubts, since it would be based on mutual self-interest. Were Britain to balk at joining armed forces, Madison continued, "it would be the dilemma of seeing our neutral commerce and navigation flourishing at the expense of hers; or of throwing us into a war against her by renewing her maritime provocations." But there should be no further delay, he cautioned:

> On the whole, I think we ought to move hand in hand with Great Britain in the experiment of awing the confederated powers into forbearance; and, if that fail, in following it by means which can not fail; and that we can not be too prompt or too decisive in coming to an understanding and concert with her on the subject.[50]

How did the President's declaration of December 2 bear upon all of this? It "distinctly indicated the intents of the United States with respect to such an interfer-

---

[47] James Barbour to Madison, December 2, 1823, James Madison Papers (Division of Manuscripts, Library of Congress), LXXII.

[48] Whitaker, *United States and the Independence of Latin America*, n. 515, refers to the letter as indicating only that for a policy of joint miliary action in conjunction with a joint manifesto there might have been "important support" in the United States.

[49] Madison to Barbour, December 5, 1823, Madison Papers, LXXII.

[50] *Ibid.*

ence," Madison explained. At best, he added, it was only a temporary measure. He thought that "a fuller manifestation of the national will" might be expedient, as well to bear out the Executive . . ., as to make the desirable impressions abroad." The declaration by the Senate, proposed by Barbour, was not broad enough. Would it not be better to have declaratory resolutions adopted by both houses instead of just the Senate? This would have the advantage of providing sanction for the President's policy, of inspiring Great Britain with "the fullest confidence in the policy and determination of the United States," and of exercising preventive effects on the Allied powers.[51] Obviously, Madison regarded the Canning offer as still very much alive and of no little concern to the United States even after December 2.

As late as December 26, 1823, Madison was still counseling a joint policy with the British, and this to President Monroe. The principal limitation, he suggested, would be to prevent the London government from usurping "a meritorious lead" in any action in behalf of our South American neighbors. "Nor ought we to be less careful in guarding against an appearance in the eyes of Europe, at which the self-love of Great Britain may aim, of our being a satellite of her primary interests." Given these precautionary policies, however, then cooperation should not only be accepted, it should be sought.[52] This particular letter is not only important for what it reveals of Madison's views on the Monroe declaration, but even more important in that it was written to the President of the United States, suggesting that the latter was thinking along the same lines.

In the records of the House of Representatives, also, there is additional evidence. Nearly two months after the famous Declaration was issued, Congressman Alexander Smyth of Virginia, in House debate on the Greek question, sought to clarify what the President had intended on December 2. Those remarks precluded our extending material aid to Greece, because it would be "going out of our way to beard the Allies: to seek a quarrel with them respecting the affairs of Europe," he explained, the effect of which would be to "make the declaration of the President . . . a falsehood."[53] To remain within the bounds of the December 2 statements, we should let England carry the torch in Europe. But we should not stand idly by if Britain is attacked by the Allies; "if she is involved in a war with the Allies, for the independence of nations, we ought to give her assurance that we will not be neutral, but will give her faithful and honorable support."[54] According to Smyth, then, while the Monroe message barred our taking the lead in settling the quarrels of Europe, it had not closed the door to an Anglo-American understanding.

By February, 1824, however, the Americans learned that there would be no rapprochement with their English cousins. Rush's November dispatch telling of Canning's explanations for dropping the project reached Washington on February 2. No longer was it necessary to speculate on the form of a policy of joint action.

The whole series of diplomatic exchanges surrounding the Monroe Doctrine have an important bearing on the formulation of American foreign policy. While they reveal a laudable determination to avert becoming a mere tail to the British diplo-

---

[51] *Ibid.*

[52] Madison to Monroe, December 26, 1823, *Letters and Other Writings of James Madison,* 4 vols. (Philadelphia, 1865), III, 354.

[53] Thomas H. Benton (ed.), *Abridgment of the Debates of Congress, from 1789 to 1856,* 16 vols. (New York, 1857–1861), VII, 660. Alexander Smyth spoke on January 26, 1824.

[54] *Ibid.*, 662.

matic kite, they also disclose a strong disposition toward a collaboration with the English. James Monroe's message of December 2, 1823, it would also appear, was not intended as a refusal of Canning's bid. Nor can it be said with complete accuracy that the pronouncement was made in the knowledge that the original offer had been abandoned. The American government had continued to act with the expectation that discussions on the project would be continued, an assumption which prevailed until February 2, 1824.

In the light of the foregoing materials, the following conclusions in regard to those statements in President James Monroe's message to Congress December 2, 1823, subsequently to be called the Monroe Doctrine, would seem to be in order. (1) The idea for a policy of joint action in Latin America evolved as much from American initiative before 1823 as from George Canning's overtures to Richard Rush in August of that year. (2) The Canning project was viewed with less hostility by the policy makers in the United States, including John Quincy Adams, than has been generally recognized. (3) The message itself appears to have been a temporary expedient—a stopgap measure intended to hold the line against the designs of Europe while the diplomatic conversations begun by Canning and Rush in London could be continued. (4) In part, it may have been a move to insure to the United States at least an equal share of the credit which might follow a joint manifesto in behalf of the former Spanish colonies in the New World. (5) It was issued with the expectation that there would be further negotiations on the British proposal for some sort of collaboration, and was not intended as a negative reply to the offer from England.

Viewed in this light, the objectives of the Monroe Doctrine seem to be very different from those alleged by students who have tried to see in its enunciation the spirit of "isolation."[55] Quite on the contrary, it would appear that the statesmen in Washington felt that isolation, in fact, was impossible. Instead of pledging themselves to a "tradition," they dedicated their efforts to the most fundamental question of all—that of American security. To achieve that end they were prepared for close cooperation with Great Britain.

[55] W. A. Bewes, "The Monroe Doctrine and Entangling Alliances," The Grotius Society Transactions, XIII (1928), 13, explains the actions of the United States as an adherence to the "tradition" of acting alone. W. P. Cresson, Diplomatic Portraits: Europe and the Monroe Doctrine One Hundred Years Ago (Boston, 1923), 335, accounts for the decision of Monroe and Adams to decline the bid as due to a realization of the extent that "the policy of their country had already been fixed by tradition." J. Fred Rippy, Rivalry of the United States and Great Britain Over Latin America (Baltimore, 1929), 119, alludes to the message as "the doctrine of American isolation."

Part II

EXPANSIONISM
AND CIVIL WAR

6 / The Mexican Fear of Manifest Destiny in California

Frank A. Knapp, Jr.

For many years historians of the War with Mexico (1846–48) have been aware that control over California was a stake in that conflict. Some scholars, however, have tended to dismiss American aspirations for the acquisition of California as constituting a significant cause of the war. Others have weighed rather heavily President Polk's ambitious program for California. Whether or not American decision makers and indeed American public opinion were seriously contemplating the acquisition of California to be the central objective in a war with Mexico, it seems clear many Mexicans believed that America's paramount objective in the war was the seizure of California. In this next article, Frank Knapp, Jr. surveys an assortment of Mexican newspapers from the early to mid 1840s and presents a persuasive thesis: in the minds of many Mexicans, Texas provided only the pretext for American belligerency; the underlying motivation for Polk's decision for war was the American design on California. Had diplomatic negotiations been successful in resolving the disputes over Texas, American expansionists would have continued to press for the acquisition of California along with New Mexico. Implications of Knapp's conclusion should be carefully considered by students.

For further reading: William C. Binkley, *The Texas Revolution* (Baton Rouge: 1952); John D. P. Fuller, "The Movement for the Acquisition of All Mexico 1846–1848," in *the Johns Hopkins University Studies in Historical and Political Science*, LIV, No. 1 (Baltimore: 1936); Norman Graebner, *Empire on the Pacific* (New York: 1955); *Frederick Merk, *Manifest Destiny and Mission in American History* (New York: 1963) and *The Monroe Doctrine and American Expansionism 1843–1849* (New York: 1966); Justin H. Smith, *The War With Mexico.* 2 vols. (New York: 1919); Richard W. Van Alystyne, *The Rising American Empire* (New York: 1960); *Albert K. Weinberg, *Manifest Destiny* (Baltimore: 1935); Shomer Zwelling, *Expansion and Imperialism* (Chicago: 1970).

Frank A. Knapp, Jr. has served on the staff of the Department of State. This article is reprinted with the permission of the University of Texas Press. From *Essays in Mexican History,* edited by Thomas E. Cotner and Carlos E. Castañeda. Copyright © 1958 by the Institute of Latin American Studies, The University of Texas.

In order to understand the causation of the war with Mexico it is necessary to penetrate the surface of a decade of complicated history surrounding the Texas question with its many ramifications. An analysis must be made of the elements which composed Mexico's seemingly unrealistic attitude toward the *fait accompli* of Texan independence and later annexation by the United States. By 1846 Mexican fear over the fate of California loomed large among these elements, for California apparently was doomed to be the first of several carbon copies cut by Manifest Destiny from the original Texas pattern. California was not only important for its potential wealth but also as the western anchor of the long northern frontier of Mexico, which in turn was believed threatened in the event of a peaceful resignation of Texas.

Although the acquisition of California was a key objective of President Polk's foreign policy and American statesmen had attempted to purchase all or a part of it since 1835, California's place among the causes of the war is still controversial ground from a strictly American viewpoint. A sampling of the views of leading historians will demonstrate the divergence of opinions.

A more recent publicist has stated that President Polk's desire to purchase California was not actually presented to Mexico "and had no part in bringing on the war. . . ."[1] Also limiting his interpretation primarily to Polk's motives, Dr. Eugene C. Barker has shown clearly that California was not involved in the outbreak of hostilities, despite the President's recognized designs on the territory, since Polk could "trust to time and immigration for the extension of American influence there, as in Oregon."[2] Professor George Garrison does not include the Mexican fear of Manifest Destiny beyond the confines of the Rio Grande as an outstanding problem between the two countries,[3] while the author of the classic account of the war, Justin H. Smith, skims lightly over this Mexican fear with the comment that "such talk was largely for effect."[4] In his earlier monograph on the annexation of Texas, Professor Smith lists the possible loss of California as one of the factors affecting the Mexican attitude toward Texas. He undermines this concession, however, with a later comment that Mexican ministers could not "rid themselves of the familiar notion" that the loss of Texas might involve an even greater loss of territory.[5]

Other writers are more equivocal. The noted historian of California, I. B. Richman, states: "Whether Polk's military and naval activity in 1845 was or was not purely precautionary, one thing is certain: If war with Mexico was to ensue, it was Polk's resolve that the acquisition of California should be its principal fruit."[6] Somewhat stronger in his evaluation, Hubert Howe Bancroft, in his *History of Mexico*, concludes a chapter entitled "Causes of the War with the United States" with the statement that two of the causes were kept in the background—"the acquisition of

---

[1] Robert Selph Henry, *The Story of the Mexican War* (Indianapolis and New York, 1950), p. 33.

[2] Eugene C. Barker, "California as the Cause of the Mexican War," *Texas Review*, II, No. 3, pp. 213–221.

[3] George Garrison, *Westward Extension 1841–1845* (American Nation Series XVII [New York and London, 1906]), p. 188.

[4] Justin H. Smith, *The War with Mexico* (2 vols., New York, 1919), I, 104.

[5] Justin H. Smith, *The Annexation of Texas* (New York, ed. of 1941), pp. 415–416, 427.

[6] I. B. Richman, *California under Spain and Mexico, 1535–1847* (Boston and New York, 1911), p. 325. In his circular to American diplomatic agents, dated May 12, 1846, Secretary of State Buchanan stated that California and other Mexican territory would be subject to indemnity to defray the expenses of a war which was not one of "conquest."—James Morton Callahan, *American Foreign Policy in Mexican Relations* (New York, 1932), pp. 159–160.

California, and the desire to extend the area of slavery."[7] In a more recent study, Bernard DeVoto declares that California was "the true begetter of the war," although he follows the reasoning of Dr. Barker in defining Polk's policy: "He wanted California. He would go to war for it if necessary but, in October '45, believed that he would not have to. He thought he could buy it; if he could not buy it, he would get it by influence—fomenting a revolution in a province known to be ripe for revolution, and then attaching it by the leverage of common interests. He expected to get it in the latter way, even if events should produce war with Mexico."[8]

Taking an opposite view, Professor N. W. Stephenson believed that Polk's primary aim was not the rectification of the Texan frontier, but California, where he "saw in imagination the germ of another Texas far beyond the mountains"; and after Slidell's failure "it was plain that the Californias could not be obtained without war."[9] No historian has come out more strongly than Professor Jesse S. Reeves, however, in aligning California at the top of the list of causes: ". . . the Mexican War was not the result of the annexation of Texas. The Mexican War was waged for the fulfillment of Polk's designs upon California."[10]

Whatever the American views on the subject, they appear to be onesided. They do not fully consider the contemporary Mexican awareness of the Yankee appetite for California, an undeniable reason that no diplomatic settlement was feasible at the Rio Grande. In the Mexican mind, the military defense of the "rebellious province" of Texas was no less a defense of California, the northern frontier, and possibly the survival of Mexico as an independent nation.

Mexican awakening to the Yankee threat to California had historic roots fed from many sources. The most obvious were events in the department during the decade corresponding to the era of frictions over Texas. Between 1836 and 1846 two major revolutions occurred in California in which American settlers were implicated.

The first came in 1836 and resulted in the local leaders' ousting of the Mexican governor. Americans were accused of taking a leading part in the financial and military aspects of the uprising with the objective of transferring sovereignty from Mexico to the United States.[11] According to a neutral observer, the Americans "had prepared a flag somewhat like that of their Union, with a single star," hoping to declare independence and then to gain admission into the United States.[12] A Mexican army officer also alleged that Captain Kennedy of the U.S.S. Peacock, then on duty along the California coast, and an American shipmaster had intervened.[13]

Quick to endorse the charges was José María Tornel, the Mexican minister of war

[7] Hubert H. Bancroft, History of Mexico (6 vols., San Francisco, 1890), V, 344.

[8] Bernard DeVoto, The Year of Decision: 1846 (Boston, 1943), pp. 194–195, 228.

[9] N. W. Stephenson, Texas and the Mexican War: A Chronicle of the Winning of the Southwest (Chronicles of America, XXIV [New Haven, 1921]), pp. 181, 184–185.

[10] Jesse S. Reeves, American Diplomacy under Tyler and Polk (Baltimore, 1906), p. 288.

[11] See Robert Glass Cleland, The Early Sentiment for the Annexation of California: An Account of the Growth of American Interest in California from 1835 to 1846 (Austin, n.d.), pp. 18–19, 18n; Callahan, op. cit., p. 136; Sir George Simpson, Narrative of a Voyage to California Ports in 1841–42 together with Voyages to Sitka, the Sandwich Islands & Okhotsk (San Francisco, ed. of 1930), p. 73.

[12] Marguerite Eyer Wilbur (trans. and ed.), Duflot de Mofras' Travels on the Pacific Coast (2 vols., Santa Ana, Cal., 1937), I, 152.

[13] Richard R. Waldron, late purser of the U.S.S. Peacock, to Powhatan Ellis, Tepic, December 30, 1836, Consular Despatches, Mazatlán, 1828–1850 (MSS), Department of State Records, the National Archives, Washington, D.C. All MSS cited herein are from Department of State Records, the National Archives.

and a powerful politician. He wrote with official authority in 1837 that the United States Navy had supported an American revolution in California—proof of the Yankee intention "to acquire possessions on the Pacific Coast." Furthermore, he predicted that the loss of Texas, if tolerated by Mexico, "will inevitably result in the loss of New Mexico and the Californias."[14] The connection between the two areas continued from this time forward.

The second of the local revolutions took place in late 1844 and was directed against another Mexican governor, General Manuel Micheltorena. Again it was claimed that a large number of Yankees had taken sides with Micheltorena against the native populace in an effort to reenact "the Texas drama" in California.[15] Although Americans had been active on both sides, the United States minister at Mexico City reported that the news of American participation had intensified the bitter anti-American feeling in the capital over the annexation of Texas.[16]

More sensational than either of the two revolutions was the seizure of Monterey in 1842 by Commodore Thomas Catesby Jones, commander of the United States Naval Squadron on the Pacific. The Mexicans never accepted this incident as conceived by an official who acted under his own impulses. To them it was a treacherous deed committed under secret governmental authority. After the Commodore's "manifesto" of permanent occupation, released at Monterey, was circulated through all the dailies in the Mexican capital, the Mexican interpretation of the episode was that "the object of the people of the United States was now not only Texas but also the Californias."[17]

Just before the war broke out in 1846, news reached Mexico of the territorial violation of Captain John C. Frémont, whose force defied the local authorities near Monterey. The official documents were sent to Mexico City and gave plausible proof that American Consul Thomas O. Larkin was collaborating with an American army officer and his detachment in an effort to unite the Yankee settlers in California for rebellion, independence, and annexation to the United States.[18] The intrusion of Frémont appeared to be a fulfillment of Tornel's foresight in 1837: "The passion of the Anglo-American people," he wrote, "their pronounced desire to acquire new lands, is a dynamic power which is enhanced and nourished by their own industry. An ill-defined line, the source of a yet unknown river, scientific explorations with the pretext of establishing monuments that shall *mark with perfect accuracy* the limits of both nations, all these have given a golden opportunity to the combined efforts of

[14] Carlos E. Castañeda (trans. and ed.), *The Mexican Side of the Texas Revolution* [1836] by *the Chief Mexican Participants* (Dallas, 1928), pp. 368, 370.

[15] Letter from a resident of Los Angeles to the editors of *El Siglo*, March 26, 1845, in *El Siglo Diez y Nueve* (México), May 22, 1845. See also Simpson, *op. cit.*, pp. 73–74.

[16] Wilson Shannon to Buchanan, Mexico, April 6, 1845, Despatches from Mexico (MSS), XII. See also Smith, *War with Mexico*, I, 87.

[17] *El Siglo*, December 25, 1842. Similar opinions may be found in *El Eco de la Justicia* (México), March 14, 1843; *El Mosquito Mexicano* (México), December 16, 1842; *Correspondencia sobre las Californias é invasión del puerto de Monterrey por el comodoro norte americano Thomas Ape* [sic] *Jones 1843* (Papeles de Californias, Núm. 6 [México, 1944]), p. 12.

[18] *El Monitor Republicano* (México), May 10, 1846; *El Zempoalteca* (Jalapa), May 15, 1846, reprinted in *El Monitor Republicano*, May 19, 1846. Even the departure of Frémont's expedition from the United States was noted in Mexico (*El Amigo del Pueblo* [México], August 23, 1845). A brief summary of the incident may be found in Rayner Wickersham Kelsey, *The United States Consulate in California* (Publications of the Academy of Pacific Coast History, I, No. 5 [Berkeley, 1910]), pp. 52–53.

the people and government to promote their plans to acquire what belongs to their neighbors."[19]

Another effective method of advertising in Mexico the spirit of Manifest Destiny toward California was via the diplomatic channel. As a Mexican historian points out, the proposal of President Jackson in 1835 for the purchase of San Francisco Bay "officially revealed for the first time the entire plan of North American conquest and at the same moment displayed the unlimited ambition of the Yankee expansionists."[20] In the years that followed, the series of attempted real estate transactions by American presidents and their secretaries of state and the relation to events in California were well understood in Mexico, thanks to the frequent reminders of the Mexican papers. A typical comment appeared in 1845: "In regard to the United States, its designs [on California] are no longer a mystery. In 1836 the citizens of the Union tried to revolutionize the province, and a year later the government offered Mexico five millions of pesos for the port of San Francisco alone."[21]

Reinforcing the schemes of Jackson, Tyler, and Polk were the American ministers to Mexico, zealous of accelerating the absorption of California. Waddy Thompson was outstanding among them for his pronounced sentiments as reflected in an often quoted despatch of 1842: "I believe that this Government would be willing to cede Texas and the Californias to us, and I am thoroughly satisfied that it is all we shall ever get for the claims of our Merchants on this Country. As to Texas I regard it as of but little value compared with California, the richest the most beautiful and the healthiest country in the world."[22] And Ben E. Green, chargé d'affaires after Thompson's departure, carried on in the spirit of his predecessor.[23]

The cumulative impression of American diplomacy was well expressed by Manuel C. Rejón when he assumed the portfolio of Foreign Relations for the Santa Anna régime in 1844. After checking the diplomatic archives to brief himself on outstanding Mexican issues with the United States, he wrote: "The documents which I found in [the archives] and other publications issued by the American press confirmed me in the opinion which I had formed that the purpose of the United States was not only to seize the department mentioned above [Texas], but all the northern territory which we hold, from Matamoros to the Sea of California."[24]

The harmful impressions of this expansionist policy, impeding and possibly preventing any amicable settlement of the Texas question, continued to work on Mexican opinion through the final effort of John Slidell to find a solution to the controversies.

[19] Castañeda (ed.), op. cit., p. 307.

[20] Vicente Fuentes Díaz, La intervenció norteamericana en México [1847] (México, 1947), p. 48. For a survey of American diplomatic efforts to acquire California, see John Walton Caughey, California (New York, 1940), pp. 262–267.

[21] El Patriota Mexicano (México), November 11, 1845. Articles on the same subject appeared in ibid., November 4 and 7, 1845. See also the translated comment of Duflos de Mofras with reference to the purchase of San Francisco Bay in El Siglo, May 25, 1845. (This extract corresponds to Wilbur (ed.), op. cit., II, 29–30.)

[22] Thompson to Webster, Mexico, April 28, 1842, Despatches from Mexico, XI. Thompson was an avowed enthusiast for the acquisition of California (Thompson, Recollections of Mexico [New York and London, 1846], p. 235) and Webster himself once wrote that "the port of San Francisco would be twenty times as valuable to us as all Texas" (quoted in Norman A. Graebner, "American Interest in California, 1845," Pacific Historical Review, XXII [February, 1953], p. 26.)

[23] Green to the Secretary of State, Mexico, April 8, 1844, Despatches from Mexico, XII.

[24] Quoted in Carlos A. Echanove Trujillo, La vida pasional é inquieta de Don Crecencio Rejón (México, 1941), p. 320.

Although it is argued that Slidell's secret instruction on the purchase of California was not presented to the Mexicans, that fact is a documentary technicality. Slidell's instructions were no secret to the Mexicans. Upon arriving in Mexico, the Minister sent an important enclosure to Washington with the following comment: "I would particularly call your attention to a handbill published on the day the news of my arrival at Vera Cruz reached this city. It would seem to indicate an acquaintance with some of the objects of my mission which cannot easily be accounted for." The "handbill" was an extra of a prominent paper of Mexico City, charging Slidell (in boldfaced type) with negotiating for

THE SALE OF TEXAS, NEW MEXICO AND THE CALIFORNIAS.[25]

Citing a New Orleans paper, another Mexican daily stated that Slidell's principal bargaining power was a letter of credit for $20,000,000 from his government to be executed in favor of Mexico "on condition that Mexico cede the Californias to the United States. . . ."[26]

Another source of Mexican fear over California's fate was the stream of Yankee immigration which began to trickle before 1830. Early warnings of the danger in this movement came from the officials of both the central and departmental governments long before it attained sizable proportions.[27] The seizure and deportation to Mexico of American and British residents in California in April, 1840, and Santa Anna's decree for expulsion of all United States nationals from California (July, 1843) were examples of ineffective measures to counter the population admixture.[28]

Although distance, internal revolts, and the Texas question spelled administrative neglect of California, alarming reports of American immigration filtered into the capital periodically. In the spring of 1844 at least three papers in the capital published the story that Governor Micheltorena had sent a special commissioner to inform the central government of the arrival of one thousand American riflemen at the California frontier.[29] About the same date a schooner proceeding from California brought news to a Mexican port that six hundred Americans had settled on the Sacramento River with the intention of "usurping the lands of the Republic."[30]

[25] Slidell to Buchanan, Mexico, December 17, 1845, Despatches from Mexico, XII, and enclosure (supplement to *La Voz del Pueblo* [México], December 3, 1845). The Mexican awareness of Slidell's instruction on California has been noted by the following: Jesse S. Reeves, "The Treaty of Guadalupe Hidalgo," *The American Historical Review*, X (January, 1905), p. 311, with a quotation of Slidell's enclosure (p. 311); Reeves, *American Diplomacy*, pp. 282–283; Thomas A. Bailey, *A Diplomatic History of the American People* (New York, 3rd ed., 1947), p. 268; Callahan, *op. cit.*, p. 152.

[26] *El Tiempo* (México), March 15, 1846.

[27] *El Siglo*, December 30, 1842; Cleland, *op. cit.*, p. 26; John Parrott to Daniel Webster, Mazatlán, April 25, 1842, Consular Despatches, Mazatlán, 1828–1850.

[28] Captain French Forrest, U.S.S. *St. Louis*, to Ellis, Mazatlán, July 14, 1840; Ellis to Forsyth, Mexico, August 20, 1840 (and enclosures), Despatches from Mexico, X; Wilbur (ed.), *op. cit.*, I, 154–156. On Santa Anna's unenforced expulsion decree, see Thompson, *Recollections of Mexico*, p. 227; Shannon to Calhoun, Mexico, October 28, 1844 (and enclosure no. 3), Despatches from Mexico, XII; Smith, *War with Mexico*, I, 73–74.

[29] *Diario del Gobierno* (México), June 12, 1844, and *La Hesperia* (México), June 12, 1844, reprinted in *El Siglo*, June 13, 1844.

[30] *La Hesperia*, July 31, 1844, reprinted in *El Siglo*, August 1, 1844.

Another report from the Pacific coast in 1845 advised that great caravans of Americans were entering California from across the Rockies, indirectly from Oregon Territory, or straight from Texas. In fact, California was another case "like Texas," the writer warned, and steps would have to be taken before the department was lost or confronted the nation with "more complicated problems than Texas."[31]

The opinions of foreigners also focused the attention of Mexicans on the danger of Yankee immigration. The pertinent comments of the French traveler, Duflot de Mofras, were translated in the Mexican press,[32] as were extracts from the book of the Spaniard Luís Manuel del Rivero, who wrote in 1842 that the aggressive and hypocritical American policy in Texas was being applied in the Yankee "invasion of California."[33] The Englishman Robert C. Wyllie, whose study of Mexican public finance in 1843 was soon translated into Spanish, argued for the colonization of California as the means of resisting American expansion.[34] Other warnings came to Mexico from the British press, which perceived that the annexation of Texas would be a precedent for California.[35]

By far the most frequent and emphatic warnings of immigration came to Mexico undiluted from the American press. Among these items were the predictions of American statemen on Manifest Destiny in the Pacific, which combined with American diplomacy to dress the popular movement in the garb of official policy. Representative Thomas W. Gilmer of Virginia was quoted as saying that "our population is invading the Pacific in an irresistible manner," and that westward expansion was as "inevitable as the current of the Mississippi."[36] Another Southern congressman made the alarming assertion that slavery would be extended to the Pacific as soon as the Texan victory was certain.[37] At the moment of the Slidell mission, a Mexican paper cited an alleged letter of Secretary of State Buchanan to President Polk, boasting that, since Texas was "already in our pocket . . . *we can at the same time continue to tighten our clutches on California and New Mexico through the emigration which we are promoting.*"[38] And after the occupation of Monterey in 1842, John Quincy Adams' speech at Braintree, Massachusetts, accusing ex-President Jackson of a grandiose design on Mexican territory stretching to the Pacific, was translated for the information of Mexican readers.[39]

The views of Jackson, whose name was anathema to Mexicans, were sometimes published to focus Mexican attention on Yankee immigration into California. He was purported to have written a letter in 1844, advocating the immediate annexation

[31] *El Monitor Constitucional* (México), May 6, 1845. See also *El Monitor Constitucional*, January 27, 1846, reprinted in *El Tiempo*, January 29, 1846.

[32] *El Siglo*, May 25, 1845.

[33] Luís Manuel del Rivero, *Méjico en 1842* (Madrid, 1844), as extracted in *El Siglo*, November 12, 1844.

[34] Robert C. Wyllie, *México: Noticia sobre su hacienda pública bajo el gobierno español y después de la independencia* (México, 1845), p. 86.

[35] Examples may be found in *El Siglo*, July 11, 1845 (a reprint from the London *Chronicle*); *Memorial Histórico* (México), February 25, 1846 (Mexican correspondent of the London *Times*); *El Tiempo*, April 6, 1846 (an English parliamentary opinion). See also Graebner, *op. cit.*, p. 18; Callahan, *op. cit.*, p. 155.

[36] Northampton (Mass.) *Gazette*, reprinted in *El Eco de la Justicia*, November 21, 1843.

[37] *Ibid.*

[38] *El Amigo del Pueblo*, November 11, 1845. The italics were supplied by the Mexican translator.

[39] *El Siglo*, December 25, 1842.

of Texas to block a California-Texas-British alliance: "How easy it would be for England to interpose a sufficient force to prevent the *emigration* of OUR CITIZENS TO THE CALIFORNIAS."[40]

Undoubtedly the strongest proof to Mexicans of the Yankee greed for California was that "the annexation of the vast territory was spoken of in the United States with an irritating insolence";[41] and the medium for this display was the American press, especially the articles fomenting emigration.

As early as 1843, one paper discussed the United States policy of grabbing Mexican provinces, a policy which gave substance to stories about the cession of California to the Union and the promotion of emigrant parties "after the fashion of those who previously went to Texas."[42] Toward the close of the same year, an Oregonian wrote to the Iowa *Herald* that many of the new settlers in the Northwest would be transplanting their homes to California, a noun which was italicized by the Mexican translator.[43]

Surveying a number of American articles on the subject, a Mexican writer declared that "a multitude of emigrants had departed in the direction of California" and judging by the Yankee reports, Texas was a finished chapter and California would be next in the book of aggression. Without precautionary measures, he insisted, "American immigration will snatch all of our departments from us, one by one, within a short time."[44]

In many instances verbatim reprints from the American press spoke for themselves without the need of Mexican editorial embellishment. At least four dailies of Mexico City translated an item in the Little Rock *Gazette* advertising the Californian colonizing expedition of Mr. Leavitt: "Mr. Leavitt, finally, speaks of the attractions and advantages which California offers to the inhabitants of the West and prognosticates that within ten years . . . that beautiful country [California] will be called '*the Great Republic of the Southwest of North America*'."[45]

From St. Louis came the story that an emigrant band headed for California had ordered the casting of cannon as part of the equipage for peaceful foreign settlement: "President Polk should keep an eye on this, if he does not want to see New Mexico and California occupied by those who emigrate before the war with Mexico can even get started."[46] The Mexican editor commented that "this article well reveals the ambitious aims of the United States of America and shows that its covetousness will not be limited to the territory of Texas."[47] And the *Diario del Gobierno*, official organ of the Mexican executive, did not overlook the notice of the big cannon accompanying the caravan to California: "The emigration which the United States is practicing toward the Californias is inconceivable; entire caravans are discovered

[40] *Ibid.*, May 25, 1844. For another letter of Jackson with the same theme, see *ibid.*, August 22, 1844.

[41] *Ibid.*, October 3, 1845.

[42] Reprinted in *El Eco de la Justicia,* March 14, 1843.

[43] *Ibid.*, December 8, 1843.

[44] *El Patriota Mexicano,* October 5, 1845.

[45] *El Amigo del Pueblo,* October 16, 1845. It also appeared in *La Esperanza* (México) and was reprinted in *El Tiempo,* April 25, 1846. The same item was extracted from the St. Louis *Reveille* and was translated in *El Patriota Mexicano,* November 14, 1845.

[46] *El Amigo del Pueblo,* November 15, 1845.

[47] *Ibid.*

en route, with only the purpose of establishing colonies; and they even carry pieces of artillery to defend themselves and the land that is *theirs by right*. Who supports that right? Is this not the beginning of a new usurpation?"[48]

Noting the avalanche of Yankee immigrants, *El Tiempo* recalled that Polk was elected in 1844 on the promise of the annexation of Texas and Texas had fallen to the United States: "Now the Californias are being dealt with. The crusade is being preached actively in the Southern States; words of the Bible are adopted to praise the fertility of its lands of milk and honey; the enterprise is painted as easy; and it is publicly announced in the American press and in *meetings*, that if the addition of Texas was the presidential question in 1844, the addition of California will be the question in 1848."[49]

Another journalist could not read "without a profound bitterness" the articles in the New York *Express* about the future American sovereignty over California. According to these writers, continuous American emigration combined with Mexican abandonment of California would bring a new star to the Stars and Stripes. Said *El Patriota Mexicano*: "The anticipated annexation of California and New Mexico, the now consummated appropriation of Texas, and the inertia and poverty of our government bring the *Express* to the conclusion that the Mexican Republic has no alternative but to be annexed en masse by the United States, or conform immediately to the idea of watching its territory pared away little by little. Although we do not endorse the prophesied total annexation of the Republic, unhappily we do not have the least bit of difficulty in admitting that the Californias will belong in a short while to our ambitious sister, and that after the Californias, she will continue to occupy all of what we call our frontiers."[50]

Describing a large emigrant band preparing to leave Missouri for California, an American paper prematurely announced that California had organized an independent government after the model of Texas. "The master carpenter of the [United States] government can now begin to construct the benches where the senators of the future state of California may seat themselves." After extracting other articles on American emigrant movements, the Mexican translator concluded the series of reprints with an extract from the New York *Express* which claimed that the same methods applied to Texas "will bring California into our hands and any other states of Mexico which we may desire."[51] A number of kindred articles in American papers, from Massachusetts to Arkansas and Louisiana, had translated second performances in Mexico and could not have been better calculated to rouse Mexican national pride, fear, and bitterness over the Texas trouble.

Joined to all sources of the Mexican fear—developments in California, American diplomacy, the bumptious boasting of American statesmen and journalists about the future acquisition of the department, and the rising wave of Yankee immigration— joined to all these sources and, in fact, springing from them were the recurring analogies between Texas and California. To Mexicans, a backing down on Texas would lead to the identical result in California. After California and New Mexico, the

---

[48] *Diario del Gobierno,* November 1, 1845, reprinted in *El Amigo del Pueblo,* November 4, 1845.

[49] *El Tiempo,* February 4, 1846.

[50] *El Patriota Mexicano,* November 14, 1845.

[51] *El Amigo del Pueblo,* November 15, 1845.

rest of the northern frontier would fall by appeasement to the ambitious sister to the north. Beyond these areas? Time and convenience of the Yankee might carry the Stars and Stripes to Tehuantepec or farther.

Usually reflecting kaleidoscopic opinions, the Mexican press was united in the belief that more was involved in Texas than Texas alone. California was about to fall prey to Yankee expansion, grieved *El Monitor Republicano,* and soon all of Mexico would be absorbed.[52] "California is entirely at the mercy of the North Americans," echoed *El Amigo del Pueblo,* and the arguments in favor of a peaceful renunciation of Texas were submerged by the disastrous precedent it would set for California, New Mexico, and the other northern departments.[53]

Civil strife in Sonora in 1845 provoked *El Siglo Diez y Nueve* to admonish that "this beautiful, extensive, and wealthy department borders upon California, the present target of the United States." The imminent Yankee invasion of California was obvious by the chain of events: a United States naval vessel insults the Mexican flag; a flood of emigrants leave for Oregon and then transfer to California; the American government sends engineers to make a reconnaissance; the Yankee press speaks blatantly of the annexation of California as an "easy and inevitable event"; travelers in that department return to the Union to give lectures on California's "wealth, weakness, and good intentions to separate from Mexico; and a crusade is prepared . . . similar to that which deprived us of Texas."[54]

By the eve of the war the Mexican press had completely fused the annexation of Texas with the impending loss of California, illustrating profusely the potential significance of appeasement in Texas. *El Zempoalteca's* analysis of President Polk's message to Congress of December, 1845, demonstrated this belief:

> How can the President of the United States dare to assert that Mexico has no injury of which to complain against them? What! The insurrection and robbery of Texas, the attack on one of our ports in the Pacific carried out by a commodore of that nation without previous declaration of war, and the effrontery with which the invasion and occupation of the Californias are proclaimed in those states . . . these are not injuries which Mexico has suffered?[55]

El Amigo del Pueblo pointed out that the implications of the Texas question could not be measured:

> Moreover, if the ambition [of the United States] is limited to the single department of Texas, the Mexican Republic would lose little now, provided the importance of Texas is little; but thereafter would follow a loss so considerable that one can scarcely estimate it.[56]

The same paper published a petition signed by "Patriotic Mexicans" under the title "Either Fight the War for Texas or Lose the Nation." This document contained related thoughts on the tragic precedent which would be set in case of retreat on Texas annexation:

[52] *El Monitor Republicano,* March 7 and 9, 1846. But almost a year earlier the same press under the title of *El Monitor Constitucional* had made the identical prediction (May 10, 1845).

[53] *El Amigo del Pueblo,* August 16, 1845.

[54] *El Siglo,* October 3, 1845.

[55] *El Zempoalteca,* January 27, 1846, as reprinted in *Memorial Histórico,* February 3, 1846.

[56] *El Amigo del Pueblo,* November 4, 1845.

> If through an incomprehensible weakness, we sanction the robbery of Texas, how can we defend the Californias, New Mexico, Chihuahua, and the other departments which the voracity of the United States already threatens? Those who today would avoid war with the United States and who would resign themselves to the loss of such a valuable part of our territory, will avoid war tomorrow when they realize that the Californias have been taken by our rapacious neighbors; and it will be recognized and established that Mexico can be robbed with impunity. . . .

Thus, a peaceful surrender of Texas would start a vicious cycle and

> once the new method of acquiring land is sanctioned . . . we ourselves would open a vast field for the insatiable voracity of our neighbors to acquire territory, which method they could place in practice freely, satisfied that after the prize was captured, an indemnity would adjust everything; and in this manner one after another of the parts of the Republic, whose possession would be of any value to them, would be appropriated.[57]

Without variation of theme other influential papers in the capital and the departments sounded the hue and cry. *El Patriota Mexicano* insisted that to listen to the proposals of American statesmen on Texas was sheer blindness:

> . . . the same persons who tomorrow, despite the most solemn agreements, will inevitably appropriate the Californias, New Mexico, and all of the department of Tamaulipas; to listen to discussions of peace from these men is to take the path of perdition . . . it is to confess that the Mexican Republic is impotent to sustain its rights and nationality; it is to submit to existence at the mercy of a foreign nation.[58]

The editors concluded with a plea against negotiation:

> Today, while our enemies are offering to treat with us, they are promoting and organizing an immediate, peaceful, but powerful invasion of our Californian territory, of which they will be owners tomorrow; and they will tell us that they did not usurp it, but admitted it into the Union; at the same time they are tracing the boundary of all the territory whose occupation they hope to legalize by virtue of a shameful treaty. . . .[59]

Somewhat later *El Tiempo* pointed out that Taylor's troops had "invaded" the territory between the Nueces and the Rio Grande on the pretext that it

> belongs to Texas. With these variations in which the philosophical [American] people indulge themselves to arrange the geographical map, well can they appropriate all of the American continent. But do Coahuila, New Mexico, and the Californias also belong to Texas? Well, the fact is that their invasion has been extended to these departments and now they do not conceal the project they have of appropriating them.
> The grand design of the United States unfurls itself into ownership of Mexican territory. Perhaps this enterprise necessitates time, but they know how to take advantage of it; they do not rest; and department after department, district after district, they will manage to plant their flag even beyond Tehuantepec.

---

[57] *Ibid.*
[58] *El Patriota Mexicano,* November 18, 1845.
[59] *Ibid.*

Therefore, the war which we fight today is not solely for the defense of our honor or a part of our territory; it is a war of independence, a national war, because on its outcome depends our existence.[60]

As in the case of stories on immigration, American papers presented Mexican writers with tailor-made articles about Texas as a preliminary to California. Under the title "Texas and California," *El Zempoalteca* warned that Texas had been a precise pattern for current events in California; and proof of this assertion came largely from the boasting way in which the American press, "especially in Louisiana, preach the occupation of California."[61]

Substantiating this claim in an article entitled "After Texas the Californias," *El Diario de Veracruz* reprinted items from the papers of New Orleans. The anti-expansionist *Tropic* denounced the scheme of events behind the acquisition of Texas: adventurous American immigrants; their discontent with alien government; advertisement of Texas' potential wealth; and finally the decision of American settlers "to convert themselves from the governed . . . into the governing." After independence and annexation, the rapacity for territory, fomented by American journalists, was being directed toward California.

The *Tropic* foresaw that the California project would follow the Texas sequence: First, the American "propensity to peregrinate" would be aroused by publicizing California. Then the flood of immigrants would follow

> and soon there will be an American population sufficiently large to repeat the game of Texas. The standard of rebellion will be raised; the [Mexican] government will be defeated; the cry of *liberty* will be lofted, and adventuresome young friends will fly in swarms to the aid of their *oppressed* compatriots in California. Destroyed by internal dissension and revolts, Mexico will not find sufficient force to reduce that unruly province to obedience; and within a short time another new "Republic of the Californias," of the so-called lone star, will reveal itself on the isolated coasts of the Pacific. Shortly afterwards we shall have the "Republic" at our doors; and then the ridiculous and absurd cry requesting the *re*-annexation of the Californias will be heard.

Mirroring the Mexican fear of a Manifest Destiny without limits, the *Tropic* predicted that the "spirit of *re*-annexation" would expand beyond the absorption of Texas and California "until the entire country has become *re*-annexed and the flag sown with stars floats over the towers of the city of the Montezumas."[62]

From a number of similar opinions in the American press, *La Hesperia* reached the conclusion that if the Yankees had their wish, the Stars and Stripes would fly over Veracruz and "the Californias will be one more state which will aggrandize the power of the Union."[63] Undoubtedly, the influence of American journalism in translation was both powerful and unfortunate.

Characteristic of the impotence of the Mexican government during this period, no positive action was taken to prevent the impending loss of California until the hour was midnight. As previously mentioned, negative and ineffective measures were taken

[60] *El Tiempo,* May 15, 1846.

[61] *El Zempoalteca,* February 10, 1846, reprinted in *El Monitor Republicano,* February 15, 1846.

[62] *El Diario de Veracruz* (Veracruz), June 7, 1845, reprinted in *El Siglo,* June 17, 1845.

[63] *La Hesperia,* March 7, 1846. See also *El Tiempo,* April 2, 1846.

against Yankee immigration, and the press and prominent officials gave frequent lip service to the need of blocking further infiltration. As late as May, 1846, one Mexican paper recommended the expulsion of all Americans from the department as the sole means of saving it for Mexico.[64]

Colonization was discussed at various times as a means of strengthening the Mexican hold, but the project of the Jesuit Macnamara to settle several thousand Irish in California was the one tangible scheme considered. It came too late and was discarded after much debate.[65] There was also talk of mortgaging California to England in order to involve the leading naval power in the preservation of Mexican sovereignty.[66]

The most concerted effort to save California, however, was the organization of a military expedition in early 1845—"Expedición a las Californias." Despite the backing of the press and Secretary of War Pedro García Conde, who realized that the Californias were "the object of the strategems of our neighbors,"[67] this gesture was as fruitless and frustrated as Mexican efforts to prepare for the eventuality of war with the United States. William S. Parrott, Polk's confidential agent in Mexico, commented sarcastically about the expedition that "the difference between receiving orders to march and of the march itself is very great in this country and especially at this time when there is not even money in the public Treasury to pay the troops in the city."[68] The failure of the expedition, however, was more concisely told in the following Mexican press report: "The expedition to California, which has been en route for six months, when will it cease to leave?"[69]

Although Mexico was unable to take adequate counteraction, the Yankee threat to California had become deeply imbedded in its national pride through ten years of the Texas question. By 1846 the impending loss of the department could not be disentangled from Mexican reasoning on Texas or from the possible loss of the entire northern frontier. In short, Texas was not an isolated issue which could be treated in a vacuum.

Whatever the American views on the role of California in the causation of the war, a more satisfactory solution is found if the scope is not limited to President Polk's motives; or to whether Slidell presented the proposed purchase of California to Mexican officials; or to the declarations of war by the two countries. A deeper insight is gained by including the Mexican interpretation of Manifest Destiny and its application to the indefinite future.

[64] El Tiempo, May 16, 1846. Typical pleas for military reinforcement of California against American immigration may be found in El Boletín Militar (México), reprinted in El Monitor Constitucional, February 4, 1846, and in the arguments of Minister of Foreign Relations Manuel Rejón before the Mexican Congress in September, 1844 (cited in Echanove Trujillo, op. cit., p. 322).

[65] See El Amigo del Pueblo, October 9, 1845; El Monitor Constitucional, May 3, 1845; Thomas O. Larkin to Buchanan, Monterey, June 16, 1846, Consular Despatches, Monterey, 1837–1848 (MSS).

[66] El Patriota Mexicano, November 28, 1845, presents an illustrative contemporary opinion of a Mexican writer.

[67] Memoria del secretario de estado y del despacho de guerra y marina, 1845 (México, 1845), p. 9.

[68] Parrott to Buchanan, Mexico, July 5, 1845, Despatches from Mexico, XII.

[69] El Siglo, October 16, 1845. See also El Amigo del Pueblo, September 11, 1845; El Patriota Mexicano, December 2, 1845; El Monitor Constitucional, February 4, 1846; El Tiempo, May 7 and 30, 1846.

From this approach it becomes quite clear that Mexicans were aware that a peaceful settlement at the Rio Grande was no guarantee against further territorial encroachment by the United States. On the contrary, they saw that negotiation would set a disastrous precedent; for California was too obviously emerging as the first copy of the Texas pattern. In turn, Mexicans seemed sincere in their anxiety that the entire northern frontier and perhaps the survival of their nation were at stake. They preferred the risk of war.

The territorial provisions of the Treaty of Guadalupe Hidalgo stand as justification for the Mexican fear of the loss of California and the northern frontier. In justification of the larger concern for the fate of Mexico, it might be pointed out that American historians have paused to explain the failure of a belated political movement to annex "all of Mexico" in 1847 and 1848.[70]

At any rate, it was not merely Mexican hindsight when Consul John Black at Mexico City reported a bit of eavesdropping soon after the end of the war: "The other day," he wrote to Buchanan, "I overheard a conversation which took place in a coffee house between six or eight Mexicans, the subject of discussion was California and the wonderful discovery of the golden region. Ah! Says one of them, who appeared to be more knowing than the rest. The Yankees knew full well, before they commenced the war, what they were going to fight for. They knew the value of that country better than we did."[71]

[70] Edward G. Bourne, "The United States and Mexico, 1847–1848," *The American Historical Review*, V (April, 1900), pp. 491–502; John D. P. Fuller, "The Slavery Question and the Movement to Acquire Mexico, 1846–1848," *The Mississippi Valley Historical Review*, XXI (June, 1934), pp. 31–48; Bailey, *op. cit.*, pp. 276–278.

[71] Black to Buchanan, Mexico, January 12, 1849, Consular Despatches, Mexico City, IX.

7 / Party Politics and the Trist Mission

Norman A. Graebner

The characteristic intimacy between domestic politics and foreign policy and between military affairs and diplomatic negotiations during wartime is well illustrated by the next article. Nicholas Trist's negotiations for a peace settlement with Mexico also illustrate the grave difficulties which an American government may encounter in repudiating a treaty, once signed, even if the treaty fails to satisfy all the conditions imposed by instructions committed to the plenipotentiary conducting the negotiations. Norman Graebner here tells the fascinating story of Trist's mission to Mexico, at once raising the intriguing question as to why Trist was ultimately discredited for his activities while his chief, President Polk, has been praised for reaching an honorable conclusion to that controversial war. Obliquely rather than directly, the article points to certain reasons which explain why it was that after a hard fought military victory over Mexico, President Polk did not insist that the United States annex all of Mexico as favored by many American expansionists.

For further reading: William C. Binkley, *The Texas Revolution* (Baton Rouge: 1952); John D. P. Fuller, "The Movement for the Acquisition of All Mexico 1846–1848," in *the Johns Hopkins University Studies in Historical and Political Science*, LIV, No. 1 (Baltimore: 1936); Norman Graebner, *Empire on the Pacific* (New York: 1955); *Frederick Merk, *Manifest Destiny and Mission in American History* (New York: 1963) and *The Monroe Doctrine and American Expansionism 1843–1849* (New York: 1966); Justin H. Smith, *The War With Mexico.* 2 vols. (New York: 1919); Richard W. Van Alystyne, *The Rising American Empire* (New York: 1960); *Albert K. Weinberg, *Manifest Destiny* (Baltimore: 1935); Shomer Zwelling, *Expansion and Imperialism* (Chicago: 1970).

On Saturday evening, February 19, 1848, there occurred in the city of Washington a simple drama with few characters, but of huge portent to the nation. Shortly after

Norman A. Graebner is Edward Stettinius Professor of History at the University of Virginia. This article is reprinted by permission of the author and the editors of the *Journal of Southern History*. Copyright 1953 by the *Journal of Southern History*.

dark a tired, though lithe and vigorous, man of frontier qualities reached the capital. Scarcely two weeks before, he had left Mexico City and had moved quickly downward through mountain passes to Vera Cruz. Ten days later his ship, the *Iris*, discharged him at Mobile. From there James Freaner, the noted "Mustang" of the New Orleans *Delta*, hastened northward to his destination. He delivered two letters at the Washington home of Mrs. Nicholas P. Trist, and then hurried to the residence of the Secretary of State, James Buchanan.[1] In his baggage was the recently negotiated treaty of Guadalupe Hidalgo.

This memorable document, by which the United States was shortly to acquire an empire in the Southwest with the magnificent harbors of San Francisco and San Diego, was the accomplishment of two men, President James K. Polk and his envoy to Mexico, Nicholas P. Trist. Their ephemeral relationship produced one of the strangest and most important episodes in American diplomatic history. So novel was it, in fact, that Philip Hone could characterize it accurately with his witty observation that the Mexican treaty was "negotiated by an unauthorized agent, with an unacknowledged government, [and] submitted by an accidental President to a dissatisfied Senate."[2] Despite its uniqueness, however, the Trist mission was completely logical, for it was the natural sequel to Polk's wartime California policy. And it was conditioned not by the conflict in Mexico, but by the exigencies of American politics.

Polk's diplomacy through the mission of John Slidell had sought the acquisition of California by purchase.[3] In his eagerness to expedite a settlement with Mexico the President had dispatched General Zachary Taylor to the Rio Grande during the spring of 1846, a move which provoked a clash of arms. The suspicion which his action created in the minds of Whig spokesmen incited an onslaught that made the Mexican War the most bitterly criticized in American history. Cried the noted abolitionist, Joshua Giddings: "With indecent haste, with unbecoming levity, under the gag of the previous question, our nation was plunged into a bloody war."[4] Thomas Corwin attacked it with venom: "It will be soon a 'bye word' a curse, a hissing, and scorn with all honest men."[5] To the query whether the United States had cause for war, Joseph Root of Ohio retorted: "Sir, I invoke the scrutiny of the Searcher of Hearts, when I declare that I believe we had not."[6] By June Giddings rejoiced that the Whig press had moved into line, and when Congress adjourned in August, 1846, Robert Winthrop of Massachusetts boasted that the Whigs in Washington were unanimous in their opposition to the administration.[7]

Nor could Polk rely on the support of his own Democratic party. The powerful

[1] Nicholas P. Trist to Mrs. Trist, February 2, 1848; Trist to James Buchanan, February 2, 1848; Mrs. Trist to Trist, February 23, 1848, in Trist Papers (Manuscripts Division, Library of Congress); Mobile *Herald*, February 13, 1848; New Orleans *Picayune*, February 13, 1848; Washington *National Intelligencer*, February 21, 1848; New York *Herald*, February 22, 1848.

[2] Bayard Tuckerman (ed.), *The Diary of Philip Hone, 1828–1851* (2 vols., New York, 1910), II, 347.

[3] For Slidell's instructions, see James Buchanan to John Slidell, November 10, 1845, in Instructions to Mexico, Department of State (National Archives), Vol. XVI.

[4] *Congressional Globe*, 29 Cong., 1 Sess., Appendix, 643.

[5] Thomas Corwin to Oran Follett, February 4, 1847, in L. Belle Hamlin (ed.), "Selections from the Follett Papers," in *Quarterly Publication of the Historical and Philosophical Society of Ohio* (Cincinnati, 1906–1923), IX (1914), 90.

[6] *Cong. Globe*, 29 Cong., 2 Sess., Appendix, 223.

[7] Giddings to Howells, June 8, 1846, in Miscellaneous Papers (Division of Manuscripts, Chicago Historical Society); Robert C. Winthrop, *Addresses and Speeches on Various Occasions* (2 vols., Boston, 1852), I, 560.

Martin Van Buren faction was lukewarm in its adherence to his leadership, while the friends of John C. Calhoun broke completely with the administration over the war issue. So harassed was Polk by congressional opposition when Congress reconvened that he confided to his diary in February, 1847:

> It is now in the third month of the Session and none of my war measures have yet been acted upon. There is no harmony in the Democratic party. . . . In truth faction rules the hour, while principle & patriotism is forgotten. While the Democratic party are thus distracted and divided and are playing this foolish and suicidal game, the Federal party are united and never fail to unite with the minority of the Democratic party, or any faction of it who may break off from the body of their party, and thus postpone and defeat all my measures. I am in the unenviable position of being held responsible for the conduct of the Mexican War, when I have no support either from Congress or from the two officers [Scott and Taylor] highest in command in the field. How long this state of things will continue I cannot foresee.[8]

Although Polk was forced to conduct a bitterly assailed war which had become burdensome to the administration, he insisted on employing American military triumphs to secure California by treaty. Whig invectives against any expansion by conquest prevented a public statement of war aims until December, 1847, but Polk privately was determined to continue the war until he could attain his territorial objectives.[9] Still American victories alone did not assure the success of his policy. The occupation of California by United States troops exerted little pressure on the Mexican government; the refusal of Congress to adopt his military measures thwarted Polk's repeated efforts to win California through a chastisement of Mexico. Perhaps a secret diplomatic mission might avail itself of the expected triumphs of General Winfield Scott on the road to Mexico City or a sudden shift in Mexican politics. By the spring of 1847, congressional trifling, added to the gloomy implications of the slavery debate on American expansionism, forced the President to seek an early peace. In mid-April he quietly dispatched Trist, weighted down with instructions, to join the army of Scott in Mexico.[10]

Trist met all the political requirements of the wartime administration. His adherence to the Democratic party dated back to Jackson's presidency, when for a time he served as Jackson's private secretary.[11] The selection of the chief clerk in the Depart-

---

[8] Milo Milton Quaife (ed.), *The Diary of James K. Polk* (4 vols., Chicago, 1910), II, 368.

[9] The tremendous discrepancy between Polk's private and public statements on California during the first eighteen months of the war has been analyzed recently by this writer. See Norman A. Graebner, "James K. Polk's Wartime Expansionist Policy," in the East Tennessee Historical Society's *Publications* (Knoxville, 1929–   ), No. 23 (1951), 32–45.

[10] For Trist's instructions see Buchanan to Trist, April 15, 1847, in Instructions to Mexico, Department of State, Vol. XVI.

[11] Trist's association with the Jackson administration is made evident by many letters in the Trist Papers. Trist supported Jackson in the election of 1828 as editor of the Charlottesville *Virginia Advocate,* but received his first political appointment in 1828 from Henry Clay to the State Department. Jackson retained him with an appointment to the Treasury Department. For a short time he succeeded Andrew J. Donelson as Jackson's private secretary. In 1833 Jackson appointed him to the more lucrative consulship at Havana where Trist remained until 1841. Louis Martin Sears has produced from the Trist Papers a brief, though excellent and sympathetic, evaluation of Trist's life and character. See Louis Martin Sears, "Nicholas P. Trist, A Diplomat with Ideals," in *Mississippi Valley Historical Review* (Cedar Rapids, 1915–   ), XI (1924–1925), 85–98.

ment of State, a position of no political importance, afforded the President the opportunity of opening negotiations without offending any faction of the party. In commissioning Trist as an executive agent, Polk left the way open for a subsequent full-fledged diplomatic mission under Buchanan should it become necessary. Since Trist, furthermore, had no standing within the party, he could not deprive the administration of full credit for any successful negotiations. The fact that Trist was destoyed by his connection with the treaty of Guadalupe Hidalgo, whereas Polk has won unending acclaim from it, indicates that these political considerations were of considerable importance.

This Virginian, Trist, was not as mediocre in ability as certain of his later critics would have us believe. Many who knew him attested to his scholarly attainments, his integrity and honor, and to his industry.[12] Schuyler Hamilton, Scott's aide-de-camp, later wrote that he had "met with few men whose conduct entitled them to so much confidence, as did that of Mr. Trist under trying circumstances."[13] He spoke French and Spanish fluently, and this accomplishment, added to a long residence in Havana as United States consul, well equipped him for his mission to Mexico. There was nothing in Trist's previous experience or his coming negotiations to merit the historian Jesse Reeves's assertion that Trist lacked the diplomatic abilities necessary for this undertaking. The treaty of Guadalupe Hidalgo was not the product of incompetence. As a diplomat Trist made a treaty of peace with Mexico at a time when American generals, politicians, the press, members of the cabinet, and the President himself believed it impossible. Perhaps few other Americans could have succeeded at the task. Trist knew the character of Mexico well, adapted himself to it, and consequently impressed its authorities favorably.

Trist lacked two important qualities, good judgment and humility. He possessed a rare measure of the intellectual quality of "abstruse investigation and searching analysis."[14] He could not, therefore, resist the inclination to fathom every secret about him, to approach each problem from every conceivable direction. Thus his letters were lengthy, verbose, and heavy in abstractions. He wrote easily and, when angered, could pour forth invectives with remarkable facility. Francis P. Blair, who knew Trist well, wrote to Martin Van Buren in August, 1847, that the Virginian would wear out even the Spanish patience, which he understood was durable enough to last a thousand years. He recalled that "Trist's letters to Jackson (almost exclusively about his own health & the physic he took & how it operated) arrived . . . to at least a thousand pages."[15] These failings have exposed Trist to criticism that has obscured the chief reason he has become an important figure in American diplomatic history. Scott recognized his real significance—that his negotiations in Mexico rather than his quarrel with the administration altered considerably the destiny of the United States. To Andrew J. Donelson the choice of Trist seemed propitious, and he assured Polk that

[12] See Edward Livingston to Martin Van Buren, March 17, 1829; W. C. Rives to Van Buren, March 19, 1829, in Trist Papers; Aaron Vail to Buchanan, October 24, 1845, in Buchanan Papers (Manuscripts Division, Pennslyvania Historical Society). Wrote Vail to the Secretary of State: "I have warmly sympathized with you for what I knew must be the toil incident to your official position, and consequently rejoiced that you had called to your aid one so able as Mr. Trist to relieve you of part of your labors."

[13] Schuyler Hamilton to Hamilton Fish, April 20, 1869, in Trist Papers.

[14] From letter of recommendation written for Trist by J. A. G. Davis, April 17, 1831, ibid.

[15] Francis P. Blair to Van Buren, August 25, 1847, in Van Buren Papers (Manuscripts Division, Library of Congress).

through his agent he would eventually announce an acceptable treaty to the American people.[16]

Since the Polk administration at the time of Trist's departure had still avowed publicly no objective beyond peace, the indemnity clauses in Trist's instructions dictated absolute secrecy. Trist slipped quietly out of Washington, impressed by the admonitions of the President. At Charleston, South Carolina, two days later, he sought an inconspicuous lodging, but reported that the fates were against him. All the omnibuses of the city belonged to some hotel; his took him to the renowned Charleston House. He left Charleston with considerable relief and continued by rail and post coach to Montgomery, Alabama, where he boarded a coastal vessel for New Orleans. One week after leaving Charleston he reported to his wife that he was "perfectly well escondido" in an obscure French *auberge* (Hotel d'Orleans), under the name of "Docteur Tarro." His knowledge of French was being employed to good purpose. Almost immediately he traveled again down the Mississippi to Southwest Pass to await the cutter *Ewing*. Only when he attempted to board his ship did he face difficulty. It required a lengthy argument with the collector of customs to keep his name off the customhouse form. After a fast trip of eight days his vessel anchored at Vera Cruz.[17] That the news of his mission shortly flooded the press was not the fault of Trist.

Polk sought above all to protect his efforts to renew negotiations from political attacks at home. His indignation was boundless, therefore, when two letters published soon after Trist's departure, showing remarkable accuracy of detail, appeared in the New York *Herald* and the Boston *Post*.[18] When the *National Intelligencer* reprinted the news, the mission became widely known at the capital. Polk interrogated his cabinet. He threatened removals. Buchanan even accused Mrs. Trist of revealing the information.[19] Although little mention was made of Trist's departure from New Orleans, a correspondent at Vera Cruz not only noted Trist's arrival for the American public, but also predicted accurately his subsequent movements. Before the middle of June the New York *Herald's* Washington correspondent had secured for his paper Polk's boundary proposals.[20]

Thomas Ritchie's Washington *Union* attempted to counter such intelligence. Polk had informed the editor confidentially of Trist's mission so that he could "shape the course of his paper in reference to it."[21] So consistent were Ritchie's denials of Trist's activities that J. C. Rives once declared that if an "opposition paper were to charge that Mr. Polk read the Bible every Sabbath, Mr. Ritchie would deny it, for fear it would make the Jury inimical to the President."[22] The administration never ceased to show its disgust for the "scribblings" of the press. William L. Marcy, the Secretary of War, termed the correspondents "gifted wiseacres who know more than

[16] Andrew J. Donelson to James K. Polk, July 15, 1847, in Polk Papers (Manuscripts Division, Library of Congress).

[17] Quaife, *Diary of Polk*, II, 478; Trist to Mrs. Trist, April 18, 25, 28, May 6, 1847; Trist to Denis Prieur, April 28, 1847, in Trist papers.

[18] New York *Herald*, April 20, 21, 1847; Boston *Post* quoted in *Niles' Register* (Baltimore, 1811–1849), April 24, 1847.

[19] M. J. R. [Trist's sister] to Trist, May 22, 1847, in Trist Papers; *Niles' Register*, May 22, 1847.

[20] New York *Herald*, June 13, 1847.

[21] Quaife, *Diary of Polk*, II, 480.

[22] J. C. Rives to Van Buren, May 12, 1847, in Van Buren Papers.

every thing some days before events transpire or exist."[23] While Polk and his cabinet fumed, the metropolitan press continued to condemn, praise, question, and outguess Trist at every turn. Any further effort of the administration to deny its war aims now became futile.

By July the administration had further cause for apprehension. News had reached Washington of the verbal feud between Trist and General Scott. When the general, motivated by an abiding distrust of the Polk administration, failed to comply with the President's instructions, Trist chose to absorb Scott's abuse of the administration. He read a lengthy lecture to the general, confiding to his wife, "If I have not *demolished* him, then I give up."[24] The letter almost drove Scott to derangement. His first impulse, he answered Trist, was to return the "farrago of insolence, conceit, and arrogance to the author," but he decided instead to preserve it "as a choice specimen of diplomatic literature and manners." He declared that Trist, armed with "an ambulatory guillotine," would be "the personification of Danton, Marat, and St. Just, all in one."[25] A few days later Scott tendered his resignation to the War Department and censured the President for sending the commissioner: "To have such a flank battery planted against me, amidst critical military operations, is a great annoyance."[26]

Washington braced itself against the expected epistolary flood, for it knew the adeptness of both men with the pen. Blair observed wittily that Scott and Trist would produce "a most voluminous, if not a luminous correspondence."[27] Marcy predicted that their writing would be "the most *piquant* & interesting in the war series."[28] To the administration the feud was especially reprehensible since many ardent Whigs interpreted Trist's presence in Mexico as an effort of the President to confine Scott's popularity. "It would appear," observed the London *Globe*, ". . . that President Polk, having made a war for 'political capital,' is not less anxious to make a peace, now he finds the capital accruing to Gen. Scott. . . . He has been sending a certain Mr. Trist to Mexico, it is said, to attempt negotiation, and—it is farther said by 'the well-informed friends of Gen. Scott—as a spy upon the public conduct of the General, and if possible to ruin him'."[29] Declared one outraged editor: "It is not a matter of every day occurrence for a government to supersede its own generals, by appointing over them civilians of neither rank nor character. Jealousy has frequently arisen at home, of successful warriors carrying the arms of their country, into distant lands; but a decent respect . . . for the dictates of justice, has prevented it from seeking its gratification by so ignoble and baseminded a resort as this."[30]

To the President, in turn, Scott's actions stemmed purely from political motivation. "The truth is," he recorded, "that I have been compelled from the beginning to conduct the war against Mexico through the agency of two Gen'ls highest in rank who

[23] William L. Marcy to P. M. Wetmore, July 26, 1847, in Marcy Papers (Manuscripts Division, Library of Congress).

[24] Trist to Mrs. Trist, May 21, 1847, in Trist Papers. Trist wrote earlier: "If I don't *finish* him I will give any body leave to say that all the time I have passed in study has been passed in vain." Trist to Mrs. Trist, May 15, 1847, *ibid.*

[25] Winfield Scott to Trist, May 29, 1847, *ibid.*

[26] Scott to Marcy, June 4, 1847, in Letter Group 94, Adjutant General, Letters Received, No. 882-S–1847, War Department (National Archives).

[27] Blair to Van Buren, July 7, 1847, in Van Buren Papers.

[28] Marcy to Wetmore, July 16, 1847, in Marcy Papers.

[29] London *Globe* quoted in New York *Herald*, August 9, 1847.

[30] New York *Courier and Enquirer* quoted in Washington *Union*, July 13, 1847.

have not only no sympathies with the Government, but are hostile to my administration."[31] Polk decided against the removal of Scott, but he instructed his fellow Democrat and close supporter, General William O. Butler, to prepare himself for the command in Mexico.[32] Privately Buchanan informed Trist that the general was being held responsible and extended to him an added assurance: "Your friends here will take care of you."[33]

Although only a reconciliation between Scott and Trist could terminate the endless review in the Whig press of the motivation behind the Trist mission, the administration was hardly prepared for the next significant intelligence from Mexico. Trist's early efforts at negotiation convinced him that he needed Scott's cooperation in making a treaty. The general's response to his overture was cordial, and soon the two men became fast friends. Scott reported to Marcy that he regarded Trist as "able, discreet, courteous, and amiable." He added: "So far as I am concerned, I am perfectly willing that all I have heretofore written to the Department about Mr. Trist, should be suppressed."[34] Similarly Trist praised Scott to the State Department. To his wife he wrote that Scott was "the soul of honour and probity, and full of the most sterling qualities of heart and head: affectionate, generous, forgiving, and a *lover of justice*."[35] When Trist suddenly became ill, Scott placed him under the care of their mutual friend, General Persifer F. Smith, sent him some guava marmalade from his personal stores, and finally made the commissioner his guest at headquarters.[36] After the American army occupied Mexico City, one officer could observe: "Mr. Trist is the only fellow-liver with the general."[37]

Quite naturally the administration viewed this arrangement as politically ominous, for it appeared to place Scott in a position of influence during any future negotiations with Mexico. For the moment Marcy thought the new friendship deserving of ridicule. "This is a changeable world in which we live," he wrote to his intimate, P. M. Wetmore. "I believe I will hereafter adopt the maxim of dealing with your friends as if you might become enemies & with your enemies as if you might become friends. Hereafter you must not expect in my letters much confidential matters unless I make you an exception."[38]

Before the end of September Whig demands for immediate peace prompted the impatient Polk to regard the Trist mission as a political liability. News of the August armistice had filtered across the nation through the New Orleans press. George W. Kendall's letter to the *Picayune* indicated that the entire negotiation looked like one

[31] Quaife, *Dairy of Polk*, III, 57–59. Marcy informed Scott that the duties of the two men in Mexico were so distinct and clear that the "most overwrought sensitiveness could not properly take the slightest exception." Marcy to Scott, May 31, July 12, 1847, in Marcy Papers.

[32] Polk to General William O. Butler, August 7, 1847, in Polk Letter Books (Manuscripts Division, Library of Congress).

[33] For Buchanan's opinions of Trist see Buchanan to Trist, June 14, July 13, 19, 1847, in Trist Papers.

[34] Trist to Scott, June 25, 1847, *ibid*; Scott to Marcy, July 25, 1847, in Letter Group 94, Adjutant General, Letters Received, No. 883–S–1847, War Department.

[35] For Trist's opinions of Scott see Trist to Buchanan, July 7, 23, August 24, 1847; Trist to Mrs. Trist, October 18, 1847, in Trist Papers.

[36] Winfield Scott, *Memoirs of Lieut.-General Scott* (2 vols., New York, 1864), II, 579–80; Scott to Persifer F. Smith, July 6, 1847, in Trist Papers.

[37] Robert Anderson, *An Artillery Officer in the Mexican War, 1846–1847* (New York, 1911), 317.

[38] Marcy to Wetmore, September 26, 1847, in Marcy Papers.

of Santa Anna's old tricks to gain time and "plan some new scheme of trickery and dissimulation." He predicted that Mexico would demand too much: " 'Give them an inch, and they'll take an ell', is applied to many people in the world—give a Mexican an inch and he'll take at least seven miles and a half."[39] The cabinet feared the implications of the unusual delay in the official reports from Mexico. Marcy expressed alarm: "The negotiations should only have lasted for a brief period—I fear the negotiators have got to writing—if so all is over—the Mexicans are the most famous people in the whole world for protracting business and both Trist & Scott are interminable writers. When they begin they never know where to stop."[40]

By October the Mexican terms, printed widely in the American press, quickly crystallized the belief that the armistice had been a hoax. The New York *Herald* warned its readers to take care when they read the proposals, or they would be thrown into convulsions.[41] Polk had no quarrel with the peaceful sentiments of his officials in Mexico, but Trist, by agreeing to submit to the administration the Mexican proposal of San Francisco and the Nueces, appeared to be ignoring his instructions. The President determined to recall him. A brief diary notation explained his action: "Mr. Trist is recalled because his remaining longer with the army could not, probably, accomplish the objects of his mission, and because his remaining longer might, & probably would, impress the Mexican Government with the belief that the United States were so anxious for peace that they would ultimate[ly] conclude one upon the Mexican terms. Mexico must now first sue for peace, & when she does we will hear her proposition."[42]

When Trist's report reached Washington the President commented again: "He had no right to depart from his instructions, and I disapprove his conduct in doing so. . . . Mr. Trist has managed the negotiation very bunglingly and with no ability. . . . I thought he had more sagacity and more common sense than to make the propositions he has made."[43] Under Polk's direction Buchanan repeated the order of recall, but he revealed privately his own embarrassment at doing so. "I am extremely sorry to be obliged to write to you this Despatch," admitted Buchanan. "It was unavoidable. You have placed us in an awkard [sic] position & the President feels it deeply." He informed Trist, however, that Polk bore no great animosity, and added a further assurance: "You may always confidently rely upon my friendship; & I hope that portion of your conduct which the President disapproved may not subject you to any public criticism."[44] Trist's recall was the product of the President's frustration, not of his antipathy.

Trist's decision to remain in Mexico was highly irregular, but his subsequent negotiations indicate that it was the proper one. It was not so viewed by the administration, partially because of its lack of knowledge of what was taking place. Communications were inadequate to keep Washington abreast of the rapidly changing political scene in Mexico that suddenly in late November made peace more than a

---

[39] Kendall's letter was widely quoted in the American press. See New Orleans *Picayune*, September 9, 1847; New Orleans *Delta*, September 10, 1847; New York *Herald*, September 18, 19, 1847; *Niles' Register*, September 18, 1847.

[40] Marcy to Wetmore, September 26, 1847, in Marcy Papers.

[41] See New York *Herald*, October 4, 5, 6, 7, 1847.

[42] Quaife, *Diary of Polk*, III, 185–86.

[43] *Ibid.*, 196–201.

[44] Buchanan to Trist [Private], October 25, 27, 1847, in Trist Papers.

possibility. The entreaties of Mexican officials, the British legation, and even Scott himself convinced Trist that on his willingness to negotiate rested all hope of peace. "I am sure you will, and I leave it to your kindness, I may almost say charity for this unhappy nation," wrote Edward Thornton, secretary of the British legation, "to lend a helping hand towards the preservation of her nationality. I look upon this as the last chance, for either party, of making peace."[45]

Early in December Trist suggested to the Mexican commissioners that he would be willing to resume negotiations on the basis of a boundary line "running up the middle of the Rio Bravo from its mouth to the thirty-second degree of latitude, and thence along that parallel to the Pacific Ocean." The Mexican authorities agreed. On December 4 Trist announced to Thornton his decision to remain in Mexico: "What is my line of duty to my government and my country in this most extraordinary position in which I find myself? Knowing as I do, that peace is the earnest wish of both, is it, *can* it be my duty to allow this last chance for peace to be lost . . .? Upon full reflection, I have come to the conclusion that my duty is, to pursue the opposite course; and upon this conclusion I have taken my stand."[46] Two days later he explained his decision to Buchanan. He assured the Secretary that his action still left the administration "perfect liberty to disavow his proceeding, should it be deemed disadvantageous to our country."[47]

Observers in Washington continued to accept a far different analysis of affairs in Mexico. Daniel Webster summed up the conventional view toward the problem of peace in Mexico when he wrote to his son in August, 1846, "Mexico is an ugly enemy. She will not fight—& will not treat."[48] Not even the seizure of the Mexican capital a year later appeared to bring peace any nearer. The London *Chronicle* predicted in November that a long time might still elapse before the United States could end the war. W. J. Hammersley, an astute political observer of Hartford, Connecticut, wrote his misgivings: "The strange people with whom we are at war, governed as they are by no ordinary rules of action, furnish us with little safe ground for

[45] See Edward Thornton to Trist, November 22, 24, 1847, *ibid.* Thornton assured Trist that certainly the actions of the Mexican government served as proof of the "sincere and anxious desire for the fulfillment of the great object which Their Excellencies the Commissioners have in view."

[46] Trist to Thornton, December 4, 1847, *ibid.*

[47] Trist to Buchanan, December 6, 1847, *ibid.* Historians have generally been critical of Trist's decision to remain in Mexico, although none has seen fit to condemn its results. Justin Smith, for example, attributed to Trist, because of his associations with Jefferson and Jackson, "queer feelings in the head that were not exactly growing pains, and produced a state of mind that was neither of heaven nor of earth." Eugene McCormac accused Trist of bad judgement and "inordinate conceit." He described Trist as a man of "small mental calibre and excessive vanity," and concluded that Trist's decision to remain in Mexico resulted from a lack of sincerity and a desire for notoriety. Jesse Reeves has treated him more kindly. He wrote simply that Polk overestimated Trist's diplomatic abilities and underestimated the task which was to confront him. Louis Martin Sears, on the other hand, has attempted to show that Trist's chief trait was devotion to duty, that his motives were genuine, and that he remained even though he knew what the probable consequences would be. Wrote Sears: "His courage under the ordeal and fortitude with which he faced its consequences reveal Trist as a character of gold." See Justin H. Smith, *The War with Mexico* (2 vols., New York, 1919), II, 127; Eugene I. McCormac, *James K. Polk, A Political Biography* (Berkeley, 1922), 490, 523, 525, 527; Jesse S. Reeves, *American Diplomacy under Tyler and Polk* (Baltimore, 1907), 312; Sears, "Nicholas P. Trist, A Diplomat with Ideals," 98.

[48] Daniel Webster to D. Fletcher Webster, August 6, 1846, in C. H. Van Tyne (ed.), *The Letters of Daniel Webster* (New York, 1902), 343.

prophecy."[49] It was inconceivable to many Americans that any Mexican regime would be permitted to conclude a peace satisfactory to the United States. "Nothing is easier than to make a revolution in Mexico," observed the *American Review* in October, "and nothing is plainer to our minds than that no chief or party in that country, who shall enter into a provisional treaty to cede away to us New Mexico and California, can hold the reins of government long enough to consummate so wicked a purpose."[50] John Parrott wrote from Vera Cruz in December that Mexico was not ready for peace, for too many areas had not been subjected to American arms. As late as January John P. Gaines, a Whig congressman from Kentucky, declared in Washington that he had met no one in Mexico who believed that Trist could make a treaty.[51] Thus Polk could deny officially all possibility of peace and base his full Mexican policy, as submitted to the Thirtieth Congress in December, 1847, on that assumption.

Trist's negotiations proved the supposition of the administration wrong. The President might have been expected, therefore, to acknowledge his error, laud Trist's sagacity, and forgive his commissioner's insubordination. It was in the final analysis Trist's superior evaluation of Mexican politics that achieved both peace with Mexico and the administration's war aims. Trist, however, was completely rejected. Although forewarned, he had become involved in the political turmoil of the American high command in Mexico and was regarded thereafter by the Polk administration as a traitor to the Democratic cause. Even before the cabinet had knowledge of his decision to remain in Mexico Trist was a marked man.

During the forties men took their political affiliations seriously. Party unity was the primary objective of such conservative politicians as Polk, and party loyalty was a mark of character. The threatened disruption of old political alignments arising from the slavery debate and the rapid economic growth of the nation greatly increased the emphasis on adherence to the party line. It was predicted, moreover, that the Mexican War would furnish presidents for the next decade, and the two leading generals were Whigs. This fear of expanding Whig prestige, unfortunately, had colored the President's conduct of the war and his relations with Scott and Taylor, both of whom were mentioned often as possible presidential candidates in 1848. It was the Executive's intense partisanship in his military policy that led to a bitter, deplorable quarrel in Mexico between Scott and three high-ranking officers. This altercation resulted eventually in a court of inquiry and unending recriminations in both the United States and Mexico. Trist became enmeshed in this controversy, chose the wrong side, and was discarded by the administration because of it.

Heading the trio in American headquarters who opposed Scott was Gideon J. Pillow, Polk's former law partner and now a volunteer major general, second in command to Scott and placed there at the suggestion of the President. Pillow was a party man above all, had headed the Tennessee delegation to the Baltimore Convention

---

[49] London *Chronicle,* November 12, 1847; W. J. Hammersley to Gideon Welles, August 1, 1847, in Welles Papers (Manuscripts Division, Library of Congress). For a similar view of Mexican affairs see New York *Herald,* May 31, July 9, September 1, December 20, 1847.

[50] *American Review* (New York, 1845–1852), VI (1847), 341.

[51] John Parrott to Marcy, December 20, 1847, in Marcy Papers; *Niles' Register,* January 8, 1848. Late in January the Washington *Union* still adhered to the view that more war would be required before a treaty could be concluded. See Washington *Union,* January 27, 1848.

in 1844, and boasted to his fellow Tennessean in the White House that he had secured his nomination.[52] Some called Pillow the President's *alter ego*; they noted that he claimed unlimited influence in the distribution of executive favors.[53] Although he lacked any great military ability, he enjoyed the full support of the administration. When he was severely criticised for ineptness at Cerro Gordo, the Washington *Union* rushed to his defense.[54]

In agreement with Pillow in matters of strategy and equally at variance with Scott was the Regular Army officer, General W. J. Worth, a New York Democrat and a friend of Marcy. His early triumphs over Taylor and other officers in matters of promotion during the north Mexican campaign exemplified the staunch support which he commanded in the War Department. Worth, like Pillow, lacked military genius. Ulysses S. Grant once described him as "nervous, impatient, and restless on the march, or when important or responsible duty confronted him."[55] Although he owed what military reputation he had achieved in the Mexico City campaign to Scott, he constantly undermined his chief and broke with him completely when it became obvious that Scott was under a ban from Washington. Colonel James Duncan, the third officer, was a close friend of both Pillow and Worth. It was the machinations of the two generals that had secured a brevet for Duncan, and finally the more substantial reward of colonel and inspector-general.[56] The promise of promotion won others to this coalition. Colonel Bennet Riley, the hero of Contreras, succumbed and was rewarded, so Scott believed, with the brevet of major general and the command of California.[57]

Scott had complained repeatedly of misstatements in the battle reports of both Pillow and Worth when a letter attributed to Pillow, but published over the signature of "Leonidas," appeared in the New Orleans *Delta*. It assigned all the credit for the victories of Contreras and Chapultepec to Pillow and predicted that they would "stand unparalleled in the history of the world."[58] This letter, moreover, ridiculed the armistice of August and indicated that both of these generals had bitterly opposed it. The repeated references to the "brave and gallant" Pillow were too much for Scott. He issued a general order directed at these officers to prevent the repetition of such offenses.

Trist was quickly caught in the whirl of this dissension. He was on good terms with Scott and at the same time was still in high standing with the administration. "Between these two facts," he recorded, "stood Gideon J. Pillow." Both Pillow and Worth had shown considerable interest in Trist as well as in his mission. When Pillow suddenly found himself in a serious quarrel with Scott, he sought to avoid the consequences by securing the "friendly services" of Trist. He wrote to Trist in October: "Will Mr. Trist do me the favour of calling to see me. I wish to see him *specially*.

[52] Gideon J. Pillow to Polk, May 29, 1844, in Polk Papers. Wrote Pillow: "I was up nearly all night last night in bringing about the *result*. I had many difficulties to encounter. But I *faultered not.* . . ."

[53] Notes in Trist Papers, 1848.

[54] Washington *Union,* June 18, 1847.

[55] U. S. Grant, *Personal Memoirs of U. S. Grant* (2 vols., New York, 1895), I, 94.

[56] Scott, *Memoirs,* II, 416–17.

[57] *Ibid.,* 417.

[58] New Orleans *Delta,* September 10, 1847, MS. copy to Trist from James L. Freaner, September 25, 1847, in Trist Papers. See also *Senate Ex. Docs., 30 Cong., 1 Sess.,* No. 65 (Serial No. 510), 320.

Please say when you can call in."[59] The general even intimated to Trist that any aid from him would bring an appointment from the President. The commissioner, however, believed Pillow to be a "barefaced impostor" and refused to intercede. Both Scott and General James Shields, Trist wrote later, warned him of an impending attack from the administration: "You don't know what party-spirit is capable of. They will torture you. They will put you on the rack."[60]

Pillow repudiated the "Leonidas" letter and was again amply upheld by the administration. Wrote the Washington *Union*: "General Pillow has been twice falsely charged with writing his own praises. As if, indeed, the pen of impartial history would not render full justice to his splendid services to his country."[61] When Scott finally placed the three officers under arrest and requested a court-martial for their trial, Pillow injected a breath of scandal into the dispute and brought it before the administration. In a letter to the President he so recounted the conversation at a July conference of officers at Puebla as to imply that Trist and Scott had attempted to bribe Santa Anna. Polk was infuriated. He wrote: "The whole cabinet and myself condemned the proceedings unqualifiedly, and resolved to have the matter investigated."[62] The President was convinced that Pillow was being abused because of his friendship for the administration. His chief concern was to prevent Pillow's name from becoming associated with the Santa Anna intrigue of July.[63] Shortly thereafter Shields arrived in Washington and offered some comfort to Polk by defending Pillow's bravery and gallantry. But he informed the President that Trist had not been present at the ill-fated conference and that no bribe had been intended.[64] The President was not convinced; he awaited further details from Pillow.

Before the end of December the Secretary of War brought more shocking news— the charges of Scott against Pillow, Worth, and Duncan. Quite naturally, the administration turned on Scott. The charges, concluded Polk, stemmed from the general's "vanity and tyrannical temper" and his "want of prudence and common sense." He believed Scott to be jealous of the Democratic generals because he had not been made the exclusive hero of the war in the American press.[65] Within two weeks the President issued orders relieving Scott of his command and substituting a court of inquiry for the court-martial. Buchanan warned him that this creation of a less severe court would be interpreted by the Whigs as a show of favoritism towards his political friends. Even the British minister observed that it would be difficult thereafter for the administration to satisfy its opposition that party considerations did not govern its relations with Scott.[66] In February, 1848, Scott received his new instructions and immediately gave the command of his army to General Butler.

[59] Pillow to Trist, October 9, 1847, in Trist Papers.

[60] Notes, 1848, in Trist Papers.

[61] Washington *Union*, November 2, 1847.

[62] Quaife, *Diary of Polk*, III, 246, 251, 263. Pillow wrote to Polk on October 28, but this letter has never been found.

[63] *Ibid.*, 253; Polk to Pillow, December 19, 1847, in Polk Letter Books.

[64] Quaife, *Diary of Polk*, III, 262–63.

[65] *Ibid.*, 266–67.

[66] Marcy to Scott, January 13, 1848, in Marcy Papers; Quaife, *Diary of Polk*, III, 293; Crampton to Palmerston, January 27, 1848, Public Record Office, Foreign Office, America, Vol. CDLXXX (Justin H. Smith Transcripts, Manuscripts Division, New York Public Library, Vol. III). Polk actually removed one member of the court when he learned that the officer was a friend of Trist. See Quaife, *Diary of Polk*, III, 301.

Trist was rejected as completely as Scott. His reconciliation with the general had made him a very dangerous member of the administration's household, and it aroused increasing disapproval in Washington. The President, therefore, interpreted Trist's refusal to pour oil on troubled waters as a personal affront. Wrote the irate Polk on December 30: "Mr. Trist, from all I can learn, has lent himself to Gen'l Scott and is his mere tool, and seems to be employed in ministering to his malignant passions, in persecuting Gen'l Pillow and others who are supposed to be friendly to me."[67] Trist's decision to remain in Mexico threw what was left of party rancor against him, for he appeared to be acting on the advice of Scott. When Polk learned of it early in January, he recognized only one explanation: "He seems to have entered into all Scott's hatred of the administration, and to be lending himself to all Scott's evil purposes. He may, I fear, greatly embarrass the Government."[68] He termed Trist's lengthy explanation of December 6 "arrogant, impudent, and very insulting to his Government, and even personally offensive to the President." His reasoning was repetitious. "It is manifest to me," he recorded, "that he has become the tool of Gen'l Scott and his menial instrument, and that the paper was written at Scott's instance and dictation."[69]

Strangely enough, Polk took no immediate action against Trist, although he knew throughout the month of January that Trist was engaged in negotiations. Jefferson Davis informed Polk before the end of December that intelligence from Mexico indicated that an American commissioner could then conclude a peace with Mexico.[70] On the following day the Washington *Union* published a report from "Mustang" of the New Orleans *Delta*, dated December 13, that Trist would probably return to the United States with a treaty. Mexican commissioners, he noted, had already arrived at the capital to confer with Trist. "Whether they have succeeded, no person as yet is apprized," he observed, "but I hope, for the interests of our country that he will, if he is so enabled, go home with the treaty in his pocket."[71] Rumors of Trist's negotiations mounted in volume throughout the month of January. Editors found themselves puzzled, however, by Polk's reticence to speak out on this subject. They knew that Trist was already in disrepute, yet the administration refused to condemn his negotiations publicly. "This discrepancy ought to be cleared up," chided the New York *Herald*. "It belongs to the personal character of the President and his cabinet to have it done." Continued silence might prove embarrassing to the administration if the treaty were based on Trist's original instructions.[72]

In his perplexity Polk concluded simply that Trist and Scott had conspired to embarrass him. Not until late in January, however, did he finally address an order to

[67] *Ibid.*, 266–67.

[68] *Ibid.*, 283, 286.

[69] *Ibid.*, 300–301.

[70] On December 31 Jefferson Davis and Lewis Cass called on the President and suggested that he confer the power of negotiation on some person immediately to conclude a treaty with Mexico. *Ibid.*, 269–70.

[71] Washington *Union*, January 1, 1848.

[72] New York *Herald*, January 27, 1848. The *Herald* stated: "Where there is so much smoke, there ought to be some fire. These rumors have continued from day to day for the last three weeks, and must mean something of some importance, in the way of negotiations between the two countries." Several days later the *Herald's* Washington correspondent wrote: "There is no direct proof that Mr. Trist has made a treaty, but there is abundance of circumstantial evidence, sufficiently strong to convince the most sceptical that a treaty has been made." New York *Herald*, February 9, 1848.

Butler to terminate any negotiation in which Trist might be engaged.[73] Even then Buchanan warned that such a letter might commit the administration to the rejection of a very desirable settlement.[74]

Following a close scrutiny of the treaty, Polk accepted it with both hands. He never again recognized Trist publicly or privately, but he showed no inclination to disqualify the product of Trist's endeavors, for the treaty contained the indemnity clauses he required. The New York *Herald* predicted with truth that Polk would be content with the "dazzling object of his ambition," California and New Mexico.[75] The administration might feel chagrin at Trist's insubordination, observed the New Orleans *Picayune*, but it would "ultimately swallow its disappointment, and California and New Mexico at the same time."[76] But Polk's hatred of Trist continued. "Mr. Trist has acted very badly," he recalled upon the receipt of the document from Buchanan. Three weeks later he wrote, "Trist has proved himself to be an impudent and unqualified scoundrel."[77] The treaty became the law of the land, but the President refused to compensate its author for his expenses in Mexico. Observed Thomas Hart Benton regretfully: "Certainly those who served the government well in the war with Mexico, fared badly with the administration. . . . Trist, who made the treaty which secured the objects of the war, and released the administration from its dangers, was recalled and dismissed."[78]

Polk gladly accepted the fruits of Trist's diplomacy to rid himself of a politically dangerous war. By 1848 the administration had extended the war so long that peace had become a prime requisite. It had learned to its dismay that it could acquire no territory from Mexico through a little war. "It was not brief, cheap, and bloodless," observed Benton, "it had become long, costly, and sanguinary."[79] Yet Polk illogically condemned the very deliberations which extricated him from this embarrassing conflict. In fact, he did nothing to stop Trist's efforts until the end of January, 1848, less than a week before the treaty was signed and a full month after the rumors of Trist's negotiations began to flood the American press. The administration was either insincere in its indignation at the commissioner's actions in Mexico, or it had determined in advance to avail itself of every opportunity for peace, even the efforts of its rejected commissioner. Certain critics of the Polk administration even believed that it purposely showed hostility toward Trist so that it could avail itself of the treaty without assuming any responsibility for the negotiations.[80]

It was within the power of the President to accept both Trist and his treaty with a minimum of embarrassment. During the lengthy negotiations in Mexico the President

---

[73] Polk revealed in his diary his confusion over Trist's actions: "The Conduct of Mr. Trist and Gen'l Scott, who seem to have entered into a conspiracy to embarrass the Government, gives me great anxiety. They have proved themselves to be wholly unworthy of the positions which they hold, and I most heartily wish they were both out of Mexico." Quaife, *Diary of Polk*, III, 312–17; Marcy to Butler, January 26, 1848, in Marcy Papers.

[74] Quaife, *Diary of Polk*, III, 313, 316.

[75] New York *Herald*, February 3, 1848.

[76] New Orleans *Picayune*, February 16, 1848; Washington *Union*, February 23, 1848.

[77] Quaife, *Diary of Polk*, III, 357–58.

[78] Thomas Hart Benton, *Thirty Years View* (2 vols., New York, 1856), II, 710.

[79] Benton wrote: "Discontent at home was disturbing to the administration; the president and cabinet were struck with terrors at the great military reputations that were growing up. Peace was the only escape from so many dangers, and it was gladly seized upon to end the war which had disappointed all calculations." *Ibid.*

[80] See Martin Van Buren, Jr., to Van Buren, February 3, 1848, in Van Buren Papers.

might have recognized the actions of his agent and thus rendered them admissible to Congress and the American people. But Polk preferred to risk congressional rejection of the settlement rather than to condone the negotiations publicly. Trist's decision to remain in Mexico considered alone should not have dictated this course of action, for his success in a difficult diplomatic situation proved the validity of his contentions. He assumed the risk of repudiation, but his negotiations had not failed. Trist's mistake lay elsewhere. He made the fatal error of siding with the administration's most dangerous political enemy, Winfield Scott. Thereafter his decision to remain in Mexico was viewed by the President as a revolt against the Democratic administration rather than an honest effort to establish peace with Mexico.

8 / Presidential Fevers

Frederick Merk

How a variety of political pressures affect presidential decision making is illustrated by the next article which is concerned with the settlement of the Oregon Question in 1846. At the same time that the American grievances with Mexico were deepening toward a state of armed conflict, President Polk was endeavoring to resolve the long standing dispute with Great Britain over Oregon. Author Frederick Merk demonstrates the process by which both the United States and Britain were ultimately willing to compromise their territorial differences in the Far West. Merk carefully dissects the complicated Oregon question as Polk inherited it in 1845 and then explains the process by which the politically divided Congress and also the President could back away from the extremists' demands for the boundary to be located along the line 54°40′ and thereby accept the compromise boundary at 49°. Among the serious difficulties in reaching this agreement was the number of presidential aspirants hoping to obtain support from the Democratic Party and the electorate to succeed Polk who had pledged himself to be a one-term president. Here is a magnificent case study of the dynamics of political compromise.

For further reading: *Ray A. Billington, *The Far Western Frontier 1830–1860* (New York: 1956); John S. Galbraith, *The Hudson's Bay Company as an Imperial Factor 1821–1869* (Berkeley: 1957); Wilbur D. Jones, *Lord Aberdeen and the Americas* (Athens: 1958); Frederick Merk, *The Oregon Question: Essays in Anglo-American Diplomacy* (Cambridge: 1967); Edwin A. Miles, " 'Fifty-Four Forty or Fight'—an American Political Legend," *Mississippi Valley Historical Review*, XLIV (1957), 291–309.

In May, 1844, three presidential nominating conventions arrived in turn in the quiet city of Baltimore, Maryland. They arrived in the order of Whigs, Tylerites, and Dem-

Frederick Merk is Professor Emeritus of History at Harvard University. This article is reprinted by permission of the editors of the *Journal of American History*. From the *Mississippi Valley Historical Review*, XLVII (June 1960). Copyright © 1960 by The Organization of American Historians.

ocrats. The Whigs established headquarters in a church, where amid religious surroundings they did their work with decorum, harmony, and speed. They ratified decisions the party bosses had made. They named Henry Clay candidate by acclamation, without even the formality of nominating speeches. They were able to adjourn in a day. The Tylerites were similarly docile. The Democrats alone authentically registered the political turbulence of the day. Their convention was wide open, virile, and discordant. It met, as the Whig press maliciously pointed out, in the Odd Fellows Hall. The hall was large, but not large enough. The weather turned hot; the place became, in the language of a reporter, a Black Hole of Calcutta.[1] It echoed for four days to leather-lunged oratory and to interminable roll calls. The nights buzzed with intrigue in smoke-filled hotel rooms. This was the first of the modernized party conventions, and it was the first to have modernized reporting. It was reported by the sensational new Morse magnetic telegraph.

Its most divisive issues, presented in the form of contending candidacies, were the annexation of Texas, the occupation of the whole of Oregon, and the protective tariff. Another troublesome issue, involving amendment to the Constitution, was the single term for the presidency. The followers of Andrew Jackson had raised this issue after the famous "bargain and corruption" election of 1825, and Jackson, as President, had repeatedly urged Congress to act on it. He had proposed to set an example himself by serving only a single term. He had been overruled by his followers, and had then relented further by favoring Van Buren for a second term. Whigs had embraced the betrayed cause. They, and their candidates in 1840 and 1844, had pledged themselves to it, and had sought to fasten on Van Buren the stigma of desertion from a great principle.

Differences at conventions are adjusted, if possible, by compromises of viewpoint, balances of interest, ambiguities of phrasing, or discreet silences that disarm contentions. Adjustment is the law of survival of parties in a nation as large and diverse as the United States. Candidates are nominated who will attract the biggest electoral vote even if not representing the highest distinction in the party; vice-presidential candidates balance the presidential. All these expedients the Democrats resorted to in 1844. They adopted an expansionist platform balancing Texas and Oregon. They pushed aside Van Buren and nominated Polk, who had offended no section. They framed a tariff plank which meant everything to everybody, and they named George M. Dallas, a protectionist and expansionist of Pennsylvania, as vice-presidential candidate.[2] They maintained a judicious silence on the issue of the single term. They relied on Polk personally to set that matter straight, as he did. In accepting the nomination he declared that if elected he would retire at the end of one term.[3]

This declaration served a number of purposes. It poured balm on wounds inflicted on Van Buren and on his delegates, who had at one time commanded a majority of the convention. It gave hope to runners-up, such as Lewis Cass and James Buchanan, of better luck at the next convention in 1848. It restored the party to an old and honored principle, entirely out of range of Whig gunfire. It exhibited Polk to the public in the attractive democratic posture of self-denial and self-restraint. It also served

---

[1] A full account of the convention is in *Niles' Register* (Baltimore), June 1, 8, 1844. See also John R. Dickinson (ed.), *Speeches, Correspondence, etc., of the Late Daniel S. Dickinson* (2 vols., New York, 1867), II, 369.

[2] Polk's interpretation of the tariff plank is in *Niles' Register*, July 6, 1844.

[3] *Ibid.*

Polk's personal preference. His pledge was the one specific commitment he made to the public in his letter of acceptance.

These tactics were not individually new. They were new in the perfection of their combination. They established a model that has served to the present day and that may serve the future. What is more, the tactics paid off. The party won the election. Polk became President. He implemented the platform, straying a little from what the convention had in mind. He did not stray from his personal pledge. He completely honored it, the only one of a number of presidents committed to the single term who did so. He gave the principle its first real testing and in so doing revealed its dangers.

A president pledging himself to a single term in effect signals the party chiefs to give thought to the succession. He invites those having ambitions in that direction to begin their preparations. The preparations consist, in a democracy, of courting the electorate. They can consist of advocating measures at variance with or even in conflict with those of the president. A president who has a second term open to him and commands eight years of actual or prospective patronage is able to restrain wide deviations from his program. A president who has cut himself off from a second term has the patronage for only four. He has, by taking the pledge, reduced by half his means of maintaining discipline in his administration.

Polk was aware of these dangers, and, in his cabinet, tried to forestall them. Whomever he invited to enter his cabinet, he asked to agree to promote no candidacy for the 1848 election by any use of patronage, and, if becoming himself a candidate, to withdraw from the family. One of the persons invited upon these terms was Buchanan, who had been an aspirant to the presidency in 1844. He was invited to be secretary of state. He cheerfully accepted, with some reservations, however, as to the conditions.[4]

Party chiefs with thoughts turned to the succession are less easily restrained in the Senate than in the cabinet. As senators they have to some extent protection against patronage withholding because of their power of confirming appointments. They have abundant opportunities, moreover, of courting the electorate by reason of the Senate's established tradition of untrammeled debate and its special authority in the field of foreign affairs. Already in Polk's day the Senate was a nursery for favorite sons.

In 1845 a foreign issue well suited to president making was before the Senate. It was the Oregon issue. It had voter appeal, as the Baltimore convention had recognized. In some respects it was more attractive than the Texas issue ever had been. It was not marred by the slavery blemish; it did not align the sections so bitterly against each other. It was directed only against the British. It promised to hold the stage a number of years, for the thesis that all Oregon was American was not likely to be soon accepted by the British. Senators from expansionist communities in championing that cause might hope to win not only immediate laurels but attentive consideration at a future convention for the highest prize a convention can bestow.[5]

At Baltimore the issue had been adroitly phrased. American title to all Oregon had been pronounced "clear and unquestionable." The territory was not to be "ceded" in any portion to England or to any other power. But the resolution had trailed off into an anti-climax. The "reoccupation" of Oregon was merely recommended to the cordial

[4] John B. Moore (ed.), *The Works of James Buchanan* (12 vols., Philadelphia, 1908–1911), VI, 110, 111.

[5] The Nashville *Union*, a Polk organ, on January 15, 1846, referred to aspirants "who believe that Texas has made one President and that Oregon may make another."

support of the Democracy of the Union.[6] In that form it had satisfied western Democrats and had seemed harmless to the southern.

Polk seemed committed to the full implications of the Oregon plank. He had declared in a pre-convention letter for the whole of Oregon.[7] In his Inaugural Address he unreservedly pronounced American title to the country of Oregon to be "clear and unquestionable," using quotation marks to indicate his source. He did, however, suggest no program of action. He left the door of exit from the platform open a little.

Several months later he offered the British a compromise. In a Washington negotiation, inherited from the Tyler administration, he offered what his predecessors had offered—a line at the forty-ninth parallel. He withheld only one item his predecessors would have allowed—the free navigation of the lower Columbia. The proposal was at once rejected, and in terms verging on the rude. It was not even taken for reference to the British government. It was, thereupon, withdrawn and the negotiation ended. The British government at once disavowed its representative. It directed him to seek a resubmission of the offer. He humbly obeyed, but Polk would not move. Polk felt that a resubmission would show too much willingness for further compromise. He doubtless realized, also, that a resubmission would infuriate the 54° 40' element in his party.

Polk next carried the issue to Congress. In his first annual message he publicly confessed his proposal and described its rude rejection. He explained, for the benefit of those who might wonder at his having made it at all, that he had felt committed by his predecessors. He assured Congress he would not make it again. Indeed, he would make no proposal. He urged Congress to serve notice of the abrogation of the treaty of joint occupation. He gravely declared that when, a year after notice, the treaty had expired, "we shall have reached a period when the national rights in Oregon must either by abandoned or firmly maintained. That they can not be abandoned without a sacrifice of both national honor and interest is too clear to admit of doubt." He asked Congress to promise donations of land to citizens of the United States who would migrate to the Oregon Country or who had already done so.[8]

This ominous message was read with unexpected calm in England. It created less excitement than the earlier Inaugural. The British public observed that the Inaugural, also ominous, had been followed by a compromise proposal and felt comforted. It cherished the hope that arbitration would be used and would save the peace. Arbitration was, in fact, twice proposed and pressed with earnestness on Polk. It was rejected with a finality that was unmistakable. Only then did the British awake to the fact that the President had ceased to waver, that his moves were now all in the same direction, and each more threatening—the cutting off of the negotiation, the proposal to abrogate the joint occupation, the recommendation of an induced migration such as was believed to have settled the fate of Texas, the rejection of arbitration. The President was evidently preparing for a showdown. When this was realized the crisis of the Oregon issue was at hand.

Polk was indeed preparing for a showdown. He had proposed a compromise. It

[6] Edward Stanwood, *A History of the Presidency* (4th ed., 2 vols., Boston, 1928), I, 215. The platform was submitted to the delegates on the last day of the convention, when many had already departed for home. It was adopted without discussion.

[7] John S. Jenkins, *James Knox Polk* (Auburn, 1851), 122.

[8] James D. Richardson (comp.), *A Compilation of the Messages and Papers of the Presidents, 1789–1897* (10 vols., Washington, 1896–1899), IV, 385.

had been spurned. The only way to treat John Bull, he believed, "was to look him straight in the eye."[9] If John Bull desired a new negotiation he must initiate it. He had wrecked the old, let him open the new. Polk sent the Foreign Office word that a new proposal would be respectfully received. It would not in itself open a negotiation. It would be examined to see whether it contained the basis for a settlement. If it seemed to him to do so it would be sent for examination to the Senate. If two thirds of the Senate decided that it contained a basis, then a negotiation could begin. The American minister in London, Louis McLane, was directed to offer no encouragement to the making of any new proposal. He might indicate to Lord Aberdeen, the British foreign secretary, if asked, merely what kind of proposal was likely to pass the screening tests of the two branches of the American government.[10]

This unusual procedure was not, as Lord Aberdeen momentarily thought it might be, a scheme to make him "eat dirt." It was a pressure device, a wringer, by use of which Polk expected to squeeze from the British a settlement satisfactory to the United States. In such a settlement the partition line must be far enough north to give the United States harbors at the Straits. The lower Columbia must be given up to the United States. It must be given up without reservation. The right of navigation which the British had enjoyed must be given up. These were terms the British had rejected for a quarter of a century. They must now propose them, themselves, and as a mere bid for a negotiation. They were unlikely to do so except under pressure.

Pressure must be initiated by abrogating the treaty of joint occupation. The treaty was a hindrance to a pressure program. It was an American recognition of British rights of presence in the Oregon Country. It obligated the United States to refrain from the exercise of any exclusive sovereignty there. It could not be ignored, as some Oregon extremists proposed.[11] It must be observed until abrogated. Such a course would demonstrate American fidelity to treaty obligations and at the same time give warning of the storm which would break over Oregon once the peace shelter was down, unless in the meantime an agreement had been reached.

Abrogation was permitted by the treaty and the method of doing it was described. A year's notice was to be given. But what authority in government would serve the notice was a detail untouched on. It was left for each side to determine for itself. By the American side it had never been determined. The Constitution was silent on it and the government had never abrogated a treaty which in its terms provided for its abrogation. The serving of notice could have been done by the chief executive in the manner of European governments. Or, it could have been done by the Senate acting in secret session, or publicly by the two houses of Congress.[12] Each of these

[9] Milo M. Quaife (ed.), *The Diary of James K. Polk during His Presidency, 1845 to 1849* (4 vols., Chicago, 1910), I, 155; Polk to Gideon J. Pillow, February 4, 1846; and Polk to William H. Polk, March 27, 1846, Polk Letter Press Copy Book, Papers of James K. Polk (Manuscript Division, Library of Congress).

[10] John Y. Mason to Louis McLane, August 12, 1845; James Buchanan to McLane, September 13, 1845; McLane to Polk, January 17, 1846, Polk Papers, Vols. 73, 74; Quaife (ed.), *Polk Diary,* I, 76; *Senate Exec. Docs.,* 29 Cong., 1 Sess. (1845–1846), No. 489 (Serial 478), 39–44; McLane to John C. Calhoun, January 3, 1846, in Chauncey S. Boucher and Robert P. Brooks (eds.), "Correspondence Addressed to John C. Calhoun, 1837–1849." American Historical Association, *Annual Report for the Year 1929* (Washington, 1930), 311.

[11] Polk was committed to this view. See a speech on it by him in *Register of Debates,* 20 Cong., 2 Sess., 129–34 (December 29, 1828), 143 (December 30, 1828), 144 (December 31, 1828).

[12] In the Tyler administration a measure serving notice was passed by the House, but it stopped there. *House Journal,* 28 Cong., 2 Sess. (Serial 462), 321.

authorities, since the days of Polk, has acted in this capacity.[13] The authority preferred by Polk was Congress. He preferred to have Congress publicly turn the screws of his pressure device. If Congress would act he could confront the British with evidence of a solid American will, legislative and executive, for a proper Oregon settlement.

Congress would act, Polk believed. In both houses it was Democratic. Its Democrats would be governed in their votes by the Baltimore platform. Even some Whigs might vote for notice in view of the summary rejection by the British of the compromise offer. Polk expected that a stout and uncompromising defense would be made in Congress of American title to Oregon, and that individuals who had reservations would withhold them so as not to damage the American case in the presence of a hostile claimant. He hoped especially that the debate would be brief, that it would end in a few weeks, and that by the close of December, 1845, the notice would be on its way to England.[14]

This was a major miscalculation. It overestimated some of the forces acting on Congress, underestimated others. One of the forces much overestimated was the zeal of the nation for expansion. This was measured in terms of the electoral vote of 1844 rather than the popular vote. The electoral vote had been clear enough—170 for the Democrats, 105 for the opposition. But the popular vote, a better gauge of public feeling, had been far from clear. Polk had carried the South, though narrowly. He had trailed the opposition in the North and even in the Northwest.[15] Other forces which were overrated were the unity to be counted on from the Democrats in Congress and the anti-British feeling to be traded on in the nation.

What were the forces underrated by Polk? They were the recently formed, the emerging, the unclear. One of them was of his own making. It was the epidemic of presidential fevers he had released in the Senate and elsewhere by his single-term pledge. Another was the expansion of New England population into the West and its effects on sectional antagonisms. A third was the bitterness created in the North by the fight over the admission of Texas and the triumph of the South in it. A fourth was the powerful current of the world peace movement. A fifth was misgiving felt by many Democrats in Congress after the 1844 election regarding some of the agreements made at Baltimore by the party delegates. Such misgiving is one of the norms of congressional behavior. On the floor of Congress an agreement, attractively packaged, as the Oregon and Texas one had been,[16] is opened. Its items are individually inspected. The price tags on them are read with dismay, especially those still to be paid; mislabelings and confused labelings such as "reannexation" and "reoccupation" are detected and denounced. Members of the party begin throwing epithets and charges at each other—"Western warriors," "slavocracy," "Punic faith." The victory celebration ends; the fight over measures begins. The debate in Congress over the notice issue was destined to be of this nature.

In the debate Democrats from the Middle West were ardent supporters of the President. They were the ones who had spearheaded the drive for Oregon in the

[13] A good brief account of treaty termination under the Constitution is John M. Mathews, *American Foreign Relations: Conduct and Policies* (Rev. ed., New York, 1938), 596ff.

[14] Quaife (ed.), *Polk Diary*, I, 338–45; *Senate Exec. Docs.*, 29 Cong., 1 Sess., No. 489, p. 46.

[15] Stanwood, *History of the Presidency*, I, 223. A considerable error appears here in the addition of the Birney vote.

[16] Polk had set the pattern of linking the two issues in his campaign letter of April 22, 1844. Jenkins, *James Knox Polk*, 120.

Baltimore convention. They represented a party constituency that was intensely expansionist, men who regarded the Oregon Country in a special sense as their own, their land of the future. They thought of it also as a land to be saved from the British, by war if necessary.[17] They were more anti-British than the Democrats of any other section of the Union. They nursed against the British bitter memories of Indian atrocities in two wars, atrocities believed to be continuing in the Far West. They had other grounds of antipathy to the British—the alleged greed of imperialism of that people, the arrogance of its governing aristocracy, and the oppressions practiced by them on the helpless of the world, expecially on the Irish. Their spokesmen professed to believe that Britain had become paralyzed in a military sense by the distresses and rebelliousness of Ireland. They found allies in such beliefs among Democrats of the border states of the South, parts of the Middle Atlantic states, and much of northern New England.

Southern Democrats on the other hand were opponents of the President's program for the most part. Cotton Democrats were especially so. They were expansionists, to be sure, but they had little interest in a crusade to acquire the frozen latitudes of the north. They were inclined to construe narrowly the Oregon plank of the party platform. They wished a partition of Oregon to be made by an amicable negotiation, and certainly not by a war. They were far from hostile to England. They were fearful of the notice proposal, and especially of its overtones in the President's message. They were apprehensive of what might happen when the peace shelter of the joint occupation treaty had come down. Allied with them in holding such views were Democrats from the commercialized and industrialized Atlantic seaboard.

Whigs were more unified than Democrats. They were hesitant about expansionism. What they saw in expansionism was the problems it would create rather than the territory it would add. They discounted the value of the Oregon Country because of its remoteness. Many of them believed, with Daniel Webster, that it would some day develop into an independent republic.[18] Others believed that it could and should be amicably divided between the United States and England. They were opposed to notice, at least to notice couched in aggressive terms. Reflecting the interests of the mercantile, the banking, and the business community they wanted peace. Some, including Webster, were Anglophiles. Others, such as Charles Sumner and Horace Greeley, were deeply influenced by the world peace movement. Nearly all objected to arming Polk with any sort of pressure weapon.

Whigs were a minority, but a strong one in Congress. They were especially strong in the Senate. They were within eight votes of equaling the Democrats in the Senate. They sympathized with Democratic conservatives of the South on a number of economic issues and were, on occasion, collaborators with them. Then, as now, conservatives in the two parties and sections were eager, and were able when joined, to shackle the wild radicals of the West. All they had to do was to cross party lines. On the Oregon issue they were especially disposed to do so.

[17] Middle Western Whigs were skeptical of the military determination of their Democratic neighbors. Thus a state convention of Indiana Whigs on January 9, 1846, resolved that while "we will have our own at all hazards" we will not, like "some of the windy democratic orators of yesterday . . . prove *soldiers in peace—citizens in war*." The Chicago *Daily Journal,* a Whig organ, reprinted these resolutions with approval on January 23, 1846.

[18] Tyler toyed with that idea as President. Richardson (comp.), *Messages and Papers of the Presidents,* IV, 258.

Men of that generation, regardless of party or section, were vehemently partisan. If they crossed party lines on occasion they clung all the more blindly on others to their political brethren. Partisanship in politics was the almost universal spirit of the age. The President was no exception to it. He was, if anything, more narrowly partisan than his period. Any Whig seemed to him probably depraved, personally as well as politically. In his *Diary* he noted two exceptions to this rule—Senator Willie P. Mangum of North Carolina and the urbane Senator John J. Crittenden of Kentucky. These two he included, even if Whigs, in the ranks of honorable men. But to do this was an extraordinary feat of tolerance on his part and it occurred only in the later years of his presidency. Such intensity of party feeling was an important force among those shaping debate on notice.

Personalities were a considerable factor in the debate. On the President's side the ones of most prominence were western Democrats. At their head was Senator William Allen of Ohio. He was a young attorney, limited in education, but endowed with some of the qualifications for frontier politics, good presence, a ready tongue, a voice that won him the name of the "Ohio fog horn," and an abundance of self-assurance and ambition.[19] He was in his second Senate term. In the Senate of that era he was in a brilliant assembly and there he shone less brightly than on the hustings. He was considered a demagogue, a ranter in debate, an advocate of rash and unsound measures. He was assigned to only the minor standing committees and even on these he always brought up the rear. In 1839 he obtained assignment to the important Foreign Relations Committee, but to the tail end of it. In the Whig Senate of 1843–1845 he had no standing committee assignments at all, though others of his party held minority berths.

In 1845, in the Twenty-ninth Congress, he rocketed suddenly to the heights. He became chairman of the Foreign Relations Committee. This was the premier Senate assignment, given normally to a distinguished Senate leader. In 1845, with foreign issues of expansionism critical in the program of the administration, it was a special prize. Its allotment to Allen under these circumstances was a sensation, indeed, something of a mystery. It is still a mystery, which the most patient investigation does not altogether solve.

A key to solving it is Senate usage. Whenever a new party succeeded to the control of the Senate and the White House, as it did in 1845, the Senate met in two sessions in the same year. One was an extra session, convened in March, for the installation of the president; the other, the regular session, convened in December. The March session lasted only a few days. It concerned itself chiefly with cabinet nominations and other executive business. It did no legislating. It could do none in the absence of the House. It dispensed, therefore, with standing committees.

The December session was the one which set up the standing committees. It acted through a president pro tempore who was the elected choice of the majority party. The vice-president was allowed no part in such proceedings. He was regarded as an outsider. Only twice in the Senate's history, and then under unusual circumstances, had he been allowed to make committee appointments.[20]

In 1845, however, all these traditions were cast to the winds. At the March session

[19] A good characterization of Allen, by a Washington correspondent of the New York *Commercial Advertiser*, appears in the issue of January 29, 1846.
[20] *Senate Journal*, 19 Cong., 1 Sess. (Serial 124), 31, 246; *ibid.*, 25 Cong., 1 Sess. (Serial 308), 27, 28.

the majority leaders arrived at a decision to have standing committees even for a matter of days. Also, they arranged to keep the vice-president always in the chair, so that no president pro tempore could be chosen.[21] Dallas, as vice-president, a 54° 40′ man, thus named the standing committees. He named a full slate of them. To the Foreign Relations Committee he named Allen as chairman, and as associates, Cass of Michigan, and Charles G. Atherton of New Hamphire, all 54° 40′ men. He named three extremists to a five-man committee, a representation out of all proportion to their strength in the Senate. This was of no immediate consequence.[22] It was of great future consequence. It anointed the extremists with the magic oil of committee seniority for the regular session.

At the regular session the Democratic leaders undertook to repeat the March procedures. They kept Dallas in the chair. A motion to allow him to name the standing committees was made by an Oregon extremist.[23] The southern Democrats, now fully aware of their danger, rebelled, kicked over the traces, joined the Whigs, and defeated the motion.[24] By way of reply the western Democrats summoned a caucus. The caucus instituted a wholly new system of setting up the standing committees—the caucus system. Allen insisted, in the ensuing distribution of places, on his right to the chairmanship of the Foreign Relations Committee on the ground of seniority gained in March. He was upheld by the other March appointed committeemen. A fourth 54° 40′ man, Ambrose H. Sevier, of Arkansas, was added. The Whigs, in their absence, were allowed one place out of five on committees. These slates were pushed through the Senate. In that way preparation was made, in the golden age of Senate history, for crises ahead in foreign affairs.

Each stage in Allen's appointment, the March and the December stage, was greeted by dismayed outcries from the Whig press. The outcries came from the East and from the West.[25] Some of the most embittered came from Allen's own state.[26] Charles Sumner, after seeing the Senator in action and hearing Senate gossip regarding his selection, wrote: "Allen, the Chairman of the Committee on Foreign Affairs, is a tall, tobacco chewing spitting loud voice ferocious blackguard. From this [Committee] he is running for the Presidency. . . . His position . . . gives him an importance that does not belong to him naturally. He obtained this through a caucus fizzle. Many of his own Party regret it very much."[27]

One of his own party who regretted it very much was Lewis Cass, the second on

[21] George M. Dallas to Sophia Dallas, March 14, 1845, Dallas Papers (Historical Society of Pennsylvania). On December 1, 1845, Dallas wrote Philip N. Dallas: "There are reasons of a peculiar nature, growing out of the weakness comparatively of the friends of the administration on the floor of the Senate, which may exact more exertion from me than would otherwise fall to my share."

[22] These standing committees served for ten days only. A full report of the proceedings is in *Journal of the Executive Proceedings of the Senate*, Vol. VI, 1841–1845 (Washington, 1887), 423, 427–28. Cass was said to have been offered the chairmanship of the committee and to have declined it. The report is of questionable authenticity.

[23] *Senate Journal*, 29 Cong., 1 Sess. (Serial 469), 7.

[24] *Ibid.*, 36.

[25] Baltimore *American*, March 14, 1845; Philadelphia *North American*, March 13, 1845; New York *Express*, March 13, 1845; New York *Tribune*, March 13, 1845. See also Allan Nevins (ed), *The Diary of Philip Hone, 1828–1851* (2 vol., New York, 1927), II, 750.

[26] Cincinnati *Daily Gazette*, March 19, 1845.

[27] Charles Sumner to [Richard Rathbone], May 14, 1846, Palmerston Papers (Broadlands, England).

the Committee. He would have liked the chairmanship himself. He had far better claims to it than Allen except that he was a newcomer to the Senate. He was an elder statesman of the party, with a record behind him of military, executive, and diplomatic service. He was an ardent expansionist and a bitter Anglophobe—a "pestilential" one, Sumner thought—and he had lost no opportunity to let this be known to his section and to the world.[28] He had been an active candidate for the 1844 nomination of the party, and he was regarded by other Senate Democrats as the leading contender for 1848—the man in front to beat. He maintained throughout the notice debate an ill-concealed rivalry with Allen for the public ear.

Another conspicuous supporter of the President was Edward A. Hannegan of Indiana. He was of Irish extraction and of better than average education. Endowed with a gift of oratory he entered the Senate in his middle thirties, in 1843. He was an intense expansionist and upheld northern and southern projects indiscriminately, but was distrustful of southern good faith toward northern. He had heard enough at the Baltimore convention to be convinced that if the South were to win Texas first, it would be content to have the whole of Texas and half of Oregon. He was to inject into the notice debate the charge of Punic faith when the South faltered in its support of Polk. He was of fiery disposition and of extravagant language. He resembled John Randolph, the Virginia orator, in these respects, and also, in his addiction to drink. Already in his Senate career his insobriety was a problem and in his later years it led to tragedy. He was the man responsible for some of the most violent scenes of the notice debate.

Lesser party champions of Polk's program came also from the West. From Illinois came Sidney Breese to the Senate and Stephen A. Douglas to the House. Both were in early stages of important careers. Breese was a tireless builder of an Illinois machine and one of the most persistent of the patronage pests pursuing the harassed Polk. Douglas was an ultra expansionist.[29] Other conspicuous party champions of the President's program came from the border states, notably David R. Atchison of Missouri and Sevier of Arkansas.

Opponents within the party to the President's program came principally from the South. They were led in the Senate by the most illustrious of southern intellects— John C. Calhoun. He was at the height of his national influence. He was remembered with gratitude in the North for having rallied southern opinion to the ratification of the Webster-Ashburton Treaty, for having enunciated a newly expanded program of nationalism at the Memphis Convention, and for having indicated a will to save the peace in the Oregon Country. Northern conservatives, even of antislavery views, were inclined to overlook his Texas and slavery transgressions on these ac-

---

[28] Van Buren wrote the following shrewd judgment of Cass in his *Autobiography*: "Long a resident of the far West, where ancient antipathies between the two Countries have not equally felt the subduing influences of increasing commerce and intercourse . . . he allowed his sense of the injuries we have received from Great Britain and his consequent denunciation of her to be inflamed in the ratio of the improvement of his chances for the Presidency." John C. Fitzpatrick (ed.), *The Autobiography of Martin Van Buren*, American Historical Association, *Annual Report for the Year 1918*, Vol. II (Washington, 1920), 495.

[29] As chairman of the House Committee on Territories Douglas reported out a bill, in defiance of his committee, calling for immediate exercise of American sovereignty over all Oregon, a bill which his committee supplanted by another conforming to the joint occupation treaty. The Douglas bill is summarized in *Niles' Register*, January 10, 1846, p. 290; the committee bill appears in *Cong. Globe*, 29 Cong., 1 Sess., 661 (April 13, 1846).

counts. Some of them joined in importuning him to return to public life in 1845 from which he had withdrawn on the accession of Polk. He had come to believe, himself, that he should return to save the nation from the Oregon folly of the President.[30] He had been at once returned to the Senate by his state legislature.

Thomas H. Benton was another Democrat of national stature opposing a radical Oregon program. He had been an expansionist for years, though never a wholly consistent one. He had advocated Texas annexation, yet at the end had opposed the treaty authorizing it. He had been a quixotic Oregon crusader, but in 1845–1846 was known to have deserted the 54° 40′ cause. He opposed militant expansionist pressures on Mexico. Sturdily independent, he was pompous, vain of his learning, and opinionated, all qualities to be exhibited in the Oregon debate. Another Democratic maverick was William H. Haywood of North Carolina, a friend and former college companion of the President.

Among Whig opponents of the President's program Webster was the leader. The opposite number to Calhoun in his party, he had recently, like Calhoun, served as secretary of state and had recent knowledge of the Oregon issue. He was suspected of being partial to the British, and this lessened the weight of his influence in the Senate. But it added to the weight of it in England. Another Whig prominent in the debate was Crittenden, the honorable Kentuckian, holder of Henry Clay's seat in the Senate.

A prompt opening of the debate on the convening of Congress was expected by Polk. In neither house was the expectation realized. In the lower a notice resolution was bottled up in committee for a month by a contest between its expansionists and a combination of southern Democrats and Whigs. A resolution was finally voted out only in the absence of part of the committee. The resolution was "naked," which meant uncovered by a peace preamble. In this form it was debated five weeks, to a total of ninety speeches, each mercifully limited to an hour.[31] At the end a notice resolution, transformed by a conciliatory amendment, was accepted and sent to the Senate.

In the Senate, Allen and his committee were promptness itself. On December 18, 1845, they voted out a resolution, also naked. But it was hastily put to bed by southern Democrats and Whigs. It reappeared on the floor on January 12, only to be whisked under cover for another month, until February 10. The votes by which this was done were a clear evidence that a majority of the Senate did not regard the early appearance of the resolution as essential.

But the 54° 40′ men were determined to appear themselves on the floor. On December 9 Cass appeared there with resolutions instructing the three standing committees on military affairs to examine at once into the state of readiness of their services for war. None of those standing committees had yet been organized or was to be for another week. But the resolutions set the stage for a resounding speech in the course of which Cass assured the Senate that a war would soon come. The British would take the notice, which he assumed would pass, as an occasion for declaring war. In such a case, Cass thought, nothing was ever gained by pusillanimity. It was

[30] See J. Franklin Jameson (ed.), *Correspondence of John C. Calhoun*, American Historical Association, *Annual Report for the Year 1899*, Vol. II (Washington, 1900), 647ff.; Boucher and Brooks (ed.), "Correspondence Addressed to John C. Calhoun," *ibid., 1929*, pp. 125ff.; also New York *Journal of Commerce*, November 3, 1845.

[31] *Cong. Globe*, 29 Cong., 1 Sess., 343–50 (February 9, 1846).

always better to fight for the first inch of the national territory than for the last. California was also in his mind. Any administration, he said, which would crown its labors of expansion by a peaceful acquisition of California, would win for itself imperishable honor. At the end of the speech an annoyed southern Whig asked what the emergency was which necessitated running ahead of the formation of the standing committees to make such an exhibit of "sublimated patriotism" and such a "splutter of patriotic emotion." Allen came to the support of Cass. He believed war was, indeed, likely, for no American government could ever honorably accept a settlement short of 54° 40′. War could be avoided only if adequate preparation was made for it, and in the United States the most effective preparation was the "preparation of the hearts of the people."[32] The themes of these two speeches—the "inevitability of war," and the "preparation of the hearts of the people"—were picked up by the Whigs and used ironically as echoes to expansionist speeches for the remaining months of the debate.

In competition with Cass, Allen sought to set up a sounding board for himself while debate on notice was held up. He brought to the Senate a resolution on European interference in the affairs of the independent states of the two Americas. The subject was before his Committee yet he undertook to score a personal triumph by submitting a resolution of his own. Calhoun objected to this as a breach of Senate rules and a beginning of premature debate on the Oregon issue. He was supported by other southern Democrats and by Whigs, and leave to introduce was denied. Later the leave was given, but the Senate at the same time ordered the resolution to be returned to the Committee, where it was thereafter kept bottled up.[33]

The time for the opening of the notice debate at length arrived. It was signaled by an extraordinary two-day speech by Allen. Sixty-three years had passed, he began, since Great Britain had acknowledged American independence. Yet the British still maintained their law, handed down judgments, carried out executions, in a vast American territory, 640,000 square miles in extent, in the Pacific Northwest. No question remained any longer as to American title to all that country. Even discussion of it was out of order. British pretensions were baseless; they were "absolute frivolity." They were, however, in character with other British aggressions on the United States—inciting savages to hack women and children to pieces, impressing American seamen, seizure of half of Maine by chicanery. One question alone remained to be answered: whether the American government had the nerve to maintain its rights, or whether it would cringe, quail, and cower before the British. If the government would stand firm, the British would not dare fight. Surrounded by embittered rivals, threatened by domestic convulsion, crippled by a parliamentary system of instability, exhausted by efforts to keep 128,000,000 colonists in subjection, they were helpless. The American people were strong. They needed only to be told that Oregon was theirs. Ask them if they are willing to surrender this large part of their country because of mere dread of invasion by a rabble of armed paupers. Ask them this "and they will give you an answer which will make the British empire tremble throughout its whole frame and foundation."[34] This was the performance of the chairman of the Committee on Foreign Relations. From its specious beginning to its melodramatic end it was the ranting of a demagogue.

[32] *Ibid.*, 30 (December 9, 1845), 45–50 (December 15, 1845), 58 (December 16, 1845).
[33] *Ibid.*, 197 (January 14, 1846), 239–48 (January 26, 1846).
[34] *Ibid.*, Appendix, 834–42 (February 10–11, 1846).

Subsequent speeches were in a pattern earlier established in the House, with western Democrats demanding all Oregon, war or no war, and southern Democrats and Whigs insisting on further negotiation and peace. Hannegan early undertook to establish three theses: first, that all Oregon to 54° 40′ is the property of the United States; second, that the American government has no power to transfer its soil to any foreign state; third, that the surrender of any of Oregon would be an abandonment of honor and character. Challenged by a southerner as to his own Texas record he replied that already in 1844 he had foreseen Punic faith from the South.[35] Cass returned to the theme of inevitable war.[36] Breese insisted that England did not dare fight, that she had never been in a more precarious state. As for his own community, its honor was involved, and rather than submit to dishonor it would endure anything war would bring.[37] In reply southern Democrats and Whigs scoffed at the thesis of the unquestionable American title to all Oregon. They reminded the western Democrats of the repeated American offers in the past to partition Oregon.[38]

But a principal anxiety of southern Democrats and Whigs was uncertainty as to the use which would be made of notice by the President. The use he had suggested in the message, and especially in its overtones, was belligerent. The message had breathed war. Yet the portion on the national defenses had breathed peace. The President had asked for no enlargement of military appropriations; indeed, the estimates had been lowered.[39] The President could by a word have removed this uncertainty. But the word was precisely the one he would not utter. It was sure to reach the British. Yet the South and the Whigs were insistent on knowing what they were voting for in voting for notice.

Over this issue the Democrats fell into a bitter internal quarrel early in March. The quarrel was set off by Haywood, the President's North Carolina friend. In a major speech he confidently predicted that the use the President would make of notice would be a reopening of the suspended negotiation. In that negotiation the President would surely accept a partition line at 49° if offered by the British. The clamor of the 54° 40′ men Haywood pronounced the noise of "selfish demagogues," interested only in "exalting little men to high places." The tactic of these men was to create a public impression that "the administration is with us."[40] The charge of Punic faith was analyzed and pronounced false.[41] The thesis of the extremists was examined point by point and its hollowness exposed. Haywood disclaimed any White House authority for these views. He relied, he said, solely on the public record.

[35] *Cong. Globe,* 29 Cong., 1 Sess., 351 (February 10, 1846), 372 (February 16, 1846), 379 (February 17, 1846). The same charge was made by Douglas in the House. *Ibid.,* 125, 126 (January 2, 1846).

[36] *Ibid.,* 425, 426 (February 25, 1846).

[37] *Ibid.,* Appendix, 378ff. (March 2, 1846).

[38] The constitutionality of congressional notice was challenged by Whig opponents of Polk and by others, who maintained that the treaty making power is the treaty terminating power. A minority report of the House Committee on Foreign Affairs set forth this thesis. *Cong. Globe,* 29 Cong., 1 Sess., 138, 139 (January 5, 1846); *ibid.,* Appendix, 363 (February 7, 1846).

[39] *Ibid.,* Appendix, 369ff. (March 4, 1846). See also Note 46, below.

[40] The administration organ, the Washington *Union,* helped to produce such an impression. It seconded Polk's pressure tactics too heartily. Its editor, Thomas Ritchie, was never admitted to the inner recesses of Polk's mind.

[41] The charge was also analyzed and refuted by Calhoun. See *Cong. Globe,* 29 Cong., 1 Sess., Appendix, 475, 476 (March 16, 1846).

The potency of this speech was indicated by the fury of the replies made to it. The speech was hardly ended before Hannegan was assailing it in a tirade that became more violent as it progressed. The President was unquestionably committed, Hannegan maintained, to 54° 40′. A denial of this was merely new evidence of southern treachery. If the President were to take the course just laid out for him the truth would come to light, and he would be in "irretrievable disgrace."

> So long as one human eye remains to linger on the page of history, the story of his abasement will be read, sending him and his name together to an infamy so profound, a damnation so deep, that the hand of resurrection will never be able to drag him forth. He who is a traitor to his country, can never have forgiveness of God, and cannot ask mercy of man. . . . I have only to add, that so far as the whole tone, spirit and meaning of the remarks of the Senator . . . are concerned if they speak the language of James K. Polk, James K. Polk has spoken words of falsehood, and with the tongue of a serpent.[42]

As Hannegan closed Allen jumped to his feet scarcely able to resist an impulse of his own to hew Haywood down. He was recognized, but the Senate was exhausted by the carnage it had witnessed and voted to adjourn.

The battle was reopened on another front. The western warriors gathered in caucus. They named a delegation, consisting of Hannegan and Atchison to visit the President and compel him to define his stand. The delegation found the President prepared; he had been warned by a southern Democrat of its coming. Hannegan, after a gingerly opening, propounded the big question. "Do you go for the whole of Oregon to 54° 40′, or do you intend to settle for 49°?" The President bristled. He would answer that question, he said, to no man. The foreign relations of the country were his charge, and it was unheard of for a President to say outside his cabinet what his foreign policy of the future would be. That was the end of the conference except for a little conversation to remove the chill from the air. As the interviewers departed Allen arrived. He proved more persistent than they; he came twice. The second time he drew from his hat a statement he wished the President to authorize him to read to the Senate: a statement that the speech of Haywood was without White House sanction; that the President had, indeed, asserted American title to 54° 40′; and that he had not changed his mind. Such a statement the President flatly refused to authorize. Allen, too, had to leave no wiser than he came.[43]

The Senate was refreshed soon after by a speech of Calhoun. In penetration of analysis and lucidity of statement it was the intellectual climax of the debate, and one of the greatest of Calhoun's career. It was critical of Polk. It began with a cold examination of the setting of Polk's request for authorization to give notice. He had expressed the conviction that no Oregon compromise acceptable to the nation was to be looked for from the British; the only course open was notice; after notice the nation must be ready either to uphold its rights or to abandon them. Notice, Calhoun said, had thus been equated virtually with war. This view of notice had been taken by western expansionists, by the community at large, and by those in the Senate, who, like himself, had for that reason opposed notice. Some moderates had, it was true, placed confidence in a general statement made elsewhere in the message, of hope for a

[42] Cong. Globe, 29 Cong., 1 Sess., 460 (March 5, 1846).
[43] Quaife (ed.), Polk Diary, I, 270–79.

peaceful settlement, and had therefore favored notice. This confidence, Calhoun believed, had been misplaced. Some moderates had believed notice was intended only as a moral weapon for obtaining an acceptable compromise. A moral weapon, Calhoun thought, could mean only intimidation, and intimidation even of a feeble nation was a hazardous tactic. Turned against a nation as great and powerful as the British it would be self-defeating. Since the message a transformation had occurred, Calhoun thought, in the state of the question. Public opinion had found time to develop on the two sides of the ocean. It had audibly and clearly demanded a compromise of the issue. It had won a favorable response from the British ministry. A large majority of the Senate favored compromise. The only question remaining was which side would take the first step in resuming negotiations. The Senate should do so by adopting a friendly form of notice. It should do so soon. Such a notice was being awaited by the British as a signal for the resumption of negotiations. In the United States it would, if adopted, end agitation and consolidate peace. Calhoun closed with a moving description of the horrors and costs of an Anglo-American war and, likewise, of the blessings of peace in a world that was being transformed in its potentialities for the happiness of mankind by the magic powers of steam and electricity.[44]

A seconding speech was made soon afterward, by Webster. It restated Calhoun's thesis in large part, but in terms more bluntly critical of Polk. It expressed uncertainty as to the wisdom of notice. It recommended simply a new negotiation without more ado. It proposed the forty-ninth parallel as the basis of a settlement. It gave friendly warning to the British that nothing more could be conceded by any party in the United States.[45]

Whigs fired challenges other than speeches at Polk. With the aid of southern Democrats they sent him repeated embarrassing requests for documents. They first called for recent correspondence exchanged between the two governments on the Oregon issue; also for correspondence exchanged between the State Department and its minister in London. The resolution was framed by Webster. It drew from Polk documents revealing his rejection of arbitration and also information concerning British naval armament. Another resolution was directed to the question whether foreign affairs necessitated increases in American naval and military forces. This brought the prompt reply that increases were necessitated by the Oregon crisis.[46] The last resolution requested the latest Oregon correspondence. It did not specifically include, as the first had done, correspondence between the American government and its London representative, McLane, of which a considerable quantity was in Polk's possession, containing reports of highly pacific Oregon conversations between McLane and Lord Aberdeen. This drew the bland reply from Polk that no correspondence between the two governments had taken place since the last transmission to Congress. Whig press reporters were aware, from information confidentially supplied by the British minister

---

[44] *Cong. Globe,* 29 Cong., 1 Sess., Appendix, 471–76 (March 16, 1846). The House of Representatives was deserted during the speech. The Philadelphia *North American,* March 26, 1846, developing a theme in the speech, criticized a demand of the extremists that the nation rally around the President. "What for? For 49°, or 54-40? For peace or war? . . . We are asked to embrace a mist—to reconcile a bundle of contradictions."

[45] *Cong. Globe,* 29 Cong., 1 Sess., 567ff. (March 30, 1846).

[46] Congress voted no increases prior to the Mexican War. Benton was opposed to increases. For an illuminating speech by him on this issue, see *ibid.,* 253 (January 27, 1846).

in Washington, of the McLane-Aberdeen conversations, and at once branded the President's reply as deliberately misleading.[47]

As the debate drew to a close Cass undertook to repair a serious breach made by Whigs in the line of 54° 40'. He hoped, doubtless, to hold also the leadership he had tried to maintain of his side. The breach had been made chiefly with the explosive ammunition that a succession of Democratic statesmen had tendered the British the line of 49°, which indicated that to them the 54° 40' claim of the United States was not at all perfect. What could be treasonable if a line, so often offered by these distinguished Americans, were taken now as the boundary? In refuting this argument Cass asserted that the line of 49° had been offered under a misconception—an early belief, founded in the error that the line had already been established in the eighteenth century under the Treaty of Utrecht by an Anglo-French commission. This error had only recently been laid bare by a historian, Robert Greenhow, who had shown that no such line had ever been drawn. Offers made in error were legal and moral nullities. Other claims to the Oregon Country the British had none. Nor did they have the power to impose a baseless claim on the United States. They were an enfeebled state.[48]

This speech roused Benton, relatively quiet till now. He could not silently permit the furthering of a presidential candidacy by a falsification of history. Himself a historian and teacher of the Senate, he believed he had a duty to set Cass straight. In a full-length address he maintained that the line of 49° had indeed been drawn under the Utrecht settlement, and that Greenhow's researches were not to be relied on. He, himself, did not appraise the claim north of 49° until after the close of the notice debate. Then he pronounced it unfounded, the exact opposite of what he had said in the Senate four years earlier. His duel with Cass, which continued, was inconclusive, but the net result of it was that the great Missouri Senator became aligned against the ultras on the Oregon issue.[49]

The debate had now run well over four months and the end was not in sight. Even the Senate had become a little breathless. One of its members observed ruefully that a debate lasting twelve nights in the British Parliament was considered a "monstrous debate." He begged that this one be closed. In London, McLane despaired. He lamented that the notice issue had ever been sent for public discussion to Congress. He believed that the Peel government was ready for major concessions to the United States, but its tenure was precarious and might end before the debate ended. He was

---

[47] The correspondent of the Philadelphia *North American* in Washington, who was the first to make this charge, was the best informed of any of the press correspondents in Washington in this period. Philadelphia *North American*, April 16, 1846. The requests to Polk are in *Cong. Globe*, 29 Cong., 1 Sess., 274–75 (January 29, 1846), 303, 304 (February 3, 1846), 510 (March 17, 1846), 656 (April 11, 1846), and for the replies see *ibid.*, 332ff. (February 7, 1846), 540ff. (March 24, 1846), 660 (April 13, 1846). See also, Quaife (ed.), *Polk Diary*, I, 208, 209, 213, 294, 296, 329. Calhoun, in supporting the request of April 11, exposed the contradictions inherent in Polk's concept that a notice could be voted by the Senate without knowledge of the state of the negotiation. *Cong. Globe*, 29 Cong., 1 Sess., 634 (April 9, 1846).

[48] *Cong. Globe*, 29 Cong., 1 Sess., Appendix 422 (March 30, 1846); Robert Greenhow, *History of Oregon and California* (Boston, 1844). The Greenhow view was upheld later by historians.

[49] *Cong. Globe*, 29 Cong., 1 Sess., 913 (May 28, 1846); *ibid.*, 27 Cong., 3 Sess., Appendix, 18 (August 18, 1842); Quaife (ed.), *Polk Diary*, I, 117.

pressing Lord Aberdeen, despite his instructions, to begin negotiations informally at once. But Aberdeen and Peel felt unable to move.[50] Even Polk was troubled. He had expected a brief debate, one that would show American unity and a sturdy faith in American claims. But the debate had loosed an avalanche of oratory, proof of sectional disunity, doubts as to the validity of the full American claim, and a disposition to challenge his own direction of foreign affairs. It had undercut his Mexican as well as his Oregon policy. It had encouraged the Mexicans to hold out against his efforts to settle American grievances by keeping alive a hope for an Anglo-American embroilment.

The Senate finally consented to a vote in April. The vote was to be on the question of the form of notice, if notice were sent. The form Allen now wanted was the one of the House. He had given up his own Senate form as unattainable. The House form relieved the President of responsibility for serving notice. It directed him to act. Another form, proposed by Crittenden, placed full responsibility for serving on the President. The Crittenden form was more conciliatory in its language, also, than the House form. It won in a preliminary test of strength by a large majority in the Senate.[51]

This moved Allen to make a speech berating the majority. He reminded them that the President had asked Congress to serve the notice. The Senate, instead of complying, had "divided, faltering, paltering, manacled, hampered by a frightful unwillingness to meet responsibility—saying, oh! we leave it all to your discretion." The Senate, Allen thought, had showed hostility to the President in foisting this responsibility on him. But the President would not shirk. He would "go behind no bush."[52] This was a reprimand questionable in taste for any senator. From one of Allen's years, in such terms, to a majority it was unbearable. It was, moreover, of a piece with the bad manners he and his associates had exhibited throughout the debate. They had resorted to browbeating. Whoever was unwilling to fight for 54° 40′ was lacking in nerve, in patriotism, must be pro-British, or even treasonable. The opponents had protested these tactics and had replied to them as they could.[53] Now at the end of the debate, Crittenden boiled over. For half an hour he administered to Allen a tongue lashing such as is seldom heard in the decorous precincts of the Senate.[54] The Senate listened in silent approval. Allen felt impelled, in reply, to refer to the "grotesque faces" Crittenden made in speaking. Whereupon Crittenden answered that he would be content to learn manners from anybody, even from a blackguard. On this note the monster debate ended.[55]

But the Senate still had its own rebuke to give Allen and his methods. By an overwhelming vote of 40 to 14 it rejected his proposed notice and approved Crittenden's.

---

[50] McLane to Buchanan, April 18, May 4, 1846, Buchanan Papers (Historical Society of Pennsylvania); McLane to Buchanan, No. 43, May 3, 1846, Despatches, England, 56, State Department Records (National Archives); McLane to Polk, May 8, 1846, Polk Papers, Vol. 74; Aberdeen to Pakenham, May 4, 1846, Aberdeen Papers (British Museum).

[51] *Cong. Globe*, 29 Cong., 1 Sess., 198 (January 14, 1846), 680 (April 16, 1846).

[52] *Ibid.*, 681 (April 16, 1846).

[53] *Ibid.*, Appendix, 370ff. (March 4, 1846); 521 (March 18, 1846).

[54] *Cong. Globe*, 29 Cong., 1 Sess., 681–83 (April 16, 1846).

[55] *Ibid.*, 682–83 (April 16, 1846).

And by a like vote it rejected him as a member of the conference committee which was to iron out differences between the Senate and House forms, though the House had named its foreign affairs committee chairman to head its conferees.[56]

The conference committee quickly reached agreement on a resolution of notice which left the President discretion to serve and was conciliatory to the British. The resolution was overwhelmingly approved by both houses and was at once dispatched by the President to the British government.[57] It effected the desired object of re-opening the negotiation.

The reopened negotiation took the form of a series of cabinet deliberations at which Lord Aberdeen pressed for concessions to the United States and was prompted from outside by McLane. Aberdeen had been personally willing to agree to a line at 49° as a basis for a boundary two and a half years before. He had failed to win over Peel and the cabinet. Now he succeeded. He got permission to propose that line, stopped short, however, at the Straits so as not to sever Vancouver Island. He was less successful with the Columbia River issue. Navigation of the river had been enjoyed by the British for half a century. Vested interests in it had become established. Yet the President had declared publicly he would agree to no continuation, and he had sent insistent warnings to McLane that any proposal continuing it would be rejected offhand. This was the sticking point in the deliberations. It was finally resolved by a compromise wherein navigation rights were retained for the Hudson's Bay Company but not for British subjects generally. Possessory rights to occupied land of the Company south of 49° were also given protection. These were the main items of a proposal, highly conciliatory, agreed to by the cabinet.[58]

What were the forces, British and American, producing these concessions? Was Polk's program of pressure among them? One force was Peel's eagerness to clear away the last of the conflicts with the United States inherited from Palmerston's days. Another was his wish to give peace protection to the great free trade experiment for which he had become responsible. A third was cabinet confidence in Aberdeen. A fourth was apprehension over the consequences of allowing the Oregon issue to slide, in the United States, into the autumn elections, and in England, into the hands of Palmerston on his expected return to the Foreign Office.[59] Another was Webster's warning that no party in the United States could accept less than the forty-ninth parallel as the basis of a settlement. Insignificant was the pressure program of Polk, and still less the fulminations of the war hawks. Peel was not a man to yield easily to intimidation.

The British proposal reached Polk on June 6. It did not meet his minimum. Its

[56] *Ibid.*, 683 (April 16, 1846), 703 (April 21, 1846). The rebuke of the Senate to Allen was unprecedented, according to the press.

[57] *Ibid.*, 717, 720, 721 (April 23, 1846).

[58] These terms were under discussion with the Governor of the Hudson's Bay Company well before the treaty project was drawn. In Sir John H. Pelly to Aberdeen, March 13, 1846, Aberdeen Papers, the Governor submitted a list of Hudson's Bay Company properties south of 49°. See also London *Times,* January 17, 1846. The navigation right of the Hudson's Bay Company was reluctantly proposed by McLane to Aberdeen as a lesser evil than a general British right. McLane to Buchanan, No. 58, July 3, 1846. Despatches, England, 56, State Department Records; McLane to Polk, May 28, 1846, Polk Papers, Vol. 74.

[59] Aberdeen to Pakenham, May 18, 1846, "Precis," p. 125, Aberdeen Papers. News of the outbreak of the Mexican War had not reached England by May 18.

Columbia River provision was short of his public prescription. Yet a rejection, without a counter offer, would lead, he believed, to war,[60] and the nation was already deep in the Mexican War. The proposal was referred to the cabinet. If the cabinet would unanimously decide that it should be sent to the Senate he would yield. The cabinet decided it should be sent, with Buchanan alone opposed. Buchanan declared he would not commit himself before knowing the nature of the President's letter of transmission. He declared that the 54° 40' men "were the true friends of the administration and he wished no backing out on the subject." The cabinet was astounded. Buchanan had been an exponent of the line of 49° throughout the preceding year. His dispatches to McLane had even been in need of stiffening. His turning to the 54° 40' men augured trouble and his remark that he wished "no backing out" was adding insult to injury. The President kept his temper and outlined what he would say in a letter of transmission. His own views, he would say, remained as they had been, but he would "conform" them to those of the Senate if that body, by a two-thirds vote, would advise him to accept the British proposal—with or without modification. If the Senate should decline to advise him, he would reject the proposal. He wished Buchanan to draft such a letter. Buchanan refused. His refusal seemed to the President designed to avoid responsibility for a compromise with a view, if compromise proved unpopular, of standing well with the 54° 40' men. At a private meeting the next day the President again asked the Secretary to draft the letter, adding that he intended to send also the correspondence Buchanan had been having with McLane. He was giving warning, perhaps, that any private reversing of gears by the Secretary would be difficult. Buchanan refused again, and objected to the sending in of the correspondence. Heated words were exchanged. A break in the relations of the two men seemed imminent.

At a subsequent cabinet meeting the President read a draft of a letter to the Senate he had himself written. It was approved by all except Buchanan. The cabinet then took the wayward Secretary in hand. It reminded him pointedly of the views he had so long been expressing. It referred, also, to his compromising dispatches. It all but suggested that this was a case of presidential fever. He responded finally to this treatment, and, in the end himself redrafted the President's letter. The letter, as agreed to, cited George Washington as having begun the practice of referring treaty issues for previous advice to the Senate. It emphasized the special appropriateness of this course on an issue so publicly and recently debated by the Senate. Then it repeated the President's formula that his own convictions were unchanged, but that he would conform his actions to those of the Senate.[61]

The Senate took up the letter and its accompanying offer in executive session. It would, under ordinary circumstances, have referred them to the Committee on Foreign Relations, and this Allen moved should be done. His motion was defeated by the overwhelming and humiliating margin of 37 to 9. Then Haywood moved to give advice to accept the offer. A hostile amendment was beaten off, following which, by a vote of

[60] The cabinet also believed the British would make use of American involvement in the Mexican War to declare their offer an ultimatum and its rejection a ground for war. McLane likewise had such fears. Quaife (ed.), *Polk Diary*, I, 445, 453; McLane to Polk, undated [May 29 to June 1, 1846], Polk Papers, Vol. 74.

[61] Quaife (ed.), *Polk Diary*, I, 451–62; Richardson (comp.), *Messages and Papers of the Presidents*, IV, 449. Buchanan had been a 54° 40' exponent prior to the Baltimore convention.

38 to 12, well above the two-thirds majority needed, the motion of Haywood was adopted.

This vote the President had expected. It corresponded with the sentiment of the Senate in the debate and with the overwhelming majority given the Crittenden notice.[62] It was not only expected, it was desired by him. The advice of the Senate was a convenient bush behind which to withdraw from the several Oregon positions he had taken.

But why did he want to withdraw? The answer is compound. He was under new pressures. One of them was the pressure of public opinion. Public opinion had undergone, during the debate, a marked change, as Calhoun had pointed out. In 1844 it could have been considered expansionist. By April, 1846, it was frowning on expansionism, at least of the war hawk variety. In February, 1846, Sumner was writing an English friend: "The war spirit has talked itself hoarse and feeble; and the conscience of the nation is awakening."[63] A New York correspondent of an English journal observed: "The rampant patriots in Congress, who threw themselves upon their war-horses and charged upon St. George with the certainty of the American people following them, have to their confusion found themselves riding all alone in their glory, whilst the nation has either forgotten them in their profound contempt or made merry at their ludicrous pranks."[64]

The President was powerfully influenced also by anxiety concerning his party. The party was breaking up over the 54° 40′ issue. Its southern and eastern wings were separating themselves from the western and falling into the arms of the Whigs. Disruption of party seemed to Polk irretrievable disaster. It had happened to the Whigs at the beginning of the preceding administration and had reduced that whole administration to impotence. This apprehension is reflected in increasingly anxious references to party dissensions in the *Diary* in the spring of 1846, in a new impatience with the 54° 40′ men whom he had earlier favored, and in a conviction that what they were primarily interested in was not 54° 40′ or 49° but '48.[65] Still another pressure on Polk, which was recent, was the war with Mexico which had come early in May. One war at a time was enough.

The advice of the Senate was promptly translated therefore into a formalized treaty which Buchanan and the British minister signed. The treaty was a copy of the British offer. It contained defects as well as virtues of the offer—technical defects destined to plague Anglo-American relations for many years.[66] Correction of these

---

[62] Moore (ed.), *Works of Buchanan*, VII, 3.

[63] Edward L. Pierce, *Memoir and Letters of Charles Sumner* (4 vols., Boston, 1877–1893), II, 378.

[64] London *Morning Post*, February 19, 1846.

[65] Quaife (ed.), *Polk Diary*, I, 261–65, 278–80, 285–88, 290, 295–300, 344, 345, 351, 352, 359–62; Roger Wolcott (ed.), *The Correspondence of William H. Prescott, 1833–1847* (Cambridge, 1925), 585; William Sturgis to George Bancroft, June 15, 1846, Bancroft Papers (Massachusetts Historical Society).

[66] The technical defects, all recognized in 1846, were inexact definition of the water boundary circling the tip of Vancouver Island, uncertainty as to the duration of the rights of navigation of the Hudson's Bay Company on the Columbia, and indefiniteness as to the kind and extent of possessory rights guaranteed to that Company. Moore (ed.), *Works of Buchanan*, VII, 3, 11; Pakenham to Aberdeen, June 13, 1846, Aberdeen Papers; McLane to Buchanan, April 18, 1846, Buchanan Papers.

seemed less important in the spring of 1846 than speed of completing the treaty.[67] The Peel government was tottering to a fall and a return of the treaty quickly to London for final approval was essential. In short order the treaty was ratified. The vote of ratification gave striking evidence of the weakness of the 54° 40' sentiment in the nation. It was 41 to 14. The ratified treaty was hurried to London where it arrived none too soon; indeed, after the Peel government had fallen though before it had given up office. Peel was able in his valedictory to hail the treaty as one of the triumphs of his administration in the cause of Anglo-American peace.

In the meantime a valedictory of another sort was delivered before the Senate. It was the resignation of Allen from the Committee on Foreign Relations. It reflected his feeling, after the crucial vote of advice to the President, that his defeats and humiliations at the hands of the Senate had made his further service on the Committee impossible. But it was by no means an admission of failure. It was meant to spark off a revolt against those in the administration responsible for the collapse of the 54° 40' cause. Allen had sought vainly to induce his Democratic colleagues on the Committee to join him in a mass resignation of protest. He referred to the treaty privately as treason and predicted an outcry against it.[68]

No outcry occurred. The Mexican War and its issues crowded the treaty out of public sight. Even the colleagues of Allen on the Committee deserted him. Cass hastened to the White House to let the President know of the attempt at a collective resignation and of his own refusal to countenance it. He assured the President that though he would vote against the treaty he would never thereafter make an issue of it.[69] Sevier actually voted for ratification. Other 54° 40' crusaders, including Dallas, abandoned the cause. Allen was defeated for re-election when his term ended and sank into an obscurity from which he emerged only briefly after the Civil War as a leader of the Ohio Greenback movement.

The debate eventuating in the treaty was of more than passing significance. It exerted for years an influence on American politics. It gave politicians warning that a pledge to the electorate of a single term is unsafe.[70] After 1848 such a pledge was never again given by a presidential candidate or a president. That relic of Jacksonian democracy disappeared. Also, the debate was significant in sowing distrust between western and southern Democrats.[71] The distrust was destined to harden as the slavery controversy deepened, and to disrupt the party on the eve of the Civil War. The debate

[67] The Washington *Union* on May 7, 1846, published under the caption "Momentous" an extract of a letter from London clandestinely supplied to it by Buchanan, discussing the probable unpleasant results for the United States of the expected return of Palmerston to the Foreign Office. The identity of the writer was withheld. The writer was A. Dudley Mann, special agent of the State Department, who was passing through London on his way to diplomatic service in the states of Germany. Mann to Buchanan, April 18, 1846, Buchanan Papers.

[68] Allen to Effie Allen, June 28, 1846, William Allen Papers (Manuscript Division, Library of Congress), Vol. 14. A discriminating biography of Allen is Reginald C. McGrane, *William Allen: A Study in Western Democracy* (Columbus, 1925). It is less satisfactory on Allen's chairmanship than elsewhere.

[69] Quaife (ed.), *Polk Diary*, I, 471, 475–77.

[70] In the Nashville *Union* of March 31, 1846, Polk's Oregon troubles were explicitly ascribed to the single-term pledge. See also New York *Journal of Commerce*, April 11, 1846.

[71] The "double dealing" of Polk and its divisive effect on his party was the theme of much Whig press comment in the spring of 1846. See especially a series of penetrating articles in the Philadelphia *North American* by its Washington correspondent, March 20, 24, 28, and June 15, 1846.

was significant, also, for the judgment it called down on Polk. It drew public attention to his shifting Oregon positions, his disingenuous tactics, and his final dodging of responsibility for the result. It projected a portrait of him on the screen as a man of short and narrow vision, of deviousness in thought and action, and of aggressiveness in dealing with other states to the point of recklessness. That portrait was by critics, to be sure, but by critics of both parties, Whigs and disenchanted Democrats. It figured in the politics of the later years of the administration and in the judgment of historians. The judgment of historians was ultimately modified, perhaps too much, by the publication of the famous *Diary*, which revealed the problems faced by the President.

But the primary impact of the debate was on its own day. The debate spread knowledge of the Oregon issue. It revealed the intrinsic weakness of the American claim to the whole of Oregon, the likelihood of a ruinous war if it were pressed to a showdown, and the irresponsibility and numerical inferiority of those pressing it. The debate gave, likewise, precious months of time to the public to reflect on this information—a major service. The magnitude of that service was dramatically shown, even as the debate closed, when a Texan boundary issue, inflamed by an order of the President to the American army to occupy the disputed region, flared into an incident, which swept Congress and the public off their feet and into the Mexican War. By giving time, by very reason of being a monster debate, this one on Oregon allowed a public opinion to form which was calm and enlightened, and which, despite presidential fevers, saved the peace in the crisis.

9 / Caleb Cushing's Chinese Mission and the Treaty of Wanghia: a Review

Richard E. Welch, Jr.

American expansionism during the 1840s was not only territorial, that is, concerned with the acquisition of new lands in the southwest and northwest, it was also emphatically commercial, concerned with a quest for export markets abroad. Whereas Democrats were by and large the prime movers behind territorial expansion, Whigs in the northeastern states pressed hard for an increasing foreign export trade. In 1843–44, President Tyler appointed Caleb Cushing of Massachusetts to lead a small American delegation to China for the purpose of putting American trade with the Celestial Empire on a legal basis for the first time. Cushing's mission reached Canton in the aftermath of the Anglo-China War (1839–42) and its settlement, the Treaty of Nanking which had placed Britain's trade with China on a legal basis. In the following article, Richard Welch describes the diplomatic negotiations which Cushing conducted with the Chinese officials and explains the resulting Treaty of Wanghia as a resounding success for Cushing's diplomacy. This American mission to China, at least in terms of its assumptions and strategy and personal style employed, served as a model for subsequent American diplomatic missions to the Far East in the 1850s.

For further reading: Mario E. Casenza (editor), *The Complete Journal of Townsend Harris* (Rutland: 1959); Tyler Dennett, *Americans in Eastern Asia* (New York: 1922); John K. Fairbank, *Trade and Diplomacy on the China Coast: The Opening of the Treaty Ports 1842–1854* (Cambridge: 1953); Kenneth S. Latourette, *The History of Early Relations Between the United States and China 1784–1844* (New Haven: 1917); Arthur J. May, "The United States and the Mid Century Revolutions," In *The Opening of an Era*, edited by Francois Fejto (London: 1948), pp. 204–213; Earl Swisher, *China's Management of the American Barbarians* (New Haven: 1953); Arthur Walworth, *Black Ships Off Japan: The Story of Commodore Perry's Expedition* (New York: 1946).

Richard Welch is Professor of History at Lafayette College. This article is reprinted by permission of the editors of the *Oregon Historical Quarterly*. From the *Oregon Historical Quarterly*, LVIII (1957). Copyright © 1957 by Richard E. Welch, Jr.

It is perhaps of some interest in these days of simmering Chinese-American relations to re-examine the way in which diplomatic contact between these two countries was first established. Surely it is time to review the part played by Caleb Cushing in "opening" China to the West. That role was at one time a matter of sharp dispute among Chinese, English and American historians, but in recent times Cushing has slipped into the amorphous shadowland reserved for "lesser historical figures."

The necessity for a trade agreement with China had been discussed in Washington for many years before any official efforts were made; by the early 1840s the eastern mercantile interest was beginning to exert considerable political pressure. Not only were New England merchants concerned with the recognition and increase of United States oriental commerce, they were increasingly anxious to secure the great harbors of San Francisco, San Diego, and Juan de Fuca Strait. Caleb Cushing, business associate and confidant of many Boston State Street merchants, was keenly aware of their desire for Pacific ports as well as improved conditions of trade with China. Their mercantile ambitions aimed at nothing less than American domination of the lucrative commerce of Asia; such a vision had, of necessity, to embrace both shores of the Pacific. Cushing's correspondence indicates that Manifest Destiny cannot be defined exclusively in terms of agrarian expansionist sentiment: the Canton trader as well as the Missouri Valley pioneer caught a glimpse of the potentialities of the vast Oregon Country.* There is a much closer connection between the China diplomacy of Cushing and the Oregon diplomacy of Polk than is generally realized. Both were in fair measure inspired by the economic interests of the vocal China merchants, and certainly the enlargement of our China Trade that followed Cushing's treaty increased American desire for a broad front on the pacific.[1]

By 1840 the situation for American traders in China had become almost intolerable. It was apparent that Chinese regulations, which tended to restrict and block commerce, must be altered in the interest of merchants of both countries. In January, 1839, a group of American merchants at Canton, only recently released from six months' imprisonment, petitioned Congress to send a commercial agent to China authorized to negotiate a treaty which would protect Americans in China from "acts of violence and aggression" on the part of Chinese officials.[2] This petition was duly referred to the House Committee on Foreign Affairs, of which Caleb Cushing was an

---

* Editorial Note: As a member of the House Committee on Foreign affairs, Cushing by 1839 had collected considerable material for the committee's "Report on Oregon Territory." Among those he asked for information were Nathaniel Wyeth, veteran of trading and commercial ventures in Oregon, and Rev. Jason Lee, then in the East to promote support for his Willamette Valley mission and interest in the Oregon Country. Their replies were published in the report (H. R. 101, 25 Cong., 3 Sess.).

For some years Cushing's and Senator Linn's reports and Irving's Astoria were "the most widely read works on Oregon . . . and were special favorites among the frontiersmen of Missouri, Iowa, Illinois and other sections of the West." Joseph Schafer, "Notes on the Colonization of Oregon," Oregon Historical Quarterly, VI (December, 1905), 385.

According to Lee's biographer, it was during the missionary's 1838–39 visit in New England that he interested Cushing's shipping firm in the possibilities of the Oregon trade. Captain John H. Couch, representing the Cushings, in 1840 arrived in Oregon on the brig Maryland, and returned in 1842 on the same firm's brig Chenamus. Couch later became a founder of Portland. See Cornelius J. Brosnan, Jason Lee (New York, 1932), 224, fn. 28.

[1] See Norman A. Graebner, Empire on the Pacific (New York, 1955), especially v–vii, 7, 217–28.

[2] H. Ex. Doc. No. 40, 26 Cong., 1 Sess.

influential member. A month later on February 7, 1839, the House, on Cushing's motion, called upon President Van Buren for "information respecting the conditions of the citizens of the United States doing business during the past year in China."[3]

Some of the more irritating of these "conditions" were 1) the restriction of trade to the single port of Canton; 2) the monopolistic privileges enjoyed by certain Chinese merchants (the co-hong merchants) in the purchase of American goods; 3) an unpublished and constantly fluctuating Chinese tariff, prone to various and elastic "extra exactions," and 4) innumerable restrictions on the personal freedom of western merchants.

With the 1840s America began to entertain a heightened interest in China and Sino-American relations. This was due to the Opium War of 1839–42 and the controversy it aroused;[4] to the increase in our trade with China; to a more widespread knowledge of the trade restrictions and exactions imposed by the Chinese; and to a growing fear of British hegemony in the ports of China, as a result of Lord Palmerston's Opium War. British imperialism had been an object of fear as well as scorn for many years, and many Americans now felt that it was only a question of time until Great Britain would attempt to control all China. England was apparently girding herself both commercially and industrially to capture and hold the markets of Asia, and to force opium on the protesting Chinese in the process. To the American people, to those in the South who grew cotton, to those in the North who manufactured it, to the merchants and shipowners who carried it to Asia (and were only now awakening to the boundless markets which might be opened), the course of Great Britain was formidable and threatening.

Great Britain, however, was not without its defenders in the United States. One of these was John Quincy Adams, who boldly insisted that the cause of the war between England and China was not opium but Chinese hauteur and arrogance. He pointed out that "the fundamental principle of the Chinese Empire was anti-commercial, and that it held itself equal to the heavenly host; while all other nations were considered tributary barbarians which should be at all times reverently submissive to the will of its despotic chief." The Opium War represented, indeed, a struggle "for equal rights of independent nations against the absurd assumption of despotic supremacy."[5]

Peter Parker, first American medical missionary to China, maintained the same opinion respecting the causation of the Opium War, and insisted that the indignities of which Britain complained had been experienced by all foreigners in China.

---

[3] When calling for an inquiry into the China Trade, Cushing had informed the House that he certainly entertained no wish to see this country join England in her recently-commenced Opium War with China. Among foreigners at Canton, it was the American alone who had shown a proper respect for the rights and sovereignty of China "in honorable contrast with the outrageous misconduct of the British there." He believed that this was a good time to make some effort to stabilize the China Trade, "but God forbid that I should entertain the idea of . . . upholding the base cupidity and violence and high-handed infraction of all law, human and divine, which have characterized the operations of the British, individually and collectively, in the seas of China." *Congressional Globe,* VIII:275. Cushing had perhaps forgotten that American traders had engaged in the opium traffic and its sizable profits.

[4] See Tyler Dennett, *Americans in Eastern Asia* (New York, 1922), 91–113, for a detailed exposition of American concern with the Opium War.

[5] *Niles' Register,* February 11, 1843, LXIII:379.

Parker's conversations with congressional and administration leaders undoubtedly helped convince many officials in Washington of the necessity for an American mission to China.[6]

Certainly the increasingly vocal demands of New England merchants for a formalization of relations with China had influence.[7] Oddly enough, however, American merchants in Canton were much less in favor of negotiations and a Chinese mission than their Boston brethren. In Canton they were reluctant to risk physical and financial security in an attempt to gain greater commercial liberties and personal immunities. The *Hong Kong Gazette* told of merchant complaints concerning injuries sustained from xenophobic mobs in Canton; yet it also reported the merchants' anxiety that the meddling of diplomats would only bring further troubles upon them. Fortunately for the expansion of American commerce, the merchants of Boston were nearer Capitol Hill, were registered at the polls, and allowed the deciding voice.

On December 27, 1842, Representative Cushing, the Boston merchants' friend, wrote President Tyler suggesting that an American mission be sent to China.[8] Three days after the receipt of this letter, President Tyler sent a message to Congress, advising that a commissioner be appointed to "reside in China to exercise a watchful care over the concerns of American citizens . . . empowered to hold intercourse with local authorities, and really, under instructions from his government . . . to address the Emperor, himself." He declared that all persons acquainted with prevailing conditions felt that this country must obtain for herself the same privileges for which the British had waged war: additional treaty ports, greater freedom of trade and residence, greater security for nationals resident in China, and bi-lateral agreement as to tariff and port regulations. Such privileges must be obtained by way of a formal treaty. Our envoy, concluded the President, should be a citizen of weight and intelligence, "adequately compensated for his services."[9]

Representative John Quincy Adams introduced into the House (January 24, 1843) a bill authorizing the suggested mission to China and appropriating forty thousand dollars to finance it. Championed by the aging but still vociferous Adams, it quickly

---

[6] More study is needed concerning the part played by American missionaries in inspiring the Cushing mission. Surely these missionaries had been unable to establish themselves in any real sense prior to that mission.

[7] The *Boston Journal* of March 7, 1843, estimated that in 1842 we shipped exports to China worth twenty-four and a half million dollars and imported Chinese goods with a total value of twenty-five million dollars, and yet China was a sealed volume. It stoutly demanded that this paradox be resolved.

[8] Cushing's discussion of the proper policy to pursue respecting China foreshadowed the Open Door Notes and policy of John Hay. In his letter to Tyler, Cushing wrote as follows: "It does not appear that England contemplates attempting to exclude other nations from similar free access to China. But it does appear that she has made the arrangement [the Treaty of Nanking, 1842] for her own benefit only, and, if other nations wish for like advantages, they must apply to China to obtain them on their own account. Is not the present, therefore, an urgent occasion for dispatching an authorized agent of the United States to China with instruction to make commercial arrangements in behalf of the United States. . . . I have information from Canton that the Chinese are predisposed to deal kindly with us, the more so as only we can, by the extent of our commerce, act in counterpoise to that of England, and thus save the Chinese from that which would be extremely inconvenient for them, viz., the condition of being an exclusive monopoly in the hands of England. . . ." Claude M. Fuess, *Life of Caleb Cushing* (New York, 1923), I:407.

[9] J. D. Richardson, *Messages and Papers of the Presidents* (Washington, 1897), IV:211–14.

passed the House,[10] but in the Senate ran headlong into the partisan politics of the day. Tyler had recently been read out of the Whig party, and many looked rather critically on the measure as a "Tyler undertaking" and expressed doubt as to its possible utility or success.

Senator Benton, a promoter of American expansion and occupation of the Oregon Country, but a sturdy enemy of all Whigs of whatever stripe, argued that the China Trade was at present sufficiently successful, and that there was no need for an expensive mission. He believed our relations with China needed no more improvement than could be obtained by authorizing one of our merchants in China to sign a treaty identical with that recently concluded by Britain at Nanking. Our citizens should not be subjected to the sight of an American minister "creeping in behind the British Minister to claim the protection of Queen Victoria's petticoats." The Missourian declared that the mission had not been proposed for the nation's benefit, but in order to allow some Tyler favorite the honor of bumping his head "nineteen times against the ground"—the famous kow-tow rite.[11] Despite this partisan sniping the appropriation passed the Senate at midnight, March 3, 1843, in the closing minutes of the session.

The necessity for a mission to China to stabilize our growing trade and put it on a more official basis was obvious, but the point raised by Benton and others, that the Sino-British Treaty of Nanking obliterated the necessity of an American treaty deserves some consideration. It should be noted that the Treaty of Nanking did not include any provision for the application of the "granted Rights" to other powers on a "most favored nation basis." That was to come later in the Anglo-Chinese Treaty of The Bogue. Furthermore, though an American naval officer, Commodore Lawrence Kearny, had been given some rather vague promises by certain Chinese provincial officials, it was not until April 1843, that the Chinese really decided to allow other foreign merchants in the four additional ports being opened to British trade. It is clear then, that in January 1843, when the bill passed the Senate, an American mission was needed, for neither the British nor the Chinese had shown any evident desire to increase the commercial liberties of America's China merchants. Chinese diplomacy of the period, as will appear, made necessary itemized, detailed definition and an official treaty basis for any rights and considerations accorded American merchants, missionaries and officials.

The choice of the commissioner who would head this first American mission to China was involved in shady politics. It appears certain that Daniel Webster hoped to give the honor to Edward Everett in order to vacate Webster's coveted post as ambassador to St. James. In a series of pathetically obvious letters, Webster urged the obdurate Everett to take this golden opportunity, but that gentlemen was completing his library and would not stir from civilized London society. The next choice of both Webster and Tyler was Cushing, who gladly accepted.

The nomination was announced during the senatorial recess. For Cushing this was most fortunate. If the Senate, which had already thrice rejected his appointment as Secretary of the Treasury, had been in session, Cushing never would have visited the Orient. Because of his adherence to Tyler and his hop-scotch politics in general,

---

[10] A Mr. Forbes concluded a disquisition on the importance of China as an American market by inquiring if anyone knew "how much of our tobacco might be there chewed in place of opium." Shortly after the bill passed, 96–59 (February 21, 1843). *Congressional Globe,* XII:325.

[11] *Congressional Globe,* XII:391–92.

Cushing had made many enemies.[12] Judging solely by his fitness for the post at hand, however, he was an excellent choice. Long interested in the China Trade and an ardent advocate of its expansion, Cushing was probably as conversant with the questions with which he would have to deal as any public man of his day.

After lengthy literary and physical preparations by the Tyler administration, the Cushing mission was finally ready to set sail in July of 1843. The squadron which was to convey our first Envoy Extraordinary and Minister Plenipotentiary to China was composed of four war vessels under the command of Commodore Foxhall A. Parker: the frigate *Brandywine*, the brig *Perry*, the sloop-of-war *St. Louis*, and the steam frigate *Missouri*. As befitting his mission to bring Progress to the East, Cushing chose the last-named as his means of transportation.

The mission got under way most inauspiciously: on July 23, as the *Missouri* came up the Potomac to take Cushing aboard, she grounded on an oyster bed, losing an officer and fifteen crewmen in the process. This tragic and perplexing misadventure occasioned a three-week delay, but Cushing finally set off, and by late August had arrived at Gibraltar. There he was again delayed, as the *Missouri* caught fire and slowly burned to the water's edge. Though all of Cushing's papers were saved, his specially designed and highly treasured uniform was lost.[13] He decided to take passage to India on a British steamer from Suez, leaving his entourage to follow him on the *Brandywine*, by way of the Cape of Good Hope. This plan was accomplished, and the two parties joined forces again at Bombay, and sailed for China.

When Cushing arrived at Macao on February 24, 1844, the political framework for his mission was altered. He had hardly set up his "miniature court" in the house of a former Portuguese governor, "creating a profound sensation by the novelty and magnitude of his Mission,"[14] when he received a long letter from Edward Everett. The latter informed him that the Chinese had agreed to admit Americans to all the concessions granted the British in the Treaty of The Bogue.[15] The right to trade at the

---

[12] John Quincy Adams confided to his diary his disgust at the appointment of Cushing: "He has not made his court to Captain Tyler in vain. His obsequiousness and sacrifice of principles lost the favor of his constituents . . . but Mr. Tyler has more precious favors in his gift, and has lavished them in profusion on Cushing." Charles Francis Adams, ed., *Memoirs of John Quincy Adams, Comprising Portions of His Diary from 1795 to 1848* (Philadelphia, 1876), XI:388.

[13] It consisted of a blue coat with gilt buttons (red and blue crystal buttons had been vetoed by Cushing as being rather "gaudy"), a white vest, white pantaloons with gold stripe, and a plumed cocked hat.

See *Niles' Register*, October 14, 1843, LXV:101–102, for interesting account of the destruction of the *Missouri*.

[14] Fuess, *Cushing*, I:194. *Niles' Register* quotes a Canton merchant: ". . . I had the honor of seeing much of his Excellency, who has spurs on his heels and mustachios and imperial, very flourishing! Although I like the man, I most heartily wish he were anywhere else but here, and am, as well as every American merchant here, in great fear. As Americans, we are now on the very *best* terms possible with the Chinese; and as the only connection we want with China is a commercial one, I cannot see what Mr. Cushing expects to do. He *cannot* make us better off— and a very few of his important airs will make us hated by the Chinese, and then we lose all the advantages we now have over the English; and though I believe Mr. Cushing to be as honest as most of politicians, yet I fear for the sake of being, as he hopes, put face to face with 'Taoukwang' [the Emperor], he will sacrifice his countrymen, and the good will of the Chinese, and lose all. . . ." *Niles' Register*, September 21, 1844, LVII:36. Extract of a letter received by *The Clarendon* of New York, dated April 16, 1844.

[15] By the treaties of Nanking (1842) and The Bogue (1843), England made peace with China and received from her a twenty-one million dollar indemnity, the cession of Hong Kong, liberty to trade at four additional Chinese ports (as well as Canton) with the right to appoint

four additional ports of Amoy, Fuchow, Ningpo and Shanghai which at first had been granted only to Britain, was now confirmed to traders and merchants of all nations on equal terms.

Yet no paths were smoothed for the American commissioner. Much to his disgust, Cushing for four months was obliged to deal exclusively and by correspondence with Ching,[16] acting Governor-General of Kwang Tung and Kwang Se provinces. Ching, though a 'second-stringer,' was no mean or pliable opponent. In his first communication, the governor, as he was instructed, attempted both to discourage Cushing from visiting Peking and persuade him of the futility of seeking a treaty:

> . . . The August Emperor, in his compassion to people from afar, cannot bear that the Plenipotentiary, having passed the ocean, should again have the toil and trouble of travelling by land and water [to Peking].
> . . . Your honorable nation is treated in the same manner as England; and, from the time of the change in the tariff . . . your nation has been bedewed with its advantages.
> The honorable Plenipotentiary ought certainly to look at and consider that the Great Emperor, in his leniency to men from afar, has issued edicts commanding the merchants and people peaceably to trade, which cannot but be beneficial to [all] nations. It is useless with lofty, polished and empty words to alter these unlimited advantages. . . .[17]

In his first exchange of letters with Ching, Cushing found himself unable to proceed to Peking, unless at the risk of "ending civility," and yet unable to discover if Peking planned to send an Imperial commissioner to the south to enter into negotiations with the American mission there. A tart communication to this effect did bring a response from Ching (April 1) stating that the Emperor would be memorialized again concerning Cushing's arrival and acquainted with his desires. Ching felt obliged to add by way of warning that "it cannot be a light matter to commence movements which may eventuate in the loss of the invaluable blessing of peace," but Cushing could credit himself with a modest gain.

On April 4, Cushing wrote another note to Ching, asking how long he might expect to wait for an answer from Peking. Ching responded that at least three months would be required for the messenger to go and return, although it actually took but twenty to twenty-two days for a letter to go from Canton to Peking at that time. Feeling the time had come to exert pressure in earnest, Cushing (following Parker's

---

consuls at each of these ports, and a promise by the Chinese to abolish all co-hong monopolies and establish a public tariff.

[16] In Cushing's correspondence with Ching, E. C. Bridgman and Dr. Peter Parker, both missionaries, were extremely helpful. Cushing had contacted them immediately upon his arrival at Macao, and spent long hours with both, trying to gain an appreciation of Chinese psychology and methods of diplomacy. As "Chinese secretaries," they subsequently served as interpreters and translators. Fuess states that Cushing, himself, was soon able not only to understand but also to speak Manchu with some fluency. Fuess, Cushing, I:426. If so, this was certainly the supreme example of Cushing's undoubted linguistic powers. It is questioned by most Chinese students of the Cushing mission.

[17] Sen. Ex. Doc. No. 67, 28 Cong., 2 Sess., 4. Cushing appreciated from the very beginning the 'blackmail' value of the projected visit to Peking. Even before the arrival of the Brandywine at Macao, he had issued a general order to the members of his staff, cautioning them always to declare that the destination of the mission was Peking. This supposed destination was throughout a Damoclesian sword held over the heads of Cushing's adversaries.

suggestion) sent a stiff communication to Ching on April 16, stating that under the circumstances, he had resolved to leave for Peking at once, in the *Brandywine*.[18] Ching replied on April 21, with less than usual inertia,[19] and in what Cushing was pleased to call a "lucid communication," that he had sent a speedy messenger to Peking who would report to the throne Cushing's "earnest request" to proceed to Peking. He added that he believed it possible that the Emperor had already appointed a commissioner to treat with Cushing, who might even now be on his way.

Though moderately pleased with this limited progress, Cushing replied firmly: "I commit myself . . . to the integrity and honor of the Chinese Government; and if, in the sequel, I shall prove to have done this in vain, I shall then consider myself . . . amply justified . . . for any determination which, out of regard for the honor of the United States, it may be my duty to adopt under such circumstances."[20] Cushing underlined his remarks by notifying Governor Ching on the following day (May 10) that the *St. Louis* and the *Perry*, which had been detained at the Cape of Good Hope, would soon arrive, and that the American fleet in Chinese waters would soon be further enlarged by the addition of the Pacific Squadron.[21]

After some further correspondence, Ching finally reported, with evident relief, that Kiying (or Kiyeng or Tsiyeng), the specially appointed Imperial commissioner, was on his way to Canton, whipping along at the speed of 500 li a day. On the thirteenth of May, Cushing received a copy of the Imperial edict appointing Kiying commissioner for the negotiation of a treaty with the United States, and enjoining the American mission to wait quietly at Macao "and by no means esteem it a light matter to agitate disorder."[22] The literary fencing match between Ching and Cushing was finally at an end, with its apparent chief result the retention of the disturbing Mr. Cushing in the south of China, far from the Imperial Court.[23]

---

[18] *Sen. Ex. Doc. No. 67, 28 Cong., 2 Sess.,* 13. In answer to Ching's subtle reference to Pottinger's conciliatory willingness to treat at Canton, Cushing replied with no little guile: ". . . The rules of politeness and ceremony observed by Sir Henry Pottinger were doubtless just and proper in the particular circumstances of the case. But, to render them fully applicable to the United States, it would be necessary for my government, in the first instance, to subject the people of China to all the calamities of war, and especially to take possession of some island on the coast of China, as a place of residence for its minister. I cannot suppose that the Imperial government wishes the United States to do this. . . ." *Ibid.*

[19] Ching was perhaps as much disturbed by the actions of Commodore Foxhall Parker's frigate as by the tone of Cushing's letter. On April 13, Cushing had ordered the captain of the *Brandywine* to pay a courtesy call at Whampoa, only twelve miles from Ching at Canton. Parker had gone straight to the waterfront at Whampoa, and fired a salute of bombastic welcome. It was not returned.

[20] *Sen. Ex. Doc. No. 67, 28 Cong., 2 Sess.,* 27.

[21] *Sen. Ex. Doc. No. 67, 28 Cong., 2 Sess.,* 66–67. Cushing informed the State Department: "The arrival of these vessels relieves me from a load of solicitude in regard to the public business; for if matters do not go smoothly with Tsiyeng [Kiying], the legation has now the means of proceeding to and acting in the North." *Ibid.,* 34.

[22] *Sen. Ex. Doc. No. 67, 28 Cong., 2 Sess.,* 30.

[23] Cushing himself was disturbed about Washington's estimate of his achievements to date. On a later occasion he felt obliged to explain to Secretary Calhoun that: ". . . if it should be suggested that it would have been better for me to have proceeded at once to the North [Peking], without stopping at Macao, I reply, that this was impracticable at the time of my arrival, with the Brandywine alone, before the southerly monsoon had set in, and without any steamer; that if at any time I had gone to the North in the view of negotiating there I should have been wholly dependent on the Chinese for the means of lodging and subsisting on shore . . . that only at Macao could I treat independently, and that here, of necessity must all the pecuniary and other

An evaluation of Cushing's efforts up to this time must include the effect of Everett's letter on his diplomatic aims and methods. Everett's communication relating that the Chinese by unilateral decree had decided to admit the Americans to all concessions granted the British, had undoubted influence on Cushing. For one thing, Cushing was persuaded to strive for a treaty which secured additional concessions for the United States, although these were not actually required by his instructions. And this consideration, in turn, tended to strengthen his belief that to deal with an Asiatic nation such as China, a stern tone, if not a high-handed manner, might be necessary.[24]

It should be remembered that the Opium War and the Treaty of Nanking, if they marked the beginning of the end of China's diplomatic insularity, did not mark its conclusion. The Chinese were desperately, if hopelessly, striving to maintain their traditional status, and were not anxious to engage in further diplomatic conversations.

Ching's pleasant conviction that he had thwarted Cushing at all turns was an erroneous one. Cushing's threatened visit to Peking, if unconsummated, had served its purpose by jarring the Chinese into accepting the necessity of negotiating a treaty. Furthermore, as he reported to Washington, the long, frustrating correspondence with Ching had quite possibly furthered the mission's chance of eventual success in another way. It had enabled the American commissioner "to say all the harsh things which needed to be said, and to speak to the Chinese Government with extreme plainness and frankness, in a degree which would have been inconvenient, if not inadmissible, in immediate correspondence with Kiying." When that gentleman wrote Cushing that "in a few days we shall take each other by the hand, and converse, and rejoice together with indescribable delight," Cushing had cause to notify Secretary Upshur that such amiable language was the "best possible augury for the success of the mission."[25]

Cushing's negotiations with Kiying present a much more agreeable picture than those with Ching. In the first place, the appointment of Kiying was taken by the Americans as a good omen, for Kiying had negotiated the English treaties and was thought to entertain relatively little anti-foreign prejudice. On the sixteenth of June, Kiying, accompanied by three Chinese officers (Hwang, treasurer of the province of the two Kwangs; Pwan, a high dignitary of state; and Chow, secretary of the mission) and their respective suites, arrived at the Chinese village of Casa Franca, to the north of the barrier at Macao. Next day they settled in the temple of Wanghia (or Wang Hiya), between the barrier and the village wall.[26]

---

arrangements of the mission be made, and the supplies obtained for the squadron. . . ." *Sen. Ex. Doc. No. 67*, 28 Cong., 2 Sess., 60; Thomas Hart Benton, *Thirty Years' View* (New York, 1856), I:521. Benton caustically comments: "So that after all it was only the fear of being whipt and starved that prevented Mr. Cushing from fighting his way to the footstool of power in the Tartar half of the Chinese Empire." *Ibid.*, 522.

[24] This point is well made by P. C. Kuo, "Caleb Cushing and the Treaty of Wanghia, 1844," *Journal of Modern History*, V (March, 1933), 37. Kuo, however, lays undue stress on the Everett letter, implies that the Treaty of The Bogue made Cushing's mission needless, and appears not to appreciate the importance of having American rights on a treaty basis. Kuo appears at one point to believe that the Everett letter determined Cushing to go to Peking (p. 37), then later implies that Cushing had never seriously intended to insist on a visit to the capital (p. 43). It is the present writer's belief that Cushing never gave particularly high priority to the Peking visit.

[25] *Sen. Ex. Doc. No. 67*, 28 Cong., 2 Sess., 40, 37, 34. Upshur had succeeded Daniel Webster as Secretary of State, and shortly would be succeeded in turn by John C. Calhoun.

[26] Niles reported: "Tsi Yeng [Kiying] very unceremoniously took possession of an immense

Some forty-eight hours later, Kiying made his first ceremonious call on Cushing. Preceded by axe-bearers and flanked on either hand by foot soldiers, Kiying was borne aloft to the meeting in a large, well-cushioned sedan chair. As Caleb Cushing later remembered it, the grand marshal of the Chinese procession carried an immense, brightly-lacquered fan, and the two commissioners (Cushing and Kiying), upon meeting, put on their hats, rather than removed them, and shook hands at rather than with each other.[27]

Cushing returned the visit the next day. He found the temple very spacious, its connecting buildings forming a series of quadrangular courtyards. As the Americans approached a band struck up, a salute was fired, and Cushing and party, supposedly both honored and awed, were ushered into the inner sanctum by Kiying, himself.

The negotiations proceeded. After some little jostling over the position and letter size for the names of their respective governments, Cushing was asked by Kiying to submit a treaty draft incorporating the desires and expectations of the United States. Tipping his hand in honest fashion, Cushing submitted such a draft, and it became the basis of the subsequent treaty.

As preface to the treaty draft, Cushing enumerated the five basic principles on which it had been prepared: 1) the United States wished to treat with China only on a basis of "cordial friendship and firm peace"; 2) the United States did not desire "any portion of the territory of China, nor any terms and conditions whatever which shall be otherwise than just and honorable to China as well as to the United States"; 3) the United States wanted "perfect reciprocity in all commercial relations, involving no export duties," but would accept the plan arranged with the English, and would only propose "such articles as may procure to the United States a free and secure commerce in the ports open to the nations of the West"; 4) the United States desired certain provisions differing from those of the British treaties, and this was due to the possession of Hong Kong by Great Britain; 5) the United States wished to insert in the treaty "a multitude of provisions in the interest and for the benefit of China."[28]

After the Cushing draft was submitted, Cushing and The Most Honorable Kiying exchanged frequent informal notes, but the detailed business at hand was largely left to Fletcher Webster (son of Daniel and secretary to the American mission), Doctor Parker and Reverend Bridgman for the Americans, and Hwang, Chow and Pwan for the Chinese. These two groups held daily conferences in the Chinese headquarters, several within the inner shrine of the temple.

---

temple dedicated to 'Our Lady of Mercy,' in the village of Wang Hiya, were he kept his state." *Niles' Register*, January 11, 1845, LXVII:299.

It is curious that two such excellent authorities as John W. Foster, one-time Secretary of State, and John Bassett Moore, one-time Professor of International Law and Diplomacy, should have emphasized the point that Wanghia was on Portuguese soil, and that consequently Cushing never set foot in China during his Chinese mission. Foster, *American Diplomacy in the Orient* (Boston, 1903), 86; Moore, *History and Digest of the International Arbitrations to Which the United States Has Been a Party* (Washington, 1898), I:419.

Even if one accepts the idea that Macao is not Chinese soil, Wanghia lies almost a mile to the north of the old barrier, Porto do Camp, built by the Chinese authorities in 1573 to mark the line between the Portuguese settlement and the Chinese province of Kwang Tung and Kwang Se, proper. See H. B. Morse, *International Relations of the Chinese Empire* (London, 1910), I:109–110.

[27] This description is based upon a conversation with Miss Margaret Cushing, recently-deceased niece of Caleb; as well as Fuess, *Cushing*, I:430–34.

[28] *Sen. Ex. Doc. No. 67, 28 Cong., 2 Sess.*, 41–42.

Cushing, sensing that the moment had come to secure success by way of concession, notified Kiying on June 25 that he was ready formally to waive the right to go to Peking, provided a satisfactory treaty was signed, and provided that if in the future any foreign envoy was received at Peking, his American equivalent should have similar privilege. Cushing appreciated that a visit to the Chinese capital—improbable at best—would delay if not imperil the negotiations for the treaty,[29] and that the time had come to graciously discard diplomatic blackjacks.

Kiying was elated at the news. He informed his subalterns that considerable latitude might be given to the various provisions of the treaty draft concerning trade rights and privileges, and now put chief emphasis upon the delivery (to himself) of a letter from President Tyler to the Chinese Emperor. The Chinese commissioner thus missed the whole point. His preoccupation with the policy of excluding foreign envoys from the court at Peking blinded him to the real issues at stake. It was, indeed, a basic difference in the respective purposes and priorities of the two commissioners which more than anything else ensured the success of the negotiations.[30]

Worthy of note, too, is the fair amount of truth in Cushing's message to Kiying respecting his refusal to "take a partial view of the subject," and his insertion of "a multitude of provisions in the interest and for the benefit of China." Apparently Kiying found these generous promises justified by the event. In any case, after certain rather minor modifications to the original draft were mutually agreed upon, the Treaty of Wanghia in its finished form was ready for signing July 3, 1844. After the lengthy deliberations between Cushing and Governor Ching as to whether there was to be a treaty, details as to its form were settled by Cushing and Kiying in but thirteen days.

Eight copies of the treaty were carefully prepared, four in each language. At a little after ten in the evening, Cushing and Kiying met in the recesses of the inner temple and solemnly inscribed their signatures to each copy in turn, while Chinese servants briskly stirred the muggy atmosphere with large bamboo fans. After two large-boned Tartars brought in the great Imperial seal and stamped all copies, the formalities were over. The China Trade had received official notice.[31]

The question of the personal relationship between Cushing and Kiying has been the occasion of much dispute among authorities on Sino-American diplomacy. Through-

[29] Cushing to John Nelson, acting Secretary of State, July 8, 1844: "[On] the question of my proceeding to Pekin[g] . . . Kiying avowed distinctly that he was not authorized either to obstruct or facilitate my proceeding to court; but that, if I persisted in the purpose of going there at this time, he had no power to continue the negotiations of the treaty." Sen. Ex. Doc. No. 67, 28 Cong., 2 Sess., 39.

Niles' Register, LXVII:299, reports: ". . . Finding the imperial commissioner had power fully to treat with him, he [Cushing] yielded his personal curiosity and pride, if he entertained any such feeling, to the consideration of his country's interests. . . . [Kiying] with equal frankness and confidence proposed to employ the American interpreters exclusively, and by so doing paid our national character, and our national representative, the highest compliment in their power."

[30] Cushing wrote that going to Peking "was but the means to an end—that end being the establishment of the commercial interests of the United States in China on a satisfactory footing of advantage, confidence, friendship, and permanency." Sen. Ex. Doc. No. 67, 28 Cong., 2 Sess., 59.

[31] The Chinese ratified the treaty and its annex on August 15, 1844, and the United States followed suit on January 17. Ratifications were solemnly exchanged at Canton on December 31, 1845, with Commodore James Biddle representing the United States. News of this exchange reached Washington almost four months later, and the Treaty of Wanghia was formally proclaimed April 18, 1846, though in fact it had been in operation for eight months.

out the entire negotiations, certainly, their communications had been marked by expressions of mutual regard and great cordiality. Kiying in his farewell letter to Cushing wrote: "While I have this opportunity to wishing you peace and happiness, I cannot repress the spontaneous goings-forth of my kind regards towards you."[32]

Later, however, an allegedly 'true translation' of Kiying's memorial report to the Emperor was published in Hong Kong. It contained but a slighting opinion of Cushing's abilities, as witnessed by the following extract:

> . . . The original copy of the Treaty presented by the said Barbarian Envoy, contained forty-seven stipulations. Of these some were difficult of execution, others were foolish demands, whilst several of the most important points of the Treaty were omitted on the list. I, your slave, corrected them one by one without daring to yield the slightest ground. . . . The sense of it was, moreover, so meanly and coarsely expressed, the words and sentences were so obscure, and there was such a variety of errors, that it was next to impossible to point them out. . . . We clearly pointed out whatever was comprehensive to reason, in order to dispel their stupid ignorance, and to put a stop to delusive hopes, while expatiating with strictness upon the most binding of the statutes; while we were obliged to polish those passages which were scarcely intelligible, so as to render the sense somewhat more obvious. . . . Only after four times altering the copies, we adopted the paper.[33]

Though this translation has been often quoted, much of it was a forgery. Kiying in his communications with the Emperor certainly did decry the draft presented by Cushing, and imply that the final treaty was largely the work of his own hand,[34] but he never went so far as to classify Cushing as a stupid ignoramus. Actually it would have been almost impossible to have concluded the threaty thirteen days after the commencement of negotiations, if Cushing's draft had not been immediately accepted in principle. Certain provisions and changes in text were indeed made by Kiying,[35] but the treaty as a whole, when checked by Cushing's original draft, is of American make. Most of Kiying's derogation of Cushing was but the result of an understandable desire to retain the favor of an ill-informed, xenophobic Emperor and avoid receipt of the silken scarf symbolic of the disagreeable necessity of self-destruction.

Cushing stayed on at Macao for nearly two months, settling the final terms of the tariff agreements (signed July 22), arranging for the removal of an American ship-

[32] Quoted by Fuess, *Cushing*, I:444. Kiying quite literally loaded Cushing with gifts during a great banquet on the night the treaty was signed. Of these gifts, the most perishable was some "succulent" Tartar cheese cake; the most interesting, a life-size portrait of Kiying, painted on a huge drop of salmon-colored silk. For President Tyler there were rare specimens of Chinese porcelain.

Cushing, in return, offered Kiying an engraved portrait of Tyler, and some books on military and naval tactics and fortifications. The Chinese were not ready, even then, to concern themselves with things military, and Kiying courteously refused the latter gifts. The portrait of Tyler was happily accepted, however, and pronounced to be the likeness of a "person of lofty stature, dignified, and of no common exterior." *Niles' Register,* January 11, 1845, LXVII:299.

[33] R. Montgomery Martin, *China: Political, Commercial, and Social* (London, 1847), I:424–32. This version first appeared in English translation in *The Friend of China,* a British newspaper published in Hong Kong. When it was first brought to the attention of Kiying, he at once declared it to be spurious and had published an official copy of his genuine report.

[34] See Kuo, "Caleb Cushing and the Treaty of Wanghia," 46–49, fn. 62.

[35] For example, Kiying pointed out to the Emperor that in the article in the treaty which purported to grant to Americans the privileges of renting property in the five ports, he had inserted a qualifying clause which made the renting of such property dependent upon the willingness of of the Chinese residents of the neighborhood to receive foreigners.

yard that was outside the treaty limits, working for the personal safety of Americans in China,[36] and writing long abstracts and analyses of the Wanghia Treaty for the information of Washington. Eventually he set sail for Mexico by way of the Philippines, and after suffering indignities from Mexican bandits, finally and gratefully debarked in New York on the last day of December, 1844, after an absence of seventeen months.

The Treaty of Wanghia has been minutely examined by David Hunter Miller in *Treaties and Other International Acts of the United States of America*.[37] However, a general summary of its more important parts helps in evaluating both the treaty and Cushing's contribution. The preamble affirmed the desire of the United States and China to establish "firm, lasting, and sincere friendship" between the two nations with this general convention of "peace, amity, and commerce." Article I enlarged upon this beneficial amity, and Article II provided that citizens of the United States resorting to China for the purposes of commerce would "pay the duties of import and export prescribed in the Tariff" annexed, and no other duties or charges whatever; and that the United States should participate in any future concessions granted to other nations by China. The United States would, in short, enjoy most favored nation treatment.

Articles III and IV made provision for the citizens of the United States to import and sell, or buy and export merchandise at the five ports of Kwang-chow (Canton), Kiyamen (Amoy), Fuchow, Ningpo and Shanghai. Article VI limited the tonnage duty that could at any time be levied on American ships—one to five mace (about fourteen to ninety cents) per ton, depending on the total tonnage.

Article XI prescribed the mode of examining goods in order to estimate the duty, and Article XII provided for regularity and uniformity of weights and measures at the five ports. Article XV abolished the hong and various other restrictions on trade in China. Article XVI provided for the collection of debts due Americans by Chinese citizens, or vice versa, through the tribunals of their respective countries; and Article XXIV arranged the mode in which complaints or petitions might be made by citizens of the United States to the Chinese government and controversies between citizens of the two nations adjusted.

Article XXVI provided for the security of merchant vessels of the United States in Chinese waters, and the "pursuit and punishment of violation of the same by subjects of China"; Article XXVIII declared that citizens of the United States, their vessels and property, should not be subject to any embargo, detention, or other molestation in China; and Article XXIX made provision for the local extradition of Chinese criminals taking refuge in the houses or vessels of Americans.

Article XXXI prescribed an elaborate process through which the United States, through its chief executive, could communicate with the Emperor, a concession which only one other nation—Russia—was allowed at that time.[38]

---

[36] Among other matters, he concerted an arrangement with the Governor-General for the erection of gates around "the foreign settlement," the establishment of sanitary regulations and an efficient police force for its protection, and the construction of a solid wall about the American factories.

[37] David Hunter Miller, ed., *Treaties and Other International Acts of the United States of America* (Washington, 1931–42), IV:626–62. An abstract of the treaty is to be found in *Sen. Ex. Doc. No. 58*, 28 Cong., 2 Sess.

[38] See *Sen. Ex. Doc. No. 67*, 28 Cong., 2 Sess., 59ff., for details concerning the manner in which Kiying vainly tried to get this point modified.

Other provisions of certain importance concerned the right of Americans resident in China "to enjoy all proper accommodation" in purchasing or renting sites, not only for the construction of houses and places of business, but also for hospitals, churches and cemeteries;[39] to employ scholars to teach Chinese; and to purchase Chinese books. Merchant ships of the United States were to be allowed to remain in a Chinese port for forty-eight hours without paying tonnage duties, or if they had paid such duties, to re-export their cargo without further charge and visit another of the five ports. There was, finally, a stipulation for the revision of the treaty after twelve years.

Articles XXI and XXV dealt with extraterritoriality, and as they subsequently proved the most controversial, deserve special attention. Extraterritoriality was no invention of Cushing's. As early as the ninth century the Chinese granted special privileges to the Arabs, who built a mosque at Canton and were governed by their own laws. In Edmund Robert's treaty with Siam in 1832 it was stipulated that American consuls were to be the exclusive judges of all disputes and suits in which American citizens were engaged *with each other*. The Portuguese at Macao had for many years been allowed complete local self-government, and there is no question but that the concession to Cushing of this privilege was a product of sorts of the recent Anglo-Chinese War.

But granting all these precedents, and the favorable circumstances created by the British, it was Cushing who obtained the first formal recognition in China of the principle of extraterritoriality in the *form* in which it would loom so large in later Chinese diplomatic history.

Cushing felt it essential to obtain from the Chinese a precise definition of the status of American citizens respecting the legal institutions of China. He secured this definition in the following two articles of his treaty: Article XXI, "Subjects of China who may be guilty of any criminal act toward the citizens of the United States, shall be arrested and punished by the Chinese authorities according to the laws of China: and the citizens of the United States, who may commit any crime in China, shall be subject to be tried and punished only by the Consul, or other public functionary of the United States, thereto authorized according to the laws of the United States";[40] Article XXV, "All questions in regard to rights, whether of property or person, arising between citizens of the United States and China shall be subject to the jurisdiction, and regulated by the authorities of their own Government. And all controversies occurring in China between the citizens of the United States and the subjects of any other government, shall be regulated by the treaties existing between the United States and such governments respectively, without interference on the part of China."

Cushing made these two articles the subject of a lengthy, detailed report to Secretary of State Calhoun:

> . . . I entered China with the formed general conviction, that the United States ought not to concede to any foreign state, under any circumstances, jurisdiction over the life and liberty of any citizen of the United States, unless that foreign state be of our family of nations; in a word, a Christian state. The states of

---

[39] This provision was included at the behest of Peter Parker. F. W. Stevens, *Life of Peter Parker* (New York, 1898), 234.

[40] Cushing pointed out to Secretary Calhoun that this clause necessitated a sizable American consular staff in China. *H. Ex. Doc. No. 69, 28 Cong., 2 Sess.,* 14–15; *Sen. Ex. Doc. No. 58, 28 Cong., 2 Sess.,*14.

Christendom are bound together by treaties, which confer mutual rights and prescribe reciprocal obligations. . . . How different the condition of things out of the
limits of Christendom. . . . As between them and us, there is no community of
ideas, no common law of nations, no interchange of good offices. . . .[41]

It was not Cushing's intention to undermine Chinese sovereignty, but to provide a
means of by-passing the quarrels which would arise, as in the famous *Terranova*
case,[42] if Americans were subject to Chinese courts and justice. The labors of various Chinese historians to present Cushing as a robber of national rights and independence are surely ill-directed. The divergence in standards of justice was very great
at that time, and the judicial institutions of the Chinese Empire neither uniform
nor centralized. Some form of extraterritoriality was necessary, and the Treaty of
Wanghia represented, in this respect, a fair and equitable adjustment of the problem.

In any discussion of the results and merits of the Treaty of Wanghia, it should be
compared with the English treaty that preceded it. The treaties of Nanking and
Wanghia were significantly different. Sir Henry Pottinger's treaty, however much it
called itself a treaty of amity, was definitely a punitive treaty. Cushing's, though perhaps more to the interest of the United States than China, does not deserve that label.
The articles of the Wanghia treaty concerning most favored nation treatment and the
rights of extraterritoriality were much more complete and definitive than their English
counterparts. So too were its provisions dealing with consulates, tariffs, and trade
accommodations. Cushing's treaty, furthermore, bluntly declared that the United
States would offer no protection to smugglers and specifically fixed the subject of
contraband goods. The article allowing Americans to employ scholars and "purchase
all manner of books" was peculiar to itself and important in that it implied that relations between Orient and Occident might involve matters beyond the boundaries of
trade, beyond the smuggling of opium, and indeed, beyond any of the nefarious relations with which the intercourse between foreigners of the lower classes and the Chinese were cursed.

In summation, the Treaty of Wanghia not only gained for the United States all
rights and privileges won by Great Britain in China (with the lone exception that
there was no physical equivalent to the British acquisition of Hong Kong), it also
established certain new principles in the field of Sino-American relations. As a legal
foundation for the conduct of trade the American treaty was definitely superior to the
British agreements. It shortly became the model for Chinese treaties executed by
France,[43] Norway and Sweden, and many of its provisions would be later claimed
and used by the English.

Though Cushing benefited largely by the diplomacy of Sir Henry Pottinger, he was

[41] *Sen. Ex. Doc. No. 58,* 28 Cong., 2 Sess., 12–13.

[42] The *Terranova* was an American ship from which a sailor was surrendered to an irate
Chinese mob supposedly to avenge the death of a Cantonese at the hands of certain mysterious
foreigners. The American merchants in Canton had forced the ship's captain to surrender the
sailor, explaining to the Chinese as they did so: "We are bound to submit to your laws while
we are in your waters; be they ever so unjust, we will not resist them." From an article in the *North
American Review* of January, 1834, cited in S. W. Williams, *The Middle Kingdom* (New York,
1883), II:460. The submissive attitude of these merchants was typical of Americans in China
until Cushing took up the question of extraterritoriality.

[43] The French treaty of August, 1844, was similar in its general outline to Wanghia with one
notable exception. It gave France a somewhat vague protectorate over all Roman Catholic missionaries and their Chinese converts.

not content to cautiously tread in his predecessor's footsteps; rather he made a distinct and individual contribution to Far Eastern diplomacy.[44]

Among the immediate effects of the treaty for China, the most important was that the Celestial Empire had escaped possible English hegemony over the ports and diplomacy of China. For while Cushing won several additional consessions from the Chinese, and won them by means approximating intimidation, the treaty nevertheless served China as commercial and diplomatic ballast of sorts.

The neo-mercantilist economists in the United States thought it doubtful whether the opening of new ports and the general expansion of foreign trade would prove of any advantage to China, herself. The *New York Commercial* was certain that China's imports would soon greatly exceed her exports, and that she would suffer an unfavorable balance of trade and find her native manufactures fatally injured by foreign competition. This view, however, was criticized even at the time as failing to consider China's primarily agrarian economy and its peculiar types of marketable manufactures.

The greatest disservice which Cushing did the Chinese was unintentional. It involved the thirty-fourth, and last article of the treaty, which stated that it might be revised after the lapse of twelve years should "modifications appear to be requisite in those parts which relate to commerce and navigation." This provision was also included in the French Treaty of Whampoa and became, via a most favored nation clause, the right of the English as well. Its disregard by the Chinese, with respect to all nations, was one of the principal causes leading to the Second Anglo-Chinese War.

The effects of the Treaty of Wanghia on the United States were uniformly beneficial. American commerce seems to have received great stimulus from the treaty. The year 1848 saw the arrival of sixty-eight American ships at Canton, twenty at Shanghai, and eight at Amoy. Britain's lead in the race for the trade and treasure of the Orient was steadily narrowed. American interests in China enlarged and multiplied, and with the trade on a more permanent and official basis, American commerce and shipping fortunes grew accordingly. In truth, it was the unspectacular, but profitable, role of the United States to follow England to China in the wake of war, and gain considerable advantage thereby. It was an honorable if safe course, and a necessary one; there was no alternative but continuing to trade without a treaty, and thus to trade on sufferance alone.

With the signing of the Treaty of Wanghia, American intercourse with China entered a new era. The initial, pioneering stage of the Old China Trade had for some time been drawing to a close, as that trade had increased in size and regularity; its termination was dramatically signalized at Wanghia. Chinese jurisdiction over foreigners, and limited, furtive American missionary labors were now to give way to freedom from personal responsibility to Chinese courts, and direct official intercourse on the basis of equality. So while it is true that the dichotomous spirit of fear and contempt which characterized the old Imperial regime still existed with nearly its old force, Wanghia did mark a transition point in the relations between the United States and China.

---

[44] That contribution might have been even greater had Cushing followed through with a half-formed intention to visit Japan on his way home. He wrote Tyler a private letter suggesting that he should be given full power to treat with Japan should the opportunity offer. Secretary Calhoun sent Cushing the necessary authorization, but Cushing on second thought decided against any "mission to Japan." See U. S. Department of State, *Instructions, China,* I, No. 23.

The extent of Cushing's primacy in effecting this transition must be at least partially a matter of personal opinion. As concerns the opening of China, there are many who would give all credit to Lawrence Kearny, in charge of the United States East India Squadron, or to the Imperial officers Ilipoo and Kiying, or to Pottinger, the British diplomat.

Kearny, however, received no reply from any responsible statesman in China acceding to his request for equal privileges for the United States, and it is extremely doubtful if his representations exercised much influence on Ilippo and Kiying whose opinions decided the question.[45] As for these Chinese officials, they only felt free to propose to the Emperor their policy of equality because Sir Henry Pottinger had vaguely, if grandly, declared at Nanking that if China should grant equal privileges to other nations, England would *not object*.[46] It seems undeniable that when Cushing landed at Macao in February, 1844, the amount and type of commercial privileges to be extended to the American "barbarians" was still to be determined and was only settled in satisfactory and permanent form at Wanghia in July, 1844.

It would be incorrect, of course, to catalog Wanghia as an example of pure Cushing policy, for it was exemplary of America's policy towards China at that time. However, because of the necessarily general quality of his instructions and the difficulties of communication between Cushing and his superiors, he was highly instrumental in the final design of this policy, and correspondingly responsible for the benefits which it brought the United States.

When looking over the correspondence conducted by Cushing, one is impressed with the keen insight of the man, his thorough acquaintance with international law, his fluency of literary expression, and his persistence in the face of difficulties. Without taking any credit from Kearny or Parker, or from Marshall and Burlingame who later so admirably secured Cushing's achievement, it can be asserted that it was this Massachusetts politician who made treaty rights of commercial privileges enjoyed on sufferance, and officially opened China to American diplomacy.

The real significance of Cushing's mission was that it did put American commercial privileges on a treaty basis. A continuation of the *de facto* arrangement, as conceived by Kearny and Kiying, would surely have been unsatisfactory and have led to further insecurity for American trade. The instability of Chinese foreign policy demanded a treaty. The treaty negotiated by Cushing gave our commercial interests in China every advantage for the prosecution of their growing trade in the face of

---

[45] The contribution of Kearny is still a most controversial question. A debate raged in the 1930s between Kearny's great-nephew, Thomas Kearny, and the Chinese scholar, T. F. Tsiang. Tsiang's discovery of certain long-hidden documents in the Chinese state archives has permitted the issue to be somewhat cleared, if to the detriment of Commodore Kearny and his admirers. See Tsiang's brilliant review of the subject in the *Chinese Social and Political Science Review*, XV: 422–42. Also Thomas Kearny's contradictory articles in the same periodical, XVI: 75–104; and finally, Tsiang's "Note in Reply," XVI: 105–109.

[46] The English view (as discussed at Nanking and specified in the Treaty of The Bogue) was, of course, this: We will accede to the Chinese suggestion that those privileges originally granted by China to us alone be extended to other nations, in order that we can lay claim in the future to any *additional* privileges granted these other nations.

The usually strongly Anglophobic Cushing in letters to secretaries Nelson and Calhoun bore "testimony to the high merits of Sir Henry Pottinger, as manifested in his negotiations with the Chinese Government," and gave convincing description of the mutual benefit accruing to both nations from the individual Chinese diplomacy of each. See, for example, *Sen. Ex. Doc. No. 67*, 28 Cong., 2 Sess., 100.

British competition. It provided for cultural contacts, international communication, most favored nation treatment, and extraterritoriality—all in terms of exemplary exactness.

Wanghia, the first treaty signed by China with a Western maritime power which was not preceded by war, marked a definite milestone—not only in the diplomatic history of the United States, but that of the Far East as well.

10 / The Civil War Blockade Reconsidered

Edwin B. Coddington

The American Civil War opened a pandora's box of new diplomatic dilemmas for the United States Government as it also did for the government of the Confederate States. The Confederacy's striving for diplomatic recognition and material assistance in Europe; the altercation produced by the *Trent* Affair in 1861; the Anglo-American dispute which arose out of England allowing the construction of naval vessels like the *Alabama* and her sister ships on behalf of the Confederacy. Perhaps there was no more complicated diplomatic controversy during the 1860s, and so little understood today, than that occurring over the operations of the Union's naval blockade of Confederate ports. In the following article, Edwin Coddington points to certain difficulties that have influenced historians' appraisal of the blockade. He concludes that the blockade, though imperfect, was an effective measure in softening and weakening the Confederacy. How the blockade was appraised by British leaders and how the Confederacy responded to this economic coercion become important parts of this story.

For further reading: Ephraim D. Adams, *Great Britain and the American Civil War* (New York: 1925); Henry Blumenthal, "Confederate Diplomacy: Popular Notions and International Realities," *Journal of Southern History*, XXXII (1966), 151–171; *Martin Duberman, *Charles Francis Adams 1807–1886* (Boston: 1961); Jay Monaghan, *Diplomat in Carpet Slippers* (Indianapolis: 1945); *Frank L. Owsley, *King Cotton Diplomacy* (Chicago: 1959) reprint edition; Robin W. Winks, *Canada and the United States: The Civil War Years* (Baltimore: 1960).

The war between the North and the South has always attracted the interest of a large band of devoted students, and yet a thorough examination of one of the more colorful and important features of that struggle has been neglected. When on April

Edwin Coddington has been Professor of History at Lafayette College. This article is reprinted with permission of the Board of Trustees, Clark University. From *Essays in History and International Relations in Honor of George H. Blakeslee.* Copyright 1949 by the Trustees of Clark University.

19, 1861, President Lincoln proclaimed the intention of the United States to institute a blockade of Southern ports,[1] he created a policy which immediately affected the nature of the conflict, as well as American foreign relations. Since a blockade is an act of war in which "the two parties in the contest must become belligerents," the Federal Government thus adopted a plan which invalidated its theory of the struggle as a purely domestic one in which the Southern "insurgents" would not be accorded the rights of belligerency.[2]

A logical but impractical application of this concept would have been the establishment of a domestic embargo, whereby Southern ports would have been closed to foreign trade by act of Congress. Under this arrangement the North could not have claimed the belligerent right to seize vessels on the "high seas bound for a blockaded port," an act which is comparable to the "right of search."[3] When the British Government learned that a domestic embargo was being considered, it became concerned and warned that such a method of excluding foreign commerce from Southern ports would have the characteristics of a paper blockade and would incur its opposition. Whether this attitude affected the decision of Northern leaders to abandon the idea of an embargo is questionable. Certainly the legal advantages of a blockade, maintained in conformity with international law, and other considerations, such as a desire to avoid the bloody excesses of civil strife and fear of reprisal, forced the United States to concede belligerent rights to the Confederacy without formal recognition.[4]

I. BRITISH REACTION TO THE BLOCKADE

A review of the blockade must revolve around the central question of its effectiveness, which includes an inquiry into Great Britain's attitude. By virtue of her position as the foremost maritime power, her reaction to the blockade assumed vital importance to its success. Should she have insisted, before recognizing its legality, upon standards of efficiency that would have permitted of virtually no violations, the Northern Government in all likelihood would have failed in this phase of its grand strategy. Fortunately for the United States this development did not occur. As relations between the North and the South became more strained after the formation of the Confederacy in February, 1861, British officials worried about the effects of a possible war on English commerce.[5] Yet when the blockade was declared "in pursuance . . . of the Law of Nations"[6] no objections were raised, for it was felt that American precedent would require it to be effective.[7] The Law of Nations in this case meant to Great Britain the definition contained in the Declaration of Paris, 1856, that: "Blockades, in order to be binding, must be effective; that is to say, maintained by a

[1] A second proclamation on April 27 extended the blockade to ports in Virginia and North Carolina. James D. Richardson, ed., *A Compilation of the Messages and Papers of the Presidents* (1896–99), VIII, 3215–16.

[2] James Russell Soley, *The Blockade and the Cruisers* (New York, 1883), 28; and James G. Randall, *Constitutional Problems under Lincoln* (New York, 1926), 59–65.

[3] Soley, *The Blockade*, 28–30.

[4] Ephraim Douglass Adams, *Great Britain and the American Civil War* (New York: Longmans, Green, 1925), I, 244–52; and Randall, *Constitutional Problems*, 65–69.

[5] Adams, *Great Britain and the American Civil War*, I, 57–75.

[6] Richardson, *Messages and Papers*, VIII, 3215.

[7] Adams, *Great Britain and the American Civil War*, I, 244, 246.

force sufficient really to prevent access to the coast of the enemy."[8] Although the United States had refused to sign the agreement, partly because the Declaration had likewise abolished privateering, its precarious diplomatic position after the outbreak of hostilities and its traditional policies guaranteed acceptance of the defintion.[9]

For several months after "early and easy acquiescence" in the blockade, the British Government gave the matter little consideration. The thinking of such men as Lord Russell, the Foreign Secretary, was affected by assumptions that the war would be of such short duration as not to cut off next year's supply of cotton, and that guarding approximately 3,500 miles of coast line would impose an impossible task on the Federal navy. Furthermore a *"regular* blockade" could not possibly prevent trade with the South.[10] The geographical factor unduly impressed the British, and the Confederates constantly tried to increase their exaggeration of its significance as part of an effort to induce the European powers to repudiate the blockade.[11]

The length of the coast line and the peculiar formation of the shore seemingly presented the blockading fleet with insuperable difficulties. A large proportion of the coast from "North Carolina to Florida on the Atlantic side and from West Florida to Galveston, Texas, was a double line, with interior channels, making it possible to travel much of the distance between the ports without frequent exposure to the open sea. . . ."[12] This advantage to the South was offset to a large extent by the arrangement of the Southern railroads, which served at all adequately only the seven largest seaports. It was to these ports (Norfolk, Wilmington, Charleston, Savannah, Mobile, New Orleans, and Galveston) that important blockade-runners directed their ships to carry on what became the bulk of Southern foreign trade during the war. It should be added that much of the total coast line was contained in the state of Florida, but that the whole area lacked rail connections with the rest of the South. The same condition existed in respect to Texas. In terms of railroads, industrial resources, agricultural development, and population, which means military potential, the vital area of the Confederacy lay between the Mississippi River and the Atlantic Ocean, bounded on the south by the Florida-Georgia line and the Gulf of Mexico, and on the north by the border states of Kentucky and Maryland.[13]

[8] Text as given in John Bassett Moore, *Digest of International Law* (Washington, 1906), VII, 562. For a slightly different wording of the text see *Official Records of the Union and Confederate Navies in the War of the Rebellion* (Washington, 1922), 2nd series, III, 299; hereafter cited as *O. R. N.*

[9] According to Jay Monaghan, *Diplomat in Carpet Slippers: Abraham Lincoln Deals with Foreign Affairs* (New York, 1945), 81–83, Secretary Seward had induced Lincoln to proclaim a blockade "in pursuance . . . of the law of nations" before the full implications of such a move were thoroughly investigated. As a result Lincoln's efforts to outlaw Southern privateering were thwarted and European recognition of Confederate belligerency, which he had ardently hoped to avoid, became inevitable. This judgment of Seward seems harsh, for it is difficult to see what other feasible course the North could have followed to prohibit commerce between the South and the rest of the world.

[10] Adams, *Great Britain and the American Civil War*, I, 246, 252.

[11] *O. R. N.*, 2nd series, III, 357, 483, 497, 622.

[12] Frank Lawrence Owsley, *King Cotton Diplomacy: Foreign Relations of the Confederate States of America* (Chicago, 1931), 250.

[13] *Dinsmore's New Railroad Map of the United States and the Canadas, Showing All the Railroads Completed and in Progress* . . . (New York, 1860); Soley, *The Blockade*, 36; Edwin B. Coddington, *A Social and Economic History of the Seaboard States of the Southern Confederacy* (Ph.D. Dissertation, MS., Clark University, 1939), chap. 5; Jefferson Davis Bragg, *Louisiana in the Confederacy* (Baton Rouge, 1941), 76, 84–87.

Assuming that its effects would prove immaterial to the British, Lord Russell did not show any active interest in the blockade until late November, 1861. He heard then that Americans planned to sink vessels filled with stones across the entrance bar of Charleston harbor. This proposal seemed to indicate the necessity of employing " 'uncivilized', if not illegal methods" to bolster the ineffectual efforts of blockading squadrons.[14] Reports of their ineffectiveness had been coming to him since the summer from British consuls resident in the South and from representatives of a Confederate diplomatic mission to Europe.[15] The "Stone Boat Fleet" affair served to confirm previous impressions of the blockade, but it likewise moved Russell to obtain an opinion from Lord Lyons, British minister to the United States. Lyons wrote:

> I am a good deal puzzled as to how I ought to answer your question whether I consider the Blockade effective. It is certainly by no means strict or vigorous along the immense extent of coast to which it is supposed to apply. I suppose the ships which run it successfully both in and out are more numerous than those which are intercepted. On the other hand it is very far from being a mere Paper Blockade. A great many vessels are captured; it is a most serious interruption to Trade; and if it were as ineffective as Mr. Jefferson Davis says in his Message, he would not be so very anxious to get rid of it.[16]

This statement presents in excellent fashion the dilemma which faced the neutral person of that day and the historian of later times in trying to estimate the effectiveness of the blockade. Those people interested in denouncing it on the grounds that it failed to meet the standards of the Declaration of Paris would find comfort in Lyons' opinion. The same satisfaction would be obtained by those who might wish to uphold the blockade. Confederate authorities and their sympathizers in England and France belittled the evidence on captured vessels and stressed the number of violations to prove the ineffectiveness and consequently the illegality of the blockade.[17] This approach to the question has been ably developed in recent years by Professor Owsley, who has gone so far as to say: "Old Abe sold America's birthright [traditional insistence upon neutral rights] for a mess of pottage."[18]

The British Government came to regard the blockade in a different light. A conditioning factor in determining its attitude was England's position as the leading naval power. Foreseeing a future war in which her situation might be reversed from that of neutrality to belligerency, leaders there decided to observe Northern efforts with indulgence.[19] Lord Palmerston, the Prime Minister, admitted that such was the case in a conversation on March 14, 1865, with Mr. J. M. Mason, head of the Confederate mission to England.[20] Sir Alexander Milne, who was in command of the North American and West Indies naval station from 1860 to March 15, 1864, refrained, in his protection of British commerce against illegal acts of the belligerents, from establishing precedents which might hamper England's use of sea power in a future

---

[14] Adams, *Great Britain and the American Civil War*, I, 253.

[15] O. R. N., 2nd series, III, 231, 246; Owsley, *King Cotton Diplomacy*, 253–56.

[16] Lord Lyons to Lord John Russell, November 29, 1861, Russell Papers, as quoted in Adams, *Great Britain and the American Civil War*, I, 254.

[17] O. R. N., 2nd series, III, 246, 263, 293, 299, 373, 379–84, 411–13, 483, 495–98, 882–89.

[18] Owsley, *King Cotton Diplomacy*, 291. See also chapter 8 entitled: "The Ineffectiveness of the Blockade."

[19] Adams, *Great Britain and the American Civil War*, I, 263.

[20] O. R. N., 2nd series, III, 1273–74.

conflict.[21] The government likewise refused to be carried away by an imposing array of statistics on violations, for, as contended in a Parliamentary debate on the blockade in March, 1862, "nearly all the alleged blockade runners were in reality merely small coasting steamers, which, by use of shallow inner channels, could creep along the shore and then make a dash for the West Indies." As a clinching argument the discrepancy of 100 per cent between the price of cotton in the South and in England was cited.[22] Actually this point proved nothing in respect to the blockade, because of the unofficial embargo on the exportation of cotton maintained by Southerners during the first year of the war. The British felt then that the normal course of trade had been seriously interrupted and that much neutral commerce had disappeared with the advent of danger.[23] Under these circumstances a liberal interpretation of the Paris definition by Lord Russell was not surprising when he wrote Lyons on February 15 that:

> Her Majesty's Government . . . are of opinion that, assuming that the blockade was duly notified, and also that a number of ships is stationed and remains at the entrance of a port, sufficient really to prevent access to it or; to create an evident danger of entering or leaving it; and that these ships do not voluntarily permit ingress or egress, the fact that various ships may have successfully escaped through it (as in the particular instance here referred to) will not, of itself, prevent the blockade from being an effectual one, by international law.[24]

The Confederates fussed and fumed over this statement, especially the phrase "sufficient . . . to create an evident danger," for to them it completely destroyed the purpose of the Paris definition. There is justification in their complaint that the British had granted the Union navy generous latitude in executing a difficult assignment with what were at first woefully inadequate forces.[25] They remained unhappy when Russell almost a year later in a communication to Mason restated the British position in more explicit language:

> It appears to her Majesty's Government to be sufficiently clear that the declaration of Paris could not have been intended to mean that a port must be so blockaded as really to prevent access in all winds, and independently of whether the communication might be carried on of a dark night or by means of small low steamers or coasting craft creeping along the shore; in short, that it was necessary that communication with a port under blockade should be utterly and absolutely impossible under any circumstances.

He ended by saying that to the British Government the Paris definition meant that "a blockade in order to be respected by neutrals must be *practically* effective."[26]

This interpretation at the time it was written constituted a fair estimate of the blockade, for by 1863 the Federal Government had established a tight enough cordon around the Southern coast to require extraordinary efforts and an unusual outlay of capital on the part of those who risked sending vessels through it. During the previous two years the navy was being built up to necessary strength. Writers on the Civil War

[21] James P. Baxter, 3rd, "The British Government and Neutral Rights," *American Historical Review*, XXXIV (October, 1928), 11.

[22] Adams, *Great Britain and the American Civil War*, I, 270.

[23] *O. R. N.*, 2nd series, III, 340; Adams, *Great Britain and the American Civil War*, I, 245–46.

[24] *O. R. N.*, 2nd series, III, 495–96.

[25] Soley, *The Blockade*, 12–18.

[26] *O. R. N.*, 2nd series, III, 688. Italics by the writer.

all agree that at the time of the two presidential proclamations no more than a few vessels were at the immediate disposal of the Federal Government. Outside of Chesapeake Bay no blockade of any sort existed until late in May, 1861, and Northern efforts at that early date proved totally inadequate and remained so for at least two months more. By no stretch of the imagination of any serious student has the blockade been considered effective by any reasonable standards until the end of 1861.[27] Some writers have declared it ineffective until two years after the beginning of hostilities, while a few of the Owsley-Scharf school of thought have refused to admit that it ever measured up to the rules established by the Declaration of Paris.[28]

Despite these conflicting opinions it would be safe to say that until the summer of 1862 the North had perpetrated a bluff which was aided and abetted unwittingly by the South and was accepted at face value by the British. Ironically, while the Confederates made futile attempts to have Great Britain denounce the blockade they pursued a policy that undermined the force of their arguments. Had it not been for a fatuous belief in the efficacy of "King Cotton" as a diplomatic weapon to force foreign recognition of their new government, the Southerners might have achieved their aims by employing their main source of wealth more realistically. There is this to be said, however: assuming that they had not been blinded by a belief in "King Cotton Diplomacy," the nature of their political thinking would probably have prevented efficient use of cotton for prosecution of their cause. The exigencies of war required a unifying control by the central government over all exports of that commodity, a development partially achieved toward the end, but inconceivable to political leaders at the outset.[29]

II. SOUTHERN EMBARGO ON COTTON

In obedience to a misguided notion of the best way to utilize the economic power of cotton, the Southern people and not the Confederate Government imposed an embargo on the export of their main cash crop. Shipment of cotton even from the plantations was prevented as a result of public sentiment inspired and backed by newspapers, the influence of important business groups, and the policies of "state and local officials and public safety committees."[30] During the summer of 1861 cotton factors, together with "insurance and warehousemen" in the various seaports, urged planters not to send that article to market. An indication of the success of the nonexportation campaign is found in the figures given for the amount of cotton which arrived at the five most important ports, Memphis, New Orleans, Savannah, Mobile, and Charleston,

[27] Soley, The Blockade, 35, 43, 84–85, 89–90, 121. See also James G. Randall, The Civil War and Reconstruction (New York, 1937), 573–74; Adams, Great Britain and the American Civil War, I, 245–46; Carl Russell Fish, The American Civil War: An Interpretation (New York, 1937), 208–9, 217; J. T. Scharf, History of the Confederate States Navy from Its Organization to the Surrender of Its Last Vessel (New York, 1887), 433–34; Owsley, King Cotton Diplomacy, 250–51, 290.

[28] Fish, The American Civil War, 217; Owsley, King Cotton Diplomacy, 253, 284; Scharf, Confederate States Navy, 488–90; Samuel Bernard Thompson, Confederate Purchasing Operations Abroad (Chapel Hill, 1935), 6, 43–47.

[29] Thompson, Confederate Purchasing, 5, 72–73, 84–99; Owsley, King Cotton Diplomacy, 34–35.

[30] Owsley, King Cotton Diplomacy, 51.

from September, 1861 to January, 1862. A little less than 10,000 bales were sent to these ports in comparison to approximately 1,500,000 bales in the same months of the previous year.[31] It might be assumed that by its failure to act the Confederate Government was unsympathetic to the embargo; actually the opposite was true. The Southern people largely through voluntary methods had accomplished all that the administration could desire in creating economic pressure abroad without incurring the dangers of diplomatic repercussions from the passage of a Confederate statute for that purpose. Talk favorable to the embargo occurred in the Confederate Congress, and bills or resolutions were introduced to enforce the unofficial policy; yet nothing came of these moves.[32]

Since the embargo had not received official sanction, Judah P. Benjamin, the Secretary of State, in the spring of 1862 had the temerity to place the blame for the greatly reduced shipments of cotton abroad on those foreign nations which had recognized an illegal blockade and had refused to send vessels through it to get Southern goods. He did admit that "as a measure of self-defense" the South had a "policy of refusing to accumulate cotton" at the various ports. He tried to shift the responsibility, however, by claiming: "The truth is that cotton was not withheld from the ports until long after the European powers had indicated their intention to respect Mr. Lincoln's interdiction of their commerce with the South." As for a policy of forcing foreign recognition of the Confederacy, he expressed indignant surprise that "the suggestion so artfully insinuated by Northern agents that cotton is kept back for the purpose of coercing foreign powers into any particular line of policy can scarcely find credence with the enlightened cabinet of St. James."[33] Secretary Benjamin wrote an excellent lawyer's brief, but bad history.

The agitation for an embargo started early in the summer of 1861 and was designed to force recognition of the Confederacy and abandonment of the blockade by means of foreign intervention. The newspapers hoped for an effectual blockade, "the stricter the better," for then the South's best customers would move more quickly in her behalf. But as long as a "sham blockade" was permitted " 'no foreigner can get any of our cotton'."[34] Such expressions received the attention of the foreign press, and the impression grew abroad that it was useless to send ships through the blockade to get cotton. Reports of British consuls resident in the South served to strengthen this idea. In an effort to discourage blockade-running the United States Government through its representatives in Europe was not averse to confirming the belief that the Confederate Government was responsible for the cotton famine.[35]

The embargo was but one of three phases in a program to use cotton as a diplomatic weapon. When it appeared that nonexportation had failed to obtain the desired reaction from England and France, the South resorted to more drastic action in the form of curtailment of production and destruction of existing supplies. In presenting to Europe its plea against the blockade, the government could claim innocence of complicity in the embargo, but such was not the case in the effort to restrict the planting of cotton and to promote its burning. Congress approved by joint resolution in March of 1862 the idea already accepted in the newspapers, farmers' conventions,

[31] *Ibid.,* 30, 43.
[32] *Ibid.,* 32–34.
[33] *O. R. N.,* 2nd series, III, 382–83.
[34] Owsley, *King Cotton Diplomacy,* 26.
[35] See *ibid.,* 29, 39–42.

and state legislatures that the forthcoming crop be curtailed. Likewise in the same month it passed a law providing for the destruction of such crops as cotton and tobacco whenever there appeared to be danger of their seizure by Federal forces. Ostensibly passed as a military measure, the statute was motivated in part by a desire to increase diplomatic pressure on England and France.[36]

Although faith in "King Cotton Diplomacy" explains much of the agitation to reduce cotton and tobacco production, other factors should be mentioned. The South struggled not only for political independence but also freedom forever from Northern economic domination by better utilization of its own resources.[37] Achievement of this goal meant among other things a fundamental change in agriculture from an emphasis on the growth of cash crops to greater production of foodstuffs. Military necessity and fear of the blockade demanded that the shift take place immediately.[38] Beginning in the summer of 1861 government officials, state legislatures, patriotic Southerners, and especially the public press exhorted farmers and planters to substitute the raising of food crops for cotton.[39] Typical of such pleas was a long editorial in the Columbus, Georgia, *Sun* which started in this fashion: "Plant Corn and be Free, or Plant Cotton and be Whipped." The paper went on to say that cotton was "still king, but like all other kings it must be fed."[40] Legislative fiat, both state and Confederate, and a public sentiment materially reduced the amount of cotton raised and stored during the war.[41] In contrast to a yield of 4,500,000 bales in 1861, the crop of 1862 came to only 1,500,000 bales.[42] Those of the next two years were approximately 500,000 and 300,000 bales respectively, while, according to one estimate, at least 2,500,000 bales were burned by the Confederate Government because its armies were forced to retreat.[43]

For various reasons, among them hatred of the blockade, the South had embarked on a program which either rendered useless at a vital period or destroyed a large proportion of its liquid capital. Mr. G. B. Lamar, banker, cotton trader, and later blockade-runner who probably reflected the opinion of other businessmen, questioned the wisdom of the embargo as early as September, 1861, when he wrote: "The *U States* has laid us under Blockade, to render our products valueless and Unavail-

[36] *Ibid.*, 45–47.

[37] Coddington, *Seaboard States,* 110–11, 186–88.

[38] E. Merton Coulter, "The Movement for Agricultural Reorganization in the Cotton South during the Civil War," *North Carolina Historical Review,* IV (January, 1927), 24.

[39] See *Savannah Republican,* July 4, 15, 1861, January 15, 1862, March 12, April 7, 1863, October 13, 1864; *Charleston Mercury,* August 27, 1861, October 8, 1863; *Charleston Courier* (Tri-weekly edition), March 27, April 1, 10, 1862, June 2, 1863; *Richmond Whig,* December 9, 1861; *Hillsborough Recorder,* April 16, 1862; Atlanta *Southern Confederacy,* November 30, 1861; *Southern Cultivator,* XX (January, 1862), 12; *ibid.* (March and April, 1862), 85; *ibid.* (May and June, 1862), 112; *ibid.,* XXI (January and February, 1863), 22; Georgia, *Acts of the General Assembly,* Reg. Sess., 1861, Resolutions, No. 12, passed December 14, 1861. See also John Christopher Schwab, *The Confederate States of America, 1861–1865: A Financial and Industrial History of the South during the Civil War* (New York and London, 1901), 277–78.

[40] Reprinted in the *Savannah Republican,* March 21, 1862.

[41] See Georgia, *Acts of the General Assembly,* Reg. Sess., 1862, No. 1; South Carolina, *Acts of the General Assembly,* Sess., 1862–63, Nos. 4619, 4620; *Richmond Dispatch,* April 10, May 4, 1863; *Charleston Courier* (Tri-weekly edition), May 6, 8, 31, 1862, April 11, June 2, 1863; *Savannah Republican,* April 20, 21, 1863; *Savannah Morning News,* October 31, 1862.

[42] *Charleston Courier* (Tri-weekly edition), December 20, 1862.

[43] Owsley, *King Cotton Diplomacy,* 51.

able to us—It is a question of policy how far we may facilitate their intentions of harming us, by withholding our produce—."[44] Gradually this point of view became accepted, and after the spring of 1862 the embargo was slowly lifted.

III. BLOCKADE-RUNNING AFTER 1862

As the embargo was abandoned, Southern and foreign merchants began to engage more actively in blockade-running, which at first was of an improvised character.[45] Not until 1863 did it assume the aspects of a well-established business which would attract the more cautious investor.[46] Practically all of the larger concerns in the seaboard states were incorporated or started operations sometime during that year,[47] for economic conditions had become ideal for this type of venture. Cotton could be bought in the South for about half its price in England, while conversely the large variety of goods demanded in the Confederacy sold for more than twice what they were worth abroad.[48] By this time, however, the increased efficiency of the Union navy resulting from acquisition of fast cruisers, many of which were converted blockade-runners, required of the companies a very heavy financial outlay. No longer were slow seagoing vessels profitable; only expensive steamers of low, long, narrow, and swift lines and with special equipment were possible. Competition between private concerns and government contractors in England depressed the price of cotton in the South and increased the prices of the desired ships.[49] Cargo-carrying capacity

[44] G. B. Lamar to C. C. Memminger, September 2, 1861, Personal Press Copy Books of G. B. Lamar, the National Archives, Division of Treasury Department Archives, Civil War Records of the Fifth Special Treasury Agency, 28F, hereafter cited as G. B. Lamar Copy Books. See Edwin B. Coddington, "The Activities and Attitudes of a Confederate Business Man: Gazaway B. Lamar," *The Journal of Southern History*, IX (February, 1943), 3, 14.

[45] See *War of the Rebellion: A Compilation of the Official Records of the Union and Confederate Armies* (Washington, 1880–1900), 4th series, II, 562, hereafter cited as O. R.; James Ford Rhodes, *History of the United States from the Compromise of 1850 to the End of the Roosevelt Administration* (New York and London, 1928), V, 396; Francis B. C. Bradlee, *Blockade Running during the Civil War; and the Effect of Land and Water Transportation on the Confederacy* (Salem, 1925), 21, 29–30; O. R. N., 2nd series, III, 371; Thompson, *Confederate Purchasing*, 43; *Richmond Dispatch*, December 2, 1863.

[46] *Charleston Mercury*, November 11, 1863.

[47] South Carolina, *Acts of the General Assembly*, Sess., 1862–63, Nos. 4650, 4651; *ibid.*, Sess., 1863, Nos. 4681, 4689, 4690, 4694; Virginia, *Acts of the General Assembly*, Adj. Sess., 1863, chap. 68; *ibid.*, Called Sess., 1863, chap. 48; Lamar to Memminger, May 6, 1863, G. B. Lamar Copy Books, 28E; *id.* to Messrs. Newman and Strasburger, May 19, 1863, and *id.* to Messrs. J. J. Hartstein [Hartstene] and C. A. Lamar, June 16, 1863, *ibid.*; *Savannah Republican*, June 17, 30, July 9, 1863.

[48] Schwab, *Confederate States of America*, 30; Rhodes, *History of the United States*, V, 396; George Gary Eggleston, *A Rebel's Recollections* (New York, 1905), 88. The goods demanded in "enormous quantities" were wool, cotton, silk, and flax textiles; iron and steel goods in a raw, semi-finished or finished condition; leather and articles manufactured from it such as shoes, boots, saddlery, harness, etc.; clothing of all kinds; liquors and wines; preserved goods and sweets; salt; drugs and chemicals; paper, manufacturers of brass, lead, pewter, tin, "together with an innumerable variety of other articles of less importance." O. R. N., 2nd series, III, 620.

[49] Soley, *The Blockade*, 156–57; Bradlee, *Blockade Running*, 79–80; Rhodes, *History of the United States*, V, 397, 401; C. A. L. Lamar [son] to G. B. Lamar, August 8, September 16, October 18, 1863, Personal Press Copy Book of C. A. L. Lamar, 28C, the National Archives, Division of Treasury Department Archives, Civil War Records of the Fifth Special Treasury Agency. C. A. L. Lamar claimed in the October 18 letter to his father that the inflated demand for ships created a situation where "boats that were contracted for 4 months ago & near being finished at a cost of 13000£ are Selling like hot cakes at from 20–25000£. . . ."

having been sacrificed to speed and shallow draught, various schemes were employed for effective use of such boats. For example, steam presses reduced the cotton to the smallest possible bulk, so that from 500 to 1,200 bales could be carried at one time.[50] A regular shuttle service developed between Confederate ports and the islands of Bermuda, Nassau, and Cuba, approximately 500 to 850 miles off the coast, to deposit Southern products at these places and pick up foreign goods which had been brought across the Atlantic in heavy freighters of "great capacity and stoutly built."[51] To insure successful evasion of the United States fleet, highly paid and skillful crews were hired to man blockade-runners; competent pilots were especially desired.[52] By adopting such methods these private companies imported immense quantities of goods but too often of the wrong type. The military requirements of the government and essential needs of civilians were of secondary importance. Instead the factors of market conditions, value per weight or size, and convenience in handling determined the articles to be brought in. As a result luxury goods such as wines and liquors, fine cloths and clothes, jewelry, and other items similar in character but useless for purposes of war became unduly prevalent in the Southern ports.[53] The army and navy frequently paid exorbitant prices for supplies.[54]

The flamboyant nature of the trade, sometimes tainted by corruption, attracted to it many unsavory characters whose speculative activities and free spending created a false sense of values and tended to undermine the morale of civilians and the men in the armed services.[55] These conditions disturbed all thoughtful and patriotic Southerners. They suggested drastic measures to abolish abuses which drained the Confederacy of its resources without adequate compensation in the form of military supplies.[56] Furthermore, the government was guilty of using inefficient methods in its purchasing operations aboard. Frequently rivalry existing between agents of the various departments or bureaus and in turn between them and representatives from the states revealed the need for "co-ordination and centralization."[57]

By means of executive orders and legislative acts beginning in September, 1863, and ending in April, 1864, the Confederate Government placed blockade-running on an efficient basis by centralizing all purchases for the trade in the hands of two offi-

[50] Rhodes, *History of the United States*, V, 397; Thompson, *Confederate Purchasing*, 91.

[51] Soley, *The Blockade*, 39. See Thompson, *Confederate Purchasing*, 8, who says that it was "discovered almost at the beginning, that the most successful method of getting supplies through the blockade was to ship them to the Sea Islands [Bermuda and Nassau] . . . , where they were reloaded into small fast steamers for running the blockade."

[52] Thompson, *Confederate Purchasing*, 43; Rhodes, *History of the United States*, V, 401. When blockade-runners were captured their pilots were never exchanged but held as prisoners of war; "and the demand for those available for service, increasing in proportion to their diminished number, there was much competition between rival blockade running companies, to the great detriment of the public service." Bradlee, *Blockade Running*, 79–80.

[53] G. B. Lamar to C. B. Baylies, November 8, 1862, G. B. Lamar Copy Books, 28E; Scharf, *Confederate States Navy*, 474. See also advertisements of sales of imported goods in Southern newspapers such as *Charleston Courier* (Tri-weekly edition), April 10, 1862, February 14, 1863; *Richmond Whig*, July 23, November 11, 1862; *Richmond Dispatch*, March 5, 1863; *Charleston Mercury*, July 23, October 31, 1863, August 17, 1864; *Savannah Republican*, September 20, 1864.

[54] Scharf, *Confederate States Navy*, 474; Thompson, *Confederate Purchasing*, 76–84.

[55] *Savannah Republican*, June 30, 1863; Eggleston, *A Rebel's Recollections*, 89; O. R., 4th series, III, 553–54; ibid., 1st series, XXVII, pt. 3, 870; Bradlee, *Blockade Running*, 80; G. B. Lamar to De Rosset[t] and Brown, June 8, 1864, G. B. Lamar Copy Books, 28G.

[56] *Charleston Mercury*, June 1, 1864; Thompson, *Confederate Purchasing*, 83–87; O. R. N., 2nd series, III, 896–97.

[57] Thompson, *Confederate Purchasing*, 22, 76–77.

cials, one stationed at home and the other in Europe. It obtained more ships, sold immense quantities of cotton on its own account, and strictly regulated the activities of private companies by forcing them to allot 50 per cent of their cargo space for government exports and imports.[58] The "new plan" was not perfect in execution, owing in large part to the frenzied opposition of the shipping interests which connived with state officials to evade the stricter controls.[59] It did increase the flow of materials for the armed services at lower costs, although luxury articles in defiance of the law still appeared at the seaports.[60] Before the full benefit of this arrangement was felt the war was over.[61]

In demonstrating Confederate successes in breaking through the blockade, figures have been given on the amount of military supplies imported, the quantity of cotton bales exported, the profits made by the blockade-running companies,[62] and the number of violations. These estimates have been cited as proof of the ineffectiveness of Northern efforts to deprive the South of military essentials. Such analyses are unconvincing because they tend to divorce a study of the blockade and its effects from a consideration of Southern wartime economy in its entirety. It is hard to imagine a conquest of the South without the establishment of a blockade, defective as it may have been. Without the blockade, overseas trade, upon which sound currency largely rested, could have been restored to normal after relaxation of the embargo. In that case the problem of Confederate finances, which appeared so insoluble until the very last, need not have assumed such immense proportions. As it was, decreasing confidence in the currency deprived the government and civilians of supplies produced in the South. To overcome this difficulty officials resorted to the impressment of goods and the tax in kind, which resulted in a tendency among farmers to reduce their production of marketable foodstuffs and thus created new obstacles.[63] Inflation disrupted the ordinary channels of trade, causing speculation which in turn accentuated the scarcity of goods and lowered morale.[64]

[58] See *ibid.*, 84–89; Confederate States of America, *Public Laws*, First Cong., Sess. 4, chap. 23; *O. R.*, 4th series, III, 80–81, 552–55.

[59] See Frank Lawrence Owsley, *State Rights in the Confederacy* (Chicago, 1925), 130–32, 136–49; Coddington, "Confederate Business Man," *loc. cit.*, 30–33. Previously the War Department had ordered private companies to reserve one-third of their tonnage for government use. *O. R.*, 4th series, III, 954. The "new plan" supplanted a loosely knit organization which had taken a year and a half to evolve. See Thompson, *Confederate Purchasing*, 23.

[60] Thompson, *Confederate Purchasing*, 97–99; Owsley, *King Cotton Diplomacy*, 287. For luxury items, see *Charleston Mercury*, August 17, 1864; *Savannah Republican*, September 20, 1864; T. C. De Leon, *Four Years in Rebel Capitals: An Inside View of Life in the Southern Confederacy, from Birth to Death* (Mobile, 1890), 281; Rhodes, *History of the United States*, V, 407; Schwab, *The Confederate States*, 244.

[61] Thompson, *Confederate Purchasing*, 126–27.

[62] *Ibid.*, 16–19, 43–45, 97–99; Owsley, *King Cotton Diplomacy*, 284–91, 574.

[63] *Richmond Dispatch*, November 6, 1863; *Southern Churchman*, March 29, 1865; *O. R.*, 4th series, II, 969; *ibid.*, III, 294–97, 595–96, 932; *ibid.*, 1st series, XLVI, pt. 2, 1289, 1297–99; *ibid.*, 1st series, XXXIII, 1128; Schwab, *The Confederate States*, 202–8; *Charleston Courier* (Triweekly edition), January 5, October 22, 1864; *ibid.* (Daily edition), January 1, 1864; *Richmond Dispatch*, March 12, August 20, 1863, October 28, 1864; *Richmond Whig*, November 3, 1863; Confederate States of America, *Public Laws*, First Cong., Sess. 3, chap. 38; Raleigh *Standard* (Weekly edition), January 20, 1864; *Augusta Chronicle and Sentinel*, November 15, 1864; *Southern Cultivator*, XXIII (February, 1865), 19–20; Broadus Mitchell, *William Gregg, Factory Master of the Old South* (Chapel Hill, 1928), 219–21.

[64] *Savannah Republican*, January 1, 1862; De Leon, *Four Years in Rebel Capitals*, 236–37; *Richmond Dispatch*, March 20, April 17, 1862, March 12, 23, April 3, 1863; *Richmond Whig*,

IV. THE EFFECTIVENESS OF THE BLOCKADE

Blockade-running met perhaps the immediate but not the basic requirements of Southern war economy. The greatest need was for all types of capital goods, which included machinery for industry, equipment for railroads, and heavy tools for agriculture. An inadequate transportation system in large measure explains the South's military failures and the loss of a will to fight. Ill-adapted by arrangement and conditon for a prolonged struggle, the railroads required significant changes to improve their efficiency. Some success was obtained in connecting lines in such large cities as Charleston and Savannah, and several new roads were built to expedite the movement of supplies, but these efforts were insufficient. Wear and tear at an extraordinary rate soon reduced many of them to a crippled condition. The government acted to prevent the collapse of the more important roads by establishing strict controls over their use and by seizing rails and equipment from abandoned lines.[65] Such steps were but palliatives and failed to remedy what became a hopeless situation.

Cut off from Northern suppliers and unable to place orders with Southern heavy industries which were engaged to capacity in the manufacture of munitions, the railroad companies could only place their hopes on Europe, but the blockade intervened. General Lawton wrote Lee in March, 1864, that "not a bar of railroad iron nor a single locomotive has been brought into the Confederacy."[66] Scarcity of rails delayed construction on the Piedmont road between Danville, Virginia, and Greensboro', North Carolina, which became the life line for the Army of Northern Virginia after General Grant had cut connections south of Petersburg in 1864.[67] For the repair of locomotives need existed for copper, pig-tin, steam gauges, cast steel, files,

---

December 9, 1862; *Charleston Courier* (Tri-weekly edition), April 5, 26, July 1, 1862, February 12, 1863; Schwab, *The Confederate States*, 135, 235–36; J. G. de Roulhac Hamilton, ed., *The Correspondence of Jonathan Worth* (Raleigh, 1909), I, 260; J. G. de Roulhac Hamilton, ed., *The Papers of Thomas Ruffin* (Raleigh, 1918–20), III, 296–97; Eggleston, *A Rebel's Recollections*, 83; *Savannah Republican*, September 20, 1862, March 20, June 4, 1863; *Charleston Mercury*, September 3, 1863; O. R., 1st series, XXXIII, 1098; G. B. Lamar to Mrs. Dr. Ries, May 29, 1862; *id.* to *id.*, June 11, 1862; *id.* to James M. Ball, October 6, 1862; *id.* to George W. Lamar, Jr. [nephew], June 29, 1863; *id.* to I. Thiveat, May 9, 1863, G. B. Lamar Copy Books, 28E.

[65] Charles W. Ramsdell, "The Confederate Government and the Railroads," *American Historical Review*, XXII (July, 1917), 795–808; U. B. Phillips, *History of Transportation in the Eastern Cotton Belt to 1860* (New York, 1908), 383, 386; Carl R. Fish, "The Northern Railroads, April, 1861," *American Historical Review*, XXII (July, 1917), 786, 788–89; O. R., 1st series, XXXVI, pt. 3, 279; *ibid.*, 4th series, I, 394, 405–6, 485–86, 617; II, 271, 348, 365–66, 393, 655; III, 392–93; *Charleston Courier* (Tri-weekly edition), November 19, 1861; *Savannah Republican*, September 27, 1861, June 20, 1862. The city of Petersburg, Virginia, at the beginning of the war was the terminal for four roads coming in from the north, east, south, and west. It soon became the big bottleneck for supplies and men sent to the Army of Northern Virginia, whose main task was to defend Richmond. Because of local opposition and fumbling moves of Confederate officials, all transportation continued to be broken at this point throughout the conflict. See Ramsdell, "The Confederate Government and the Railroads," *loc. cit.*, 796–98; O. R., 4th series, I, 394, 405–6, 485–86.

[66] O. R., 1st series, XXXIII, 1237. Not a single bar of railroad iron was rolled in the Confederacy. See *ibid.*, 4th series, III, 1092.

[67] *Ibid.*, 4th series, III, 227.

and other small but vital items. Only a small supply of these materials came through the blockade.[68] The financial statements of various railroads, while creating the illusion of prosperity, furnish further evidence of rapid deterioration of physical assets. The accumulation of huge surpluses at first puzzled contemporary observers, but the reasons were soon revealed by the companies themselves. In 1863 the directors of the East Tennessee and Georgia Railroad Company, acknowledging the impossibility of procuring engineers, cars, iron, and materials to make repairs, decided to distribute among stockholders funds annually reserved for such purchases. Another company admitted an improved financial status, but the directors wanted to build up a rehabilitation fund to be spent after the war and thus refused to declare an unusually large dividend.[69] In its desperation for supplies, by 1864 one of the principal corporations of Virginia allowed the fare for passengers to be paid in tallow or its equivalent in some other product.[70] Although other reasons explain the decline of the railroads, such as lack of man power, continued use of the facilities to capacity, and destructive raids of the enemy,[71] the blockade remained the primary cause. The effects of this situation on the economy are almost too obvious to mention. Military efficiency was impaired, and maldistribution of goods and foodstuffs resulted in more suffering among city dwellers than among those in the country.[72]

Similar conditions affected manufacturing concerns to the detriment of the war effort. As in the case of the railroads, many companies were seemingly more prosperous than ever, if dividends were considered as the sole criterion. Many complaints were voiced against the high prices charged by manufacturers for their goods and the huge financial surpluses accumulated by them. It was little realized at first that the inability to replace worn-out machinery largely accounted for illusory profits. The experience of the Battersea Company, a textile concern in Petersburg, Virginia, typifies affairs elsewhere. It reported that "the expenditure of a large amount [of money] will be necessary in order to place the mill and machinery in a condition to meet the competition that will arise on the resumption of trade with the world on the reopening of the ports; but no part of the profits of the company has been set apart for this purpose."[73]

Textile manufacturers not only suffered from deterioration of machinery but lacked sufficient quantities of oils and other items used in production. More impor-

[68] Ibid., 1092.

[69] Charleston Courier (Tri-weekly edition), December 4, 1862, April 7, 1863; Augusta Chronicle and Sentinel, March 21, 1863. For other annual reports see Richmond Dispatch, March 20, October 26, 1863, December 21, 1864; Virginia, Documents, 1863–64, passim; Savannah Republican, March 12, 1863; Atlanta Southern Confederacy, May 17; August 24, 1863; South Carolina General Assembly, Reports and Resolutions, Annual Sess., 1863, 52–65; Charleston Courier (Tri-weekly edition), May 2, 1863.

[70] Richmond Dispatch, December 21, 1864.

[71] Ibid., April 7, 1863; Charleston Mercury, August 31, 1864; O. R., 1st series, XXXVIII, pt. 2, 929; ibid., pt. 5, 584; ibid., XLIV, 792; ibid., 4th series, II, 485; ibid., III, 1093.

[72] Coddington, The Seaboard States, 181, 184; Charles W. Ramsdell, Behind the Lines in the Southern Confederacy (Baton Rouge, 1944), 96.

[73] Virginia, Documents, 1862–63, No. 27, p. 4. For protests against high prices for manufactured articles and financial conditions of concerns, see also Richmond Whig, March 12, December 13, 1862; Hillsborough Recorder, May 7, 1862; Charleston Courier (Tri-weekly edition), April 26, May 1, 10, 15, November 8, 15, 25, 29, December 13, 1862; Charleston Mercury, June 1, 1864; Virginia, Documents, 1862–63, No. 22, pp. 3–4, 6, 27; ibid., No. 28; Mitchell, William Gregg, 208, 211, 219–21, 232–35.

tant, the scarcity of raw wool increased after 1862, for several reasons. The Texas crop of that year was poor, and that of 1863 failed to reach the Mississippi before communications were severed by the capture of Vicksburg and Port Hudson. Little wool was obtained throughout the rest of the South or by importations from England.[74]

Since Southern industry could not meet the demands of civilians and the government for cotton and woolen goods, people resorted to homespuns. This development in turn created a need for hand looms, spinning wheels, and cards. The market was never sufficiently supplied with the last item, an instrument used to comb raw cotton or wool, because machines to make hand cards were run through the blockade with great difficulty. It then became the practice of many individuals to send wool or cotton to a factory where special machines did the work. Again the blockade limited the amount of such equipment available.[75] Inadequate manufacturing facilities and the blockade deprived the South of many other commodities which, if considered separately, were rather unimportant but assumed significance when studied in relation to all factors involved in a sound economy. The production of foodstuffs depended upon proper maintenance of farm tools and machinery. The plantation blacksmith usually had little difficulty in keeping plows and hoes in order, but the repair of reapers and threshers was a different matter, for new parts were unobtainable. With no usable threshing machines available, some farmers resorted to crude methods of beating the heads of wheat on barrels and then letting the wind blow away the chaff. One writer blames the lack of good harvesting, threshing, and grinding facilities for much of the flour shortage.[76] In an age of poor refrigeration, the preservation of meats, butter, and eggs depended upon salt; manufacturers also used it to preserve green hides and to set the color of cloth dyes. Faced with a serious deficiency, state governments took steps to encourage its production. The principal Southern source of salt, the immense wells of Saltville, Virginia, could not be developed as expected largely because of inadequate transportation facilities.[77] Last but not least of the scarce articles which affected economic life in countless ways, barrels and nails may be mentioned.[78]

[74] *Charleston Mercury,* June 1, 1864; Charles W. Ramsdell, "The Control of Manufacturing by the Confederate Government," *Mississippi Valley Historical Review, VIII* (December, 1921), 239–40; *Southern Cultivator, XX,* 24, 210; *ibid., XXI,* 81.

[75] Bell Irvin Wiley, *Southern Negroes, 1861–1865* (New Haven, 1938), 59; *Southern Cultivator, XXI* (March and April, 1863), 64; *Richmond Whig,* November 12, 1862; Atlanta *Southern Confederacy,* November 16, December 10, 1862; *Charleston Courier* (Tri-weekly edition), October 28, 1862, April 14, 1863; Raleigh *Standard* (Weekly edition), April 22, 1863, advertisement; *Hillsborough Recorder,* June 4, 1862, advertisement. The shortage of hand cards was a subject of great concern to the state governments, always conscious of civilian needs. The production of homespuns depended upon the availability of cards, which were made of scarce materials—leather and wires. For an example of some of the primary sources examined, see Georgia, *Acts of the General Assembly,* Reg. Sess., 1862, Resolutions, No. 8, November 21, 1862; *ibid.,* No. 3; *ibid.,* Reg. Sess., 1863, No. 1; Allen D. Chandler, ed., *Confederate Records of the State of Georgia* (Atlanta, 1909), II, 360–63, 395, 666–67; South Carolina General Assembly, *Reports and Resolutions,* Annual Sess., 1863, First Annual Report of the Auditor of South Carolina, November 12, 1863, 151; North Carolina, *Public Laws,* Adj. Sess., 1862–63, Resolutions, January 26, 1863; Virginia, *Senate Journal and Documents,* 1863–64, No. 14.

[76] Wiley, *Southern Negroes,* 52–53.

[77] Ella Lonn, *Salt as a Factor in the Confederacy* (New York, 1933), 17–18, 20, 35, 78–79, 85–87, 90, 96–104, 107–9, 139–59, 211–14, 223, 229.

[78] G. B. Lamar to W. J. Anderson Company, December 31, 1862, G. B. Lamar Copy Books, 28E.

V. THE BLOCKADE: DEFECTIVE BUT IMPORTANT

The dislocation of Southern economy by the blockade could have been more complete. The suspicion grows that the Northern Government did not choose to make it airtight. An examination of Union policies in respect to the land blockade established by law and presidential proclamation, July 13 and August 16, 1861, respectively, reveals among various factors in a complicated situation a strong desire to obtain Southern products, even if it meant in the end the restoration of almost unrestricted commercial intercourse.[79] It has been estimated that nearly 450,000 bales of cotton came from "the blockaded South by way of Nassau, Bermuda, Tampico, Vera Cruz, Matamoras, and Belize."[80] It may be that "powerful private industries" in the North which pressed for the resumption of trade with the enemy in the Mississippi Valley[81] were allowed also to obtain cotton shipped through the blockade. There is the suggestion that in its anxiety to prevent recognition of the Confederacy and the building of a Southern navy in British shipyards the Northern Government refrained from greater efforts against blockade-running as a sop to English commercial interests.[82] The policy of permitting licensed trade within areas occupied by Union forces along the Atlantic and Gulf coasts opened the way to illicit traffic with the enemy and operated against the purposes of the blockade.[83]

A knowledge of these loopholes in the execution of the program to isolate the South from the rest of the world serves to increase uncertainty in the minds of many students about the effectiveness and thus the legality of the effort. Further study may confirm these doubts, but on the basis of present evidence it would seem that even an imperfect blockade was an important element in weakening Southern economy under the stress of war. The complete story of the blockade in all its ramifications has yet to be told.

[79] E. Merton Coulter, "Commercial Intercourse with the Confederacy in the Mississippi Valley, 1861–1865," *Mississippi Valley Historical Review*, V (March, 1919), 378–93.

[80] Owsley, *King Cotton Diplomacy*, 289.

[81] Coulter, "Commercial Intercourse with the Confederacy," *loc. cit.*, 393.

[82] Monaghan, *Diplomat in Carpet Slippers*, 195, 306–8, 371–72.

[83] Richard S. West, Jr., *Gideon Welles: Lincoln's Navy Department* (New York, 1943), 243–44; Scharf, *Confederate States Navy*, 445–46.

Part III

AN AMERICAN IMPERIALISM

11 / The Expansion of the Marketplace and Capitalist Foreign Relations

William Appleman Williams

Until quite recently few students of American foreign relations took seriously the Marxist economic interpretation of imperialism, at least to the extent of relating the Marxist models to America's historic experience. Charles A. Beard's explorations of America's emerging national interests, published during the 1930s, had emphasized the concern of American capitalists with finding overseas markets for the export of domestic agricultural and industrial surpluses. However, not until the 1950s, when William Appleman Williams and his students at the University of Wisconsin began their researches was there a systematic attempt to demonstrate how the American economy, with its various pressure groups, served as an active force on the peacetime operations of American foreign relations. The quest for new markets in South America and Asia was designed to eliminate the distress caused by cyclical, recurring depressions. Government policies presumably reflected the spirit and endorsed the programs of dominant economic groups at home. The development of a merchant marine, the acquisition of colonies in the Caribbean and the Pacific, increased appropriations for an enlarged navy; and the creation of a healthy climate for encouraging private investments abroad all seemed to fit snugly into a unified capitalist, imperialist foreign policy not qualitatively at odds with the Marxian or Beardian models. In the selection that follows, Williams spells out in a general fashion the bases for this economic interpretation of American foreign policy.

For further reading: Charles A. Beard, *The Idea of National Interest: an Analytical Study of American Foreign Policy*, written in collaboration with G. H. E. Smith (New York: 1934) and *The Open Door at Home: A Trial Philosophy of National Interests,* written in collaboration with G. H. E. Smith (New York: 1934); Lloyd Gardner, *Economic Diplomacy of the New Deal* (Madison: 1964); Thomas C. McCormick, *China Market* (Chicago: 1967); Carl P. Parrini, *Heir to Empire: United States Economic Diplomacy*

William Appleman Williams is presently Professor of History at Oregon State University. This chapter from his *Great Evasion* is reprinted by permission of the Quadrangle Books, Inc. Copyright © 1964 by William Appleman Williams.

1916–1923 (Pittsburgh: 1969); William A. Williams, *The Great Evasion* (Chicago: 1954), *The Roots of the American Empire* (New York: 1969), and *The Tragedy of American Diplomacy* (Cleveland: 1959).

Marx never prepared a separate, formal study of capitalist foreign relations, and no one has ever collected his scattered discussions of the subject into one co-ordinated volume. V. I. Lenin's famous essay on *Imperialism* is a significant document in its own idiom, but it has little value as a basis for evaluating Marx. The same is true of the neglected study by Nikolai Bukharin, *Imperialism and World Economy*, although it provides a somewhat better outline of Marx's own ideas. It seems wise, therefore, to review the main elements of Marx's analysis as he offered it in his own studies of capitalism.

One of the central features of capitalism, Marx argued, was its splitting of the economy into two principal parts. This "cleavage between town and country" was not complete, of course, but the reciprocal relationship between them was heavily imbalanced in favor of the town, or Metropolitan, sector. Marx was here following Adam Smith, the master theorist of capitalism, as well as the facts he gathered in his own study of the system. This was one of the most important instances in which the theory and the practice of capitalism coincided.

Another such example involved the continued expansion of the marketplace, first within a country and then beyond its boundaries. The never-ending necessity to accumulate additional surplus value, or capital, a process which was essential for the system as well as to the individual businessman, meant that this market "must, therefore, be continually extended." Without such expansion the economic system would stagnate at a certain level of activity, and the political and social system based upon it would suffer severe strains leading either to a caste society upheld by force or to revolution. Hence "the real task of bourgeois society," Marx explained, "is the establishment of the world market . . . and a productive system based on this foundation."

As it crossed the national boundary, this process transformed "the cleavage between town and country" into "the colonial system." The town became the developed, industrial Metropolis, while the country became the backward, underdeveloped society. It follows both logically and from the evidence that the periodic crises created and suffered by capitalism intensified the drive to expand the market. "The conquest of new markets and the more thorough exploitation of the old ones," Marx pointed out, served as the principal means whereby the internal crisis in the Metropolis "seeks to balance itself."

Concerning both the normal and the crisis situations, Marx was typically succinct and non-euphemistic in describing the central feature of this expansion of the marketplace. "The favored country recovers more labor in exchange for less labor." It is worth re-emphasizing, moreover, that Adam Smith reached the identical conclusion, and based his entire theory and strategy of capitalist success on this essentially imbalanced relationship between the Metropolis and the country society.

Such expansion of the marketplace is directly and explicitly relevant to an understanding of American foreign relations. It offers, to begin with, a good many insights into the major periods of American diplomacy. The first of these eras began in the middle of the eighteenth century and culminated in the 1820's. The increasing British efforts after 1750 to control and limit the existing American marketplace, its further agrarian expansion westward, and its increasing share in international trade, led to a confrontation with the colonists that lies at the heart of the American Revolution.

Similar British attempts to restrict American territorial expansion after independence had been won, and to set limits upon America's international trade (which antagonized the surplus-producing farmers as well as other groups), promoted and accelerated and intensified the nationalism which led to the War of 1812. And the American push into the Floridas, and into the trans-Mississippi region, was obviously expansionist in origin and purpose. The vision of a great trade with South America and Asia, while not as central to these movements as the concern for land, was nevertheless a significant part of the continuing pressure to expand the marketplace that culminated in the Trans-Continental Treaty of 1819 with Spain.

Throughout this period, moreover, the same underlying thrust to expand the marketplace defined the basic character of American policy toward the Indians. The drive to dispossess the natives of their land, and the campaign to remove all restrictions on trade with the various tribes, combined to drive the Indians further westward while at the same time subverting any efforts to integrate them as full citizens into the white man's society and weakening their ability to resist further encroachments.

In a similar way, Marx's emphasis on the expansion of the marketplace offers major —and in many respects still unexploited—perceptions concerning the struggle between various elements of the country during the 1840's and 1850's to organize the marketplace along one of three alternate axes: a North-South, a South-West, or a North-West alliance. The psychology of fear that became so apparent in all sections of the nation on the eve of the Civil War, for example, is directly related to this increasingly intense conflict.

Farmers in the region north of the Ohio River not only manifested an active desire to control the national government and the Western territories for their own benefit, but developed a corresponding antagonism toward other groups and regions which appeared to be blocking their attempts to win that predominance. Southerners expressed similar hopes and fears, as did still other groups in the Northeastern part of the country. As the economic integration between the Northeastern "town" and the food-producing Northwestern "country" became stronger than an earlier relationship between the Eastern Metropolis and the Southern raw material producing "country," Southerners increasingly defined themselves as members of a potentially independent system sustained and strengthened through connections with non-American Metropolitan areas.

The formerly regional conflicts thus gradually changed into a struggle between two giant sections over the issue of which was to control the trans-Mississippi West. Both blocs viewed that area as what today would be called an underdeveloped, potentially neocolonial resource that would guarantee their respective prosperity and security. At bottom, both sections viewed slavery as an economic phenomenon that would determine the outcome of the marketplace struggle for final victory. Ultimately, of course, slavery became both a symbol of that conflict and a moral and ideological banner for both sides. If slavery be said to have caused the Civil War, however, it must also be said that it did so more in its economic sense than in its moral respect. For the general response to the abolitionist minority (both positive and negative) was grounded in the economic fears of Northerners and Southerners who saw themselves first of all as combatants in a desperate struggle to control the continental marketplace.

The postwar conflicts between the Eastern Metropolis and the Southern and Western agrarian sectors of the economy can most fruitfully be approached as a clear illustration of the validity of the emphasis placed on "the cleavage between town and country" by Smith and Marx. This provides by far the most accurate guideline to any understanding and interpretation of the Granger, Alliance, and Populist movements. Even a viable psychological interpretation of these protest movements must be grounded upon such a structural analysis.

The general drive to expand the marketplace during these same years of the late nineteenth century provided the primary energy for the American economic move outward into Europe, Africa, Latin America, and Asia. That expansion has been sustained and intensified in the twentieth century. Nobody but Americans thrust world power upon the United States. It came as a direct result of this determined push into the world marketplace. John D. Rockefeller's comment on the policy of Standard Oil typifies the attitude of both centuries. "Dependent solely upon local business," he explained in 1899, "we should have failed years ago. We were forced to extend our markets and to seek for export trade."

Since the farmer was a capitalist entrepreneur (a vital consideration often neglected or discounted in narrowly psychological interpretations of his behavior), Marx's analysis provides an insight into the policies and actions of the agrarians that most commentators have overlooked. If Marx is correct, that is, then the evidence ought to reveal the farmers participating in the expansionist movement as their production outran domestic consumption. The documents show precisely that: the American farmer's concern with overseas markets played a significant part in initiating and sustaining the momentum of the idea and the practice of such expansion.

Beginning in the early 1880's, the farmers' turn to export markets led directly to diplomatic encounters with England, France, Austria-Hungary, and Germany. It also prompted specific urban business interests, such as the railroads, the flour millers, the meat packers, and the implement manufacturers, to follow the lead of the farmers and undertake their own expansionist efforts. And, more generally, urban business leaders increasingly looked to agricultural export figures as a reliable index of general economic activity.

Politicians likewise responded, and the campaign for reciprocity treaties drew almost as much suport from certain agrarian groups (as with Secretary of State James G. Blaine's efforts in 1890 to win reciprocity agreements with Cuba and other food-importing nations) as from the manufacturers. This involvement in the world marketplace also played a central role in the agrarian campaign for unlimited coinage of silver at a ratio of 16 to 1. The farmers, and their leaders like William Jennings Bryan, argued that free coinage would free America from economic control by Great Britain and other European powers and give the United States economic supremacy in the world marketplace. This militant and expansive economic nationalism, which stemmed directly from the experience of the farmers in having to deal through Liverpool and London, not only provided a surprising amount of support for building a new and big navy and taking Hawaii, but was a very significant factor in the coming of the Spanish-American War.

Marx's particular emphasis on foreign policy as a way to generate recovery in the context of economic crisis is also verified by American behavior. The trans-Appalachian depression that developed between 1808 and 1811, and which hit the farmers hard, had a direct causative connection with the agitation that elected the War Hawks and led to the War of 1812. Expansion into Mexico began in the downturn after the War of 1812, and matured into an imperial clash ultimately involving war during the panics and the depression of the late 1830's. The same pattern appears in the late 1860's and the 1870's, though it is somewhat camouflaged by taking the form, at least primarily, of the North's extension of its economic control over the South and the West.

Americans again began to react more explicitly and generally to depressions by turning to economic expansion during the business troubles of the 1880's, a decade when surplus production began to pose a problem in some industries as well as in agriculture. This response crystallized during the panic and depression of the 1890's and prompted the appearance of a good many general theories about the necessity of such expansion. Such ideas played a double role: they served as an explanation of what was happening, and they offered a solution for the difficulties of the system. As a result, they were a primary causative force in the imperial expansion of the period.

This emphasis on overseas economic expansion, through both exports and investments, was an integral part of the New Deal program for recovery from the Great Depression. And it was the central theme of the discussions during 1943–1945 concerning the best way to handle the depression that was expected to develop at the end of World War II. The same approach has been increasingly emphasized during the series of postwar recessions. The New Frontier's stress on the expansion of exports and the creation of regional markets tied to the American system is candidly explained and defended as a solution for the specific difficulties of the domestic economy and the more general problems incident to the breakdown of the nineteenth-century imperial system.

Marx recognized and understood that the imperial relationship that evolved out of such economic expansion could take several forms. One of these is colonialism, which involves the seizure or conquest of empty, or lightly populated, real estate and the subsequent transfer of other people into the new area. It is accompanied by direct and extensive controls over the new society, as well as over the displaced or conquered population. Americans take great pride, of course, in denying any colonial blemish upon their historical record. This case is debatable even if colonialism is defined or thought of, as it usually is by Americans, as involving action across the open sea.

But there is no serious justification for making the crossing of water a necessary condition of colonialism. The essential definition is the control of territory and resources, and the displacement, re-establishment, and control of human beings. American policy toward the Indian, and toward the Negro from 1650 to 1863, certainly satisfies those criteria and therefore belies the assertion that the United States has never been a colonial power. It is customary and accurate to talk about the Negro during those years as a slave, but slavery is only the most extreme form of colonial exploitation. In any event, the Negro was transported across the sea in the course of being colonized.

There was also a significant degree of colonialism involved in the economic and political controls exercised by the American Metropolis over the Western territories. Jefferson's attitude toward the non-English settlers in the region acquired through the Louisiana Purchase is symbolic, not only of the discrepancy between his rhetoric and his policy, but also of the general attitude of the East toward the new settlements across the mountains. The foreigners could acquiesce or leave, Jefferson announced; otherwise force would be used against them.

The process by which the settlements beyond the Appalachians were ultimately accepted as full members of the federal commonwealth does not offer as great an exception to the usual colonial pattern as latter-day Americans are inclined to assume. For one thing, the final agreement to admit such areas as states was not achieved without overt resistance by the territories against being treated as colonies. The agitation of the 1780's, for example, had a great deal to do with overcoming Easterners who wanted to handle the trans-Appalachian region as a colony in the traditional British manner.

In the final plan, moreover, the Metropolis was given many explicit controls over a territory until it was admitted as a state, and these opened the way for outsiders to establish their power and authority in less formal ways. It often took a generation (if not longer) for the new state to break free of the resulting institutionalized influence. Nor was statehood granted by the Metropolis with any noticeable dispatch. After the Civil War, for example, only two territories (Nebraska and Colorado) gained legal equality during a period of twenty-four years. As might be imagined, this artificial and protracted delay reinforced and intensified other causes involved in the West's antagonism and resistance toward outsiders.

A second kind of imperial relationship that Marx recognized and discussed is the form of administrative colonialism evolved by the British in India during and after the 1850's. This pattern is characterized by the effective control by an outside minority, through force and the threat of force, of alien territory and population, and by its concurrent establishment of economic predominance. It does not involve, as with colonialism per se, the large-scale transfer of population under the direction and control of the Metropolis. There is emigration from the Metropolis, but it is strictly limited both in numbers and direct function. Its object is to provide a military force in being in support of the leadership necessary for the effective control and management of the political economy of the subject society. The emigrants thus comprise an absolute and a relatively small group of army and naval personnel, political administrators, and economic directors. The success of the system, and of the agents of the Metropolis, is measured by the degree to which absentee control of crucial decisions is institutionalized within a framework of native selfgovernment in local affairs, and routinely maintained domestic political and social peace.

American administrative colonialism appears most classically in the cases of Cuba and the Philippines. All the features of the system were apparent: the colony's own internal cleavage between town and country, its imbalanced, limited, and skewed development, and the improvement purchased at the price of drastic costs in human and material resources, and in harmful consequences to the social fabric itself. The same pattern, with variations appropriate to the circumstances, has emerged in American relations with Liberia and many Latin-American countries, such as Nicaragua and Guatemala. And the current American relationships with Okinawa, South Korea, and Vietnam follow the main outlines of such administrative colonial empire.

The third principal form of the imperial relationship emerges in the evolution of the inherent nature of the marketplace connection between a Metropolis and a backward, underdeveloped region or society. It arises out of the imbalance between the two societies which produces the situation so aptly described by Adam Smith: "The revenue of a trading and manufacturing country must, other things being equal, always be much greater than that of one without trade or manufactures. . . . A country without trade and manufactures is generally obliged to purchase, at the expense of a great part of its rude produce, a very small part of the manufactured produce of other countries." Or as described by Karl Marx: "The favored country recovers more labor in exchange for less labor." Or, to phrase it in the language of our own time, the price received by the underdeveloped country for its goods and services does not suffice to pay for the goods and services it requires to initiate and sustain its own development. For that matter, in many cases the prices set by the Metropolis for such goods decline so much that the loss to the underdeveloped country is not even made up by grants or loans provided by the Metropolis.

Even under the most favorable circumstances, therefore, the gap between the rich and the poor remains constant or decreases only in tiny and sporadic increments. At worst (and more usually), the increases take the form of creeping impoverishment in the poorer nation. Or, as Marx put it, in a kind of increasing misery and increasing proletarianization. It is essential to realize that, whatever the evidence indicates as to increasing misery within the Metropolis, the facts of the world capitalist marketplace support Marx's analysis. He was correct. The poor are poorer and more miserable.

While force is periodically employed, and formal agents from the Metropolis occasionally take a direct hand in managing the affairs of the weaker society, neither action is a routine, institutionalized part of this variant of the imperial relationship. British historians have recently used the phrases, "the imperialism of free trade" and "informal empire," to describe this pattern, and their suggestions seem astute, accurate, and convenient. As Marx clearly understood, the system evolves from the basic capitalist conception of the market and the marketplace as the Metropolis expands into the backward area.

The marketplace is an integrated, two-way relationship involving access to raw materials as well as export markets for goods, services, and investment capital. Marx understood these reasons that lay behind the expansionist arguments developed by American farmers and industrial leaders. They pointed out the marginal utility of foreign operations and explained why it was rational to sell at a loss overseas in order to avoid the economic and social costs of shutting down when the domestic demand was satisfied. In addition to saving capital and avoiding labor unrest, such practices offered an effective strategy for entering and winning control of foreign markets.

American foreign relations since 1895 provide the central historical illustration of this kind of imperial expansion. The informal empire of the United States in the twentieth century offers an example of the character, dynamism, and consequences of the capitalist marketplace that is even purer in form and substance than the one provided by British expansion after the middle of the nineteenth century. The famous Open Door Notes of 1899 and 1900 were consciously and brilliantly formulated on the assumption that America possessed the necessary and overwhelming economic power vis-à-vis other advanced industrial powers, as well as the weaker, poorer countries, and on the conviction that Adam Smith was correct in holding that such strength would enable the United States to control the world marketplace if it was defined as a fair field with favor to none.

Given this belief in the fundamental economic preponderance of their system, American policy-makers designed their imperial strategy with a view to creating and maintaining the conditions which would enable their nation's power to produce the desired economic and political victories. Since they viewed war as the great disrupter of economic progress, and as the nightrider of political and social regression, their broad objective was to establish rules of the game which would prevent the struggle in the marketplace from becoming a trial by arms.

The Open Door Notes sought to do this in Asia (and, later, in other regions, such as

Africa) by committing America's industrial rivals to the following principles of policy and action: (1) a prohibition on further division and colonization of such areas as China; (2) existing and subsequent regulations within established spheres of interest to apply equally to all competitors; and (3) equal opportunity to be afforded to all rivals in all future economic activity.

While the strategy did not succeed in preventing subsequent wars, it is crucial to realize that the United States entered such conflicts to defend and to re-establish the Open Door Policy. In an important degree, moreover, America was drawn into those wars because of antagonisms arising out of the effectiveness of its performance within the limits set by the principles of the Open Door Policy. This was true in the positive sense of American economic penetration and influence in the world marketplace after 1900, as well as in the negative sense that the Open Door Policy appeared to competitors as an obstacle to their own progress. In this respect, at any rate, the policy was effective enough in its actual or potential economic operation to subvert its political and military objectives.

The evolution and adoption of the Open Door Policy involved one of the truly majestic ironies of American—and perhaps even Western—history. Men like Theodore Roosevelt and Henry Cabot Lodge initially favored a vigorous kind of administrative colonialism as the proper strategy of American expansion. Not unjustly, therefore, they came to be known as Imperialists. Their critics and opponents, men like Andrew Carnegie, William Jennings Bryan, and Edward Atkinson, claimed and were known by the label of Anti-Imperialists. This likewise was true and fair enough as a description of their position on traditional colonialism, or even formal and extensive administrative colonialism.

But the Anti-Imperialists were actually men who understood and advocated the very kind of informal empire that Adam Smith and Karl Marx maintained was created by the inherent imbalance of the marketplace relationship between the advanced industrial Metropolis and the poor, backward, agrarian societies. To begin with, the Anti-Imperialists argued that the economic and other institutional requirements of colonialism or widespread administrative colonialism would slow down and limit the accumulation of capital at home, would progressively limit essential bourgeois freedoms, and would breed social unrest. They added that such a strategy of expansion would also encourage and sustain resistance movements in the dependencies and lead to wars with other advanced nations. Taken together, such consequences would be very apt to subvert economic and political liberty at home, and might even bring about the destruction of the empire itself. To avoid such dangers, yet enjoy the necessary expansion of the marketplace, the Anti-Imperialists rested their strategy of empire on the very principle that Adam Smith advanced.

The Anti-Imperialists and Smith were correct. The Open Door Policy worked magnificently for half a century—surely as effectively as the European forms of colonialism and administrative colonialism. American economic power expanded throughout the world, into the other advanced countries as well as into the underdeveloped regions (including European colonies and spheres of interest), and came ultimately and literally to dominate the world capitalist marketplace. And, measured either in absolute terms or relatively against the performance of the older patterns of empire, the United States was required to employ but small amounts of force between 1900 and 1950 in order to maintain its imperial relationship with the weaker countries. Within the assumptions of the system, American economic power was deployed with considerably more astuteness, and managed with more finesse and sophistication, than either its advocates or its critics are often prone to admit. In addition to the huge profits returned to the United States, the result was the creation of a pattern of domestic politics within the "country" side of the empire that sustained pro-American rulers in power for the great majority of the years since 1900.

But Karl Marx was also correct. The inherent drive within the advanced countries to accumulate capital and to expand and control the marketplace, and the resulting increasing proletarianization and misery in the subject half of the empire, has led to more and increasingly violent conflict. American entry into World War I was at bottom predicated upon the conclusion, reached by both top economic and high political leaders, that the United States could not risk being excluded from what appeared to be the probable reorganization of the world marketplace on terms that would seriously restrict, if not actually subvert, the operation of the Open Door Policy.

Both the Allies and the Central Powers had made it clear by 1916 that they would transform a military and political victory into an economic system strongly favorable to themselves. Wilson's emphasis on his famous Fourteen Points, and his insistence on the Covenant of the League of Nations, involved far more than transcendental idealism. Those programs were designed to apply the axioms of the Open Door Policy to the world and, through the crucial Article X of the Covenant, to guarantee their observance for an indefinite future. The same considerations, even more explicitly avowed, lie at the heart of American involvement in World War II and the Cold War.

America's increasing opposition to Germany and Italy began not with the attacks on Czechoslovakia or Poland, but in connection with basic Axis economic policy (such as barter agreements in place of open marketplace transactions) as early as 1933, and in reponse to German penetration of Latin-American economic affairs during that decade. Germany's increasing resort to force to extend the sway of such ideas and policies, and others including racial persecution, carried the economic and ideological conflict into the military arena before Japan's attack on Pearl Harbor. From the very beginning, moreover, American leaders openly acknowledged that the tension with Japan was created by the decision to uphold and enforce the principles of the Open Door Policy in China and southeastern Asia in the face of Japanese expansion.

Antagonism toward the Soviet Union involved the same issues in an even more central and unqualified manner. This struggle, which had begun in 1917 and 1918, involved an outright rejection by the Soviets of the cardinal principles of the capitalist marketplace. The United States never fully reconciled itself to this withdrawal by Russia from the capitalist world. In the more narrow and explicit sense, this opposition manifested itself at the end of World War II in an openly proclaimed American determination to preserve and institutionalize the principles of the Open Door Policy in northeastern Asia and in eastern Europe. The Soviet Union's avowed willingness to negotiate particular and more limited rights for the capitalist world in those regions was never explored in any serious, sustained manner. The United States defined the choice as lying between an acceptance of the principles of the Open Door Policy or a condition of opposition and antagonism.

None of this means (in any of the three instances) that the United States entered upon war simply to make money. Certain freedoms and liberties are essential to capitalists and capitalism, even though capitalists and capitalism are not essential to freedom and liberty. There is no discrepancy, therefore, in going to war for a free marketplace and going to war to defend, secure, and even extend the particular freedoms and liberties associated with such a marketplace political economy. But if either war had been fought solely for those freedoms and liberties, then the condition of the underdeveloped part of the world would have been quite different as early as 1920. And its circumstances would have changed much more rapidly, and with considerably less violence against the advanced Metropolitan countries, after the victory in 1945.

Hence none of these actions involved either a series of terrible conspiracies or a kind of narrow, crude economic motivation or determinism on the part of American leaders or their constituency. All parties had a sincere and practical commitment to the kind of freedom inherent in the Open Door Policy per se, and in the informal empire constructed by the United States between 1898 and 1950. The issue is not how bad or evil Americans were, but rather the far more profound and human theme of their tragic inability to realize their desire for peace and freedom so long as they decline to modify seriously the principles of possessive individualism that lie at the heart of capitalism.

As far as America's informal empire itself is concerned, the case of Cuba serves perfectly—if horribly—to illustrate the validity of Marx's analysis. Or, for that matter, the accuracy of Adam Smith's argument. To Marx's axiom about who takes more labor from whom, add his principle that "violent eruptions are naturally more likely to occur in the extremities of the bourgeois organism than in its heart," and top it off with his conclusion that the ideals of the capitalist fight a generally losing battle with the economic axioms of the system. The result is a definition of, and a set of major insights into, the principal features of Cuban-American relations from 1895 to the present. Marx was not primarily concerned to predict when the convulsion would occur, or who would ride its first wave. He was engaged in explaining what would happen, and why it would occur, if the Metropolis continued to act on the principles of the marketplace in its relationships with a colonial or otherwise dependent society. The origins and evolution of the Cuban Revolution, and the nature and course of its confrontation with the United States, verify the central themes of his analysis.

The Cuban missile crisis of 1962 offers an international example of Marx's fundamental argument that a change in the forces of production ultimately causes a change in the relations of production. In the confrontations of war and cold war, of course, the means of production are ultimately defined in military terms. During the years that the United States enjoyed a monopoly or a significant advantage in nuclear weapons, from 1945 to 1955, it unilaterally established and in large measure maintained the ground rules for international relations in the atomic age.

There were exceptions, particularly in China, that provided clear warnings that this vast preponderance of productive power did not provide the United States with an ability to control every situation. The policy was based on a far too narrow, and even typically marketplace, defintion of power. It provided an excellent illustration of the way in which the mind concerned with commodities discounts the significance of people. The instruments of power were confused with the sources of power.

The signs indicating the dangers in this outlook were largely ignored until the Russians developed the same productive forces and the same instruments of power. Even then, however, the evidence continued to be generally discounted for a considerable period. Americans continued to make a fetish of producing the commodity of the atom and hydrogen bombs, arguing quite irrationally that the power to kill everybody twice or thrice gave them more security than only being able to do so once. The situation took on the characteristics of a macabre extension of the national attitude toward buying multiple automobiles. Thorstein Veblen might have discussed the phenomenon under the heading of the urge to conspicuous annihilation.

Then came the Cuban Revolution. It was an example of the impotence of nuclear supremacy that could not be evaded or rationalized away. American control of the island had been too obvious for too long a time, and the absurdity of vaporizing the revolution in order to save trade and investments was so evident as to be humorous despite the frustration. Americans sensed, when they did not realize it more explicitly, that the revolution was the product of their own administrative colonialism and informal empire. Even the Pavlovian exercises in explaining it as the work of a communist conspiracy were feeble and generally unimpressive examples of casuistry.

The first direct attempt to destroy the revolution employed the strategy of using conventional weapons inside what was thought to be the womb of safety provided by nuclear predominance. But the strength of the revolution foiled that American effort to combine superficial morality and rhetorical righteousness with secret malice. The subsequent nuclear showdown with the Russians was a direct consequence of that unsuccessful effort to square the circle. Cuban leaders became convinced that the United States would try again with vastly greater forces. This may not have been true, but they declined to risk their revolution on the word of an American administration that had already acted differently than it had talked.

On the surface, it is true, the productive forces of the United States emerged triumphant in the resulting confrontation with the Soviet Union. "The other fellow blinked," as the story goes. But as Secretary of State Dean Rusk later acknowledged, the United States for the first time caught a glimpse of the true nature of nuclear reality. The Soviets withdrew their missiles, but the United States gradually realized that it, the world's greatest Metropolis, had become a colony. A colony, that is to say, of the vast forces of production that it had created and put on the marketplace.

For in a profound sense, the increasing recognition of the necessity of co-existence that dates from the Cuban missile crisis stands as proof of Marx's central thesis that the productive forces will ultimately determine the relations of production. No single entrepreneur can impose his will on the economic marketplace if he is blocked by an element of comparable strength, save at a price so dear as to be self-destructive. Neither can one superpower impose its will upon the international nuclear marketplace if it is matched by another super-power, save at the cost of the very influence it is seeking to enlarge. There is considerable evidence, moreover, that one of the main reasons Soviet leaders placed their weapons in Cuba was to dramatize this truth to the United States.

It is conceivable that, despite that encounter, the United States will continue trying to prove Marx wrong by sustaining the essential structure and attitudes of the Cold War. That approach reveals a powerful inherent propensity to devolve into nuclear war. It is a dynamism that is not effectively checked, let alone redirected, by mere changes in the rhetoric or the means employed in connection with the existing policy. Even if the policy somehow avoided nuclear war, America would not really have proved that Marx was wrong. Another decade of cold war, even more sophisticated and more gentlemanly cold war, would destroy capitalism in any meaningful—let alone American —sense. The result would be a form of non-violent, totalitarian state managerialism that would make C. Wright Mills's power elite look like the founding fathers of Jacksonian Democracy.

These considerations may serve to clarify a generally misunderstood aspect of

Marx's theory and analysis. To accept the proposition that changes in the forces of production lead inexorably to changes in the relations of production is not to accept as a corollary that those changes will inevitably take one course or pattern. Marx held that men make their own history within the limits they create for themselves, but he never abstracted intellect or volition from man himself.

He acknowledged, for example, that it was possible for an advanced capitalist country to make the transition to socialism without a violent social upheaval. "We do not deny that there are countries, like England and America, . . . where the worker may attain his object by peaceful means." Even if co-existence is thought of wholly within a Marxian framework, which is most certainly not necessary, it is false to assume or fear that the result is pre-ordained by some inexorable superhuman law. To accept the necessity of co-existence is not to bow fatalistically to the idea that everyone has to embrace communism as defined and practiced by Lenin, Stalin, Mao, or Khrushchev. Those models comprise but a tiny percentage of the alternatives. The acceptance of co-existence actually opens up a wide range of possibilities, whereas the insistence on trying to preserve the conventional wisdom of the Cold War drives America deeper into a cul-de-sac.

Within a year after the Cuban missile crisis created some recognition of these considerations and possibilities, the perceptive and courageous Senator George McGovern boldly challenged American leaders to adapt their ideas and their policies to the new reality. "We need," he said, "a thoroughly honest discussion and debate, not so much about competing weapons systems, but rather about the basic postulates of our defense strategy. . . . What is the mounting arms race doing to our freedom and the quality of our lives? . . . Are we following a blueprint for peace or racing toward annihilation?" He then bluntly asserted that "the United States now has a stockpile of nuclear weapons in excess of any conceivable need." Nor did he shrink from pointing out that the national fetish concerning nuclear commodities had failed to prevent the rise of structural unemployment, and that it had left America with a shopping list of urgent social and humanitarian needs that would take years—if not decades—to fill.

In the realm of foreign affairs, at least, the United States has not proved that Karl Marx was wrong. America has been a colonial power. America has practiced administrative colonialism on a significant scale. America has built an informal empire of massive proportions. And America is now face to face with the proof of Marx's thesis that such empires create their own increasingly effective opposition both from within and from without.

It would appear to be the greater part of wisdom, to say nothing of safety, to admit that Marx was right. That would enable us to invest our intellectual and psychological and moral capital in an imaginative effort to adjust our foreign policy to the very reality we have done so much to create. We could begin, for example, by getting straight on the actual and limited power of money. True, money can buy some governments some of the time. But money cannot even buy some governments all of the time, let alone all of the governments all of the time.

This limitation arises from the nature of governments. Governments are made of and by people. This is the case whether or not other people make their governments in the same way we Americans make ours. And money does not buy people. It only buys their labor or the product of their labor. Hence when they produce a new government, all we have to show for our money is the old-model government which has been dropped from the assembly line.

Having come to terms with the limited power of money to buy success in foreign affairs, we might then confront the problem of how best to transcend the inequities of the international capitalist marketplace. Here the first problem is to relax enough to stop reading the headlines as though they were bulletins on the state of our manhood. This is a magnificent epoch. Billions of people are beginning to control their own societies for the first time in centuries. We should relax enough to be exhilarated when they break another link in their chains, and to respond with sympathy to their efforts to cope with their difficulties and to realize their own aspirations. Once we relax, some of our blood might move out of our fright glands back into our heart and our head. We might even begin to realize that we can respect people even if we cannot buy them. We might even establish a dialogue with them.

It is often asserted, of course, that we have nothing to learn from the underdeveloped and developing nations. This is an argument based on the assumption that they are obsessed with emulating the United States and other advanced industrial nations, and are thus doing little more than repeating all our mistakes in rapid-fire sequence. Their struggle to escape scarcity is deemed irrelevant to our effort to cope with plenty.

This analysis is relevant only as long as we define our future as a projection of our own past. Only as long, that is, as we do not transcend the limits of our existing marketplace society. But this is precisely what we must do if we are to recognize and overcome the new kind of scarcity we confront as we begin to master the traditional economic scarcity.

We have not transcended scarcity per se. For that matter, we still have many vital decisions—choices—to make concerning how to use the great productive powers we have created. We cannot instantaneously do everything that is possible, let alone everything that will become possible. We have only reached the point where we can begin to deal intelligently and responsibly and democratically with those choices, and the point where we can define the new and different and vastly more difficult kinds of scarcity. This is precisely what Marx was at such pains to point out to us when he argued that capitalism would create the means of conquering economic scarcity, but would not know what to do with that power.

This new kind of scarcity concerns the lack of humaneness and community in relationships between human beings. It is not literally new, of course, but it seems new to us because capitalism defined achievement so narrowly in terms of economic scarcity that we pushed the far more vital issue into the background. Economic success became the definition of life. And it is here, in connection with the scarcity of humaneness in human relationships, in the shortage of community, that the underdeveloped and developing countries can offer us insights and assistance.

They do so merely by existing in their poverty. Once we recognize and accept Marx's point about the scarcity of community under capitalism, for example, we enable ourselves to accept the simple and elementary truth that our existing approach to helping the poor countries perpetuates the scarity of community. Community is defined by humane human relationships, not by marketplace calculations of profit and loss. Consider Cuba. It tells us that people are still able to commit themselves to the idea and the ideal of the *general* welfare, and to act on that commitment. Cuba tells us that it is better to make a revolution than to give up and accept conditions that offer no serious hope for the future. And Cuba tells us that the humane response to that commitment and that effort is respect, not scorn, and generous help, not embittered and spiteful opposition. And all of these things we need most desperately to relearn.

The poor countries offer us a second kind of assistance because they do have their own traditions and institutions and practices of community. The point is not so much that we should adopt, or even adapt, their particular concepts. That may in some cases be an intelligent approach, but the real help they offer us lies in providing a constant reminder of the idea and the ideal of community. We have so long neglected, and even denied, our own images and practices of community that we need all the encouragement we can find to support our groping efforts to recover and revitalize those traditions.

Other reactions to the validity of Marx's analysis of the capitalist marketplace, and its manifestations in American foreign affairs, lead to dangerous consequences. One such alternative is to define foreign relations in terms of space. This is a continued evasion of the problem, however, because the exploitation and development of space will be conditioned in large measure by events on earth. The other principal approach is to continue the struggle to sustain the existing pattern of capitalist foreign relations. But this offers two equally dismal probabilities. Either the effort will culminate in isolating the United States from a developing world community, or it will eventuate in a nuclear catastrophe.

The cost of continuing the effort to prove Marx wrong is thus exorbitant even by capitalist standards. Indeed, it would seem time to honor the old capitalist axiom of cutting our losses and investing our capital in a more promising venture.

12 / The Background of Cleveland's Venezuelan Policy: A Reinterpretation

Walter LaFeber

Among the serious international crises involving the United States during the 1890s, perhaps none was so multi-faceted as the Venezuelan Boundary Dispute with Great Britain which reached its climax in 1894–96. United States interest in this South American dispute reached such feverish pitch that some contemporary observers expected that war would surely occur between the two English speaking nations. Walter LaFeber's article which follows endeavors to analyze the reasons behind the hard bargaining posture which President Cleveland and his Secretary of State, Richard Olney, assumed in their communications with the British. Because of the economic depression during the 1890s, American rhetoric addressed to London was intended to make it unmistakably clear that the United States would not fail to support a South American country in time of need. Leaders in the government and business community of the United States firmly endorsed the hard-line policy of the Cleveland Administration, for they assumed that such support for Venezuela's claim might assure the United States the lion-share of profits in future trade with South American nations.

For further reading: Thomas A. Bailey, "America's Emergence as a World Power: The Myth and the Verity," in *Pacific Historical Review*, XXX (1961), 1–16; Foster R. Dulles, *The Imperial Years* (New York: 1956); Paul S. Holbo, "Presidential Leadership in Foreign Affairs: William McKinley and the Turpie-Foraker Amendment," in *American Historical Review*, LXX (July, 1967), 1321–1335; William L. Langer, *The Diplomacy of Imperialism 1890–1902* (New York: 1935); Ernest R. May, *American Imperialism: A Speculative Essay* (New York: 1968) and *Imperial Democracy* (New York: 1961); Allen Nevins, *Grover Cleveland: A Study in Courage* (New York: 1933); Dexter Perkins, *The Monroe Doctrine 1867–1907* (Baltimore: 1937); David M. Pletcher, *The Awkward Years: American Foreign Relations Under Garfield and Arthur* (Columbia: 1961); *Julius W. Pratt, Expansionists of 1898* (Baltimore: 1936).

Walter LaFeber is Professor of History at Cornell University. This article is reprinted by permission of the author and also the editors of the *American Historical Review*. From the *American Historical Review*, LXVI. Copyright © 1961 by Walter LaFeber.

The policy that Grover Cleveland's second administration formulated in the Venezuelan controversy of 1895–1896 was a direct answer to British encroachments on United States interests in Latin America. Political and business leaders believed these American interests to be economic, strategic, and political. The economic influence on the shaping of Cleveland's policy in this dispute has not received sufficient attention. After the 1893 depression paralyzed the domestic economy, United States attention focused increasingly on Latin America; indeed, it is significant that the controversy occurred during the depths of that business crisis.

American interests, both economic and strategic, were threatened during the 1893–1895 period by ominous British moves in Brazil, Nicaragua, the disputed area in Venezuela itself, and the small island of Trinidad off the Brazilian coast. During the same years Germany and France menaced United States advantages in Brazil and the Caribbean. Gravely concerned, the State Department finally forced a showdown struggle on the issue of the Venezuelan boundary. By successfully limiting British claims in this incident, the United States won explicit recognition of its dominant position in the Western Hemisphere.

This essay attempts to trace two developments: that international dangers motivated the Cleveland administration in formulating its Venezuelan policy; that the economic crisis arising out of the 1893 depression provided the context and played an important role in this policy formulation. This is not to say that the economic influence was the only motivating force, but that this factor, relatively overlooked by previous writers on the subject, greatly shaped the thinking of both the Cleveland administration and key segments of American society.

Five considerations should serve to establish the validity of this interpretation: timing played a key role in that the year 1895 witnessed a convergence of forces which brought the United States into the controversy (after the argument had simmered over half a century) and led it to assert control over the nations of the Western Hemisphere; the Cleveland administration and the American business community viewed foreign markets, especially those of Latin America, as providing a solution to the domestic depression; policy makers in Washington believed the Monroe Doctrine to be important primarily for what Secretary of State Richard Olney called its "practical benefits," that is, its potential strategic and economic benefits,[1] the State Department acted unilaterally in the affair, cared little for Venezuelan opinion or advice, and hoped to benefit American interests primarily, not Venezuelan; neither the political situation in the United States nor the newly discovered "psychic crisis" of the 1890's played important roles in key American decisions.

The events leading to the Venezuelan crisis were silhouetted against the somber and ominous background of the 1893–1897 depression. Economic crisis had threatened the United States since 1890 and 1891, when only unexampled American exports had averted financial trouble.[2] Despite these huge exports, American prices and

---

[1] Olney to Thomas F. Bayard, July 20, 1895, Department of State, Instructions to Great Britain, State Department Archives, National Archives [hereafter cited as SDA]. The note is also in *Papers Relating to the Foreign Relations of the United States* [hereafter cited as FR] (2 vols., Washington, D. C., 1896), I, 545–62.

[2] Alexander Dana Noyes, *Thirty Years of American Finance* (New York, 1898), 158–59, 200. The best accounts of the effect this depression had on the American economy are Charles Hoffman, "The Depression of the Nineties," *Journal of Economic History*, XVI (June 1956), 137–64; E. H. Phelps Brown with S. J. Handfield-Jones, "The Climacteric of the 1890's," *Oxford Eco-*

wages continued their long downward swing which had begun in 1873. By late 1892 and early 1893 business observers recognized that the American economic system had reached a point of maturity which disrupted its relations with the markets of the world.[3] Panic struck the weakened nation in the spring of 1893 when the Philadelphia and Reading Railroad and the National Cordage Company collapsed.

Political and social uprisings, which were renewed and intensified by the economic breakdown, forced the Cleveland administration not only to face the problem of reviving a glutted industrial system, but to do so before radical political forces paralyzed the administration's initiative. Labor unrest manifested itself in the marches of Coxey's and Hogan's armies of the unemployed on Washington—marches which highly dramatized the fact that the great American frontier no longer attracted, but even repelled the discontented of the nation—and in the nearly successful attempt of the socialist wing of the American Federation of Labor to control that body. The threat posed by restless farmers (and many businessmen) in the West and South compounded the danger of labor dissatisfaction. Among others, James J. Hill and the assistant chairman of the Kansas State Democratic Committee warned Cleveland in 1893 that all the "isms" that had plagued society in the past were "now appearing in an organized and most formidable manner."[4]

Cleveland quickly reacted by calling a special session of Congress to repeal the Silver Purchase Act of 1890. The President hoped that the repeal would stabilize the country on a gold standard. Though this action had little immediate effect on the economy, the administration's reasons for the repeal pointed the way for further ameliorative action. Cleveland and his advisers assumed that the economic problems stemmed not from the lack of circulating medium (as the Populists and silverites charged), but from bad monetary laws and overproduction. Since a powerful Populist-silver bloc in Congress could sidetrack any legislation that would carefully regulate and restrict the amount of paper money, the administration emphasized overproduction as the causative factor of the depression. This, in turn, led to a quest for foreign markets.[5]

In a speech to the New York Chamber of Commerce in November 1893, Secretary of the Treasury John G. Carlisle explained the administration's belief that the gold standard and an expanded foreign trade went hand in hand. Carlisle declared that "our commercial interests are not confined to our own country; they extend to every quarter of the globe, and our people buy and sell in nearly every market of the civilized world. . . . Without exception these prices are fixed in the markets of countries

nomic Papers, new ser., IV (Oct. 1952), 266–307; Frank S. Philbrick, "The Mercantile Conditions of the Crisis of 1893," *University Studies of the University of Nebraska*, II (1894–1902), 299–320; W. Jett Lauck, *The Causes of the Panic of 1893* (Boston, 1907); Gerald Taylor White, "The United States and the Problem of Recovery after 1893," doctoral dissertation, University of California, Berkeley, 1938.

[3] Noyes, *Thirty Years of American Finance*, 200. For a summary of the factors influencing the new manifest destiny, see Samuel Flagg Bemis, *The Latin American Policy of the United States: An Historical Interpretation* (New York, 1943), 123–24.

[4] Hill to Cleveland, June 24, 1893, and J. B. Crouch to Cleveland, June 23, 1893, Grover Cleveland Papers, Manuscript Division, Library of Congress.

[5] Alfred Vagts believes the monetary situation directly affected Cleveland's Venezuelan policy since the policy not only silenced silverite expansionists temporarily, but also attempted to keep England away from Venezuelan gold fields which American interests had claimed. Alfred Vagts, *Deutschland und die Vereinigten Staaten in der Weltpolitik* (New York, 1935), 510, 1257.

having a gold standard." Carlisle's *Annual Reports* and many of Cleveland's public statements emphasized the administration's belief that foreign trade provided a key to America's economic revival and that the gold standard was necessary for such trade.[6]

Two other developments motivated the Cleveland administration to view enlarged foreign trade as a means to end the depression: the withdrawal of British investments and the closing of the American frontier. American political and business leaders believed the exodus of British capital from the United States to be a basic cause of the panic.[7] When the repeal of the Silver Purchase Act failed to attract new foreign investments, the administration and the business community turned to the hope of a large foreign trade surplus as a replacement for the withdrawn capital. Such a trade balance would not only provide fresh capital to invigorate stagnant American industries, but newly found markets would revive these industries to a point where they would again be appealing to outside investors.[8]

Cleveland and others in influential positions coupled this view of foreign capital with the belief that a mature American system had finally absorbed its western frontier. They view this occurrence with alarm.[9] Cleveland made special mention of this in his annual message in 1893 and later attempted to reopen western lands that had been claimed by speculators.[10] Obviously, if the closed frontier had been a leading cause in the glutting of the home market, the Republican protective tariff had to be revised. The Democrats thus proposed a tariff that they believed would stimulate the movement of domestic surpluses into world markets.[11]

[6] Quoted in James A. Barnes, *John G. Carlisle: Financial Statesman* (New York, 1931), 299–302. See especially Carlisle's *Annual Report* of 1894 in which he declared that American "prosperity . . . depends largely" upon the ability of the United States to sell its "surplus products in foreign markets at remunerative prices." *Annual Report of the Secretary of the Treasury* (Washington, D. C., 1894), lxxii–lxxiii. See also Cleveland's letter to the Chicago Businessmen's Meeting, quoted in *Commercial and Financial Chronicle*, Apr. 20, 1895, 690; the President's letter to J. M. Stone, governor of Mississippi, Apr. 26, 1895, Cleveland Papers; and Carlisle's letter to Secretary of the Interior Hoke Smith, Aug. 11, 1894, *ibid*.

[7] *A Compilation of Messages and Papers of the Presidents, 1789–1897*, ed. James D. Richardson (10 vols., Washington, D. C., 1900), IX, 402; R. H. Inglis Palgrave, "An English View of Investment in the United States," *Forum*, XV (Apr. 1893), 191–200. *Banker's Magazine*, XLIX (Aug. 1894), 97–98, supplements Cleveland's and Palgrave's views.

[8] See again Carlisle's remarkable analysis in his 1894 *Annual Report*, lxxii–lxxiii; see also A. D. Noyes, "Methods and Leadership in Wall Street Since 1893," *Journal of Economic and Business History*, I (Nov. 1931), 3–4. A lack of markets for capital, not a lack of capital, caused the 1893–1897 depression in the United States. The administration paradoxically attempted to attract foreign capital at the same time American investors placed their money in foreign markets. (See the discussion of United States investments in Latin America below.) This attitude can probably be traced to such vital sections of the American economy as railroads and cotton and wheat exporters—groups that believed the London Stock Exchange to be the best indicator of economic prosperity. Also, these years marked the early stage of the transitional period when control of the international money market swung from London to New York.

[9] See Lee Benson, "The Historical Background of Turner's Frontier Essay," *Agricultural History*, XXV (Apr. 1951), 59–82; Herman Clarence Nixon, "The Precursors of Turner in the Interpretation of the American Frontier," *South Atlantic Quarterly*, XXVIII (Jan. 1929), 83–89; John R. Procter, "America's Battle for Commercial Supremacy," *Forum*, XVI (Nov. 1893), 320–22.

[10] *Messages and Papers of the Presidents*, ed. Richardson, IX, 454, 661–662.

[11] *Ibid.*, 459; *Annual Report of the Secretary of the Treasury* (Washington, D. C., 1893), lxxx–lxxxi; see also Vagts, *Deutschland und die Vereinigten Staaten*, 1257.

In this desire to reinvigorate production instead of redistributing goods, Cleveland asked for a tariff bill that would include a long list of free raw materials.[12] He believed that if these industrial essentials entered the United States tariff-free, "the world [would] be open to our national ingenuity and enterprise." He related this hope of world markets to the growing labor unrest by noting that "the limited demand for . . . goods" on a "narrow market" inevitably led to industrial stagnation.[13] Carlisle expressed it more succinctly: "The demand for labor would steadily grow with the extension of trade."[14]

Cleveland's two congressional leaders, William L. Wilson of West Virginia in the House and Roger Q. Mills of Texas in the Senate, shared these opinions. Wilson introduced the tariff by observing that it had been devised "in the shadow and depression of a great commercial crisis." He declared that the free raw materials clauses would lead to "the enlargement of markets for our products in other countries, the increase in the internal commerce and in the carrying trade of our own country." All these factors would "insure a growing home market." In effect, Wilson believed that the United States had to rebuild its home market by enlarging its foreign market.[15] Mills echoed Wilson's statements, then added a new note by declaring that Great Britain would have to suffer economic setbacks since she blocked the path of America's economic manifest destiny. Mills believed that the British "saw with alarm the triumph of Mr. Cleveland as the representative of commercial expansion."[16] Many other congressmen repeated these arguments during the tariff debates.[17]

A group of protectionist senators gathered support to defeat the House bill and to substitute a quasi-protectionist measure of its own. This tariff measure resulted mainly from the lobbying of several trusts and from political and personal hatred for Cleveland. But during the congressional debate, the President continually reiterated the importance of the raw materials provisions. In disgust, he finally allowed the bill to become law without his signature, though only three free raw materials remained in the measure.[18]

The American business community followed the example of the administration in attempting to devise new means of expanding its foreign commerce. The depression reached its deepest trough in 1894–1895 as exports, especially staple agricultural products, failed to revive the economy. Business circles recognized this condition and called for drastic measures. The *Banker's Magazine* declared, "Small exports and agri-

[12] See the excellent observations by Frank W. Taussig in "Rabbeno's American Commercial Policy," *Quarterly Journal of Economics*, X (Oct. 1895), 109.

[13] *Messages and Papers of the Presidents*, ed. Richardson, IX, 459. It is important to note that Cleveland had wagered his political life on the tariff issue in his first administration, but did not emphasize this raw materials argument as he did after the 1893 depression struck. See *ibid.*, VIII, 589, 776.

[14] *Annual Report of the Secretary of the Treasury*, 1893, lxxx–lxxxi.

[15] *Congressional Record*, 53 Cong., 2 sess., XXVI, pt. 9, Appendix, 193–96 (Jan. 8, 9, 1894); Frank W. Taussig, *The Tariff History of the United States* (7th ed., New York, 1923), 309; Festus P. Summers, *William L. Wilson and Tariff Reform* (New Brunswick, N. J., 1953), 172–74.

[16] Roger Q. Mills, "The Wilson Bill," *North American Review*, CLVIII (Feb. 1894), 235–44.

[17] See *Congressional Record*, 53 Cong., 2 sess., XXVI, pts. 1, 2, 945 (Jan. 17, 1894), 776 (Jan. 12, 1894), 643 (Jan. 10, 1894), 1422 (Jan. 25, 1894), and Appendix, 79 (Jan. 16, 1894).

[18] See esp. *ibid.*, 53 Cong., 2 sess., XXVI, pt. 8, 7712 (July 19, 1894). Cleveland's letters sharply criticizing protectionist senators are in *Letters of Grover Cleveland, 1850–1908*, ed. Allan Nevins (New York, 1933), 363, 365–66.

cultural depression are, therefore, now the chief remaining obstacles to a return of general prosperity."[19] The *Commercial and Financial Chronicle* concurred, stating that the "abnormal situation of the Treasury and of our foreign trade" had halted the growth of prosperity "several times" in 1894.[20] Perhaps Henry W. Cannon, president of the Chase National Bank, best summarized the American business community's position when he wrote in February 1895, "It is necessary, in order to restore complete prosperity, that we should compete in the markets of the world with our goods and commodities."[21] The New York correspondent of the *Economist* bluntly warned in September 1895: "Either goods or gold must go abroad to pay for our purchases there, and thus far this autumn our shipments . . . have not equalled expectations."[22] One authority explicitly prescribed the cure. A. S. Heidelbach, the senior member of a large international banking firm in New York, declared that in order to stop the gold outflow, merchandise exports would have to exceed merchandise imports by "at least" $350,000,000 per year. Some disputed his figures, but few disputed his solution.[23]

Unfortunately for the prospects of such a trade surplus, American agriculture, the main prop of the export trade, could not bear such a burden. Though the volume of exports for the 1894 fiscal year had been surpassed only twice before in American history, the four leading staples of the export trade—breadstuffs, provisions, cotton, and oil products—had decreased in value by almost six million dollars. This occurred because in order to find markets their producers had to accept extremely low prices, in some cases the lowest in history.[24]

Several astute observers, however, saw hope in these export tables. Worthington C. Ford, chief of the Bureau of Statistics, published an article in the summer of 1895 entitled "The Turning of the Tide."[25] Ford demonstrated that while exports of farm staples had slumped, American manufactured exports had rocketed to all-time highs. He emphasized this change by noting that the United States had imported less food in 1895, but that "more raw materials for domestic industries" had arrived.

Business journals quickly drew the lesson from such trade figures. *Banker's Magazine* and *Bradstreet's*, among others, declared that American agriculture could no longer compete with the newly exploited grain lands of Argentina and Russia.[26] The former journal foretold the consequences for the American economy: henceforth

---

[19] *Banker's Magazine*, XLIX (Nov. 1894), 326; see also *Bradstreet's: A Journal of Trade, Finance and Public Economy*, Feb. 16, 1895, 99. Henry L. Bryan of the State Department sent newspaper clippings to Ambassador Bayard in London (Aug. 23, 1895) which illustrated the great interest in increasing American export trade. Even some protectionist papers pointed out the need for more exports and thus opposed revising the 1894 tariff. Thomas F. Bayard Papers, Manuscript Division, Library of Congress.

[20] *Commercial and Financial Chronicle*, Jan. 5, 1895, 9.

[21] J. Sterling Morton, William M. Spring, and Henry W. Cannon, "The Financial Muddle," *North American Review*, CLX (Feb. 1895), 129–56, esp. 151. Another banker and merchant, A. B. Farquhar, said essentially the same thing to his good friend Cleveland (Nov. 9, 1894, Cleveland Papers).

[22] *Economist*, Sept. 21, 1895, 1244.

[23] Alfred S. Heidelbach, "Why Gold Is Exported," *Forum*, XVIII (Feb. 1895), 647–51; see also *Yale Review*, IV (Aug. 1895), 136; *Commercial and Financial Chronicle*, Mar. 30, 1895, 542–43.

[24] *Ibid.*, July 21, 1895, 93–95.

[25] Worthington C. Ford, "The Turning of the Tide," *North American Review*, CLXI (Aug. 1895), esp. 188–95.

[26] *Banker's Magazine*, XLVIII (Mar. 1894), 649–50; *ibid.*, XLIX (Dec. 1894), 31–32; *Bradstreet's*, Apr. 27, 1895, 259; *ibid.*, Oct. 26, 1895, 674; *Economist*, Mar. 3, 1894, 273.

the United States must depend upon "our future manufacturing supremacy over Europe" rather than upon American "producers of food, feed, and raw materials." When this occurred, the business community's dream would be realized. There would be no more booms followed by depressions, but "slow and steady improvement . . . and our surplus manufacturing capacity turned to the production of goods we may be able to export hereafter at reduced cost and thus keep all our industries permanently employed, as England does, having the world's markets in which to unload any accumulation."[27]

In his article Ford further observed that this change in the nature of American trade had "political consequences," for it meant that the United States would need markets in the underindustrialized nations of Latin America and Asia rather than in Europe.[28] Translating these words into action, the American business community began systematically opening Latin American markets. Business journals devoted much space to the promotion of a Nicaraguan canal; *Bradstreet's* called for the immediate formal abrogation of the Clayton-Bulwer Treaty.[29] American investment, composed mainly of surplus capital accumulated from the home market's collapse, flowed into Latin America in increased amounts during the 1893–1898 period. New steamship lines, heavy investments in Latin American railroads, the movement of American bankers into Santo Domingo, and the expansion of the Guggenheim interests in Mexico exemplified this southward advance of the dollar.[30] The investor moved southward with a minimum of fanfare, but the manufacturer invaded Central and South America with the cheers of commercial manifest destiny ringing in his ears.[31]

James G. Blaine's intense interest in Latin American markets and tranquillity, symbolized by the Pan-American Conference of 1889, had directed American commercial attention to the southern nations. But the stagnation of 1893–1895 increased and sharpened the business community's interest. Before 1893 Blaine had led, and the businessmen had willingly followed. But after 1893 the businessmen played at least an equal role in focusing attention southward and in some instances blazed paths that the State Department then followed in formulating Latin American policies.

This intensified expansion of American industrialists into Latin American markets can be illustrated by three developments: the growth of and interest in expositions held in the southern United States, the development of commercial museums, and the formation and growth of the National Association of Manufacturers. Encouraged by such business journals as *Dixie* and the Chattanooga *Tradesman*, the South held several large industrial expositions during the depression.[32] The chairman of the

---

[27] *Banker's Magazine*, XLIX (Nov. 1894), 326–28; *ibid.* (Oct. 1894), 249. See especially the article in the Baltimore *Sun* of May 27, 1895, by Frederic Emory, a member of the State Department. Emory explained how manufactured products would have to replace raw materials as the backbone of United States exports. Copy in Bayard Papers.

[28] Ford, "Turning of the Tide," 93–95.

[29] *Economist*, Sept. 7, 1895, 1179; *Bradstreet's*, Dec. 28, 1895, 820.

[30] Bureau of American Republics, *Special Bulletin* (Washington, D. C., Aug. 1896), 839–42; *ibid.* (May 1896), 626–27; *ibid.* (Sept. 1895), 145; James Morton Callahan, *American Foreign Policy in Mexican Relations* (New York, 1932), 508; *Bradstreet's*, Jan. 5, 1895, 14. By 1897 American investments in Cuba, the West Indies, Central and South America (excluding Mexico) amounted to $108,000,000. Cleona Lewis, *America's Stake in International Investments* (Washington, D. C., 1938), 606; see also Hoffman, "The Depression of the Nineties," 156–57.

[31] See *Bradstreet's*, Apr. 27, 1895, 270; *Banker's Magazine*, XLIX (Mar. 1895), 498; *Public Opinion*, XVII (May 17, 1894), 159.

[32] The *Tradesman* believed that "if the South shall push her advantages . . . her ports will soon have a monopoly of many lines of trade with the West Indies, Central and South America." Quoted in *Bradstreet's*, July 7, 1894, 430.

Atlanta Exposition of 1895 informed Secretary of State Olney that "the foreign trade idea is the basic and uppermost feature of the Exposition."[33] Olney and his predecessor in the State Department, Walter Quintin Gresham, encouraged this exposition, while President Cleveland and several members of his cabinet found time to visit it.[34]

The full bloom of the commercial museum movement appeared in the flowering of the Philadelphia Commercial Museum in 1894–1897. New York City soon followed this example. Secretaries of State Gresham and Olney again displayed much interest. Speaking at the opening of the Philadelphia museum in June 1897, Olney declared that economic solidarity in the Western Hemisphere was "inevitable." American industrialists strove to make this prediction come true, for the president of the museum, William Pepper, wrote Olney in 1895 that he was "surprised and gratified at the rapid spread of interest" shown by United States industrialists.[35]

After the panic struck, the most publicized and concerted movement for the systematic opening of Latin American markets arose from the formation of the National Association of Manufacturers in January 1895. The depression operated as a direct cause of this movement, and the association's first convention met for the avowed purpose of enlarging the Latin American trade of the United States.[36] Three themes dominated that convention: the need for foreign, especially South and Central American markets; a strong anti-British feeling, revealed in bitter references to British control of international trade and finance; and the hope that the federal government would provide favors to American businessmen which would encourage overseas economic expansion.[37] After the convention the NAM sent a group of American industrialists and financiers to inspect potential market areas in Latin America. In 1897 the association established its first sample warehouse in Caracas, Venezuela.[38]

By late 1895 a concise economic analysis had led both the American business community and the administration to the conclusion that the United States industrial system needed more Latin American markets. Such a conclusion suggested that any expansion of European (especially British) influence in the area endangered not only America's security, but also its economic and political well-being.

In 1894 and 1895 these dynamic American policies clashed with expanding European claims in Brazil, Nicaragua, and Trinidad, a small island off the Brazilian coast. A revolution erupted in Brazil in September 1893. Rebels, led by promonarchist

[33] J. W. Avery to Olney, Nov. 8, 1895, Richard Olney Papers, Manuscript Division, Library of Congress.

[34] Public Opinion, XVIII (Apr. 25, 1895), 436–37; Bradstreet's, Dec. 21, 1895, 808.

[35] Pepper to Olney, Aug. 2 and Nov. 29, 1895, Olney Papers; Philadelphia Commercial Museum, The Philadelphia Commercial Museum: What It Is, Why It Is (Philadelphia, 1899); Olney's speech is dated June 2, 1897 (Olney Papers). For testimony to Gresham's interest in the commercial museum movement, see Pepper to Bayard, Aug. 11, 1895, Bayard Papers.

[36] See Albert Kleckner Steigerwalt, "The National Association of Manufacturers: Organization and Policies, 1895–1914," doctoral dissertation on microfilm, University of Michigan, 1953, 24–26, 381; also National Association of Manufacturers, Purposes of the National Association of Manufacturers (Philadelphia, 1896).

[37] For the best summary of these themes, see Steigerwalt, "The National Association of Manufacturers," 41–42, 51–53.

[38] National Association of Manufacturers, A Commercial Tour to South America, Apr. 25, 1896; National Association of Manufacturers, Sample Warehouse for American Goods in Caracas, Venezuela (2d ed., Philadelphia, 1897).

groups, hoped to end the four-year-old republic and restore the empire. But most important for American-Brazilian commercial relations, the insurgents included elements desiring to abrogate Brazil's reciprocity treaty with the United States—the most important one the United States possessed.[39] The rebels planned to cut off all outside aid to the besieged government by blockading the harbor of Rio de Janeiro; indeed, they had placed all their hopes of success in this one embattled area. Secretary of State Gresham did little more in the early months of the revolution than promulgate the rule that American merchants and traders could continue their commerce with Rio harbor unless their ships crossed the line of fire.[40]

Suddenly, in December 1893, the revolutionary cause grew stronger when a key Brazilian admiral, known for his promonarchist views, defected to the insurgents. Thus reinforced, the rebels announced that they would prevent all incoming trade from unloading in Rio harbor. This meant that all foreign ships would encounter "lines of fire." When German and British business interests endorsed the new rebel stand, the State Department feared that if the insurgent policy succeeded, American trading interests would lose their favored position.[41] Influenced by urgent letters from United States exporters, especially Crossman Brothers of New York and Standard Oil President William Rockefeller, and guided by his own fervent belief that American industry needed more foreign markets, Gresham reversed his position in early January 1894.[42] Sending a strong naval force to Rio harbor, the Secretary of State instructed the commander to protect with force the landing of American goods. This was accomplished, and the revolution collapsed. American congressional leaders, applauding Gresham's policy, portrayed Great Britain as the culprit in the rebellion. The republic had not only been saved from a monarchist-inspired plot, but United States commercial interests (as the American minister to Brazil was quick to point out) had preserved intact their private inroads into the Brazilian market. The German minister to Brazil remarked, "The American dollar started to roll in order to break off the monarchist point of the revolution."[43]

Several months after the failure of this revolt, Gresham peacefully but firmly ejected British interests from the Mosquito Indian reservation in Nicaragua. This reservation occupied a crucial area, for it governed the eastern entrance to the proposed Nicaraguan canal. During the summer of 1894 the British hesitated leaving the region as they claimed that under an 1860 treaty they had obtained rights to protect the Indians

[39] American action in the Brazilian revolt of 1893–1894 is analyzed in detail in Walter LaFeber, "American Depression Diplomacy and the Brazilian Revolution 1893–1894," *Hispanic American Historical Review*, XL (Feb. 1960). See also James Lawrence Laughlin and H. Parker Willis, *Reciprocity* (New York, 1903), 208.

[40] Gresham to Thomas S. Thompson, American minister to Brazil, Nov. 1, 1894, Instructions to Brazil, SDA.

[41] Gresham to Bayard, Dec. 18, 1893, Instructions to Great Britain, SDA.

[42] Gresham to Isidor Straus, Jan. 6, 1894, Letterbooks, Walter Quintin Gresham Papers, Manuscript Division, Library of Congress; Rockefeller to Gresham, Jan. 4, 1894, Area 4 file, Navy Department Archives, National Archives [hereafter cited as NDA]. For Gresham's ardent belief in the need of foreign markets for the American industrial glut, see Gresham to Wayne MacVeagh, May 7, 1894, and Gresham to Judge Charles E. Dyer, May 2, 1894, both in Letterbooks, Gresham Papers; also Matilda Gresham, *Life of Walter Quintin Gresham, 1832–1895* (2 vols., Chicago, 1919), II, 797–98. For an opposing view of Gresham, see Vagts, *Deutschland und die Vereinigten Staaten*, 1918.

[43] *Ibid.*, 1699–1700. On the effect of the American action, see *ibid.*, 1700; Lawrence F. Hill, *Diplomatic Relations between the United States and Brazil* (New York, 1932), 208.

from Nicaraguan injustices. Gresham disagreed and exerted continuous pressure on the British Foreign Office; in the fall of 1894 the British surrendered their position.[44]

The American press disliked England's reluctance to leave this key area. When in the spring of 1895 British warships blockaded the Nicaraguan port of Corinto, American public and official opinion became aroused. An injury to a British citizen suffered during the 1894 trouble brought about the blockade. The State Department admitted the British right of blockade when it announced that the Monroe Doctrine had no relevance to the situation.[45] But American press and business circles, concerned over the future safety of an American-owned canal, deprecated the possibility that Great Britain would continue to rule over four million dollars worth of mushrooming American investment in bananas, timber, and inland trade in the reservation area.[46] Gresham shared this alarm, for although he disavowed the pertinence of the Monroe Doctrine, he nevertheless expressed deep concern to American Ambassador Bayard in London.[47] Then, with two strokes, the Secretary of State brought the reservation under United States control. First, Gresham implicitly agreed to protect the expanding American investments in the territory from Nicaraguan injustices. Second, he informed the British ambassador in Washington that henceforth the State Department would assume Britain's duties of guarding the rights of the Mosquito Indians.[48] By doing so, Gresham replaced England's control with that of the United States.

As Venezuelan matters moved to a climax in 1895, other British actions increased American apprehension. The Foreign Office attempted to force Nicaragua to reopen the delicate reservation problem. Though the outstanding points were soon settled, Alvey A. Adee, Second Assistant Secretary of State, told Olney that this irritation was "an important indication of the drift of British policy."[49] England further worried Washington by occupying the island of Trinidad; it hoped to use this uninhabited jut of rock off the Brazilian coast as a cable station. The American press loudly supported Brazil's protests. Adee wrote Olney that "the newspaper men are wild about the Trinidad business."[50] Under scrutiny of the State Department, Brazil and England reached an agreement in 1896.

[44] Gresham to American minister to Nicaragua, Lewis Baker, June 13, 1894, Instructions to Central America, SDA; Gresham to Bayard, May 2, 1894, Letterbooks, Gresham Papers; Bayard to Gresham, May 28, 1894, Dispatches from Great Britain, SDA.

[45] This episode and the reaction of American policy makers is best outlined in a "memorandum" prepared for Olney dated August 10, 1895, in the Olney Papers. See also Gresham to Bayard, Apr. 24, 1895, Instructions to Great Britain, SDA.

[46] See *Review of Reviews*, XI (June 1895), 621–22; W. T. Stead, "Jingoism in America," *Contemporary Review*, LXVIII (Sept. 1895), 338; *Public Opinion*, XVIII (May 9, 1895), 502.

[47] "Memorandum" enclosed in State Department's files with cable from Baker to Gresham, Dispatches from Central America, Apr. 13, 1895, SDA.

[48] See especially Gresham's actions in restoring the rights of the Maritime Canal Company in Nicaragua and the protection he gave two American citizens who should have been dealt with by Nicaraguan law for attempting to lead a revolution in the reservation against Nicaraguan authorities: *Nicaraguan Canal . . .* (*Senate Executive Document*, No. 184, 54 Cong., 2 sess., 1897), 96–97; Gresham to Baker, Aug. 4, 1894, Instructions to Central America, SDA; see also Wilfred Hardy Callcott, *The Caribbean Policy of the United States, 1890–1920* (Baltimore, 1942), 77–78.

[49] Note penned by Adee on dispatch from Baker to Olney, Nov. 18, 1895, Dispatches from Central America, SDA.

[50] Adee to Olney, Aug. 2, 1895, Olney Papers.

Britain's multiplying claims in the Western Hemisphere caused Adee to exclaim to Olney in August 1895 that the British were playing a "grab game" throughout North and South America.[51] But France also gave the State Department concern. In mid-1895 France and Venezuela severed relations over the French minister's alleged insult of the Venezuelan government. The United States stepped into the dispute and attempted to restore diplomatic connections. Bayard explained the State Department intervention when he wrote in August 1895 that the dispute was "of present interest" when viewed in "connection with the status of the existing Anglo-Venezuelan Boundary dispute."[52]

This situation had cooled when France attempted to occupy some 155,000 square miles of Brazil shortly after gold was discovered in the region. France had previously claimed the area, but had never forcibly tried to govern it. Olney and Bayard watched proceedings closely and even discussed the contingencies that might occur in case the United States assumed "a supervision of Brazilian boundaries, should French interests or ambitions prompt their invasion."[53] French and American interests also clashed in Santo Domingo. France demanded that the customs houses of the Caribbean nation guarantee a reparation payment which the French had demanded as a result of the murder of one of their citizens. A group of New York bankers shared the control of these customs houses and quickly asked for State Department aid. When a French naval squadron arrived at Santo Domingo, American Secretary of the Navy Hilary Herbert promptly instructed United States warships to proceed to the area and "watch carefully" over American interests. Fortunately the matter was soon adjusted.[54]

Congress and the Cleveland administration responded vigorously to these European encroachments. The character of this response can be briefly analyzed in the following incidents and personages: a congressional debate in the winter of 1894–1895 on the best means of protecting and expanding American commerce abroad; the naval appropriation debates of 1895 and 1896; a speech by Don Dickinson in May 1895; recognition by influential Americans that the Orinoco River was a vital pawn in the Venezuelan boundary dispute; Olney's concepts of American economic needs and power; statements of Cleveland and Olney during the Venezuelan boundary negotiations.

In the winter of 1894–1895 Congress became the center of an extended debate over American expansion into commercial and strategic areas and over the evolution of an anti-British policy. Henry Teller, leader of the Senate's silver bloc, sounded the keynote when he called England "our great commercial antagonist."[55] Conservative

[51] Adee to Olney, Aug. 19, 1895, *ibid.*

[52] Bayard to Olney, Aug. 8, 1895, Dispatches from Great Britain, SDA. German financiers were active in Venezuela during the 1890's (Vagts, *Deutschland und die Vereinigten Staaten,* 1525–29). Olney, Gresham, Cleveland, and key personnel in the State Department paid little attention to this infiltration, judging from their papers and diplomatic correspondence.

[53] Bayard to Olney, Oct. 25, 1895, Dispatches from Great Britain, SDA.

[54] Explanatory memorandum sent by Santo Domingo's chargé in Washington to the State Department, Feb. 5, 1894, Confidential Correspondence, NDA; Secretary of the Navy to Rear Admiral R. W. Meade, Mar. 9, 1895, *ibid.* German and American interests had clashed in Santo Domingo and Haiti before 1893. The State Department became active in pressuring Germany out of the area only after 1897. See Vagts, *Deutschland und die Vereinigten Staaten,* 1707–1709, 1788–93.

[55] The essence of the debate is in the *Congressional Record,* 53 Cong., 3 sess., XVII, pt. 1, 157–626, *passim* (Dec. 1894–Jan. 1895).

Nelson Aldrich of Rhode Island concurred as he warned that "there is a commercial warfare . . . going on among the great nations of the world for enlarged markets" and added that the United States could not "sit down silently and submissively."[56] In the House, Leonidas F. Livingston of Georgia proposed a resolution requesting Cleveland to invoke "friendly arbitration" to solve the Venezuelan-British Guiana boundary dispute. When weak opposition to the proposal appeared, William J. Coombs of New York quickly silenced it by replying, "Large American interests will be promoted by a friendly settlement of this question." Livingston added that the Orinoco River played a crucial role in the problem. Great Britain's claims endangered this waterway, which provided "the key to more than one-quarter of the South American continent." Livingston capped his argument by bluntly remarking, "This relates to a matter on our [sic] continent. Our trade and other relations with those people are involved in this settlement."[57] It is difficult to find much altruistic concern for Venezuela in this debate.

During this and the 1895–1896 session, Congress passed naval appropriation measures that provided money for the continued construction of the new American battleship fleet. The first three battleships had been authorized in 1890, and another had been added in 1892. Congress accelerated the construction program in 1895 and 1896 when it authorized the construction of five more battleships. Significantly, Congress provided money to begin building these vessels even though the Treasury suffered from an acutely depressed condition.

The cry for both commercial expansion and protection against British encroachments appeared frequently in these naval debates. Senator Orville Platt of Connecticut noted the importance of the frontier's closing when he declared: "It is to the ocean that our children must look, as they have once looked to the boundless West." Senator Anthony Higgins of Delaware urged the building of more battleships with the argument that the necessity of United States commercial expansion would have serious implications for the potency of the Monroe Doctrine and "the suzerainty of the American Republic over both American hemispheres."[58] Robert Adams, Jr., of Pennsylvania, an important member of the House Foreign Affairs Committee, was more specific: he announced that the Monroe Doctrine had become not only a political principle, but a notice to all nations that the American people would brook "no foreign interference either in the political affairs or the commercial relations of this hemisphere." Adams observed that Gresham's intervention in Brazil showed how the United States would have to uphold its new interpretation of Monroe's dictum.[59] J. Fred Talbott of Maryland, chairman of the House Naval Affairs Committee, declared that the American navy had to dominate the Western Atlantic and Eastern Pacific; if anyone disagreed with this proposition, he "was not worthy to represent his people in this Congress." Talbott pointed to the enemy when he said, "Great Britain never arbitrates with anybody except one who is ready to fight her."[60] John

---

[56] *Ibid.*, pt. 3, 1889 (Feb. 7, 1895).

[57] *Ibid.*, 1832–34. William Scruggs, former United States minister to Venezuela, had been hired by the latter country to interest the United States in the dispute. Livingston's introduction of the House resolution was one result of Scruggs's work. The interesting fact, however, is the argument used to support the resolution in debate.

[58] *Ibid.*, 3045, 3109; see also *ibid.*, 1950, 2259, 3043.

[59] *Ibid.*, 2307, 3106.

[60] *Ibid.*, 2310–11.

Van Voorhis of New York added that the United States could take care of itself, but that he wanted battleships to protect Latin America from Great Britain.[61] By 1896 such arguments had silenced almost all previous opposition to the building of a battleship fleet.[62]

Perhaps a speech delivered in May 1895 by Don Dickinson, a leader of the Democratic forces in Michigan and a close friend of President Cleveland, provided the most widely publicized commercial argument for American action in the Venezuelan dispute. One student of this episode calls Dickinson's speech "the most notable incident . . . indicating the desire of the Cleveland Democrats to assert their own lusty patriotism."[63] It should be emphasized, however, that Dickinson's address was more than a reflection of internal political pressure on the Cleveland foreign policies. The speech was important because it symbolized a wide and strongly held opinion that the United States had to obtain additional foreign markets. In a flaming peroration that summarized the speech, Dickinson declared, "We need and must have open markets throughout the world to maintain and increase our prosperity." He realized that such American expansion would conflict with "the settled policy of Great Britain." Consequently, Dickinson asked that England's "extraordinary claims and movements" be watched closely in Nicaragua and Venezuela.[64] The President applauded the speech in a personal letter to Dickinson.[65]

Cleveland had become interested in the Venezuelan dispute in early 1895, the importance of the Orinoco River especially attracting his attention. When Dickinson made a midnight call on the hard-working Chief Executive in April 1895, Cleveland displayed a large map showing the controversial boundary area. He explained that Great Britain had not previously formally included the mouth of the Orinoco in its territory, but recently the British Foreign Minister had entered such a claim. Cleveland expressed alarm since the control of the river meant the control of a rich section of the South American interior trade.[66]

The State Department shared the President's concern, for it also realized the importance of the Orinoco for American commerce. In late 1894 Venezuela closed the river in an alleged effort to end smuggling. By quickly exerting diplomatic pressure to reopen the waterway, Gresham demonstrated that the United States valued the Orinoco.[67] Venezuela took advantage of this incident to send a diplomatic note to Washington that stressed the dire consequences for American commerce if England

---

[61] *Ibid.*, 3105–3106.

[62] This is illustrated by the action of the Quaker bloc in the House. Prior to 1896 this group opposed battleship appropriations. In the 1896 debates, however, one of the Quaker leaders, John B. Robinson of Pennsylvania, rose, quoted Tennyson's vision of universal peace, and then asked for four battleships. *Ibid.*, 3249.

[63] Nelson W. Blake, "The Background of Cleveland's Venezuelan Policy," *American Historical Review*, XLVII (Jan. 1942), 267.

[64] Clipping in Cleveland Papers from *Detroit Free Press*, May 10, 1895.

[65] Cleveland to Dickinson, July 31, 1895, Cleveland Papers.

[66] Note that this visit occurred before Dickinson's speech in May. Allan Nevins, *Grover Cleveland: A Study in Courage* (New York, 1933), 631. Nevins is one of the few historians who have given the Orinoco River any significance in explaining American concern in the dispute. For Cleveland's anxiety over the Orinoco, see his *Presidential Problems* (New York, 1904), 182–83.

[67] See P. F. Fenton, "The Diplomatic Relations of the United States and Venezuela," *Hispanic American Historical Review*, VIII (Aug. 1938), 299–329; *Bradstreet's*, Apr. 27, 1895, 257.

gained control of the river's entrance.[68] Then, on April 5, 1895, the British formally claimed the Orinoco's mouth. Between this date and May 25 events moved rapidly. Cleveland told Dickinson of his concern over the control of the river; Gresham asked Venezuela to restore diplomatic relations with England in order that the United States would "be in a position" to mediate; and the President began an urgent search to find "someone . . . of a much higher grade than is usually thought good enough" to send to the vacant ministerial post in Venezuela. Gresham finally began composing a long note on the subject which he planned to send to Great Britain, but death cut short his task.[69] Olney picked up and supercharged this growing American concern, then exploded it in the British Foreign Office with his note of July 20.

The real origins of the boundary dispute dated from 1841, but the United States entered the controversy much later, in 1883 and 1886, and then only briefly. The State Department made the British-Venezuelan controversy a three-cornered affair only toward the close of Gresham's term of office.[70] Olney, former Attorney General, replaced Gresham upon the latter's death in May 1895. He possessed two beliefs that must be understood to comprehend American action in the dispute. First, he had a clear conception of the 1893 depression as a "labor revolution" which had resulted from the introduction of machine technology. With these new means of expanded production, more markets had to be found if Olney were to fulfill his hope of restraining this "revolution" to what he termed "peaceful and moderate channels."[71] Second, he believed that the United States had emerged from its century of internal development as a full-fledged world power. The natural corollary of this was that the United States could now exert its will almost any place in the world, particularly in the Western Hemisphere. As Olney stated this concept, "It behooves us to accept the commanding position" the United States occupies "among the powers of the earth."[72]

Olney embodied these beliefs in his July 20, 1895, note on the Venezuelan boundary question to British Prime Minister Lord Salisbury. The Secretary of State posited that American "honor and . . . interests" were involved in the controversy. He then tried to fit the Monroe Doctrine into the dispute. Historians might demonstrate that

[68] Seneca Haselton to Gresham, Jan. 15, 1895, Dispatches from Venezuela, SDA. William L. Scruggs also widely publicized the importance of the Orinoco in *The Monroe Doctrine on Trial* (Atlanta, Ga., 1895), 24–25.

[69] On April 5, 1895, Bayard learned from Lord Kimberley, the British Foreign Minister, that England claimed land inside the mouth of the Orinoco (Bayard to Gresham, Apr. 5, 1895, Dispatches from Great Britain, SDA). Gresham began drafting a note to England on the subject sometime during the last part of that month. There are good reasons to believe that Gresham's note would have been nearly as blunt and boastful as Olney's. As early as January 1895, Gresham told Bayard that Britain's position on the Orinoco question was "contradictory and palpably unjust" and that if England continued to encroach on Venezuelan territory "we will be obliged . . . to call a halt." Gresham to Bayard, Jan. 16, 1895, Instructions to Great Britain, SDA. For Cleveland's reaction, see Nevins, *Grover Cleveland,* 631; *Letters of Grover Cleveland,* ed. id., 392; Cleveland, *Presidential Problems,* 251–52.

[70] For the background of the boundary dispute, see Dexter Perkins, *The Monroe Doctrine, 1867–1907* (Baltimore, 1937), 44–60.

[71] Significantly, Olney changed his mind about the depression's causes between June 1893 and 1894. In 1893 he believed the panic resulted from a cyclical movement in the economy. See his remarks prepared for Harvard commencement dinner, June 28, 1893, Olney Papers; clipping from Philadelphia *Daily Evening Telegraph,* June 20, 1894, *ibid.*

[72] Richard Olney, "International Isolation of the United States," *Atlantic Monthly,* LXXXI (May 1898), 577–88; speech at national opening of the Philadelphia Commercial Museum, June 2, 1897, Olney Papers.

Olney made a poor fitting and that the doctrine, as defined by past use, did not apply to the question. This, however, does not lead to an understanding of either Olney's intentions or the aims of the Cleveland administration's foreign policy. Olney advanced the argument that American interests as well as Venezuelan territory were at stake. In essence, he interpreted the Monroe Doctrine as the catchall slogan that justified protecting America's self-interests. If the Monroe Doctrine had never existed, Olney's note would have been penned anyway; only the term "American self-interest" would have been substituted for the doctrine.[73]

Declaring that the United States had political and commercial stakes in Latin America, the Secretary of State proceeded to proclaim the ideal of extending the American form of democracy to the world in sentences that resemble those of Wilson in 1917. He interrelated American interests with the Orinoco River since it controlled "the whole navigation of the interior of South America." Of vital significance is the context within which Olney placed these points, for he emphasized that the Monroe Doctrine was positive as well as negative. Not only did the doctrine formulate the rule of European abstinence from the Western Hemisphere, but "It aimed at also securing the practical benefits to result from the application of the rule." Olney then defined these benefits as "popular self-government" in Latin America, the commercial and political relationship of South and Central America to the United States, and the unencumbered use of the Orinoco. The Secretary of State climaxed this argument with the blunt assertion that if necessary these benefits could be secured and preserved by American force: "Today the United States is practically sovereign on this continent, and its fiat is law upon the subjects to which it confines its interposition."[74]

When Lord Salisbury challenged these claims, Cleveland rephrased the American argument in his special message of December 17, 1895. The President first defined the Monroe Doctrine as a statement of self-interest. He then declared that the doctrine had to be maintained since it was "essential to the integrity of our free institutions and the tranquil maintenance of our distinctive form of government." Phrasing his message candidly, Cleveland warned that if Great Britain continued its course in the boundary dispute, the United States would regard this action "as a willful aggression upon its rights and interests."[75]

The causes and intentions of the administration's policy are given in a personal letter from Cleveland to Bayard. The President emphasized two points. He wrote that the Monroe Doctrine had been invoked because of "its value and importance *to our government and welfare,* and that its defense and maintenance involve its application when a state of facts arises requiring it" [Cleveland's italics]. The President next strongly disclaimed any idea that internal political pressure, especially jingoism, had inspired the American action; such influence was "entirely irrelevant to the case and . . . had absolutely nothing to do with any action I have taken."[76]

Throughout the ensuing negotiations, the United States acted unilaterally. Venezuela did not know that Olney had penned his July note until the newspapers printed

[73] For an opposite view of the involvement of American interests, see Perkins, *Monroe Doctrine,* 155, 180.

[74] Olney to Bayard, July 20, 1895, Instructions to Great Britain, SDA; the note is in *FR,* I, 545–62.

[75] *Messages and Papers of the Presidents,* ed. Richardson, IX, 656–58.

[76] Cleveland to Bayard, Dec. 29, 1895, Cleveland Papers; the letter is also in *Letters of Grover Cleveland,* ed. Nevins, 417–20.

the text. Even after this, the Cleveland administration did not consult Venezuela.[77] When, in January 1896, Great Britain proposed a court of arbitration that included a Venezuelan representative, Olney countered with an offer excluding Venezuelan membership. The Secretary of State took the same position when he opposed including the Latin American nation in the negotiations. He argued that he did not care to have Venezuela "consulted at every step."[78] Olney succeeded in including his plan for the court of arbitration in the treaty signed by England and the United States in November 1896. When the Caracas government learned of this, it demanded and obtained a representative on the tribunal. Even then Venezuela so intensely disliked both the treaty and the manner in which Olney had carried on negotiations that the legislature ratified the pact only after police ended threats of street rioting in Caracas.[79]

The United States obtained its two principal objectives: England submitted the dispute to an arbitral commission, and in the final disposition Venezuela retained control of the Orinoco River. But most important, by submitting its case to arbitration, England recognized Olney's claim of American dominance in the Western Hemisphere.

American historians have offered three interpretations to explain the Cleveland administration's policy in the boundary dispute. The most popular explanation states that domestic political attacks "must explain both the seriousness with which the administration came to consider a distant boundary dispute and also the aggressive tone which the Olney note and the Cleveland message displayed."[80] A second thesis traces the policy's roots to Olney's bellicose, stubborn temper.[81] A third interpretation declares that a "psychic crisis" struck influential segments of American opinion in the 1890's and that a new spirit of manifest destiny emerged from this "crisis."[82]

There can be little doubt that Cleveland took domestic political pressures into account, but defining these pressures as major causative elements leaves key questions unanswered and raises many others. Cleveland's bellicose policy could not have permanently won any political enemies to his side. The Republican jingoists and the Democratic silver bloc led the cheering for the December 17 message. Neither of these groups would have agreed with Cleveland on national political objectives. The President actually alienated many of his strongest supporters, especially the eastern financiers who had once saved the gold reserve, and who, at Cleveland's request,

---

[77] See esp. George B. Young, Intervention under the Monroe Doctrine: The Olney Corollary," *Political Science Quarterly*, LVII (June 1942), 251–52, 260, and Arthur P. Whitaker, *The United States and South America: The Western Republics* (Cambridge, Mass., 1948), 160–61.

[78] Olney to Bayard, Jan. 22, 1896, Olney Papers. Bayard was very bitter at Olney's exclusion of Venezuela. See Bayard's personal memorandum, undated, but written sometime during March 1896 (Bayard Papers).

[79] Young, "Intervention under the Monroe Doctrine," 276–78; London *Times*, Feb. 5, 15, 1897.

[80] Blake, "Background of Cleveland's Venezuelan Policy," 275–76. Blake acknowledges that Cleveland did not "surrender to political pressure" and that "he became personally convinced that the Monroe Doctrine was at stake and that it was his duty to maintain it." But Blake then adds the statement quoted above. Bemis, *Latin American Policy of the United States*, 119; Vagts, *Deutschland und die Vereinigten Staaten*, 510–11.

[81] Charles Callan Tansill, *The Foreign Policy of Thomas F. Bayard, 1885–1897* (New York, 1940), 776; see also Vagts, *Deutschland und die Vereinigten Staaten*, 1918.

[82] Richard Hofstadter, "Manifest Destiny and the Philippines" in *America in Crisis*, ed. Daniel Aaron (New York, 1952), 173–200, esp. 176, 178.

repeated the rescue operation shortly after the December message.[83] In other words, the administration's Venezuelan policy attracted groups that were irreconcilable in domestic politics, while repelling the administration's staunchest supporters. War might have united the nation behind him, but Cleveland certainly did not want to turn the controversy into an open conflict.

No reliable proof exists which shows that Cleveland hoped to benefit personally from the episode. It is extremely doubtful that with his conservative conception of the Chief Executive's duties and responsibilities he would have broken the third term tradition even if he had possessed the support. E. C. Benedict, who handled Cleveland's investments in stocks and bonds, testified three weeks before the Venezuelan message that the President had repeatedly said that he was "impatient" to end his term in office.[84]

An interpretation that stresses Olney's bellicose character misses two important points. First, Gresham worked on a diplomatic note concerning the Venezuelan situation several months before Olney assumed the top position in the State Department. Second, Cleveland probably initiated the dispatch of the Olney note, reworked the draft, and heartily endorsed his Secretary of State's language. The President played an extremely important part in the formulation of the policy, especially during the crucial incubation period of April-July 1895.[85]

A thesis which emphasizes that Cleveland bowed to the pressure of jingoism and a mass psychological need for vicarious excitement does an injustice to Cleveland. The President's greatest assets were his courage and a strong character.[86] After all, Cleveland defied public pressures exerted for Hawaiian annexation, the application of the Monroe Doctrine in the Corinto dispute, and compromises in the silver repeal act and the 1894 tariff. There is no reason to believe that he suddenly bent to the winds of jingoism in 1895, unless he had better reasons than pleasing irreconcilable political enemies. It would be difficult, if not impossible, to put Cleveland and Olney in the social groups that supposedly were undergoing this psychological dilemma.

Olney and Cleveland acted as they did because they feared that United States interests were in jeopardy. Both men said this at the time, and there is no reason to doubt their word. Such danger emanated from actual or threatened European encroachments in Latin America. This expansion not only endangered both areas held vital for American strategic purposes and existing or possible political democracies in the Western Hemisphere, but it also threatened present and potential commercial markets for American products. Both the administration and the business community proclaimed these markets to be necessary for American economic and political health. They reasoned that increased shipments of industrial products to less developed regions would have to replace faltering agricultural products as the staple of American export trade; and, as a member of the State Department observed in 1895, "It has been the task of Mr. Cleveland's foreign policy to prepare the way" for these manu-

[83] *Wall Street Journal*, Dec. 21, 1895. Two weeks before the special Venezuelan message, Henry Villard personally pleaded with the President to prevent American "arguments with Europe" until the treasury reserve was restored. Vagts, *Deutschland und die Vereinigten Staaten*, 512, 1702.

[84] *Wall Street Journal*, Nov. 27, 1895.

[85] Cleveland, *Presidential Problems*, 257–59; *Letters of Grover Cleveland*, ed. Nevins, 392; Bemis, *Latin American Policy of the United States*, 119.

[86] Nevins rightly emphasized these traits in his *Grover Cleveland*.

factured goods.[87] One may speculate that Cleveland referred to both economic and security problems when he told a close friend late in 1896 that the Venezuelan affair was not a foreign question, but the "most distinct of home questions."[88] As Olney realized, the mature power of the United States could be used to harvest what the Secretary of State called "the practical benefits" of the Monroe Doctrine. Then these "home questions" could be solved.

[87] Unsigned article by Frederic Emory in Baltimore *Sun,* May 27, 1895, sent to Bayard, May 28, 1895, Bayard Papers.

[88] George F. Parker, *Recollections of Cleveland* (New York, 1909), 195. This conclusion differs from Vagts's belief that Cleveland's policy was one of "negative imperialism" or what Vagts describes as "eager for rule but not for gain." *Deutschland und die Vereinigten Staaten,* xi, 1416, 1701, 1702. It should be noted, however, that numerous and influential voices of the American business community applauded Cleveland's vigorous use of the Monroe Doctrine to challenge British expansion in Latin America. Many of these businessmen based their support on the hope of increased commercial expansion into Latin America once British power was weakened in the area. See Walter LaFeber, "The American Business Community and Cleveland's Venezuelan Message," *Business History Review,* XXXIV (Winter 1960), 393–402.

13 / A Balance Sheet of the Philippines

Rufus S. Tucker

Historians have long wondered why the United States acquired the Philippines following the Spanish-American War. From a political and strategic perspective, the Philippine Islands stood as hostage-outposts of American territory in the western Pacific, and even Theodore Roosevelt came to acknowledge that the territory could not be defended readily by American arms. Some Americans in 1899, however, justified the acquisition of the Archipelago on grounds of anticipated economic benefits that would flow to the United States. In the following article, Rufus Tucker presents a classic indictment, challenging the economic argument with empirical data derived from statistics during the first two decades of American ownership. If his argument is sound, his conclusions may very well apply to other economically and technologically undeveloped colonies under imperial rule. The student might well wonder why it was that if American ownership was a political liability as well as an economic burden, the United States Government and many Americans seemed genuinely reluctant, if not outright opposed, to severing the political connection that tied the Philippines to the United States during the early years of the Twentieth Century.

For further reading: *Howard K. Beale, *Theodore Roosevelt and the Rise of America to World Power* (Baltimore: 1956); Charles S. Campbell, Jr., *Special Business Interests and the Open Door Policy* (New Haven: 1951); Raymond Esthus, "The Changing Concept of the Open Door 1899–1910," *Mississippi Valley Historical Review*, XLIV (December, 1959), 435–454 and *Theodore Roosevelt and Japan* (Seattle: 1966); Charles Neu, *An Uncertain Friendship: Theodore Roosevelt and Japan 1906–1909* (Cambridge: 1967); Paul A. Varg, *Missionaries, Chinese and Diplomats: The American Protestant Missionary Movement in China 1890–1952* (Princeton: 1958).

The late Rufus S. Tucker served as an economic analyst with the General Motors Corporation, 1936–1954. He had earlier served in the Federal Government and as an economic consultant for private corporations. This article is reprinted by permission of the editors, *Harvard Business Review*. From the *Harvard Business Review*, VIII (1929), 10–23. Copyright 1929 by the President and Fellows of Harvard College; all rights reserved.

As far as the writer is aware, no study of this question has ever been made from an economic point of view or with any attempt to check theories by statistics. Certain persons interested in their own welfare have emphasized some aspects of the problem; persons of an altruistic bent have emphasized others; and the majority of the comments made in the press or on the floors of Congress have been based on crude mercantilistic and imperialistic fallacies.

In this study the economic benefits, real or alleged, from the possession of the Philippines have been set off against the costs, direct and indirect, and the conclusion is reached that the costs far outweigh either present or prospective benefits. The economic benefits fall into four classes: (1) a market for exports, (2) a source of materials, (3) a center of distribution for trade with Asia, (4) a field for investment. The employment of American citizens in the islands involves an income of negligible proportions, and this is more than offset by the payment by the United States of the salaries of 6,000 Philippine scouts and of the expenses of Filipino cadets at West Point and Annapolis. The strategic value of the Philippines to the United States from the military point of view is a question which can not be ignored in any discussion of the relations between the Philippines and the United States.

MARKET FOR EXPORTS

Exports of merchandise from the United States to the Philippines in 1927 amounted to $69,522,000, including $128,000 of foreign goods reexported, on which American merchants made a middleman's profit. The value of goods carried in American vessels was $45,353,000, on which American ship owners earned the freights, which probably amounted to about 7% of the value of the cargoes.

The net gain on these transactions is harder to state. How much should be deducted from the invoiced values on account of the cost of materials and labor? Going back a step, how much profit did the producers of the raw materials make, and how much wages did their laborers earn? Even more important, how much profit and wages would these manufacturers, laborers, and producers of raw materials have made if they had been compelled to find a market for their goods and services elsewhere than in the Philippines? Only the difference, if any, between the profits actually made and the profits that might have been made elsewhere can properly be credited to the trade with the Philippines. Doubtless in some cases this difference was great, in others negligible. If the trade with the Philippines were wiped off the map to-morrow there would be only a slight readjustment of industry in the United States. A few concerns specializing in the Philippine trade might have to go out of business, but it is very likely that the persons involved might turn to other branches of industry, producing goods or services for domestic consumption or for sale to other countries, and make just as good profits and wages as they had been making when producing goods for the Philippines. The theory of international trade now universally accepted by economists teaches that if other nations captured our trade with the Philippines, our exports to other nations would increase or our imports from the Philippines and the rest of the world would decrease (using the terms "exports" and "imports" to include invisible items such as services and investments as well as merchandise) or both these results would ensue, so that a balance would inevitably result. There would be an increased export of American goods to other countries than the

Philippines and an unusual domestic production of some goods now imported. If, however, our trade with the Philippines disappeared not because of foreign competition but because of their inability to purchase, there would be no compensating increase in the rest of our trade. In view of the fact that our exports to the Philippines were in 1927 only 1.43% of our total exports and that our total exports are usually reckoned to be less than one-eighth of our total production, it is obvious that the decrease in the nation's profits and wages that might result from losing all of the trade of the Philippines would be infinitesimal, although some concerns now engaged in that trade would suffer serious inconvenience, and the slight loss to the nation might be more than made up by corresponding gains.

Moreover there is very little likelihood of our losing all of our market in the Philippines, even if there were a change of sovereignty, unless there should be a war between the Philippines and the United States or such unfriendly relations that the Filipinos would establish discriminating tariffs or refuse for patriotic reasons to buy our goods; and experience has shown that tariffs and patriotic boycotts are not as a rule effective for long against the appeal of superior goods at attractive prices. The justification for this statement is apparent to any one who will study carefully the figures of our trade with foreign countries and with the Philippines. These statistics show that out of 109 foreign countries and colonies separately reported in our annual reports of foreign commerce in 1927, 15 foreign countries,[1] and also Porto Rico and Hawaii, each bought more goods from us than the Philippines did, and 35 foreign countries and every one of our own other overseas possessions bought more in proportion to their population. In the case of nine foreign countries[2] and four United States colonies their imports from the United States formed a larger proportion of their total imports than was the case with the Philippines in the latest year for which comparative figures are available. Limiting the comparison to tropical and Far Eastern countries we find that out of 63 such, seven[3] bought more United States goods than the Philippines and 20[4] bought more in proportion to their population, while in eight[5] of them the proportion of their total imports from the United States was greater than the Philippines. Moreover, a comparison of the five-year period 1910–14 and the five-year period 1923–27 shows that our exports to the Philippines have increased only 168% in value while our exports to the rest of Asia increased 373%, to Oceania 277%, to the West Indies 167%, to South America 209%, and Africa 248%. During all this time products of the United States were admitted free of duty into the Philippines, while goods from other countries were required to pay duties averaging about 20%. Partly as a result of this discrimination the proportion of Philippine total imports from the United States rose from about 45% to about 60%.

Before the Tariff Act of 1909 the greatest proportion of Philippine imports coming

[1] United Kingdom, Canada, Germany, France, Japan, Cuba, Italy, Netherlands, Mexico, Australia, Argentina, Belgium, China, Spain, and Brazil.

[2] Honduras, Haiti, Nicaragua, Dominican Republic, Mexico, Panama, Salvador, Canada, Cuba; also Porto Rico, Hawaii, Virgin Islands and Guam.

[3] Japan, Cuba, Mexico, Australia, Argentina, China, and Brazil; also Porto Rico and Hawaii.

[4] Cuba, Dutch West Indies, Panama, British Honduras, Australia, Dominican Republic, British West Indies, Honduras, Argentina, Costa Rica, Uruguay, Nicaragua, Mexico, Chile, Venezuela, Salvador, Dutch Guiana, Colombia, Union of South Africa, British Malaya; also Hawaii, Virgin Islands, Porto Rico, Guam and Samoa.

[5] Honduras, Haiti, Nicaragua, Dominican Republic, Mexico, Panama, Salvador and Cuba; also Porto Rico, Hawaii, Virgin Islands, and Guam.

from the United States was 19%; for three years immediately preceding this Act the proportion was 17%. Immediately after its passage the proportion doubled. Inasmuch as the Philippine tariff has not been changed since 1909 the later gains of American trade are probably due in large part to other causes, such as those which have enabled American exports to overcome foreign competition in other Far Eastern markets.

The tariff preference is not, however, of much consequence with respect to a large part of our trade with the Philippines, as is proved by the fact that we export to Japan much more of many kinds of goods without any tariff preference. Our exports to Japan in 1923–27 were four times as valuable as our exports to the Philippines, and four-fifths as great per capita. There are 327 classes of goods separately enumerated in the statistics of exports from the United States to Japan and only 291 classes of exports to the Philippines, in at least 112 of which we exported greater values to Japan than to the Philippines in both 1924 and 1925. These are the most recent years for which the figures have been published in a form convenient for comparison. The value of the goods in these classes in 1925 was $15,049,000 or 22% of the total exports of the United States to the Philippines, which plainly can compete with the products of any other nation on equal terms. To these may be added some 24 other groups which are freely sold at present in foreign markets in the Far East and consequently need have little fear of foreign competition in the Philippines. These articles formed an additional 18% of the United States exports to the Philippines in 1925. And of course the other classifications of the export statistics include many products which the United States can export against foreign competition. Consequently it would be safe to assert that at least one-half of the United States products now sold in the Philippines do not depend on tariff preference for their market.

Allowing for the rise in wholesale prices the actual increase in the quantity of American goods consumed was only between 70 and 75% in 13 years. The low consumption of American goods (under $6 per capita) results from the low purchasing power of the natives, which is typical of the natives of tropical countries. Since there is very little prospect of increasing their individual productivity to any great extent, their demand for United States goods in the future is not likely to increase much more rapidly than their numbers.

The population of the Islands increased from 7,635,426 in 1903 to 10,350,730 in 1918, and is believed to have been 11,921,600 in 1928. This means an annual growth of between 1.6% and 2.0%, or a doubling in between 35 and 42 years, if continued. The density is now 104 per square mile, compared with 107 in the Dutch East Indies (exclusive of New Guinea), where climatic and racial conditions are similar. Allowing for both the increase in prices and the increase in population between 1910–14 and 1923–27, the per capita consumption of American goods increased about 55%, partly as a result of increased individual purchasing power but mainly as a result of a developing preference for American goods, which was encouraged if not wholly caused by the tariff.

It is very likely that even if the Philippines became independent the United States would retain an important place in their markets. Trade that has been flowing in certain channels is not easily diverted, the Filipinos speak English more than any other language but their own and are accustomed to American fashions, their factories and plantations are equipped with American machinery, and their monetary and banking system is closely linked with ours. In the absence of specific discriminating legislation, which there is no reason to expect unless the Filipinos should gain their independence by force, American exporters could still carry on a good business. It is possible, although very unlikely, that the virtual subsidy which was given to them by the United States Tariff Act of August 5, 1909, would be repealed; under this act and subsequent tariff acts all goods exported to the Philippines are exempt from United States internal revenue duties. This exemption amounted to about $1,677,000 in 1927. Since, however, a similar exemption is given to all exports to foreign countries it is unlikely that this would be repealed or seriously modified. Congress seems convinced that selling goods for export at a lower price than that charged at home is better than taking a chance of not selling them at all. In fact, the argument for such an exemption is stronger in the case of goods exported to foreign countries than in the case of goods exported to dependencies, since it is always more difficult to shift a tax onto foreigners, and the attempt to do so may result only in losing their trade, whereas in the case of domestic or subject consumers it is possible to deprive them of any alternative source of supply and thereby compel them to pay the tax.

The preceding considerations show that, if the Philippines remained as prosperous after separation from the United States as they are now, our exports to them would in all likelihood be at least half as great as at present. Unfortunately it is almost certain that they would not be so prosperous, and their imports from all countries, including the United States, would decline on account of their lower purchasing power. The loss of their privileged position in our markets, and the necessity of financing their own government unassisted, would certainly reduce their ability to pay for imports. Consequently, it is to be expected that independence would reduce their consumption of American goods even in the cases where American goods can compete successfully with foreign goods.

SOURCE OF TROPICAL MATERIALS

Imports of merchandise from the Philippines in 1927 amounted to $115,685,000 besides a very small amount of foreign goods transshipped in the Philippines. The value of goods carried in American vessels was $66,681,000 on which American ship owners earned the freight, probably amounting to less than 7%. These imports were all admitted free of duty, unless they contained foreign materials to the value of more than 20%, or were shipped via a third country. If they had come from a foreign country the duties collectible would have been more than $45,350,000. How much, if anything, would be added to the retail price if duties were paid, no one can tell. In other words, it is impossible to say how much this exemption benefits United States consumers or Filipino producers or how much the United States producers or consumers or the United States Treasury lose by it. In the case of sugar the cost to the American consumer is partly offset by a gain to the American producer, but the other tariffs affecting the Philippine trade represent an uncompensated loss of $22,000,000 to either the American consumer or the government. It is certain that some of the goods would have gone elsewhere if the United States duty had been imposed. In 1927, 25% of the exports of the Philippines did go to foreign countries, and there is nothing to prevent them from going wherever they can command the best price. It is also certain that in many cases they could not command a profitable price elsewhere.

Tobacco, cigars, and cigarettes sent to the United States pay the United States stamp duties, but the total receipts on this account ($366,000 in 1927) are handed over to the Philippine government. This is a gratuitous subsidy at the expense of United States smokers, exports from the United States to the Philippines being exempt from United States internal revenue duties and the proceeds of Philippine internal revenue duties levied on them being retained by the Philippine government.

It seems obvious that self-interest would cause the Filipinos to attempt to continue sending their goods to the United States unless we raised our tariff against them or unless communication was interrupted during a war. However, communication is probably more apt to be interrupted if the Islands remain under our flag than if they are independent—in the first case any enemy possessing bases in the Far East would be certain to attack Manila, while in the second he might find it expedient to observe Philippine neutrality. In either case it would be unwise to count on drawing any supplies from the Philippines during a war in the Pacific, since the distance from Manila to San Francisco is over twice as long as the distance from New York to Liverpool, and the western third of the route is wholly within striking distance of Japan or Japanese possessions. Even if the war were with some other power than Japan such a long line of communication would be hard to maintain. Prudence would dictate building up sources of supply nearer home.

A large part of the Philippine exports to the United States would be unable to bear the duties imposed on foreign goods by the United States tariff. It seems certain that of the total of $115,685,000 that came to the United States in 1927 the following would have come in very much smaller quantities, if at all:

Coconut Oil	$24,284,000
Coconut Meat	2,841,000
Sugar	47,887,000
Embroideries	3,853,000
Tobacco & Cigars	4,029,000
	$82,894,000

Of the foregoing, the coconut oil might be replaced by an increased import of copra, but the loss of a protected market for the other articles would mean a direct reduction in exports to the United States, which, because of the comparatively high cost of production in the Philippines, could not wholly or even largely be made up by sales to other countries. This would be a loss to the Philippines but not to the United States; adequate supplies of these goods could easily be obtained elsewhere, and if necessary the American tariff could be reduced to attract such supplies. The only loss to the United States would be in the reduced purchasing power of Filipinos, which would affect exports to the Philippines, but this loss would be less than the gain from customs duties or, if the tariff were reduced, the saving to American consumers.

Before the Tariff Act of 1909 was passed, only 40% of the exports from the Philippines came to the United States; recently the proportion has been about 70%. These ratios may indicate what would happen if all tariff privileges were abolished, but they are not conclusive, for the reason that even before 1909 the American tariff gave Philippine goods a 25% preference. In 1927 the principal Philippine exports that were not almost wholly dependent on the United States market were manila hemp, tobacco products, maguey, lumber, copra cake, copra meal, and hats.

In 1927 our imports from the Philippines were 1.85% of our total imports of merchandise. In that year we imported more, respectively, from China, Japan, India,

British Malaya, Mexico, Cuba, Brazil, and four other countries. In the latest year for which comparative figures are available there were seven foreign countries that sent to the United States a larger proportion of their total exports than the Philippines, viz: Guatemala, Honduras, Nicaragua, Panama, Colombia, Cuba, and Mexico; likewise Porto Rico and Hawaii. During the past decade (comparing five years 1910–14 with 1923–27) imports from the Philippines have increased 421%, from British Malaya 939%, Dutch East Indies 811%, Hongkong 427%, Kwangtung 3300%, Japan 341%. These figures show that the foreign trade of countries and colonies is affected much more by their geographical and economic conditions than by their allegiance. On account of their propinquity it is more economical and prudent for us to develop sources of tropical products in Mexico, the West Indies, and Central and South America—even in West Africa—than to attempt to build up a source over 6,000 miles away, unless that can be done as a business proposition without subsidies, protective tariffs, or preferential freight rates.

There are a few materials for which we depend mainly on the Philippines as a source of supply. They are shown in the following table, with the ratio which imports from the Philippines bore to total imports of each class of goods in 1926 and the alternative sources, if any:

Sawed cabinet woods	70.0%	Japan, Cuba, Guatemala, Mexico, Nicaragua
Oil-cake and oil-cake meal (coconut or copra)	93.7%	Japan, Trinidad & Tobago, French Oceania
Coconut meat, desiccated or prepared	60.2%	Ceylon, Colombia, Germany, British Malaya, British India
Copra, not prepared	59.7%	British Malaya, French Oceania, British Oceania
Coconut oil	100.0%	Netherlands, British India, United Kingdom
Cigars and cheroots		Mexico, Cuba
Cordage	60.4%	Cuba, Netherlands, Belgium
	57.6%	England, Netherlands, Belgium,
Manila or abaca	99.6%	
Buttons, pearl or shell	89.0%	England, Japan, Italy

All of these except oil-cake and meal, copra, and manila are protected by the United States tariff; if this protection were removed it is likely that other countries would furnish a larger part of the supply except in the case of manila, of which the Philippines have a natural monopoly. It is possible that an independent Philippine government might impose an export tax on manila, but we could injure them so severely by tariff retaliations and by using substitutes that it is unlikely that they would make it very high and it is even less likely that they would discriminate against the United States.

It was widely suggested that the recent British attempt at a monopoly of rubber could be fought by developing rubber plantations in Mindanao. This would not, however, require American sovereignty in Mindanao. Besides, those American interests that have looked into this matter have found other more attractive and available places, such as Liberia, Mexico, Brazil, and the Dutch East Indies.

It has recently been stated in the press that the War Department believes that for strategic reasons development of rubber sources in Central America, Porto Rico, South America, and West Africa is preferable to development in the Philippines. The few existing plantations are small and all raise either coconuts or hemp besides the rubber; the largest area devoted to rubber is 1,625 acres. A recent American government commission reported that there were 1,500,000 acres of possible rubber land in the Philippines, but labor enough to develop only 500,000 acres. The Philippine government is now attempting to encourage rubber-growing by small farmers, as in the Dutch East Indies where small growers produce most of the crops. As soon as the recent American investments in Liberia, Mexico, Yucatan, and the Dutch East Indies result in bearing trees there will be no more danger of a rubber monopoly. The recent downward course of rubber prices bears out this statement.

DISTRIBUTION CENTER FOR ASIATIC TRADE

It was hoped, when the United States first took the Philippines, that they would be a valuable trading outpost for our trade with China and other Far Eastern countries. This hope has not materialized. Although the amount of United States goods sent to China, *et cetera*, via the Philippines is not separately stated in either the United States or Philippine statistics of foreign trade, it is possible by a process of comparison to be certain that the total value of United States goods sent to all Asiatic countries from the Philippines did not exceed $581,000 in 1924, $1,000,000 in 1923, and $1,420,000 in 1922. There is no reason to believe that the actual amounts anywhere nearly approached these maximum sums. As a matter of fact, since the steamship service from the United States to Japan and China is better than that to the Philippines, or from the Philippines to those countries, there is no advantage in routing goods via Manila.

Hongkong and Shanghai have a great advantage over Manila in the trade with China in that it is possible to transfer goods directly from the transoceanic steamers to small coasting or river vessels or to land vehicles in which they can be carried to their destination, whereas Manila is over 600 miles away across a stormy sea. Hongkong and Shanghai also have easier access to sources of fuel. In recent years there have been more Americans engaged in business in Shanghai than in Manila.

An important fact not generally realized is that by the shortest route Manila is 172 miles further from San Francisco than is Hongkong, and 834 miles further than Shanghai; Manila is 243 miles further from Seattle than Hongkong and 921 miles further than Shanghai. Even on the southern route, via Honolulu, the distance to Manila is only 90 miles less than to Hongkong and is 437 miles greater than to Shanghai. The commonly used Mercator maps give a very false impression of relative distances. Manila is, however, fairly well situated for trade with the Dutch East Indies and French Indo-China in the case of goods that can be transshipped without too great cost. Possibilities for trade of this sort seem to be slight and are at present diminishing. In recent years the ports of Cebu, Iloilo, Jolo and Zamboanga have been increasing in importance in foreign trade, for the reason that it is cheaper in many cases to ship goods directly to and from them instead of via Manila. In fact, exports of Philippine products are shipped directly from some 20 smaller ports, not ports of entry, for the same reason. This indicates that transshipment at Manila has disadvantages even for trade with near-by islands and presumably still greater disadvantages for trade with foreign countries and possessions. If the United States coastwise laws were extended to the Philippines, as has been so often proposed, all hope of developing a transshipment trade to foreign countries and colonies would of course be destroyed.

The further suggestion has been made that factories or mills established under American auspices could produce goods in the Philippines for export to near-by countries. In so far as these factories might make up native raw materials this is a reasonable proposition, but if they are to use United States or other foreign materials it is hard to see how they can compete with China or Japan, where labor is either cheaper or more skillful and where coal is available and the climate better adapted to industry. In any case, if they succeeded in producing, say, cheap textiles, they would by that much cut down the market for the same goods produced in the United States and now sold in the Far East, so that the benefit to the United States would be hard to see.

It is said that if Japan got control of the Philippines the United States would be cut off from China. This, of course, would be true in time of war; it would be equally true even if Japan did not possess the Philippines, because there is a perfect screen of Japanese islands at present, extending from Japan to the equator.

FIELD FOR INVESTMENT

The Philippines have attracted considerable American capital and may do so in the future. The present status is unsatisfactory, United States investors not caring to undertake the risks of an insurrection or of sabotage. The fact that the Islands were independent or under a foreign flag would not necessarily deter American investors. At the present time there is no less than $12,555,000,000 of United States capital invested in industries in foreign lands, including over $1,000,000,000 in Asia and $4,652,000,000 in Latin America. It is not the sovereignty that counts, but the prospects of profit combined with reasonable safety. Of course, a country disturbed by riots or in which foreigners are arbitrarily taxed is discouraging to investors; and, if it is certain that the Philippines can not maintain a stable government or will discriminate against Americans, American capital will not go in. However, the world is wide, and good investments can be found elsewhere, as for example, Firestone's recent acquisitions in Liberia and Yucatan. But there is no reason to believe that an independent Philippine Government would discriminate against American capital, since to do so would be contrary to their own economic interest.

The Finance and Investment Division of the Department of Commerce prepared four or five years ago an estimate of American investments in the Philippines, which has been partly revised by the Bureau of Insular Affairs. It is as follows:

Philippine government bonds	$61,294,000
Municipal bonds	6,875,000
Manila Railroad bonds	15,500,000
Philippine Railway Co.	8,549,000
Manila Electric Corporation	18,000,000
P. I. Tel. & Tel. Co.	1,500,000
Sugar, hemp, tobacco, copra	25,000,000
Trading concerns	5,000,000
Miscellaneous	10,000,000

The income from these investments is probably around $7,000,000 or $8,000,000. No one can say how much more or less the same amount of capital would have yielded if invested elsewhere or how investment would be affected by independence. The tax-exempt feature of the municipal and insular bonds makes them worth more to the holder, but this gain is at the expense of the United States Treasury while the benefit accrues to the Philippine Treasury. This is another concealed subsidy and amounts to over $300,000 per annum. In addition to the value of the tax-exempt feature it is, of course, certain that the Philippine government would have to pay a high rate of interest to attract American investors if they were a foreign country. In fact their bonds are practically guaranteed by the United States government. By virtue of these circumstances the Philippine people save about $3,000,000 a year in interest on their bonds, while the United States assumes a contingent liability which can not be expressed in figures.

If the United States withdrew from the Philippines there would be a moral obligation to continue this guarantee on outstanding government and municipal bonds, so that the greater part of these investments would be safe. Investments in purely local enterprises, especially sugar, tobacco, and copra, would be severely injured and might become worthless. It is not thought however, that this fact imposes any obligation on the United States, since these investments were in no way guaranteed; the case is analogous to tariff reductions affecting so-called "vested interests."

STRATEGIC VALUE

The strategic value of the Philippines in case of a war with Japan has been much stressed by some persons. There is a difference of opinion among military men on two points: First, could the Philippines be held against attack? Second, could they be of assistance to the United States in the defense of Hawaii and the Pacific Coast? The first point is of purely academic interest. Conceding that the Philippines could be made impregnable by providing proper armament and garrisons, it is yet a practical certainty that Congress would not authorize the necessary expenditures or that, if one Congress should do so, subsequent Congresses would allow the garrison and equipment to run down. Moreover, the Naval Limitation Treaty of 1921 forbids us to increase our fortifications or establish new bases on the Islands at least until 1936. In their present state few military or naval men would maintain that they could be long defended, although some believe that Corregidor could be held until relief arrived. In discussing this point I do not wish to argue that there is any real reason to expect such a war. It would be disastrous to both nations, no matter which won. But it is obvious that the possibility of such a war's occurring would be much less if the United States did not possess a colony so near Japan as the Philippines, since there would be less possibility for jingoes in either nation to stir up false alarms.

As to the second point, it is not ordinarily considered good strategy to establish an outpost behind the enemy base, but that is exactly the position of Manila with respect to Japan. The shortest route to Manila passes within 150 miles of Yokohama, and every other feasible route passes within 200 miles of a Japanese colony or mandate. Many of these Japanese possessions contain harbors that could be used by submarines or airplane carriers.

In his evidence before the Senate Committee on Territories and Insular Possessions on March 1, 1924, Secretary of War Weeks states, "I want to make this quite clear . . . that if I were going to view this question entirely from military or other benefits to the United States I would say, 'let the Philippines go.'" He believed, however, that the United States should maintain a base for naval and commercial operations in the Far East. According to the testimony of General MacIntyre and Admiral Jones the maintenance of such a base, even if compatible with Philippine independence, would cost as much as or more than the present status. Such a base might be convenient for military operations in China. It is doubtful whether it would be of any value to the United States trade or important to United States prestige. Our trade with Europe and the southern part of South America, as well as our prestige in those regions, is very satisfactory, although we have never had naval bases there. Moreover, we maintained gunboats in China before we ever owned the Philippines. In case of intervention in China the large volume of our trade with that country would give us ample ground on which to insist on being allowed to participate, even if we had no territory nearer than Alaska and Hawaii, and if other countries maintain guards in Peking and Shanghai we can do so as well.

SUMMARY OF COSTS OF OCCUPATION

The cost of our occupation of the Philippines is very hard to reckon, since a large part of the expenditures of the army there would be required even if the army were located in the United States and also because some expenses are incurred in the United States which would not be necessary if the Philippines were not under our flag. Another very important consideration is the amount of revenue lost by the United States government and the amount of Philippine taxes paid by United States citizens by reason of the privileges granted to the Philippines in our customs and internal revenue laws. Still another question is whether the purchase price and the cost of subduing the insurrection should be included and whether interest should be reckoned on these expenditures. According to the Chief of the Bureau of Insular Affairs, annual disbursements of the army and navy in the Philippines in recent years have been around $12,000,000, but only the cost of the Philippine Scouts ($2,000,000) was properly chargeable to our possession of the Islands, since the other items would continue even if the United States withdrew. To this sum he added pensions, retirement pay, et cetera, of Philippine citizens and the amount of United States internal revenue duties turned over to the Philippine treasury. He stated, however, that "if we should retain in the islands a naval and commercial base, there would probably be no saving."

The average annual appropriations by Congress on account of the Philippines in recent years have been as follows:

1906–1914	$2,736,570.30
1914–1919	2,181,476.50
1919–1924	1,943,106.50
1924–1929	1,827,351.50

These amounts do not include appropriations for "insular possessions" in general, of which a large part was available for the Philippines, nor the ordinary expenses of army and navy forces stationed in the islands. However, the expenses of the Bureau of Insular Affairs are included so far as they are covered by specific appropriations, since the greater part of the work of this Bureau has to do with the Philippines.

To these appropriations must be added the sums annually paid to the Philippine treasury, representing the proceeds of United States internal revenue stamps on tobacco imported from the Philippines. These sums ranged from $258,097.63 in 1916 to $1,425,283.67 in 1920 and have averaged annually, since the latter date, $705,678.

Customs duties on goods imported from the Philippines are turned over to the Philippine government. Since 1909 they have been unimportant: about $60,000 in 15 years. They amounted to a total of $3,650,000 in the eight years 1902–1909, to which must be added the benefit received by Filipino exporters from the fact that their products were taxed 25% less than competing foreign products. This is incapable of exact measurement, but did not exceed $1,200,000 and may not have been even that much of a burden to American consumers. Since 1909 Philippine goods have paid no duty, with the theoretical exception of rice which has been exempt since 1913, and goods made of foreign materials. The duty imposed on the same quantity of similar goods from foreign countries in 1927 would have been over $45,350,000 which may be regarded as partly a subsidy to Filipino producers, partly a relief of taxes to the American consumer, and partly a withdrawal of protection from the American producer. It seems likely that the increased cost to the American consumer of Philippine products which are not produced in the United States was about $22,000,000 in 1927.

Philippine government and municipal bonds are wholly exempt from United States income tax. The value of this exemption to the Philippines is over $300,000 a year; the loss of revenue to the United States may be less but it is probably more than that. In addition to the direct value of the tax exemption the Philippine people save at least $3,000,000 in interest because of their improved credit derived from being under the United States flag.

Exports to the Philippines are exempt from the United States internal revenue duties. This exemption amounted to about $1,677,000 in 1927. Possibly it should not be regarded as a cost of possessing the Philippines, most exports being similarly exempt when sent to foreign countries. It does, however, put the Filipinos in a favored position when compared with American citizens, since the proceeds of the only taxes they pay go wholly to the support of their local government, while American citizens have to contribute to their states and to the federal government in addition.

It is evident at any rate that the annual cost of the Philippines to the American taxpayer is at least $26,000,000, not including interest on the purchase price and cost of conquest. The Bureau of Insular Affairs has stated that the total cost to the United States Treasury up to 1924 was about $505,000,000, or $19,000,000 a year, again excluding interest and making no allowance for tariff preferences, but of course the expenditures during the insurrection were higher than now. How much should be added to cover the increased military and naval establishment required by the colonial policy and the consequent hostility of foreign nations no one can say. It must be enormous as is plainly shown by two considerations: First, the chief pretext for ill-feeling with Japan is our possession of the Philippines; second, the chief reason for our disagreement with Great Britain concerning the tonnage of cruisers required for our defence is the necessity of having large enough bunker capacity to travel freely between Hawaii and the Philippines. There are also some extra expenses incurred by our consular and diplomatic services because of the necessity of protecting Filipino interests abroad. If accounts were drawn up on a strictly business basis the United States government would have to charge the Philippines annually with about $800,000 as interest on the purchase price, and at least $10,000,000 as interest on the cost of conquest (after the end of the war with Spain). These costs were met originally by bond issues in part, but can not be separated from the general debt.

SUMMARY OF GAINS TO THE UNITED STATES

The pecuniary benefits to the United States from control of the Philippines are briefly summarized in the following paragraphs. These are benefits to the United States citizens or corporations; the benefits to the United States government and to citizens not directly interested in the Philippines can not be stated in money. The government gets a small share (not over 10% on the whole) of the increased income of its taxpayers, and each citizen benefits theoretically by the prosperity of his neighbors and those with whom he has business relations. Unfortunately the distribution of benefits is in no way correlated with the distribution of costs. The expenditures of the government certainly exceed its tax receipts, and, while some people profit by importing and exporting to the Philippines, other equally estimable citizens suffer from the competition of Philippine goods or have to pay more for their own purchases in order to protect the Philippine trade. Consequently, the net benefit of the Philippines to the United States, aside from the dubious strategic value, seems to be limited to the few persons who have direct connections with the Philippines.

Commercial Profits
The net profit on exports to the Philippines is somewhere between zero and $3,000,-000, taking into account the profit which might have been made by selling these goods elsewhere. Similar calculations would disclose net profits on imports from the Philippines to be probably somewhere between zero and $2,000,000. Freight charges earned by American vessels certainly did not exceed $10,000,000, from which the usual deduction should be made for wages, interest, et cetera, and for possible earnings elsewhere.

Profits from Investments
The total American capital invested in the Philippines is reckoned to be about $152,000,000, of which $68,000,000 are in tax-exempt government bonds. There is nothing to prevent American investment in the Islands if they were independent, although in that case the amount of tax-exempts would decline, and on account of United States sovereignty the investors in bonds are content with much less interest than they would otherwise require. Investors in sugar and other protected industries gain by access to the protected American market, but what they gain is at the expense of American consumers, producers, or taxpayers. Under the present tariff it is likely that their net gain from United States sovereignty does not exceed $2,000,000, assuming that their property would not be destroyed by an independent government and that anarchy would be avoided.

Profits from Personal Service
It was reckoned that the 484 Americans in government service and the three or four thousand other Americans receiving salaries in the Philippines did not average over $3,000 apiece. Doubtless if they were working at home they could earn at least

$2,500 on the average. Some of them would still be employed under an independent government. Assume that 3,000 would leave and lose $500 apiece on an average, the total loss would be $1,500,000.

The total gain from United States sovereignty to all classes of United States citizens adds up to less than $10,000,000 a year, which represents all the economic gain susceptible of numerical expression, including some that is made at the expense of other Americans. The potential value of the Philippines as a source of rubber and the possible danger of interference with the supply of manila hemp, coconut products, and pearl buttons can not be even approximately expressed in dollars, depending as it does on so many hypothetical factors. On the whole it would seem that the occupation of the Philippines brings no additional income to the United States Treasury but subjects it to an annual charge of at least $4,000,000—nearer $15,000,000 if interest on the cost of acquisition is included—but the saving to the Treasury from letting the islands go would not exceed $4,000,000 and would be much less than that if a naval base were retained in Manila harbor.

BENEFIT TO FILIPINOS

The citizens of the Philippines benefit much more than the Americans. They have a privileged position in our market, are relieved from all expense in connection with external matters, are exempt from our immigration laws, and many of them are on the United States pay-roll. The value of these privileges is roughly as follows:

Tariff privileges	$25,000,000 to $45,000,000
Pay and allowances of Philippine Scouts	2,000,000
Other expenditures of army or navy in the Philippines	10,000,000
Other Filipinos in U. S. employ, pay, and allowances	2,200,000
Earnings of Filipinos in U. S. and Hawaii, above what they could earn at home (56,000 at $100 each)	5,600,000
Proceeds from U. S. internal revenue	700,000
Value of exemptions from U. S. internal revenue	1,500,000
Value of exemption of bonds from income tax	300,000
Value of implied guarantee of bonds	3,000,000
Miscellaneous	700,000
Total	$71,000,000

The actual increase in the income of Filipino citizens because of tariff privileges and United States government employment is of course impossible to ascertain exactly, but the lowest possible estimate of the total benefit received by them is $40,000,000 which is one and one-half times the total amount now raised by taxation in the Philippine Islands. About $17,000,000 of this is received in such form as to permit the Philippine government to avoid otherwise necessary increases in taxation; the remainder ($23,000,000 or more) is received by individuals or business concerns.

CONCLUSION

The value of American occupation to the Filipinos is very great, very likely greater than the total cost to the American taxpayers, except the extra naval expenditure they occasion, but it is a question whether Americans desire to be taxed to benefit Filipinos and whether it is socially desirable or morally right that they should be. It is at least certain that, if the United States tariff were applied to imports from the Philippines, the producers of embroideries, furniture, coconut oil, pearl buttons, sugar, and cigars would be very seriously injured; and, if the American army were withdrawn, not only the natives enrolled in the Philippine Scouts but also a large number of merchants and others would lose their principal means of livelihood. On the other hand, withdrawal would mean an annual saving to the United States government of at least $4,000,000 in addition to a sum many times as large saved from naval expenditures and a still further saving of approximately $22,000,000 annually to the American consumers of Philippine products other than sugar. It seems obvious that so far as material advantages are concerned not only is the present arrangement much more beneficial to the Philippines than to the United States, but also the cost to the United States far exceeds the commercial benefit derived or likely ever to be derived.

14 / Dollar Diplomacy in Nicaragua, 1909–1913

Dana G. Munro

The policies which the Taft Administration pursued in Central America and China, known generally as Dollar Diplomacy, were based on definite political and economic assumptions. In the Far East, the program aspired to restrain Japanese and Russian expansion so that America's trade would enjoy unhampered access to the markets of China. To further this goal, selected American bankers were encouraged to participate in an international financial consortium which would provide loans for the purpose of building railroads in China, currency stabilization, and in other respects strengthen China. The notion was that each national member of the consortium would have an equal stake in the venture thus discouraging the domination of China by any single foreign power. In Central America, Dollar Diplomacy operated toward the end of providing maximum security for the developing American strategic life line—the still unfinished Panama Canal. Security, it was believed, would develop from political stability, and American policy aimed at encouraging such stability by promoting economic assistance through private loans and investments to the countries of Central America. In the following article, Dana G. Munro provides a case study of how Dollar Diplomacy operated in Nicaragua.

For further reading: Charles D. Ameringer, "The Panama Canal Lobby of Philippe Bunau Varilla and William Nelson Cromwell," *American Historical Review*, LXVIII (1963), 346–363; Peter Calvert, *The Mexican Revolution 1910–1914: the Diplomacy of Anglo-American Conflict* (Cambridge, England: 1968); Naomi W. Cohen, "Ambassador Straus in Turkey 1909–1910: A Note on Dollar Diplomacy," *Mississippi Valley Historical Review*, XLV (June, 1958), 632–642; Herbert Croly, *Willard Straight* (New York: 1924); Dora A. Graber, *Crisis Diplomacy: A History of United States Intervention Policies and Practices* (Washington: 1959); Dana G. Munro, *Intervention and Dollar Diplomacy in the Caribbean 1900–1921* (Princeton: 1964); Charles Vevier, *The United States and China 1906–1913: A Study of Finance and Diplomacy* (New Brunswick: 1955).

Dana G. Munro has served as Professor of Latin American History and Director of the Woodrow Wilson School of Public and International Affairs, Princeton University. This article is reprinted with the permission of the author and of the editors of the *Hispanic American Historical Review*. From the *Hispanic American Historical Review*, XXXVIII (May, 1958). Copyright © 1958 by Duke University Press.

Much of the hostile feeling caused by our interventions in the Caribbean arose from misconceptions of what we were trying to do. This is especially true in the case of the Taft administration's "Dollar Diplomacy." There is still a rather wide-spread impression that dollar diplomacy meant sending Marines to Caribbean countries to collect debts and to support bankers and concession hunters in unfair business deals. Most historians have realized that the primary objectives of the policy were political rather than economic, but many of them have felt that it was carried out in a way that helped American financial interests at the expense of the countries where we intervened. Whether this is true can be determined only by an examination of particular cases. It may be possible to throw some light on the question by examining the outstanding example of dollar diplomacy during the Taft administration—the intervention in Nicaragua.

The troubled situation in Central America was one of the first matters that demanded attention when Philander C. Knox became Secretary of State in March, 1909. Knox's predecessor, Elihu Root, had taken a lively interest in Central American affairs, and in 1907, with the help of Mexico, he had persuaded the five governments of the Isthmus to sign a series of treaties providing for the settlement of disputes through a permanent Central American court and outlawing the interference in one anothers' affairs which had been a chief cause of disorder. Unfortunately the two most powerful rulers in the Isthmus, Manuel Estrada Cabrera of Guatemala and José Santos Zelaya of Nicaragua, paid little attention to these provisions. The two men feared and hated each other, and each had allies among political leaders in other republics. In 1908, Estrada Cabrera and the President of El Salvador fomented a revolution in Honduras, where the government was friendly to Zelaya, and a general war was prevented only by the urgent representations of the United States and Mexico and the interposition of the new Central American court. Zelaya then attempted to subvert the government of El Salvador. In the first months of 1909, the Nicaraguan dictator's frankly expressed ambition to unite Central America under his own leadership seemed the chief obstacle to the success of the efforts of the United States and Mexico to maintain peace, and warships of both countries were patrolling the west coast of Central America to discourage the departure of filibustering expeditions from Nicaraguan ports.

The immediate responsibility for dealing with the situation, under the new administration, seems to have fallen to Huntington Wilson, who had been Third Assistant Secretary of State under Root and who now, as Assistant Secretary, became the chief officer of the Department after Knox himself. Wilson was a career diplomat, but he had never been south of the Rio Grande, and he did not have the tolerant sympathy and genuine liking for Latin Americans that had made Root successful in dealing with them. He had the help of the veteran Second Assistant Secretary, Alvey A. Adee, and after the first months he had the advice of the newly-established Latin American Division, which was headed for a time by Thomas C. Dawson, who was an able career diplomat with much Latin American experience. Wilson himself, however, seems to have made the important decisions, especially during the frequent and extended periods when he was Acting Secretary in Knox's absence. It was probably Wilson who formulated the plan of action that Knox laid before the new cabinet at two of its meetings in March, 1909, and then informally took up with the Mexican government.[1]

[1] For a brief summary of what took place at the Cabinet meetings, see M. A. De Wolfe Howe, *George von Lengerke Meyer* (New York, 1919), pp. 427–428.

The plan contemplated the holding of a new conference on Central American affairs from which Zelaya's government would be excluded. This would draw up a treaty under which the United States and Mexico would join with the other Central American states in active measures to assure peace. Specifically, the treaty would guarantee the neutrality of Honduras, provided for in the 1907 treaties but repeatedly violated. Honduras' weakness and her central position had always made her a battleground for her neighbors, and throughout her history she had rarely had a government that did not owe its existence to outside intervention. If she could be kept neutral, it would be difficult for the armies of the other states to attack each other. To discourage internal strife within Honduras, Knox proposed that the United States should set up a customs collectorship like that which had existed in the Dominican Republic since 1905.

These proposals reflected two ideas that were to play an important part in the Taft administration's Central American policy. One was the State Department's belief that Zelaya was chiefly responsible for the failure of the 1907 treaties. Probably Estrada Cabrera had been equally guilty of attempting to foment revolutions in other countries, but the Guatemalan dictator had shown some respect for foreign opinion by acting secretly, while pretending to co-operate with the United States, whereas Zelaya had sought to build up his prestige by being conspicuously offensive to the American government. He had made life unpleasant for American diplomats at Managua by a series of petty insults and annoyances, and there had been an especially bitter dispute over his refusal to arbitrate the Emery Claim, which arose from the cancellation of a timber concession held by a North American company. Just one week after taking office, Knox had withdrawn the American Chargé d'Affaires from Managua as an indication of displeasure at Zelaya's attitude.

The other idea was the belief that American customs collectorships would solve many of the worst problems of disorderly Caribbean states. Projects for collectorships were to play an important part in the Caribbean policy of the United States under Taft and under Woodrow Wilson. The customs duties were by far the most important source of income in Latin American countries, and it was thought that honest and efficient collection would make weak governments stronger by providing them with more adequate funds. Customs collectorships would also afford security for American loans, and thus make possible the railroad and port construction that were clearly needed if the poorer Caribbean countries were to attain the prosperity that was essential for political stability. At the same time, they would make possible the elimination of European financial influence. The State Department had been impressed by the apparent success of the Dominican collectorship, which had relieved the government at Santo Domingo from the importunities of its foreign creditors and had provided money for better administration and for public works, even though the loan that should have gone with it had not materialized.[2] The presence of American customs officials, and the belief that the United States would protect them, had made for political stability because it was no longer possible for revolutionists to seize a port and use the revenues there. Even after experience in Santo Domingo had shown that efficient collection of revenues was of little use without prudence and honesty in their expend-

---

[2] Delays in approving the loan contract caused the bankers to lose interest in the loan, and the bonds were consequently given directly to creditors in payment of their claims. Some money for public works was made available later, when bonds still in the Dominican government's possession were sold to the sinking fund.

iture, and that revolutionists could learn new techniques, many officers in the State Department seemed convinced that American customs control was almost a panacea for Caribbean political ills.

Knox's plan called for an active intervention in Central American affairs which neither the United States nor Mexico had up to that time been willing to consider. Secretary Root, in his efforts to promote peace, had been careful to avoid any appearance of coercion, and he had enlisted the help of Mexico precisely because joint action would allay suspicion that the United States sought to control the Isthmus for its own selfish ends. The Mexican government, when Knox's plan was submitted to it, was unwilling either to use force to maintain the neutrality of Honduras or to consent to North American financial control in that country. Furthermore, Porfirio Díaz considered Zelaya a personal friend and was unwilling to exclude him from any new conference.[3] Díaz' misgivings about the direction in which American policy was developing increased when he received an erroneous report that the admiral commanding the joint naval force on the Central American west coast had asked one of the Mexican gunboats to fire on a Nicaraguan filibustering craft.[4] After some discussion, he reluctantly agreed to the establishment of a financial commission in Honduras, if Mexico were represented on it, and to the holding of a new Central American conference, if Nicaragua were allowed to participate. His representatives made it clear, however, that the Mexican government would not go beyond the use of moral influence in dealing with Central American problems. The State Department regarded this reply as a rejection of its proposals, and made no further effort to reach an understanding.

The proposed conference was abandoned, but the State Department went ahead with its project for a customs collectorship in Honduras. The British government had for some time been pressing for payments on the Honduran foreign debt, which had been in default for many years, and the United States, inspired probably by a desire to prevent the increase of British financial influence, had been opposing the proposed settlement. It could hardly continue to encourage Honduras to refuse payment, without offering a reasonable alternative. Wilson consequently made persistent efforts to interest American bankers in the idea of a refunding loan which would not only take care of the British debt but also provide the occasion for setting up a customs collectorship, and, in the summer of 1909, J. P. Morgan and Company took up the business and negotiated an agreement with the British bondholders. Many months later they signed a loan contract with the weak and somewhat reluctant Honduran government, and on January 10, 1911, the United States and Honduras signed a treaty placing collection of the customs in the hands of an official nominated by the bankers and approved by the President of the United States. Opposition both in Honduras and in the United States Senate made it impossible to carry out this project but in the meantime events in Nicaragua had made that country rather than its northern neighbor the chief object of the State Department's attention in Central America.

Zelaya had shown a disposition to come to terms after the United States withdrew its diplomatic representative, and had agreed to arbitrate the Emery claim. For a time, too, there were fewer complaints about his filibustering activities, partly per-

[3] Most of the correspondence about these negotiations is in Numerical Case 18920 in the State Department files in the National Archives. There are other papers in Numerical Cases 18432 and 6369.

[4] For this incident see Numerical Case 18432/107, 127.

haps because President Taft ordered the Navy to use force to stop them if necessary.[5] On the other hand, the State Department was displeased when Zelaya negotiated a large loan with the Ethelburga Syndicate of London in May, 1909, and it tried unsuccessfully to prevent the sale of the bonds in London and Paris.[6] In the summer there were reports that Zelaya was preparing to resume his attacks on El Salvador and was attempting to interfere in the internal affairs of Costa Rica.[7] The State Department consequently hardly attempted to conceal its sympathy for a revolt that broke out at Bluefields on the East Coast of Nicaragua in October, 1909.[8]

Zelaya's opponents had made repeated efforts to overthrow him in the years before 1909. In Nicaragua virtually every citizen, from the humblest worker to the intellectual, was an ardent member of one of the two parties that had fought each other since independence. Politics was largely a matter of locality: León and the districts in the western part of the Lake region were predominantly Liberal, while Granada, to the Southeast, was the Conservative center. Zelaya, who had set up a Liberal government in 1893 after thirty years of Conservative rule, had many enemies in his own party, but he still had much popular support. He had easily suppressed several Conservative revolts in the Lake region in the years before 1909. It was somewhat more difficult to deal with an uprising on the East Coast, especially when his own forces at Bluefields took part in it.

The East Coast is cut off from the lake region, where most Nicaraguans live, by a broad belt of jungle where travel is exceedingly difficult. There is some communication by way of the San Juan River, but rapids in the river and a treacherous bar at its mouth make the journey so dangerous that many people before the days of the airplane preferred to avoid it by going from Bluefields to New Orleans and from there to Panama and Corinto. The inhabitants of the East Coast were English-speaking West Indian Negroes, with a number of North American and European business men and a few Nicaraguan officials and other recent immigrants from the interior. Many of them had long been unhappy under the rule of the distant government at Managua, and Zelaya had increased the discontent by granting monopolistic concessions with little regard to local interests. Native and foreign banana planters especially resented the exclusive privileges that he had given to a subsidiary of the United Fruit Company. In the first months of 1909 there had been much talk of revolution and a few unsuccessful efforts to enlist the help of the United States Government.[9]

The leader of the October revolt was Juan J. Estrada, whom Zelaya had appointed as governor of the East Coast, in spite of past political differences. Estrada was a Liberal, but most of the participants were Conservatives, some of them Nicaraguans living on the Coast and other people who came to Bluefields to take part in the movement. Funds were obtained from local American business men, and Estrada Cabrera furnished a limited amount of arms and supplies. The evidence available gives little support to the allegation, made later, that the United States Government instigated the revolution, but it is clear that the American consul at Bluefields, Thomas P. Moffat, gave it his enthusiastic personal support after it started.

[5] Secretary Meyer's diary indicates that the Navy had such instructions early in March. Howe, loc. cit. Formal instructions to stop all expeditions across the Gulf of Fonseca were sent at the State Department's request on April 24. Numerical Case 18432/101A.

[6] The correspondence is in Numerical Case 5691.

[7] Numerical Cases 4598/96, 19865, and 6775/664, 708.

[8] See Wilson's memorandum of Oct. 21, 1909, Numerical Case 6369/226.

[9] Numerical Case 6369/110, 131.

Wilson, who was Acting Secretary of State, was also inclined to give the revolutionists any possible encouragement, but more levelheaded officials in the Department insisted on a formal neutrality.[10] The American government's attitude changed in November when Zelaya ordered the shooting of two Americans named Cannon and Groce, both of them commissioned officers in the revolutionary army, who were seized while allegedly placing mines in the San Juan River. The execution seemed the more outrageous because Zelaya spared a Frenchman who was in the same party. Wilson wanted to retaliate by occupying Corinto and possibly Managua, but this idea was abandoned, apparently because it was thought that armed intervention would require the approval of Congress.[11] Instead, Knox broke off diplomatic relations. In a note made public on December 1, he described Zelaya's regime as a "blot on the history of Nicaragua" and openly expressed sympathy for the revolution.[12]

Zelaya had to go. His supporters realized that they could hardly keep the Liberal party in power if the United States openly supported the revolution, and his Mexican friends joined with the party leaders in advising him to resign. Porfirio Díaz, when he realized that the murder of Cannon and Groce might lead to American intervention, had suggested that the United States and Mexico offer their good offices for the restoration of peace in Nicaragua under a new president, but the State Department had received this suggestion with a marked lack of enthusiasm. Though President Taft assured Díaz that he wished to act in harmony with him,[13] the Chargé at Washington was apparently not even told in advance of the contents of Knox's note of December 1,[14] and Root's old friend the former Ambassador Creel got a cold reception when Díaz sent him to Washington to propose that the two governments co-operate in the pacification first of Nicaragua and then of all Central America. The officials with whom he talked thought that his proposals revealed a purpose to set up a sort of joint protectorate over Nicaragua with Mexico in the leading role, and to continue the Zelaya faction in power under a new president.[15]

This suspicion was not diminished when Zelaya resigned on December 16 and José Madriz, who had been Creel's candidate, was elected by the Congress as his successor. The United States did not recognize the new administration and declared that it would deal informally with both parties on an equal basis. It nevertheless offered a warship as a meeting place for peace negotiations which Madriz proposed immediately after his inauguration. Unfortunately the rebels' emissary was drowned on his way to the conference; and soon afterward a military victory which opened the way for an invasion of the interior made the Estrada faction less willing to discuss a settlement.

The improvement in the rebels' prospects seems also to have caused the State Department to consider what it would do if Estrada won. Up to this time its policy had

[10] Wilson's memorandum of Oct. 21, cited above, and Counselor Hoyt's memorandum of November 19 (Numerical Case 6369/346) are two of several papers in the State Department's files that support this statement.

[11] See the rough drafts and memoranda filed in Numerical Case 6369 after enclosure /323.

[12] For the text of the note, see *Foreign Relations*, 1909, p. 455.

[13] Numerical Case 6369/320A.

[14] The Mexican Minister of Foreign Affairs told the press that Knox's action came unexpectedly while Mexico was awaiting a reply to the peace plan. See the clippings enclosed with a despatch of Dec. 3, 1909, from Mexico City, Numerical Case 6369/777.

[15] Memoranda about Creel's call on Knox on Dec. 14 and his conversation with Wilson on Dec. 20, Numerical Case 6369/400, 400 2/9, 400 3/9.

apparently been motivated by its irritation at Zelaya's repeated violations of the 1907 treaties and at his attitude toward the United States, rather than by any thought of doing in Nicaragua what it was already trying to do in Honduras. Wilson now asked the Latin American Division to prepare two letters to be handed to the Department by Estrada's agent at Washington when the revolutionists should enter Managua. One would request immediate recognition, and the other, besides promising to hold free elections and to punish the murderers of Cannon and Groce, would express an intention to request an American loan. The Department's Latin American experts doubted the propriety of immediately recognizing a revolutionary government, in view of the provisions of the 1907 treaties, and they realized that a public request for a loan might endanger the new government, but the letters were nevertheless prepared.[16] They were never used because Estrada's invasion of the interior was a disastrous failure.

A month later, the revolution seemed about to collapse. Moffat reported from Bluefields that Estrada's situation appeared hopeless and Admiral Kimball, who commanded the numerous warships that had been sent to both coasts to protect American lives and property, recommended immediate recognition of Madriz.[17] The danger of further fighting in the interior seemed so remote that the American government withdrew most of its forces, including several hundred Marines who had been kept under disagreeable conditions on a transport in Corinto Harbor for the preceding three months. Wilson and his advisers were nevertheless in no mood to change their attitude toward Madriz. They thought that a Liberal victory would hurt the prestige of the United States and strengthen the influence of Mexico, which was reported to be helping the Nicaraguan government with arms and money.[18] It would also cause further trouble in Central America by strengthening the hand of what Dawson described as the "anti-Cabrera factions" in other countries. They had no illusions about Estrada Cabrera's loathsome despotism or about the sincerity of his professed friendship for the United States, but they looked on his enemies as opponents of their own policy of maintaining peace on the basis of the 1907 treaties.[19]

Obviously unable to find a more effective course of action the State Department told both Nicaraguan factions on March 26 that it would not recognize any government that did not have full control of the country and that did not give positive assurances of free elections, of punishing the murderers of Cannon and Groce, and of abiding by the provisions of the 1907 Treaties. It added that it would also expect the new government to subscribe to additional provisions that had been shown necessary by experience—a vague statement that may have contemplated new measures to assure Central American peace, or the establishment of a customs collectorship in Nicaragua, or both. When this statement of policy had no effect, Wilson asked Dawson to recommend further steps, and Dawson proposed that Madriz be definitely told that he would not be recognized, because his government was unconstitutional and because of his unsatisfactory attitude. Dawson thought that this action might compel Madriz and the Mexicans to come to terms with the United States. If it did not, he suggested that

[16] The text and the accompanying memoranda are in the State Department's Decimal File, in the National Archives, 817.00/1373. Hereafter, unless otherwise indicated, references are to the Decimal File. Many papers in the latter part of 1909 were indexed both under Numerical Cases and Decimal File numbers.

[17] 817.00/832, 843.

[18] See Minister Merry's despatch from Costa Rica, Feb. 12, 1910, 817.00/776.

[19] This feeling about the "anti-Cabrera" factions was expressed in Dawson's memorandum to Wilson of April 19, 1910, 817.00/906.

the United States should seize the customhouse at Corinto in order to collect an indemnity for the murders and the sum due on the Emery Claim. He suggested, however, that this action might be delayed until after the Pan American Conference that was to meet at Buenos Aires in July, and he frankly admitted that it might simply cause more "wars and confusion" in Central America.[20] Perhaps because of his own doubts, his recommendations were not followed. When the Central American Court of Justice offered its mediation to the Nicaraguans a few days later, the State Department welcomed the proposal with an eagerness that suggested that it was ready to grasp at anything that offered a way out of its dilemma, and was evidently disappointed when both parties turned down the offer.[21]

The turning point came in May, 1910, when Madriz' forces attempted to end the war by an attack on Bluefields. The capture of the rebel capital was prevented by the captain of the U. S. S. Paducah, who forbade any fighting in the city and landed men to enforce his order. This action would seem high-handed today, but in the first years of the century both American and European naval officers frequently prevented fighting at Caribbean ports when foreign lives and property were in danger. The American Navy had in fact been ordered in January to take similar action at Greytown, where it would have benefited Madriz.[22] At Bluefields, the effect on the Liberal army was disastrous, for it had to remain inactive in the unhealthful jungle, far from any base of supplies. The American commander also required the bulk of the Conservative forces to move out of the town, but they were in a better position with a secure base behind them.

The Liberals were able to capture the Bluff, where the Bluefields customhouse had been, but they gained little from this victory because the State Department asked the Navy not to permit them to interfere with ships going into the harbor or to collect duties on goods destined for territory under rebel control. Soon afterward, when Madriz attempted to blockade the port, the American government again interfered. The Liberals' only effective warship was the former British steamer Venus, which had sailed from New Orleans, ostensibly as a merchant ship, a few weeks earlier. The federal authorities at the port had detained her for a time, but had finally had to release her because there seemed to be no legal ground for refusing clearance. When she appeared off Bluefields as a warship, the American government took the position that it had been deceived as to her real purpose and refused to permit her to establish a blockade. The Liberals' whole plan of action was consequently frustrated, and when their land forces were defeated in several battles on the outskirts of the city the campaign had to be abandoned.[23]

The American government's action at Bluefields has been severely criticized as an improper and unfair interference with Madriz' effort to end the war. Though Knox and his advisers stoutly maintained that what they had done was justified under international law and practice, it seems clear that their hostility to Madriz, as well as their desire to protect foreign interests, influenced their action. It seems less probable that

[20] Memoranda of April 19, 1910, 817.00/906, 907.

[21] Knox to the President of the Central American Court of Justice, May 3, 1910. Foreign Relations, 1910, p. 744; and Hale to Moffat, May 6, 1910, 817.00/920.

[22] Numerical Case 6369/594, 626. The American commander did not act on these orders because a British commander had already forbidden fighting in the port.

[23] The most important documents about the events of May, 1910, are printed in Foreign Relations, 1910, pp. 745 ff. There is additional correspondence about the Venus, which Madriz renamed the Máximo Jerez, in file 817.00, beginning with enclosure 879.

they thought that their interference would actually help the rebels to win the war. Madriz was in full control of the interior, and even after the failure of the attack on Bluefields the American naval commander and the American consul reported that Estrada had no chance of defeating him without outside help. Moffat, in fact, thought that lack of money and quarrels among the leaders might cause the revolution to collapse at any moment.[24]

At any rate, the State Department clearly had no plans for further action. Reports that intervention was being considered were officially denied.[25] Knox did indeed ask J. Reuben Clark, the Assistant Solicitor, to draft a resolution by which Congress would have authorized the President to set up a free and stable government in Nicaragua,[26] but he probably realized that opposition in the Senate would make it useless to present it. Senator Stone had already introduced a resolution demanding an investigation of the Nicaraguan situation, and in presenting it had referred to reports that American bankers had formed a syndicate to refund the Nicaraguan debt and set up a customs collectorship.[27] The talk about intervention alarmed the other Central American governments, but their representatives and President Díaz of Mexico were politely rebuffed when they urged that the United States consider the recognition of Madriz.[28] For the time being, the American government remained formally neutral. In August we find Adee still insisting that the State Department "serve the same sauce for the Estrada gander as for the Madriz goose."[29]

The reverse at Bluefields and the continuing hostility of the United States hurt Madriz more than the American officials realized. The Conservatives in the interior were encouraged to resume their resistance, and in August, when Estrada's army again invaded western Nicaragua, the Liberal government fell. The leaders of the revolution entered Managua on August 28. On the same day, the revolutionists' agent at Washington cabled Estrada the text of a message that the American government wished to receive from him giving assurances about the policy that he would follow and in particular undertaking to contract a loan secured by a customs collectorship.[30] Estrada was reluctant to commit himself, but he needed the moral support of the United States and on September 10 he sent the required message.

The position of the new regime was precarious. The always bitter feeling between the political parties had been increased by the civil war. The Liberals were unquestionably the majority party, and they could be expected to seize the first opportunity to return to power. Few of them were willing to support Estrada because the movement that he headed was primarily a Conservative one; and at the same time, because he was a Liberal, Estrada had few friends among the leaders of the revolution. These leaders, however, were divided into rival factions. One was led by Emiliano Chamorro, who had a strong following in Granada, the Conservative stronghold, and another by Luis Mena, a man of humble origin who had distinguished himself as a

[24] Moffat's report of June 12, 1910, 817.00/1053. For Commander Gilmer's opinion see 817.00/1084.

[25] New York Times, June 1 and June 3, 1910.

[26] 817.00/1486, 1487.

[27] Congressional Record, 61st Cong., 2nd Sess. Vol. 45, pp. 9058–9059 (June 25, 1910.)

[28] 817.00/1194, and Foreign Relations, 1910, pp. 752, 754.

[29] Memorandum about shipment of arms on Panama Railroad steamers; 817.00/1284.

[30] The State Department also cabled the text to the Consul at Managua on September 1, 1910, 817.00/1370A.

general in the war. A third group, somewhat more moderate in its attitude, was made up of followers of Adolfo Díaz, a civilian businessman who had taken a leading part in raising money for the revolution. Though Estrada had been promised the presidency, because the Conservatives could not start the revolution without his help, some of the other leaders were already plotting to replace him.

These rivalries were the first problem that confronted Dawson when he went to Nicaragua in October, 1910, to help the new government to carry out the measures to which Estrada had agreed. Dawson's instructions were to urge a free election "at the earliest possible date,"[31] but he soon realized that this was impracticable and he consented to the typical Central American device of a constitutional convention, which could set up a government and also give legal effect to the other measures that the United States wished to see adopted. He persuaded the Nicaraguan leaders to agree that Estrada should serve as president and Díaz as vice president for a two-year term. Their successors were to be chosen at a popular election, in which the official candidate would be selected by a committee consisting of Estrada, Díaz, Chamorro, Mena, and a prominent Conservative named Fernando Solórzano—an important provision, because the official candidate, in Nicaragua, was always the successful one. It was hardly a democratic arrangement, and events were to show that it was not even a practical one, but it was perhaps the best that could be devised at the time. It was also agreed that a new constitution would abolish the monopolies which had been one of the most objectionable features of Zelaya's regime, and that Nicaragua and the United States would set up a commission to adjudicate claims arising from this action and all other unsettled claims against the government. To provide funds for payment and for public works, Nicaragua would ask the American government's help in obtaining a customs-guaranteed loan. Finally, the murderers of Cannon and Groce would be punished. These undertakings were embodied in a series of documents that were known as the "Dawson pacts," and the new government formally communicated them to Dawson in a note dated November 5.[32] A constituent assembly chosen at an election in which the Zelaya liberals took no part, unanimously elected Estrada and Díaz as president and vice president, and the United States formally recognized their government when it was inaugurated on January 1, 1911.

The new American Minister, Elliott Northcott, was instructed to negotiate a treaty providing for the customs collectorship and an agreement for the claims commission, and he pressed both matters vigorously. The Claims Commission played an important part in the State Department's financial program, because it would presumably eliminate one of the most troublesome problems that confronted Caribbean governments in their relations with foreign powers. When diplomatic claims were presented, the creditor's government usually accepted the claimant's view of the amount due, and the weak Caribbean states, often the victims of sharp practice or unable to produce their own records of the transactions, found it difficult to resist their demands. The United States was frequently embarrassed by the difficulty of determining whether an American claim really merited its support. The proposed commission would provide an impartial and competent tribunal which might be expected to protect the interests

[31] Adee to Dawson, Oct. 11, 1910, *Foreign Relations*, 1910, p. 763.
[32] For the note, see *Foreign Relations*, 1911, pp. 625–627. The agreements are printed *ibid.*, pp. 652–653.

of all parties.[33] The claimants would be more likely to accept the awards if funds were available from the proposed loan and the customs.

Nicaraguan public opinion was strongly averse to foreign financial control, but the new government was in no position to withstand the Legation's pressure and it wanted the proposed loan. A decree setting up a claims commission, which would be a Nicaraguan court but would have two members appointed by the Secretary of State of the United States and one named by Nicaragua, was approved by the Constituent Assembly in April, 1911.[34] A loan treaty, very similar to the pending treaty with Honduras, was signed on June 6,[35] and was immediately presented to the United States Senate, with a message from President Taft emphasizing its importance as part of a broad plan for the financial rehabilitation and the political stabilization of all Central America. Like the Honduran treaty, it met with strong opposition, and the President's repeated requests for immediate ratification were disregarded.

The treaty with Honduras had been negotiated to conform to an agreement that had previously been worked out with the Honduran government by the bankers. In Nicaragua, the treaty was negotiated first, with the idea of awarding the loan to the bankers who made the best proposal.[36] While it was being negotiated at Managua, Ernest H. Wands, whom the State Department had selected to act as financial adviser to Nicaragua, made a study of the country's financial needs. He also discussed the proposed loan with several bankers in New York, and found that there would be no difficulty in selling the bonds. Speyer and Company, who had been associated with the Ethelburga Syndicate that handled the loan for Zelaya in 1909, seemed eager for the business,[37] and Brown Brothers and Company, who had a large interest in the still unpaid Emery Claim, asked Senator Penrose to intercede with the State Department on their behalf.[38] Both firms were apparently ready to make a loan without insisting on a customs collectorship,[39] but the State Department showed no interest in this idea. Aside from the fact that the interest would have to be higher if the security were less adequate, a collectorship seemed desirable as a means of assuring peace and sound financial administration.

There is no indication that the State Department took any active part in Wands' negotiations with the bankers, but after Wands decided to accept a proposal from Brown Brothers and J. and W. Seligman and Company, Knox asked a New York lawyer who had no connection with either firm to make a careful study of the contracts from the standpoint of the interests of Nicaragua.[40] He had taken the same action in the case of the contracts with Honduras, for he realized the importance of forestalling any accusation that he was helping American bankers to make undue profits at the expense of a Central American government. Under the contracts,

[33] For a discussion of this matter by a man who was an officer of the State Department's Latin American Division and later Minister to Nicaragua, see George T. Weitzel, *American Policy in Nicaragua, Senate Document 42*, 64th Cong., 1st Session, p. 19.

[34] *Foreign Relations*, 1911, p. 631.

[35] For the text, see *Foreign Relations*, 1912, pp. 1074 ff.

[36] Knox explained this to the Senate Committee on Foreign Relations on May 24, 1911, *Foreign Relations*, 1912, p. 594.

[37] Northcott to Knox, Feb. 25, 1911, 817.51/112.

[38] Penrose to Knox, Jan. 26, 1911, 817.51/99.

[39] See Northcott's telegram cited above and the Latin American Division's memorandum of Feb. 21, 1911, 817.51/113 for Speyer's offer, and Wands' letter of July 19, 1911, 817.51/176 for Brown Brothers'.

[40] 817.51/202.

signed on September 1, 1911, the bankers agreed to buy $12,000,000 of five per cent bonds at 90½ per cent of their face value. The proceeds would be used to refund the government's debts, to stabilize the currency, and to meet half of the cost of much needed new railroad lines to the Atlantic Coast and the coffee region of Matagalpa. The remainder of the cost of the railway would be met by the bankers, who would receive in return first mortgage bonds covering the full amount of their contribution and also all of the common stock in the railroad corporation, while the government received non-cumulative, six per cent preferred stock for its contribution. To make the enterprise more attractive, the railroad company was to be given large land-grants along the right of way.[41] The terms of the loan seemed fair, in view of conditions in the money market, and the provisions in connection with the proposed railroads, which would have been profitable to the bankers if all had gone well, were perhaps not unreasonable in view of the risks involved.

There was no possibility that the treaty could be ratified before the United States Congress reconvened in December, and it seemed important to make a start toward Nicaragua's financial rehabilitation in the meantime. One of the most urgent problems was a reform of the currency. The depreciated and fluctuating paper money inherited from the Zelaya regime was a serious handicap to trade, and an important part of Wands' plan was the establishment of a National Bank which would issue new currency on a gold basis. To make this possible, the bankers agreed in a separate contract signed on September 1 to buy one-year, six per cent Nicaraguan treasury bills to the amount of $1,500,000. To secure these, the customs collectorship was to be established at once, under officials appointed by the Nicaraguan government on the nomination of the bankers and after approval by the Secretary of State of the United States. The State Department's files do not show who proposed this temporary arrangement or what part American officials played in its formulation. The bankers later asserted that they accepted it much against their own inclinations,[42] but it is not clear who, if anyone, exerted pressure on them. Officially, the State Department took the position that it had no connection with the short-term loan, and Knox wrote the bankers that his approval of the nomination of the new collector general of customs did not indicate that they would be accorded any support or protection that was not accorded to any legitimate American enterprise abroad.[43] In dealing with the Nicaraguans, however, there was no pretense of lack of interest in the contracts, and the legation at Managua vigorously urged their ratification by the Constituent Assembly.

While the financial program was being worked out, the flimsy political structure set up by the Dawson pacts began to collapse. In April, 1911, when the first constituent assembly, under Chamorro's influence, voted a constitution that greatly curtailed the president's powers, Estrada dissolved it and ordered the election of a new one. This did not improve his situation because Mena, who was Minister of War, was able to pack the new assembly with his own adherents. Estrada then attempted to stage a coup d'état, by arresting Mena and calling on the Liberals for support, but his

[41] The texts of the loan contracts and of later contracts that will be mentioned below were published in the annual *Memorias* of the Ministry of Hacienda y Crédito Público of Nicaragua and also in César Arana's *Compilación de contratos celebrados con los banqueros de Nueva York, con el Ethelburga Syndicate de Londres, y con el Banco Nacional de Nicaragua, Inc.*, 3 volumes, Managua, 1928. There are also copies in the State Department's files in the National Archives.

[42] This statement appears in a cable to their representative in Nicaragua, a copy of which was sent to the State Department by Mr. Mallet-Prevost on June 12, 1912, 817.51/446.

[43] 817.51/256.

plan miscarried and he was forced to resign. Adolfo Díaz thus became President on May 8, 1911, but Mena, through his control of the army, was the real ruler. Díaz found this situation so humiliating that he repeatedly threatened to resign if he did not get more support from the United States,[44] but the American legation gave him little real help, and seemed, in fact, to prefer to work through Mena, who controlled the assembly votes that were needed for the ratification of the financial measures that the United States wished to see adopted. Díaz was consequently compelled not only to co-operate with Mena but to support the latter's presidential ambitions.

Besides the loan contracts, the pending financial measures included a series of amendments to the claims commission decree that had been passed in April. The State Department realized that the cancellation of all of Zelaya's concessions, some of which were valid under Nicaraguan law, would work an injustice on American investors and would cause it trouble in Washington. Concession-holders were already writing to their senators urging that the loan treaty be amended to protect their rights. The Department therefore proposed that no concessions be annulled until the Claims Commission had declared them illegal, and that those which were not illegal should if necessary be expropriated, with compensation. Díaz protested that this would mean that few concessions could be cancelled, but he reluctantly agreed to submit the proposed changes to the Assembly.[45]

Mena evidently hoped that the American government's desire for the approval of its projects might be turned to his own advantage. In September, 1911, he told the American Chargé d'Affaires that some of his followers in the Assembly would not vote to ratify the loan contracts unless they were permitted to elect him as president for the term beginning in 1913, and he asked the Chargé's opinion about this project. Though it was clear that such action would violate the Dawson pacts and would be vigorously opposed by other political groups, the legation was instructed to say that the American government would not concern itself with political questions until the financial legislation had been approved.[46] Mena apparently construed the failure to object to his plan as a tacit consent, for his followers went ahead with his election and then approved the loan contracts and the new claims commission decree. Mena nevertheless promised the legation that he would not accept the election until the American government had expressed its opinion.[47] The Assembly's action, and the American government's failure to take a stand for or against it, encouraged renewed agitation and talk of uprisings among the political groups opposed to the Minister of War. Díaz, unhappy as he was about his own position, thought that the chances for peace would improve if the United States accepted the election, but the State Department for several months deliberately kept the Nicaraguan leaders uncertain about its attitude in the hope of making them more amenable to its suggestions for further financial reforms.[48]

The financial situation clearly needed attention, for it had been growing worse rather than better ever since the revolutionary government took office. Though the

[44] 817.00/1591A, 1611, 1677.

[45] Most of the correspondence about the Claims Commission is printed in Foreign Relations, 1911, pp. 625 ff.

[46] Gunther to Knox, Sept. 5 and Sept. 29, and Adee to Gunther, Sept. 30, 1911, Foreign Relations, 1911, pp. 666–668.

[47] Gunther to Knox, Oct. 7, 1911, 817.00/1702.

[48] This attitude was spelled out in a telegram sent to the American Minister on June 7, 1912, 817.51/464.

Dawson pacts had provided that all claims should be submitted to the proposed commission, the government had paid out great sums to Conservatives who alleged that they had suffered losses under Zelaya. It had dissipated the money left in the treasury by Madriz and much of its current revenue, and was now unable to meet the salaries of its employees or other necessary expenses. The customs collectorship, which started work in December, 1911, offered no immediate relief, because the customs receipts had to be set aside for payment on the bankers' short-term loans and on the Ethelburga bonds. The internal revenues had been counted on to provide money for the regular budget, but these had been reduced to insignificance by graft and bad administration. Worst of all, when foreign experts began to work out the details of the currency reform, they found that large secret issues of paper money had increased the amount outstanding by fifty per cent since Wands had studied the problem. Much, though not all, of this state of affairs could be attributed to officials whom Mena had forced Díaz to appoint and whom the President could not control.

If the whole project of financial rehabilitation were not to collapse, the government would have to have more money for the currency reform and some help in meeting current expenses. Brown Brothers and Seligman consequently agreed in March, 1912, to make a new short term loan of $755,000 for these purposes and to extend for one year the maturity of the 1911 treasury bills. As security they took a lien on all the stock of a company to which the government transferred the railroad line running from the chief cities of the interior to Corinto. They were to manage this company as long as the government owed them money, and they were given an option to buy 51 per cent of its stock. The loan made it possible to go ahead with the currency reform, so that new money, maintained at par with the American dollar, was in circulation early in 1913. The arrangement about the railroad seemed to many Nicaraguans merely another step in the process by which the bankers were obtaining a stranglehold on Nicaragua's economic life, but it is difficult to see how the bankers could have made further loans, at a time when the approval of the pending treaty seemed increasingly doubtful, without protecting their own interests. The idea of selling the railroad seems to have originated with the Nicaraguan government.[49]

In May, 1912, the bankers, on behalf of the Nicaraguan government, signed an important agreement with the London Council of Foreign Bondholders. Under this, the interest on the Ethelburga bonds was reduced from six to five per cent so long as the customs collectorship continued, and about $1,500,000 from the proceeds of the bonds, which had been held in London for eventual use in railroad building, was released to the Nicaraguan government. The agreement meant that the customs collectorship would probably continue indefinitely even though the treaty with the United States were not ratified.

Both the treaty with Nicaragua and that with Honduras were still in the hands of the Senate's Committee on Foreign Relations, where they were encountering opposition from the Democrats and the Republican insurgents. Knox had made extraordinary efforts to win votes for both of them,[50] but in March, 1912, when he visited Nicaragua, he was so impressed by the situation there that he was ready to sacrifice the Honduran treaty if he could obtain approval of the Nicaraguan one.[51] All of his efforts were in vain, for on May 8 the Committee defeated by a tie vote a motion for

[49] Gunther to Knox, December 20, 1911, 817.77/12.
[50] Early in 1912, for example, he wrote a personal letter to every Senator, 817.51/297A.
[51] See his telegram to the Department from Managua, March 11, 1912, 817.51/386.

a favorable report. There was thus little further hope for the large loan on which all of the plans for Nicaragua's financial rehabilitation were based.

Meanwhile the political situation had continued to deteriorate in Nicaragua. It is not clear that the American government could have prevented the catastrophe that ensued, but it seems strange that it should not have foreseen the consequences of its failure to take a stand on Mena's election. Probably it was uncertain what course to take, for as late as June, 1912, the State Department told George T. Weitzel, who had succeeded Northcott as Minister, that it continued "to regard this whole question in the spirit of the Dawson agreements" and attached "full value" to Mena's promise to relinquish the presidency if the United States asked him to do so. If it seemed necessary, the Minister might say just enough to preclude the possibility that the Department's silence might be interpreted as meaning a change in its attitude.[52] In defense of the State Department it should be noted that Mena could claim the support of three of the five leaders who under the Dawson pacts were to choose the official candidate to succeed Díaz,[53] so that his election would have been in accord with the pacts if it had been by popular vote rather than by action of the Constituent Assembly. Furthermore, a refusal to accept his election could probably have been made good only by a much more energetic intervention in Nicaragua's internal affairs than the administration at Washington then wished to contemplate.

By June, 1912, Mena's position was growing weaker because several members of the Assembly had shifted their allegiance to Chamorro. Mena apparently suspected that Díaz might also turn against him, and on July 29 he attempted to seize the fort at Managua, which was commanded by an officer loyal to the President. Failing in this, he fled to Granada, where he had already stored most of the Government's arms and ammunition. Much of the army followed him, and the Liberals soon began to join the revolt. Díaz at once asked that the American government "guarantee with its forces security for the property of American citizens in Nicaragua and that it extend its protection to all the inhabitants of the Republic."[54] A small force of Marines was landed and some thousands more were ordered to proceed to Nicaragua as fast as possible.

Before they could arrive, the situation grew more alarming. A rebel attack on Managua was repulsed, after four days of destructive bombardment, but the capital's communications with the outside world were cut off when the Liberals at León seized that city and massacred the government's garrison. On August 20, fifty American Marines and bluejackets who were attempting to go from Managua to Corinto were attacked by a mob at León and forced to abandon their train and return to Managua on foot. All foreigners in the country clamored for protection, and the position of the Americans working in the customs and the National Bank and the railroad seemed especially dangerous. President Taft likened the situation to the Boxer rebellion in China, and he would have sent an infantry regiment to Nicaragua if the War and Navy Departments had not both objected.[55]

The army was not needed, for by the first week in September there were enough Marines in Nicaragua to open the railroad line from Corinto to Managua and to en-

[52] Telegram of June 7, 1912, 817.51/464.

[53] Díaz, Fernando Solórzano, who had been elected Vice President on the ticket with Mena, and Mena himself.

[54] *Foreign Relations,* 1912, p. 1032.

[55] 817.00/1904, 1939, 1940A.

able the United States to consider what it could do to restore peace. Wilson, who was Acting Secretary of State throughout the period of the revolt, wanted to take vigorous action against Mena, in the hope of restoring some of the prestige that the American government had lost, in his opinion, as the result of recent disturbances in Cuba and Mexico and Panama and "anti-imperialist activities" in the United States Senate. He consequently persuaded President Taft to authorize the publication of a statement denouncing the revolutionists and promising support to the constituted government of Nicaragua.[56] This did much to discourage the rebels, whose operations were already hampered by the Marines' control of the railroad line and by the fact that the American commander had forbidden another attack on Managua. Mena, who was seriously ill, surrendered to Admiral Sutherland at Granada.

The Liberals still held León, and a Liberal named Zeledón was entrenched in a reputedly impregnable position on a hill overlooking the railroad between Managua and Granada. Weitzel thought that the Marines should compel Zeledón to evacuate this position to assure the free use of the railroad, but Admiral Sutherland, who had repeatedly commented unfavorably on the inactivity of Díaz' army, had no desire to do the Nicaraguan government's fighting for it.[57] At the insistence of the State Department, however, the Navy instructed him to act. When the Nicaraguan government's own forces failed to take the hill, after some days of not very vigorous efforts, the American Marines stormed it on October 4, losing four dead and seven wounded in the battle. Three more Americans were killed in street fighting at León on October 6, in spite of the Liberals' previous promise to surrender the city.

The war was over. The greater part of the Marines remained in Nicaragua only long enough to restore order in the towns along the railroad and to prevent the Conservatives from avenging themselves on their opponents in the first flush of victory. Weitzel insisted, however, that at least 100 Marines be left at Managua because he thought that a complete withdrawal would be "construed as the tacit consent of the United States to renew hostilities."[58] This legation guard was to be an important factor in Nicaraguan-American relations in years to come.

When the revolution ended, less than three months remained of Díaz' presidential term. The Dawson pacts had stipulated that his successor should be chosen at a popular election, and Wilson suggested that this should be supervised by the United States. He thought that representatives of "the worst elements" should be excluded as candidates, but that it was important for the United States to make it clear that it was not hostile to the Liberal party, though it did oppose Mena and the Zelayistas who were "enemies of the peace and welfare" of Nicaragua.[59] Weitzel, however, thought that any attempt at supervision would be unwise. He pointed out that real elections were unknown in Nicaragua, and that there was neither enough time nor available personnel to set up an organization that could assure fair play.[60] An election without supervision would of course mean a victory for the official candidate. How to select this candidate was a problem, because the committee that should have made the

[56] Wilson to the President, August 30, 1912, 817.00/1940A. The text of the statement, issued by the Legation at Managua, is printed in *Foreign Relations*, 1912, p. 1043.

[57] Weitzel to the Secretary of State, Sept. 20, 1912, 817.00/2205, and Sutherland's radiogram to the Navy Department, Sept. 23, enclosed with Navy Department's letter to State Department, Sept. 26, *ibid./*2016.

[58] Weitzel to the Secretary of State, Dec. 14, 1912, *Foreign Relations*, 1912, p. 1069.

[59] Wilson to Weitzel, Sept. 25, 1912, 817.00/2017A.

[60] Weitzel to the Secretary of State, Oct. 9, 1912, *Foreign Relations*, 1912, 817.00/2081.

selection under the Dawson pacts could hardly act when two of its five members were in exile, and the revolutionary leaders who were still in Nicaragua could not agree among themselves. Chamorro was probably the choice of a great majority of the Conservatives, but he was opposed by the group in the government that wanted to re-elect Díaz. Furthermore, his long record as a militant revolutionist made him particularly unacceptable to the Liberals, who would be more inclined to remain peaceful under a tolerant chief executive like Díaz. Weitzel consequently persuaded Chamorro to withdraw in Díaz' favor, in return for a promise of appointment as Minister to Washington.[61] When the election was held, the Liberals refused to participate, and Díaz was chosen as President for the four year term beginning on January 1, 1913.

The revolution made the financial situation worse than ever. The bankers had given Díaz some help during the war, by agreeing to a $100,000 loan from the new National Bank and by turning over part of the customs collections that should have been applied to the reduction of their earlier loans. They were promised in return an option on the 49% of the railroad stock not covered by their existing option, but this was rejected by the Nicaraguan Congress. They also insisted that the National Bank take over the collection of the internal revenues, an experiment that failed because the Bank could not get co-operation from the local police. They were reluctant to advance any more money, because they could obtain no information about the policy of the administration that was soon to take office at Washington, and early in 1913 Díaz threatened to break off relations with them and to turn to British bankers for aid. The local British bankers, who resented the competition of the new National Bank and opposed the currency reform because it interfered with their exchange speculations, had probably encouraged this idea, but it was vigorously opposed by the State Department.[62] Early in March, 1913, Brown Brothers and Seligman finally agreed to release for four months the customs receipts that would otherwise have been paid to them. This enabled the Díaz government to survive while Secretary Bryan was painfully reaching the conclusion that he would have to continue his predecessor's policy in Nicaragua.[63]

Another legacy to the incoming administration at Washington was the Chamorro-Weitzel Treaty, signed February 8, 1913. Under this, the United States was to buy for $3,000,000 an option to build an interoceanic canal through Nicaragua and a right to establish naval bases in the Gulf of Fonseca and on the Corn Islands. The American government probably had little real interest in the idea of a second canal[64] or in the proposed bases, but Weitzel thought that the treaty would be helpful as an indication that Díaz still had the support and confidence of the United States.[65] Later, when Secretary Bryan revived the idea of buying the canal option, both governments seemed interested in it principally as a means of solving some of Nicaragua's financial problems, but the treaty as it was negotiated by Weitzel provided that the $3,000,000 should be used for education and public works rather than for current needs. The

[61] The writer obtained this information from well-informed sources in Nicaragua in 1914. Weitzel did not report this agreement to the State Department, but his despatch of Nov. 5 shows that he took a hand in the selection of the conservative ticket. *Foreign Relations*, 1912, p. 1063.

[62] 817.51/522A.

[63] For a good account of Secretary Bryan's policy see Selig Adler's article, "Bryan and Wilsonian Caribbean Penetration," *HAHR*, XX (May, 1940), pp. 198–226.

[64] See General Goethals' opinion as expressed in his letter to the War Department on January 4, 1913, 817.12/8.

[65] Memorandum to Assistant Secretary Phillips, Jan. 9, 1917, 817.51/914.

treaty was rushed to the United States Senate, but no action was taken before the session ended on March 4.

The amount of the indemnity for the murder of Cannon and Groce, which had hardly been discussed since the fall of Madriz, was also settled in February, 1913, by the Nicaraguan government's agreement to pay $10,000 in each case. The claims were not actually paid until 1918, but in the meantime the State Department continued the small allotment that it had been making out of its own funds to Groce's Nicaraguan widow.[66]

With this review of what happened in Nicaragua between 1909 and 1913, we should be in a position to consider the question whether Dollar Diplomacy in that country helped American financial interests to make improper profits at the expense of the local community. The principal charges, of course, were directed against the New York bankers. Many Nicaraguans, who saw their customs service and their railroad and the new National Bank being managed by foreigners, had the impression that the bankers were systematically taking over everything of value in the country; and even the Nicaraguan government frequently complained that the bankers were unwilling to give the government desperately needed help except on onerous terms. The amount of money that the two firms obtained from Nicaragua up to March, 1913, was nevertheless very small. What they received was six per cent interest on the $1,500,000 loan of 1911 and six per cent interest plus one per cent commission on the $755,000 credit opened in March, 1912. The purchase and resale of part of the railroad and bank stock, from which they made a larger profit, took place during the Wilson administration.

The bankers had gone into the business because they hoped to handle a large bond issue and to go into partnership with Nicaragua in building the proposed railroad to the Atlantic Coast. It might be argued that the arrangement about the Atlantic railroad would have been a one-sided one if the line had been built and had proved a financial success. On the other hand, it would have been unreasonable, and in fact improper, to ask banking institutions to undertake a venture that did not seem likely to be profitable, and the State Department, as we have seen, made a special effort to make sure that the contracts were not unfair or injurious to Nicaragua. The enterprise was at best highly speculative, for renewed political disorder could easily have made the railroad unprofitable and could even have made the security offered by the customs collectorship of doubtful value. One suspects, indeed, that the fascination of cooperating with the American government in a constructive enterprise in a strange country outweighed sound business judgment in leading the bankers into it. When the larger plan fell through, with the rejection of the loan treaty, the bankers would seem to deserve credit rather than condemnation for continuing to help Nicaragua with the currency reform and with her fiscal problems, which involved an expenditure of time and effort that could hardly have been justified by any expectation of further profits.

Other American financial interests seem to have benefited little from the State Department's program. The greater part of the American capital in Nicaragua in 1909 was invested in concessions granted by Zelaya, which the State Department at first encouraged the revolutionary government simply to annul, but then arranged to have passed on by the Claims Commission. The correspondence about the establishment of the Claims Commission strongly suggests that the American government was

[66] The correspondence about the claims is in Decimal File 317.112G 89.

more interested in the adjustment of claims on terms favorable to Nicaragua and in a way that would make it unneccessary for the American or other governments to press them, than it was in collecting money for American claimants. The Commission itself could certainly not be accused of undue generosity to foreigners. North American claimants were awarded $538,749 for claims aggregating $7,576,564. Other foreigners who submitted their claims, in spite of the fact that several European governments objected to the whole procedure, fared little if any better. Nicaraguans, on the other hand, were awarded $1,217,650 for claims amounting to $5,491,533.[67] For several years no funds were made available for the payment of any but the very smallest awards, most of which were to Nicaraguans. Even the Emery Claim, which because of the arbitral procedure was technically a debt owed to the government of the United States, went unpaid so long as the Taft administration was in office.

It seems evident in fact that those who directed American policy were less interested in the protection of American investors than in the attainment of their political objectives. They thought that the customs collectorship and other financial reforms would promote peace and better government in Nicaragua. Since they were confident that decent, law-abiding people in Nicaragua would see this, and that opposition could come only from "professional revolutionists" and other groups that had a vested interest in disorder and governmental corruption, they had few scruples about using force to impose their ideas. Apparently they had little thought of establishing any permanent political control. When Estrada, in February, 1911, proposed a virtual protectorate, under which the United States would have co-operated in holding elections and suppressing revolutions, he received a friendly but non-committal reply.[68] Díaz also urged a North American protectorate in December, 1911, with a similar result.[69] The officials of the State Department, whatever their personal views, realized that such an arrangement would meet with strong opposition in the United States Senate and from public opinion in both countries.

Whatever we may say about the Taft administration's motives, however, the result of its policies was clearly unfortunate. It is true that the ousting of Zelaya and the intervention of 1912 gave Nicaragua several years of rather uneasy peace, and for a time strengthened the hands of the United States in its efforts to obtain respect for the 1907 treaties. Wars between the Central American republics became a thing of the past and revolutions within the various countries were discouraged by the fear of North American interference. In Nicaragua itself, the customs collectorship and the currency reform helped to improve the government's financial condition, though not until the United States had furnished additional help under the Bryan-Chamorro canal option treaty and imposed additional controls through the financial plan of 1917. On the other hand the policies which the Taft administration inaugurated, and which the Wilson administration continued, were unfair to the Nicaraguan Liberals and caused distrust and resentment in other American countries.

The intervention left the United States committed to the support of a minority government in Nicaragua. The legation guard of one hundred Marines, which was

[67] For a résumé of the Claims Commission's work, see Otto Schoenrich's article, "The Nicaraguan Mixed Claims Commission," *American Journal of International Law*, IX (1915), pp. 858–869. Judge Schoenrich was President of the Commission.

[68] Weitzel to Knox, Feb. 25, 1911, and March 4, 1911; and Wilson to Weitzel, April 21, 1911, *Foreign Relations*, 1911, pp. 655–656, 658. Weitzel's despatch of Feb. 25, which is not printed in full in *Foreign Relations*, is filed under 817.00/1540.

[69] *Foreign Relations*, 1911, pp. 670–671.

kept at Managua after the 1912 revolt, became a symbol of the determination of the United States not to permit this government to be overthrown by revolution and its presence enabled the Conservatives to remain in power, by running elections in a way that gave the Liberals no chance to win. This situation grew increasingly embarrassing to the State Department, but for more than ten years the Department could not make up its mind either to intervene more actively in Nicaragua's affairs in order to compel the holding of a free election, or to invite a revolution by simply withdrawing the Marines. After the Marines were withdrawn in 1925, there was a bloody civil war which culminated in another, and from our standpoint a much more unfortunate, American intervention.

Part IV

AMERICAN
LEADERSHIP IN
WORLD AFFAIRS

15 / Diplomacy and War Plans in the United States, 1890–1917

J. A. S. Grenville

Recently, historians of American foreign relations have turned their attention to the activities of military and naval staff officers in influencing foreign policy. The work of intelligence gathering organizations as well as of planning staffs in the army and navy have become the subject of a substantial number of books and articles. In the next article, the English historian, John A. S. Grenville, asks some provocative questions with regard to how the American army and navy responded to the country's emergence as a great world power during the early Twentieth Century: How did the United States Government expect to defend its recently acquired territories located on the outer perimeter, namely the Philippine Islands? How well were strategic plans of the army and navy coordinated with the general decision-making process operating within the Executive Branch of government responsible for foreign policy? Grenville's article presents much valuable information, but of equal importance it offers valuable suggestions for further research concerning the important relationships between military-naval planning and foreign policy.

For further reading: W. R. Braisted, *The United States Navy in the Pacific 1897–1909* (Austin: 1958); Kenneth Bourne, *Britain and the Balance of Power in North America 1815–1908* (Berkeley: 1967); A. E. Campbell, *Great Britain and the United States 1895–1903* (London: 1960); Charles S. Campbell, Jr., *Anglo-American Understanding 1898–1903* (Baltimore: 1957); John A. S. Grenville and G. B. Young, *Politics, Strategy and Diplomacy: Studies in American Foreign Policy 1873–1917* (New Haven: 1966); William Livezey, *Mahan on Sea Power* (Norman: 1947); Seward, Livermore, "The American Navy as a Factor in World Politics 1903–1913," *American Historical Review*, LXIII (July, 1958), 863–879 and "Theodore Roosevelt, the American Navy and the Venezuelan Crisis of 1902–1903," *American Historical Review*, LI (April, 1946), 452–471.

John A. S. Grenville is Professor of International History at the University of Leeds. This article is here reprinted with the permission of the author and of the Royal Historical Society of London. From the *Transactions of The Royal Historical Society, Fifth Series,* Volume II.

In 1890 America was at peace, the golden age appeared to be at hand; unfettered by the miseries of European strife, in prosperous rather than splendid isolation, the American people confidently looked forward to an even more exciting future.[1] But a new age of danger was rapidly approaching; the nineteenth-century conditions of American safety—geographical isolation, the British fleet, as it turned out, the 'hostage' of Canada in American hands, and the balance of power in Europe—were passing away. The era which had seen the new world fattening on the follies of the old was coming to an end; soon the follies of the old world impinged on the peace and prosperity of the new. Within three decades the contest for world power fought out in Europe, and the rise of the youngest of the great nations, Japan, was to endanger the safety of the United States. Yet few Americans recognized the full import of these changes and the need for fresh policies.

In the conduct of foreign affairs one of the most essential considerations must always be to adjust policy, sometimes rapidly, to changing conditions. Now we know that the American people remained overwhelmingly isolationist in sentiment long after Washington's admonition to avoid entangling alliances had lost its validity. What, however, of America's leaders? How well did they perceive the new configuration of power and politics which faced America in the twentieth century? Much study has been devoted to this subject; but the contribution to American foreign policy of those men, the generals and admirals, whose very business it was to consider in concrete terms the shifting balance of world power, is virtually an unknown chapter, although this contribution was an important one. From the recently opened records of the United States Army and Navy Departments we may now attempt to answer one vital question, namely, how far strategic advice was responsible for the new rôle played by the United States in world affairs during the first two decades of the twentieth century. In the search for what Kennan has called "the realities" of American policy a few weeks spent examining the military records are worth many years of theorizing.[2]

Until the 1890's the American armed forces were considered not so much as the country's first line of defence against outside aggression, but as a police force to subdue troublesome Indians and Mexicans. In 1890, the same year as the Kaiser sensed the coming age of *Weltpolitik*, a number of men in America tried simultaneously to awaken the American people to the dangers. The intellectual giant among them was Captain Alfred Thayer Mahan.

When he published, in 1890, his *Influence of Sea-Power upon History*, Mahan was a lecturer at the Naval War College. He believed that the American continent was threatened both from the West and from the East. Germany with her expanding population and boundless energy, he thought, would sooner or later attempt to colonize South America, while the teeming millions of China and Japan might burst across

[1] The research for this paper was undertaken while I was a member of the research seminar of Professor Samuel Flagg Bemis at the University of Yale during the session 1958–59 under the auspices of the Harkness Fund of the Commonwealth Fund. I wish to express my indebtedness to the Fund, to Professor Bemis for his wise counsel, and to the historical sections of the United States Army and Navy Departments, especially to Admiral E. M. Eller for his courtesy in enabling me to examine hitherto security-classified records.

[2] The first book to do this, although not all the essential documents were available to the author, is William R. Braisted's scholarly and excellent study, *The United States in the Pacific, 1897–1909* (University of Texas Press, 1958). W. Schilling's *Admirals and Foreign Policy, 1913–1919* (unpublished Yale University Ph.D. thesis, 1956), and J. A. S. Grenville and G. B. Young, *Politics, Strategy and American Diplomacy* (Yale University Press, 1966), are also useful.

the barrier of the Pacific Ocean. With the construction of the isthmian canal across Central America, the Caribbean, he also prophesied, would become one of the great life-lines of trade and consequently a region of intense international rivalry. He warned that, unless the United States possessed a dominant fleet when the canal was built, the canal would prove a source of danger rather than of safety and welfare. The United States must therefore not rest content until she controlled the canal itself, and guarded the approaches to it with a powerful fleet of battleships.[3] Behind the advocacy of the annexation of Cuba and Hawaii lay not so much a growing American imperialism as a concern for the safety of the isthmian canal and the American continent.

The same conclusion had been reached in the same year (1890) by a group of naval officers called together by Secretary of the Navy Benjamin Tracy. They advocated an ocean-going battleship fleet in place of the floating coastal batteries, which the American battleships of those days virtually were. In the years which immediately followed, Mahan's ideas were translated into political action by a number of younger politicians, of whom the most prominent were Theodore Roosevelt and Henry Cabot Lodge. Before 1898 these proponents of the so-called 'large policy' did not so much seek to lay the basis of an American empire overseas as to provide for the safety of the American continents in the new realities of power and politics as revealed to them by Mahan.

Theodore Roosevelt's opportunity to shape policy came when Cabot Lodge and his supporters persuaded President McKinley to appoint him Assistant Secretary of the Navy. In the Navy Department "T. R." had, as he would have put it, a "bully time"—but according to an entry in the private diary of Secretary of the Navy Long, Teddy went about his business like 'a bull in a china shop'.

Hitherto, in the absence of other evidence from the Naval archives, it has been customary to credit Roosevelt with a large share of responsibility for the war with Spain and especially for the involvement of the United States in the Far East through the acquisition of the Philippines. Was it not Roosevelt who on 25 February 1898 sent the famous telegram to Commodore Dewey to prepare for an attack on the Philippines? This decision has rightly been regarded by historians as a momentous step in United States policy, and it was therefore tempting to look on it as part of a great expansion of America overseas, brought about, or plotted, as some would have it, by Roosevelt, the supporters of the 'large policy' and Commodore Dewey.

This view, as I have already tried to show, does not fit in with the actual objective which the proponents of the large policy had in mind—the defence of the American continents. Nor does it fit in with the evidence discovered in the Navy Department archives. Incredible as it may seem, the attack on the Philippines was a secondary consideration, a by-product of the war with Spain.

The idea of attacking the Philippines was neither Roosevelt's nor Dewey's but the brain-child of a young naval lieutenant, William Warren Kimball, whose name ought to have, but certainly has not yet, found its way into the history books. In 1896, that is before Roosevelt had joined the Navy Department, Kimball had drawn up a war plan providing, in the even of a conflict with Spain, for a simultaneous attack on the Spanish possessions in the Caribbean and in the Pacific. The main theatre of War was designated as Cuban waters. An attack on the Philippines was

---

[3] For Mahan's views on these points see especially his *The Interest of America in Sea Power Present and Future* (Boston, 1897).

intended as a secondary, almost incidental, operation, to be undertaken merely to humiliate and embarrass Spain. In 1898 Kimball's general plan, in the absence of another, won Navy Secretary Long's and Roosevelt's approval. Here then is a most striking example of how a war plan, drawn up by a young naval officer, altered the course of history.[4]

It was Kimball's plan which Roosevelt set in motion on 25 February 1898. Only after Dewey's victory at Manila Bay on the glorious first of May did the exponents of the 'large policy' suddenly become converts to the 'larger policy' of carrying the American flag across the Pacific. In the decision to retain the Philippines they played an important rôle, but strategic considerations and a number of officers, members of a newly created Strategy Board, played the greater part.

Shortly before the outbreak of hostilities, Long had recognized that the organization of the Navy Department made it difficult to conduct war operations efficiently. The hydra-headed administration consisted of six boards, over each of which presided a naval officer, jealously guarding the power of his own department. It was not always easy to move a ship in time of peace, as the commanding captain was liable to receive quite contradictory orders from more than one bureau chief. Such a division of command would have proved disastrous in wartime. But Secretary Long despaired of reforming the system radically, and so, in March 1898, he created instead a special Strategy or War Board, composed at first of Roosevelt and three bureau chiefs, Captains Crowninshield and Barker, and Commander Clover. After Roosevelt's departure Mahan and Admiral Sicard joined the Board, replacing Captain Barker and Commander Clover. The Board's task was to act in a purely advisory capacity. Yet from this modest beginning developed the General Board, whose members exerted a decisive influence on the overall American strategic planning, down to the American entry into the First World War.

In May 1898 the Board sought to strengthen Dewey's position at Manila. After the news had reached them that Admiral Camara was collecting the remnants of the Spanish fleet, whose destination, they feared, might be the Philippine Islands, the Board advised Secretary Long to secure Dewey's lines of communication by the acquisition of the island of Guam. In May 1898 McKinley ordered troop transports to Manila and to Guam to support Dewey. Thus the exigencies of war drove America into a deeper Far Eastern commitment. When eventually the armistice of 12 August 1898 brought the war to an end, the United States found herself in occupation of Cuba, Puerto Rico, Guam and the Philippines. But whereas the military situation in the Caribbean reinforced a concept of American policy long cherished, the state of affairs in the Pacific was brought about largely by the adoption of Kimball's war plan and the strategic advice of the War Board during the course of the conflict. No concept of American diplomacy lay behind the occupation of a part of the Philippine archipelago and the consequent American involvement in Far Eastern rivalries.

President McKinley now faced the entirely new and unexpected problem of what to do with the Spanish possessions in the Pacific. The American Commissioners sailing for Paris to negotiate a peace were given clear instructions to implement American

---

[4] War with Spain 1896. General Consideration of the War, the Results desired and the consequent kind of operations to be undertaken. Plan by W. W. Kimball, Lt. U.S. Navy, Staff Intelligence Officer, June 1, 1896. Navy Department, National Archives, Washington. See also Braisted, *ibid.* For a recent discussion, see John A. S. Grenville, "American Naval Preparations for War with Spain, 1896–1898," *Journal of American Studies*, II (1968), 33–47.

policy in the Caribbean as stated before the war, that is to secure Spain's renunciation of sovereignty over her Caribbean possessions, but their instructions concerning the Philippines were vague. The War Board had warned that their occupation constituted a major burden for the United States, and McKinley was reluctant to assume it. Nevertheless, other considerations besides strategic ones led McKinley in the succeeding months to insist on the acquisition of the whole of the Philippine archipelago.

By an extraordinary coincidence the Far East had become the cockpit of European rivalries just at about the same time as the Cuban-Spanish-American War. Germany, not content with a gradual growth of economic influence in China, had proceeded to rob the Manchu Empire of Kiaochow. This greed ushered in a new era of European imperialism in China. Russia grabbed Port Arthur, and Britain, to restore the balance, took over Weihai-Wei from the Japanese. By the summer of 1898 the partition of China seemed probable. Special American business interests were much alarmed by the development and from the winter of 1897 onwards bombarded the State Department with petitions. America's great market of the future, they believed, lay in China. The possession of the Philippines appeared to them a providential base, from which America might make her influence felt on the mainland of Asia.

Then the exponents of the "large policy" added their voice to the general clamour. Less than a week after the battle of Manila Bay, Cabot Lodge hailed Dewey's victory as giving the United States "a foothold in the East," and as offering vaster possibilities "than anything that has happened to this country since the annexation of Louisiana";[5] while Roosevelt enthusiastically replied from the troopship that was carrying him to Cuba that the war must not be concluded before Cuba, Puerto Rico and the Philippines were taken from Spain. Another influential member of the group, Cushman K. Davis, Chairman of the Senate Foreign Relations Committee, ardently desired to see the United States keep the Philippines, and was anxious lest a weak President and the Peace Commissioners in Paris, surrounded by "sexless cosmopolites" and engaged in "guzzling" and "guttling," as he put it, might lose sight of America's real interests.[6]

McKinley spent his time earnestly praying for an answer to the puzzling problem of the Pacific, while Cabot Lodge went in and out of the White House talking hard at him. As the President saw it, the United States had assumed responsibility for the Philippines and could neither escape the white man's burden nor hand the rebels over to the vengeance of Spain. Moreover, if the United States withdrew from the Philippines, the islands would no longer remain in the hands of a weak power. The presence of Admiral Diederichs' German squadron, the ships of the other European powers, and of Japan, served notice that, if America gave them up, one of these countries would try to grab them. At first McKinley was inclined to limit American demands to the island of Luzon, but in the end, having first convinced himself that the Almighty and the American public demanded that the United States flag should remain there, he gave way to these various pressures and instructed the Peace Commissioners to demand the whole of the Philippines. When on 6 February 1899 the Senate, by a narrow margin, confirmed the treaty of peace, the United States became a Far Eastern power.

During the next five years, that is from 1899 to 1903, the Administration endeavoured to adjust American policy to the entirely new state of affairs brought about by

[5] John A. Garraty, *Henry Cabot Lodge* (New York, Knopf, 1953), p. 197.
[6] Garraty, *op. cit.*, p. 199.

the war with Spain. An army was despatched to suppress the Philippine rising, and Cuba became a protectorate at the same time. With consummate skill Secretary of State John Hay sought to strengthen America's position by diplomatic means. The only European power with possessions and naval forces in the Caribbean was now Great Britain. Fortunately it so happened that Britain, hard pressed by Russia and France, was just at this time trying to concentrate her military and naval forces; and the British Cabinet was thus ready to lend a more sympathetic ear to American aspirations. By the Hay-Pauncefote treaty of January 1902, Hay not only secured British assent to the exclusive American control over the projected isthmian canal but also in reality the British recognition of American predominance in the Caribbean. The treaty paved the way for Roosevelt's coup in Panama a year later.[7]

The problem confronting Hay in the Pacific and in China was infinitely more grave. In this vast region the United States not only faced a friendly Britain but also other European great powers as well as Japan, each one of them powerful enough to despatch America's weak military forces to the bottom of the ocean. Hay's well-known Open Door Notes of 1899 and 1900 thus were intended to preserve America's interests in China by purely diplomatic means. By enunciating as the two principles of United States policy the support of equal commercial opportunity and the maintenance of the integrity of China, and by seeking to give these principles some international sanctions Hay, like President Monroe before him, had announced to the world the United States' intentions without possessing the necessary military force to implement them. But whereas America's military power caught up with President Monroe's doctrine, the same was not true of the Hay doctrine. The acquisition of the Philippines and Hay's notes in effect led the United States into a Far Eastern quandary, from which there seemed no escape until some four decades later America's China policy lay in ruins.

The great need to build up America's military might in this new era of American policy was not lost on the more far-seeing men of McKinley's generation, but only when a President, acutely conscious of the realities of force that underlie diplomacy, entered the White House did the executive provide real leadership to the nation. That moment came when Roosevelt succeeded to the Presidency in 1901. Roosevelt never ceased to strive to convince Congress and the nation that the defence of America's interests required above all a large fighting fleet, and that the determination and ability to go to war was the best guarantee of peace.

The younger naval and army officers also did battle against a military machine that seemed totally inadequate for modern needs. The war with Spain had underlined the need for adequate staff work and the success of the War Board had pointed the way for the future. Among the most persistent advocates of a general staff for the Navy was Captain H. C. Taylor. He had first laid plans for such a staff before Roosevelt in May 1897; now in 1900 he brought the idea once more to the attention of Secretary Long. Long, however, was reluctant to risk a fight with his entrenched bureau chiefs, hesitant about allowing the professional officers wide powers outside civilian control, and rightly dubious whether Congress could be brought to approve the scheme. Consequently he compromised, and in March 1900 created a Board, known as the General Board, which possessed no executive functions, but was to serve as a purely advisory council which was constitutionally confined to considering

[7] See J. A. S. Grenville, "Great Britain and the Isthmian Canal, 1898–1901," *American Historical Review,* lxi (1955).

such problems of strategy as the Secretary of the Navy might refer to it.[8] Under the dynamic leadership of Admiral Dewey, its first President, the Board, whose other members were the President of the Naval War College, the Chief of the Bureau of Navigation and the Chief of Naval Intelligence, soon outgrew these limitations. It became the chief military council of the nation, advising successive Presidents on the grand strategy which the country must follow to preserve her present interests and to provide for her expanding needs in the challenging future. The influence of the Board on America's foreign policy was profound. Just as Mahan had dominated strategic thought in the 1890's, so Dewey was the intellectual giant who bestrode the years from 1900 until, in 1914, a stroke curtailed his effectiveness. His service to the nation during the war of 1898 is well known and was lavishly rewarded by his countrymen, but his infinitely more important contribution to national policy in later years still remains to be recognized by the historian.

The army was until the outbreak of the First World War very much the weak sister of the services. The defence of the United States was regarded primarily as a naval problem, yet the garrisoning of the outlying American possessions involved the army also in new responsibilities. Weak in numbers, the army had hitherto coped successfully with Mexicans and Indians, but had been caught woefully unprepared by the war with Spain. With no strategy board to co-ordinate their efforts, the chiefs of the army bureaux at the War Department had proved quite unequal to the crisis.

Just as in the navy, however, a few able and young army officers were alive to the need to reorganize the War Department. Elihu Root, appointed Secretary of War in 1899 to still their complaints and to meet the criticisms of Congress investigating the scandals of 1898, was finally responsible in 1903 for the creation of a General Staff. His staff borrowed the prestige of the Prussian name without allowing it to enjoy any of its power. Indeed he leant rather more heavily on the ideas of an Oxford Professor, Spenser Wilkinson, who in 1890 had written a remarkable book, *The Brain of an Army*. The influence of the Army General Staff on American strategic and foreign policy before the First World War was in fact very slight. Yet it became obvious that some degree of army co-operation would be necessary if the navy was to play its rôle, since the defence of naval bases was a problem requiring the help of soldiers. To meet this need the year 1903 also saw the creation of the Joint Army and Navy Board, presided over by the indomitable Dewey. As if an omen for the future, the first years of inter-service co-operation proved a lamentable failure.

These three staff organizations were charged with the responsibility for formulating America's strategic policy in the new picture of power and politics. Their success would depend in large part on their ability to assess the probable development of international relations accurately. Unfortunately the cardinal truth escaped them. They failed to recognize that the growing rivalries of Europe in the Caribbean aided the United States in pursuing a policy of dominance, while in the Pacific it undermined United States security. The doctrine laid down by the strategists from first to last, on the other hand, declared that until the United States possessed a fleet powerful enough to be divided between the two oceans, the battlefleet would have to be stationed on the Atlantic seaboard ready to enforce the Monroe Doctrine and to meet any conceivable European threat of invasion.

Every naval officer had taken to heart Mahan's teaching that economic rivalries

[8] Harold and Margaret Sprout, *The Rise of American Naval Power*, (Princeton University Press, 1946), p. 247.

were the true cause of global conflict, and then, by a process of applying "the precepts of history," it seemed a logical conclusion to regard Germany and England as the ultimate mortal foes of the United States. All naval war plans of the period were based on an application of Mahan's 'doctrines', however absurd the conclusion to which they led. Consequently this slavish imitation of Mahan's historical techniques helped to warp American strategic thought.

Roosevelt was an outstanding *Realpolitiker*, regarding as worthless a policy which was not backed by force to maintain it and if necessary by threat of war. His estimate of the Kaiser's ambitions made it appear likely to him that one day Germany would attempt to colonize portions of South America. Consequently he approved of the policy of retaining the undivided battlefleet in the Atlantic Ocean. His diplomacy, moreover, sought in a more forceful way than Hay's to secure for the United States every strategic vantage point in the Caribbean. With this end in view he took advantage of a revolution in Colombia to occupy the territory through which the Panama Canal was destined to run. At the same time he seconded with great vigour and considerable success the policy of the General Board for a large battleship fleet.

During the first three years of his office, Roosevelt, strangely enough, paid scant attention to the Far East. He was content to leave the Philippine difficulties to his Secretary of War, Taft, and the Chinese question to Hay. Russia rather than Japan appeared to be menacing the open door in China, and the conclusion of the Anglo-Japanese alliance in 1902, an alliance which ultimately proved disastrous to Anglo-American interests in the Far East, was welcomed in Washington as tending to uphold the integrity of the Manchu Empire. The strategists, moreover, took a decidedly unrealistic and rosy view of America's Far Eastern position. The early war plans of 1903 and 1904 providing for the defence of the Philippines were intended to meet a European foe rather than Japan. The General Board had then decided on the establishment of a first-class naval base in the Philippines, and selected Olongapo in Subic Bay as the most suitable site, and the Joint Board added its agreement.[9] The fact that Olongapo could not be defended from the land side did not perturb the strategists at this time, as the probable enemy, Germany, could only operate with naval forces. The General Board also looked forward to the establishment of a naval base on the coast of China, so that in the event of a partition, America would be able to make her weight felt. The policy of the strategists, however, ran counter to Hay's diplomatic efforts, and although Hay in the winter of 1900 did enquire about the possibilities of leasing Samsa Bay, he was happy enough to allow the matter to drop on learning of Japanese objections. But marines were nevertheless stationed in the Philippines for several years in readiness for the seizure of a Chinese base. Hypnotized by the prospects of America's future needs in China, the General Board, incredible as it may seem, was still pressing for an American coaling-station on the Chinese coast as late as November 1905.[10]

While the strategists advocated a policy in the Far East outdated by rapidly changing events there, Roosevelt speedily recognized that American interests in China were deeply affected by the outbreak of the Russo-Japanese war. Just as in the Caribbean,

[9] Records of the Joint Army and Navy Board, National Archives, Washington, 9 Dec. 1903, 19 Dec. 1903.

[10] General Board Correspondence, United States Navy Department, 25 Nov. 1905, for a summary of strategic policy on this point and for the reaction of the State Department to naval demands.

where America's safety depended on the divisions in Europe, so in the Pacific, American security had in reality been founded on the balance of power which the rivalry of Japan and Russia had provided. During the early stages of the war Roosevelt favoured and admired Japanese prowess, David fighting Goliath. Japan's smashing naval victories and the efficiency of her army soon led him to view the situation differently. His decision to accept the rôle of mediator and to bring about peace was certainly founded on the belief that America's interests required the maintenance of the balance of power in the Far East. It could not, however, be done; military realities and the growing antagonisms of the European powers had permitted Japan to gain a predominant position. Britain, hoping to save her Yangtze interests by placing them under Japanese protection, renewed the Anglo-Japanese alliance in 1905 and 1911, while Russia turned her attention once more to the Balkans and was content to sign secret treaties with Japan at China's expense, which allowed Japan the lion's share of the bargain. Consequently the United States was powerless to alter the course of events on the Asiatic mainland. Yet Hay's notes had committed the United States to the policy of maintaining Chinese integrity. This was a dilemma which no amount of diplomatic skill and finesse could solve. Worse still any insistence on the part of the United States that Japan desist from spreading her co-prosperity sphere might lead to a Japanese attack on America's Pacific possessions.

Soon after the conclusion of the Russo-Japanese war, the strategists took a hard new look at the strategic problems of the Pacific. The result of their deliberations was hardly encouraging. Gone were the days when they thought America might share in the partition of China. Indeed, now it appeared that the Philippines could hardly be held in the face of a Japanese attack. Yet it took another four years before strategic policy was adjusted to the new military realities. From 1905 until 1909, it was Roosevelt who led the strategists rather than the strategists who guided the Administration.

The navy in the Philippines had selected Olongapo as the site for a naval base, but the army now declared that they could not defend it. The reduction of Port Arthur had shown that without adequate land defence a naval base was useless. The army therefore suggested Manila and its Bay with Corregidor Island as the most suitable site for a naval base capable of defence. Dewey, however, stubbornly rejected Manila Bay as impracticable from a naval point of view. Not even Roosevelt's personal intervention ended the inter-service bickering.[11] The General Board and the Joint Board had fallen on evil days. In the end, in 1909, the navy declared that no suitable site for a first-class naval base could be found in the Philippines and that accordingly Pearl Harbour in the Hawaiian Islands should be developed. Clearly the strategists had come to the conclusion that the Philippines were virtually impossible to defend.[12]

Roosevelt had, however, already anticipated this result of the discussion two years earlier, when he referred to them as America's heel of Achilles. While the sailors despaired, the diplomats were left with the thankless task of trying to appease Japan without sacrificing China. From 1905 to 1917 they negotiated a number of interesting agreements with Japan, which in substance allowed Japan a free hand on the mainland, while in phraseology they paid lip-service to the "open door" and "Chinese integrity." The Taft-Katsura conversation of 1905 was the first of these, it was fol-

---

[11] Joint Army and Navy Board, 6 Nov. 1907, 29 Jan. 1908, 31 Jan. 1908, 19 Feb. 1908.
[12] General Board Correspondence, 24 Feb. 1909. Joint Army and Navy Board, 5 Mar. 1908, 8 Nov. 1909.

lowed by the Root-Takahira agreement of 1908, and finally by the controversial Lansing-Ishii agreement of 1917. In truth these agreements were of little value. The Japanese Government had no intention of precipitating a conflict with the United States by attacking the Philippines as long as the United States did not impede their programme on the Asian mainland. They were ready, moreover, to give every conceivable paper assurance on the "open door" and Chinese independence, but this did not restrain them one iota from furthering their own aggressive aims. However laudable or cynical the intentions of American diplomats may have been, American policy in the Far East made very little impression on international developments there in the years from 1906 to 1917.

Roosevelt and the strategists were nevertheless rightly perturbed by the defenceless position of America's possessions in the Pacific Ocean. In such a situation it seemed the height of folly to injure sensitive Japanese pride by humiliating Japanese immigrants on the western seaboard. Roosevelt did his best to smooth over the crisis in American-Japanese relations caused by the problem of oriental immigrants, but not before, for the first time in their history, a Japanese war scare swept over the American people.

Theodore Roosevelt, whose grasp of the strategic realities underlying diplomacy was better than that of any President before the outbreak of the Second World War, believed that only a large navy could guarantee the safety of America's insular possessions in the Far East and gain respect for the country among the great nations of the world all arming to the teeth. He now redoubled his efforts to win Congressional approval for new naval construction. He got two new battleships a year, having asked for four, and in February 1907 secured Congressional approval for the construction of the first American Dreadnought. In battleship strength, with sixteen first-class battleships, America had already gained a safe margin of superiority over Japan. He sent the fleet around the world to show the American flag in the Pacific (Dec. 1907 to Feb. 1909) and he dealt with American-Japanese differences in a conciliatory but firm way. These were the elements of Roosevelt's Far Eastern policy from 1906 until he left the White House in 1909.

His successor Taft sought to meet the problem by the new expedient of substituting the dollar for guns in the Far East, and law for brute force in the world at large, while Wilson was forced during his first five years of office to focus his attention on the European catastrophe.

The two great war plans, worked out by the strategists during these years, were entirely defensive in character. They were denoted by a colour to represent a possible enemy, Orange for Japan, Black for Germany. While the Orange plan is chiefly of academic interest and showed just how defenceless the United States' position in the Pacific was, the Black War Plan with its subsequent amendments proved a vital influence on America's defense policy during the years which preceded the American entry into the First World War. Together they represent a tremendous advance in American strategic planning and are in fact the first modern war plans in American history.

War Plan Orange was completed in 1914.[13] It showed a realistic grasp of the Pacific situation. Logistics dominated the problem as the naval strategists saw it. If the means were lacking to insure the arrival of the full naval strength in the area where the decisive battle of the war would be fought, the national calamity would be as

[13] War Plan Orange, War Portfolios, United States Navy Department.

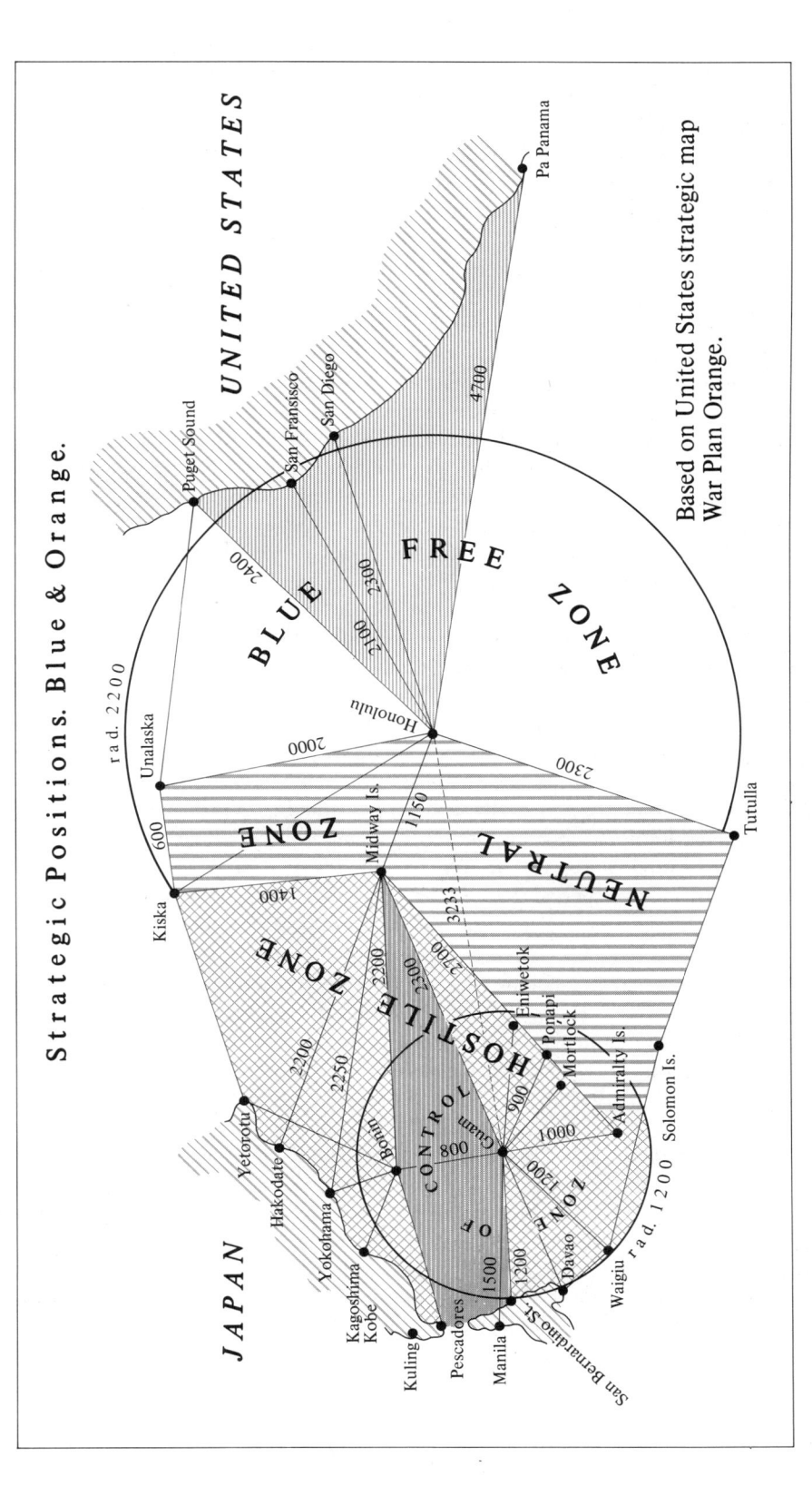

Strategic Positions. Blue & Orange.

Based on United States strategic map
War Plan Orange.

great as if the fighting fleet were inferior to the enemy. The naval experts calculated that by way of the "Panama Canal," Pearl Harbour, Midway and Guam, it would take the first section of the United States fleet sixty-eight days to reach Manila, whereas the Japanese fleet and troop transports would arrive in the Philippines eight days after having left Japanese ports. This gave the Japanese full control of the western Pacific for sixty days if the Panama Canal could be utilized by the United States fleet and, if not, full control for 104 days. The defence of the Philippines thus depended on the army plan of defence on Corregidor Island. The army mission was to hold out for at least sixty days, and the navy mission to engage the Japanese navy in battle on its arrival in the western Pacific, in order to relieve Japanese pressure on the Philippines. Guam was held to be the vital strategic point of control, and the navy believed that the decisive battle would be fought within a 1,200-mile radius of that island.

So much for the plans, now what were the realities of the situation? The strategists frankly confessed that the plan departed from usual procedure in not taking account of actual conditions, but in assessing that well before the war the reforms they proposed were instituted. In 1914 the position was bleak indeed. Congress had approved appropriations for the construction of a battleship fleet superior to the Japanese. The United States fleet, however, was unbalanced, for Congress had ignored the persistent requests of the General Board, passed on to them by the Secretary of the Navy, for adequate personnel to man the ships and for the necessary auxiliary ships, cruisers, destroyers, transports, ammunition ships and above all colliers on which the movement of the fleet depended. In 1914 the battleship fleet could hardly reach San Francisco, let alone make a voyage of 10,000 miles from their Atlantic base to the Philippines. Moreover, the construction of defences, docks, and the establishment of garrisons on the United States Pacific islands had been neglected. The army in the Philippines could not hope to resist a Japanese assault for sixty days, while Guam, Midway and Hawaii were virtually defenceless and Pearl Harbour as yet could not even dock a battleship. War Plan Orange thus underlined the fact that for many years to come the United States was incapable of fighting Japan. Accordingly, American diplomacy during this period had to be, and was, shaped on this assumption, as illustrated by the famous Lansing-Ishii Agreement. But what of the Black War Plan?[14]

Here, from the strategic point of view the situation was reversed, for Germany rather than the United States suffered the handicap of long lines of communication. As against this, the strategists had to face their own estimate that a large German army of three-quarters of a million men could be transported to the West Indies and the United States. It was thus held that the mission of the United States fleet, based on Guantanamo, Cuba, and its advanced base, Culebra, Puerto Rico, was to meet the German fleet in the Atlantic, once it had passed into the zone of control at a radius of 500 miles from Culebra, and to prevent a German landing in the West Indies or on the American mainland. The chances of American success were rather gloomily rated about even. Clearly the strategists failed to recognize the enormous problems involved in endeavouring to send an army with all its supplies across the Atlantic Ocean. As yet geographical isolation still provided the North American mainland with a considerable degree of protection.

These two great war plans Orange and Black were completed before the outbreak

---

[14] War Plan Black, War Portfolios, United States Navy Department.

of the First World War, and the historian approaches the 1914–1917 period with some very interesting questions. We would like to know how far the war modified pre-war plans, at what stage in the war the strategists drew up plans to co-operate with the allies, when precisely were the first army and navy plans drawn up to enable the United States to fight in Europe, what were the long-term objectives of the strategic planners, and to sum up, how far the nation had been brought to a state of preparedness before entering the war. The most important naval and army records for the period of the Wilson Administration are now open to some historians and provide the answers to these fascinating problems.

As it turned out, when Congress in their investigation of 1920 addressed themselves to the problem of discovering how far the nation was prepared for 1917, they were asking the wrong question, and the answers they received from naval officers carefully hid the fact. From 1914 until February 1917 the General Board and the General Staff of the Army were preparing not for the First World War but for the war which would follow it. The revision of the Black War Plan on 1 January 1915 recognized, it is true, that as long as the Central Powers and the Entente were locked in battle, there was no threat to the Monroe Doctrine, and that in defence of American citizens maltreated by the Central Powers America might be forced to fight Germany.[15] But there was no thought of joining in the allied war effort; in effect the United States' war effort was limited to meeting any hostile German cruisers in the Atlantic. "No other objective exists for the American fleet," in the words of the war plan, "unless an expeditionary force is sent against German South Africa"! The Black War Plan was amended from time to time during 1916 and 1917 to provide for a variety of emergencies against a German fleet operating in the West Indies, and the purchase of the Danish West Indies was recommended by the Board in August 1916 to complete the defensive American position in the Caribbean.

Wilson pursued a lonely policy of trying to preserve America's neutral rights and of bringing the war to a close before the balance of power in Europe was destroyed. As late as February 1917 he shocked his Secretary of State, Lansing, by refusing to agree that an allied victory was necessarily a good thing. The Secretary of the Navy, Josephus Daniels, was deeply in sympathy with these pacific views, and while building up the United States navy, looked forward to a general disarmament after the European war was over.

In the summer and autumn of 1915 the General Board examined American naval needs in the light of the World War. Their views were adopted by Wilson. The General Board called for a navy second to none and recommended a building programme of battleship and auxiliary ships over a five-year period which would realize this aim. The great naval Act of 1916 gave this plan Congressional sanction. But it is of cardinal importance to recognize that neither Wilson nor the strategists had recommended the construction of such a fleet in order to prepare the nation for intervention in the European War. In their memorandum of 6 August 1915 the General Board gave as their reason for the need of a large navy the problems that would face the United States when the war in Europe was concluded. "History shows," the General Board wrote, "that wars are chiefly caused by economic pressure and competition between nations and races . . . . At the close of the present war it is not improbable that the defeated belligerents, with the connivance and perhaps participa-

---

[15] War Plan Black, War Portfolios, United States Navy Department.

tion of the victors, may seek to recoup their war losses and to expand at the expense of the new world. On the other hand, perhaps soon, the victor may challenge the United States. . . . The naval policy should therefore make the United States secure in Western Atlantic, the Caribbean and the Pacific Oceans at the earliest possible moment."[16] Even in August 1917 the Board could still write: "A new alignment of powers after the present war must not find our fleet . . . unprepared to meet possible enemies . . . to act singly or jointly with all their naval powers against us."[17] In the eyes of the strategists the United States had no friends in the world, only jealous rivals.

Perhaps the cardinal error of the strategists during the First World War was their failure to recognize the submarine menace. According to the General Board memorandum of 9 November 1915, "The deeds of the submarines have been so spectacular that in default of engagements between the main fleets undue weight has been attached to them . . . . Yet at the present time, when the allies have learned in great measure to protect their commerce, as they learnt a few months earlier to protect their cruisers from the submarine menace, it is apparent that the submarine is not an instrument fitted to dominate naval warfare."[18] By 1917 they belatedly recognized that the issue of war hung on the success with which the allies could cope with German submarines. Every destroyer had to be pressed into service to convoy the allied supplies and the United States had less than fifty in commission at the outbreak of war.

And so it was that Wilson's passionate desire for peace, a mediated peace which he held was necessary to save "white civilization," and a grave strategic error on the significance of the submarine led the nation in 1916 to make a great military effort which was peculiarly ill-suited to the needs of 1917. Until February 1917 no thought whatever had been given to co-operating with the allies on land or on the high seas. Not even a rough plan existed to provide for the eventuality of sending an American expeditionary force to Europe. The war plans held in readiness by the army included an American invasion of Canada (1912–13) and also envisaged such possibilities as an attack on New York by Great Britain (March 1915) and the defence of the Pacific coast from a Japanese invasion (February 1915–March 1917).[19] The first plans for an American expeditionary force to Europe, not drawn up until February 1917, were based on the possibility of invading Bulgaria through Greece, and of invading France in the rear of the German armies in alliance with Holland.[20] All these plans were only fit for the waste-paper baskets of the War Department. Consequently the full impact of American intervention was delayed for many months. Wilson had not provided the leadership to prepare the nation effectively for a war which until the very last he regarded as disastrous, while the strategists had failed to consider eventualities which their President virtually refused to envisage.

I have attempted to provide a general and brief survey of the interaction of war plans, strategic planning and diplomacy for the momentous period in American history

[16] General Board Correspondence, 6 Aug. 1915.

[17] *Ibid.,* 29 Aug. 1917.

[18] *Ibid.,* memorandum on General Policy, 9 Nov. 1915, Josephus Daniels Papers, Library of Congress, Washington.

[19] Army War Plans, National Archives, Washington, reference to folios Canada, Great Britain, and Japan.

[20] Army War Plans, reference to folio Germany, memorandum, 3 Feb. 1917.

from 1890 to 1917. Looked at as a whole, these years witnessed a great change in diplomatic and strategic thought. Strategic concepts had vitally influenced American foreign policy in time of peace. But it is curious that practically the only offensive war plan to be found, Lieutenant Kimball's, coincided with the period when American power was only beginning to entitle the United States to be considered as a great power. The most striking characteristic of American war planning from 1903 until 1917 is that it was conceived in terms of defence, and also that the possibility of an alliance with Britain or any other power was given no consideration whatever. The military men continued to regard as absolutely axiomatic Washington's admonition against entangling alliances. But for a brief period their outlook remained entirely isolationist. Isolationism indeed was to most Americans not a "policy" but a part of the American way of life.

16 / National Interest and American Intervention, 1917: An Historiographical Appraisal

Daniel M. Smith

American intervention in the First World War has given rise to many historical interpretations. Did President Wilson and his advisers decide in favor of American belligerency because of German submarine attacks on American ships and cargoes in violation of prevailing international law? Or, as some revisionists have contended, did Wilson favor intervention in 1917 because of his genuinely unneutral, pro-allied inclinations, as urged by militant bankers and munitions makers who had developed a financial stake in the allied cause? During the last three decades, historians have gained access to documentation in the American National Archives and to huge private collections of papers pertaining to the Great War 1914–18. In the process, several fresh reexaminations of American intervention have been published. Not only have historians exploited much fresh documentation, they have also brought to their task fresh insights and new hypotheses, thus drastically altering the earlier explanations. Those rather simplistic interpretations fashionable in the 1920s and 1930s, both traditionalist and revisionist, have given way to a view of a President Wilson less the moral idealist and more appreciative of *realpolitik,* with an awareness of America's relationship to a world balance of power. In the following historiographical analysis, Daniel Smith suggests some of the reasons for the changes in scholarly explanations of American intervention in 1917.

For further reading: Thomas A. Bailey, *The Policy of the United States Towards the Neutrals 1917–1918* (Baltimore: 1942); George F. Kennan, *The Decision to Intervene* (Princeton: 1958) and *Russia Leaves the War* (Princeton: 1956); Richard W. Leopold, "The Problem of American Intervention, 1917: an Historical Retrospect," *World Politics,* II (1950), 403–425; *N. Gordon Levin, *Woodrow Wilson and World Politics* (New York: 1968); Victor S. Mamatey, *The United States and East Central Europe 1914–1918: A*

Daniel Smith is Professor of History at the University of Colorado. This article is reprinted from the *Journal of American History,* LII with the permission of the Managing Editor. Copyright © 1965 by the Organization of American Historians.

Study in Wilsonian Diplomacy and Propaganda (Princeton: 1957); *Ernest R. May, *The World War and American Isolation 1914–1917* (Cambridge: 1959); *Arno J. Mayer, *Political Origins of the New Diplomacy 1917–1918* (New Haven: 1959); Charles Seymour, "The House-Bernstorff Conversations in Perspective," in *A Study in Diplomatic History and Historiography,* edited by A. O. Sarkissian (London: 1961), pp. 90–106.

In the two decades since 1945 several significant studies have been published on American involvement in World War I. These works have advanced beyond the revisionist debates of the 1930s to a more balanced consideration of economic, psychological, and political factors. Also they study the causes of hostilities within the context of developments in the principal European belligerent countries. An important aspect has been the investigation of considerations of the national interests in the decision of the United States to enter the great conflict in 1917.[1] The purpose of this essay is to examine these recent studies, with an especial concentration on the theme of the national interest and its influence on American foreign policy makers.

In 1950 Richard W. Leopold published a stimulating article on the historiography of the American involvement in World War I.[2] He pointed out that scholars had not achieved a consensus on the problem and that a general study had not been published since 1938. Until then the historical debate that began almost with President Woodrow Wilson's war message could be categorized into two schools. One was the "submarine" school, best represented by Charles Seymour, which contended that the nation had entered the war primarily because of violations of neutral rights and international law and morality by the ruthless German submarine campaigns. Another school comprised the unneutrality group, with Charles C. Tansill as the latest spokesman, that emphasized the patent American unneutrality in favor of the Allied Powers.[3]

---

[1] Only a few of the reviews in the major historical journals of the works examined in this paper commented to an appreciable extent on the emergence of the national interest theme, Ernest R. May, *Mississippi Valley Historical Review,* XLIII (June 1956), 147–48, pointed out that Edward H. Buehrig's study was important as a contribution to a more realistic appraisal of Wilsonian diplomacy; Julius W. Pratt, *American Historical Review,* LXIV (July 1959), 1023–24, called the Smith study of Lansing a "partial answer" to the role of balance-of-power concepts in the 1917 intervention; and Richard L. Watson, Jr., *ibid.,* 973–75, gave the best review from that point of view to the May volume.

[2] Richard W. Leopold, "The Problem of American Intervention, 1917: An Historical Retrospect," *World Politics,* II (1950), 405–25. Richard L. Watson, Jr., in "Woodrow Wilson and His Interpreters, 1947–1957," *Mississippi Valley Historical Review,* XLIV (Sept. 1957), 207–36, examines recent literature, and especially the Wilson centennial outpouring, on the domestic and foreign policies of the Wilson administration. Ernest R. May, in two short articles, makes perceptive comments on the major currents of interpretation on American involvement in 1898, 1917, and 1941. He describes himself, Arthur S. Link, and others as moving away from earlier "What went wrong" approaches to a Rankean "What happened" emphasis. See May, "Emergence to World Power," John Higham, ed., *The Reconstruction of American History* (New York, 1962), 180–96; and *American Intervention: 1917 and 1941* (Service Center for Teachers of History, Pamphlet 30, 1960).

[3] Charles Callan Tansill, *America Goes to War* (Boston, 1938); Charles Seymour, *American Diplomacy During the World War* (Baltimore, 1934) and *American Neutrality, 1914–1917* (New Haven, 1935). Tansil ignored the issue of American security and global aspects of the war.

During World War II, Leopold noted, a new interpretation emerged that the basic motive for intervention in 1917 had been to protect the nation's security against the menace of possible German victory and a disturbance to the balance of power, and to preserve Anglo-American domination of the North Atlantic. In 1943 Walter Lippmann maintained that the submarine issue had been merely the formal occasion for war, while "the substantial and compelling reason . . . was that the cutting of the Atlantic communications meant the starvation of Britain and, therefore, the conquest of Western Europe by imperial Germany."[4] While acknowledging that Wilson officially had justified hostilities on the basis of submarine violations of American neutral rights, Lippmann contended that this would not have sufficed as a rationalization if most Americans had not realized, intuitively or consciously, that a German victory would imperil American security. In another wartime book the newspaperman Forest Davis advanced a similar explanation.[5] As Leopold observed, however, scholars remained skeptical of these interpretations that seemed to project the fears of 1941 into the 1917 era, and at most viewed them as insights requiring extensive research and study. Diplomatic historian Thomas A. Bailey, for example, commented that there had been no rushing into war to redress the power balance and save the Allies in 1917, as seemingly they were winning; only after it was in the war did America realize the dire Allied plight.[6]

The diplomat and historian, George F. Kennan, published in 1950 a volume of essays on recent American diplomacy in which he recognized that there had been high American officials in World War I cognizant of the need to preserve a favorable balance of power against the disturbing possibility of a German triumph. Kennan concluded, however, that such a realistic approach had not been shared by the great majority of citizens; instead, the nation plunged into war on the narrow grounds of defending neutral rights and then turned the struggle into a moralistic-legalistic crusade to remold the world order.[7] The more detailed study, *Ideals and Self-Interest in American Foreign Relations,* published in 1953 by Robert Endicott Osgood, in general substantiated that interpretation.[8]

He disclaimed having a particular thesis to offer. Seymour dismissed political and economic factors as peripheral and attributed the war entry primarily to outraged sentiment at submarine warfare and a determination to protect American lives and property on the high seas. Harley Notter, *The Origins of the Foreign Policy of Woodrow Wilson* (Baltimore, 1937), 642–43, 647, 650, concluded that by 1917 Wilson viewed Germany as a danger to the peace and security of America and the world, but that the United States entered the war only because of intolerable violations of its neutral rights. A slim volume by Samuel R. Spencer, Jr., *The Decision for War, 1917* (Rindge, N.H., 1953), adhered to the submarine thesis while stressing the *Laconia* sinking and release of the Zimmermann telegram in Feb. 1917 as events in the transition to full hostilities. Also see Barbara W. Tuchman, *The Zimmermann Telegram* (New York, 1958).

[4] Walter Lippmann, *U. S. Foreign Policy: Shield of the Republic* (Boston, 1943), 33–37

[5] Forest Davis, *The Atlantic System: The Story of Anglo-American Control of the Seas* (New York, 1941), 240–46.

[6] See Thomas A. Bailey, *Woodrow Wilson and the Lost Peace* (New York, 1944), 12–13, and *A Diplomatic History of the American People* (6th ed., New York, 1958), 594n. Richard W. Van Alstyne, *American Diplomacy in Action* (rev. ed., Stanford, 1947), 255–56, 289, conceded, on the other hand, that while the majority of citizens had not been aware of balance of power arguments, some persons including high officials had been influenced by such considerations.

[7] George F. Kennan, *American Diplomacy, 1900–1950* (Chicago, 1951), 64–66, 70–74. Also see Edward Mead Earle, "A Half-Century of American Foreign Policy: Our Stake in Europe, 1898–1914," *Political Science Quarterly,* LXIV (June 1949), 168–88.

[8] Robert Endicott Osgood, *Ideals and Self-Interest in American Foreign Relations* (Chicago, 1953). Approximately one third of this study is devoted to the Wilson period.

Osgood acknowledged the plausibility of the Lippmann thesis and in his study, based on printed materials, he recorded similar views held by a number of Americans in 1914–1917.[9] As a *New Republic* editor Lippmann had written several articles[10] contending that American security was involved in the continuation of the existing balance of power, as had the American diplomat Lewis Einstein in 1913 and 1914.[11] Other prominent Americans publicly advanced arguments that vital national interests would be threatened by a German victory. Theodore Roosevelt mixed with such views a type of belligerent moralism that advocated hostilities in 1916 in order to uphold national honor and save civilization from the new barbarians.[12]

Several of Wilson's advisers, Osgood wrote, analyzed the meaning of the war to America from a balance-of-power view. The list included Colonel Edward M. House; Robert Lansing, Counselor and then Secretary of State in mid-1915; the ambassador to Britain, Walter Hines Page; and James W. Gerard, ambassador to Germany. These men envisioned a German conquest in Europe as a threat to American security in the western hemisphere and analyzed the war in terms of the national interest in Anglo-American naval predominance in the Atlantic. Yet such considerations, though increasing their willingness to support neutrality policies favorable to the Allies, did little more than quicken events which led the United States into the war. That was because the advisers did not really expect Germany to win and therefore their recommendations to the President did not advocate intervention on the grounds of an endangered security. Events did not seem to pose the clear alternative of fighting Germany or confronting a nearly certain later attack by that power, so it was easier to follow the line of submarine violations of honor and morality and to enter the war on that popular basis.[13] In any case, Osgood concluded, it would be difficult to prove that these advisers had any appreciable influence on the idealistic Wilson, for the President was in nearly complete control of foreign affairs and was unusually independent of counselors.[14]

Osgood thus seemed reluctant to accept the implications of his own findings, that presidential assistants had taken a realistic approach toward the European war. Furthermore, Osgood tended to concentrate on the question of immediate security. These advisers saw the national interest in a broader sense as embracing not only security but economic interests and a favorable postwar position. Osgood's own reasoning strongly suggests that House, Lansing, and others might not have recommended to Wilson considerations of honor, morality, and ideology as justifications for belligerency if they had not viewed Germany as a menace to broadly defined national interests. Later studies also have revealed that Wilson was capable of a more realistic approach to the war and that he was far more receptive to advice and dependent on counselors than previously assumed.

Osgood and Kennan undoubtedly have been correct that there was little evidence

[9] *Ibid.,* 115–34.

[10] Walter Lippmann, *Annals of the American Academy of Political and Social Science,* LXVI (1916), 60–70; *Stakes of Diplomacy* (New York, 1915), preface; and *New Republic,* X (Feb. 17, 1917), 59–61.

[11] Lewis Einstein, "The United States and Anglo-German Rivalry," and "The War and American Policy," *National Review,* LX (Jan. 1913), 736–50 and LXIV (Nov. 1914), 357–76.

[12] Osgood, *Ideals and Self-Interest,* 135–53. Also see Howard K. Beale, *Theodore Roosevelt and the Rise of America to World Power* (Baltimore, 1956).

[13] Osgood, *Ideals and Self-Interest,* 154–71.

[14] *Ibid.,* 172–75.

of popular apprehensions of a direct German threat in 1914–1917. Much evidence exists, however, that an influential minority viewed imperial Germany askance. Since 1898 American military and naval leaders increasingly envisioned Germany as offering a threat to American security in the western hemisphere. The Navy General Board in 1901 recommended purchase of the Danish West Indies because "In view of the isthmian canal and the German settlements in South America, every additional acquisition by the United States in the West Indies is of value."[15] In testimony before the House Naval Affairs Committee in 1914, Admiral Charles Vreeland justified naval expansion as needed to cope with Germany and Japan.[16] A Navy General Board estimate of 1910, recirculated in February 1915, concluded that only Germany, driven by population pressures and rivalries in Latin America and the Far East, could undertake singlehandedly war on the United States and was therefore the most probable potential enemy.[17] The War Department also had defensive war plans drawn with Germany as the theoretical opponent.[18] A lengthy War College paper, 1909–1910, by Captain Paul B. Malone, described Germany as the most serious economic competitor of the United States, in contact and conflict with America both in Latin America and China. Although the author did not flatly predict hostilities he commented that, in the past, war had been the virtually inevitable result of such conflicting interests.[19]

The historian Alfred Vagts has attempted to explain the fact that navalists in Germany and the United States, from the late 1890s to 1914, viewed each other as a probable opponent on the grounds that each needed an excuse to justify large naval expansion programs.[20] He concluded that actual commercial competition between the two states was small and that each power lacked coaling stations and naval cruising range for an attack on the other. Talk of rivalry in both countries primarily reflected the propaganda efforts of big navy advocates. No doubt a degree of validity must be accorded Vagts' interpretation, but the evidence indicates that the apprehensions were genuine and were shared by many leading civilians. On the other hand, apparently

[15] General Board No. 187, 31–01, Vol. 1, 374, Report of Nov. 12, 1901, Naval War Records Office (Arlington, Virginia). Unclassified. Rumors of German endeavors to acquire the Galapagos Islands caused the Navy and War departments on several occasions to object to the State Department on the grounds of proximity to the Panama Canal; similar objections were made against possible German acquisition of Haiti's Mole St. Nicholas, in 1910 and 1912. See correspondence of April 25, 28, 1911, State Department File Number 822.014G/177, 178; Aug. 25, 1910, June 27, 1912, ibid., 838.802/5, 12 (National Archives).

[16] Harold and Margaret Sprout, The Rise of American Naval Power, 1776–1918 (Princeton, 1942), 311–13. The Navy League centered its none too successful propaganda before 1914 for a more powerful navy on the German menace to the Monroe Doctrine. See Armin Rappaport, The Navy League of the United States (Detroit, 1962), 31–66.

[17] War Portfolio No. 1, Atlantic Station—approved by the General Board, Oct. 19, 1910 and reissued in Feb. 1915, Naval War Records Office.

[18] No. 9433, War Materials Division (National Archives). Still classified as confidential in 1960.

[19] "The Military Geography of the Atlantic Seaboard, Considered with Reference to an Invading Force," War College Division, General Staff, 6916–1, War Materials Division.

[20] Alfred Vagts, "Hopes and Fears of an American-German War, 1870–1915." Political Science Quarterly, LIV (Dec. 1939), 514–35, and LV (March 1940), 53–76. Fritz T. Epstein, "Germany and the United States: Basic Patterns of Conflict and Understanding," G. L. Anderson, ed., Issues and Conflict (Lawrence, Kansas, 1959), 284–314, concludes that German-American friction prior to 1914 reflected psychological differences rather than actual clashes of interest.

there were no official interchanges in the 1910–1917 period between the two defense departments and State in regard to American national interests in the outcome of a general European war. Officials in all three departments apparently shared similar appraisals of the situation, and perhaps informally discussed it, but no effort was made to plan and coordinate policy to cope with the danger.[21]

The decade before World War I witnessed a slowly maturing conviction among informed Americans that Germany was a potential enemy and Great Britain a natural ally of the United States. Editorials in the *New York Times* envisioned Germany as hostile, thus requiring an American navy of at least comparable size, and repeatedly expressed confidence in an enduring Anglo-American community of interest.[22] From 1898 the American periodical press also occasionally printed articles expressing distrust of Germany's expansionist tendencies. *Munsey's Magazine* in 1901 featured a comparison of the German and American navies and called for greater naval preparations to cooperate with Great Britain in meeting the German challenge in the western hemisphere.[23] Articles from English journals on the theme of German naval threats to the United States were reprinted in American publications.[24] Comparisons of the American and German navies were drawn and parity was strongly recommended.[25] A 1909 article in *The Independent* by Amos S. Hershey, professor of Political Science and International Law at Indiana University, depicted Germany as menacing both world peace and American interests in the Far East and Latin America. To meet that danger Hershey advocated a defensive Anglo-American alliance. He wrote prophetically: "the people of the United States could hardly remain neutral in a war between Germany and Great Britain which might possibly end in German naval supremacy. . . . A blockade of the British Isles by German cruisers and submarine mines, or the loss involved in the danger to contraband trade would be severely felt in this country."[26]

Understandably, the general conflagration which began in 1914 increased the

---

[21] Based on the author's perusal of State-Navy files in the National Archives, and on a recent article by Fred Greene, "The Military View of American National Policy, 1904–1940," *American Historical Review*, LXVI (1961), 354–77. Greene points out that the army and navy staffs often complained of lack of policy guidance from the State Department before 1940 and were compelled to try to define basic national interests themselves as guidelines for defense plans. J. A. S. Grenville, in "Diplomacy and War Plans in the United States, 1890–1917," *Transactions of the Royal Society*, 5th Series, XI (London, 1961), 1–21, notes that American strategic war plans, revised in 1915 and 1916, were defensive in character and were designed not to cope with the current war but to meet the threat of the victor after the war in Europe was over. Also see Ernest R. May, "The Development of Political-Military Consultation in the United States," *Political Science Quarterly*, LXX (June 1955), 161–80.

[22] New York *Times,* July 17, Aug. 20, 26, 1898; Feb. 18, 1899.

[23] Walter S. Meriwether, "Our Navy and Germany's," *Munsey's Magazine,* XXIV (March 1901), 856–73.

[24] See *American Monthly Review of Reviews, XIX* (Jan. 1899) 86–88; *Living Age,* CCXXIX (June 1, 1901), 583–86; *ibid.,* CCLXXVIII (July 12, 1913), 67–81.

[25] *Harper's Weekly,* XLVII (March 14, 1903), 428–29; *New York Times,* Feb. 20, 1905; W. G. Fitz-Gerald, "Does Germany Menace the World's Peace?," *North American Review,* CLXXXIV (April 19, 1907), 853–60.

[26] Amos S. Hershey, "Germany—The Main Obstacle to the World's Peace," *Independent,* LXVI (May 20, 1909), 1071–76. For a similar analysis by a well-known English journalist writing for *Fortnightly Review,* see Sydney Brooks, "Great Britain, Germany and the United States," reprinted in *Living Age,* CCLXII (July 31, 1909), 259–66.

conviction of a number of Americans that Germany was in fact a menace and that American interests could best be secured through an Allied triumph.[27] In the 1916 annual volume of the American Academy of Political and Social Science well-known scholars and pundits presented several papers that emphasized that United States security was involved in the preservation of British sea power.[28] To help focus the widespread interest in 1916 in the preparedness question, the editors of *The Independent* printed an outline of pro and con arguments, prepared by Preston William Slosson, entitled: "Resolved: That the United States should enter the Great War on the side of the Entente Allies." The affirmative side asserted among other arguments that a Teutonic victory would endanger the future security of the American people.[29]

These references to public opinion do not indicate that a majority of citizens in 1917 supported intervention on the grounds of vital national concerns. However, the evidence does reveal that for over a decade a number of educated and informed persons were exposed repeatedly to warnings that Germany challenged the security and the economic welfare of the nation. The existence of these attitudes probably made it inestimably easier to condemn Germany on moral and ideological grounds after 1914 and facilitated eventual war entry on the basis of a defense of neutral rights.

Edward H. Buehrig, as Osgood a political scientist, made an important contribution to the "national interest" school in a subtle study entitled *Woodrow Wilson and the Balance of Power*.[30] Based largely on printed sources and a few manuscript collections, the volume explained the American intervention in the war in 1917 as resulting from the German challenge to Britain's position as the dominant sea power. If Americans had been accustomed to viewing foreign relations in terms of practical power issues the ultimate war entry possibly might have been based squarely on considerations of security and economic connections. As it was, Germany and the United States were soon entrapped in complicated questions of neutral rights and drifted into war because of different attitudes toward British control of the seas. The United States accepted the British role as beneficial to its interest; Germany felt compelled to challenge it with every available weapon. Consequently, even though a bilateral German-American war was highly improbable, an Anglo-German struggle which threatened to alter drastically Britain's position posed serious questions to America's trans-Atlantic connections and created tensions culminating in war.[31]

The submarine issue was a point of departure for an evolving American policy toward the war. Without it, of course, German-American relations would have been smoother. American neutrality was in practice favorable to the Allies, but Germany decided to use fully the submarine weapon in 1917 because it alone seemed to promise victory. Probably no other course by the United States, short of cooperation with Germany to challenge the British blockade in order to renew substantial American trade with the Central Powers, could have averted unrestricted U-boat warfare.

[27] For example, see *New York Times* editorials of Oct. 14, 19, 1914, Nov. 29, 1916, and letters Oct. 16, 18, Nov. 10, 1914.

[28] See articles by S. N. Patten, George Louis Beer, and Walter Lippmann, in *Annals of the American Academy of Political and Social Science*, LXVI (1916), 1–11, 60–70, 71–91. Dissenting views were also voiced.

[29] *Independent*, LXXXVI (May 8, 1916), 228.

[30] *Woodrow Wilson and the Balance of Power* (Bloomington, 1955).

[31] *Ibid.*, viii–ix, 16–17.

Germany naturally resented the American munitions trade with the Allies but, except as a moral justification, it played no important role in German decisions. What
really was sought was to reverse British control of the seas and markets. To have
satisfied the Berlin government by effecting a major change in neutral trade would
have harmed important American economic interests and would have meant a
disturbing replacement of British power with German.[32]

Wilson in 1915 adopted the policy of holding Germany fully accountable for losses
of American lives and ships by submarine attacks around the British Isles in order
to defend the traditional American concept of neutral rights and "freedom of the
seas." He chose to uphold international law, and thereby to defend a conception of
the national interests, for Americans had long believed that the nation's security was
closely connected with the preservation of the world legal structure. In speeches
advocating defensive military preparations in 1916, Wilson clearly developed that
theme: the United States had to defend legal principles and support the international
community. Germany's lawless methods of warfare affected American security, the
President implied, dependent as it was on maintenance of national honor and rights
and the preservation of the structure of international law and morality.[33]

When the *Sussex* controversy in 1916 made imminent the prospect of entering the
war over the submarine issue, Wilson turned to diplomatic intervention in hopes
of avoiding hostilities. The House-Grey Memorandum, negotiated earlier by Colonel
House with British Foreign Secretary Sir Edward Grey, provided that at a time
propitious for the Allies Wilson was to propose a conference to terminate the war;
if Germany declined or rejected a "reasonable" peace, the United States "probably"
would enter the struggle on the Allied side. The refusal of Britain and France to invoke the plan, which Wilson had hoped would end the war before America should
be forced in, compelled the President to seek other means for mediation.[34]

In May 1916 President Wilson addressed the League to Enforce Peace and advocated a universal association of nations that would accord with America's national
interest by preserving world free trade and access to markets ("freedom of the seas")
and would protect all nations through territorial guarantees. This global organization,
said Wilson, could prevent future wars by substitution of conferences for force, and
the United States could facilitate the transition by making it known that its power
would be thrown onto the international scales in behalf of peaceful means of adjustment. Buehrig analyzed the address as revealing not only Wilsonian idealism but
also his interest in maintaining a stable world balance of power. Clear indications
that the British government would not aid in promoting a negotiated peace caused
Wilson in late 1916 to turn to other avenues for peace.[35] Wilson moved beyond
considerations of a balance of power to a community of power when in December
1916 he requested statements of belligerent war aims and early in 1917 appealed for
"peace without victory." The President thereby completed a shift from the initial
policy of defense of maritime neutral rights to mediation efforts and a just peace on
which to build a new community of nations. When Germany subsequently launched
unrestricted submarine warfare and abolished not only all neutral rights but also
made clear the determination to dictate a conqueror's peace, Wilson took the nation

[32] *Ibid.,* 79–84, 90, 102–05.
[33] *Ibid.,* 106–08, 117–21, 149.
[34] *Ibid.,* 172–73, 228, 230–35.
[35] *Ibid.,* 238–46.

into war. He had no real choice, Buehrig concluded, either from the standpoint of maritime legal rights or of future world peace and stability.[36]

In Buehrig's view, Wilson in shaping American policy lacked neither astuteness nor an appreciation of balance-of-power concepts. The idealistic element in his policy finally received the major emphasis, over realistic considerations, because the President's temperament so required. The need to adjust policies to the requirements of an American public not trained to appraise world affairs in practical terms was also a probable factor.[37]

The Buehrig study has made at least two important contributions. In contrast to Osgood he defined the American concept of the national interests as comprising not only immediate but long-term security, economic interest in freedom of the seas, and the desire for world order and safety through preservation of an international regime of law. Buehrig also has carefully analyzed the elements of Wilsonian policies and thereby detected, along with idealistic elements, indications of a realistic consciousness of the balance of power and concrete American interests involved in the war.[38]

In an early volume in the New American Nation series, *Woodrow Wilson and the Progressive Era*, Arthur S. Link subscribed to the "submarine" school in interpreting the entry of the United States into World War I.[39] He recognized that House and Lansing had viewed realistically the European struggle, but he maintained that the two advisers "had only an incidental influence" on the President. In the ultimate analysis it was Wilson who, influenced by public opinion, had determined the American course. To mid-1916 Wilson had followed a neutrality course benevolent toward the Allies because of his moralistic appraisal of the war, German violations of international law, and the apparent greater readiness of Great Britain to make a reasonable peace. When he became convinced that the Allies in fact did not desire a fair settlement but sought, as Germany, a conclusive victory, he moved toward a genuinely impartial position. If Germany had not violated the *Sussex* pledge by unrestricted submarine warfare early in 1917, there would have been no war between the two countries. Considerations of finance, economic ties, ideology, or security were not involved in the presidential decision. War finally came because the submarine assaults on American lives and shipping left Wilson no feasible alternative.[40]

As he continued his multi-volume study of Wilson, Link seemed to modify his views

[36] *Ibid.*, 260–66.

[37] *Ibid.*, 274–75.

[38] Buehrig noted that Robert Lansing held balance-of-power concepts about the war, but he asked to what degree this was submerged by an ideological view of the struggle. *Ibid.*, 135–37. That question was answered, at least partially, by Daniel M. Smith's *Robert Lansing and American Neutrality, 1914–1917* (Berkeley, 1958), and "Robert Lansing and the Formulation of American Neutrality Policies, 1914–1915," *Mississippi Valley Historical Review*, XLIII (June 1956), 59–81. Lansing, on the basis of his private diaries, was depicted by Smith as combining ideological considerations with a concern for the nation's economic and security interests in the war, and to have concluded in July 1915 that on both grounds a German victory should be prevented, by an American intervention if necessary. Smith shows that Lansing helped shape the basic neutrality policies in the early months of the war and thereafter was a strong advocate of a firm approach toward the submarine issue. Lansing rarely spoke directly to Wilson of security interests, apparently because of an appreciation of the President's psychology, but he did to Colonel House. He also recommended measures to Wilson based on concrete economic considerations, and he couched other suggestions in idealistic terminology.

[39] Arthur S. Link, *Woodrow Wilson and the Progressive Era 1910–1917* (New York, 1954).

[40] *Ibid.*, 279–81.

of the causes of American intervention. In 1957 his Albert Shaw Lectures on Diplomatic History were published as *Wilson the Diplomatist*.[41] The interpretation generally followed that of the earlier volume: a genuinely neutral America adjusted to British measures, but the U-boat campaigns were opposed for legal and moral reasons.[42] By early 1917, however, after failure of efforts to halt the war short of total victory for either side and thereby to preclude American involvement and establish the basis for a stable postwar world, Wilson apparently decided to effect a diplomatic withdrawal. Continuation of the war, he foresaw, would cause further deterioration of neutral rights. The President seemingly was willing to retreat on strict account- ability and perhaps would have accepted a new U-boat campaign against armed merchantmen or all belligerent vessels except passenger liners. The German decision to attack all shipping, neutrals included, forced Wilson to break diplomatic relations.[43]

Link thus considered the submarine issue to have been the immediate cause of hostilities, but he concluded that the agonized Wilson reluctantly accepted full hostilities in 1917, as opposed to armed neutrality or a limited naval war, only because of other factors. One of the most important of these, though supported by little direct evidence, was Wilson's "apparent fear that the threat of a German victory imperiled the balance of power and all his hopes for the future reconstruction of the world community."[44] Wilson seems not to have apprehended a serious German danger to the United States nor did he seek to preserve the old balance of power. Yet the Allies appeared to be on the verge of losing the war and that would mean German conquest and the end of Wilsonian hopes for a new world order. He remarked to Colonel House that Germany seemed to be a madman who required restraining— and he apparently thought that only through American armed intervention could a Central Power victory be avoided and American prestige among the Allies enhanced so that a just peace could be achieved. The President undoubtedly also was affected in the war decision by an aroused American public and by the reiterated counsel of his close advisers.[45]

In the preface of the third volume in the Link biography, *Wilson: The Struggle for Neutrality*,[46] the author expressed the hope that in this study of the first fifteen months of neutrality he had purged his mind of preconceived interpretations and could let the men and events speak for themselves. He would appear to have suc- ceeded admirably in this exhaustively researched volume. Realistic apraisals of the war by House and Lansing had an important effect on Wilson's mind. House, as Lansing, was favorably inclined toward the Allies and feared the militaristic and expansionist tendencies of Germany. As a result, the Colonel advised Wilson to acquiesce in Allied war measures and to oppose those of Germany. Yet House did not want a sweeping Allied victory, only one sufficient to check Teutonic ambitions and still leave Germany powerful enough to block Russian imperialism.[47] President Wilson, after initial

---

[41] *Wilson the Diplomatist: A Look at His Major Foreign Policies* (Baltimore, 1957).

[42] *Ibid.*, 32–35, 40–54.

[43] *Ibid.*, 70, 80–82.

[44] *Ibid.*, 88.

[45] *Ibid.*, 89–90.

[46] Arthur S. Link, *Wilson: The Struggle for Neutrality, 1914–1915* (Princeton, 1960). An excellent first chapter discusses American public opinion and the role of belligerent propaganda. Link finds invalid the assumptions of many writers that most Americans were irrationally pro-Ally and that German propaganda was generally inept and ineffective.

[47] *Ibid.*, 45–48.

sympathy for the Allies, achieved a large degree of impartiality on the question of war guilt. As the war continued, Wilson was increasingly persuaded that the greatest opportunity for a just and lasting peace would come from an indecisive conclusion of the war. As he told a newspaperman, however, while "I cannot regard this [a sweeping Allied triumph] as the ideal solution, at the same time I cannot see now that it would hurt greatly the interests of the United States if either France or Russia or Great Britain should finally dictate the [peace] settlement."[48] Wilson thus indicated, by the close of 1914, a realistic view that the preferable result of the war would be a deadlock which would preserve the existing power structure and facilitate a just peace, but that American interests would not be adversely affected by a decisive Allied triumph. As far as American policy was concerned, however, both moral and practical considerations required maintenance of neutrality.

The fourth volume in Link's series, *Wilson: Confusions and Crises,* necessarily lacks the unifying themes present in the earlier volumes. Among other topics, domestic and foreign, it narrates America's relations with the belligerents through the *Sussex* crisis. The section on the House-Grey Memorandum, based on heretofore unexploited sources including French materials which the author could not directly quote or cite, is particularly valuable. Link depicts the divergence of motives behind the scheme: House, believing that intervention in the war was almost inevitable, was prepared to go far in assuring the Allies of American backing, whereas the President apparently contemplated only peaceful mediation. He believes Grey did not take his "understanding" with the Colonel very seriously, as he doubted the possibility of American intervention, and was aware that the Allied governments were adverse to a negotiated peace and sought a decisive triumph over the Central Powers.[49]

These interpretations reveal that Link is constantly reevaluating the materials as he continues his biography of Wilson. Wilson is now seen as not only the moralist and idealist, but also as aware of balance-of-power arguments, responsive to the advice of realistically-inclined counselors, and to a considerable degree framing the American course on the basis of practical considerations of the national interest. Completion of the biography and the concluding judgment of Link can only be awaited with great interest.

The centennial of Wilson's birth in 1956 occasioned a number of commemorative essays and books. Osgood and Buehrig restated their evaluations of Wilsonian neutrality;[50] Charles Seymour reiterated the submarine thesis,[51] and William L. Langer concurred.[52] Two short and unfootnoted but well-researched biographies were

---

[48] *Ibid.,* 49–56.

[49] Arthur S. Link, *Wilson: Confusions and Crises, 1915–1916* (Princeton, 1964), 111–13, 130, 138–40.

[50] Edward H. Buehrig, "Idealism and Statecraft," *Confluence,* V (Oct. 1956), 252–63; Robert E. Osgood, "Woodrow Wilson, Collective Security, and the Lessons of History," *ibid.,* (Jan. 1957), 341–54.

[51] Charles Seymour, "Woodrow Wilson in Perspective," *Foreign Affairs,* XXXIV (Jan. 1956), 175–86. In an article, "The House-Bernstorff Conversations in Perspective," A. O. Sarkissian, ed., *Studies in Diplomatic History and Historiography in Honour of G. P. Gooch* (London, 1961), 90–106, Seymour acknowledged that House had some fears of a German threat to American security and that his pro-British sentiments affected his interest in mediation schemes. Seymour credited the protracted and confidential House-Bernstorff negotiations in 1915–1916 with helping to postpone war until the final crisis in 1917.

[52] William L. Langer, "From Isolation to Mediation," Arthur P. Dudden, ed., *Woodrow Wilson and the World of Today* (Philadelphia, 1957), 22–46.

published by John A. Garraty and John M. Blum. Garraty described American neutrality as decidedly pro-Ally, because of Wilson's biases, but the President's views and emotions precluded him from either accepting a German victory or intervening in the war. Wilson eventually lost much of his faith in the Allies and attempted to mediate in late 1916, but was forced into the conflict by the submarine issue.[53] Blum believed that Wilson lacked a realistic appraisal of the war's meaning for American interests and that the country entered the conflict only because of unrestricted U-boat warfare.[54] A generally persuasive and solidly-based psychological study, *Wilson and Colonel House,* was published by Alexander L. and Juliette L. George, that pointed out that while Wilson undoubtedly was familiar with the balance-of-power concept, his psychological aversion to frank considerations of power and self-interest made it difficult for him to frame policies clearly based on such grounds.[55] Two years after the centennial, Arthur Walworth published a two-volume biography of Wilson that, while well-researched, hewed to the Seymour interpretation and made little new contribution to understanding the causes of involvement.[56]

The first extensive exploration of the formulation of German policy toward the United States appeared in Karl E. Birnbaum's *Peace Moves and U-Boat Warfare.*[57] His book, concentrating on the *Sussex* crisis and after, does not focus on American policy making but it does have important implications for American diplomatic historians. He found that not only did German policy oscillate between peace moves and intensification of submarine warfare but that a third course was also pursued of trying to manage issues with the United States so that even full underseas warfare would not lead to hostilities.

In the *Lusitania* and *Arabic* crises full compliance with Wilson's demands was precluded by official skepticism of the President's impartiality and by German public opinion, which was embittered at the American war trade and hopeful of the power of submarine warfare.[58] As 1915 ended, Chancellor Theobald von Bethmann-Hollweg came under great military and public pressures for full underseas warfare. Bethmann, deeply fearful of the dire consequences of hostilities with America, was hampered in resistance by the weakness of Kaiser Wilhelm II and by his own lack of energy and will.[59] The *Sussex* pledge, therefore, was only a temporary triumph over the U-boat enthusiasts.[60]

The Chancellor initiated a peace move in late 1916 in the hope of either forcing a general peace conference or of creating an atmosphere of reasonableness that would prevent hostilities with the United States when more drastic submarine warfare

[53] John A. Garraty, *Woodrow Wilson: A Great Life in Brief* (New York, 1956), 96–97, 99, 112, 116–17.

[54] John Morton Blum, *Woodrow Wilson and the Politics of Morality* (Boston, 1956), 96, 100, 129.

[55] Alexander L. and Juliette L. George, *Woodrow Wilson and Colonel House: A Personality Study* (New York, 1956), 159–60.

[56] Arthur Walworth, *Woodrow Wilson* (2 vols., New York, 1958). For an interesting survey of modern American foreign policy by a French scholar, see Jean-Baptiste Duroselle (trans. by Nancy Lyman Roelker), *From Wilson to Roosevelt: Foreign Policy of the United States, 1913–1945* (Cambridge, 1963). Duroselle attributes involvement to Wilson's desire to establish a just peace and a stable and progressive postwar world society.

[57] Karl E. Birnbaum, *Peace Moves and U-Boat Warfare* (Stockholm, 1958).

[58] *Ibid.,* 28–32, 36–37, 39.

[59] *Ibid.,* 51–53, 58–61.

[60] *Ibid.,* 78–79, 86.

began. The overture failed and when Wilson asked on December 18 for a statement of belligerent war goals, the Berlin government gave it an evasive, negative reply because both the military and civilian officials distrusted the President's motives and suspected collusion with the Allies. Unfortunately, in Birnbaum's view, the quick reply to Wilson's overture doomed the policy of trying to create a rapport sufficiently strong to avoid hostilities over a new underseas campaign. This was the final failure of Germany's American policy.[61] At the decisive conferences at Pless on January 9, 1917, the military and naval leaders unanimously insisted on unrestricted underseas warfare as the best hope for victory, whereas the Chancellor merely recited his past objections before deferring to the military view. Birnbaum believes that even at this date a more vigorous objection by Bethmann, analyzing the probable results of unrestricted warfare and the effects of an American entry, might have swayed the Kaiser and have postponed the decision at least long enough to try to cushion its impact on Wilson.

German vacillation between peace efforts and the submarine panacea finally broke down in a decision for the latter because of doubts over Wilson's neutrality and goals, and the growing primacy of the shortsighted military voice within the German government. Although the author disavowed in the preface any intention of answering the question of whether German-American hostilities were avoidable, in his conclusions he attributed considerable weight to German skepticism of Wilson engendered by the pro-Ally nature of American neutrality and the different attitudes of Washington toward Allied as opposed to German infractions of international law.[62] In that sense Birnbaum suggests a partial answer to the question if a more impartial American neutrality would not have strengthened the hands of German moderates in resisting pressures for unrestricted U-boat warfare.

The latest one-volume study of the neutrality period is Ernest R. May's *World War and American Isolation*.[63] Utilizing multi-archival research in Europe and the United States, May has examined the evolution of policies from the British and German perspectives as well as the American. He pointed out that in both Great Britain and Germany questions of policy toward neutral America were intertwined in domestic politics. In comparison with the Birnbaum study, May developed in greater detail the story of domestic German political pressures on foreign policy.

British Foreign Secretary Grey successfully shaped the English course in the first six months of the war by proceeding cautiously and considerately in applying maritime measures so that Anglo-American friendship would be preserved and strengthened. Even when Grey had lost the ability to control events because of mounting public pressures in England for a more drastic blockade, he had helped establish a moral basis of friendship capable of surviving a more trying period.[64]

In Germany Bethmann "fought long and hard against reckless opponents, only in the end to fail."[65] May thus gave a more favorable appraisal than did Birnbaum and Link, who portrayed the Chancellor in less flattering terms as failing to make a serious effort either to comprehend Wilson's peace objectives in 1916, to develop a

[61] *Ibid.*, 270.

[62] *Ibid.*, 31, 336–38.

[63] *The World War and American Isolation, 1914–1917* (Cambridge, 1959).

[64] *Ibid.*, 18–19, 21–25, 32–33. May has concluded that American economic retaliation in late 1916 would not have been fatal to Britain, which by then had developed alternative sources of munitions supplies. *Ibid.*, 321–22.

[65] *Ibid.*, [vii].

reasonable German peace move, or to subject Admiralty claims for the submarine to close scrutiny and refutation.[66] May depicted the harried Chancellor as convinced that the submarine could not defeat England and that war with the United States would be disastrous for Germany. He could not force abandonment of the U-boat weapon, however, because of the fanatical attitude of the navy admirals, the submarine enthusiasm of the German public, and the pressures of the conservative political parties and press. Caught in a dilemma, complicated by reliance on the vacillating Kaiser, the Chancellor temporized and delayed, making enough concessions to the United States to avoid war in the *Lusitania, Arabic,* and *Sussex* crises and yet endeavoring to permit the navalists use of the submarine just short of that point. At best, therefore, Bethmann could only postpone a decision for war with America.[67] By the fall of 1916 the new supreme army command of Field Marshal Paul von Hindenburg and General Erich F. W. Ludendorff had come to dominate Wilhelm, and Bethmann could no longer control the Reichstag. Hence when the army leaders joined the admirals in insistence on unrestricted underseas warfare as the one reliable hope for victory, the Chancellor was compelled to acquiesce. Any other course would have meant his immediate political demise.[68]

In concurrence with Buehrig and other writers, May described American neutrality as generally benevolent toward the Allies. Yet permission of belligerent loans and the arms trade were not deliberately unneutral but merely reflected America's view of international law and its trade interests. Legal and moral factors also were involved in the different American policies toward the British blockade and the submarine zone, but "the central difference in the two cases was a matter of national interest and not of either law or morality." Wilson could be satisfied that he had complied with the requirements of international law and morality and had served the national interests.[69]

May agreed with previous writers that House and Lansing viewed a triumphant Germany as a future threat to American security. House repeatedly warned Wilson in late 1914 and after that Germany would never forgive America for its pro-Ally attitude and if it won the war would hold the United States accountable and might challenge the Monroe Doctrine in South America. The Colonel did not desire a smashing Allied victory, however, for that would leave Russia free to expand.[70] As for Wilson, May stated that "He does appear, however, to have shared the view of Lansing and House that Germany was an enemy. He hoped that she might be too exhausted by the European war to turn immediately upon the United States, but he was not sanguine."[71] Wilson in late 1915 admitted to House that a victorious Germany might well take the western hemisphere as its next target, and his speeches for

[66] Link, *Wilson the Diplomatist,* 79–80. In *The Struggle for Neutrality,* 399, 401–03, 553, Link portrayed Bethmann more favorably as compelled by his precarious position to temporize in regard to U-boat warfare.

[67] May, *World War and American Isolation,* 197–205.

[68] *Ibid.,* 288–89, 413–15.

[69] *Ibid.,* 45–53. Although Link in the earlier volumes, described American neutrality to 1916 as benevolent but legally neutral toward the Allies, in *The Struggle for Neutrality,* 687, 691–92, he emphasizes the essential impartiality of American policies. Wilson acquiesced in Allied maritime measures, as required by trade, sympathy, and neutrality, but he also sought an adjustment to German submarine warfare by narrowing an initial condemnation of the U-boat as a weapon to mere insistence on the safety of American lives aboard belligerent liners. Thus the Oct. 21, 1915 protest to Britain was "fair warning" not to expect a benevolent neutrality. Neither side could reasonably complain that Wilson was against it.

[70] May, *World War and American Isolation,* 77–78.

[71] *Ibid.,* 169.

military preparedness in 1916 revealed a deep apprehension for the future security of the Americas. The President differed from these advisers primarily in his emotional attachment to peace. Consequently, although Wilson accepted the judgments of House and Lansing for a firm policy toward Germany, caution and pacifist inclinations caused him to follow a course of patience and delay, hoping for a "miraculous deliverance" from his dilemma. Additionally, Wilson's caution reflected his consciousness of the divided state of American public opinion, military weaknesses of the United States, and the hope of playing a role of peacemaker in the European war.[72]

Ruthless use of the submarine was the only kind of German action that could have engendered German-American hostility, as Germany lacked other means to affect directly American interests. Wilson could have accepted German underseas warfare in early 1915, just as he had British actions, but he instead chose to condemn it. Other alternatives were rejected apparently because the U-boat campaign violated international law and morality, and because it endangered important American economic interests in the war trade with the Allies.[73] After the *Lusitania* crisis American national prestige was fully committed to the strict accountability policy and diplomatic flexibility was greatly circumscribed. If only moral principles and economic interests had been involved, some possibility of compromise would have remained; what prevented Wilson and his advisers from considering such, however, was apprehension that prestige would be lost by a retreat or a compromise. House conceived of prestige in reference to the diplomatic influence of the American government. Lansing saw it also as closely connected to domestic public confidence in the administration, while Wilson thought of prestige as affecting national pride and involving moral purposes.[74] To the American leaders the concept of national interests thus included not only security but legal, economic, and prestige factors as well.

The unrestricted submarine campaign in 1917 caused Wilson to respond with a decision for war apparently in large part because of his concern for the nation's prestige and moral influence as a great power. Acceptance of the new U-boat war would have been a surrender in the light of past American declarations and seemed impossible to Wilson, not so much now on the grounds of immediate economic or security considerations, but because of the damaging blow American prestige and influence would have suffered. Each succeeding crisis with Germany had seen American prestige more deeply committed; and the submarine issue had become a symbol of Wilson's dedication to uphold international law and the rights of humanity.[75] Full belligerency, rather than armed neutrality, was chosen because of the President's growing distrust of Germany, his desire to unite the American people, and his belief that the nation's role in the war would be limited militarily. May concluded that Wilson had held balance-of-power ideas but that they were subsidiary to his idealistic desire for a just and lasting world peace. Although Wilson has been criticized by some historians for not taking the nation into war to protect its security, May believes it difficult to find fault with Wilson's statesmanship. Not perceiving an immediate danger to America from a German victory in the war, Wilson realistically coped with

---

[72] *Ibid.,* 167–78.

[73] *Ibid.,* 137–42. Contrary to Link, May viewed the Feb. 10, 1915 strict accountability note as initially intended to cover loss of American lives on belligerent as well as American merchant ships.

[74] *Ibid.,* 156–59.

[75] *Ibid.,* 426–27.

the only endangered national interests, economic and prestige, and idealistically sought to promote world peace through a new international order.[76]

The problem of the role of the national interests in the neutrality period receives at least a partial answer in the studies by Buehrig, Link, and May. The evidence that Wilson was more realistic than portrayed in the past, and that he was aware of and held to some degree balance of power and national interest concepts, is too extensive to be dismissed as a mere selection of isolated statements from the larger corpus of Wilsonian materials. Contrary to previous interpretations, the works of Buehrig, Link's recent volumes, and May reveal that Wilson often was influenced by his realistic counselors, and that he shared much of their evaluations of the meaning of the European war. Secretary Lansing had the clearest conviction that American security would be menaced by a German victory and might require intervention to avert that possibility. House and Wilson generally believed that the outcome of the war most favorable to American and world interests would be a peace short of total victory for either side. May pointed out that both the Colonel and Wilson foresaw that a victorious Germany would probably threaten the position of the United States in South America. Yet as Buehrig, Link, and May agree, balance of power and other considerations caused Wilson and House in 1915 and 1916 to try to mediate the war and thus to avoid American involvement and to preserve the existing equipoise. When the President finally did take the nation into the conflict in 1917, it was not because he feared an immediate German menace to American security.

How, then, were concepts of the national interest involved in the American war entry? Buehrig saw the answer in a Wilsonian balance of power concern being transformed into reliance on a community of power concept to protect American interests and preserve a just future peace. The unrestricted submarine announcement of 1917 precipitated war because of past policy stands, and because Germany was seen as a menace to the new world order envisioned by Wilson. Link portrayed Wilson as driven into acceptance of full hostilities over the submarine issue because of fear of a German victory endangering the balance of power and precluding realization of his idealistic and moralistic hopes for world reconstruction. May placed the emphasis on the prestige factor, which in a sense combined both national interests (security, economic, and diplomatic influence) and moralistic ideas of national honor and duty.

The more simplistic explanations of American involvement in the European war, current in the 1920s and 1930s, whether on the narrow grounds of a defense of legal neutral rights or of unneutral economic ties with the Allies, no longer suffice. The Buehrig, Link, and May studies make that conclusion abundantly clear. Just as clearly, the hypothesis that the United States went to war in 1917 to protect its security

---

[76] *Ibid.*, 433–37. Richard W. Leopold, *The Growth of American Foreign Policy* (New York, 1962), has usefully synthesized recent scholarship on the neutrality era. He views Wilson's acquiescence in the Allied maritime system as necessitated by America's economic and other national interests, and by the impossibility of maintaining an absolutely impartial neutrality when challenged by conditions of modern warfare (pp. 299, 303). The President, despite some evidence of pro-Ally feelings and balance-of-power concerns, "steered a course which was dictated solely by what he thought . . . to be best for America" (p. 311). The resultant economic ties with the Allies did not make war inevitable; only the German declaration of unrestricted submarine warfare, based on hopes of victory and not on resentment of America's role, left no alternative but entry into the war (pp. 303, 336). See also Leopold's "The Emergence of America as a World Power: Some Second Thoughts," John Braeman and others, eds., *Change and Continuity in Twentieth-Century America* (Columbus, 1964).

against an immediate German threat lacks persuasiveness. It appears that a complex of factors, including legitimate economic interests, some fear of a German victory and long-term threat to the western hemisphere, moral and legal reactions to the submarine, a very sensitive awareness of the involvement of American prestige, and especially Wilson's determination to promote a just and enduring postwar system, underlay American policies and the war entry in 1917. Defined as meaning more than immediate security needs, the authors reviewed agreed that the concept of involved American national interests had a large place in Wilsonian policies and war entry. At least as important, however, if not more so, were moral and idealistic factors.

17 / The Paris Education of Woodrow Wilson

Charles Seymour

Without much question, the first important American historian who made American diplomacy during the First World War a matter of central concern was Charles Seymour. Beginning in the early 1920s and continuing almost to his death in 1963, Seymour was a devoted scholar, a trenchant critic, a principal curator of documentation for the World War papers at the Yale University Library. He was also a man who encouraged younger scholars to undertake research in this field. Seymour set lofty standards for his own work and insisted on the same rigor when criticizing the scholarship of fellow historians. In his article which follows, Seymour describes President Wilson's various activities during the Paris Peace Conference and contends that Wilson obtained a substantial education in international affairs; that some of his ideas changed drastically, but, more important, he developed considerable flexibility and a willingness to compromise fundamental principles.

For further reading: *Thomas A. Bailey, *Wilson and the Peacemakers* (New York: 1947); Clarence A. Berdahl, "Myths About the Peace Treaties of 1919–1920," *American Scholar*, XI (Summer, 1942), 411–423; Paul Birdsall, *Versailles Twenty Years After* (New York: 1941); John A. De Novo, "The Movement for an Aggressive American Oil Policy Abroad 1918–1920," *American Historical Review*, LXI (1956), 854–876; Robert H. Ferrell, "Woodrow Wilson, Man and Statesman," *Review of Politics* XVIII (April, 1956); Lawrence E. Gelfand, *The Inquiry: American Preparations for Peace* (New Haven: 1963); *Arthur S. Link, *Wilson the Diplomatist* (Baltimore: 1957); Arno J. Mayer, *Politics and Diplomacy of Peacemaking: Containment and Counterrevolution at Versailles 1918–1919* (New York: 1967); Robert E. Osgood, "Woodrow Wilson, Collective Security and the

The late Charles Seymour served as Professor of History and President of Yale University. This article is reprinted with the permission of the author's son, Charles Seymour, Jr., and of the Managing Editor of the *Virginia Quarterly Review*. From the *Virginia Quarterly Review*, XXXII (1956), 578–593. Copyright © 1956 by the *Virginia Quarterly Review*, The University of Virginia.

Lessons of History," *Confluence*, V (1957), 341–354; Harry Rudin, *Armistice 1918* (New Haven: 1943); Seth P. Tillman, *Anglo-American Relations at the Paris Peace Conference* (Princeton: 1961).

No character in history or even on the Shakespearean stage has undergone a greater variety of interpretative renderings than Woodrow Wilson at the Paris Peace Conference. Depending upon the biographer and the climate of the day in which the story is told, Wilson appears as hero or simpleton, the courageous defender of justice against the intrigues of nationalistic greed, or the cowardly compromiser surrendering the principles for which the free men who trusted him and his leadership had fought and died. Even with the passing of the years, which is supposed to provide perspective, and with the opening of stores of rich firsthand materials for research, there has been no approach even to an approximate unanimity of judgment.

During the decade that followed the Treaty of Versailles opinion was primarily and not unnaturally affected or determined by personal emotion and political affiliation. The eulogistic pictures of Creel and Tumulty, the better documented but almost equally uncritical histories of Dodd and Ray Stannard Baker, betray the personal hold which Wilson had on the writer, who was caught in close-range adoration of his subject. The President suffered thereby. However worthy he might be of the pedestal which they sought to build, their bias was obvious and their passionate praise unconvincing.

The rather blind vigor of this portrayal of Wilson's service at the Paris Peace Conference derived its impetus in part as a reaction to the more effective although hardly better justified criticism passed on the President by Maynard Keynes. The latter's "The Economic Consequences of the Peace," a polemic of persuasive quality, sought to expose the inevitable disaster that must result from the reparations policy embodied in the treaty. His arguments were irrefutable on the economic ground; but he could not restrain his brilliant and mordant pen from a striking personal sketch of Wilson, almost a caricature, which caught the popular attention. This portrait of the "poor, bamboozled President . . . a blind and deaf Don Quixote" has never been entirely obliterated. Its persistence is only partly due to the brilliance of its imagery; as in all good caricatures, it rests upon a substratum of fact. But it is set forth in misleading phrases too witty to be true.

A dozen years later this picture was adapted with skill and in more detail by another Englishman, Harold Nicolson, in his "Peacemaking." It is drawn with less harshness but in an equally critical tone. He gives full credit to the loftiness of Wilson's political homiletics and he emphasizes the corresponding disappointment in his failures of execution. Like Keynes he harps upon the President's "tinge of revivalism, a touch of methodist arrogance, more than a touch of presbyterian vanity . . . the active belief that God, Wilson, and the People would triumph in the end." With some justification Nicolson excoriates the amateurishness, imprecision, and improvisation characteristic of Wilson's methods of negotiation; and he concludes the confession of his own disillusionment with the verdict that "the prophet was a dry and uncertain man . . . not in the least prepared to enforce his own prophecy." The surrender of Wilson's principles, which Nicolson stresses, his complacent sacrifice of the Fourteen Points, he attributes to the President's mesmerized confidence in the League of Nations as a panacea. "He immured himself within the Ark of the Covenant."

These opinions found hospitality in the American mood of the thirties, which was impregnated with the dominant isolationism of the time and the consciousness of the impotence of the League of Nations manifested by events in Manchuria, Ethiopia, and the Rhinelands. But with the renaissance of German military power and aggressive temper, interpreters of Wilson such as George Noble and James Shotwell, although careful to avoid any return to emotional adulation, found in his policy at Paris the only sure protection against international bankruptcy. This reaction developed with increasing strength as the necessity of world organization became obvious during the course of the Second World War. The beautifully balanced biography of Herbert Bell, the careful studies of Birdsall and Bailey, emphasized not merely the prophetic quality of the President, at which earlier critics had sneered as an aspect of mere sermonizing, but credited him with a high degree of achievement in the face of serious obstacles. "With all his mistakes," writes Birdsall, "Wilson emerges as the only man of real stature at Paris."

This conclusion emanating from the new idealism of the early forties and the reaction against isolationism has obviously not achieved a permanent endorsement. The disillusion that followed upon the military defeat of Germany, the onset of the cold war, have again altered the trend of opinion and given rise to renewed criticism of Wilson. Not only is the President depicted as ineffective in negotiation but his principles are dismissed as forming an inadequate or impracticable basis for international relations. Thus Hajo Holborn in his objective and incisive "Political Collapse of Europe" stresses the weakness of the Wilsonian program because of the generality of its tenets and the contradictory aspects of its dogmas. "More serious," writes Holborn, "was Wilson's ingrained belief that his abstract ideals would blot out certain realities of political life."

In his "American Diplomacy" George Kennan is equally critical and more caustic. The President's primary deficiency, he believes, was an inability to grasp the necessity of a balance of power as basis for a stable European system. Thus, in his disregard of the essential, Wilson forgot his own principle of "justice even to those to whom we do not wish to be just." Blindly he helped to enforce upon Germany a disastrous peace of humiliation which led to his own "tragic and historic failure." The final result, in Kennan's opinion, was "the sort of peace you get when you allowed war hysteria and impractical idealism to lie down together in your mind . . . when you indulged yourself in the colossal conceit of thinking that you could suddenly make international life over into what you believed to be your own image."

Thus the pendulum swings, according to the push and pull of political philosophy or personal predilection. And the variation in the estimate of Wilson's achievement at Paris is the more confusing because of the contradictory qualities in the President's own temperament. Depending upon which of the traits or moods is emphasized, this or the other interpretation can take reasonable form. "I have never known a man," said Colonel House, "so changeable in his disposition. Anything you might say of him, good or bad, could be true at one time or another."

But in all the variety of verdicts passed upon Woodrow Wilson one quality has not received the emphasis which it deserves. He was eminently educable. Contrary to popular belief he was surprisingly ready to learn his lesson, provided he were allowed to make up his own mind in an atmosphere of reason, and always assuming that his emotional hostility was not aroused by an impertinent adviser, a violent opponent, or an ineradicable prejudice. He was proud of his capacity for rational change of mind. "I should be ashamed of myself," he insisted in explaining his *volte face* on the preparedness issue, "if I had not learned something during the course of the past year."

Wilson's whole political career, indeed, was marked by development from one position to another, not infrequently with such rapidity as to permit the change to appear revolutionary. We may note his shift from the hands-off attitude of *laissez-faire* to the doctrines of the New Freedom, wherein government was to assume active responsibility for the maintenance of freedom. He did not fear to make the leap from "peace without victory," before the United States entered the European war, to "force without stint or limit" in the attainment of complete triumph when our troops were on French soil.

This capacity for adaptation to changing circumstances or to his own better understanding of them, whether we regard it as admirable or otherwise, demands attention if Wilson is to be evaluated objectively. With few exceptions his biographers have accepted the general conviction of his political colleagues that he was "obstinate" or "firm," depending upon the point of view of the individual, but in either case adamant. Once his mind was made up, they felt, it was useless to argue. "The President," asserted Keynes, "was capable of digging his toes in and refusing to budge . . . but he had no other mode of defense." He lacked the "capacity for adjustment to circumstances," Nicolson concludes. "It was his spiritual and mental rigidity which proved his undoing."

Such generalizations might be multiplied. They form a curious misreading of Wilson's temperament and mentality. Upon occasion he could be unyielding, no one more so. But he could also shift his position. It is impossible rightly to appreciate his achievement at Paris as well as his apparent failures there unless we perceive, first, how much he had to learn and, next, how much he actually did learn. Thus, as touching the larger issues underlying the settlement, he came to recognize that self-determination was not an absolute principle and was by no means capable of universal application. Another reality he finally accepted was that in any system of international organization effective control must be in the hands of the great Powers. The most important lesson of all, which it is likely he never honestly acknowledged to himself, was that no firm dividing line could be drawn between right and wrong in world politics and that there must be discovered, accordingly, a reasonable adjustment among the conflicting demands of sovereign states. Without such compromise no settlement could be achieved.

Even the enthusiastic hero-worshippers of Wilson will admit that he had much to learn when he undertook to lead the American delegation to the Peace Conference. Of political Europe he knew nothing at first-hand. Previous to his landing at Brest on December 13, 1918, he had never been on the continent, except for a brief vacation in Italy some fifteen years previous. He knew something of the English Lake District as a casual tourist, but he lacked any personal contact with British political leaders. The gaps in the President's information on contemporary conditions in Europe shocked his advisers on the *George Washington*. He found it hard to believe that there were three million Germans in northern Bohemia. ("Why, Masaryk never told me that.") He was opposed to German annexation of Austria because it would make for Catholic control of Germany. Very early in the negotiations of the Peace Conference he promised Orlando full support of the Italian claim to the Brenner frontier, apparently unaware of the injustice thereby imposed upon the homeland of Andreas Hofer.

This lack of specific information was of less significance than Wilson's naïve confidence in his own capacity, with the help of expert advisers, to frame an adequate settlement and the extent of his distrust of any other leadership. His determination to attend the Conference in person and as an active participant is an indication of this self-confidence. He persisted stubbornly in this decision, although it destroyed the possibility of calling a preliminary conference immediately after the armistice for the prompt settlement of military terms and the revival of stable economic conditions. This was unfortunate. It can be argued that the naïveté underlying his bold crusade to Paris ultimately paid dividends, that whatever good was to be found in the treaties resulted from his own conduct of negotiations. So much is averred by the historians of the forties, although it runs counter to the conclusions of some of his most astute counselors. But right or wrong in his decision Wilson undertook his personal venture in an atmosphere of ignorance. He believed, apparently, that he had merely to proclaim his principles in person in order to rally the common people to their support. Clemenceau was not far from the mark in referring to Wilson's "generous artlessness" (*noble candeur*).

The ingenuous quality of his attitude found expression in the President's confidence in popular feeling and the rather sinister purposes he imputed to European political leaders. "We shall be the only disinterested people at the Peace Conference," he insisted, in talking with his American advisers, "and the men whom we are about to deal with do not represent their own people." Thus the American delegation must assume the leadership and see that the Conference was "prepared to follow the opinions of mankind and to express the will of the people rather than that of their leaders." This innocent reliance upon the wisdom of popular judgment and rather arrogant emphasis upon the validity of his own rôle as its prophet were naturally strengthened by the hysterical acclamation which he received from the vast throngs that greeted him in the European capitals.

It should also be noted that Wilson undertook his adventures at Paris with little in the way of a specific program. He enjoyed always the excitement of improvisation and seemed unappreciative of the dangers involved therein. Many of his most effective oratorical effects had been achieved under the spur of the moment. At Princeton he never worked out the essential details of his quadrangle plan with the consideration necessary to success. When he entrusted Colonel House with the responsibility of representing him at the armistice conference, in response to the latter's request for a program the President said: "I have not given you any instructions because I feel you will know what to do." Colonel House endeavored to provide a precise interpretation of the Fourteen Points, which had not been designed as a chart for peace negotiations and were ill-suited to that purpose; but Wilson took little interest in this attempt at specification. The harsh criticism leveled by Maynard Keynes at the President for his failure to define exactly the principles of his program and their pertinence is not entirely without justification. "He could have preached a sermon on any of them or have addressed a stately prayer to the Almighty for their fulfilment; but he could not frame their concrete application to the actual state of Europe."

In view of such lack of experience and with these personal handicaps, the final extent of success which Wilson achieved bears witness to abilities that more than counterbalanced his defects. In his own mind, as he set forth for Paris, the creation of a League of Nations had become the dominating goal of the Conference. This was to be his main accomplishment; and this he actually accomplished. The successful completion of the Covenant, at least in its initial form, and its approval by the plenary Conference on February 14, called for capacities that Wilson possessed in great measure—clarity of thought and expression, imaginative courage, persuasive rhetoric. His leadership in the committee that drafted the Covenant was compelling. He was entirely at home in the process of developing constitutional forms. His mental agility was obvious in the skill with which he fulfilled the functions of chairmanship.

Moreover, in this congenial task Wilson enjoyed the most competent and sympathetic support. Lord Robert Cecil brought to the committee intense enthusiasm and a first-class brain. The wisdom and rich experience of Jan Smuts and his liberal attitude captured the President's respect and confidence. Beside him sat Colonel House, foreseeing snags and deftly indicating their avoidance. Representatives of the lesser nations, statesmen of ability such as Venizelos and Hymans, proved warmly co-operative, seeing in the League an enfranchisement from the control of the great Powers. Whatever weaknesses might later be discovered in the Covenant it was bravely and happily conceived. Wilson's sense of triumph, when after securing its unanimous approval by the Conference he sailed for the United States, was exalted.

This clear-cut success was not to be repeated in the more specific areas of negotiation, in which Wilson did not enjoy similar advantage. His world leadership might have been better protected if he had not returned to Paris and had given his attention to the cultivation and persuasion of the Senate. The other problems of the peace might safely have been left to his lieutenants. If they yielded too much of the Wilsonian program, the President in distant Washington could disavow them. From February on, the settlement need not have suffered from his personal absence from Paris. His own reputation would have remained untarnished. His political supporters at home would have taken heart. But the education which he had already begun in the Paris negotiations would have been incomplete.

Even during the first triumphant progress of the Covenant of the League Wilson had been learning lessons. Verbal imprecisions could be dangerous and phrases carried hidden dangers. Thus the popular interpretation of "Open covenants openly arrived at" was, he discovered, obviously impracticable. No reasonable person ought ever to have believed that peace negotiations could be carried on as a public forum. But the secrecy of the Council's discussion and the inadequacy of the information given out to the Press created the impression that at the very start Wilson had surrendered one of his points to the forces of European darkness.

At this early stage of negotiation he also began to learn the necessity of compromise. Before any agreement could be reached upon the Covenant of the League, the problem of the disposal of the German colonies had to be faced. Emotionally and rather absent-mindedly Wilson had taken for granted that they would not be restored to Germany. On the way to Paris, influenced by a suggestion from George Louis Beer, he expressed the opinion that they "should be declared the common property of the League of Nations and administered by small nations. The resources of each colony should be available to all members of the League." The rather vague idea of mandates was sharpened by General Smuts' pamphlet which advocated a similar type of trusteeship; although Smuts planned it not for the German colonies but for territories formerly belonging to Russia, Austria-Hungary, and Turkey. The British Dominion leaders disliked Wilson's proposal and were loath to modify their determination to annex the colonies. The struggle that followed was sharp. It was settled by Smuts' ingenious plan of three types of mandated territory which the President accepted, albeit with a certain absence of grace. The extent of the concessions made on each side is indicated on the one hand by the charge that the mandates were merely a camouflage for annexation, as compared on the other hand with Herbert Bell's conclusion that Wilson "had scored a real triumph."

The importance of what the President yielded in the discussion of mandates was obscured by his success in winning approval of the Covenant on February 14. He himself was unconscious of any significant capitulation. But when in March he returned from his hasty trip to Washington, he was shocked to discover that for the settlement of the issues henceforth before the Conference a process of give-and-take was unavoidable. During his absence he had left to Colonel House the responsibility for the conduct of United States policy. The latter was not in a position to make definite concessions, even if he had so desired. He kept Wilson informed by constant telegrams of every step in the negotiations. And contrary to the opinion of the more idealistic Wilsonians he was not inclined "to give the greedy ones all they want." But House realized more clearly than Wilson the necessity of coming to terms on the problems of reparations and of French security as to which the President's ideas of justice were not likely to be accepted intact. By the development of his personal relations with the European leaders he had prepared the ground for compromise.

Upon his return to France Wilson gave no hint to House of the distress which his sudden and belated appreciation of this condition of affairs aroused. But to his wife the President expressed himself in explosive terms. The American case, he felt, was in grave danger of being given away. He must gird himself for the combat necessary to salvage his program. It is likely that he never recovered absolute confidence in House, although he continued to use him and to regard him as his second-in-command up to the close of the Conference. In the ensuing process of compromise into which despite his abhorrence of the word Wilson was drawn, House served as his chief agent.

The procedures of negotiation were carried on in the intimate conversations of Wilson, Lloyd George, and Clemenceau who, together with the less authoritative Orlando, replaced the Council of Ten as the controlling body of the Conference. The nature of these conversations has been differently presented by various historians. Extreme critics have regarded their complete secrecy as in itself a denial of Wilsonian principles. Better instructed students have recognized that no more rapid or effective method of negotiation could have been devised. The majority of writers have emphasized the atmosphere of belligerent conflict which, they assume, characterized the discussions. They have phrased the decisions taken in the terms of "victory" or "defeat." Such an impression is given by Keynes on the one hand and by Ray Stannard Baker on the other. The Council is depicted as a battleground. This portrayal is denied by Tardieu, who certainly attended more meetings of the Four than Keynes and is better qualified to bear witness. But it is confirmed by another Frenchman, Gabriel Terrail, who although he wrote as early as 1922, was supplied with numerous unpublished and authoritative documents. Under the pseudonym of Mermeix he gave to his small volume on the Peace Conference the significant title: "Le Combat des Trois."

Clearly there was sharp expression of conflicting views and policies in the Council of Four. But if these meetings had constituted merely a battleground Woodrow Wilson would never have completed his Paris education or accepted a practicable basis of agreement. He would never have learned his lesson of compromise. For the President, once he entered a conflict, once his Covenanter's blood was aroused, would never yield to the violence of irrational opposition. He merely stiffened under threats. But in an atmosphere of sweet reasonableness, of what he liked to term "common counsel," he was ready to listen, to evaluate, to adjust. The tone of the discussions of the Four was conducive to such an atmosphere; so much is made clear from the recently published notes of those conversations as set down by Paul Mantoux, the official interpreter of the Conference.

Mantoux' notes throw new light upon our understanding of the process of negotiation. They cover the first of the early discussions, which are not included in the more formal minutes of Lord Hankey. They were not designed for general distribution and they stand unrevised. They reflect the genius of Mantoux as interpreter and his learned understanding of the problems under discussion. Through these pages we can today follow the give-and-take of the vital negotiations and appreciate the balance of factors that finally made possible a decisive conclusion. Without the most careful analysis of Mantoux' notes no verdict of permanent value can be passed upon the peacemakers of 1919.

Whatever the irritations and frustrations which Wilson experienced in the discussions of the Four, it is clear that there he came to understand certain basic realities. No single one of the chiefs of state was going to secure his program *in toto*. A number of the primary demands of each Power would have to be satisfied. The alternative to compromise between the maximum demand and the minimum necessity, in the case of each state, was the break-up of the Conference with a trail of consequences that could not be foretold. This disaster each of the three dominant leaders of the Conference was determined to avoid. To help prevent it Wilson soon came to recognize that he would have to make large concessions.

Another lesson was borne in upon him without overmuch delay. This was the inevitable interplay of domestic and international politics. The decisions finally taken at Paris must be made in the light of political conditions in each of the home countries. The three leaders were not free agents. In a world supposedly made safe for democracy they were subject to the overlordship of democracy. They could offend their parliamentary majorities back home only at the cost of endangering or destroying their own position.

This fact was brought very close to Wilson upon his return to Paris. He carried with him various demands for amendment to his Covenant which in the opinion of his shrewdest advisers were essential to its ultimate approval by the United States Senate. Certain of these amendments, notably that which dealt with the Monroe Doctrine, would raise opposition in Europe. If he were to have support by the British and French in this matter so close to his heart, he could not refuse to understand the political exigencies which they also faced.

Thus his attitude on reparations was affected by French and British national sensibilities as well as by the emotional appeal of General Smuts. His own advisers made clear to him that failure to establish a definite lump sum for reparations, within the terms of the pre-Armistice Agreement, was bound to vitiate the economic aspects of the settlement. But neither Lloyd George nor Clemenceau could afford to disappoint and infuriate their constituencies by agreeing to the relatively modest sum advocated by the Americans. Of this fact Wilson became rationally persuaded. Hence his reconciliation to the postponement of setting a specific sum and to the device of flexible arrangements under a Reparations Commission.

This adjustment was not easy for the President to accept and it intensified the April crisis during which he ordered the *George Washington* to be readied to take him home, a futile and rather petulant gesture which did not alter the basic necessity of compromise. Even more difficult for him was French insistence upon the separation of the Rhinelands from the German Reich, which Wilson as well as Lloyd George rightly regarded as both impracticable at the moment and fatal to a permanent peace in the future. Clemenceau was wise enough to accept their protests. But his exposition of the need of special protection for France against fresh German attacks was impressive. It sufficed to induce Wilson to approve a lengthy period of occupation of the Rhinelands by Allied troops and their permanent disarmament. The old Tiger's persuasive rhetoric also availed surprisingly to secure Wilson's endorsement of the special tri-partite treaty of guarantee, which provided for British and American military assistance in case of German aggression. To many idealists this treaty appeared as a confession of distrust in the League of Nations. But the President's conviction that the assurance of French security demanded special measures of this sort was sincere.

Wilson's developing sense of political realities became manifest also in his acquiescence in Japanese demands in the Shantung settlement. Both sentimentally and politically he paid a high price for this decision, which his most loyal supporters disapproved. But he would have paid a higher price if he had given stubborn support to the Chinese position. Time and again the Japanese had yielded to his appeals in one or another issue; they could fairly ask some tangible token of appreciation. Their withdrawal from the League would not have been fatal. But their co-operation was needed in order to avoid political and financial confusion in the Far East. Nor, in the end, would the Chinese have been better off if Wilson had blocked Japanese claims. His final decision, which enemies in the Senate were to capitalize viciously, was made to appear as surrender to barefaced blackmail. But he reached that decision on reasonable grounds and with clear appreciation of the consequences.

Other instances of the President's enlarging comprehension of conditions that could not be changed and must be faced might be multiplied. One of the most striking is found in his attitude on the northern frontiers of Bohemia where, after he had discovered the impressive German population inhabiting the Sudetenlands, he might have been expected to invoke the principle of self-determination and insist upon their incorporation in the German Reich. On the contrary, he became so thoroughly convinced that the new Czechoslovak state needed a strong frontier that he did not even support the suggestions of his experts for lopping off the more obviously nationalistic German districts. Elsewhere in decisions upon territorial issues he finally realized that there were no absolutes. During the May discussions of the Austro-Jugoslav frontier, specifically the Klagenfurth Basin, one of his experts was called in to sit by the President in the Council of Four. In response to the American proposal a counter-suggestion was made by the Italians. Turning to his adviser, Wilson asked in a low tone, "Does that seem a reasonable compromise?" Six months earlier the word would have shocked him.

Not less notable is his acceptance of the necessity and the wisdom of throwing responsibility for the maintenance of international tranquility and protection from revolutionary discontent upon the great Powers. At the outset of his crusade his distrust of the motives of those Powers was such as to bring his support to the lesser nationalities. The maintenance of the control formerly exercised by the great Powers through the Balance of Power, he insisted, "had always produced only aggression, and selfishness, and war." To the principle of balance as contrasted with what he called the "community of interest" he was always opposed. But the realities of power, as he finally appreciated, could not be disregarded. Thus in May, when the smaller nations were protesting the provisions designed to protect minorities, as constituting an infringement of their sovereignty, Wilson in full plenary session asserted that ultimate control must rest in the hands of the great Powers. They had won the war and they were, in the final resort, the guarantors of the peace. But what he failed to grasp, even at the end of the Conference, was that a relative balance of power must always be a matter of critical significance. Indeed, if the League were to be a practical success in operation, there must be the balance that Wilson still denied.

His Paris education was thus by no means complete. It had enabled him to accept various decisions on the basis of demonstrated facts. But it had produced no revolution in his temperament, nor had it touched his basic principles. More obviously, his appreciation of European realities was still uneven. His mistaken appeal to the Italian people in the Fiume crisis was evidence of a continuing optimistic simplicity. Equally unreal was his naïve confidence that the deficiencies of the settlement would be obliterated through the operation of the League of Nations. He waved a casual good-bye to the Freedom of the Seas which, League or no League, was an issue always pregnant with factors of Anglo-American discord. The contradiction between the disarmament demanded in his Fourteen Points and the eventual and unilateral disarmament imposed upon Germany in the treaty did not offend him. Nor was he sensitive to the obvious fact that any permanent political settlement would demand the firm economic foundation that was not provided at Versailles.

Wilson's high rank as statesman, as distinguished from political prophet, would be more solid if he had been able to admit such deficiencies. He would also have gained not merely in reputation but in political position had he frankly attributed his decisions to the necessities of fact and not attempted to clothe them in idealistic principle. His conviction of the needs of French security, for instance, was entirely honest. In his defense of the treaty he would have been on stronger ground by explaining and emphasizing his conversion.

An open avowal that various aspects of his original program could not be applied because of practical reasons would have saved him from the charge of hypocrisy and would actually have strengthened his plea for ratification. Such an attitude would have permitted him, in his struggle with the Senate majority, to contend that the final decisions taken at Paris were not the result of compromise or failure to protect American interests, but emerged from a realistic understanding of political possibilities. They fell short of idealistic hopes. But they were the best that circumstances permitted.

18 / The War-Guilt Question and American Disillusionment, 1918–1928

Selig Adler

Isolationism and nationalism were deeply accentuated in American society during the interwar decades by a rather widespread disillusionment with the nation's record of participation in the First World War. Many Americans adopted a view that Wilsonian policies had served no useful purpose; that American intervention in 1917 had been one tragic, unnecessary mistake. The postwar disillusionment, as Selig Adler describes in the following article, was advanced by the rash of revisionist historical writings published during the 1920s. Adler's article clearly illustrates the relationship of ideas and intellectual history to American foreign relations. Moreover, it suggests that the revisionist historiography expressing a later generation's reaction to the First World War exercised an influence upon governmental policies during the interwar decades.

For further reading: Joseph Brandes, *Herbert Hoover and Economic Diplomacy: Department of Commerce Policy 1921–1928* (Pittsburgh: 1962); Warren I. Cohen, *The American Revisionists* (Chicago: 1967); John P. Diggins, "Flirtation with Fascism: American Pragmatic Liberals and Mussolini's Italy," *American Historical Review*, LXXI (1966) 487–506; L. Ethan Ellis, *Frank B. Kellogg and American Foreign Relations 1925–1929* (New Brunswick: 1961); *Herbert Feis, *The Diplomacy of the Dollar; First Era 1919–1932* (Baltimore: 1950); Robert H. Ferrell, *American Diplomacy in the Great Depression: Hoover-Stimson Foreign Policy 1929–1933* (New Haven: 1957) and *Peace in Their Time* (New Haven: 1952); Joseph C. Grew, "The Peace Conference of Lausanne 1922–1923," *Proceedings of the American Philosophical Society*, XCVIII (1954), 1–10; *Elting E. Morison, *Turmoil and Tradition: A Study of the Life and Times of Henry L. Stimson* (Boston: 1960); Harold G. Moulton and Leo Pasvolsky, *War Debts and World Prosperity* (Washington: 1932).

Selig Adler is Professor of History at the State University of New York at Buffalo. This article is published with the permission of the author and of the Editor, *Journal of Modern History*. From the *Journal of Modern History*, XXIII (1951), 1–28. Copyright 1951 by The University of Chicago Press.

The time is ripe for a critical examination of the impact of first World War revisionism upon American thought. We are now in the sixth year of "peace," and it was in 1922 that a veritable avalanche of literature appeared, to reverse the earlier verdict of exclusive German guilt. Samuel F. Bemis has raised the question: "Will the new revision help to lose the second peace as the first revision helped to lose the first peace?"[1] Harry Elmer Barnes is now working on "neorevisionism."[2] Hence a study of the gigantic shift of opinion which took place in the United States after November 11, 1918 not only should be helpful in explaining the growth of isolationist sentiment but should also aid in the evaluation of the emerging literature on the more recent conflict.

The story of "Die Kriegsschuldfrage in Amerika" must begin by measuring the effect on American opinion of four years of "rainbow books," imported and domestic propaganda, Wilsonian idealism, and the "over-there" spirit. Even the professional historians, with few exceptions, by 1918 explained the war as a plot against civilization by the Central Powers.[3] Many members of the American Historical Association had written wartime propaganda. The already venerable Albert Bushnell Hart joined the National Security League and wrote *America at War: a Handbook of Patriotic Education*.[4] George Lincoln Burr, fresh from reading before the American Historical Association his presidential address on "The freedom of history," donned khaki and helped drill his students on the Cornell campus.[5] The list of prominent historians who wrote pamphlets for George Creel's Committee on Public Information is long and impressive.[6] James T. Shotwell headed the National Board for Historical Service. Prominent American historians formed part of the "Inquiry" which advised Wilson at Versailles. From the point of view of the extreme revisionists, it was "Clio's debauch in the arms of Uncle Sam."[7] Hence the charge that the American historical guild had a vested interest in both the "Entente epic" and the treaties of peace.

Few would deny today that the Allied case in the first World War was overstated. Andrew C. McLaughlin told a British audience that, before America could be united in the fight for democracy, it had been necessary to know: "Who began this war? We wanted to know authoritatively, documentarily, unequivocally—and we found out."[8] In December 1918 William Stearns Davis' *Roots of the War* began to appear in serial form in the *Century*. The American public learned that by July 1914 the German war lords had declared everything in readiness at the Potsdam council and William II started on "the greatest of human adventures," lured on by the same

[1] Samuel F. Bemis, "Revisonist historiography for the second World War," *Journal of Modern History*, XIX (1947), 55–59.

[2] See pamphlet distributed by the author entitled *The Struggle Against the Historical Blackout* (2d ed. rev. and enl.; n.p., n.d.).

[3] Harry Elmer Barnes, *A History of Historical Writing* (Norman, Okla., 1937), p. 279.

[4] C. Hartley Grattan, "The historians cut loose," *American Mercury*, XI (1927), 416, 420.

[5] *Ibid.*

[6] *Ibid.*, pp. 421–22. According to Grattan, Creel stated that he had twenty-five hundred historians on his list of potential propaganda writers (p. 423).

[7] *Ibid.*, p. 430.

[8] Andrew C. McLaughlin, *America and Britain* (New York, 1919), p. 15. Munroe Smith, of Columbia, later to become one of the chief opponents of revisionism, in *Militarism and Statecraft* (New York, 1918), p. 199, compared collective action against Germany to collective action against a claim-jumper in a mining camp.

dream of glory which had motivated conquerors from Xerxes to Napoleon.[9] Carleton J. H. Hayes's *A Brief History of The Great War* appeared in 1920, with much the same thesis. Hayes did recognize "international anarchy" as a remote cause of the conflict, but, he wrote, the German ruling class alone precipitated the war.[10] Charles D. Hazen's 1920 edition of *Modern Europe* spoke in even stronger terms of the "sinister and brutal challenge" of Germany to civilization.[11] William Roscoe Thayer became in later years the bête noire of the revisionist writers. Thayer had been a Harvard classmate and close friend of Theodore Roosevelt. During the war he had written the famous pamphlets, *Volleys from a Noncombatant* and *Germany vs. Civilization*.[12] In his 1919 presidential address to the Cleveland meeting of the American Historical Association on "Fallacies in history," he found many occasions to remind his colleagues of "German frightfulness."[13]

Probably the most important reason for the kaleidoscopic changes in interpretation after 1920 was the unexpected opening of the sources. The revolutionary leaders of the defeated powers were willing to expose the innermost diplomatic secrets of their monarchical predecessors. Germany and Austria felt that they had nothing to lose in the eyes of the world. Moreover, Soviet Russia was anxious to bare diplomatic intrigue so as to discredit the 1914 capitalistic "warmongers" of all the powers. In the United States, the *Nation* and the *New Republic* received this material as soon as it was printed and promptly digested it and dispensed it to the American intelligentsia. The editors of these magazines, Oswald Garrison Villard and Herbert Croly, were both liberals who had supported Wilson and then turned against him. Bitterly disillusioned by the Versailles settlement, they used the material from the Russian archives to impeach the motives of England and France. Thus the *Nation* warned its readers that only if you discredit these Russian sources is it possible to "go back undisturbed to one's comfortable belief in the unique and unprovoked responsibility of our late enemies."[14] In September 1919 the socialist coalition government published a three-volume *Austrian Red Book of 1919*, containing 352 documents.[15] Within a year an English translation was available. Edited by the able Dr. Roderich Gooss, these docu-

---

[9] *Century*, XCVIII (1919), 432. Davis' *Europe since Waterloo* (New York, 1926) maintained virtually the same thesis of war responsibility as did his *Roots of the War*.

[10] Carleton J. H. Hayes, *A Brief History of the Great War* (New York, 1920), pp. 1–17. W. S. Davis, in reviewing this book for the *American Historical Review*, XXVI (1920), 91–93, stated that, while "revelations" from Europe concerning the war might modify important secondary matters, they may not "swerve our judgment as to the greater things."

[11] Charles D. Hazen, *Modern Europe* (New York, 1920), p. 690.

[12] Grattan, "The historians cut loose," *loc. cit.*, p. 416.

[13] *American Historical Review*, XXV (1920), 179–90.

[14] *New Republic*, XVIII (1919), 347–51, contained much recently uncovered Russian material. *Nation*, CVII (1918), 807–8, apparently accepted *Ambassador Morgenthau's Story* (Garden City, 1918). The turn to revisionism began with "Some outstanding diplomatic revelations," *Nation*, CIX (1919), 161, followed by "More revelations from Russia," *ibid.*, CIX (1919), 235–36, from which the above quotation is taken.

[15] Austria, Foreign office, *Diplomatische Aktenstücke zur Vorgeschichte des Krieges 1914: Ergänzungen und Nachträge zum Österreichisch-ungarischen Rotbuch* (3 vols; Vienna, 1919). The English translation, *Austrian Red Book of 1919*, was published in 1920. The *American Historical Review*, XXV (1919–20), 337–38, called the attention of the profession to the publication of these documents and also pointed out that Gooss, in *Das Wiener Kabinet und die Entstechung des Krieges* (Vienna, 1919), had thrown doubt on the Wangenheim-Morgenthau story of the Postdam council of July 5, 1914.

ments "revealed the reckless diplomacy by which Austria dragged Germany into a World War which Austria did not want, but which she was willing to risk in her determination to put an end to the danger which menaced her from the side of Serbia."[16] The villain now seemed to be not William II but the Austrian foreign minister, Count Leopold von Berchtold. Hard upon these revelations came reports of the extraction by Karl Kautsky of important material from the Berlin archives.[17] Despite the fact that Kautsky proved that Germany had not plotted the war, his emphasis upon the kaiser's marginalia on the diplomatic correspondence possibly influenced the American public more than did the sober facts. In this display of "royalty revealed in Unterhosen,"[18] the kaiser called the British a "pack of base hucksters," and the Serbs "rabble" that must be crushed. Moreover, references to "ruthless action on our part" were hardly designed to convince the American mind of the essentially pacific intentions of the German emperor.[19]

Probably the greatest impression on American thinking in the early postwar years came from people who had worked with the Russian sources. Within a matter of months after the Bolshevist coup of November 1917, Pravda began to reveal the imperialist and militarist aims of the tsarist government by printing archival material.[20] An important impact on opinion in this country came in 1921 when the American press carried full extracts from the von Siebert publications.[21] B. von Siebert had been a counselor in the Russian embassy at London. He clandestinely copied secret papers and either sold or gave them to the Germans.[22] These documents helped break down the exclusive guilt theory by showing strenuous Entente efforts to make their coalition strong enough to defy, if necessary, the Triple Alliance.[23] Shortly thereafter,

---

[16] Sidney B. Fay, The Origins of the World War (2d ed., 2 vols. in 1; New York, 1932), I, 10.

[17] Soon after the armistice the German provisional government authorized Kautsky to go ahead with the work. Ready in May 1919, publication was postponed. Die deutschen Dokumente zum Kriegsausbruch was published in four vols. in Charlottenburg in November 1919. Count Max Montgelas and Walter Schücking had been put in charge of publication in September 1919, but the proof was read by Kautsky. The English edition is Outbreak of the World War: German Documents Collected by Karl Kautsky, published by the Carnegie Endowment for International Peace (New York, 1924).

[18] Sidney B. Fay, "New light on the origins of the World War. I. Berlin and Vienna, to July 29," American Historical Review, XXV (1920), 617.

[19] "Some private notes of Wilhelm II," Living Age, CCCIV (1920), 63–67.

[20] Fay, Origins, I, 10. As early as April 1918 Seymour Cocks published The Secret Treaties and Understandings (London, 1918), which told English readers of many secret commitments concerning Italy, Constantinople, Asiatic Turkey, and the left bank of the Rhine. The story of the Russian crown council of February 8, 1914, concerning the question of the Straits, and other important documents, was published in Russian from December 1917 to February 1918. In 1919 Émile Laloy published an abridged edition of these treaties, Les documents secrets publiés par les Bolcheviks. For the story of Herman Bernstein's publication of the "Willy-Nicky" correspondence in the New York Herald in September 1917, and subsequently in January 1918 in book form, see S. B. Fay, "The kaiser's secret correspondence with the tsar, 1904–1905," American Historical Review, XXIV (1918), 48–72.

[21] J. W. Headlam-Morley, "Russian diplomacy before the war," Quarterly Review, CCXXXVII (1922), 155–76.

[22] Fay, Origins, I, 38.

[23] Ibid. B. von Siebert, Diplomatische Aktenstücke zur Geschichte der Ententepolitik der Vorkriegsjahre (Berlin, 1921); published by G. A. Schreiner, after being rearranged, as Entente diplomacy and the world (New York, 1921). Headlam-Morley, loc. cit., p. 158, suggests that perhaps von Siebert was the agent of the German foreign office and that Wilhelmstrasse was in possession of these documents even before 1914.

the publication of René Marchand's *Un Livre Noir* seemed to offer convincing proof of Franco-Russian responsibility for the war. These two volumes were the work of a French newspaper correspondent, whose chief contribution was to make available to the Western world much of the Soviet material.[24] The publication of *Un Livre Noir* resulted directly in the December 1923 revisionist speech in congress of Senator Robert L. Owen on the causes of the war.[25]

One of the major blunders of Anglo-French policy after 1918 was the delay in releasing their war material. The policy is understandable because there had been no overturn of government and all stable states are naturally reluctant to publish confidential material of the recent past. Yet the Russian, Austrian, and German policies should have forced a change in the usual rules. This was especially true after *Die Grosse Politik* began to appear in 1922. This set of forty stout volumes, completed in 1927, was backed by the guarantee of its three eminent compilers that no documents of importance had been omitted or concealed.[26] Compared to this magnificent output, the French published nothing of major importance until the late nineteen twenties. Not until 1926 did the British release the first volume of *British Documents on the Origins of the War, 1898–1914*. By that date, world-wide revisionism was so well organized that the extremists used these Allied documents as ammunition in their own cause.[27] All this gave Germany an enormous advantage in the historical battle. Time and again the Germans asserted that they had put their cards on the table and challenged the Allies to do the same.[28]

Before the Treaty of Versailles had been completed, the leaders of the defeated powers were writing their memoirs to the accompaniment of substantial royalties for the American copyrights. Four years of Allied propaganda now began to bear strange

[24] Fay, *Origins*, I, 37. The full title is: *Un Livre Noir: Diplomatie d'avant-guerre d'après des documents des archives russes, novembre, 1910—juillet, 1914* (2 vols.; Paris, 1922–23). See reviews by S. A. Korff in *American Historical Review*, XXVII (1922), 796–98, and XXVIII (1923), 747–48. In 1924 Friedrich Stieve, *Der diplomatische Schriftwechsel Iswolskis, 1911–1914* (4 vols.; Berlin, 1924), threw further light on Russian origins of the war. This book and Stieve's *Das russische Orangebuch über den Kriegsausbruch mit der Turkei* (Berlin, 1926) were frequently quoted by American writers. For a complete discussion and evaluation of the Bolshevist "revelations" see Fay, *Origins*, I, 10 ff.

[25] Robert L. Owen, *The Russian Imperial Conspiracy, 1892–1914* (New York, 1927), foreword, pp. vii–viii.

[26] Johannes Lepsius, Albrecht Mendelssohn-Bartholdy, and Friedrich Thimme (eds.), *Die grosse Politik der europäischen Kabinette, 1871–1914: Sammlung der diplomatischen Akten des auswärtigen Amtes* (40 vols.; Berlin, 1922–27); see Fay, *Origins*, I, 36, and review in *American Historical Review*, XXVIII (1923), 543–48, and XXX (1924), 136–41.

[27] Harry Elmer Barnes in *Nation*, CXV (1927), 161–63. "From the French archives, a few documents were published by Professors Bourgeois and Pagès, as a French Senate Report on *Les Origines et Les Responsabilités de la Grande Guerre*" (Fay, *Origins*, I, 38). These were published in book form with some material from the Kautsky documents in Paris in 1921. In 1929 the first of *Documents Diplomatiques Français* of the Ministère des affaires étrangères appeared in Paris.

[28] Compare the following statement of leading Germans quoted in the *New York Times*, February 27, 1927, that the German documents have been published: "We await an equally open answer to our profession from the whole world." As late as April 12, 1947 a reviewer in the London *Times Literary Supplement* stated that the judgment rendered in *The Origins of the World War* would have been different if Fay had written on the basis of either British or French documents without knowledge of the German sources. Fay replied in the issue of June 14, 1947, stating that all the new material published since 1928 had not caused him to change his mind on essential points: "There is hardly a word in my final chapter of conclusions that I want to alter."

fruit. The issues of the war had been personalized in countless editorials and cartoons. The American people were now quite eager to read what the archdemons had to say for themselves. Although their direct influence is conjectural, they did form another medium through which the Central Powers could state their case before the bar of American public opinion.[29] Far more important were the positive steps taken in Germany to influence world opinion on the question of war guilt. In 1921 a German newspaper predicted: "The campaign against war responsibility is the wedge which will allow us to force open the Treaty of Versailles."[30] "Die Kriegsschuldfrage" became a German national fetish, which was pursued with Teutonic thoroughness. There was more incentive for the German historians to write upon this vexed subject than for any other group. Everything was to be gained, nothing to be lost. Thus they took the war-guilt clause of the Treaty of Versailles[31] and turned a historical question into a political issue. In so doing, the Germans made the most successful case of historical propaganda on record.

Even before Article 231 had been written, Hans Delbrück, heading a committee of well-known historians, compiled a *White Book* which stated that the charge that Germany had started the war was "historically incorrect and morally unjustifiable."[32] The victors disregarded this book, and Germany was forced to agree to the war-guilt dictum. The basis for much of Germany's future action was laid in May 1919, when Count Ulrich von Brockdorff-Rantzau replied to Georges Clemenceau's invitation to settle accounts. Brockdorff-Rantzau admitted some responsibility on the part of the imperial government but insisted that Russian mobilization had taken the question from diplomatic into military hands. He demanded an impartial tribunal to measure the guilt of all powers concerned.[33] While the majority of Americans who read Brockdorff-Rantzau's defiant words were angered rather than convinced, it should be noted that a month earlier the *New Republic* had insisted that all powers were guilty in 1914 and that the efficient cause of the war had been Russian mobilization.[34]

As the war began to fade into the background, the American historical profession renewed the traditional ties with Germany which had been forged by a line of scholars from George Bancroft to William E. Dodd. Despite the strain of the war years, there was still strong, if concealed, admiration for German scholarship. In July 1920 the *American Historical Review* assured its readers that, while the war had reduced German historical productivity, the famous libraries and seminaries were still intact.[35] Friedrich Meinecke had survived the war at Freiburg and had called upon his colleagues to abandon the paths of Heinrich von Treitschke and to return to

---

[29] For an excellent appraisal of Entente memoirs and recollections see Fay, *Origins*, I, 21–32.

[30] Quoted in Pierre Renouvin, *The Immediate Origins of the War* (New Haven, 1928), p. 3.

[31] "The Allied and Associated Governments affirm, and Germany accepts, the responsibility of Germany and her allies for causing all the loss and damage to which the Allied and Associated Governments and their nationals have been subjected as a consequence of the war imposed upon them by the aggression of Germany and her allies" (Art. 231).

[32] *Deutschland schuldig? Deutsches Weissbuch über die Verantwortlichkeit der Urheber des Krieges* (Berlin, 1919). English translation: *German White Book Concerning the Responsibility of the Authors of the War* (New York: Carnegie Endowment for International Peace, 1924).

[33] *New York Times,* May 8, 1919.

[34] *New Republic,* XVIII (1919), 348–51.

[35] Antoine Guilland, "German historical publications, 1914–1920," *American Historical Review,* XXV (1920), 640–59. Guilland taught history at the École polytechnique fédérale at Zurich.

the objectivity of Leopold von Ranke. Samuel B. Harding noted that this statement removed somewhat that "distrust of German historical scholarship."[36] When the Austrian writer, Alfred Franzis Pribram, published an English translation of his work on the Austro-Hungarian secret treaties, it was edited by Archibald C. Coolidge, of Harvard.[37] The final volumes of Ludwig Pastor's great work on the papacy were eagerly welcomed by American scholars.[38] So the *rapprochement* was made, and by 1924 Erich Brandenburg's work on pre-1914 diplomacy, written from German manuscript sources, was well received.[39]

One must be careful to differentiate between the works of the German scholars of the old school, who, despite stout prejudices, usually maintained their integrity, and the postwar crop of "national" writers, who were already influenced by fascist ideology. The situation was made more difficult because "Die Kriegsschuldfrage" was the one issue which united practically all the Germans. Hence the great difficulty in differentiating in this country between sound scholarship and the pure propaganda of The League of German Patriots, who in 1921 appealed to all Christians to repudiate "the great lie."[40] Often in the material emanating from Germany there was a deluding mixture of fact, fiction, and outright falsehood. The majority of Americans were unable to separate the wheat from the chaff. Count Max Montgelas, perhaps the most influential of all German writers of the period on American public opinion, was a man of moderate views. After thirty-five years of military service, he retired in 1915 because of differences with the high command. Following a stay in Switzerland, he returned to the fatherland in time to participate in the earliest dissent against the "Diktat" of Versailles.[41] Henceforth, Montgelas devoted himself to writing and speaking on the vexed question. In 1925 Knopf published an English translation of the count's first book on the subject, *The Case for the Central Powers*.[42] Montgelas argued that, unlike the Russian and French prewar designs, Germany had no aims incompatible with the peace of Europe. When Wilhelmstrasse agreed to a "local" war on July 5, it was thought that the risk of a general conflict was negligible. After Serbia's reply, Germany believed even a local war to be unnecessary. Montgelas admitted the political error of Germany's declaration of war on Russia but insisted that Russian mobilization made this inevitable.[43] As time went on, Montgelas, like so many other revisionists, tended to work for a complete German vindication.

The existence of so many German societies preoccupied with the question of war guilt made it difficult for any German to keep a judicial balance on the subject. In July 1923 Die Zentralstelle für Erforschung der Kriegsursachen began publication

[36] Review in *American Historical Review*, XXV (1920), 266–68.

[37] Alfred F. Pribram, *Die politischen Geheimverträge Oesterriech-Ungarns, 1879–1914* (Vienna, 1920), English translation: *The secret treaties of Austria-Hungary, 1879–1914*, ed. A. C. Coolidge (2 vols.; Cambridge, 1920–21).

[38] Review by G. L. Burr in *American Historical Review*, XXVII (1921), 112–15.

[39] Erich Brandenburg, *Von Bismarck zum Weltkriege: die deutsche Politik in den Jahrzehnten vor dem Kriege* (Berlin, 1924); reviewed by S. B. Fay in *American Historical Review*, XXX (1925), 362–65.

[40] *New York Times*, Mar. 26, 1921.

[41] Count Max Montgelas, *British foreign policy under Sir Edward Grey*, trans. W. C. Dreher, ed. Harry Elmer Barnes (New York, 1928), foreword, p. vi.

[42] Translated by Constance Vesey; the original, *Leitfaden zur Kriegsschuldfrage*, was published in Berlin in 1923.

[43] Summary of conclusions in Montgelas, *Case for the Central Powers*, pp. 200–203.

of the monthly *Die Kriegsschuldfrage*.[44] This magazine became a clearing house for world-wide revisionist scholarship. In its earlier days, under the editorship of Alfred von Wegerer, it maintained as high objective standards as might be expected from any periodical founded to disseminate one point of view. Much more purely propagandist in nature was the *Arbeitsausschuss deutscher Verbände,* which constantly incited German public opinion on the question.[45] Unquestionably, this violent dissent, rational and irrational, had its influence on American public opinion. Along with other factors, it helped produce a "guilt complex" in regard to Allied treatment of Germany.[46]

Another distinct factor in the growth of American revisionism was the French literature of exposure. French and even British writers exerted greater influence on American revisionism than did the Germans. Perhaps this paradox can be explained by the fact that public opinion tended to discount everything "made in Germany." When, however, French and British writers asserted that their own countries had started the war, it attracted and held American attention. The great majority of Americans had never realized the cleavages on the war issue in either France or Britain. With a national penchant for idealism rather than realism, we envisaged a unity among our "associated powers" which never existed. So, when Fernand Gouttenoire de Toury published *Poincaré a-t-il Voulu la Guerre?* (Paris, 1920), it shocked the American readers. The next year, Alfred Pevet winnowed much French testimony, with the conclusion that Raymond Poincaré and René Viviani had deceived their countrymen as to the origins of the war.[47] Poincaré was forced in lectures at the Sorbonne to defend himself from repeated French charges that he had conspired with Russia to light the torch of war.[48] To be sure, the overwhelming majority of Frenchmen believed the classical story of July 1914, but it was the case of

---

[44] Published until 1930 as *Die Kriegsschuldfrage: berliner Monatshefte für internationale Aufklärung.* After January 1930 it appeared as *Berliner Monatshefte.* See discussion of German organization for revisionism in Harry Elmer Barnes, *World Politics in Modern Civilization* (New York, 1930), pp. 454–58.

[45] *Ibid.,* p. 455. The Steuben Society of America, which disseminated much of this material, had its beginnings at a small meeting in a private home in New York in May 1919. The growth of the new organization was phenomenal. Part of its avowed program was a revision of American opinion on German guilt, and the usual isolationist devotion to the maintenance of "the independence of the United States." The semiofficial organ of the society began publication as *Issues of To-day,* Oct. 16, 1920. Later the name was changed to the *Progressive.* The files of this publication form a prime source for an understanding of the war-guilt problem and the growth of isolationist sentiment after 1920. In many respects the *Progressive* played an American counterpart to *Die Kriegsschuldfrage* in collating revisionist material. Publication was discontinued in 1930.

[46] In each important country there were prominent dissenters from the conventional point of view. While the Germans and Austrians who held their own country to blame were fewer than their French and British prototypes, one should mention Richard Grelling, who during the war wrote *J'Accuse* (Lausanne, 1915) and published in Paris in 1925 *Le Campagne 'Innocentiste' en Allemagne et le Traité de Versailles.* The New Republic, XXVII (1921), 83, estimated the influence of F. W. Foerster, *Mein Kampf Gegen das Militaristische und Nationalistische Deutchland* (Stuttgart, 1920). Similar views are ascribed to H. von Gerlach in *New York Times,* October 12, 1919. In postwar Austria, Heinrich Kanner in *Kaiserliche Katastrophenpolitik* (Vienna, 1922) and *Der Schlüssel zur Kriegsschuldfrage* (Munich, 1926) blamed the Central Powers in a more scholarly way. Kanner was the former editor of a Vienna Socialist daily.

[47] Alfred Pevet, *Les responsables de la guerre* (Paris, 1921).

[48] Raymond Poincaré, *Les origines de la guerre* (Paris, 1921).

the man biting the dog who made the headlines. When Jean Longuet, leader of the French moderate Socialists, called Poincaré and William II equally guilty, it was well noted in this country.[49] Many of the charges against Poincaré were based on the testimony of the Russian ambassador, A. P. Izvolski, and on the latter's letters to his chief, S. D. Sazonov.[50] At the very least, it was widely asserted, Poincaré had foreseen the war and had done nothing to stop it. Frederick Bausman thoroughly absorbed the writings of the French revisionists.[51] Lewis Gannett, who wrote the celebrated article in the *Nation* (October 11, 1922), "They all lied," was influenced by the same sources.

Because of language, British revisionism had an unusually great influence on American writers. Prior to 1919 it was largely overlooked in this country that there had been a minority in England who thought the war unnecessary. Their tongues and pens loosened by the peace, the British antiwar group turned to history to justify their course. Some of this literature found its way to America in time to become an important factor in the general collapse of Wilsonian idealism. Americans were surprised to learn that former Lord Chancellor Loreburn had said in 1915: "We went to war in a Russian quarrel because we were tied to France in the dark."[52] The shock was greater to American than to British public opinion, partly because England had allowed such wartime books as Edmund D. Morel's *Truth and the War* (London, 1916) to be printed. It had been, however, a criminal offense to send a copy out of the realm.[53] Morel was one of the liberal M.P.'s who had resigned at the outbreak of the war. His writings during the conflict had landed him in prison, but after the armistice he became editor of *Foreign Affairs*.[54] Francis Neilson was even more directly influential in America. A widely traveled critic and author, he had been interested in such liberal movements as the single tax and agrarian reform. Like Morel, he had resigned his seat in parliament. In 1916 Neilson's *How Diplomats Make War* was published in New York. It is significant to note that the book was edited by Albert Jay Nock, who was a pioneer American revisionist, and was printed by B. W. Huebsch and Company, a firm which specialized in revisionist literature. In 1917 Neilson married Mrs. Edward Morris, widow of the Chicago meat baron. Together they subsidized the *Freeman* magazine, which partly explains its strong revisionist views.[55]

From 1919 to 1921 the literary critic, Irene Cooper Willis, published a series of books in England with the suggestive titles, *How we went into the war, How we got on with the war,* and *How we came out of the war.* Although Knopf's American edition did not appear until 1928, Miss Willis' debunking of the "holy-war" idea and Sir Edward Grey's "liberalism" had long before left its mark on American think-

---

[49] *New York Times,* July 31, 1921.

[50] B. E. Schmitt, "Where did the guilt lie?" *Saturday review of literature,* III (1926), 311–12. *Recollections of a foreign minister: memoirs of Alexander Iswolsky,* trans. C. L. Seeger (Garden City, 1921). For some of Izvolski's indiscretions see Maurice Paléologue, *La Russie des tsars pendant la grande guerre* (3 vols.; Paris, 1922), I, 27.

[51] Frederick Bausman, *Facing Europe* (New York, 1926), pp. 97–98, 104–5.

[52] Quoted in Ferdinand Schevill, "Professor Barnes on war guilt," *Christian century,* XLIII (1926), 778–80. See also Earl Loreburn, *How the war came* (London, 1919).

[53] Frederick Bausman, *Let France explain,* pp. 64–65.

[54] Albert Jay Nock, *The myth of a guilty nation* (New York, 1922), p. 60. By December 20, 1919 the *Nation* (CIX, 812) was quoting Morel and the French revisionist, Georges Demartial.

[55] *Nation,* CXVIII (1924), 131.

ing.[56] The Very Reverend William Ralph Inge, dean of St. Paul's, pictured Germany as the lamb which had been attacked by the Entente wolf.[57] On December 12, 1922 the noted historian, George Peabody Gooch, read a paper before the British Institute of International Affairs. He frankly termed the late conflict as one "not of right with wrong, but of right with right."[58]

During the early twenties the British Labor party used revisionism in its rise to power. Pamphlets were distributed to assail the Treaty of Versailles on the grounds that it was based on the false premise of German war guilt.[59] The National Labour Press published Miss Willis' books. The British pioneer revisionists, representing a small fragment of opinion, had tremendous influence upon the American revisionists. Lewis Gannett called Morel's *Ten Years of Secret Diplomacy* a "little classic."[60] Senator Robert L. Owen in 1923 acknowledged his debt to the British pioneers on the floor of the Senate.[61] Albert Jay Nock had been "converted" by Morel and Neilson. Frederick Bausman, Harry Elmer Barnes, Charles A. Beard, and John K. Turner printed a list of Englishmen to whom they were indebted for ideas.[62] In attempting to explain why the same Americans who were attracted to Neilson and Morel rejected the work of the British "orthodox" historians, one must turn to the *Zeitgeist* of the "jazz age." The new and the bizarre had strong appeal to the individualism of the "lost generation." As W. J. Ghent cogently noted in 1926: "Vociferous and sweeping denunciation of existing beliefs, customs, standards, and institutions is the current mode, and 'revisionism' is merely one of its phases."[63] Along with behavioristic psychology, Freudianism, and impressionistic art, revisionism formed part of the general revolt against the older nineteenth-century values. Regardless of what a defense of Germany connoted after 1933, in the twenties it was the revisionists who were the "liberals."

The end of the war coincided with the rapidly growing popularity of weekly journals of opinion. The *Nation*, the *New Republic*, the *Freeman*, and the *Dial* specialized in revisionism. Their editors and their brilliant group of young associates were liberals or, in rare cases, Marxists. Deeply hurt by Theodore Roosevelt's abandonment of the Progressive party, many of this group had turned to Wilson for leadership in the cause of liberalism. By 1919 they had broken with the president. They blamed him for tangled Russian relations, for the severe wartime curtailment of civil liberties, and for failure to stay domestic reaction by a liberal program of postwar adjustment. Above all, they accused Wilson of betraying his own fourteen points at Versailles. Weekly they wrote that isolationism was gone forever; yet they opposed the League of Nations as a plot to perpetuate Anglo-French imperialism. These liberal writers used

---

[56] *England's Holy War* (New York, 1928). For the direct influence of the author on Barnes, see the latter's *World Politics*, pp. 391 ff.

[57] "Who made the war?" *Spectator*, CXXIX (1922), 197–98.

[58] George P. Gooch, *Recent Revelations of European Diplomacy* (London, 1927), p. 206.

[59] "War guilt myths," *Living Age*, CCCXV (1922), 218–22.

[60] "They all lied," *Nation*, CXV (1922), 353–57.

[61] U.S., *Congreessional Record* (68th Cong., 1st sess., Dec. 18, 1923), LXV, Part I, 375.

[62] Bausman, *Facing Europe*, p. 98. Barnes's acknowledgment can be found in his preface to Montgelas, *British foreign policy under Sir Edward Grey*, p. x, n. 1. See also Charles A. Beard, *Cross Currents in Europe Today* (Boston, 1922), p. 273, and John K. Turner, *Shall it be again?* (New York, 1922), *passim*. Turner wrote after one striking quotation, "This from an Englishman" (p. 233).

[63] W. J. Ghent, "Menckenized history," *Outlook*, CXLIII (1926), 286–90.

revisionism as a weapon to combat imperialism and reaction. Thus the first purveyors of revisionism to the American people were journalists rather than historians. The torrent of documents and monographs based on fresh archival or manuscript material came so fast that professional historians had great difficulty in accommodating their views to the new evidence. This situation was somewhat clarified by the publications of Sidney B. Fay, the first American historian to use the sources in a scientific manner.

The outbreak of the war found Fay teaching at Smith College. He was one of a small group of historians who resisted the tide of public opinion.[64] "I was convinced," he wrote in 1948, "that we in the U.S. were being fed a great deal of silly propaganda arising from war hatred and hysteria, and that some day documents would be published which would allow sober historians to arrive at a more just estimate. Lacking these documents, I wrote nothing on the subject during the war years."[65] In the meantime, Fay prepared himself for what was to be his life's work by devoting a month of his course on modern European history to a minute study of the British edition of the "rainbow books" of the various belligerents.[66] Shortly after the war, J. Franklin Jameson, editor of the *American Historical Review,* assigned the "Willy-Nicky correspondence" and the Kautsky documents to the Smith professor for review. On the basis of this material, Fay wrote four articles, entitled "New light on the origins of the World War." The first of the series was published in the July 1920 issue of the *American Historical Review.*

These "New light" articles launched American scientific "revisionism." Source material became naturally much more abundant after these pioneer essays had been printed, and some views have since been altered, amplified, or abandoned. Yet, with the material at hand, Fay demolished the legend of the Potsdam conference, showed that the Austrian policy of 1914 was not dictated by Germany, and demonstrated how the military leaders had doublecrossed both "Willy" and "Nicky." Although much of the bellicose spirit of that fateful July emanated from St. Petersburg, Germany had been mainly responsible for the growth of militarism, had sent a precipitate ultimatum to Russia, and her generals had ruled that mobilization means war. "In a wider sense," he argued, "these new documents do not in any way relieve Germany of the main responsibility."[67] Considering the very limited circulation of the *American Historical Review,* it is questionable how much influence Fay's articles had outside the historical guild. This was an unfortunate development because, unlike Fay, many of the popular writers sensationalized and interpreted beyond the documents at their disposal. While Fay might have had a nostalgic sympathy for the prewar Germany of his *Wanderjahre,* he was always the scientific historian who arrived at his conclusions not from one sensational telegram or hearsay evidence but from an exhaustion of the available sources. If Fay's conclusions changed in the years between the writing of his articles and the publication of his definitive work, the change was made in the light of evidence which he believed trustworthy. During the mid-twenties when popular revisionism was outrunning the documents, Fay tried to "put on the brakes." At the Williamstown Institute of Politics he stated that Germany did not plot the war but that it came largely "by her own stupidity and by the reckless and

---

[64] Fay to writer, Aug. 25, 1948.
[65] *Ibid.*
[66] *Ibid.*
[67] "New Light on the origins of the World War. II. Berlin and Vienna, July 29 to 31," *American Historical Review,* XXVI (1920), 37–53.

adventurous policy of Austria."[68] If the war was precipitated by Russian mobilization, this step came only after Germany had lost the confidence of the Entente by wholesale deceit in regard to her relations to Austria.[69] While Fay was thus exercising caution and moderation, a host of amateurs was abandoning the sound "divided-guilt" thesis in an attempt to portray the war as a Franco-Russian plot.

In order to understand the avalanche of ultra-revisionist literature which appeared in 1922, it is necesary to consider the activities of the publishing firm of B. W. Huebsch and Company. The founder, Benjamin W. Heubsch, had begun his career as a lithographer's apprentice. Like many others of German-Jewish descent, he cherished a love and respect for the German liberal, idealistic tradition. A militant liberal, he resented the war that meant "farewell to reform." In 1948 Huebsch thus explained the origin of his firm's connection with revisionist publications:[70]

> My publishing course . . . was not deliberately planned; it had its origins in my anti-militarism. . . . I was influenced, too, by the utterances of sober students of public affairs which revealed the gulf between governmental statements of the causes of the war and the truth. I became satisfied, too, of the relations between war and private profit. And as we went along I became aware of how the red herring of propaganda was drawn across the path of public opinion. . . . Thus I was sympathetic to such works as Neilson's "How Diplomats Make War," Veblen's "Imperial Germany and the Industrial Revolution," and, later, Turner's "Shall it Be Again."

During the period of American participation in the war Huebsch had several un-pleasant experiences with the exclusion of his books from the mails.[71] After the armistice, Heubsch went frequently to Germany and, along with Knopf, seems to have had first choice of the German literary output suitable for American export.[72] Putting all these facts together, it is possible to understand why B. W. Huebsch and Company played such an important part in the dissemination of revisionist opinion.

On March 5, 1920 the *Freeman* made its bow to the literary world. The new periodical, destined for a life of four years, formed a cross-current of ultra-revisionism. Subsidized by Mr. and Mrs. Francis Neilson, edited by Albert Jay Nock, printed by Huebsch, it had, as part of its alleged "radical" program, a new understanding of the origins of the late war.[73] The editorial policy of the *Freeman*, which was consciously modeled after the pattern of the London *Spectator*, owed most to Nock. The latter had been raised in Brooklyn, had studied at St. Stephens College (now Bard College) had spent some time in Brussels before the war, and had been an associate editor of the *Nation*. While Nock passed for a crusading liberal in the twenties, late in life he moved to the extreme right. His hatred of the New Deal passed far beyond the bounds of good taste.[74] Nothing will better illustrate the complexity of the revisionist

[68] Quoted in *New York Times,* Aug. 7, 1924.

[69] *Ibid.*

[70] Benjamin W. Huebsch to writer, Dec. 13, 1948.

[71] *Ibid.*

[72] Donald Friede, *The Mechanical Angel* (New York, 1948), p. 97.

[73] *Nation,* CXVIII (1924), 131.

[74] See article on Nock in *Current Biography* (1944). Nock's *Memoirs of a Superfluous Man* (New York, 1943) is very revealing.

coalition than adding to Nock's story the fact that Benjamin W. Huebsch was later to become president of Manhattan Lodge, B'nai B'rith, and treasurer of the American Civil Liberties Union.[75]

Nock's *Myth of a Guilty Nation* originally appeared as a series of articles in the *Freeman*. He was among the first American writers to abandon the "divided-guilt" argument in favor of an assertion that German responsibility for the war was negligible. Nock stressed Entente preparedness to wage war against the Central Powers as evidence of Allied aggression. Taken in its entirety, the book shifted the blame for the war to the French and Russians.[76] *The Myth of a Guilty Nation* is a classic example of poor historical workmanship. Nock was unacquainted with Fay's findings, he quoted repeatedly out of context, and about a quarter of the book was filled with material handpicked by Junker propagandists from the Belgian archives.[77]

In the very same year, 1922, Huebsch published John Kenneth Turner's *Shall it be Again?* The book was dedicated "To the lads who will come under the next draft." This verbose selection of four hundred and forty-three pages of undigested half-truths bore many resemblances to the works of some of the "disillusionist" writers of the thirties. Turner, strangely enough, hated both Woodrow Wilson and Wall Street. Together, he believed, these two evil forces had led the country into a war fought for the sake of bolshevism. Whereas his contemporary revisionists were interested in war-guilt and argued that American entry into the war was a result of Allied duplicity, Turner argued that Wilson wanted to fight to save the banking interests. The "profits of patriotism" resulted in twenty-one thousand new millionaires.[78] Judged by the canons of historical method, the book is ridiculous. Yet the *Nation's* reviewer wrote, "If it be biased, it is biased only in favor of America's most cherished principles."[79]

Frederick Bausman, also in 1922, launched the "first comprehensive American attack on the Entente propaganda."[80] Bausman was then in the late prime of a successful life as a lawyer, judge, and occasional writer. If we accept his own testimony, his British-born mother "taught him that nothing was so glorious as the British crown or so reverend as the Anglican bishop in his lawn sleeves."[81] Bausman's chief motiva-

---

[75] *Who's Who in the East* (1948), s.v. "Huebsch, Benjamin."

[76] "I do not by any means wish to escape the responsibility of saying that I think the German Government's share of guilt . . . inconsiderable" (preface, p. 5).

[77] *Current biography* (1944), s.v. "Nock, Albert Jay." Munroe Smith, "A typical brief for Germany," *New York Times*, July 16, 1922. *La Follette's magazine* for April 1922 began instalment publication of Nock's book and advertised it as "a concise, scholarly and pungent presentation of incontrovertible and deadly facts" (p. 63).

[78] P. 388. The present writer has been unable to find anything on Turner's background or subsequent career, except that he had written against Porfirio Díaz's dictatorship in Mexico, seemed to belong to the muckraking school, and lived for many years in California. His 1919 articles in the *Nation* presaged many of his later views. His *Hands off Mexico* (New York, 1920) was published by the Rand School of Social Science. Like Scott Nearing and others of the Rand School of socialist thought, Turner associated American entry into the League of Nations with a Wall Street conspiracy to extend American imperialism (p. 5); yet, in 1941 Turner wrote *Challenge to Karl Marx* (New York, 1941).

[79] Review by E. H. Gruening in *Nation*, CXV (1922), 667–68.

[80] Barnes, *A History of Historical Writing*, p. 286.

[81] Bausman, *Facing Europe*, preface, p. vi. *Who Was Who in America, 1897–1942* (Chicago, 1942), I, 70 contains a sketch of Bausman. He was an associate justice of the supreme court of the state of Washington, 1915–16, and he died in 1931.

tions were travel in prewar Germany, an unbridled dislike of France, and the reading of the newly published documents.[82] Because of failure to procure an American publisher, *Let France Explain* was printed in London.[83] On the eve of the Ruhr occupation, Britain welcomed the news that France had armed Russia and had drawn England into the war. Bausman had much sympathy for the former kaiser who "had to decide . . . whether his nation should be overrun by Cossacks or be saved by his hurling her forces through a neutral state which did not like Germany."[84] Four years later Bausman published *Facing Europe*. While this second effort was "more mature and mellow,"[85] the former jurist had now turned anglophobe.

In the fall of 1922 Lewis S. Gannett of the *Nation* brought home to the American intelligentsia the nature of French and Russian responsibility for the war. He was the first popular writer to digest the new documents and to present the results in plausible and palatable form. Gannett was a thirty-year-old Quaker pacifist who had rounded out his Harvard education with some work in imperial Germany.[86] While employed in Paris by the American Friends Service Commission, his interest in revisionism was aroused by Jean Longuet and Boris Louvaine.[87] Here, too, he encountered the advance guard of the Russian "revelations." On his return to New York he became an associate editor of Oswald Garrison Villard's *Nation*. Material poured into his office from all parts of the world, and, aided by his fluency in French and German, Gannett put the pieces together. The result was two epoch-making articles: "They all lied" and "Documents in diplomatic deceit," both published in the *Nation* of October 11, 1922. With pointed pen, Gannett struck hard at the "grim legend" that Germany had plotted the war. Unlike Nock, Turner, and Bausman, he had read Fay's work. Gannett still placed the major responsibility upon the Central Powers but emphasized the contributory guilt of Entente diplomats and generals, who with "criminal casualness . . . played their parts in that terrible week."[88]

Despite the fact that Charles A. Beard lived long enough to become a pioneer second World War revisionist, in 1922 he was fairly moderate in his conclusions. As a result of a series of Dartmouth lectures, Beard published *Cross Currents in Europe Today*. He was severe on Poincaré for making Russian commitments "fraught with such agony for mankind."[89] Yet "no one is more responsible than William II

---

[82] See Bausman's *Let France Explain,* preface, pp. 5–7.

[83] Barnes, *World Politics,* p. 473.

[84] Bausman, *Let France Explain,* p. 204.

[85] Noted by Barnes, *World Politics,* p. 473.

[86] *Ibid.,* p. 468. *Who's Who in America* (1948–49), *s.v.* "Gannett, Lewis."

[87] Lewis S. Gannett to writer, Sept. 4, 1948. In 1916 Gannett translated from the German Alfred H. Fried's *The Restoration of Europe* (New York, 1916). In the translator's foreword (p. xii) Gannett wrote that a true peace must be based on the reality of divided guilt.

[88] Gannett, "They all lied," *loc. cit.,* p. 255.

[89] *Cross Currents in Europe Today,* p. 27. For evidence that at the close of the war Beard favored a strong League of Nations, see Frederic A. Ogg and Charles A. Beard, *National Governments and the World War* (New York, 1919), pp. 589–91. The preface to this book is dated Dec. 12, 1918. Within a matter of months, Beard seems to have joined Villard, Croly, and other American liberals who turned against the League because of the "imperialistic" parts of the Treaty of Versailles. For the influence upon Beard of Fay's work and the publication of German archival material see his article, "The recent war," *New Republic,* XXV (1920), 114–15. Beard's future isolationism was presaged by the following quotation from his *Cross Currents in Europe Today,* p. 265: "It is the course of allowing Europe to set its own house in order under the stress of its own necessities and experiences. Its statesmen know Europe better than any agents sent out from Washington."

for encouraging Austria to light the European fire."[90] Three years later Beard had moved to a point where he assigned France and Russia "a Titan's share" of the guilt.[91] When, however, Barnes later tried to vindicate Germany entirely, Beard dissented. The latter pointed to the inconsistency of the German militarists parading as "injured innocents . . . which presents such a strange contrast to their words and deeds before 1914."[92] Beard did not base his isolationism on the premise that in 1917 we had intervened on the wrong side.

Until late in 1923 the historical question of the origins of the European war or reasons for American participation did not enter in any large measure into the halls of congress. When Representative M. Alfred Michaelson (Republican insurgent from Illinois) moved in 1921 to investigate "why the Yanks came in 1917," he was shouted down with cries of "scandalous" and "treasonable."[93] Two years later, Senator Robert Latham Owen of Oklahoma brought the entire matter to the attention of his colleagues in such a way as they were long to remember. Owen was a Virginia-born lawyer who in early manhood became interested in Choctaw and Cherokee affairs.[94] One of the first of Oklahoma's senators after her admission to the Union, Owen belonged to what was then the liberal wing of the Democratic party. Following his cosponsorship of the Federal Reserve Act of 1913, he went along with his party on the war and the treaty. He even wrote a book about the war, castigating William II.[95] In the summer of 1923 Senator Owen went to Europe, where he read Marchand's *Un Livre Noir* and the von Siebert material. He continued to pursue the subject until he was convinced that the Allies "had greatly deceived the people of the United States . . . [and] . . . the theory that the war was waged in defense of American ideals was untrue."[96] He then determined to speak at length in the senate on "Secret diplomacy of Europe."

This important speech was delivered on December 18, 1923. Read only in part, its more than forty thousand words were incorporated into the *Congressional Record*. Owen asserted that documents now "out of hiding" destroyed forever the premise of exclusive German guilt. From this tenable statement, he turned to accuse Russia and France of starting the war. If the United States wished peace, it must first right the great wrong done the German people.[97] So strong were Owen's accusations of Entente

[90] *Ibid.,* p. 76.

[91] Charles A. Beard, "Viscount Grey on war guilt," *New Republic,* XLIV (1925), 172–75.

[92] Charles A. Beard, "Heroes and villains of the World War," *Current History,* XXIV (1926), 730–35.

[93] "America's war responsibility," *New Republic,* XLVII (1926), 270–71. On May 20, 1921 Michaelson introduced a resolution to investigate statements of M. Gabriel Hanotaux and Sir Gilbert Parker concerning their parts in spreading propaganda in the United States prior to April 1917. Speaking for the resolution, May 26, 1921, Michaelson said that it would appear that we were "duped by an unscrupulous combination of wealth that, through its kept literary harlots, seduced the noble patriotism of the American citizenry in order to enrich themselves" (U.S., *Congressional Record* [67th Cong., 1st sess., May 26, 1921], LXI, Part II, 1814).

[94] Edward Elmer Keso, *The Senatorial Career of Robert Latham Owen* (abstract of thesis, George Peabody College for Teachers [Nashville, 1937]; abstract of "Contributions to education," No. 190), pp. 1–5.

[95] *Where is God in the European War?* (New York, 1919). After 1919, however, there were a few portents of his future position. Owen wanted to feed the Germans immediately after the war, he was unusually suspicious of England's designs on Egypt, and he demanded a "square deal" for Turkey (Keso, *Senatorial career,* pp. 8–9).

[96] Owen, *Russian imperial conspiracy,* foreword, p. vii.

[97] U.S., *Congressional Record,* LXV, 355–99. According to the *Progressive,* X (1927), 3, Owen's speech was subsequently translated into Spanish, Italian, French, and German.

guilt that even the *Nation* was forced to remind him of Austria's share in the tragedy.[98] As long as Owen was in the senate, he pressed for an inquiry into the responsibility for the war by a committee of experts.[99] After Owen's retirement from the senate, he turned increasingly isolationist, pacifist, and anti-Russian. The thesis of his *Russian Imperial Conspiracy, 1892–1914* is that Russia and France plotted the war and artfully staged it so that the world would think Germany guilty.[100] The United States had a clear duty to make retribution to the German people, who were the innocent victims of a conspiracy. Senator Owen's story is a conspicuous example of the "guilt-complex" factor in the revisionist movement.

A matter of days after Owen's initial speech of December 18, 1923 the brethren of the American Historical Association gathered at Columbus, Ohio. The vexed question was duly weighed at an important section meeting. J. V. Fuller, of Wisconsin, argued that Bismarck's policies had created the bellicose atmosphere. As part of the same panel, Bernadotte E. Schmitt, of Western Reserve, entered a controversy which was to absorb much of his time and energy for fifteen years. Schmitt had a Virginia-Tennessee background, had been in Oxford before the war as a Rhodes scholar, had written *England and Germany, 1740–1914,* and had served in the war.[101] Schmitt held that the basic cause was the existence of the two alliances "rather than the bellicosity of this or that power."[102] The conflict was all the more tragic because both coalitions "were formed in the interests of peace, and were, originally at least, defensive in character."[103] The military cliques, not the responsible statesmen, wanted war. All the diplomats were bluffing, and, fearing that their hands might be called, they sanctioned military measures short of war. This situation provided the opportunity for the German militarists to start the fighting.[104] Schmitt's paper was hailed by the revisionists, but before long they were to dub him a turncoat.[105]

In 1920 Harry Elmer Barnes was professor of the history of culture at Clark University. While he was doing some summer teaching at the University of Oregon, a colleague called his attention to the first of Fay's "New light" articles. The result was a sudden conversion. There was little in Barnes's previous career to suggest his rise as a revisionist of international fame. He had even written a pamphlet for the National Security League.[106] Like many other young American liberals, Barnes

---

[98] "Set the war truths free!" *Nation,* CXVIII (1924), 247.

[99] *New York Times,* Feb. 20, 1924.

[100] P. 204.

[101] For the influence of Schmitt's Oxford years on his point of view see Bernadotte E. Schmitt, *England and Germany, 1740–1914* (Princeton, 1916), preface. The author regrets that the limitation of this paper to the years 1918–28 prevents a consideration of Schmitt's outstanding two-volume work, *The coming of the war, 1914,* which was published in New York in 1930.

[102] Quoted in the *New York Times,* Dec. 29, 1923. Because Schmitt used Russian material which had not been available when Fay wrote, this paper marked a definite advance in interpretation of the causes of the war (see Barnes, *In Quest,* p. 293).

[103] The paper was published as "Triple Alliance and Triple Entente, 1902–1914," *American Historical Review,* XXIX (1924), 450.

[104] *Ibid.,* p. 471.

[105] For a full, but by no means unbiased, account of Schmitt's relations with the extreme revisionists see Barnes, *In Quest,* pp. 293–331.

[106] Barnes was born in Auburn, New York, in 1889, of English and Dutch ancestry. After graduating from Syracuse University in 1913, he did graduate work at Columbia in the heyday of the school of the "new history." He received his Ph.D. degree in 1918. The same year found him acting as statistician for the war department. Barnes wrote the present writer, Aug. 25, 1948, that he was responsible for getting Earle E. Sperry the assignment to write the wartime pamphlet,

turned to revisionism as a means of discrediting reaction and economic imperialism. Once in the midst of the fray, Barnes, to use his own words, "kept on because nobody likes to quit under attack and I persisted until the battle was won against all except the 'bitter-enders'."[107]

Barnes's formal entry into the war-guilt question was his 1922 review of Raymond Turner's *Europe Since 1870*. Although this first review was strongly revisionist in tone, Barnes did not attract national attention until two years later.[108] In 1924 Herbert Croly was still editor of the *New Republic*. Angered by the publication of a revised edition of Charles D. Hazen's *Europe Since 1815* without substantial change in the treatment of the war, Croly assigned Barnes the review of the new text. The forthcoming article was destined to be the longest book review in the *New Republic*'s history.[109] Barnes spared no words in criticizing Hazen for not revising his 1916 views in the light of the new evidence and accused both Hazen and Turner of letting personal bias outweigh the facts. Barnes called Hazen "innocent of the sources," and the latter replied in a lengthy polemic.[110]

The Barnes-Hazen feud had not died down before Barnes threw a still greater bombshell in his article "Assessing the blame for the world war." Strangely enough, in view of the *New York Times*'s vigorous stand against even mild revisionism, this article was published in the *Times's Current History*. Barnes was invited to prepare the essay by the editor, George Washington Ochs-Oakes, who was a brother of Adolph Ochs.[111] In this, his first constructive writing on revisionism, Barnes did not move too far from the Fay-Schmitt verdict of divided guilt. Barnes, in 1924, assigned the blame to Austria-Hungary, Russia, France, Germany, and England in the order named.[112] Editor Ochs-Oakes had taken the precaution of sending a manuscript copy of the article to Albert Bushnell Hart, who was chairman of the board of associates of *Current History*. Hart's dissent, published with Barnes's article, was weak and illogical. Instead of going after the vulnerable parts of Barnes's conclusions, Hart compiled a weak series of reasons why an opinion "forged by the fires of war" should not be

---

The Tentacles of the German Octopus. In 1919 he collaborated with Stephen Pierce Duggan and others to publish *The League of Nations* (Boston, 1919). Barnes wrote chap. ix and took the usual 1919 approach to the war. At Potsdam the German militarists and expansionists plotted a "sudden, vigorous and well-nigh successful assault upon the foundations of modern civilization and world order" (p. 162).

[107] Barnes to writer, Aug. 25, 1948.

[108] See "History and international good-will," *Nation*, CXIV (1922), 251–54, 402.

[109] Harry Elmer Barnes, "Seven books of history against the Germans," *New Republic*, XXXVIII (1924), Part II, 10–15; Barnes to writer, Aug. 25, 1948; Barnes, *World Politics*, pp. 470–71.

[110] *New Republic*, XXXVIII (1924), 284–86. Frank M. Anderson, in his review of Hazen's revised edition (*American Historical Review*, XXIX [1924], 768–69) defended Hazen's unmodified treatment: "It simply means that for so short an account there is no special occasion to modify."

[111] The *New York Times* owned *Current History* in 1924. George Washington Ochs-Oakes was a chevalier of the Legion of Honor and a stout defender of the League of Nations (Barnes, *In Quest*, p. 122). Probably Ochs-Oakes merely wished to capitalize on the interest created by Barnes's review of Hazen.

[112] Harry Elmer Barnes, "Assessing the blame for the World War," *Current History*, XX (1924), 171–95.

changed.[113] Quite understandably, the venerable Harvard professor became the target of much revisionist criticism.

Barnes later asserted that his 1924 article "started off revision in any general sense in this country."[114] Certainly, the popular revisionists now had a leader with professional training, unlimited energy, and utter fearlessness. Moreover, Barnes occupied the chair of historical sociology at Smith College. In the middle twenties, sources and monographs on the war appeared in such abundance that, by making the proper selection, one could build almost any "frame of reference" and fortify it with enough facts to make it plausible. So Barnes began to revise his revisionism. He was soon convinced that, while the acts of the Central Powers made the war possible, those of the Entente made it inevitable.[115] On March 14, 1925, he announced that new evidence compelled him to believe that France and Russia were tied for first place in the revised order of "guilt." Therefore, no honest American could wish to collect German reparations based on Article 231 "any more than he could wish to see an honest man hang."[116]

Shortly after Barnes's "new departure" on the question of war guilt, he lectured at a conference held in Olivet, Michigan. The Rev. Charles Clayton Morrison, editor of the *Christian Century*, heard him speak and was impressed. He invited the professor to prepare a series of articles for his magazine. Morrison was quite surprised when the subsequent "fan mail" brought in more letters "than the combined previous correspondence of his whole editorial career."[117] Later in the series, Barnes publicly repudiated his former thesis of divided guilt and charged "the sole and direct responsibility of Russia and France for the European war in 1914."[118]

The following year, Barnes expanded his *Christian Century* articles into a large book, entitled *The Genesis of the World War*.[119] This work attracted wide attention not only because of its controversial conclusions but also because it was the first American book written from the sources. Prewar Germany, argued Barnes, was not so nationalistic as France, so imperialistic as England, or so militaristic as France or Russia. From 1911 on, France and Russia engaged in secret diplomacy to foment the war which was necessary for their respective aims—the recovery of Alsace-Lorraine and control of the Straits. In other words, Germany was the somewhat simple victim of a gigantic Entente plot. When this generalization was promptly challenged, Barnes answered that he had five thousand documents to prove his case.[120] No wonder that the editor of *Die Kriegsschuldfrage* wrote that it would be "scarcely possible to provide a better book than this one."[121] John Haynes Holmes was satisfied that "we know

---

[113] Albert Bushnell Hart, "A dissent from the conclusions of Professor Barnes," *Current History*, XX (1924), 195–96. Barnes later stated (see H. E. Barnes, "The revisionist viewpoint corroborated," *Christian Century*, XLII [1925], 1476–78) that Ochs-Oakes had sent the manuscript of Barnes's 1924 article to ten reputable historians, and all but two had concurred in the findings. See *New York Times*, May 4, 1924, for a general dissent to Barnes's conclusions.

[114] Barnes to writer, Aug. 25, 1948.

[115] Harry Elmer Barnes, "Liquidating war illusions," *Nation*, CXX (1925), 154–55.

[116] *New York Times*, Mar. 15, 1925.

[117] Barnes to writer, Aug. 25, 1948.

[118] "Russia and France start the war," *Christian century*, XLII (1925), 1370–75.

[119] Barnes, in a letter to the writer, Aug. 25, 1948, stated that the Genesis was originally intended to be a reprinting of the articles in the *Christian Century*, but the project grew into a book.

[120] *New York Times*, May 27, 1926.

[121] Barnes, *In Quest*, p. 420.

now . . . Germany was the victim and France and Russia, the arch conspirators."[122]

There were, of course, many historians, writers, and leaders of public opinion who were unwilling to accept Barnes's radical conclusions. The result was the exchange of many bitter words and polemics on both sides. The lines had been forming since the end of the war, but it was Barnes who defined the issue in the United States. The controversy in America reached its zenith in the years following the publication of Barnes's *Genesis*. Preston Slosson called the *Genesis* "no judge's verdict but the brief of a rather emotional advocate."[123] Slosson pointed to Barnes's habit, when short of documents, of using secondary works of doubtful category to clinch his arguments. The first of Barnes's feuds to attract national attention was with Bernadotte E. Schmitt. On the basis of his 1923 Columbus paper, Barnes had prematurely welcomed Schmitt into the revisionist camp and had even sent him an advance copy of his 1924 article in *Current History*.[124] On April 3, 1926 the two men aired their differences before the Chicago Council on Foreign Relations. The encounter was unexpectedly tame, but, when Schmitt read Barnes's newest article in *Die Kriegs-schuldfrage*, he answered him in *Foreign Affairs*.[125] This article was an allout attack on Barnes's findings. Schmitt charged that the Smith professor had not examined the documents himself and that he had distorted, omitted, and selected facts. Barnes had applied historical criticism only to evidence which did not suit his conclusions.[126] When Barnes replied in a biting polemic, Schmitt made no public retort.[127]

Until his untimely death on the last day of 1929, Edward Raymond Turner was perhaps Barnes's most formidable opponent. Turner, born in Baltimore in 1881, had received his doctorate at Hopkins and, after a sojourn at Michigan and Yale, had returned in 1925 to his alma mater as professor of European history. Like Schmitt, Turner had been convinced even before 1914 that German militarism would lead to a world-wide conflagration.[128] As Barnes began to attract national attention, Turner wrote a number of open letters of protest to important journals and newspapers.[129] He called Barnes the "most vociferous advocate" of the absurd charge that the war had been an Entente plot. The *Genesis*, according to Turner, was an "unimportant and flimsy work . . . which . . . contains so many errors in statement and from omission that the task of evaluation and disentangling the truth from the false is much like preliminary work in a garden choked and tangled with weeds."[130] The following

---

[122] *Unity*, July 12, 1926, quoted in Barnes, *In Quest*, pp. 418–19. William L. Langer stated in a review of Izvolski's correspondence: "When all is said and done this correspondence still formulates the most serious indictment of Franco-Russian pre-war policy and lends considerable color to the theory that there was a conspiracy against the peace of the world" (quoted by Barnes, *ibid.*, p. 35).

[123] *American Historical Review*, XXXII (1927), 319–21.

[124] Harry Elmer Barnes, "Mr. Bernadotte Everly Schmitt and the question of responsibility for the outbreak of the World War," *Progressive*, X (1926), 86–101. This article has a complete account of the growing differences between the two men after 1924.

[125] *Progressive*, X (1926), 86.

[126] Bernadotte E. Schmitt, "July, 1914," *Foreign Affairs*, V (1926), 132–47.

[127] Barnes, *In Quest*, p. 331.

[128] Turner to the editor of the *Times*, Nov. 30, 1928, *New York Times*, Dec. 3, 1928. Preston Slosson, who knew Turner well, wrote the writer on December 1, 1948, that, while Turner was a specialist in English history, he wrote and taught in the field of modern European history and that his interest in the war-guilt question probably grew out of his teachings and writings.

[129] Much of this material is reprinted in Barnes, *In Quest*, pp. 206–26.

[130] Unmarked and undated clipping, quoting a letter from Turner to the editor of the *Saturday Review of Literature*, sent to the author by Preston Slosson.

month the Hopkins professor stated his views in *Current History*. Reaffirming Germany's liability in strong language, Turner asserted that revision in the United States was instigated by Germans desirous of escaping just punishment and by communists eager to discredit capitalism.[131]

If Barnes's critics influenced him at all, it was only to send him still further in the same direction. He freshened his views by almost annual summer pilgrimages to the German founts of revision.[132] In July 1927 he was the guest of honor at a banquet sponsored by the Union German societies. Barnes took the occasion to announce that he had now uncovered evidence to prove not only that Germany was innocent in 1914 but that her course of action had been most honorable.[133] Barnes returned to America fortified by interviews with the ex-kaiser, the former crown prince, Leopold von Berchtold, Count Alexander von Hoyos, Gottlieb von Jagow, and Alfred Zimmermann. One result of these interviews was a symposium in *Current History* on the question "Did Germany incite Austria in 1914?"[134] Barnes wrote the leading article, and his manuscript was sent to prominent German and Austrian survivors of 1914 who were to comment on his remarks.

In 1928 Barnes published *In Quest of Truth and Justice*, a recapitulation of arguments on both sides. He admitted that the *Genesis* had not attained wide distribution because of lack of co-operation by booksellers.[135] The new book was therefore to be distributed by the National Historical Society "because it has the largest and most relevant list for mail order distribution among the type of citizens most likely to be immediately interested in the book."[136] Before final publication of *In Quest*,

---

[131] Raymond Turner, "Germany's war guilt reaffirmed," *Current History*, XXV (1927), 648–55. In an attempt to stem the tide of opinion which regarded the war as an Entente conspiracy, Clarence W. Alvord offered an interesting synthesis on the question of war guilt in "Historical science and the war guilt," *American Mercury*, XI (1927), 324–26.

[132] Barnes, "Mr. Bernadotte Everly Schmitt and the question of responsibility for the outbreak of the World War," *loc. cit.*, p. 90.

[133] *New York Times*, July 22, 1927. It is interesting to note that the *New Yorker Volkszeitung*, quoted *ibid.*, July 26, termed Barnes's remarks as "childish."

[134] *Current History*, XXVIII (1928), 619–40. Michael T. Florinsky and James T. Shotwell contributed dissenting opinions to the German and Austrian assertions. See also the interesting symposium in *Current History*, XXVIII (1928), 961–98 on the question "Was Germany responsible for the World War?"

[135] Barnes, *In Quest*, preface, p. vi.

[136] *Ibid.*, p. vii. The National Historical Society had been founded in 1915 and was incorporated under the laws of the District of Columbia. The purposes of the society were to aid diffusion of American history, "inculcate patriotism; promote the peace of righteousness among nations," and promote co-operation among historical organizations (unidentified pamphlet and "press notice" in the vertical files of the Grosvenor Library, Buffalo, New York). It is interesting to note that, judged by stamped markings in the Lockwood Memorial Library's (University of Buffalo) copy of Bausman, *Facing Europe*, the National Historical Society took over the copyright of this isolationist book from the Century Co. The present writer is now engaged in further investigation of this society as an important agency in spreading isolationist literature in the twenties. He has found that this organization was in the forefront of the movement to "purge" American history texts of British and internationalist leanings. There is strong presumptive evidence of German-American influence in the society. On July 1, 1927, the National Historical Society took over publication of the *Progressive* which had been the semiofficial organ of the Steuben Society. Until publication was suspended in 1930, both societies worked together to make the *Progressive* a leading organ for the dissemination of anti-British, isolationist, and extreme revisionist thought.

Barnes read the proofsheets of Fay's *Origins of the World War*.[137] Nevertheless, he specifically reversed his 1924 stand and did his best to give Austria-Hungary a clean bill of health. He insisted that whatever the Dual Monarchy had done was done only in the interest of self-preservation, while Russian aggression came from the desire for prestige and material gain.[138] Barnes argued that, morality aside, Germany could not have been guilty because she had nothing to gain by war. Thus, as the ex-crown prince had told him, unless one assumed that German policy was controlled by idiots, if Wilhelmstrasse had really wanted war they would have chosen a crisis previous to 1914 when the Entente was much weaker.[139] In later years Barnes admitted that Germany in 1914 had not been a "helpless lamb in the midst of a pack of howling wolves."[140] Yet she worked for peace in 1914 not because she particularly believed in it but because *Realpolitik* mandated such a policy. In 1948 Barnes wrote that he had seen no new evidence that did anything but strengthen his former convictions.[141]

As the 1920's wore on, revisionism became steadily more international in character. Every important country in the Atlantic world had prominent writers on both sides of the question. Thus it is impossible to evaluate the American phase of the controversy without further consideration of the international cross-currents of revisionist literature. *Die Kriegsschuldfrage* encouraged revisionists in the United States, France, England, and Italy and publicized their writings. Thus one can find listed in the index of *Die Kriegsschuldfrage* Demartial, Alcide Ebray, and Caillaux from France; Gooch and C. R. Beazley from England; Fay, M. H. Cochran, Barnes, John Haynes Holmes, and even Drew Pearson from the United States.[142] In addition, there was the ever increasing horde of German writers on the subject, including serious historians, outright propagandists, and monarchical apologists. The agitation was continuous, but, like the Nazi propaganda mill of the next decade, the output was greater for special occasions.[143] Conservative elements in general, including many professional historians, wished vindication to come through an international tribunal of scholars, and there were many abortive actions in this direction during the period under discussion.

Former Chancellor Wilhelm Marx's article on "The responsibility for the war" was widely discussed in the United States in the early months of 1926. Marx, leader of the moderate Centrist group, told his readers that the war-guilt question united all Germans. He followed the familiar technique of first admitting that all had sinned and then, from this premise, pressing the case against the Entente. Marx's chief target was Alexander Petrovich Izvolski, who was the Russian ambassador to Paris after 1909. "This dangerous man" wanted Russian hegemony over the Balkans and Constantinople. The war came because unscrupulous French leaders gave him *plein pouvoir*. By 1914 Germany had been surrounded by a "ring of fire" and fought

[137] Barnes, *In Quest*, preface, p. viii.

[138] *Ibid.*, p. 51.

[139] *Ibid.*, p. 52.

[140] Harry Elmer Barnes, "The World War of 1914–1918," in Willard Waller (ed.), *War in the Twentieth Century* (New York, 1940), pp. 39–99.

[141] Barnes to writer, Aug. 25, 1948.

[142] See, for instance, John Haynes Holmes, "Ein Urteil nach zehn Jahren: Woodrow Wilson, Amerika und der Weltkrieg," *Die Kriegsschuldfrage*, IV, 552–69.

[143] See *New York Times*, May 11, 1924, for charges that the Germans released important source material bearing on the war just when reparations were due. The *Times* reasoned that this was done to show the world that Germany was paying the price of defeat, not of guilt.

to break this "deadly embrace." Marx concluded that only a condemnation of the Treaty of Versailles could ensure "the future happiness of humanity."[144]

The German entry into the League of Nations, on the morrow of Locarno, intensified the campaign.[145] The German religious leaders attempted, in vain, to interest the World Alliance for International Friendship through the Churches in the subject.[146] A million Germans petitioned Foreign Minister Gustav Stresemann for the creation of an impartial tribunal on the grounds that historians of all countries had found Germany innocent.[147] In 1927 even the German moderates distinctly accelerated their time table on the exploitation of the war-guilt question. Very possibly they wished to impress thousands of American Legionnaires who visited Germany after a celebration in France of the tenth anniversary of American entry into the war.[148] President von Hindenburg at the dedication of a war memorial at Tannenberg for the first time publicly denied German war guilt.[149] He repeated the familiar demand for a new impartial tribunal to settle the question.[150] P. J. Philip reported to the *New York Times* that "mysterious agencies are pouring out into other countries pamphlets to prove how Germany did not do it and there seems no way of stopping the outflow."[151] A prominent German banker demanded in *Current History*: "We yielded to President Wilson's famous fourteen points; and what advantage did they take of it! Americans indeed have cause to hear us generously and to do Germany justice."[152] By 1929 the nationalists were pressing for penal action against any German who perpetuated "Die Kriegsschuldlüge." The Germans had largely won the battle of history, and they were ready to pass from the "injured innocent" role of the twenties back to the "fire-eating" stage.[153]

Harry Elmer Barnes observed in 1930 that more good books had been written in France against Article 231 than in Germany and Austria combined.[154] While the actual number of French revisionists was but an infinitesimal fraction of the entire population, they wielded tremendous international influence. The official organ of French revisionism was *Evolution*, founded by Victor Margueritte and edited by Armand Charpentier. Margueritte began by attacking the French generals, and then in 1925 in *La Dernière Guerre* (Paris, 1925) he opened fire on the statesmen.[155] Closely allied with this group was Alfred Fabre-Luce, son of a leading French

[144] Marx, "The responsibility for the war," *Foreign Affairs*, IV (1926), 177–94. Compare Marx's article with Raymond Poincaré. "The responsibility for the war," *Foreign Affairs*, IV (1925), 1–19; see also appraisal of both articles by Sidney B. Fay, "Who started the war?" *New Republic*, XLV (1926), 185–86.

[145] Despatch of Edwin L. James from Paris to *New York Times*, Jan. 18, 1926.

[146] *Ibid.*, Mar. 29, 1926. This request was refused on the ground that it was a political question at a meeting of the World Conference of Churches at Berne (*ibid.*, Sept. 1, 1926).

[147] *Ibid.*, Oct. 28, 1926.

[148] Despatch of Edwin L. James from Paris to *New York Times*, Sept. 27, 1927.

[149] *Ibid.*, Sept. 19, 1927.

[150] *Ibid.*, The *New York Times* correspondent noted that Jewish rabbis and war veterans were conspicuous by their absence at this celebration.

[151] *Ibid.*, Oct. 16, 1927.

[152] Arthur von Gwinner, "Who were the war criminals of 1914?" *Current History*, XXVI (1927), 241–44.

[153] Austria played a relatively minor part in the war-guilt controversy after 1920. Barnes (*World Politics*, pp. 456–57) believed this to have been partly due to socialist influences. For the influence of Italian revisionism see *ibid.*, p. 463.

[154] *Ibid.*, p. 443.

[155] *Ibid.*, p. 462.

financier. In his book *La Victoire* (Paris, 1924), Fabre-Luce developed the widely quoted formula that the actions of the Central Powers had made the war possible, while those of the Entente made it inevitable.[156] Georges Demartial, former French director of colonial affairs, wrote *La Guerre de 1914: Comment on Mobilisa les Consciences* (Rome, 1922), in which he pinned exclusive guilt on his own country and on her allies. When Demartial wrote an article for *Current History* in 1926 outlining his views, he was suspended from the Legion of Honor for five years.[157] "L'affaire Demartial" aroused a limited amount of interest in the United States, and some thought him "a second Zola, martyred as a result of his courage and belief."[158]

The opposite extreme of French opinion can be gauged by a 1919 statement of Poincaré: "Not only did . . . [the Germans] declare war, but they sought it, wished it, and precipitated it."[159] Somewhere in between, but distinctly closer to Poincaré than to the revisionists, was the Société de l'Histoire de la Guerre. The editor of its quarterly,[160] Pierre Renouvin, occupied the chair of war history at the Sorbonne. In 1928 the Yale Press published an English translation of Renouvin's *Immediate Origins of the War*. This balanced, scholarly work placed much of the blame on the Austrian declaration of war against Serbia. This "local war," Renouvin insisted, the Central Powers alone wanted, and the step was premediated, with the calculated risk discounted.[161] Renouvin's work was well received in American scholarly circles and somewhat offset the writings of the French revisionists. In *Foreign Affairs* Poincaré noted the effect of German and Soviet propaganda on the minds of "well-meaning" and "high-standing" Americans. He recapitulated the case against Germany and warned: "Against these unalterable truths the gates of hell themselves shall not prevail."[162] "Behind the impression that bites into the consciousness of mankind during a generation," wrote the *New York Times* of Poincaré's conclusions, "there is bound to be a reality."[163] Yet, because of the wide dissemination of French revisionist views in America, Demartial, Fabre-Luce, and Margueritte had greater influence upon American public opinion than had their conservative fellow-countrymen.[164]

In the late twenties English revisionism built upon the foundation which had been laid by E. D. Morel, Francis Neilson, and Irene Cooper Willis. Barnes dedicated his *In Quest of Truth and Justice* to C. Raymond Beazley, of the University of

---

[156] Quoted in *Nation*, CXX (1925), 155.

[157] Georges Demartial, "France's responsibility for the World War," *Current History*, XXIII (1926), 787–93; *New York Times*, May 20, 1928. Demartial was a frequent contributor to *Die Kriegsschuldfrage*.

[158] Faith E. Wilcox, "French war historian's expulsion from Legion of Honor," *Current History*, XXVIII (1928), 641–43. Alcide Ebray (*A Frenchman Looks at the Peace* [London, 1927]) was less vehement than some of the other revisionists.

[159] Quoted in *New York Times*, Mar. 24, 1919.

[160] The quarterly, founded in 1923, was the *Revue d'Histoire de la Guerre Mondiale*.

[161] Pp. 354–55.

[162] Poincaré, "The responsibility for the war," *loc. cit.*, p. 19. Fay wrote that Poincaré's "most severe critics have been his own countrymen—Pevet, Judet, Fabre-Luce, Converset, Morhardt, Victor Margueritte, Lazare, and a host of lesser lights" (*Origins*, I, 24).

[163] Editorial, Sept. 14, 1925.

[164] For the influence of French revisionism on Barnes see his *World Politics*, pp. 461–62. Few Americans understood the connection between world-war historiography and politics in France. Thus it was the radical Socialist paper, *L'œuvre*, which published parts of Georges Louis's diary asserting that Poincaré had instructed Ambassador Maurice Paléologue to tell the Russians to be obstinate (*New York Times*, Nov. 17, 1924).

Birmingham. Yet Barnes admitted that the English revisionists were far more influential in the United States than in their own country, where the "Grey myth" remained almost impregnable.[165] Originally, almost all historians had placed very little direct war guilt on England. With that almost masochistic urge to blame one's own country that was so typical of many of the revisionists, British writers began to list Sir Edward Grey among the "guilty." Frederick C. Conybeare suggested that England went to war to deal with German navalism and commercial and colonial expansion.[166] Henry W. Nevinson, famous British war correspondent, wrote of Article 231 that it was "a lie of such grossness that I wonder the hand which first wrote it did not wither."[167] G. Lowes Dickinson, whose *International Anarchy* was published in New York in 1926, was more moderate. This well-known British writer believed that all the powers shared the responsibility but that France and Russia had been particularly aggressive. The great majority of British historians stoutly resisted the onslaught of world-wide revisionism. Yet this fact made less impression upon American public opinion than did Ramsay MacDonald's 1928 speech before the Reichstag on war guilt or the publication of Arthur Ponsonby's *Falsehood in War-Time*.[168] Moreover, British postwar disillusionist writers and speakers frequently expressed anti-American sentiments, just as our own "lost generation" were often chronic anglophobes. Certainly the general disillusionment which often expressed itself in a desire for the bizarre aided the extreme revisionists rather than the moderate scholars.

In many respects the year 1928 was a landmark in world-war historiography. Soon the great depression, the rise of the dictators, and the fighting in China were to turn American interest from the question of who started the last war to the problem of how to stay out of the next conflict. Moreover, the publication of Fay's *The Origins of the World War* did much to stabilize American opinion on the question. Probably even today the overwhelming majority of American writers and teachers of history who concern themselves with this problem do not seriously differ from Fay's findings of over twenty years ago. In the seven years which elapsed between the publication of his "New Light" articles and the appearance of his definitive work, Fay became a sort of legend. Few historical books have ever been awaited so eagerly as was this work. Extreme revisionists, so-called "bitter-enders," and moderates alike waited anxiously for a confirmation of their divergent opinions.[169] From the American point of view, all other scholars in the field were suspect. Fay, on the other hand, was a respected member of the guild with a reputation for unimpeachable integrity. Here at last those Americans who were interested in the subject might find a guide out of the darkness created by years of controversy and the ever accumulating mass of documents.

When the long-awaited two volumes appeared late in 1928, all sides claimed

---

[165] Barnes, *World Politics,* p. 461.

[166] *Ibid.,* p. 459.

[167] "The great revision," *Saturday Review of Literature,* III (1926), 309–11.

[168] *New York Times,* Oct. 16, 1928. Ponsonby was a member of a distinguished British family who became a Laborite M.P. in 1922. His book was published in New York in 1928.

[169] Harry Elmer Barnes, "The revisionists vindicated," *Current History,* XXIX (1928), 443–48. Barnes asserted here that close friends and fellow-historians put great pressure on Fay "to discomfort the revisionists and to vindicate the timid, the evasive, the slothful and the somnolent." See also Barnes, *World Politics,* pp. 478–508.

victory. The dispute among the reviewers revolved mostly around the twelve final pages into which Fay condensed his conclusions. Barnes promptly invited all the "timid but sincere and candid" brethren in the American Historical Association to climb "aboard the revisionist toboggan."[170] While hailing Fay as a revisionist, Barnes asserted that the concluding chapter was a sort of *non sequitur* to the more "revisionist" evidence in the foregoing pages. Barnes also criticized Fay for being too harsh on Austria-Hungary and strongly dissented from the verdict that "NONE of the Powers wanted a European War."[171] William L. Langer, whom Fay was soon to join at Harvard, reviewed the volumes for the *Nation*. Langer was excellently prepared for this assignment, as he had studied in Vienna after the war and was himself working on the prewar European alliances.[172] He pointed out that, like the revisionists, Fay held that hasty Russian mobilization made war inevitable. Like Barnes, Langer thought that Fay was too severe on the Ballplatz but that a careful reading of the conclusion would tend to explain away some of Austria's culpability.[173]

As Fay wrote at the time, the reader generally finds in a book not the author's meaning but what he himself seeks.[174] Hence W. P. Cresson held that only in the concluding chapter of the *Origins* was there any fuel for revisionist thought.[175] Preston Slosson, of Michigan, covered the book for the *American Historical Review*. Although known to lean toward the Schmitt-Turner school, Slosson praised the work as "comprehensive, authoritative, impartial, and well proportioned."[176] He distinctly refused to put Fay among the revisionists because he had rejected the heresy of his "unwelcome allies of the 'extreme left' " and had refused to regard the war as a Franco-Russian conspiracy. Moreover, Fay held Count Leopold Berchtold more guilty than any other one man in precipitating the conflict.[177] On the other hand, the veteran historian William MacDonald reasoned quite differently. Inasmuch as Fay had argued that, but for the assassination, there would have been no war, MacDonald said this meant that the ultimate cause was Serbian nationalism.[178] In a letter to the *New York Times*, Raymond Turner attacked the contention of the revisionists that the *Origins* upheld their point of view, and he claimed an essential victory for the conservative historians.[179] Pierre Renouvin thought Fay's work deserving of an entire article in *Foreign Affairs*. The French professor praised Fay's sound methods and restrained judgments. Yet he felt that Fay failed to realize that, regardless of Germany's ultimate intentions, the Triple Entente was forged on the anvil of Berlin's warlike words and preparations.

[170] Harry Elmer Barnes, "The twilight of the myth-mongers," *Living Age,* CCCXXV (1928), 270–71. Fay had kept in the public eye by critical professional reviews and occasional articles. One of the very few times in the intervening years between the publication of his articles and the completion of his definitive work that he attempted a synthesis was in an article in *Die Kriegsschuldfrage,* IV (1926), 900–903.

[171] *World Politics,* p. 506; *History of Western Civilization* (2 vols.; New York, 1935), II, 605.

[172] Langer was soon to publish *The Franco-Russian Alliance, 1890–1894* (Cambridge, 1929) and *European Alliances and Alignments, 1871–1890* (New York, 1931).

[173] *Nation,* CXXVII (1928), 622–23.

[174] Fay to editor of *New York Times,* Dec. 13, 1928.

[175] *American Journal of International Law,* XXIII (1929), 714–16.

[176] *American Historical Review,* XXXIV (1929), 336–40.

[177] *Ibid.*

[178] Review in *New York Times,* Nov. 18, 1928.

[179] *New York Times,* Dec. 3, 1928. For a debate between Turner and Fay as to the meaning of the latter's conclusions see *ibid.,* Dec. 11, 13, 1928.

Renouvin admitted that Russian actions complicated the crisis, but he regretted that Fay had accepted the "axiom" that "mobilization meant war."[180]

Perhaps the most effective summary of what American historians had come to believe about war origins at this time was written by M. H. Cochran.[181] "Each of the governments of 1914 was trying to reach certain goals, without war if possible. None of them wanted war for war's sake, yet none of them would let the opponent win without armed struggle. Since the most direct method of winning the game was an attack on the opponent, each of them suspected the other of planning an overwhelming attack." Somewhere along this line of reasoning American professional opinion had come to rest when Hitlerian Germany made many people wipe their glasses and re-examine the documents in the rays of the fresh spotlight that the present always plays upon the past.

To some extent the debate over the American entry in 1917 paralleled the war-guilt controversy. In a larger measure, however, the traditional story of 1917 was not seriously assailed until the revisionist point of view had made a deep impression upon American thought.[182] Important source material on American entry was made available much later than the European documents. As a victorious country and, unlike England and France, with no German and Russian accusations to answer, the United States did not rush to open archival and manuscript material.[183] Yet, as revisionism made progress, it was bound to raise questions about our own part in the war. Albert Bushnell Hart sensed this in his reaction to Barnes's 1924 article: "If Barnes is right, Roosevelt was wrong. Wilson was wrong. Elihu Root was wrong. Ambassador Page was wrong, everybody was wrong."[184]

A distinct part of this early disillusionment came from Europe. Thus Munroe Smith, while traveling on the continent in the summer of 1921, was amazed to hear that many Europeans believed that we had fought to save our capitalist loans.[185] Working on hunches rather than on source material, John Kenneth Turner's *Shall it be Again?* asserted that America entered the war because the financial and banking interests could not stomach a German victory. While engaged in the perhaps not unpleasant task of eulogizing Wilson in the *Nation*, Oswald Garrison Villard wrote that when the late president decided for war, "he was acclaimed with joy by every

---

[180] "How the war came," *Foreign Affairs*, VII (1929), 384–97.

[181] "Historiography and war guilt," *Political Science Quarterly*, XLIII (1928), 76–89. For the impact of revisionism on the general current of American thought, the following quotation from a letter of Henry White, Sept. 24, 1926, is significant: "It is quite getting to be recognized in this country that Germany was not solely responsible for the war, although of course she could have stopped it, and Berchtold lied to the old Emperor of Austria to get him to approve of the declaration of war against Serbia" (quoted in Allan Nevins, *Henry White* [New York, 1930], p. 489).

[182] For what the leftists thought of American motives in 1917 see Scott Nearing, *The American Empire* (New York, 1921), pp. 146–48; and Harold Stearns, *Liberalism in America* (New York, 1919), pp. 132–35. But Senator Owen, in his speech of Dec. 18, 1923, said: "America was justified in entering the war regardless of who was responsible for willing the war" (*Congressional Record*, LXV, 375).

[183] For a summary of how important American material was released see Bernadotte E. Schmitt, "American neutrality, 1914–1917," *Journal of Modern History*, VIII (1936), 200–211. For the revisionist demand for the release of American war material, see T. St. John Gaffney, "Open the American war archives," *Progressive*, X (1926), 41–42.

[184] Hart, "A dissent from the conclusions of Professor Barnes," *loc. cit.*, p. 196.

[185] *New York Times*, July 16, 1922.

munition-maker, every war profiteer, every agent of big business."[186] Again and again leading bankers were forced to issue statements denying their share in the American declaration of war. These early attacks, however, were sporadic. Harry Elmer Barnes was the real connecting link between the war-guilt controversy and revision of the story of American entrance. While Barnes was at Clark University, one of his students was C. Hartley Grattan. After several years of college teaching, Grattan broke into print in 1925 with an attack on the "Walter Hines Page legend." If the ambassador was a great patriot, wrote Grattan, then "the definition of American had better be revised."[187] About the same time Barnes himself digressed from his principal theme to a consideration of pre-1917 American foreign policy. Barnes did not think German submarine warfare one iota more vicious than English violation of American neutral rights.[188] While he had some reservations about a complete economic interpretation of Wilson's policies, "unquestionably from 1915-1918 the enormous power of American finance and industry was directed almost solely toward the defense of the allied powers and support of their subtle propaganda."[189] In the *Genesis,* Barnes went back to the submarine theory; for he argued that it was "the unneutrality, lack of courage, or maladroitness of the Washington authorities in regard to English violations of international law which produced the German submarine warfare that actually led us into war."[190] Nevertheless, Barnes was not then an isolationist. While he called Wilson the supreme architect of the "holy-war legend," he admitted that both American idealism and the League of Nations drew nourishment from his memory.[191]

Strangely enough in view of later events, Charles A. Beard strongly dissented from Barnes's interpretation of American entry into the war. "Given a German victory," wrote Beard in 1926, "and given the present world position of the United States, does anyone not obsessed by pacifist ideas or German sympathies think for a moment that Potsdam would not challenge Washington in full panoply before the lapse of many years?"[192] On the other hand, the *New Republic's* reaction to Barnes was to demand the opening of American archival material in order to determine: "What was it? A crusade to defend civilization against the military barbarism of the Huns? . . . Who were responsible for this belief, by what means was it diffused, and to what extent was it justified?"[193] In 1928 Barnes noted that the problem of

---

[186] "Woodrow Wilson: a supreme tragedy," *Nation,* CXVIII (1924), 156–58. Robert M. La Follette, campaigning for the presidency in 1924, helped spread similar ideas. At St. Louis on Oct. 14, 1924, he asserted that in 1917 J. P. Morgan and his associates "turned loose the press and agencies of propaganda to drive us into the war" (*Nation,* CXIX [1924], 477). La Follette charged that the international bankers tried to force American ratification of the Treaty of Versailles to involve us "inextricably in the intrigues and wars of Europe" (*ibid.*).

[187] *American Mercury,* VI (1925), 39–51. Compare this statement with William E. Dodd's review of Burton J. Hendrick, *The life and letters of Walter H. Page* (2 vols.; Garden City, 1922), in *American Historical Review,* XXVIII (1923), 566–70; see also *World's Work,* XLII (1921), 346–60, for the strength of the Page tradition in the United States.

[188] "Why America entered the war," *Christian Century,* XLII (1925), 1441–44.

[189] *Ibid.,* p. 1443.

[190] *Ibid.,* p. 595. By 1935 when Barnes published his *History of Western Civilization,* he seems to have been influenced by the growing popularity of the munitions-bankers theory of American participation (see II, 605).

[191] *World Politics,* p. 367.

[192] "Heroes and Villains of the War," *loc. cit.,* p. 735.

[193] "America's War Responsibility," *New Republic,* XLVII (1926), 270–71.

American entry into the war had still not received adequate treatment. So he again examined the question, and this time veered back in the direction of economic determinism. By 1917, Great Britain had overdrawn her American credit, and the bankers were experiencing difficulty in floating additional private loans. It was time for the federal treasury to take over.[194] Yet Barnes was astute enough to realize that Wilson was more influenced by cultural affinity to England than by material considerations. The paradox was resolved by explaining that Wilson was vain and that when big business made the press and country want war, Wilson could not resist the temptation to lead the crusade.[195] Thus was the stage set for the 1929 publication of Grattan's *Why We Fought*—the pioneer work of the disillusionist school of writers.

Finally, to what extent was revisionism responsible for the growth of isolationism? Before this query can be answered, certain observations are in order. There was a marked increase in isolationist sentiment in the twenties. The reasons for this attitude, so measurable in Democratic party politics after 1920, are complex. Revisionism was unquestionably one of the factors. By 1929 it would have been difficult to believe that, a decade before, a historian had written that isolationism conflicted with the realities of modern life and had vanished forever.[196] In order to understand one cause for the change which had taken place in the minds of so many Americans, it is necessary once more to follow the general trend of the war-guilt controversy.

Frederick Bausman wrote in 1922 of the A.E.F. that "there never went to battle legions with so little desire to bring back anything for themselves or their native land."[197] As a result of the victory, Germany was pouring gold marks into Allied coffers, yet the money did not come back to the United States as payment for debts but went in large measure to support French armies of occupation.[198] In *Facing Europe*, Bausman was even more pointed and bitter. The Allies had beguiled us into the war and then, in their newly found strength, had become a menace to the safety of the United States. Only the Scandinavian countries still respected the United States, and that was because we had never helped them. He classed Europe as "disorderly, envious, and quarrelsome" and predicted that some day England would attempt to crush us as she had all her erstwhile friends in the past.[199] Albert Jay Nock in the *Myth of a Guilty Nation* wrote that the Treaty of Versailles, conceived "in the pure spirit of the victorious Apache, has, in practice, utterly broken down."[200] Lewis Gannett, in the same year, warned that Europe, enmeshed in a new series of secret treaties, was plunging toward another catastrophe. "And yet, if there be any hope in the world, must it not be precisely in this process of slowly cleaning the lies out of our minds and starting fresh?"[201] The influence of the war-guilt question on Charles A. Beard is striking. He had been one of the leading liberal internationalists. In 1918 he collaborated in writing a book which asserted that isolationism was gone

[194] *In Quest*, p. 104.
[195] *Ibid.*, p. 102.
[196] C. F. Lavell, in review of A. C. McLaughlin's *America and Britain*, *American Historical Review*, XXIV (1919), 740–41.
[197] *Let France explain*, p. 63.
[198] *Ibid.*, preface, p. 7.
[199] Pp. 9, 322.
[200] Preface, p. 7.
[201] Gannett, "They all lied," *loc. cit.*, p. 357.

forever and that a League of Nations held out the only hope for world peace.[202] soon thereafter he was writing reviews for the liberal journals which showed strong revisionist tendencies. While Beard was never willing merely to shift villains and place the entire blame on the Entente powers, he warned that the *Kriegsschuldfrage* must make us "regard with cold blood all the quarrels of Europe."[203] When Senator Owen enlightened the senate on war guilt, he still showed some evidence of his former pro-league stand. Yet he admonished his colleagues that the war had left problems "that the people of Europe themselves must work out. They can not be advised from America."[204]

Barnes, who belonged to the liberal wing of the revisionist coalition, genuinely favored international co-operation and organization. He insisted, however, that a realistic American foreign policy could be built only upon a true understanding of the nature of the war. Thus Barnes classed the league as "a league of victors" and compared the Washington conference (1921–22) to a group of sportsmen who agreed not to use flintlocks in their fall shooting.[205] The net result was an isolationist impression upon Barnes's readers and audiences because he put the war-guilt question above everything else. Barnes's frequent contradictions were partly due to the fact that, while he disliked "international anarchy," he felt that the war still would not have come unless the Russians and French had planned it.[206] So no good could come of any existing arrangements until the Treaty of Versailles was nullified.[207] Gradually, Barnes dropped much of his internationalism, and his writings in the late twenties read much like the minutes of an "America First" meeting.[208]

The "liberal" journals of opinion almost always used the war-guilt question to preach isolation. The *New Republic* gleefully quoted a British magazine to the effect that the German guilt myth had been framed during the war "when we wanted to get the Americans into it."[209] The *Nation* called for "a juster historical assessment" of the war in order to "force a deep revulsion of American feeling."[210] Georges Demartial told America that the idea that the League of Nations existed to prevent war was a "humorous suggestion."[211] The *New Republic*'s review of Fay's *Origins* asked: "Is there any lesson for Americans in this record? Yes! . . . The constitutional limitations upon the President should not be circumvented by the negotiations of 'personal' agreements . . . if public opinion permits such precedents, it will not be long before a virtual autocracy will be established by the Executive."[212]

By the time that Herbert Hoover moved into the White House, attended by the final glow of postwar prosperity, the war-guilt question had made a deep impression

---

[202] Frederic A. Ogg and Charles A. Beard, *National Governments and the World War* (New York, 1919), p. 589.

[203] Beard, "Heroes and villains of the world war," *loc. cit.,* p. 735.

[204] U.S., *Congressional Record,* LXV, 372.

[205] "Liquidating wartime illusions," *Christian Century,* XLII (1925), 1506–10.

[206] "The genesis of the world war," *New Republic,* XLVIII (1926), 246–49.

[207] *Ibid.*

[208] "A revised verdict on guilt of nations for the world war," *Current History,* XXVI (1927), 676–98; *World Politics,* p. 44.

[209] "The living lie," *New Republic,* XLIV (1925) 189–90.

[210] "Set the war truths free," *Nation,* CXVIII (1924), 247.

[211] "France's responsibility for the World War," *loc. cit.,* p. 792.

[212] Edward M. Earle, "A wise and upright story of war responsibility," *New Republic,* LVII (1928), 73–75.

upon the American mind. Germany again enjoyed a decent respect in the opinion of mankind. Only unprecedented *Schrecklichkeit* would convince America that Nazi brutality was not just Act II of the same play. Much of American thought and policy in the 1930's was due to the general impression that we had been "taken in" once before. The most startling events in the history of modern times were necessary to make us sing: "There will be blue birds over the white cliffs of Dover."

19 / The Professional Diplomat and His Problems 1919-1939

Gordon A. Craig

In any reasonably comprehensive collection of articles dealing with American foreign relations, there should be at least one selection addressed to the status of diplomats in the Twentieth Century. Although the following article by Gordon Craig emphasizes the declining importance of diplomats in several European countries after the First World War, many of the tendencies observed by Craig also applied to American envoys. The article suggests that the decline was not a phenomenon limited to any single government but was part and parcel of the emerging "new diplomacy." Implicitly, decisions concerning foreign policy were too important to be left to the professional diplomats. After all, for the generation that came of age during the 1920s and 1930s, the professional diplomats were made the scapegoats for the catastrophe that was the Great War 1914–18. Perhaps the technological improvements in transportation and communication also tended to downgrade the importance of professional diplomats by facilitating the transmission of dispatches between foreign office and diplomatic representatives abroad thus eliminating or at least sharply reducing the discretionary responsibility of diplomats within the national decision-making process.

For further reading: *Robert P. Browder, *The Origins of Soviet-American Diplomacy* (Princeton: 1953); David D. Burks, "The United States and the Geneva Protocol of 1924: A New 'Holy Alliance'?" *American Historical Review*, LXIV (1959), 891–905; *Gordon A. Craig and Felix Gilbert, editors, *The Diplomats 1919–1939* (Princeton: 1953); Lewis Einstein, *A Diplomat Looks Back* (New Haven: 1968); Waldo Heinrichs, *American Ambassador: Joseph C. Grew and the Development of the United States Diplomatic Tradition* (Boston: 1966); *George A. Kennan, *Memoirs 1925–1950* (Boston: 1967); John C. Vinson, *The Parchment Peace: The United States Senate and the Washington Conference 1921–1922* (Athens: 1955); Gerald Wheeler, *Prelude to Pearl Harbor: the United States Navy and the Far East*

Gordon A. Craig is Professor of History at Stanford University. This article is reprinted with the permission of the editors of *World Politics*. From *World Politics*, IV (January, 1952), 145–158. Copyright 1952 by *World Politics*.

1921–1931 (Columbia: 1963); William A. Williams, "The Legend of Isolationism in the 1920's," *Science and Society,* XVIII (1954), 1–20.

One of the recurring themes in those books on the diplomatic prehistory of the second World War which have come to us from the former enemy countries is the plight of the professional diplomat, whose training and knowledge convinced him that the policy of his government was leading straight to disaster but whose advice was seldom solicited and never followed. The memoirs of Erich Kordt, of Herbert von Dirksen, and of Rudolf Rahn, the books of Elisabetta Cerruti, Mario Donosti, and Filippo Anfuso[1] include abundant and circumstantial evidence of the lack of influence exercised in matters of high policy by the permanent staffs of the Foreign Offices of Germany and Italy and by their agents in the field. In his study of the origins of the Pact of Steel, Mario Toscano has described the desperate efforts made by Attolico, the Italian ambassador in Berlin, to convince his political superiors in Rome of the inadequacies and dangers of the projected alliance with Germany.[2] Those efforts failed; and they were certainly resented by the "realists" in Rome, who had long since reached the conclusion that foreign policy was too important to be left in the hands of professional diplomats. The same conclusion had been reached in Germany; and it was persisted in until the collapse of 1945. As early as 1936, the German foreign service had been deprived of most of its former prerogatives in the processes of policy formulation and execution. Ernst von Weizsäcker, the State Secretary for Foreign Affairs from 1938 until 1944, says in his memoirs: "Amateurish and irregular reports were often preferred to the official ones. Decisions were taken without the Foreign Minister or the Foreign Office having had a say in the framing of them. The carrying out of the decisions was entrusted to the most various quarters . . . The foreign service had been degraded to the level of a mere technical apparatus."[3]

We could dismiss all of this evidence of the diminution of the influence of expert advice in modern diplomacy as being nothing more than an interesting sidelight on the nature of totalitarian regimes if it were not for one thing that is sometimes forgotten. And that is that the experience of the professional diplomat in Germany and Italy finds striking parallels in the diplomatic practice of the democratic states of Europe in the interwar period. In both Great Britain and France especially, the neglect and abuse of the resources of expert diplomacy was a recurrent phenomenon in the years 1919–1939; and, when the new Fay or Schmitt or Seymour appears to write a comprehensive history of the origins of the second World War, he will have to compose at least a lengthy footnote on the subject. The political scientist who is willing to relate the experience of history to current problems will probably wish to do more than that, for some of the more unhappy features of prewar British and French practice are recognizable—in somewhat exaggerated forms—in the conduct of foreign relations in our own country at the present time.

[1] Erich Kordt, *Nicht aus den Akten,* Stuttgart, 1950; Herbert von Dirksen, *Moskau,* Tokio, London: *Erinnerungen und Betrachtungen zu 20 Jahre deutscher Aussenpolitik,* 1919–1939, Stuttgart, 1949; Rudolf Rahn, *Ruheloses Leben,* Düsseldorf, 1950; Elisabetta Cerruti, *Visti da vicino,* Milan, 1951; Mario Donosti, *Mussolini e l'Europa: la politica estera fascista,* Milan, 1945; Filippo Anfuso, *Roma Berlino Salò,* Milan, 1950.

[2] Mario Toscano, *Le origini del Patto d'Acciaio,* Florence, 1948, especially pp. 170–80.

[3] *The Memoirs of Ernst von Weizsäcker,* Chicago, 1951, p. 106.

I

"The art of diplomacy," Harold Nicolson has written, "as that of water-colours, has suffered much from the fascination which it exercises upon the amateur."[4] The years after 1919 were years in which the political leaders of the Western states found that fascination irresistible, and in which, undeterred by their lack of previous experience in the arts of diplomacy, they took into their hands "delicate work for which a life's training is no sure guarantee of success, and for which sciolism is an almost certain presage of failure."[5] Their successful penetration into what had formerly been the preserve of diplomats of career is, of course, easily explained. Even in normal times, career diplomats are not beloved in democratic states, where foreign affairs seem, at the very least, to be a distraction from the true business of the nation and, at the worst, a source of constant trouble and danger, and where men who make a career of dealing with foreign affairs are apt to be viewed with grave suspicion. "On n'aime pas," Jules Cambon has said, "ces porteurs de secrets que sont les ambassadeurs."[6] In 1919 this vague suspicion had been greatly strengthened by the prevailing conviction that the secret diplomacy which was their stock in trade had been the principal cause of the recent war. When Woodrow Wilson announced in the Fourteen Points that "diplomacy shall proceed always frankly and in the public view," his demand was accorded widespread approval; and, in March 1918, a speaker in the House of Commons proclaimed the doom of the professional caste when he declared:

> The old ambassadorial system has failed and is discredited in the eyes of most people. After the war, the old diplomacy of Court and upper classes will be, in the eyes of most people, obsolete and inadequate. . . . Difficulties between nations should no longer be settled in conclaves of Ambassadors.[7]

The cry of the times, then, seemed to be for new diplomatic methods and new diplomatic personnel, and the political leaders of the Western states were quick to respond to what they considered to be the popular desire. Conclaves of ambassadors at the Quai d'Orsay, the Wilhelmstrasse, and the Ballplatz—names now of sinister connotation—gave way to "frank and friendly conversations" in such charmingly unconventional places as the golf course at Cannes, the bosom of the Lago Maggiore, the mountain tavern at Thoiry, and a certain mossy log on the banks of the Potomac. The correctly dressed and distressingly uniform diplomats, who had until now held the center of the stage, ceded their places to a succession of politician-diplomats with such striking and memorable characteristics as plus-fours, Scots brogues, shaggy coiffures, white linen neckties, underslung pipes, and various kinds of umbrellas. The new dispensation was dignified by the name "diplomacy by conference" and was celebrated in a much-read essay by Sir Maurice Hankey, who in the early years served as impresario for the entertainment.[8]

If we consider the case of Britain alone, it is easy to demonstrate that the new

[4] Harold Nicolson, *Curzon: The Last Phase, 1919–1925*, New York, 1939, p. 54.

[5] A. L. Kennedy, *Old Diplomacy and New*, London, 1922, pp. 363–64.

[6] Jules Cambon, *Le diplomate, Paris*, 1926, pp. 10–11.

[7] *Parliamentary Debates:* Commons, CIV (1918), 846.

[8] Sir Maurice Hankey, "Diplomacy by Conference," *The Round Table*, XI (1920–1921), 287–311.

diplomacy created serious problems for the Foreign Office, the agency constitutionally charged with the conduct of Britain's foreign relations, and made its position embarrassing and at times almost insupportable. Think, for instance, of the four long years of insult and injury suffered by it at the hands of Mr. Lloyd George. Lloyd George's contempt for the diplomatic profession and its conventions was well known, for he made little attempt to conceal it. "I want no diplomats," he said during the course of the war. "Diplomats were invented simply to waste time. . . . It is simply a waste of time to let [important matters] be discussed by men who are not authorized to speak for their countries."[9] He showed that he meant this during the Paris Peace Conference. He went to that gathering, it is true, surrounded by clouds of experts from the Foreign Office and from other government departments; but he made singularly little use of them. He seems to have been irritated by their habit, when consulted, of producing closely argued analyses bristling with statistics. In any event, he soon relegated the Foreign Secretary and his staff to the limbo already tenanted by Mr. Lansing and his,[10] while he himself retired with Wilson, Clemenceau, and Orlando to see what intuition could do to solve the intricate problems of the peace.

When it appeared subsequently that intuition had not been enough and that the formulae devised by the Council of Four had postponed, and minimized, but certainly not solved, acute differences of opinion between the European Powers,[11] Lloyd George was not dismayed, nor was his faith in his own diplomatic talents shaken. He set out bravely to solve all the problems created by the Treaty of Versailles. That this should be done by methods tested by experience—by careful soundings of opinion in other capitals, by the tedious, but always useful, exchange of formal correspondence—does not seem to have occurred to him. "I wish the French and ourselves never wrote letters to each other," he said in 1920. "Letters are the very devil. They ought to be abolished altogether. . . . If you want to settle a thing, you see your opponent and talk it over with him. The last thing you do is write him a letter."[12] According to this prescription, Lloyd George acted in the years 1919–1922, meeting his opponents at San Remo and Spa and Cannes and Genoa and, when the occasion demanded greater intimacy, at his breakfast table at 10 Downing Street. At these meetings, without prior, or even subsequent, consultation with the Foreign Office, he decided policy, negotiated claims, and made commitments to foreign governments. At the Spa Conference, for instance, he gave promises of protection to the Polish Government which had not been authorized by the Cabinet and of which the Foreign Office and His Majesty's representative in Warsaw were given no intimation until after they had been discussed in the popu-

[9] Kennedy, Old Diplomacy, pp. 364–65.

[10] If this seems an exaggeration, it should be remembered that, even in such an important matter as the treaty in which Great Britain and the United States guaranteed to come to France's aid in the event of future German aggression, the Foreign Secretary was not consulted. Only after the Treaty of Guarantee had been drafted in accordance with Lloyd George's personal instructions and been approved by Wilson and Clemenceau was Mr. Balfour informed of it.—Lord Hardinge of Penshurst, Old Diplomacy, London, 1947, p. 241.

[11] See, for instance, "Is There a New Diplomacy?", Fortnightly Review, CXI (1922), 711. Formula-making became a characteristic feature of Lloyd George's diplomacy. His latest biographer says: "Failure to reach agreement or to do no more than expose divergencies to the world could, as a rule and for the moment, be veiled in intentional obscurity by drafting a dextrous formula, an art in which his secretaries became proficient."—Thomas Jones, Lloyd George, Cambridge, Mass., 1951, p. 180.

[12] Lord Riddell, Intimate Diary of the Peace Conference and After, London, 1933, p. 206.

lar press.[13] The Foreign Office, with reason, came to expect the worst of the Prime Minister's peripatetic activities; and Curzon said sadly at the time of the Genoa Conference: "When I reflect that the P.M. is alone at Genoa with no F.O. to guide him . . . and when I recall the whole trend of his policy for the past three years—I can feel no certainty that we may not find ourselves committed to something pregnant with political disaster here."[14] The results of Genoa were startling, but not as calamitous as Curzon feared; but the apprehension of the Foreign Secretary was nevertheless justified. A year later, indeed, disaster was very narrowly averted, as Lloyd George's stubborn refusal to listen to Foreign Office advice in Eastern affairs and his unfortunate habit of encouraging the Greeks by winks and nods brought Britain to the verge of war at Chanak.

It is not intended to suggest here that the eclipse of the Foreign Office in the Lloyd George period was permanent. Indeed, in Curzon's last years in that office and in the years when Austen Chamberlain was Foreign Secretary, the Foreign Office resumed its normal position in the conduct of British policy. It cannot, however, be denied that Lloyd George's methods had created unfortunate precedents. The Prime Minister cannot be expected to stay out of foreign affairs, for he is ultimately responsible for policy. But perhaps never before Lloyd George had the Prime Minister interfered so directly, so frequently and so secretly with the actual day-by-day business of foreign relations—that is, with the implementation of formulated policy and with the varied tasks of negotiation. And this kind of interference was repeated sporadically, and generally with unfortunate effects, in the years that followed, reaching its highest point in the years 1937–1939. Here we need cite only a few examples. During the crisis created by the French occupation of the Ruhr in 1923, when the Foreign Office was maintaining a position of studied neutrality in the double hope of restraining the French and preventing the victory of extremism in Germany, an ill-timed visit of Mr. Baldwin to Paris and an injudicious *communiqué* issued without Foreign Office knowledge created the impression that Britain was supporting French policy without reservation. This debacle led the British ambassador in Berlin to suggest that "it might be wise to apply to British Prime Ministers the rule governing the peregrinations of a Lord Chancellor and forbid their leaving England."[15] The rule, of course, was not invoked, as the subsequent wanderings of Ramsay MacDonald attest. Concerning these, we need note only that Mr. MacDonald, like other amateur diplomats, was apt to make imprecise but enthusiastic promises to his opposite numbers abroad and then to forget to tell the Foreign Office about them. There was an embarrassing business, for instance, in 1932, when MacDonald had talks at Bessinge with Tardieu, Bruening, and Stimson concerning the policy to be followed at the Lausanne Conference. The Germans argued later that the Prime Minister had promised to support their claim to equality of treatment in armaments. Mr. MacDonald didn't think he said that at all. The Foreign Office had no way of telling whether he had or not, for they had received no record of the talks.[16]

The Foreign Office was never, perhaps, reduced to the "mere technical apparatus" that the German Foreign Office became under Hitler. But throughout the period it was

[13] Kennedy, *Old Diplomacy*, p. 337.
[14] Nicolson, *Curzon*, p. 245.
[15] *An Ambassador of Peace: Lord d'Abernon's Diary*, London, 1929, II, 285.
[16] R. D. Butler and E. L. Woodward, eds., *Documents on British Foreign Policy, 1919–1939*, second series, III, 123, 517 n.

subjected to more interference than any other service department[17]; it was often by-passed; periodically it was inadequately informed of meetings between economic experts, military advisers, and labor officials and deprived of any opportunity of evaluating the findings of such meetings; and, with distressing frequency, the right of its permanent staff to be considered as *the* expert advisers on foreign policy was contested or ignored. There was a recurring tendency on the part of the political leaders of the state, when matters of high moment were pending, to believe that the professionals in the Foreign Office were incompetent to deal with them, because of narrowness of view, dependence upon traditional concepts, or lack of "realism." Lloyd George believed this; Ramsay MacDonald believed it; and it became dogma with Neville Chamberlain.[18] Mr. Chamberlain, indeed, revived some of the more unfortunate methods of Lloyd George and carried them further—for, in justice to Lloyd George, it must be admitted that he never contested the views of his Foreign Secretary in the presence of a foreign ambassador, as Chamberlain did in a meeting with Eden and Grandi in 1938.[19] Like Lloyd George, Chamberlain preferred to find his advisers on foreign policy outside the Foreign Office[20]; and it is perhaps fitting that he should have included among them Lord Lothian, who, as Lloyd George's secretary in an earlier period, had announced that the Foreign Office "had no conception of policy in its wider sense."[21] It is doubtless fitting also that, in pursuance of such wider policy, Chamberlain should have tried his hand at "diplomacy by conference," although his travels, it is true, were restricted by circumstances to Germany, and although the fractiousness of his host rendered them less pleasant than the junkets of his predecessors.

The emphasis placed here on the British experience should not leave the impression that the French were unaffected by these developments. After the second World War, a commission was established by the French Constituent Assembly to investigate

[17] See, for instance, Curzon's views on this in Nicolson, *Curzon,* p. 60 n.

[18] The word "realism," with all its variants, was used with remarkable frequency by Chamberlain and by other British officials who associated themselves with his policy, often to differentiate their views and objectives from those of Eden, Vansittart, and others who had no faith in the policy of appeasement. The Germans and Italians were quick to realize that the word possessed persuasive, if not magic, qualities when introduced into conversations with the British, and they came to rely upon it heavily, as the diplomatic correspondence of the period shows. See, for instance, *Documents on British Foreign Policy,* third series, I, 22, 28, 49, 109, 257, 273, 307, 345, II, 133, 385; *Documents on German Foreign Policy: From the Archives of the German Foreign Ministry,* Washington, 1919, and continuing, series D, I, 221, 264. See also Chamberlain's letter of 16 January 1938 to Mrs. Morton Price in which he says: "As a realist, I must do what I can to make this country safe."—Keith Feiling, *Life of Neville Chamberlain,* London, 1946, p. 323. The German ambassador in Paris spoke in July 1938 of French anxiety over "the dreaded realism of the British."—*Documents on German Foreign Policy,* series D, I, 1168.

[19] See Galeazzo Ciano, *L'Europa verso la catastrofe,* Verona, 1948, pp. 249 *et seq.*

[20] Feiling, *Chamberlain,* p. 327. According to a German memorandum of 11 October 1938, a "confidential agent of Neville Chamberlain" informed a member of the Dienststelle Ribbentrop in London that "in all future moves [i.e., negotiations between Britain and Germany] it was important that all major questions should be dealt with direct, thus bypassing the Foreign Office."—*Documents on German Foreign Policy,* series D, IV, 306. Since February 1938, Lord Vansittart, formerly permanent Under-Secretary for Foreign Affairs, had held the office of Diplomatic Adviser to His Majesty's Government. The title had little meaning, and Vansittart once said, in a private interview: "Nobody asks my advice and, when it is tendered, it is ignored."

[21] Riddell, *Intimate Diary,* p. 219.

the "political, economic, diplomatic, and military events" that contributed to the collapse of 1940. The first summary report of that commission makes specific reference to the personal diplomacy of heads of states and political ministers.

> After the conclusion of the treaties of 1919 [it reads], ministers had the habit of multiplying their contacts with their colleagues in other countries. The abuse of direct conversations opens the door to numerous dangers. Engagements are taken too easily. They are often improvised. It is better to define the course of a negotiation by a note which has matured in the silence of the ministry than by chance exchanges which are likely to be imprecise.[22]

This passage doubtless has reference to the kind of improvisation that took place at Geneva, where—after Germany's entrance into the League—the foreign ministers of the Great Powers met four times a year. The unnecessary frequency of these meetings had a stultifying effect upon normal diplomatic work, since the Foreign Office was placed in the position of waiting anxiously to see what decisions were made by the ministers. The ministers themselves, being politicians, were always anxious to reach decisions, since it seemed important to be able to record some success before they went home; and they were likely, in consequence, to "pluck the fruit before it was ripe."[23] Nor was it only the Geneva activities which gave concern to the permanent staff at home. There were other and more dangerous *tête-à-têtes*. M. Philippe Berthelot, the Secretary-General of the Quai d'Orsay, was never, for instance, able to learn from M. Briand precisely what the latter had promised to Herr Stresemann at Thoiry in 1926.[24] And no one has ever been able to discover what M. Laval did, or did not, promise Mussolini in January 1935, although that mystery had an undoubted effect in disrupting the co-ordination of Anglo-French policy in the Stresa period.[25]

II

The French report cited above dwells upon one other development that demands at least brief consideration in any discussion of the diplomatic methods of this period—and that is the decline of the position and the authority of the ambassador. Traditionally, the ambassador—apart from what are known as his duties of representation—had a twofold function. He was supposed, in the first place, to communicate the wishes of his own government to that court at which he was resident and to use his trained judgment and experience in negotiation to secure their fulfillment. He was expected in the second place to send home objective reports on the political, economic, and social conditions of the country in which he was stationed. With the invention of the telegraph, and later of the telephone, the importance of the ambassador as a

[22] Commission d'Enquête parlementaire sur les événements survenus en France de 1933 à 1945: *Rapport de M. Charles Serre, député au nom de la Commission d'Enquête parlementaire,* Paris, 1951, p. 86.

[23] Weizsäcker, *Memoirs,* p. 69.

[24] André Géraud, "Diplomacy, Old and New," *Foreign Affairs,* XXIII (1944-1945), 267.

[25] L. B. Namier, *Europe in Decay: A Study in Disintegration, 1936-1940,* London, 1950, p. 17. See also Joseph Paul-Boncour, *Entre les deux guerres: souvenirs sur la IIIe républic,* Paris, 1945-1946, III, 14-16.

negotiator declined[26]; and it has been reduced even more by the recent tendency of governments to send special missions and "men of confidence" to foreign capitals to hold conversations which could often be conducted quite effectively by the resident diplomatic agents. The ambassador's importance as a trained observer of foreign conditions has diminished also, although for reasons that are more difficult to explain. In view of the issues at stake in the 1930s, for instance, it might be supposed that the situation reports of ambassadors and other agents abroad would have been read with interest in London and Paris and weighed carefully when policy had to be defined. This does not always seem to have been the case.

Two examples may be cited to illustrate this. As early as the fall of 1935, the French consul general in Cologne and other French agents in Germany were sending circumstantial reports to Paris with evidence that clearly pointed to an imminent German reoccupation of the Rhineland.[27] French governmental circles nevertheless expressed surprise and consternation when Hitler actually did send troops into that area in March of the following year. Again, when Robert Coulondre, the French ambassador in Moscow, visited the Commissariat for Foreign Affairs immediately after the Munich settlement, Potemkin, the Vice-Commissar, said to him: "My poor friend, what have you done? For us I see no other way out but a fourth partition of Poland." On the basis of this warning, Coulondre reported to Paris on 4 October 1938 that a Russian *rapprochement* with Germany could now be expected.[28] There was, however, no indication in the long months that followed that anyone in Paris was concerned about, or even envisaged, any such possibility. Coulondre's message had as little effect as Attolico's warnings to Rome a year later.

The failure to pay proper attention to reports from missions abroad can, of course, be explained in several ways. The tremendous increase of incoming correspondence in all foreign offices in the 1930's[29] probably forced overworked departmental staffs to give priority to cables which required action and to defer the analysis of situation reports to a later time which sometimes never came. The commission appointed by the French Assembly has suggested also, that, in the period under review, the rapid increase of a departmental staff composed largely of men who had never served in the field tended to raise an "impassable barrier" between France's agents abroad and those charged with the formulation of her policy. "Too often," their report reads, "the ministers were informed of events abroad only through the medium of established functionaries of the ministry . . . functionaries who made their career almost exclusively in the offices of the Quai d'Orsay,"[30] and who, in consequence, lacked knowledge and judgment to appreciate the reports reaching their desks.

However valid these two explanations may be, they should not lead us to exclude a third. In any country and at any time, political ministers have a tendency to seek to

---

[26] Sir Horace Rumbold speaks of "this age of rapid communication, of what I would call the telegraphic demoralization of those who formerly had to act for themselves and are now content to be at the end of a wire."—*Recollections of a Diplomatist,* London, 1902, I, 111–12. See also Cambon, *Le diplomate,* pp. 13, 118–19.

[27] Commission d'Enquête parlementaire: *Rapport,* pp. 86–87. See also the testimony of Jean Dobler, *ibid., Témoignages et documents recueillis,* II.

[28] Robert Coulondre, *De Staline à Hitler,* Paris, 1950, p. 165.

[29] "In 1913, the number of dispatches &c. received at the Foreign Office was 68,119. The figures for the years 1935–38 were 169,248 in 1935, 187,878 in 1936, 201,323 in 1937, 223,879 in 1938."—*Documents on British Foreign Policy,* first series, I, iii.

[30] Commission d'Enquête parlementaire: *Rapport,* pp. 86–87.

impose their pre-conceived notions of foreign affairs upon the agents in the field; and they are apt, moreover, to place greatest confidence in those representatives abroad whose reports confirm their own views. German diplomats in the nineteenth century frequently complained that they were expected only to tell Bismarck that he was right; Hitler's ambassadors learned that it was dangerous to depart from the line established in the *Reichskanzlei;* and this sort of thing was certainly neither unknown nor unimportant in British and French diplomacy between the wars. The difficulty, in short, was not always that reports were not read, but that they were read and rejected, sometimes with intimations of punishment for future nonconformity. In 1922, a high official in England—and one attached neither to the Foreign Office nor to the War Office—sought to effect the recall of Brigadier General J. H. Morgan from the Inter-Allied Control Commission in Germany, because he persisted in reporting, in the teeth of denials from England, that the Germans were defying the disarmament provisions of the Versailles Treaty.[31] In 1938, a member of the French embassy staff in Moscow received a stinging reprimand from Paris because he had reported, with statistics to support his opinion, that the Russian army was stronger than it was the fashion in Paris to believe and was well equipped with tanks and aircraft.[32]

It is worth remembering that, if some British and French ambassadors of this period were men of mediocre attainments, independence of judgment and clarity of view were not always expected or rewarded. In the 1920's, Jules Cambon said to his brother Paul: "Are you aware that nowadays we could not serve as ambassadors?"[33] In the late 1930's, the Cambons would have been very rare birds indeed, for the approved diplomats were men like Perth in Rome and Henderson in Berlin, the latter of whom especially never reported anything that did not echo and reinforce the opinions and policies of Neville Chamberlain and who was probably kept in Berlin because he followed this practice.[34]

III

If we relate the deficiencies of British and French diplomatic practice to the known results of the policies of the two governments—and surely there is a logical relationship—it is difficult to avoid the conclusion that they were ill-advised in their cavalier treatment of professional diplomacy after 1919. Yet these by-products of the so-called "new diplomacy"—the practice of by-passing the Foreign Office, of failing to consult it or to keep it informed in important matters, and of giving preconceived ideas priority over intelligence from the field—have attracted little criticism and attract little today, although they are still very much a part of democratic practice in foreign affairs.

A brief reference may be permitted here to current American experience. In this country the word "diplomat" is even more a hissing and a reproach than it was in Britain immediately after the first World War; and the average citizen seems willing

[31] J. H. Morgan, *Assize of Arms: The Disarmament of Germany and Her Rearmament, 1919–1939,* New York, 1946, pp. xvi-xvii.

[32] Coulondre, *De Staline à Hitler,* pp. 126–27, 129.

[33] Géraud in *Foreign Affairs,* XXIII, 267.

[34] "The Makers of Munich," *Times Literary Supplement* (London), 29 September 1950, p. 607.

and eager to believe the worst of the Foreign Service. In this atmosphere of popular antipathy, the State Department has lost much of its former authority as the central agency for the administration of foreign affairs in this country. Functions formerly reserved to it have been farmed out all over the government, to the Pentagon, the ECA and the Treasury, to the Secretaries of Commerce and the Interior and to the Attorney General, to the Bureau of the Budget and the Export-Import Bank and other agencies. Some of this delegation of authority can, of course, be justified by the specialized nature of problems which have arisen since the end of the war; but the co-ordination of the activities of multiple agencies is always difficult, and in this case leaves much to be desired. The State Department is often placed in the awkward position of having to assume responsibility for actions taken without its knowledge.

In addition to this, in the field of political negotiation, this country has not escaped the evils of abrupt and inexpert intervention by officials whose experience has been confined to the domestic field; and—in view of Mr. Truman's expressed wish, not so long ago, to send Mr. Vinson to Moscow—we cannot be sure that we will not see more of this in the future. Finally, it would be difficult to contend that we are sufficiently conscious of the importance of encouraging integrity on the part of our Foreign Service Officers in the field. Who today can say how many of our representatives abroad feel compelled to adjust their judgments to preconceived notions at home or to the vagaries of congressional opinion? It was, after all, only four months ago that fragmented and unrelated passages from a diplomatic report written from China in 1944 were read before a congressional committee in an apparent attempt to prove their author sympathetic to Communism[35]; and other examples could be cited of the unfortunate and increasing tendency to force diplomats to explain and justify their past judgments before ill-informed, and essentially irresponsible, committees. This, at least, is something that the British and French never came to; and in 1918, when popular criticism of professional diplomacy was at its height, a British Foreign Secretary expressed very clearly the dangers of such procedure.

> If [said Mr. A. J. Balfour in the House of Commons] you are going to ask Foreign Office officials . . . to expend some of their energy in getting ready for cross-examination, you will really be destroying the public service. . . . They are not accustomed to it and they ought not to be accustomed to it. They are not trained for it, and they ought not to be trained for it. . . . I beg the House to remember that any system that keeps constantly before the eyes of the civil servants of this country the fear of examination, cross-examination and re-examination by gentlemen who may be described as professional politicans, would be most disastrous in the public interest.[36]

It is possible, of course, that the professional diplomat is an anomaly in democratic society and that we must seek new forms and procedures of foreign relations which are more fitting to this type of political community. That is a subject upon which a historian would be reluctant to embark. He can only suggest, on the basis of the interwar experience of the two great democracies of Western Europe, that flagrant neglect of the resources and conventions of professional diplomacy have in the past had unfortunate results.

[35] John S. Service, " '. . . pertinent excerpts . . .'," *Foreign Service Journal* (October 1951).
[36] *Parliamentary Debates*: Commons, CIV (1918), 876.

20 / The Department of State and American Public Opinion

Dexter Perkins

Public opinion in a democratic country may exercise a profound influence in shaping or circumscribing foreign policy. Historians and social scientists are far from agreed as to how public opinion on a given issue takes form. But many historians would probably concur in the view that every American president and his advisers constantly endeavor to estimate the force of public opinion when they decide on some given course of action. Dexter Perkins's article which follows suggests that during the 1920s and 1930s, each presidential administration responded to what it perceived to be a national public consensus by imposing rather tangible limitations on American commitments in world affairs. If public opinion influences the fundamental directions that foreign policy takes, then how is public opinion itself conditioned; how does government evaluate a strong drift of opinion germane to foreign policy; and what can account for the substantial changes that often occur in public attitudes towards international affairs, as Perkins readily acknowledges actually occurred between the 1920s and the 1940s?

Dexter Perkins has been Professor of History at the University of Rochester and at Cornell University. This article is reprinted with the permission of the Princeton University Press. From *The Diplomats, 1919–1939*.

The study of social history, highly desirable and fruitful, has led in some instances to a distorted concentration on trends and movements, and to an undue minimization of the part played by highly individual decisions. In American foreign policy, as elsewhere, the importance of resolutions taken *in camera* by a few persons is not to be disregarded. Yet in a fundamental sense, the diplomatic history of the United States does not resemble the diplomatic history of Europe. Essentially, the professional diplomat has always played a subordinate role. There are few Légers, few Vansittarts, few Holsteins in the record of American action. Occasionally, we have a House, or a Hopkins, or a Harriman—a non-professional—who plays a significant role; and, in the 1930's, a career diplomat, Sumner Welles, had great influence. But, for the most part (and the longer the perspective the truer is the generalization), men of this type are rare. The elements in the formation of policy are at once more subtle and more complex than they are in many other states. We may, therefore, before describing the diplomacy of the 1920's, properly examine the various factors that enter into it.

In a sense that is true in no such degree in other nations, American diplomatic action has been determined by the people. There were ardent debates on foreign policy in the first days of our national history. There have been such debates ever since. Uninstructed though the average citizen may be in the facts of international life, he still has an opinion with regard to them. If he does not know, he thinks he knows. And this conviction on his part is one that cannot be disregarded. Nor do those who conduct our affairs in the main desire to disregard it. The democratic tradition is deeply rooted in our history. The men who stand at the levers of control are almost always men with substantial political experience. Their habits, their prepossessions, their convictions all lead them to pay heed to the voice of the great body of citizens, to shape their decisions with that voice in mind.

This does not mean that the minutiae of diplomatic action can be determined by the masses. Nor does it mean, if we are careful in our use of terms, that "public opinion," in the sense of a carefully thought-out view of a specific problem, is the fundamental factor. It means, rather, that the general sentiment of the people lies at the root of every great issue. There have been times when the mood of the American people was essentially militant. The government has responded to this militancy. There have been times when the mood was essentially one of withdrawal, of *reculement* as the French would put it. The government has responded to this mood likewise. Presidents have been powerless to withstand these deep-seated feelings. President McKinley was a man of peace, yet he was swept into war. President Franklin D. Roosevelt was certainly by conviction no isolationist, yet his first administration was essentially isolationist in spirit. This over-mastering popular emotion rationalized, perhaps, into convenient slogans, often influences policy. To say this is not to praise or condemn. It is simply to state a fact. One may believe, if one is a convinced democrat, that in the main the popular instincts are sound. Or one may be cynical enough to distrust them. The important thing is to recognize that they exist.

But once this essential generalization has been made, there are others that need to be added to it. So far as individuals make policy, the balance of influence in the United States is always tipping, now this way or that, now to the executive, now to the legislature, and rarely to the professional diplomat. For example, there have been many Presidents of the United States who have exercised a remarkable personal influence on diplomatic action. This was true of Polk, of Theodore Roosevelt, of Woodrow Wilson, of Franklin D. Roosevelt, to mention only a few. But there have also been Presidents who delegated a large part of their power to their Secretaries of State. Except perhaps at the beginning of his administration, Lincoln did so. Grant did so. Harding and Coolidge did so. The role of the Chief Executive in foreign policy is a shifting thing, now great, now small, depending upon the type of individual happening to hold the office.

It is the same way with Secretaries of State. Some have been strong personalities, the true makers of policy. Others have recorded the views of Presidents, or depended upon their professional staffs. The one thing that is certain is that no definite and fixed role can be assigned to the Secretary under our constitutional system.

But we cannot end here. The conduct of American diplomacy is substantially affected by our constitutional forms. It is not, of course, merely that the legislative body, through the treatymaking power, participates in the formation of policy. In other states some control of foreign affairs can be exerted by the law-making power. What is more important is that, under our type of government, there is no certainty of harmony between the executive and the legislature. Under the parliamentary system with cabinet responsibility there naturally exists between the government of the day and its majority in parliament an intimate and cooperative relationship. But in the United States the Congress does not feel bound to pay any very extraordinary deference to the views of the executive, and its attitude is all the more likely to be critical if the Congressional majority is, as it may be under our system, of a different political complexion from that of the executive. Furthermore, the chairmen of the great committees, especially the chairman of the Senate Committee on Foreign Relations, may be veterans in political life, and men of strong convictions who feel no obligation to take their views from the other end of Pennsylvania Avenue. They may insist not only on being consulted but on being heeded.

Let us look for a moment at the manner in which these generalizations apply to the period under examination in this essay. It is the period of the Harding, Coolidge, and Hoover administrations, from 1921 to 1933. First, as to the mood of the American people. When the Harding administration entered power, the country had just emerged from a great war. There had been much disillusionment and a severe letdown from the mood of exaltation induced by the leadership of Woodrow Wilson. The question of the role of the United States in world affairs had been under constant and vigorous debate. On the whole, I think it fair to say, the country had reacted against a policy of extensive commitments in the world at large. In the struggle over the League, there was so much pettiness and partisanship that it is difficult to discover its essential meaning. Yet it seems reasonable to say that between the President and his opponents there was a real issue involved and that this issue centered upon that part of the Covenant which projected the United States most deeply into the international scene. Article 10, with its pledge of territorial sovereignty and political independence, may or may not have been, as Wilson claimed, the heart of the whole matter. But, if one reads the Senate reservation to that article,[1] one becomes convinced that there was a real and fundamental question at stake, the question whether the United States should participate in the fullest sense in the development of a system of collective security for the maintenance of peace. And the answer that the American people gave, with the election of Harding to the Presidency, was that they did not care much about the matter. This renunciation must not be understood as implying that the withdrawal of the United States from world affairs was to be

---

[1] The Senate reservation reads as follows: "The United States assumes no obligation to preserve the territorial integrity or political independence of any other country by the employment of its military or naval forces, its resources, or any form of economic discrimination, or to interfere in any way in controversies between nations, including all controversies relating to territorial integrity or political independence, whether members of the League or not, under the provisions of Article 10, or to employ the military or naval forces of the United States, under any article of the treaty for any purpose, unless in any particular case the Congress, which, under the Constitution, has the sole power to declare war or authorize the employment of the military or naval forces of the United States, shall, in the exercise of full liberty of action, by act or joint resolution so provide." D. F. Fleming, *The United States and the League of Nations* (New York, 1932), p. 433.

anything like total, or that there was not much devotion to the peace ideal as an abstraction. It merely means that the American mood was not one in which a sense of world responsibility played a dominant part.

Moreover, the mood of 1920 was the mood of virtually all of the period we shall consider. The immense prosperity of the United States, and the profound reaction from that prosperity, both concentrated American attention upon domestic rather than foreign matters. Those who conducted the foreign affairs of the nation, while often far ahead of public opinion in the breadth of their vision and in their sense of the large role which the country ought to play, had to take account of that essential fact.

As to the role of the Executive, neither President Harding nor President Coolidge was fitted to assume the function of leadership in the field of foreign affairs. Harding was an easy-going man of very mediocre intellectual gifts, if the word gifts may be used at all, and when he thought at all he thought in stereotypes. Coolidge was congenitally cautious, incapable of powerful or effective leadership, essentially the exponent of the laissez-faire philosophy. Neither exercised any really powerful influence on the diplomacy of the period. The same thing cannot be said of Herbert Hoover. Few Presidents were more conscious of their responsibilities than he, and, as we shall see, in some essential matters the opinion of the Chief Executive was of great significance during his administration.

The Secretaries of the period we are examining present an interesting picture, and interesting contrasts. Charles Evans Hughes, Secretary from 1921 to 1925, was undoubtedly one of the ablest men who ever held that office. His personal role in the formation of policy was a most important one. Secretary Kellogg, on the other hand, was much less disposed to initiate action of any kind, much more conscious of the limits imposed upon him by public opinion and by the Congress. Henry L. Stimson, Hoover's Secretary of State, was a man of powerful and strongly-held convictions, but was compelled in some matters, as we shall see, to defer to his chief.

All three Secretaries had to consider the legislative branch. The great concentration of powers inevitable to the waging of the first world war had inevitably led to a reaction, and the Congresses of the 1920's were in many respects jealous of their own position, and none too disposed to defer to the Executive. Despite the obstacles thrown in his way, Hughes often succeeded in by-passing the legislators, and in shaping policy by his own personal force. Kellogg was exceedingly deferential to Senators, and he had to deal with a man of great force, and of capacity superior to his own, in William E. Borah, chairman of the Senate Committee on Foreign Relations. Stimson was, on the whole, on good terms with the Senate, and was more confined by the views of his chief than by the opposition of the legislature. Yet on some questions, as we shall see, he could make little headway over Congressional resistance. The pattern, in other words, changed with each Secretary of State.

As for the permanent personnel of the Department, it is not easy to estimate its role. But it seems fair to say that Hughes dominated his department, Kellogg was often much influenced by his professional advisers, and Stimson, like Hughes, had strong views of his own. From all of which it can be understood how difficult it would be to write the diplomatic history of this period in terms of any single personality.[2]

---

[2] It is relevant to remark that in the brief period between 1921 and 1933 there were no less than six Under-Secretaries of State. No single fact indicates more strikingly the contrast between the American and the European diplomatic scene.

Since the personal interpretation of American foreign policy is denied to us by the facts of the American scene, it seems wise to center our examination of the 1920's about certain key ideas. Such emphasis is wholly justified. For whatever may have been the case before 1914, the relations of the United States with the great communities of the West are, in the period with which we are dealing, of great significance to the world as a whole.

II

Let us choose, as the first theme for our examination, the attitude of the United States towards the idea of collective security, as it was reflected in the three administrations from 1921 to 1933. First of all, it is necessary to reiterate that the opposition to the famous Article 10 of the Covenant was nothing more or less than opposition to the collective security idea. That article was designed by its framers to prevent physical aggression on the part of one state against another. The members of the League agree, it read, "to respect and preserve as against external aggression the territorial integrity and existing political independence of all members of the League." This was not, as has sometimes been said, a freezing of the *status quo*. It was a prohibition on the alteration of the *status quo* by force. But it involved, and involved very deeply, the notion of common action against an aggressor, and it became the focus of the most fundamental attacks upon the Covenant itself. While the materials for a judgment are not so satisfactory as we might desire, it seems clear that a majority of the Senate were not ready to accept such an obligation, and when President Wilson attempted to make an issue of the matter in the election of 1920, he utterly failed. The great vote for Harding in that year showed, so it seems to me, that the mass of the people, to put it mildly, attached no very great positive importance to this central idea—if, indeed, they apprehended it at all clearly.

It seems clear, too, that Mr. Hughes, soon to become Secretary of State, was not enamored of the collective security idea, either. He was not a foe of the League idea in general but, as his correspondence shows, he thought of it in quite a different way from Wilson. "There is plain need for a league of nations," he wrote, "in order to provide for the development of international law for creating and maintaining organs of international justice and machinery of conciliation and conference, and for giving effect to measures of international cooperation which may from time to time be agreed upon."[3] There is not a word in this interesting statement with regard to the machinery of coercion. It is, moreover, abundantly clear that he was opposed to Article 10. Indeed, he expressed such opposition as early as March of 1919, and this position he consistently maintained. Whether or not the treaty was to be ratified by the new administration, there seems no reason to believe that Hughes was ready to fight for the principle of common action against aggression. In point of fact, however, the question was never discussed in the early days of the Harding regime. For so bitter was the opposition of the irreconcilable Republicans to the whole Wilsonian edifice that Hughes, despite his own desire to see the Versailles pact ratified with reservations, was obliged to abandon this idea, and to abandon it even in the face of the assurances that he had offered to the American people in the campaign of 1920

[3] C. E. Hughes to Senator Hale, July 24, 1919, quoted in M. J. Pusey, *Charles Evans Hughes* (2 vols., New York, 1951), I, 397.

that a vote for Harding was a vote for entry into the League under reasonable conditions.[4]

Despite the rebuff administered by the new administration to the idea of collective security, the idea itself showed a remarkable vitality. This is not to say that it was ever close to general acceptance in the 1920's; such a proposition, I think, cannot be maintained. But there were important discussions of the problem, and we should understand these discussions before we can examine the American attitude with regard to them.

First of the attempts to strengthen the machinery of the Covenant was the Draft Treaty of Mutual Assistance of 1923. This treaty gave to the Council considerably greater power than that conceded in the League constitution itself. It permitted that body, for example, in case of the outbreak of hostilities to designate the aggressor nation, and bound the contracting parties to furnish each other mutual assistance against the nation so designated, on a basis determined by the Council itself. It assumed that both military and financial aid would be accorded the aggressed state, and implied that an international force would be created to give effect to the obligations of the treaty. It sought at the same time to limit the operation of sanctions by declaring that in principle no state in a continent other than that in which the operations would take place would be required to co-operate in military, naval, or air operations.[5] The Draft Treaty was transmitted to the various governments by the Fourth Assembly, and comment invited.

There is little reason to believe that there was ever much chance of the adoption of this ambitious scheme, even by the members of the League. Indeed, the opposition to more extensive commitments than those of the Covenant had been expressed by not a few states in the deliberations which preceded the drafting of this instrument, and in the Fourth Assembly itself. In the debates at Geneva, indeed, it is possible to discern a distinct reaction against the idea of collective security, a reaction by no means wholly due—perhaps not even chiefly due—to the attitude of the United States. Nevertheless, it is interesting to observe the extremely cold tone in which Mr. Hughes replied to the note of January 9, 1924, in which the Draft Treaty was presented to the American government. Delaying his answer until June 16, and expressing a "keen and sympathetic interest" in "every endeavor" for the reduction of armaments, an end towards which the treaty was directed, he pointed out that wide powers were given to the Council of the League of Nations. "In view of the constitutional organization of this government," he declared, "and in view of the fact that the United States is not a member of the League of Nations, this Government would find it impossible to give its adherence."[6]

The reference in this note to the constitutional obligations of the United States deserves a word of comment. What Hughes is talking about is perfectly clear. Obviously effective action under any agreement looking to the application of collective measures for the maintenance of peace can, under our form of government, only be taken by the Congress of the United States. But this is not to say that the Executive

[4] For a discussion of this point see Pusey, *Charles Evans Hughes*, II, 431–434.

[5] For a scholarly discussion of the mutual assistance treaty, see B. S. Williams, *State Security and the League of Nations* (Baltimore, 1927), pp. 151–182. See also Gordon A. Craig and Felix Gilbert, eds., *The Diplomats, 1919–1939* (Princeton, N.J., 1953), chs. i sec. 3, iv sec. 3, and x sec. 1.

[6] *Foreign Relations*, 1924, I, 79.

cannot enter into an engagement which would bind Congress to act. Many another treaty, and not merely a treaty of the type we have been discussing, can be made effective only by affirmative action of the legislative branch. The question is not constitutional but moral. When an obligation is incurred, it is morally imperative that the Congress should carry it out. It should not be incurred, of course, unless there is good reason to believe that it would be honored. But it is quite unnecessary to speak, as did Mr. Hughes, as if our governmental forms prevented the signature by the United States of agreements for the maintenance of peace.

Practically speaking, we repeat, the Hughes note was not of very great importance. The Draft Treaty was probably doomed from its inception. The point to be made is that in this instance the Secretary showed no enthusiasm for—indeed no interest in—the idea of collective security.

The Secretary was to take a still more drastic stand with regard to the Geneva Protocol.[7] In 1924 the European diplomats tried their hand once again at the problem which the Treaty of Mutual Assistance had failed to solve. The result was the Geneva Protocol for the Pacific Settlement of International Disputes. This Protocol erected an elaborate system for the solution of international difficulties, first by extending the compulsory jurisdiction of the Court of International Justice, and, second, by providing for the settlement, either by the Council of the League or by compulsory arbitration, of all disputes which did not fall within the jurisdiction of the Court. At the same time it made it possible to define an aggressor with more precision than was possible in the Covenant, and bound the signatories to participate loyally and effectively in the application of sanctions, but with the proviso that aid should be given by each state "in the degree which its geographical position and particular situation as regards armament allows." It is important to note that the Geneva Protocol was unanimously approved by the Fifth Assembly of the League on October 2, 1924.

The Geneva Protocol has a far greater significance than the Draft Treaty. The leaders of the greatest states of Europe were at the meetings of that famous Assembly of 1924, Ramsay MacDonald for Great Britain, Eduard Herriot for France. The Protocol was launched at a favorable moment and under favorable auspices, with the end of a period of tension in the relations of France and Germany, and in an atmosphere favorable to constructive achievement. It is true that the position was somewhat altered by the fall of the Labor government in November of 1924. Still, without overstressing the matter, it is possible to say that, on the mere basis of the significance of the instrument, the attitude of the United States toward the Protocol was bound to be of considerable importance.

The *Foreign Relations of the United States* for 1925 contain a very remarkable account of conversations on the subject between the Secretary and the British ambassador in Washington. The first occurred on January 5, 1925. It is important to quote this document, recorded in a memorandum by Mr. Hughes himself. It was Sir Esmé Howard who opened the conversation. Declaring that "it was a cardinal point in British policy to maintain friendly relations with the United States, and to cooperate with this Government wherever possible," he added that

[7] For a discussion of the protocol, see Williams, *State Security and the League*, pp. 182–205, also D. H. Miller, *The Geneva Protocol* (New York, 1925), and P. J. Noel Baker, *The Geneva Protocol for the Pacific Settlement of International Disputes* (London, 1925); and Craig and Gilbert, eds., *The Diplomats, 1919–1939*, chs. i sec. 3, iv sec. 3, and x sec. 1.

"there might be interference with this policy if contingencies should arise in which through the operation of the Protocol the British Government was brought into opposition to the interests of the United States." "On the other hand," he continued, "it seemed to the British Government that it would not be well to throw out the Protocol entirely. . . ." "The only alternative to such a competition in armament with all its possible consequences would seem to be the adoption in some form of such an arrangement as the Geneva Protocol proposed."[8]

In reply to these observations the Secretary took what can only be described as a rather high tone. "There were," he remarked, "two aspects, at least, of the Geneva Protocol which might give concern to this Government." "If the Protocol were taken as having practical value and actually of portending what it set forth," said Hughes, "there would appear to be a proposal of a concert against the United States, when the Powers joining in the Protocol considered that the United States had committed some act of aggression, although the United States might believe itself to be entirely justified in its action, and in fact be acting in accordance with its traditional policies. The Secretary said that he did not believe that such a concert would actually become effective but he supposed that the Protocol must be taken as it is written and in this view the United States would be compelled to view it with disfavor. The Secretary said there was another class of cases where the action of the United States itself might not be involved but that of some other country with which the United States had trade relations, and the action of the Powers who had joined in the Protocol might turn out to be inimical to the interests of the United States in such relations with the country in question." Alluding still further to the possibility of collective action against some other nation, Mr. Hughes went on to remark that "there was one thing he believed could be depended upon, and that was that this Government from its very beginning had been insistent upon the rights of neutrals and would continue to maintain them." He "did not believe that any Administration, short of a treaty concluded and ratified, could commit the country against assertion of its neutral rights in case there should be occasion to demand their recognition."[9]

All this could hardly be described as encouraging. But Mr. Hughes went further. He declined at one and the same time to approve or to disapprove the Protocol. He intimated that the British sounding was a mere maneuver and excuse for inaction, and expressed the hope that if other governments did not approve of the Protocol, they should deal with the matter from the point of view of their own interests and not put the responsibility on the United States. To the suggestion that the matter might be handled by a reservation on the part of the British, he declared that he would not wish anything to be said that might imply that this way of dealing with the problem might be satisfactory to the United States.

It is difficult to describe this commentary of Mr. Hughes as other than a dash of cold water thrown in the face of Sir Esmé. Indeed, it is hard to see how the tone could have been much more intransigent and unconciliatory. Nor was the effect of this interview diminished three days later when the British ambassador returned to the State Department and was told that the Secretary had consulted with the President and that the Chief Executive approved the point of view previously expressed.[10] And

[8] *Foreign Relations*, 1925, I, 16–17.
[9] *Foreign Relations*, 1925, I, 17.
[10] *Foreign Relations*, 1925, I, 19.

it is worth noting that the position then assumed was in no sense due to any particular political pressure. The date, it will be noted, was January 1925. The presidential elections were over, and the Republican party had been brilliantly victorious. It may be that Mr. Hughes believed that he was expressing the mood and temper of the American people. It is certain that he was not acting on the basis of any particular exigency of the moment.

On the other hand, it is by no means clear that the action taken by the Secretary was a determining factor in the final collapse of the effort to strengthen the League through the Protocol. The British elections of November 1924 brought the Conservatives into power with an overwhelming majority, and the new Secretary of State for Foreign Affairs was not an enthusiast for the arrangements that had been worked out at Geneva. The Dominions, when consulted, also were disposed to avoid the rather sweeping commitments contained in the League proposals.[11] True, the position of the United States afforded an excellent argument against these new commitments, and the British government made a good deal of this argument in its memorandum of March 1925.[12] But the most that can probably be said is that the position assumed by Mr. Hughes reinforced a point of view that the London government might have assumed in any event. It is useless to speculate, of course, on what would have been the course of events in the 1920's if the United States had wholeheartedly accepted the engagements of the Covenant itself.

The dislike of the League idea, it must be stressed, did not, in the secretariat of Mr. Hughes, prevent the taking of steps which expressed American interest in the idea of peace. There was, for example, in 1923, a proposal put forward by the administration for American adhesion to the protocol creating the Court of International Justice.[13] Such a proposal was consonant with American traditional thinking, which connected peace, not with power, but with orderly process. But this proposal got nowhere. When the United States Senate in 1926 voted to adhere to the protocol, it did so with reservations that created new problems and that carried the whole controversy with regard to the Court over into the Roosevelt administration.[14]

But let us return to the movement for collective security. The failure of the Protocol was followed by the very significant negotiations, lasting through a great part of 1925, that finally resulted in the treaties of Locarno. By these treaties specific agreements strengthening the principles of collective security were approved in place of generalized understanding. Thus the French, British, Italian, Belgian, and German governments entered into engagements by which the territorial *status quo* with regard to the frontiers between France and Germany and Belgium and Germany were guaranteed, and by which the countries concerned mutually undertook in no case to attack each other or resort to war against each other. They also agreed to settle all disputes arising between them by resort to arbitration, and to extend mutual assistance to one another against any one of their number which resorted to war in violation of the pact. The Eastern frontier settlements of Versailles, that is, the frontier between Germany and Poland and Germany and Czechoslovakia, were not similarly guaran-

---

[11] See some of their comments in Williams, *State Security and the League*, pp. 310–320. See also Craig and Gilbert, eds., *The Diplomats, 1919–1939*, ch. 1, note 91.

[12] Williams, *State Security and the League*, p. 306.

[13] On the World Court question, see D. F. Fleming, *The United States and the World Court* (Garden City, 1945).

[14] *Ibid.*

teed. But treaties of arbitration were drawn up between Germany and Poland and Germany and Czechoslovakia, and these treaties were buttressed by antecedent agreements between France and Poland and France and Czechoslovakia to give each other immediate aid and assistance in case of an unprovoked recourse to arms. The Locarno agreements, signed at the end of 1925, represent the high-water mark of the movement for collective guarantees in the period between the wars.[15]

By the time the Locarno treaties were under discussion, Secretary Hughes had laid down his charge at the State Department and had been succeeded by Secretary Kellogg. The new director of American foreign policy was a man of far less force than his predecessor, far less likely to adopt any initiative in the field of foreign policy. Yet the very fact that the Locarno agreements were regional in their character was calculated to relieve the United States of any embarrassment with regard to them. To such partial understandings the American government could have no such objections as pertained to the strengthening of the Covenant. Mr. Kellogg, of course, when informed of what was going on, firmly declined to have anything to do with any guarantee.[16] But President Coolidge speaking in July of 1925 gave the negotiations his blessing,[17] and in his message of December 1925, the cautious Chief Executive declared that the recent agreements "represent the success of the policy on which this country has been insisting . . . of having European countries settle their own political problems without involving this country," and went on to suggest that the way was now clear for the reduction of land armaments, while underlining the fact that this was primarily a European problem.[18]

III

The question of American participation in the movement for the reduction of land armaments was, in due course, to take another turn. In no little time the American government began to participate in discussions at Geneva looking to such reduction. But, since the climactic moves in this discussion came in the early 1930's, it will be convenient to postpone discussion of this subject for a moment, and to examine first that remarkable movement which culminated in the famous Kellogg Pact, or the Pact of Paris, for the maintenance of peace.[19] This pact, finally signed on August 28, 1928, was a simple pledge on the part of the contracting parties "not to have recourse to war as an instrument of national policy, and to settle all disputes arising between them by peaceful means." At first blush this compact looks like a denial of the very principle of collective security, a substitution of peace by promises for peace by common action. But whoever studies the background of the Kellogg Pact in detail will, I think, come to a somewhat different conclusion. For the

---

[15] For a convenient summary see Williams, *State Security and the League,* pp. 206–226. See also G. Glasgow, *From Dawes to Locarno* (New York, 1926).

[16] *Foreign Relations,* 1925, I, 21.

[17] See the *New York Times,* July 4, 1925.

[18] The *New York Times,* December 9, 1925.

[19] On the Kellogg Pact, see the full discussion in *Foreign Relations,* 1928, I, 1–234. See also J. T. Shotwell, *War as an Instrument of National Policy and Its Renunciation in the Pact of Paris* (New York, 1928), D. H. Miller, *The Peace Pact of Paris: A Study of the Briand-Kellogg Treaty* (New York, 1928), and D. P. Myers, *Origins and Conclusion of the Paris Pact. The Renunciation of War as an Instrument of National Policy* (Boston, 1929).

friends of the Pact were by no means always clear on the matter of sanctions. Mr. S. O. Levinson of Chicago, who very early espoused the idea of the outlawry of war and who was one of those who pressed it most tenaciously throughout the 1920's, though certainly not depending on force as the essential element in his own view of the problem, at one time seems to have believed that in flagrant violations of a no-war pledge force might be used.[20] Senator Borah, who had a great deal to do with the promotion of the Kellogg Pact, on one occasion declared that it was "quite inconceivable that this country would stand idly by in case of a grave breach of a multilateral treaty to which it was a party."[21] Statements such as these ought not, it is true, to be given an exaggerated importance. They certainly do not represent the prevailing mood or conviction of the two men just mentioned, both of whom seem to have had a naïve faith in the power of public opinion. But neither can they be entirely disregarded. To this fact must be added another. Some of the friends of the Pact were quite clear as to what they hoped would flow from it. Believing in the principle of collective action against aggression, they took the view that once the treaty was ratified there would arise, almost inevitably, a demand that it be "implemented." And this demand, they hoped, would in due course lead the United States into closer relations with the League of Nations. If once the principle that war was inherently illegal, as well as immoral, were accepted, a way would be found by which the American people would take action in support of the principle they had affirmed. This point of view appears most clearly in Professor Shotwell's interesting book on *War as an Instrument of National Policy*.[22] But one can find it in many other pronouncements of the period as well.[23]

Perhaps the most interesting thing about the Pact of Paris, however, is the illustration it affords of the way in which American foreign policy on occasion comes up from the grass roots rather than down from the State Department or its Secretary. It is a well-known fact that the initial step in the negotiations that led to the Pact came from a proposal of the French Foreign Minister Aristide Briand, made on April 6, 1927, to enter into a bilateral treaty for the renunciation of war. This proposal, incited by Professor Shotwell on a visit to Paris, passed almost unnoticed at the time, and was indeed completely ignored by Secretary Kellogg. The situation was in some degree changed when Nicholas Murray Butler, then president of Columbia University, in a letter to the *New York Times,* called attention to the significance of the Briand offer, and when Professor Shotwell and Professor Chamberlain put the idea in the form of a draft treaty. In June of 1927, the French government presented a formal proposal to the United States.[24] Still the administration hesitated, indeed the State Department declared that no such compact was necessary, and that it would not even be desirable.[25] But the outlawry of war proposal aroused an increasing interest, and the crucial factor in securing official consideration for it was doubtless the attitude of Senator Borah, the powerful chairman of the Senate Committee on Foreign Relations. On December 27, 1927, Borah introduced a resolu-

---

[20] See J. E. Stoner, *S. O. Levinson and the Pact of Paris: A Study in the Techniques of Influence* (Chicago, 1943), esp. pp. 27 and 185.

[21] See Shotwell, *War as an Instrument of National Policy,* p. 224.

[22] *Ibid.,* pp. 254ff.

[23] See, for example, Miller, *The Peace Pact of Paris,* and J. B. Whitton, *What Follows the Pact of Paris* (New York, 1932).

[24] Shotwell, *War as an Instrument of National Policy,* p. 72.

[25] *Ibid.*

tion calling for the outlawry of war, the establishment of an international code, and of an international court by the decisions of which the nations of the world should be bound to abide.[26] On the very next day, Secretary Kellogg, in a note to the French government, proposed that "the two governments, instead of contenting themselves with a bilateral declaration of the nature suggested by M. Briand, might make a more signal contribution to world peace by joining in an effort to obtain the adherence of all of the principal powers of the world to a declaration renouncing war as an instrument of national policy."[27] Thus were initiated the negotiations that finally led to the Pact of Paris.

I do not think it desirable to trace these negotiations in detail. There were substantial obstacles to be overcome. The French were by no means enthusiastic about the alteration of their original proposal, and they feared that the proposed agreement might weaken the structure of the League of Nations, and the machinery of sanctions embodied in the Covenant. Other difficulties soon arose. The British, in particular, seemed to fear that their freedom of action in certain parts of the world might be limited by the proposed engagement. Matters ended happily, however. By making it clear, as he did in a speech of April 28, 1928, that the Pact did not affect the right of self-defense, Mr. Kellogg calmed the apprehensions of the critics, and at the same time (having regard to the flexibility of the term self-defense itself) whittled away some of the significance of the Pact itself.[28] By the spring of 1928, with a Presidential election coming on, there was only one course of action to be followed, and that was to press matters to a conclusion. And so the Pact was signed.

What effect did the Pact have on American diplomacy in the years that followed? The first attempt to invoke it concerned a dispute between China and Russia in 1929 and need not concern us here save to remark that the appeal made by the American government exposed the United States to a severe rebuff from the Soviet Union.[29]

The fiasco which resulted in this particular case led Mr. Stimson to meditate on possible means by which the Kellogg Pact might be made more effective. Thus arose the idea of consultation, or of a consultative pact.[30] This idea was discussed with the French ambassador in the fall of 1929.[31] It also came up at the London naval conference of 1930. At that conference the French again brought it forward and threw out the hint that the reduction of their own naval armament might be facilitated by some understanding on the matter. The Secretary was at first cold to the suggestion since it smacked of a diplomatic bargain, and President Hoover was still more opposed. But, as the conference proceeded, it appeared possible that the French and the British might agree on some strengthening of their association under the Covenant of the League, and Stimson played with the idea of encouraging such a strengthening by some agreement for consultation. On March 25 he issued a somewhat cryptic statement to the press on the matter, intimating that some positive step might be taken. He seems at this moment to have had the support of the American delegation of which

---

[26] The resolution is found most easily in Shotwell, *War as an Instrument of National Policy,* pp. 108–109.

[27] *Foreign Relations,* 1927, II, 626–627.

[28] The speech is in the *New York Times,* April 29, 1928.

[29] The voluminous correspondence is in *Foreign Relations,* 1929, II, 186–435.

[30] For this whole matter of consultation, see R. M. Cooper, *American Consultation in World Affairs for the Preservation of Peace* (New York, 1934).

[31] See *Foreign Relations,* 1929, I, 59–64.

he was the head. There was, however, less enthusiasm in Washington; the President was distinctly nervous with regard to the matter and feared the reaction in the Senate. He was, indeed, strongly opposed to any generalized engagement to consult. Though he gave his approval to a watered-down version of consultative clause in the naval treaty, the project was, in the last analysis, abandoned.[32]

But Stimson was tenacious of the general objective. When the Manchurian crisis broke in the fall of 1931, he maintained close contact with the League, even to the extent of permitting the American representative at Geneva to sit in on meetings of the Council, and of sending General Dawes to Paris to participate at arm's length in the League deliberations. There was an American member on the commission which the League appointed to investigate the situation and make recommendations, and the League and the United States co-operated in the winter of 1932 in proclaiming the so-called Stimson doctrine by which it was declared that there could be no recognition of an illegal situation arising out of the violation of the Kellogg Pact. In the course of the year 1932, moreover, both party nominating conventions declared in favor of the principle of consultation,[33] and Stimson underlined the desirablity of accepting this principle in a speech of August 8.[34] Nonetheless, no formal engagements were entered into during any part of the period which we are reviewing.

Taken all in all, however, it cannot be said that the American government, between 1921 and the advent of the Roosevelt administration, had gone very far towards the acceptance of the idea of collective security. There was very distinctly a difference between the attitude of Hughes and the attitude of Stimson,[35] but the difference was by no means so wide as practically to affect the policies of the European nations. On the whole, the dogma of freedom of action dominated American policy during the period, and none was more deeply attached to it, it should be said, than was President Hoover.[36] It seems likely that in this respect he expressed the dominant opinion of the nation.

Interesting as it is to speculate on "what might have been," in summarizing the attitude of the United States in the years under review, all that can really be said is that the general line of policy was unfavorable towards common action against an aggressor, but that the Kellogg-Briand Pact, by branding war as immoral, reflected something of the sentiment of the American people, and may have provided a basis for the more active diplomacy of the United States at a later period.

IV

The dislike of the administrations of this period for the League idea is well illustrated in the manner in which they dealt with the problem of reduction of armaments. There was, at the end of the war, an immense sentiment for such reduction, and Mr. Hughes, in the very first year of his administration of the State Department, boldly capitalized on such sentiment. The Washington Arms Conference of 1921–1922 was, in many ways, a great diplomatic achievement. Though the British would

[32] See *Foreign Relations*, 1930, II, *passim*, esp. pp. 36–92.
[33] Cooper, *American Consultation in World Affairs*, p. 58.
[34] *Ibid.*, p. 59.
[35] Stimson was disposed to acquiesce in sanctions against Japan in 1931.
[36] See President Hoover's recent article in *Collier's, The National Weekly*, for April 19, 1952, p. 57.

have liked the credit for calling it, Mr. Hughes insisted on garnering that credit for himself. He electrified all observers when, at the very outset, he laid down a plan for the scrapping of a substantial part of existing building programs and for the establishment of fixed ratios in capital ships and aircraft carriers. He secured that parity with the British which American opinion (for no very clear reason, it must be conceded) demanded, and he persuaded the Japanese to accept a subordinate position. He brought about these striking results without what the enemies of the League would have described as "entanglement." The nearest approach to such an entanglement, indeed, was a Four Power pact, consultative in nature, with regard to "the regions of the Pacific." (Somehow or other, such a pact could, even in 1922, be regarded as innocent if it applied to the Orient.) In the course of the negotiations, moreover, assisted by the pressure exercised by the Dominions, and especially by Canada, he broke up the Anglo-Japanese alliance which had existed since 1902. But this story is not for us to tell here in detail.[37] The point is that the American theory with regard to arms reduction was essentially different from the thesis upheld by many influential Europeans, and especially by the French. To the latter, the building of a system of external security was a condition precedent to the reduction of armaments, and it was only under very heavy pressure that the Quai d'Orsay yielded even on the partial limitation of naval armaments at Washington. But American statesmanship stoutly insisted that there was no necessary connection between the curtailment of armed forces and a network of treaties to punish aggression. It succeeded, in this particular instance, in making its point of view prevail by giving up, in the face of Japanese pressure, the right to fortify Guam and the Philippines. In other words, it abdicated so far as the use of force in the Far East was concerned. No doubt, as was frequently maintained at the time, because of the state of American public opinion, it would have been impossible to secure funds for such fortifications in any case. But however this may be, the significant thing is that the American outlook on the whole question of armaments was so very different from that involved in acceptance of the League.

The success of the Washington Conference in the field of naval armament was to be repeated and extended in the administration of President Hoover. For a time after 1922 it seemed as if the rivalry of the United States and Great Britain, partially exorcised so far as capital ships were concerned, was to break out in new construction of vessels of inferior tonnage. An attempt to come to an agreement in 1927 in a conference at Geneva aborted, largely because the preparations for the conference were inadequate and because the admirals were allowed a very important, if not a central, role in the negotiations. But at London in 1930, the three Great Powers, the United States, Great Britain, and Japan, came to an agreement which limited ships of every kind and which was, indeed, a remarkable achievement.[38] It ought, perhaps, to be said parenthetically, that one of the reasons for the success of both the Washington and London conferences was the appointment of influential Senators as members of the American delegations. This specific is not infallible, but it has frequently proved efficacious in smoothing the way to successful negotiation.

The naval agreements of the period seemed at the time to be remarkable achievements. In the short run they were rightly so regarded. But they did not survive

[37] The best brief account of the Conference is in A. W. Griswold, *The Far Eastern Policy of the United States* (New York, 1937), pp. 269–332.

[38] The London negotiations are given in much detail in *Foreign Relations*, 1930, I, 1–186.

the tensions of the 1930's, and their long-time effects were certainly not entirely happy. The United States was for a time lulled into a false security and neglected its naval establishment, failing to build up to the agreed quotas. The British were compelled at London, or in the negotiations preceding London, to reduce their cruiser strength in order to propitiate the American government, and this was to be a serious handicap in the 1940's. Naval disarmament was an expression of the temper of the 1920's and of a distinctively American point of view. But it was very far from affording a long-time guarantee of peace, and it contributed little to the stabilization of Europe. It is for this reason that I have dealt with it so summarily.

Let us turn to examine the American role in the effort carried on from 1925 to 1933 to reduce land armaments. As early as 1925, eschewing the very cautious view of the matter expressed by Secretary Hughes, and responding, no doubt, to the pressure of powerful elements in American opinion, Secretary Kellogg permitted the United States to take part in the deliberations of the Preparatory Commission on Disarmament that assembled at Geneva. For years a long discussion went on in this Commission which finally culminated in the Geneva Conference of 1932. In this conference bold proposals were put forward for the curtailment of land armaments as well as sea armaments, and in June of 1932 President Hoover presented a sweeping program which laid the emphasis on the abolition of "offensive weapons."[39]

But firmly, at all times, the United States adhered to its idea of no entanglement, of making no engagements that might tie its hands. And, equally firmly, the French insisted that such engagements were essential to any understanding. Thus the arms conference was to end in a fiasco; the way was blocked to any concrete accomplishment, and though the attitude was slightly changed when the Roosevelt administration came into power, the advent of Hitler in Germany dimmed the prospects of any accord. The world, instead, was to march down the long road to war.

Let us summarize at this point the policies of the United States with regard to peace and security as they relate to Europe. We shall have to begin by saying once again that these policies were narrowly circumscribed by public opinion. There are those who believe that if the American government had been able to take part wholeheartedly in a program of military guarantees the catastrophes of the 1930's might have been avoided. Certainly, in this year of grace 1953, the assumptions of American diplomacy are based on the idea of such guarantees. But different times, different manners. Neither Secretary Hughes nor Secretary Kellogg ever believed in the principle of collective action, and Stimson, believing in it more, had to contend with a President who was deeply set against any such conception. It is easy, if one will, to bewail the situation. But it is perhaps more judicious merely to recognize the fact that in democratic countries it is not possible to proceed in defiance of, or in opposition to, a powerful body of opinion.

V

Let us turn from the questions of politics to the principal economic problems that vexed the administrations of the 1920's. And here the two principal matters to be considered are the war debts[40] and reparations. On the former a position had been

[39] See *Foreign Relations*, 1932, I, 180–182.

[40] On the war debts, see especially H. G. Moulton and L. Pasvolsky, *War Debts and World Prosperity* (Washington, D.C., 1932).

taken at Paris by President Wilson from which it was impossible at any time in the next fifteen years to depart. This position was that the cancellation of the debts could not be considered. It is obvious that, in assuming this position, Wilson was interpreting American opinion. It would have been impossible to take any other course. In the wave of postwar nationalism most Americans saw only that they had come to the rescue of the Western democracies in a great war, that they had played a decisive part in the winning of that war, and that the United States had little to show, in the way of material gain, for the immense sums of money that had been expended and for the loss of American lives. The suggestion that they should now forgive borrowings which had been understood to be such at the time they were made was hardly to be tolerated.

Accordingly, the Harding and Coolidge administrations were bound to base their own policy on the position assumed by the previous administration, and to turn a deaf ear to European appeals for a scaling down of both the war loans and reparations. The American attitude was first defined in an explicit manner, that is, by legislation, in the winter of 1922. The act of February 9 of that year created a special War Debt Commission to preside over the liquidation of these debts into long-term obligations. The Secretary of State, the Secretary of the Treasury, and members of both Houses of Congress were to constitute this commission. The original act narrowly confined the Commission as to the terms on which refunding could take place. No new bonds were to be issued the date of maturity of which was later than June 15, 1947, and the rate of interest was not to be fixed at less than 4¼ per cent.

The legislation of 1922 produced no great enthusiasm in the breasts of our European debtors for refunding, and it was indeed fundamentally vulnerable. For as the rate of interest fell in the United States so that the American government could borrow at a rate substantially lower than that of the war years, it seemed unreasonable to exact a high rate from other governments. It was also apparent, as time went on, that if interest payments were to be added to principal, there was little chance of arriving at agreements which stipulated for the complete discharge of the debt by 1947. The Congress was therefore obliged to enact a much more flexible statute in the winter of 1923, which gave far more latitude to the Commission. It was undoubtedly influenced to that end by the negotiations with Great Britain which took place in January of the same year. Secretary Mellon was chairman of the Debt Commission, and it does not appear that the American Secretary of State took the leading part in the discussions. The first of these discussions, carried on for the British by Stanley Baldwin, who came to America for that purpose, ended in a deadlock. The problem was complicated, moreover, by the wholly unauthorized assurances of George Harvey, our ambassador in London, as to the rate of interest that the United States would demand, and as to the possibility of floating a tax-free loan in the United States.[41] Hughes had good reason to lament the good old American custom which confided the charge of the most important embassies to political supporters of the administration. But, in due course, an arrangement was arrived at, the rate of interest reduced, and the period of payments extended to 62 years, and this agreement was approved by the Congress. The method adopted, that is, legislative approval instead of the negotiation of a treaty, undoubtedly made easier the arrival at an accord, and is an

[41] Pusey, *Charles Evans Hughes*, II, 585.

interesting example of a method, which was to be more and more employed in the future, of circumventing the Senate.

Other debt agreements followed. It was the French who were the most obdurate in negotiation, and who were particularly insistent that the war debt problem be linked up to the question of reparations. Against any such proposition the War Debt Commission and the State Department alike took a very strong and unyielding stand. No connection between the two subjects was admitted, though it was obvious, of course, that if Germany defaulted on reparations, the burden of repayment of the debts would fall squarely upon the taxpapers of the debtor nations, and would, to some extent, at least, create a new situation. The first flurry with the French took place in 1925. When the French went home without an agreement, and in a good deal of a huff, the Italian government, nicely calculating the moment for a deal, took up the thread of its own negotiations, and, for reasons that are somewhat obscure, emerged with a settlement that reduced the average rate of interest on the Italian obligations to something like .4 of one per cent. A new effort at dealing with the French was undertaken in 1927, and in a much more favorable climate of opinion. Though the French continued to press for a recognition of the relationship between debts and reparations, an agreement was signed and payments began to be made.

In these negotiations for debt refunding, the principal burden was borne by the Treasury. But it was not so with reparations. Here the State Department played an important role, and this was particularly true under Secretary Hughes.

At Paris in 1919, it was impossible to arrive at any settlement with regard to Germany's payments to the victors. The problem was, at best, a very complicated one, and it was rendered more complex by the strong public feeling in both France and Great Britain. The exaggerated hopes of the mass of people had been encouraged by the politicians, and economic realism flew out the window. Accordingly, what was done was virtually to adjourn the settlement of the matter, to entrust the determination of Germany's indebtedness to a Reparations Commission set up by the treaty, which should by May 1, 1921, following certain principles laid down in treaty, determine the facts of the situation. In the meantime Germany was compelled to make certain types of payment, which we do not need to examine in detail.

Originally, it was expected that the United States would be one of the five nations represented on the Commission, and that the American member would be chairman. But the treaty of Versailles failed in the Senate, and when a separate treaty was negotiated with Germany, the Senate tacked on a reservation by which the representation on any of the numerous bodies functioning under the pact was forbidden, unless the explicit consent of Congress had been given. Mr. Hughes thus found himself in a most embarrassing situation. He could, of course, and did, appoint "unofficial" representatives to the Commission. But these individuals could wield very little authority; they could not vote on any issue. As a consequence, the control of the Commission gravitated into the hands of the French, and the attitude assumed became more and more rigorous. On a problem where the relatively objective attitude of the United States might have been of very great value, it became of almost no value at all.

The hamstringing of the State Department did not prevent Mr. Hughes from taking an active interest in the reparations question. At the outset of his term of office he was approached by the German government and asked to mediate the reparations question, and to fix the sum to be paid by Germany to the Allies.[42] This hot potato the Secretary naturally laid down hastily enough, but he urged that the German government itself formulate proposals that would form a proper basis for discussion. This suggestion was promptly accepted, and an offer made to pay a sum of 50,000,000,000 gold marks, present value, which would have amounted to something like four times this sum in annuities. The very afternoon it was received, the German proposition was submitted to the British and French ambassadors, and in the conversation that ensued Mr. Hughes raised the question whether a point had not been reached where it was better to take the proposal as a basis for further negotiations.[43] But the various European governments concerned remained obdurate. And on May 2 the word went forth to Berlin that the United States "finds itself unable to reach the conclusion that the proposals afford a basis for discussion acceptable to the Allied Governments."[44] The first American effort at a solution of the reparations question had met with failure.

As is well known, the reparations question became more and more aggravated in 1922, and the French government in particular manifested a more and more rigid point of view. The situation was shaping up towards sanctions and military pressure on Germany in the fall of the year. Very obviously, this development the Secretary profoundly deplored. Indeed, in December of 1922, he held a long conversation with Jusserand in which, in none too gentle a tone, he pointed out the difficulties to which further coercive measures by France would surely lead.[45] Moreover, there was germinating in his mind as early as September a proposal that the reparations question be taken out of the field of emotional debate, and submitted to the examination of financial experts, and this idea, too, he presented to Jusserand. On the other hand, he rejected as impracticable a proposal that came from Ambassador Houghton in Berlin, and which looked towards easing the general international tension by canceling the war debts in exchange for measures of disarmament, and a pledge on the part of the great nations of Europe not to go to war without a public referendum.[46] At the end of December, in a step only less remarkable than the dramatic proposal for arms reduction at the Washington Conference in November 1921, he laid bare to the public his views on the reparations question, in a speech before the American Historical Association at New Haven. The speech, it is true, indicated no concessions on the part of the United States. But it contained a key idea, which the Secretary stated as follows, "Why should they (the Allies) not invite men of the highest authority in finance in their respective countries—men of such prestige, honor and experience that their agreement upon the amount to be paid (by Germany), and upon a financial plan for working out the payments, would be accepted throughout the world as the most authoritative expression obtainable. I have no doubt that distinguished Americans would be willing to serve on such a commission."[47]

At the time that it was pronounced, the New Haven speech produced no effect whatever. On January 2, Britain dissenting, the Reparations Commission declared Germany to be in default, and authorized sanctions against her. Not many days

[42] Foreign Relations, 1921, II, 41.
[43] Foreign Relations, 1921, II, 48.
[44] Foreign Relations, 1921, II, 54.
[45] Foreign Relations, 1922, II, 187ff.
[46] Foreign Relations, 1922, II, 181.
[47] Foreign Relations, 1922, II, 199–202.

later the French moved into the Ruhr, and there began one of the most disastrous political moves of the postwar decade.

During the summer and early fall of 1923 the situation in the Reich deteriorated in sensational fashion. There was, in Hughes' opinion, nothing that the United States could do that would not make the situation worse; any suggestion in favor of Germany would, he felt, irritate the French and weaken the force of the suggestion that he had made at New Haven. Only experience could alter the situation and provide a means of settlement. And experience did precisely that. Slowly the French, in the face of British and American criticism and German passive resistance, yielded ground. They haggled over terms of reference to be laid down for the committees of experts and sought to limit the conclusions of the inquiry in time. But Hughes stood his ground, and at last he had his way. On November 23, 1923, the Reparations Commission approved of an inquiry of the type the Secretary had suggested, and two committees of experts were appointed to consider means of balancing the budget and stabilizing the currency and to investigate the amount of German capital that had been exported abroad. Since the Commission itself appointed the members of the committees, the limitation that the Senate had appended to the treaty of peace with Germany with regard to official representation on international bodies was of no effect, and that body was neatly outflanked.

The deliberations of these committees, appointed in November 1923, resulted, of course, in the Dawes plan. It is not possible to analyze that plan here. But it is important to note the part which Hughes played in seeing that its recommendations were carried into effect. Ostensibly going to Europe as President of the American Bar Association (a camouflage that seems a bit ineffective), he visited the various capitals of Europe and lent his influence to persuading the governments concerned to accept the program that General Dawes and his associates had laid down. He appears to have had his greatest difficulties in France, where Premier Herriot, himself not unfavorable to the plan, was mortally afraid of the hostile influence of Raymond Poincaré. But he saw both Herriot and Poincaré and made it clear that rejection of the scheme would have a very unfortunate effect.[48] Whether his role was decisive it is not possible to say. But, at any rate, the Dawes plan was put into effect.

Of course the new arrangements did not last long. They had to be revised in 1929 when the same technique of committees of experts was again employed. And then came the depression of 1929, forcing still further readjustments.

These readjustments we must for a moment examine if only for the light they throw on the character of American foreign policy in general. As the depression deepened, it became increasingly clear that the whole structure of international indebtedness erected in the postwar years rested on a flimsy foundation. The crisis came in 1931, with the collapse of the Austrian bank, the Credit-Anstalt, and a serious deterioration in the economic situation of Germany. Though Congress was not in session, and though his only recourse was to telegraph Congressional leaders in both Houses, the President came forward with a proposal for a year's moratorium on reparations and war debts alike. In his recent memoirs Mr. Hoover declares that this proposal was his own.[49] Certainly there have been few examples of more forthright action on the part of the Chief Executive, and no one will deny that the decision took political courage. Even so, it was necessary to attenuate its effects by

[48] Pusey, *Charles Evans Hughes*, II, 591–592.
[49] *Collier's*, May 10, 1952, p. 72.

declaring that no question of cancellation was involved, and by stating (somewhat illogically, it must be confessed) that the question of German reparations was a "strictly European problem."

The President's bold initiative did not alter the fundamentals of the situation. It was accepted by the French only after some diplomatic haggling, and it did not prevent an increasing agitation for the reduction of German reparations. The European conference which met at Lausanne in the summer of 1932 reduced the obligations of the Reich to a minimum, while at the same time drawing up a "gentleman's agreement" which stipulated that these reductions would not go into effect if the United States persisted in maintaining its attitude with regard to the war debts. What followed is no part of our story, except to say that both reparations and war debt payments had broken down entirely by 1934. The essence of the matter is that here was a problem that the diplomats simply could not settle, one in which the prejudices and resistances of the masses were more powerful than any appeal to intelligence could be. And outside the gesture of the Hoover moratorium, it is to be stated that American statesmanship in the last years of the debt question was never ready to face up to explaining to the American people the cold realities of the situation.

There is a peripheral aspect of this question of war debts and reparations that deserves a word of attention. The tariff attitude of the United States in the 1920's and early 1930's was in glaring contrast with its position on the refunding of the war obligations. It is an extraordinary commentary on the architects of American policy that they seem to have been so oblivious of the fact that if Europe were to pay up, it would be necessary to tear down, or at least to lower, customs barriers. Yet Secretary Hughes appears to have been little interested in the tariff act of 1922, and Secretary Stimson, though apparently more clearly aware of the problem, offered no effective resistance to the still higher tariff bill of 1930. The co-ordination of economic and political factors in the evolution of American diplomacy would, in any case, have been difficult; but in this one phase, at any rate, it does not seem even to have been attempted.

It is further to be noted that the edifice erected in the 1920's, the edifice of the naval treaties, of the Kellogg Pact, of the Dawes plan and the Young plan, was virtually completely to collapse in the 1930's, and here again the principal reasons were economic. When economic collapse came, an economic collapse for which the uncontrolled inflation in the United States must be regarded as a heavy contributing cause, the diplomats found their work in large degree undone. In the face of popular pressures based on economic discontent, they were powerless to prevent the deterioration of the general international situation in the 1930's.

The central question raised by this essay is, then, the question as to where, in the last analysis so far as America is concerned, foreign policy is made. And the conclusion is one suggested by the first pages of this text. It is made by the people, to no inconsiderable degree. It functions only within a frame of reference which they prescribe. Today, we seem to have embarked upon courses of action entirely antithetic to those of the 1920's. Then the thought was all of keeping American freedom of action, of avoiding Leagues and treaties which implied commitments. Today we think in terms of massing collective strength against a new menace, of alliances, of common action, and warning to aggressors that aggression will meet with punishment. Such policies are today dictated by the public mood, or are at least consistent with it. But the statesmen of the 1920's labored in a different climate of opinion, and were circumscribed by the prejudices which were typical of that climate. In the long run, they failed to erect a structure of peace. Will the formulas of the 1950's make success possible where it was not possible three decades ago? That is a question, not for the historian but for the prophets.

21 / Congressional Isolationists and the Roosevelt Foreign Policy

John C. Donovan

Those Americans who favor restricting presidential initiative in the conduct of the nation's foreign relations would do well to heed the findings of John C. Donovan in the following article. He perceives the Congressional pre-occupation during the 1930s with a magic legislative potion that somehow would keep America out of foreign entanglements and wars while at the same time making it all but impossible for American statesmen to consider the means to lessen international tensions in Europe and Asia. In other words, Congressional isolationism is interpreted as weakening the efforts of President Roosevelt and his associates to bring about a possible peaceful solution to the crises then besetting the world. Donovan also expresses some interesting observations on the conservatives and liberals who constituted the isolationist coalition in the Congress. In effect, his article suggests the need for many studies in depth showing both positive and negative influences of the Congress in the formulation of American foreign policy.

For further reading: Robert A. Devine, "Franklin D. Roosevelt and Collective Security," *Mississippi Valley Historical Review*, XLVIII (1961), 42–59; Alton Frye, *Nazi Germany and the American Hemisphere* (New Haven: 1967); Arthur D. Morse, *While Six Million Died: A Chronicle of American Apathy* (New York: 1968); Julius W. Pratt, *Cordell Hull 1933–1944*, 2 volumes in *The American Secretaries of State and Their Diplomacy*, edited by Samuel Flagg Bemis and Robert H. Ferrell (New York: 1963); Armin Rappaport, *Henry Stimson and Japan* (Chicago: 1963); Joachim Remak, "Friends of the New Germany: The Bund and German-American Relations," *Journal of Modern History* (March, 1951), 38–41; *Arthur P. Whitaker, *The Western Hemisphere Idea* (Ithaca: 1954); John Wiltz, *In Search of Peace: The Senate Munitions Inquiry 1934–1936* (Baton Rouge: 1963).

John C. Donovan has served as Professor and Chairman of the Department of Government and Legal Studies at Bowdoin College. This article is reprinted with the permission of the editors of *World Politics*. From *World Politics*, III. Copyright 1951 by *World Politics*.

In the 1950's, as in the 1930's, there are Congressional efforts to limit executive discretion in the conduct of foreign affairs. Senators Taft and Wherry have generated a debate over the President's authority to send armed forces abroad, which is reminiscent of the debate over the neutrality legislation of the earlier decade. The time has therefore come when a more just appreciation of President Roosevelt's leadership in foreign affairs may be possible and when such an evaluation may be useful.

Before an attempt is made to evaluate the foreign policy of Franklin Delano Roosevelt some attention should be paid to the Congressional views of isolationism that limited the formulation of American foreign policy in the decade prior to World War II. The efforts of the new revisionist school of American history, under the leadership of the late Charles A. Beard, to assess American foreign policy exclusively in terms of executive responsibility have shown less than adequate appreciation of the role that Congress plays in the making of American foreign policy. Any evaluation of the Roosevelt foreign policy that fails to consider the part played by the Congressional isolationists in the formulation of our foreign policy in the 1930's will leave something to be desired. The following article is an introductory effort based on detailed analysis of the role of Congress in the making of neutrality legislation, suggesting certain basic information which ought to be weighed by those who are interested in reaching a final evaluation.

I

American isolationism found expression in the 1930's in two very different groups in Congress. One group, in which Senators Hiram Johnson and William E. Borah provided the most effective leadership, firmly opposed American support of the program of collective security, insisting that the end product of the struggle for power in Europe would always be war and that there was nothing United States influence could do to alter the process or the result. Consequently, they argued, the government of the United States should concentrate its attention on the primary problem of making American democracy work at home with some consideration given, of course, to the problem of continental defense. Since war in foreign areas, and especially in Europe, was an inevitable feature of "power politics," the best opportunity for protecting American interests, according to this view, lay in the field of international law where a scrupulous adherence to our rights and duties as a neutral would keep the nation from involvement in foreign controversies, the outcome of which had no bearing on the future course of American democracy. John Bassett Moore and Edwin M. Borchard were the outstanding intellectual spokesmen for this view, and their advice was gladly and frequently given to Congressional groups studying the problem of keeping the nation "unentangled" and free from "foreign commitments."

The other Congressional group, led by Senators Nye, Clark, and Vandenberg, while agreeing on the futility of American participation in experiments in international political co-operation, considered it essential that the Congress frame neutrality legislation relinquishing many of the traditional rights of a neutral under international law. The purpose of this neutrality legislation would be to avoid any risks which might be involved in carrying on foreign trade in time of foreign war.

Whereas the Johnson-Borah group wanted to insist on American rights to trade in time of foreign war, the second group was anxious to abandon many of these traditional rights as a means of avoiding political involvement in foreign "quarrels." But both groups shared the popular disillusionment concerning American participation in the First World War. Both groups felt that American participation in that war had been based on an erroneous decision encouraged principally by: (1) huge private loans by American firms to Britain and France; (2) armament firms which were in a position to profit from a bigger war; (3) Allied propaganda; and (4) an unneutral and naive American President who thought (a) that the outcome of the war had implications for the future of the United States, and (b) that the war might conceivably be turned to constructive ends. Operating in this general atmosphere of disillusionment (in which practically nothing was made of the fact that it was the peace and not the war that had been lost) and encouraged by the Nye munitions investigation, sympathy was developed for the notion that the United States ought to enact legislation which would automatically rule out the mistakes of "last time."

In addition to sharing the general feeling of disillusionment concerning the purposes for which World War I had been fought, by 1935 the two Congressional isolationist groups were united in their suspicion of, and opposition to, the foreign policy of the Roosevelt administration. The abortive efforts of the President to obtain a discriminatory arms embargo in 1933 and adherence to the World Court in January 1935 alerted these groups to guard against the possibility of another "unneutral" President leading the nation down the road to collective security and international co-operation. They wanted no part of a policy which might mean taking sides in the "eternal quarrels" of those foreign nations indulging in the "sordid game of power politics." Hence, the theory developed that legislation restricting executive discretion in the conduct of foreign affairs would help to keep the nation out of foreign wars.

As has been pointed out, the Nye-Clark-Vandenberg theory of isolationism advocated the abandonment of traditional neutral trading rights in time of foreign war as a means of preventing "incidents" at sea and as a means of avoiding economic involvement in foreign wars. It is obvious that the logical extension of this theory would lead to the point where the nation would be asked to give up foreign trade in order to keep free of war. As a matter of fact, however, there were very few isolationists of any variety who were prepared to carry the Nye-Clark-Vandenberg theory that far. First to object, and this might have been expected, was the Johnson-Borah group, also isolationist but extremely proud, which considered it ignoble for a powerful, self-respecting nation to so restrict its own legitimate activities.

Thus, when the Congress of the United States eventually faced the terrible dilemma of how to keep out of war without abandoning foreign commerce, the natural answer was found in the famous "cash-and-carry" formula, whereby it was possible to keep the trade and transfer the risk. This problem was thoroughly aired and debated in Congress and on public platforms during 1936 and 1937, and in the latter year a cash-and-carry compromise resolution was adopted, embodying a principle the Nye-Clark-Vandenberg group favored and the Borah-Johnson group disliked, with much more executive discretion written into the legislation than either isolationist group preferred.

From that time on, both isolationist groups concentrated their efforts on retaining the arms embargo which they considered to be the symbol of American "neutrality." And as the aggressive designs of Nazi Germany became the more explicit and menacing, the Roosevelt administration gradually prepared to press for repeal of the arms embargo as a means of discouraging German aggression, and when that effort failed, as a means of strengthening the armed might of Britain and France in the war against Germany.

II

In any complete and thorough study of the making of American foreign policy from 1935 to 1939 which seeks to shed light on who was responsible for what, it will be necessary to consider the very important role played by Congress in the formulation of legislation designed to keep the nation out of war. It will be imperative in any such study to recognize the fact that the idea of designing this legislation was of Congressional origin. Obviously, the whole effort to restrict executive discretion, which lay at the heart of this legislation, was, and could only have been, a Congressional undertaking.

At the outset of the neutrality experiment in 1935, the Administration tried to outflank the Nye-Clark-Vandenberg isolationist bloc by offering its own proposal for neutrality legislation, the purpose being to secure provision for a *discretionary* arms embargo. But Congress wrote the first neutrality law in 1935 including a *mandatory, non-discretionary* arms embargo provision, which the President did not want and said that he did not want. And so the Chief Executive was immediately placed in a defensive position from which he tried repeatedly to obtain as much leeway as possible for the exercise of executive discretion.

Not until the spring of 1939, however, would the Administration risk an outright frontal attack on the arms embargo, the cornerstone of the Congressional isolationist edifice. Even then, the remainder of the Administration's proposal was composed for the most part of features designed to maximize its appeal to legislators of isolationist persuasions.

It is quite possible, of course, that both the Administration and the Congressional isolationists overestimated the strength of popular sentiment in favor of keeping out of war by means of legislation. We do at least know that the isolationist bloc in the Senate invariably deemed it necessary to resort to the use of the filibuster threat, the minority weapon *par excellence,* in order to win concessions for their point of view. When the voting on neutrality legislation came, as it usually did come, in the midst of a legislative docket already crowded with major proposals (frequently dealing with problems of domestic recovery and reform), the Administration leaders in Congress were understandably sensitive to the threat of filibuster. In such a situation it is not surprising that the Administration was willing to compromise with the isolationist bloc. As a result, until the autumn of 1939 (after general war had broken out in Europe) it was next to impossible to tell whether majority support for the Administration's views was or was not within its reach.

In any case, it is a matter of record that the isolationist groups, within and outside Congress, were strong enough and clever enough and were in a sufficiently strategic position to win substantial concessions from the Administration from 1935 through 1939. And, in evaluating Congress' responsibility for the theory that we ought to try to keep out of war by means of legislation, one of the striking facts is the immense amount of time that was devoted to discussion *within the limits* established by this theory. It is almost as if the Congressional mind had erected a mental block prohibiting serious consideration of any measures that might have been taken to try to prevent the outbreak of war. To anyone who feels at all sympathetic toward this latter objective, the worst feature of the neutrality laws and the whole neutrality debate in the 'thirties is the extent to which they diverted attention from this aspect of the problem. It is ironic that a people who pride themselves on their ability to experiment should have so confined their thinking on this most challenging of all problems within such narrow limits.

It is probably useless to speculate on what might have been accomplished if Congress had been able to call a halt and bring about a fundamental re-examination of the whole complex issue. But, of course, it was extremely difficult to call a halt once "neutrality" had assumed the guise of an emotional symbol. Once placed on an emotional level, rational discussion was at a serious disadvantage, and expanding the limits within which rational discussion of the issue might be carried on was probably out of the question.

Psychologically, the existence of neutrality legislation had a decidedly unfortunate effect on popular thinking, which tended to assume that a difficult problem had been solved by means of drastic legislation. The existence of legislation that had as its purpose keeping the nation out of war tended to create the comfortable illusion that Americans were safe over here in their own land despite wars in Europe and Asia. It is hardly too much to say that neutrality legislation became the American Maginot line.

In addition to deluding the American people, neutrality legislation had the further unfortunate effect of misleading potential aggressor nations by giving them reason to assume that the United States was indifferent to the use of war as an instrument of national policy. Henry L. Stimson made the point extremely well in his testimony before the Senate Committee on Foreign Relations in 1939 when he said:

> . . . the American people are not insensible to cruelty and aggression. Nor are they so unintelligent that under conditions of today they cannot distinguish an aggressor nation from its victim . . . Moreover, they are not a constitutionally timid people, nor are they smitten with such an inferiority complex as to make them wish their Government to avoid decisions which are really necessary to their own future interests. And this is the trouble, that the form of this statute today tends to make the outside world believe each one of these fantastic falsehoods and to guide their own policy in the light of that belief.[1]

III

Finally, in November 1939, after war had broken out in Europe, the Roosevelt administration succeeded in its effort to remove the arms embargo provision from American neutrality legislation, replacing it with a cash-and-carry provision on arms. Thus, two months after the outbreak of general war in Europe, the President proposed and Congress accepted the revision of neutrality legislation in a manner calculated: (1) to aid that group of belligerents which shared the Western democratic tradition and whose existence was considered essential in the interests of American security; and (2) to reduce the possibility of "incidents" at sea involving American

---

[1] *Neutrality, Peace Legislation and Our Foreign Policy: Hearings before the Committee on Foreign Relations,* U. S. Senate, 76th Congress, 1st Session, 1939, p. 7.

ships, goods, and lives, as a means of avoiding entanglement as a belligerent in the European war.

Revisionist historians, unfortunately, are likely to concentrate their attention on this second purpose to the utter exclusion of the first. And, of course, looking at the 1939 Neutrality Act exclusively in terms of the second purpose, it is perfectly clear that the measure had isolationist aspects which proposed to keep this country from becoming involved in the Second World War for causes which allegedly led us into the First World War. There can be no doubt that the American people in the autumn of 1939 did not want their nation to become a belligerent in the European war.

However, when we look at the same act from the point of view of the first purpose and, specifically, when we view the provision that repealed the arms embargo and replaced it with a cash-and-carry provision, the conclusion is inescapable that the President and Congress, apparently supported by majority opinion, had decided to support the cause of Britain and France in the war against aggressive and expanding German Fascism. Thus, the decision of November 1939 was equally and significantly a decision *away from* isolationism, and this was a decision made by the President, the Congress, and the American people in the usual manner.

The decision was made in the autumn of 1939, shortly after Germany invaded Poland, to place the extensive productive capacity of the United States behind the cause for which Great Britain and France were already fighting. In this connection the fact is apt to be overlooked by revisionist historians that the isolationists in Congress apparently had no objection to placing all of our commerce, *except* arms and ammunition, on a cash-and-carry basis, although they knew perfectly well that such a policy would benefit Great Britain and France immensely. In the autumn of 1939, most Americans left it to the future to decide what should be done when Britain and France had exhausted their own financial resources, but for the present the American nation consciously, deliberately, and by the normal, democratic procedures decided to become economically involved in the European war.

IV

Those who intend to make the effort to evaluate the Roosevelt foreign policy will do well to note the strong support which the philosophy of isolationism mustered in "progressive" and "liberal" quarters throughout the 1930's. It is one of the startling paradoxes of this period that many of the most enthusiastic supporters of the New Deal domestic program were outspokenly critical of the Roosevelt administration's foreign policy. Charles A. Beard was, of course, the outstanding intellectual spokesman of this brand of American progressivism, but he certainly did not stand alone. In Congress the Western progressives were lined up against the President's foreign policy almost to a man. When the crucial vote came late in October 1939 to repeal the arms embargo, Senator Norris of Nebraska was the only outstanding Western progressive or independent who voted to repeal the arms embargo. Senators Wheeler, Frazier, Nye, Shipstead, Lundeen, Hiram Johnson, La Follette, and Borah—all of whom in the past on many occasions had helped the President form a majority against the dissident conservative wing of his own party when domestic issues were at stake—were joined in opposition to the Roosevelt foreign policy.

As a matter of fact, it might be rather difficult to understand the strength of American isolationism in the 'thirties unless one were aware of the isolationist predilections of an influential branch of American progressivism during the same period. When one has come in contact with a full-blown version of isolationist-progressive doctrine, he realizes at once the powerful appeal it offered to men who cherished the "democratic dream." Fortunately, the Beards have left us a full statement of the philosophy of "Continental Americanism" in *America in Midpassage,* a book that reveals most of the assumptions on which the thinking of the isolationist-progressives was based. In this book, the Beards undertook to define this school of thought, and the definition is worth quoting at some length. At the heart of the continentalist philosophy, the Beards write,

> . . . was the idea that through domestic measures, adopted by the democratic process, vast improvements could be and should be effected in American civilization, where at least one-third of the nation was ill-housed, ill-clothed, ill-nourished, and ill-educated; moreover, that this civilization could be defended in its continental home under prudent policies by small but appropriate military and naval establishments. Associated with the vision was the conviction that American democracy should not attempt to carry the Atlas load of the White Man's Burden in the form of imperialism all over the earth, or assume that it had the capacity, even with the best of good-will, to settle the difficult problems of European nations encrusted in the heritages of their long and sanguinary history. Its theories and sentiments were enclosed in such phrases as: let us keep out of the next world war mind our own business; till our own garden; create the wealth; substitute abundance for scarcity; establish a sound and efficient domestic economy; make America a work of art.
>
> Although owing to the lack of a precise name, this . . . school of foreign policy was often described as isolationist by its critics, its defenders disowned the connotations of the kind of isolationist creed sponsored by Henry Cabot Lodge, Warren G. Harding and Calvin Coolidge. They likewise refused to be battened down by the name "nationalist," with its chauvinist and militarist associations. . . . Surrendering shop-worn reliance upon imperialist pressures, moneylending, and huckstering abroad, they turned to the efficient, humanistic use of national resources and technical skills as a means for making a civilization on this continent more just, more stable, and more beautiful than anything yet realized.[2]

Who can doubt that here was a view for Americans who lived in the light of the democratic dream? This was the kind of thinking that most appealed to a good many American progressives in the decade before the Second World War. And yet, it is quite clear, the view was *restricted* to *Americans* who lived and worked for the ideal. Beardians might protest that their philosophy was not isolationist and their emphasis on domestic reform was not calculated to win the devotion of a Lodge, a Harding, or a Coolidge. They might also protest that their philosophy was not nationalistic, and who can doubt that it was shorn of its chauvinist and militarist connotations? But, protests notwithstanding, this was pre-eminently a philosophy of isolationism grounded in the rich soil of American nationalism.

It was certainly a doctrine without appeal to internationalists with its assumption that America lacked the capacity to solve the difficult problems then facing mankind

[2] Charles A. and Mary Beard, *America in Midpassage,* New York, Macmillan, 1939, pp. 452–53.

and, therefore, had no obligation to join in trying to solve them. At this point we need to remind ourselves that, according to the "continentalists," we Americans have a primary obligation to keep democracy alive and flourishing in "our own garden." There was the further assumption, not expressed here by the Beards, that the problems of the rest of the world, whatever their outcome, could not appreciably alter the future course of American democracy. Despite the protests of the Beards and their followers, this was obviously and, indeed, *openly,* a nationalist philosophy with its challenge to make the American civilization "a work of art." Instead of engaging in the perpetual quarrels of Europe (and the war against Hitlerism was, of course, another in the endless series of foreign quarrels), Americans ought to apply "the efficient, humanistic use of national resources and technical skills" in order to build on this continent a civilization "more just, more stable, and more beautiful than anything yet realized."

This was clearly a vision to inspire Americans of progressive faith. In fact, so passionately was the faith held that men were encouraged to think of it as a dream intended *solely* for Americans. Combined with this faith in national democracy was an equally passionate hatred of war. Pacifism as a strand of American isolationism is a subject deserving careful analysis in its own right. And the normal pacifistic hatred of war for its own sake joined hands in the 'thirties with an equally profound fear of what might happen to our own democracy if we prepared to fight for democracy. Hatred of war, that is, pacifism, was one element in American isolationism, and the fear that war would bring totalitarianism was another. One hated to get involved in a war allegedly waged against totalitarianism when involvement seemed certain to bring about the establishment of totalitarianism at home. This was the worst charge the American progressive-isolationists could hurl at the Roosevelt foreign policy—that fighting totalitarianism would accomplish nothing worth while abroad and would precipitate the collapse of democracy at home. It was hard for many liberals in the 'thirties to see that the time might not be far off when they would have to participate in war (inherently an illiberal device) in order to give liberalism a chance to survive.

Charles A. Beard was typical of American progressives in general in his devotion to the objectives toward which the domestic New Deal was moving. Thus we find the following evaluation in *America in Midpassage:*

> It was well within the circle of factual description to say that in his numerous discourses Franklin D. Roosevelt discussed the basic human and economic problems of American society with a courage and range displayed by no predecessor in his office; that he thrust their challenges into spheres hitherto indifferent or hostile; that he set in swift circulation, through the use of the radio, ideas once confined to groups more or less esoteric; that he both reflected and stirred the thought of the nation to the uttermost borders of the land. And in doing this he carried on the tradition of humanistic democracy which from colonial times had been a powerful dynamic in the whole movement of American civilization and culture—economic, political, literary, scientific and artistic.[3]

Eight years later Dr. Beard was to conclude that, when this same President passed on, the way had been paved for an American Caesar to destroy the American democracy, so long in the building. He reached this conclusion after observing and

[3] *Ibid.,* p. 948.

studying Franklin D. Roosevelt as leader of the nation during the Second World War. In *President Roosevelt and the Coming of the War*, Dr. Beard asserts that if the precedents established by Franklin Roosevelt's conduct of foreign relations are to stand unmodified,

> . . . the Constitution may be nullified by the President, officials, and other officers who have taken the oath, and are under moral obligation to uphold it. For limited government under supreme law they may substitute personal and arbitrary government—the first principle of the totalitarian system against which, it has been alleged, World War II was waged—while giving lip service to constitutional government.[4]

It is almost as though Dr. Beard were seeking to convince us that the progressive-isolationists were correct in the first place in asserting that intervention in World War II would inevitably lead to the destruction of democracy at home. And, as a result, Dr. Beard has left those who still cherish the vision and share the democratic dream (broadened in its applicability) in a terrible dilemma. Are the survivors of the Second World War to believe that another generation has been duped, misled, and unnecessarily led to slaughter? Are we to believe that Franklin Roosevelt, in pursuing the objectives of American foreign policy, either distorted or destroyed "the tradition of humanistic democracy" which had long been "a powerful dynamic in the whole movement of American civilization and culture"?[5]

For those who would seek to evaluate the Roosevelt foreign policy, the obvious fact has to be faced that American democracy was not destroyed in the process of fighting World War II, as many progressive-isolationists feared that it would be. Instead, the American democracy today shows signs of strength and vigor that would have seemed impossible in, let us say, 1932. More than that, a society of free men exists in Great Britain and France and the rest of Western Europe today, although the future of such a society also was in doubt in 1939 and was even more doubtful in the summer of 1940. So, far from destroying "democracy" at home and abroad,

---

[4] Charles A. Beard, *President Roosevelt and the Coming of the War, 1941*, New Haven, Yale University Press, 1948, p. 584. For a detailed listing of the charges against President Roosevelt's conduct of foreign relations, see Chapter XVIII of the same book. A brief observation on Beard's charges may be in order. Professor Beard seems to assume that Franklin Roosevelt created all the precedents for the use of executive power in foreign relations. Actually when Edward S. Corwin first published *The President's Control of Foreign Relations* (Princeton, Princeton University Press, 1917), thirty years before Beard constructed his criticism, he found ". . . an unlimited discretion in the President in the recognition of new governments and states, an undefined authority in sending special agents abroad, of dubious diplomatic status, to negotiate treaties or for other purposes; a similarly undefined power to enter into compacts with other governments without the participation of the Senate; the practically complete and exclusive discretion in the negotiation of more formal treaties, and in their final ratification; the practically complete and exclusive initiative in the official formulation of the nation's foreign policy." (Pp. 205–6.)

[5] The most complete and carefully reasoned refutation of Beard's thesis to appear up to this time is Basil Rauch's *Roosevelt, From Munich to Pearl Harbor*, New York, Creative Age Press, 1950. Rauch is convinced on the basis of his examination of the evidence that Beard's interpretation of the Roosevelt foreign policy is grounded on "omissions, distortions, and falsifications." If this evaluation seems harsh, the writer can only add that his analysis of the 1935–39 period would support essentially the same evaluation of Beard's *American Foreign Policy in the Making, 1932–1940*, New Haven, Yale University Press, 1946. See John C. Donovan, "Congress and the Making of Neutrality Legislation, 1935–1939," unpublished doctoral dissertation, Harvard University, 1949.

the policies of the Roosevelt administration evidently had something to do with keeping it alive in the world and may also have helped to invigorate it. Those who would undertake to evaluate the Roosevelt foreign policy will find it difficult to be critical of its purposes and accomplishments.

V

The major criticism, then, will probably be raised with respect to the methods used by the Roosevelt administration in formulating and carrying out that foreign policy within a system of democratic controls. And at this point, a study of the making of neutrality legislation in the years 1935 to 1939 will produce valuable evidence. In fact, it will not only throw light on some of the methods used, but it also will illuminate the general setting in which decisions were made, thus increasing our understanding of *why* they were made in the way they were made.

A careful study of the making of neutrality legislation will show, for example, that the President did indeed deliver addresses from time to time that must have been encouraging to American isolationists. The evidence also will show that the President was less than candid in explaining the objectives of American foreign policy on several occasions. On the other hand, the record also includes abundant evidence showing that the Roosevelt administration tried with fair consistency to obtain neutrality legislation which would leave a maximum of discretion in the hands of the Chief Executive in the conduct of foreign relations. And there was nothing very mysterious or secret about the Administration's efforts in this respect, as a reasonably careful reading of the *New York Times* will show.

It was certainly no secret that the Administration tried (and failed) to obtain legislative authorization for a discriminatory and discretionary arms embargo in 1933 and again in 1935. The evidence also is quite clear that the neutrality law in 1935 represented definite acquiescence on the part of the Chief Executive in a policy he did not favor and did not believe would work. It is worth remembering that in signing the act, the President warned that situations might develop in which the "wholly inflexible provisions" of the act might drag the nation into war instead of keeping us out.

The record also reveals that by 1936 the Roosevelt administration had discovered that the possibility of additional discretionary authority for the Chief Executive lay within the field of conditional contraband, and that the Administration then tried to obtain legislation embodying the normal-trade quota principle as a means toward the desired end. By 1937 the Administration shifted position slightly to favor the cash-and-carry principle, which was growing in popularity, again in order to retain as much discretion as possible for the Chief Executive in the conduct of foreign affairs.

The record also contains the "Quarantine" speech of October 5, 1937, which was both a candid and clear statement by the President in behalf of collective action against aggressors. The loud reaction to that speech in isolationist quarters suggests one of the major reasons for less frankness in a number of other Presidential statements on foreign policy.

Not only was the general orientation of the Administration's foreign policy no great mystery, there was also impressive support for the President's contention that a maximum of discretion was rightfully his in the conduct of foreign relations. The Supreme Court's decision in the case of the *United States* vs. *Curtiss-Wright Export Company* in December 1936 had an immediate effect on Congressional thinking that was helpful to the Administration. The Court's opinion in the *Curtiss-Wright* case recognized ". . . the very delicate, plenary and exclusive power of the President as the sole organ of the federal government in the field of international relations— a power which does not require as a basis for its exercise an act of Congress."[6] This special power of the President in the area of foreign affairs sprang from the fundamental difference between the powers of the federal government in respect to foreign affairs and those in respect to domestic affairs, the Court explained.

> It is quite apparent (the opinion continued) that if, in the maintenance of our international relations, embarrassment—perhaps serious embarrassment—is to be avoided and success for our aims achieved, congressional legislation which is to be made effective through negotiation and inquiry within the international field must often accord to the President a degree of discretion and freedom from statutory restriction which would not be admissible were domestic affairs alone involved.[7]

But apparently most of the isolationists in Congress retained their faith in a greater degree of legislative control of foreign policy than either the President or the Court was willing to admit. And the constant effort of the legislative branch, and especially of the isolationist group in Congress, to tighten the restrictions on executive discretion doubtless accounts in large measure for the unwillingness of the Chief Executive and the Secretary of State to deal with the question of American neutrality policy always in complete frankness.

On several occasions during 1938, the Administration abandoned opportunities to press for repeal of the arms embargo, evidently not wishing to stir up an acrimonious debate on foreign policy. In the first half of 1939, precious months slipped away before the Administration openly campaigned for repeal of the embargo provision. This was due in part to poor support from Senator Pittman, the supposed leader of the Administration forces in the Senate on this particular issue. This was not the first time that Senator Pittman had proved to be a less than satisfactory legislative lieutenant. And furthermore, the President was still reluctant to risk a divisive Congressional debate in view of the unsettled world situation.

The President and his Congressional supporters were unable to convince at least a determined minority in Congress that there was real danger of general European war in 1939. As a result, the first session of the Seventy-sixth Congress adjourned in the summer of 1939 without modifying the Neutrality Act of 1937, except for the cash-and-carry section which was allowed to expire on May 1, 1939. The Congress of the United States, relying on its own judgment, was apparently convinced that war in Europe was not imminent, although by that time the President and the Secretary of State had pleaded vigorously that the danger was acute.

After the German invasion of Poland in September 1939, the Roosevelt administration moved swiftly and surely to bring about repeal of the arms embargo. In September 1939 the situation in Europe had clarified enough to make it difficult to accept the notion that Germany only wanted to gather "all the Germans" into the

---

[6] 299 US 304 at 320.
[7] *Ibid.*

fatherland. By that time, the Administration was so thoroughly convinced of the urgent need to strengthen Britain and France militarily in order to protect the interests of American security that there was no longer a disposition to compromise with Congressional isolationists on the central issue. Furthermore, since Congress had been called into special session, the revision of neutrality legislation was the only task on the docket, and public support for the Administration's program was no longer a question mark.

But even in this case, neither the President nor the Secretary of State frankly and openly stated the reasons for the arms embargo repeal to Congress and the American people. The final evaluation of the Roosevelt foreign policy will almost certainly be critical of the Administration for its failure to clarify the issues behind this key decision in foreign affairs. If it had been in the interests of American security to strengthen Britain and France in a war with German Fascism, then the leader of the nation should have made the issue as clear as he could. And yet it is to be hoped that the final evaluation will not be based on the assumption that a kind of cynical, Machiavellian cunning prompted this lack of frankness. The evaluation of the Roosevelt foreign policy would be neither complete nor fair if it were to omit the fact that a well-organized, well-led, and extremely vocal opposition stood ready to use any frank statement from the Chief Executive on American foreign policy as ammunition against that foreign policy.

And it would be a mistake to assume that the President was cautious simply because he did not care to lose a debate. Here we must consider the fact that most of the leaders of the opposition were unconvinced even in October and November 1939 that German aggression constituted a threat to American security. On the other hand, the President had certain constitutional obligations and responsibilities as Commander-in-Chief that Congress did not share, and he was convinced in his own mind that such aggression *did* threaten American security. The historian in weighing the factor of the President's special responsibilities as Chief Executive and Commander-in-Chief will also note that the President had to assume most of the burden of trying to create a semblance of national unity in a time of grave international upheaval. It was doubtless a matter of grave concern to him that a bitter and prolonged debate on foreign policy might serve to widen the breach at home, a possibility that would be expected to delight the leaders of the German, Italian, and Japanese war machines. Individual congressmen, on the other hand, could be expected to pursue their prerogative to criticize with less sensitivity to the broader implications.

It is important to note, in this connection, that throughout this period the President in his difficult and delicate relations with Congress had to be constantly on guard,

> . . . to avoid what Tolstoy called "the irrevocable act." He now carried a heavy share of the responsibility for the future history of the world. If he were to go before the Congress with a request for action on an issue of international importance and were defeated, it would involve more than gleeful editorials in the *Chicago Tribune* and possible losses for the Democratic party at the next election; it could well involve utter, world-wide disaster.[8]

Finally, attention ought to be paid to the fact that despite the overwhelming desire of the American people to stay out of war, the decision was freely made in November 1939 by the Congress in the usual manner, and apparently with the majority of

---

[8] Robert E. Sherwood, *Roosevelt and Hopkins*, New York, Harper, 1948, pp. 132–33.

American people concurring, to revise our neutrality legislation in a way that would provide assistance to Britain and France against Nazi Germany. It is to be hoped that the future historian in making his evaluation of American foreign policy will avoid the temptation to oversimplify the independent creative role that is left to executive leadership in a modern democratic and constitutional setting. A study of the making of American foreign policy in the 1930's will reveal the extent to which such leadership is hedged in by public opinion and by the restrictions imposed on independent executive action by the presence of a national legislature which is jealous of its prerogatives.

Not only public opinion and the legislative branch restrict executive action. Also, the historian must consider the tendencies and traditions, the general consensus (the ideology, if you wish) of the people. The truth of the matter will be more nearly approached if the historian heeds the observation that:

> . . . the men who are popularly said to "make history" are dealing with highly intractable material, that this material which includes the wills of their fellowmen, can be moulded only in accordance with certain existing trends, and that the statesman who fails to understand, and refuses to comply with, these trends dooms himself to sterility.[9]

Possibly we can make the phrase "tendencies and traditions" less ambiguous in the present case. Briefly, it is extremely doubtful that a future historian would dare to speculate that an "unneutral" President, intent upon foreign adventures as a means of surmounting domestic difficulties, would have had any chance of success in trying to take the United States into the Second World War on the side of Nazi Germany. President Roosevelt left his own great mark on history as an influential world leader, but he was also representative of, and reflected, the wills and efforts of millions of his fellow-countrymen, and he was unable to move except in the direction, and largely at the pace, they wanted to go.

[9] E. H. Carr, *Conditions of Peace*, New York, Macmillan, 1942, p. 6.

Part V

THE
RESPONSIBILITIES
OF A
SUPERPOWER

22 / War Came at Pearl Harbor: Suspicions Considered

Herbert Feis

American intervention in the Second World War has already inspired numerous historical commentaries. Orthodox or traditional interpretations have generally supported and defended the policies of the United States Government, advancing the view that President Roosevelt and his advisers sincerely attempted to keep America out of the Second World War. Responsibility for American involvement accordingly is placed on the aggressive acts of the Axis powers. By contrast, revisionist historians have insisted that America had no fundamental interest in the outcome of the war; that American intervention was quite unnecessary; and moreover that American intervention ultimately occurred because the policies pursued by the Roosevelt Administration provoked the Japanese Government into attacking American territories in the Pacific. Various revisionists have maintained that President Roosevelt personally favored American involvement in the war and only sought some avenue which would afford moral justification for belligerency. Herbert Feis's article which follows discusses several of the charges aired by the revisionists and the evidence which revisionists have assembled to support their allegations.

For further reading: Charles A. Beard, *President Roosevelt and the Coming of War 1941* (New Haven: 1948); Robert J. C. Butow, *Tojo and the Coming of the War* (Princeton: 1961); Wayne S. Cole, "American Entry into World War II: A Historiographical Appraisal," *Mississippi Valley Historical Review*, XLIII (1957), 595–617; *Herbert Feis, *The Road to Pearl Harbor* (Princeton: 1950); Robert H. Ferrell, "Pearl Harbor and the Revisionists," *Historian*, XVII (1955), 215–233; *William Langer and S. Everett Gleason, *The Challenge to Isolation 1937–1940* (New York: 1952) and *The Undeclared War 1940–1941* (New York: 1953); Basil Rauch, *From Munich to Pearl Harbor* (New York: 1950); Paul W. Schroeder, *The Axis Alliance and*

Herbert Feis has had a long and distinguished career of service in the Department of State. More recently, he has been affiliated with the Institute for Advanced Study at Princeton, New Jersey. This article is reprinted here with the permission of the author and of the editors of *The Yale Review*. From *The Yale Review*, XLV. Copyright © 1956 Yale University Press.

Japanese-American Relations (Ithaca: 1958); Charles C. Tansill, *Back Door to War: The Roosevelt Foreign Policy 1933–1941* (Chicago: 1952); *Roberta Wohlstetter, *Pearl Harbor: Warning and Decision* (Stanford: 1962).

Ten years after victory, we look ruefully at the way the world has gone. It is right and natural to search out any errors of judgment or faults of character that have led us to our present pass. But such self-scrutiny can go awry if governed by a wish to revile rather than a wish to understand. Unless we are alert, that could happen as a result of the suspicions that have come to cluster around the way in which the United States became engaged in the Second World War—torch-lit by the Pearl Harbor disaster.

The more recently available sources have added but little to our knowledge of the events that led to our entry into the war. The books of memoirs written by Japanese witnesses have told us something more, especially about the struggle within the Japanese Government. But in my reading, while they may improve our knowledge of details, they do not change the fundamental view of this experience or its main features. In American and British records still kept secret there may be information or explanations that would do so. But even this I doubt. With no new great revealing facts to display, and no great new insights to impart, the most useful service would seem to be to act as caretaker of what is known, and in particular to deal with certain warped comments and inferences that seasonally must feel the straightening edge of evidence.

Of all the accusations made, the one most shocking to me is that Roosevelt and his chief advisers deliberately left the Pacific Fleet and base at Pearl Harbor exposed as a lure to bring about a direct Japanese attack upon us.

This has been diffused in the face of the fact that the Japanese High Military Command conference before the Imperial Throne on September 6, 1941, resolved that "If by the early part of October there is no reasonable hope of having our demands agreed to in the diplomatic negotiations mentioned above, we will immediately make up our minds to get ready for war against America (and England and Holland)." This is September 6. The plan for the attack on Pearl Harbor was not approved and adopted until October; and Secret Operation Order #1, the execution of the plan, was not issued until November 5. The presence of the Pacific Fleet at Pearl Harbor was not a lure but an obstacle.

The literature of accusation ignores or rejects the real reasons why the Pacific Fleet was kept in Hawaii. It must do so, since one of the main reasons was the hope that its presence there would deter the Japanese from making so threatening a move south or north that American armed forces might have to join in the war. It scorns the fact that the American military plans—to be executed in the event that we became engaged in war—assigned vital tasks to this Pacific Fleet. A mind must indeed be distracted if it can believe that the American Government could, at one and the same time, use the Pacific Fleet as a target and count on having it as part of its main defending force.

A variant of this accusation, which at least does not require such a willingness to believe the worst, might also be noted—that despite ample knowledge that Pearl

Harbor was about to be attacked, the American Government purposefully left it exposed and allowed the event to happen.

Those who do not find such an idea at odds with their view of the sense of duty and regard for human life of President Roosevelt and his chief advisers can find striking points about the occurrence that may be construed to correspond with this conception. How they glare out of the record in hindsight: Ambassador Grew's warnings; Secretary Hull's acute gleam put into words at least three times in Cabinet Councils in November that the Japanese attack might come "at any moment, anywhere"; the intercepted Japanese messages telling of the Japanese effort to secure minute information as to the location of the ships of our Pacific Fleet in the Harbor; carelessness in checking up on the protective measures taken by the local commanders; failure to use the chance to give an effective last-minute warning to Hawaii. How else, it is asked, can these be explained except in terms of secret and conscious purpose?

However, just as hindsight makes the failure of perception plain, so it also makes it understandable—but only by bringing back to mind the total circumstances. That can be done here only in the barest way. Up to then Japanese strategy had been wary, one small creeping step after another, from Manchuria to North China into China and down into Indo-China. American military circles came to take it for granted that it would go on that way. Then there was the fact that Japan's basic objectives lay to the south and southeast; there and there only it could get what it needed—raw materials, oil, and island bases to withstand the attack from the West. Expectation already set in that direction was kept there by impressive and accurate intelligence reports of movements under way. Against this flow of preconception, the signs pointing to Pearl Harbor were not heeded.

Such features of contemporary thinking within the American Government explain, though they do not excuse, the failure to discern that Pearl Harbor was going to be attacked. To think the contrary is to believe that the President and the heads of the American Army, Navy, and Air Force were given to deep deception, and in order to have us enter the war were ready to sacrifice not only the Pacific Fleet but the whole war plan for the Pacific. This, I think, is the difference between history and police court history.

I have taken note of these accusations that have been built about the disaster at Pearl Harbor because they appeal to the sense of the sinister which is so lively in our times. But I am glad to turn to ideas and interpretations of broader historical import.

The first of these is that Roosevelt and the Joint Chiefs of Staff were obligated by secret agreements with Churchill and their British colleagues to enter the war at some time or other, in one way or other. Therefore, it is further supposed, the American authors of this agreement had to cause either Germany or Japan, or both, to attack us.

This view derives encouragement from the fact that the American Government *did* enter into a secret agreement about strategy with the British. The accord, known as ABC–1 Staff Agreement, adopted at Washington in March, 1941, set down the respective missions of the British and American elements in the event that the United States should be at war with Germany or Japan, or both; and subsequently the American basic joint war plan, Rainbow–5, was adjusted to fit this combined plan of operations. An attempt was made at a similar conference in Singapore soon after to work out a more detailed United States-British-Dutch operating plan for the Pacific.

This attempt failed; but the discussion that took place there left a lasting mark on American official thinking, for the conferees defined the limits on land and sea beyond which Japanese forces could not be permitted to go without great risk to the defenders.

The ABC–1 agreement did not place the Roosevelt Administration under *political* obligation to enter the war against either Germany or Japan, not even if Japan attacked British or Dutch areas in the Far East. Nor did Roosevelt give a promise to this effect to Churchill when they met at Newfoundland in August, 1941. Up to the very eve of the Japanese assault the President refused to tell the British or Dutch what we would do. In short, the Government kept itself officially free from any obligation to enter the war, certainly free of any obligation to thrust itself into the war.

But I do think this accord conveyed responsibilities of a moral sort. After ABC–1 was adopted, production of weapons in the United States and the British Commonwealth took it into account; and the allocation of weapons, troops, ships, and planes as between threatened areas was based on the expectation that the United States would carry out the assignments set down in the plan.

Thus, it may be fairly thought, Roosevelt and his administration were obligated to try to gain the consent of Congress and the American people to play the part designated in the joint plans if Japanese assaults crossed the land and sea boundaries of resistance that were defined at these joint staff conferences. In the last November weeks when the end of the diplomatic talks with Japan came into sight, and General Marshall and Admiral Stark were asked what measures should be taken in face of the threatened Japanese advances, they advised the President to declare the limits defined at Singapore, and to warn the Japanese that we would fight if these were crossed. There is much reason to think this would have been done even had the Japanese not struck at Pearl Harbor and the Philippines, and this boundary would have been the line between peace and war. But this reaffirmation was made not as a measure required to carry out a secret accord, but because it was believed to be the best course.

A variant explanation of the way we dealt with Japan runs somewhat as follows: that Roosevelt was determined to get into the war against Germany; that he had to find a release from his public promises that the United States would not enter "foreign wars" unless attacked; that his efforts to do so by unneutral aid to Britain and the Soviet Union had failed because Hitler had refused to accept the challenge; and so he sought another door into war, a back door, by inviting or compelling the Japanese attack.

This interpretation, with its kick at the end, twists the record around its own preconception. The actions taken did not flow from a settled wish to get us into war. They trailed along the rim of necessity of the true purpose—which was to sustain resistance against the Axis. How many times the American Government refused to do what the British, French, Chinese, Russians, Dutch asked it to do, because it might involve us in actual combat!

This slant of reasoning about American action passes by the course of Japanese conduct which aroused our fears and stimulated our opposition: the way in which, despite all our pleas and warnings, Japan pressed on. By not recognizing that these Japanese actions called for American counteraction, it excuses them. Thus our resistance is made to appear as nothing else but a deceitful plot to plunge us into war. Furthermore, it dismisses as insincere the patient attempt to calm Japan by diplomatic talks, by offers to join in safeguarding its security.

There were influential individuals in the Roosevelt Administration who wanted to get into the war and indifferent as to how we got into it. Of these, Secretary of the Interior Ickes was, I believe, the most candid, at any rate in his diary entries. Secretary of the Treasury Morgenthau and his staff also had a positive wish that we should engage in war—but against Germany, not against Japan, for that might have brought a diversion of forces to the Pacific. Secretary of War Stimson thought that it would not be possible for Great Britain to sustain the fight unless we entered it; but toward the very end, particularly as it was becoming plain that the Soviet Union was going to survive the Nazi assault, he began to wish for delay. However, time and time again the memoirs and diaries record the impatience of these officials, and those who thought like them, with Hull's caution and Roosevelt's watchful indirection.

The most genuine point made by those who dissent, one that merits thorough analysis, is that the American Government, in conjunction with the British and Dutch, refused to continue to supply Japan with machines and materials vital to it—especially oil. It is contended that they thereby compelled Japan to resort to war, or at least fixed a time period in which Japan was faced with the need of deciding to yield to our terms or go to war.

In reflecting upon this action, the reasons for it must not be confused with the Japanese response to it. Japan showed no signs of curbing its aggressive course. It paid no heed to repeated and friendly warnings that unless it did, the threatened countries would have to take counter-measures. As when on February 14, 1941, while the Lend-Lease Act was being argued in Congress, Dooman, Counsellor of the American Embassy in Japan and known to be a firm and straightforward friend of that country, carried back from Washington the message for the Vice-Minister for Foreign Affairs: that the American people were determined to support Britain even at the risk of war; that if Japan or any other country menaced that effort "it would have to expect to come in conflict with the United States"; and that the United States had abstained from an oil embargo in order not to impel Japan to create a situation that could only lead to the most serious outcome. Japan's answer over the following months had been to force its way further into Indo-China and threaten the Dutch East Indies.

This sustained proof that Japan was going on with its effort to dominate Asia, and the alliance pledging it to stand by Germany if that country got into war with the United States, made a continuation of trade with Japan an act of meekness on our part. Japan was concentrating its foreign purchases on products needed for war, while reducing civilian use by every means, and was thus accumulating great reserve stocks. These were enabling it to maintain its invasion of China without much strain, while continuing to expand its war-making power. Had *effective* restraints—note that I do not say *total* restraints—not been imposed, the American Government would have been in the strange position of having declared an unlimited national emergency, of calling upon the American people to strengthen their army, navy, and air force in great urgency, while at the same time nourishing the opponent that might have to be met in battle. This was a grave, if not intolerable responsibility.

It is hard to tell how squarely the American and British Governments faced the possible consequence of their restrictive measures. My impression is that they knew the danger of war with Japan was being increased; that Japan might try to get by force the means denied it. The Japanese Government served plain warnings that this game of thrust and counterthrust might so end. These were soberly regarded, but did not weaken the will that Japan was not to have its way by threat.

Mingled with the anxiety lest these restrictive measures would make war more likely, there was a real hope that they might be a deterrent to war. Conceivably they would bring home to the Japanese people that if it came to war, they might soon run out of the means for combat, while the rapid growth of American military strength would make it clear that they could not in the end win. And, as evidence of these probabilities became plain, the conciliatory elements in the Japanese Government would prevail over the more militant ones.

This almost happened. But the reckless ones, those who would rather court fatality than accept frustration, managed to retain control of Japanese decision. The pressure applied by us did not prevent war, and may have brought the time of decision for war closer. The valid question, however, is not whether the American Government resorted to these restrictions *in order* to drive Japan to attack; it is whether the American Government failed to grasp a real chance, after the restraints had begun to leave their mark in Japanese official circles, to arrive at a satisfactory understanding that would have averted war. Twice, in the opinion of some qualified students of the subject, such a chance emerged, or at least appeared on the horizon of diplomacy. Were they real opportunities or merely mirages or decoys?

The first of these was the occasion when in the autumn of 1941, the Japanese Prime Minister, Prince Konoye, sought a personal meeting with the President. It is averred that the President's failure to respond lost a chance to avert the war without yielding any American principle or purpose. Some think the reason was that American diplomacy was inflexible, dull in its insight, and too soaked in mistrust. Others, more accusatory, explain the decision by a lack of desire for an agreement that would have thwarted the design for war.

Since there is no conclusive evidence of what Konoye intended to propose or could have achieved, comment on this subject must enter into "the boggy ground of what-might-have-been." Some observers, including Ambassador Grew, believe that Konoye could have made a real, and an irreversible, start toward meeting American terms. It will always be possible to think that this is so. But to the Americans in authority, the chance seemed small. Konoye was a man who in every past crisis had allowed himself to flounder between criss-crossed promises; hence there was good reason to fear an attempt at deception. Such glimpses as we have of what he might have proposed do not support the view that he could have offered a suspension or end of the fight against China. His freedom to negotiate would have been subject to the conditions stated by those who had controlled Japan's course up to then—their price for allowing him to go to meet the President.

Even so, to repeat, it is possible that skilled and more daring American diplomacy might have handled the meeting so as to get a satisfactory accord; or, failing that—and this is the more likely chance—to bring about so deep a division within the Japanese circle of decision as to have prevented warlike action. These alluring historical queries will continue to roam in the land of might-have-been.

But the risks were great. The echoes of Munich and its aftermath were still loud. The American Government might have found itself forced to make a miserable choice: either to accept an accord which would have left Japan free to complete its conquest of China and menace the rest of Asia, or to face a deep division among the American people. Any understanding with Japan that was not clear and decisive would have had unpredictable consequences. The Chinese Government might have felt justified in making a deal following our own. The Soviet Union, at this time just managing with the greatest effort and agony to prevent German victory, might also have chosen to compromise with Hitler rather than to fight it out. Speculations such as these must leave the subject unsettled. But in any case I think it clear that the American decision was one of judgment, not of secret intent. Konoye was not told that the President would not meet with him; he was told that he would not do so until more progress had been made toward defining what the Japanese Government was prepared to propose.

The same basic question had to be faced in the final crisis of negotiation in November, 1941: whether to relax restraints on Japan and leave it in a position to keep on trying to control much of Asia in return for a promise not to press on farther for the time being.

The opinion that the Japanese truce offer made at this last juncture accepted the main purposes and principles for which the American Government had been standing may be summarily dismissed. It was ambiguously worded, it was silent about the alliance with Germany, and it would have required the American Government to end its support of China—for the last of its numbered five points read: "The Government of the United States undertakes to refrain from such measures and actions as will be prejudicial to the endeavors for the restoration of general peace between Japan and China." This scant and unclear proposal was at once deemed "entirely unacceptable." Furthermore, there seemed little use and much possible damage in making a counter truce-offer of the same variety. The intercepted Japanese messages stated flatly that this was Japan's last and best offer. They told of the swift dismissal of a much more nearly acceptable one that Nomura and Kurusu asked their superiors in Tokyo to consider. A deadline had been set. Thus it was all but sure that the reduced counter-offer which had been patched together in Washington would be unheeded. But it might shake the coalition to which by then the opponents of the Axis had pledged their lives and national destinies.

This seems to have been the thought uppermost in Hull's mind in recommending to the President that the counter truce-offer be withheld. As set down in his historic memo of November 26, he had been led to this conclusion by the opposition of the Chinese, the half-hearted support or actual opposition of the British, Dutch, and Australian governments, and the further excited opposition to be expected because of lack of appreciation of the importance and value of a truce. This I believe to have been the true determining reason for a decision reluctantly taken. Even if by then Japan was genuinely ready for reform, the repentance had come too late. The situation had grown too entangled by then for minor measures, its momentum too great. Germany-Italy-Japan had forced the creation of a defensive coalition more vast than the empire of the Pacific for which Japan plotted. This was not now to be quieted or endangered by a temporary halt along the fringe of the Japanese advance.

Even though these reasons for dropping the idea of a truce may seem sufficient, they leave the question why the American Government could not have given a softer and less declaratory answer. Why had it to give one so "bleakly uncompromising"? It could have said simply that the Japanese offer did not convey the assurances that would warrant us and the alliance for which we spoke to resume the shipment of war materials to Japan and end our aid to China. Why was it deemed advisable or essential at this juncture to state fully and forcibly our maximum terms for a settlement in the Pacific? Was it foreseen that, scanned with mistrust as it would almost surely be, this would be construed as a demand for the swift abandonment of Japan's whole program? Was it done, as the accusation runs, with the deliberate intent of banning any last chance for an accord? Of propelling the Japanese attack?

That this was not the reason I am as sure as anyone can be on a matter of this sort; but I can offer only conjecture as to what the inspiring purposes were. Perhaps to vindicate past actions and decisions. Perhaps a wish to use the dramatic chance to put in the record a statement of the aims for which the risk of war was being accepted, and of the basis on which the Americans would found the peace when the time came. Such an idea was in accord with the usual mode of thought of the men in charge of the Executive Branch of the Government and of most of the American people. It gave vent to the propensity exemplified in Hull to find a base in general principles meant to be at once political standards and moral ideals. After long caution, it appealed as a defiant contradiction of the Axis program. All this, however, is surmise rather than evidenced history.

But I think it is well within the realm of evidenced history that the memo of November 26 was not in any usual sense of the word an ultimatum. It did not threaten the Japanese with war or any other form of forceful punishment if our terms were not accepted. It simply left them in the state of distress in which they were, with the prospect that they might later have to submit to our requirements. The Japanese Government could have, as Konoye and Nomura pleaded with it to do, allowed the situation to drag along, with or without resuming talks with the American Government. Its power to make war would have been depleted, but neither quickly nor crucially. The armed forces and even the position in China could have been maintained.

Notably, the final Japanese answer which ended negotiations on December 7, 1941, does not accuse the American Government of confronting it with an ultimatum, but only of thwarting the larger Japanese aims. Part 14—the clinching part of this note—reads: "Obviously it is the intention of the American Government to conspire with Great Britain and other countries to obstruct Japan's efforts toward the establishment of peace through the creation of a New Order in East Asia, and especially to preserve Anglo-American rights and interests by keeping Japan and China at war. This intention has been revealed clearly during the course of the present negotiations. Thus, the earnest hope of the Japanese Government to adjust Japanese-American relations and to preserve and promote the peace of the Pacific through coöperation with the American Government has finally been lost."

This is a more nearly accurate description of the purposes of the American Government under Roosevelt than those attributed to it by hostile and suspicious American critics. Our Government did obstruct Japanese efforts, believing them to be unjust, cruel, and a threat to our national security, especially after Japan became a partner with Hitler's Germany and Mussolini's Italy and bent its efforts toward bringing the world under their combined control.

This determination stood on the proposition that it was better to take the risks of having to share in the suffering of the war than of finding ourselves moved or compelled to fight a more desperate battle against the Axis later on. The American Government, I believe, knew how serious a risk of war was being taken. But in its addresses to the American people it chose to put in the forefront the perils we would face if the Axis won, and to leave in the background, even to camouflage, the risks of finding ourselves plunged into wars which during the election campaign it had promised would not occur. Whether any large number of Americans were fooled by this, or whether most of them, in reality, were content to have the prospect presented that way rather than in a more blunt and candid way, I do not know.

This essay in interpretation has compelled me to recall and stress the aggressive Japanese assault—though I should have been glad to let that slip into the past. The passage of time does not alter facts, but it can bring a fuller and calmer understanding of them. It frees the mind for fairer appreciation of the causes and circumstances which impelled Japan along its tragic course and which impelled us to resist it. For both countries there are many common lessons. One of them is that continued friendliness requires mutual effort to relieve the other, to the extent it can, of deep cause for anxiety—the Japanese people of their anxiety over the means of living decently, the American people of anxiety about their security and power to defend the free world. Another is that they must both feel, speak, and act so honestly and steadily that their view of each other will be cleared of mistrust, and brightened by trust.

23 / Unconditional Surrender Reconsidered

John L. Chase

In 1943, President Roosevelt announced that the United States, and, in effect, the United Nations were committed to continuing the Second World War until the Axis governments would agree to an unconditional surrender. Roosevelt's announcement served notice that the terms of peace were not negotiable, its principles not subject to compromise. Though advocating unconditional surrender, Roosevelt in no way embraced the notion of a harsh, vindictive or punitive peace settlement. Probably no decision by the United Nations affecting the Axis powers has proved so controversial then and now as the decision for unconditional surrender. In the following article, John Chase explains the many long- and short-range advantages that could accrue to the United States and the United Nations from the policy of unconditional surrender. He suggests that the tactical, immediate benefits to be derived while the war was still in progress served to cut off public discussion of peace terms. Here is a reasoned defense of this policy.

For further reading: Anne K. Armstrong, *Unconditional Surrender: The Import of the Casablanca Policy Upon World War II* (New Brunswick: 1961); Robert J. C. Butow, *Japan's Decision to Surrender* (Stanford: 1954); Robert Divine, *Second Chance: The Triumph of Internationalism in America During World War II* (New York: 1967); Herbert Feis, *Roosevelt, Churchill, Stalin: The War They Waged and the Peace They Sought* (Princeton: 1957); Oscar J. Hammen, "The Ashes of Yalta," *South Atlantic Quarterly*, LIII (October, 1954), 477–484; Ruth B. Russell, *A History of the United Nations Charter: The Role of the United States 1940–1945* (Washington: 1958); John L. Snell (editor), *The Meaning of Yalta* (Baton Rouge: 1956).

Of all American policies during the period of World War II, that of unconditional surrender toward the Axis Powers appears to have given rise to the most controversy and adverse comment. Secretary Hull has revealed that he opposed it, the psycholog-

John L. Chase has been a member of the staff, United States Office of Education in the Planning, Evaluation and Reports Section. He has also taught at the University of North Carolina. This article is reprinted with the permission of the editors of the *Political Science Quarterly*. From the *Political Science Quarterly*, LXX (June 1955).

ical warfare specialists obviously had difficulties with it, and even Mr. Churchill has commented on it at least twice—and with somewhat confusing effect.[1] In the United States the prominent military analyst Hanson Baldwin took exception to the policy some time ago in a book,[2] and more recently he has returned to the attack in an article aimed at a wider audience.[3] Plainly, the issues involved are by no means dead, and perhaps cannot even be laid to rest easily.

In spite of the frequency of previous discussions of the subject, there is in them something not entirely satisfactory from the scholarly point of view. In the first place, much of the adverse comment has been made in the heat of the immediate post-war period, and seems to be related directly to the authors' satisfaction or indignation with post-war American policy in Germany.[4] Secondly, the dispute over the consequences has left one really important aspect of the problem untouched— namely, the way in which it grew out of the actual historical context of the times, and especially President Roosevelt's reasons for endorsing it. Thus little attention has been given to the problem of understanding a major problem in American foreign policy as an American decision. Finally, a good deal has been published recently on the war period, and some of this new material is relevant to the problem involved. For all of these reasons, it is thought worth while to reconsider the policy.

I. THE ORIGINS OF "UNCONDITIONAL SURRENDER"

In his *Atlantic* article Mr. Baldwin repeats, with some new material, the earliest recollection of Mr. Churchill that he first heard the term "unconditional surrender" from the lips of the President at the joint press conference held by the two leaders at Casablanca. Relying also on the study by Matloff and Snell,[5] Mr. Baldwin declares that "unconditional surrender was laid down as a *diktat*—a one-man decision— without any study of its political or military implications and was announced publicly and unilaterally at a press conference to the surprise of the nation's chief ally, Great Britain."[6]

As Mr. Churchill subsequently acknowledged, his first recollection of the episode proved somewhat inaccurate. Elliott Roosevelt, who was present at the conference as an aide to his father, first challenged the "suprise" nature of the announcement when he wrote that at a luncheon *prior* to the press conference, the President tried out the slogan on the Prime Minister. He stated that

> . . . it was at that lunch table that the phrase "unconditional surrender" was born. For what it was worth, it can be recorded that it was Father's phrase, that Harry Hopkins took an immediate and strong liking to it, and that Churchill, while

[1] Secretary Hull's comments may be found in his *Memoirs* (New York, 1948), pp. 1570 *et seq.*; James Warburg's views seem to represent those of some of the psychological warfare specialists, as in his *Germany—Bridge or Battleground* (New York, 1946), Appendix II, pp. 259–265; Mr. Churchill's statements will be cited in detail later.

[2] *Great Mistakes of the War* (New York, 1949), pp. 14–25.

[3] "Churchill Was Right," *The Atlantic*, vol. 194, no. 1 (July 1954).

[4] This view is naturally strongest among the Germans themselves. See Baldwin, *Great Mistakes*, pp. 22–23.

[5] Maurice Matloff and Edwin M. Snell, *United States Army in World War II. The War Department: Strategic Planning for Coalition Warfare, 1941–1942* (Washington, 1953).

[6] Baldwin, "Churchill Was Right," p. 27.

he slowly munched a mouthful of food, thought, frowned, thought, finally grinned, and at length announced, "Perfect! And I can just see how Goebbels and the rest of 'em 'll squeal."[7]

Mr. Churchill subsequently took note of this variant account, and stated that later research in his own files confirmed Elliott's impression that the whole matter had been discussed previously. Apparently it was even earlier than Elliott believed, however, for Mr. Churchill prints a report of his to the Deputy Prime Minister and War Cabinet, dated January 20, 1943, in which he stated:

> I would like to know what the War Cabinet would think of our including in this statement to the press a declaration of the firm intention of the United States and the British Empire to continue the war relentlessly until we have brought about the "unconditional surrender" of Germany and Japan. The omission of Italy would be to encourage a break-up there. The President liked this idea, and it would stimulate our friends in every country.[8]

Mr. Churchill adds that, in the Cabinet discussion which followed receipt of his message, it was not the principle itself which was questioned, but the possibility of making the exception in favor of Italy. The Cabinet definitely opposed any such exception. Mr. Churchill continues that he had neither record nor recollection of any conversation with the President on the matter subsequent to his receiving the views of the War Cabinet. He makes it clear that both he and the President approved the official communiqué, which had been prepared by the various staffs, and which contained no reference to unconditional surrender, and that the War Cabinet had also approved this.[9]

Mr. Churchill confesses his surprise at hearing the President use the phrase at the press conference. He says that "It was natural to suppose that the agreed communiqué had superseded anything said in conversation," and that General Ismay, who was well acquainted with his thoughts, was also surprised.[10] But he quotes the President's own explanation, as given by Robert Sherwood, as finally disposing of the matter:

> Roosevelt himself absolved Churchill from all responsibility for the statement. Indeed, he suggested that it was an unpremeditated one on his own part. "We had so much trouble getting those two French generals [DeGaulle and Giraud] together that I thought to myself that this was as difficult as arranging the meeting of Grant and Lee—and then suddenly the press conference was on, and Winston and I had had no time to prepare for it, and the thought popped into my mind that they had called Grant 'Old Unconditional Surrender' and the next thing I knew I had said it."[11]

Sherwood comments that for some reason or other the President liked to cultivate the impression of himself as "a rather frivolous fellow who did not give sufficient attention to the consequences of chance remarks."[12] As applied to this particular case,

[7] Elliott Roosevelt, *As He Saw It* (New York, 1946), p. 117.

[8] Winston S. Churchill, *The Second World War: The Hinge of Fate* (Boston, 1950), p. 684.

[9] *Ibid.,* pp. 685–686.

[10] *Ibid.,* pp. 686–687.

[11] Quoted in part by Churchill, *ibid.,* p. 687, and in Robert Sherwood, *Roosevelt and Hopkins: An Intimate History* (New York, 1948), p. 696. It is somewhat strange that in his book Hanson Baldwin recognizes the error in Churchill's first recollection and the correctness of Elliott Roosevelt's account, while in his article he does not. The point would seem to be important enough to emphasize, even in a popular account.

[12] Sherwood, *op. cit.,* p. 696.

however, two well-known facts have to be weighed against the accuracy of any such characterization. One is the fact that the President spoke from notes, and these—which were not allowed to be quoted—contained the following statement:

> The President and the Prime Minister . . . are more than ever determined that peace can come to the world only by a total elimination of German and Japanese war power. This involves the simple formula of placing the objective of this war in terms of an unconditional surrender by Germany, Italy, and Japan. Unconditional surrender by them means a reasonable assurance of world peace, for generations. Unconditional surrender means not the destruction of the German populace, nor of the Italian or Japanese populace, but does mean the destruction of a philosophy in Germany, Italy and Japan which is based on the conquest and subjugation of other peoples.[13]

It might be suggested that the President's notes also may have been composed only a few minutes prior to the press conference, so that their existence does not disprove the unpremediated nature of the phrase. As against this, however, we have the evidence of Churchill's own memorandum to the War Cabinet, dated January 20, and including the vital phrase, while the press conference did not occur until four days later.[14] The evidence seems incontrovertible, therefore, that the President had been thinking about the phrase for at least several days before the public announcement.

A second reason mentioned by Sherwood for believing the President's selection of the phrase to have been a carefully considered one is his determined resistance to any modification of it. Objection to it came from many sources: from Secretary Hull, from some of the American psychological warfare specialists, from the War Department, from the British Foreign Office, and even, after the Teheran Conference, from the Soviet government.[15] Despite all the pressure, however, the President clung determinedly to his position, and would not consent to any modification of the principle. Plainly, then, as Sherwood says, the announcement was no casual slip of the tongue, but "very deeply deliberated," and "a true statement of Roosevelt's considered policy."[16] Further, "One thing about Roosevelt's statement is certain. . .—he had his eyes wide open when he made it."[17]

Since the President insisted on retention of the policy over so much opposition, it seems clear that in his own mind it must have served some very basic function, or have entailed some very definite advantages. Careful analysis of the available records indicates that the slogan did, in fact, have such a basic function in the over-all development of American policy, and there were very considerable advantages in it from the President's point of view. The main function, briefly stated, was to impose a damper on premature discussion of the post-war settlement, and the advantages related to three areas, the existing German government and the German people, the policy of the Soviet government, and the attitude of the American people toward the winning of the war. In the following sections the relevance of the policy to each of these subjects is examined in greater detail.

[13] *Ibid.,* pp. 696–697.
[14] Elliott Roosevelt, *op. cit.,* pp. 117–121.
[15] Hull makes his own lack of agreement clear, and also mentions other examples of opposition to the phrase in his discussion, *op. cit.,* pp. 1570 *et seq.*
[16] Sherwood, *op. cit.,* p. 696.
[17] *Ibid.,* p. 697.

II. UNCONDITIONAL SURRENDER AND THE GERMAN GOVERNMENT

The most immediate and obvious bearing of the unconditional surrender policy was its relation to Germany and the ending of the war. Sherwood has stated the President's view on this point as follows:

> What Roosevelt was saying was that there would be no negotiated peace, no compromise with Nazism and Fascism, no "escape clauses" provided by another Fourteen Points which could lead to another Hitler. (The ghost of Woodrow Wilson was again at his shoulder.) Roosevelt wanted this uncompromising purpose brought home to the American people and the Russians and the Chinese, and to the people of France and other occupied nations, and he wanted it brought home to the Germans—that neither by continuance of force nor by contrivance of a new spirit of sweet reasonableness could their present leaders gain for them a soft peace. He wanted to ensure that when the war was won it would stay won.[18]

Sherwood goes on to explain that it was particularly important for the President to stress the uncompromising nature of American policy toward the Nazis at this time because of the "uproar over Darlan and Peyrouton," and the fears of the enemies of Fascism everywhere that this might indicate an American willingness to compromise and to accept less than the total defeat of the enemy.[19] This interpretation of the policy stresses primarily its importance as a statement of the attitude: No negotiated peace with existing enemy governments!

An additional, complementary interpretation of the policy, also bearing on Germany, has been suggested by Wallace Carroll, formerly Deputy Director of the Overseas Branch of the Office of War Information. He quotes an anonymous source—a person present at the Casablanca Conference, as having been told by the President that

> . . . he wanted to rule out any pledge or offer like the Fourteen Points and still convey to the enemy peoples the idea that they would be treated generously by the Allies. He thought that the story of Grant and Lee at Appamatox would convey this idea . . . what he especially wanted to bring out was Grant's gesture in letting the Confederates keep their horses. The President felt that this incident from American history would help the enemy peoples to realize that they were facing chivalrous foes who did not desire to impoverish them or humiliate them, but who would treat them with magnanimity. *That is, he meant to reassure the peoples of enemy countries about Allied intentions, not to terrorize them.*[20]

To those who have associated the President with the Morgenthau Plan, this hypothesis will seem both novel and improbable. Nevertheless, it is borne out by a number of the President's later statements, of which the following is typical: "In our uncompromising policy we mean no harm to the common people of the Axis nations. But we do mean to impose punishment and retribution in full upon their guilty, barbaric leaders."[21]

[18] *Ibid.* Sherwood's interpretation is borne out by the President's remarks on two subsequent occasions. See Samuel I. Rosenmann, *Public Papers and Addresses of Franklin D. Roosevelt* (New York, 1948), 1943 volume, Item 10, pp. 59–60; and 1944–45 volume, Item 55, p. 210.

[19] Sherwood, *op. cit.,* p. 697.

[20] Wallace Carroll, *Persuade or Perish* (Boston, 1948), p. 309. Italics mine.

[21] Hull, *op. cit.,* p. 1571.

The foregoing statement was made in February 1943. Late in August of the same year, in what seemed a clear reference to the Atlantic Charter, the President declared:

> Except for the responsible fascist leaders, the people of the Axis need not fear unconditional surrender to the United Nations. . . . The people of the Axis-controlled areas may be assured that when they agree to unconditional surrender they will not be trading Axis despotism for ruin under the United Nations. The goal of the United Nations is to permit liberated peoples to create a free political life of their own choosing and to attain economic security.[22]

That the policy did not exclude the probability of generous Allied action was also emphasized by the President in his exchanges with Hull. On two occasions the President said that the best definition of the policy was exemplified by Lee's surrender to Grant. Lee had relied upon Grant's fairness, and Grant had responded with a generous gesture. On one occasion the President added that "both the German people and Russia" should be told what this "best definition" meant.[23] On the other, the President added the apparently contradictory thought: "That is the spirit I should like to see abroad—but it does not apply to Germany. Germany understands only one kind of language."[24]

But, taken in its context, the latter statement makes clear that what the President meant was that the Germans would misconstrue as a sign of weakness any magnanimous gesture *in advance* of unconditional surrender. Is it possible to disagree with him in this?

The similarity between the President's view and that of the Prime Minister on this point should be clear from the following explanation by Mr. Churchill:

> The term "unconditional surrender" does not mean that the German people will be enslaved or destroyed. It means however that the Allies will not be bound to them at the moment of surrender by any pact or obligation. There will be, for instance, no question of the Atlantic Charter applying to Germany as a matter of right and barring territorial transferences or adjustments in enemy countries. . . . If we are bound, we are bound by our own consciences to civilization. We are not bound to the Germans as the result of a bargain struck. That is the meaning of "unconditional surrender."[25]

It only remains to point out that, so far as the example of Lee's surrender to Grant was concerned, the example did nothing to clarify the President's intention. One reason is that the President's recollection was, unfortunately, somewhat erroneous. As Carroll has explained,

> . . . the President bungled the announcement of the decision. The correspondents at Casablanca were not permitted to quote his words directly and it is therefore impossible to ascertain exactly what he said. From the newspaper accounts it appears that he may have mentioned Grant, but he forgot to mention Lee and the horses. Those American correspondents and newspapers which sought to explain what he had in mind assumed that he referred to Grant's letter to General

---

[22] *Ibid.*

[23] *Ibid.*, p. 1574. The President repeated the illustration at considerable length in a press conference late in July 1944. *Cf.* Rosenmann, *op. cit.*, 1944–45 volume, Item 55, pp. 209–211.

[24] Hull, *op. cit.*, p. 1576.

[25] Churchill, *Hinge of Fate,* pp. 690–691.

> Buckner. . . . Grant's demand for unconditional surrender at that time had not
> been tempered by an act of magnanimity. Consequently, Allied propagandists,
> who received all their news of the Conference from the press, never got the point
> of the generous gesture to the defeated foe.[26]

Carroll adds that when the President again used the example in his exchanges with Hull, "Secretary Hull forgot to pass it on to the Office of War Information."[27]

It seems clear, then, that so far as Germany was concerned the unconditional surrender policy was intended to inform the world—Germans, Americans, and everyone else—that the Allies would accept nothing less than the complete defeat of existing enemy governments, and would not bargain or compromise with them. Both the President and Mr. Churchill agreed on this, and both went out of their way to explain that this did *not* mean a policy of unnecessary harshness or vindictiveness toward the common people of the Axis nations.

So much, then, for the President's purpose where Germany was concerned. The question has often been raised as to the effect of the policy in Germany, and the allegation has been made that the policy unnecessarily prolonged the war.[28] This question is probably too large to be discussed in detail here, but a few pertinent considerations may be mentioned. The first and most obvious point is that there is no necessary connection between the unconditional surrender formula and the "Morgenthau Plan," which in point of time came almost two years later. Either one could have been adopted without the other, although most of the critics treat them as identical.[29] But it seems evident that one could accept unconditional surrender without accepting Mr. Morgenthau's ideas—as in fact Secretary Stimson appears to have done.

A second point is also worth consideration. Many of the critics of the policy appear to place overly great emphasis on the effect of mere propaganda alone, divorcing stated aims of policy from the effects of actual wartime conditions. Allen Dulles, however, in commenting upon American policy in Germany, couples the two significantly when he says:

> Our propaganda consisted of the slogan "unconditional surrender," and was
> coupled with the bombing of German cities, high civilian casualties and the de-
> struction of thousands of workers' dwellings. That this type of bombing came only
> from the west made a deep impression on the German masses who ascribed it to
> a deliberate difference in policy between East and West. They overlooked the
> fact that Russian aviation was not adapted to that type of bombing. . . .[30]

Dulles' point is, it seems to me, well taken. The critics decry unconditional surrender, but do not suggest that our strategy with respect to bombing should have been different. The implication is that a mere difference in words would have been greatly to the American advantage. It seems hard to believe that Goebbels would

---

[26] Carroll, *op. cit.*, pp. 310–311. A transcript of the press conference, corroborating Carroll's observation, is printed by Rosenmann, *op. cit.*, 1943 volume, Item 6, pp. 37 *et seq.*

[27] Carroll, *op. cit.*, p. 317.

[28] This is Hanson Baldwin's view, in both his book and later article.

[29] Baldwin states that "The Casablanca policy came to logical fruition in the Morgenthau 'pastoral Germany' policy at Quebec. . . ." *Great Mistakes*, p. 24. For a fuller discussion of the Morgenthau Plan and the Quebec conference, see the author's "The Development of the Morgenthau Plan through the Quebec Conference," *Journal of Politics*, vol. 16, No. 2 (May 1954).

[30] Allen W. Dulles, *Germany's Underground* (New York, 1947), p. 168.

have had any greater difficulty countering such a policy than he had with the actually existing one. The argument strains credulity a bit too far.

It is interesting to note Churchill's response to this kind of criticism. "It is false to suggest," he wrote, "that it [i.e., unconditional surrender] prolonged the war. Negotiation with Hitler was impossible. He was a maniac with supreme power to play his hand out to the end, which he did; and so did we."[31]

Finally, admitting that the present discussion is not conclusive, Sherwood's comment is pertinent that

> It is a matter of record that the Italians and the Japanese were ready to accept unconditional surrender as soon as effective force was applied to their homelands. Whether they might have done so sooner, or whether the Germans might ever have done so, under any circumstances whatsoever, are matters for eternal speculation.[32]

III. UNCONDITIONAL SURRENDER AND THE SOVIET GOVERNMENT

So important an aim as unconditional surrender must also, obviously, have been considered for its bearing on other Allies, and particularly the Soviet government. In this connection it should be recalled that only six months prior to the Casablanca Conference the United States had intervened forcibly in the Anglo-Soviet treaty negotiations. At the outset of these negotiations, Churchill had been willing to pledge British support for a guaranty of Soviet territorial acquisitions made during the period of the Nazi-Soviet pact. But the President, with Woodrow Wilson and the secret treaties of World War I clearly in mind, had intervened to prevent any discussion of commitments with regard to territorial issues in post-war Europe.[33] Nevertheless the question, so long as it was not finally disposed of, was bound to hang heavily over the future, and to exert an unsettling effect on the policies of all the Allies. One of the major consequences of the unconditional surrender policy was to reinforce the ban on any such premature discussion, and to forestall any further demand to reach a territorial settlement, which the United States could not support, before the ending of the war.

The policy also had another important bearing on the relations of the two Western Powers to Russia. It may be recalled that in May of 1942 the United States and Britain had made a rather tenuous promise to the Soviets to open a second front in Western Europe in 1942.[34] Subsequently, some misunderstanding developed over the implementation of this commitment. In August 1942, Mr. Churchill felt it necessary to make a special trip to Moscow to explain to Stalin why the front could not be created that year.[35] Following his visit, and in part as the result of a curtailment of western supplies to Russia made necessary by the planned invasion of Africa, the Soviets became very uncommunicative. In October there were indications, according to Mr. Churchill, that the Russians feared a British attempt to negotiate a separate

[31] Sherwood, *op. cit.*, p. 696.

[32] *Ibid.*, p. 697.

[33] *Ibid.*, pp. 401 *et seq.*; Churchill, *The Second World War: The Grand Alliance* (Boston, 1950), pp. 528 *et seq.*; and Hull, *op. cit.*, pp. 1165 *et seq.*

[34] See Sherwood, *op. cit.*, p. 577, and Churchill, *Hinge of Fate*, pp. 341–342.

[35] Churchill, *Hinge of Fate*, pp. 472–502.

peace with Germany. In November, a combination of rain and German reinforcements caused the western campaign in North Africa to bog down.[36]

In the light of these developments, and accompanying Russian suspicion, it was perhaps not surprising that Stalin found it impossible to leave Moscow to participate in the Casablanca Conference. His reply to the urgings of Roosevelt and Churchill made it clear that he still felt that the next western move should be ". . .a second front in Europe. . .by the joint forces of Great Britain and the United States of America in the spring of the next year."[37]

At the Casablanca Conference itself, western strategy for the rest of 1943 was agreed upon by the combined staffs and political leaders. General Marshall and Harry Hopkins wanted the main objective to be the invasion of northern France, but they were overruled.[38] Instead, it was agreed to advance on Sicily next, and to secure the Mediterranean lines of communication and air bases. It did not require very careful reading between the lines of the Combined Chiefs' report on "The Conduct of the War in 1943" to perceive that the invasion of Western Europe had again come off second- or even third-best.[39]

In view of this background, one can better appreciate the force of Wallace Carroll's argument that the policy of unconditional surrender was designed to take the sting out of the further postponement of the European front. In his opinion,

> The Russians had been displeased by the failure of the British and Americans to open a "second front" in Western Europe in 1942, and it seemed likely at Casablanca that they would be still more displeased when they learned that the decision had been taken to invade Italy, ruling out the possibility of a western front in 1943. The announcement of a policy of no compromise and no bargaining by the western Allies would therefore help to counter Russian suspicions.[40]

Carroll goes on to argue that the Russians agreed to unconditional surrender as "basic policy," and wanted to modify it later only because they considered it "bad tactics" to insist on it "in public."[41] Without it, Soviet suspicions of treachery and double-dealing could not have been allayed; "with it, they [i.e., the Western Allies] exposed themselves to a few gentle complaints that they were being unnecessarily stern in their propaganda."[42]

Carroll's interpretation is borne out in all respects not only by the facts already cited, but also by two remarks of the President as reported by his son Elliott, who was present at the time. The first occurred at the previously mentioned luncheon with Mr. Churchill:

> Father, once his phrase had been approved by the others, speculated about its effect in another direction.
> "Of course, it's just the thing for the Russians. Unconditional surrender," he repeated . . ., "Uncle Joe might have made it up himself."[43]

[36] Ibid., pp. 569, 575, 577 and 660–667.

[37] Ibid., pp. 662 et seq. and 667.

[38] Sherwood, op. cit., pp. 674–675.

[39] The official agreement of the Combined Chiefs is given by Churchill, Hinge of Fate, pp. 692–693.

[40] Carroll, op. cit., p. 312.

[41] Ibid., p. 333.

[42] Ibid., p. 334.

[43] Elliott Roosevelt, op. cit., p. 117.

The second was a conversation between the President and his son, in which Mr. Roosevelt discoursed philosophically about the disagreements on invasion strategy between the American and British chiefs, and the nature of the agreement reached:

> . . . Father was to tell me about the rocky path the Combined Chiefs had travelled to reach the plan for the invasion of Sicily; he was to complain, but philosophically, about the continuing British insistence on striking Europe from the south rather than from the west; he was to note his misgivings as to Stalin's attitude when the news arrived of a further postponement of the invasion cross-channel; he was to comment that "Wars are uncertain affairs. To win this one, we must maintain a difficult unity with one ally by apparently letting another down. To win this war, we have been forced into a strategic compromise which will most certainly offend the Russians, so that later we will be able in turn to force a compromise which will most certainly offend the British. The compelling needs of war dictate a difficult course."[44]

Finally, one might note that the official communiqué of the conference made a great point of Stalin's having been invited to join the other two leaders. It added that

> The President and Prime Minister realized up to the full the enormous weight of the war which Russia is successfully bearing along her whole land front, and their prime object has been to draw as much weight as possible off the Russian armies by engaging the enemy as heavily as possible at the best selected points. Premier Stalin has been fully informed of the military proposals.[45]

The evidence on this aspect of the policy now seems conclusive. Unconditional surrender served the important function not only of reinforcing the ban on premature discussion of post-war territorial issues, but also of reassuring the Russians that, in spite of necessary delays over the opening of the second front, it was still the Western determination to press on unremittingly to victory, in fulfillment of Allied commitments, as soon as the physical forces could be assembled to do the job.[46]

It only remains to point out that from the standpoint of satisfying the Russians the policy was not, and indeed could not be, completely satisfactory. Nothing short of the second front itself could have been. Stalin's reply to the conference message of Roosevelt and Churchill made this crystal-clear. He said: "It is my understanding that by the decisions you have taken you have set yourselves the task of crushing Germany by the opening of a Second Front in Europe in 1943 and I should be very obliged for information concerning the actual operations planned for this purpose. . . ."[47]

But it seems evident that the policy did convince the Russians of the Western determination to get on with the war as fast as possible, and in this respect the

---

[44] *Ibid.*, p. 109.

[45] Rosenmann, *Public Papers*, 1943 volume, Item 7, p. 50.

[46] Professor William L. Langer has expressed essentially the same view as follows: ". . . the Soviet leaders were quite as suspicious of their Allies as we were of them. Whether sincerely or otherwise, they took the line that refusal to open a second front was an indication of unwillingness to crush the Nazi power or permit Communist Russia an unqualified victory. It was this mutual suspicion and constant recrimination more than anything else that lay behind the demand for unconditional surrender. . . ." "Turning Points of the War: Political Problems of a Coalition," *Foreign Affairs*, vol. 26, No. 1 (October 1947), p. 84.

[47] Sherwood, *op. cit.*, p. 701.

policy, as President Roosevelt hoped, averted a threat to Allied unity at a crucial moment.[48]

The subsequent record of Soviet pronouncements with regard to unconditional surrender bears out this interpretation. Stalin endorsed the policy in his Order of the Day of May 1, 1943.[49] Soviet objections to it were not voiced until the Teheran Conference. By that time, however, the Western Allies were fully committed to the opening of the western front, so that the Russians may well have figured that the policy had served its main immediate purpose. It is a notable fact that even at Teheran the Russian objections were based upon tactical considerations, and that their situation was in this respect less happy than that of the Western Allies, whose tactical problem was to convince the Germans of their deadly seriousness, not of their humaneness.[50] On the whole it can be said that at the time it was announced, and until the tactical, propaganda argument could seem more important, the Soviets accepted unconditional surrender as the President apparently hoped and felt they would. In this respect the policy was clearly successful, and achieved what it was designed to do.

IV. UNCONDITIONAL SURRENDER AND AMERICAN PUBLIC OPINION

The final advantage of the policy in the President's mind undoubtedly lay in the fact that it helped to preserve American unity of feeling, both within itself and in relation to our major Allies. This emerges clearly not only from the President's own remarks, but also from those of persons close to him. So far as the President's own thoughts are concerned, his clearest explanation of the policy was in his address to the White House Correspondents' Association, two and a half weeks after the Casablanca Conference.

In that speech the President referred to his talks with American servicemen abroad, and to their concern "about the state of the home front." Diplomatically the President suggested that the reports of grumbling over petty discomforts, the self-seeking and the profiteering were "gross exaggerations," and that "the people as a whole in the United States are in this war to see it through with heart and body and soul." The President felt that the faultfinders and "pettifoggers" could not obscure the fact that "one of the major battles of the war" was impending in North Africa, and that this fact revealed "not merely cooperation but active collaboration between the United Nations." He mentioned the likelihood of heavy casualties, and the necessity for facing this prospect with the same courage as that of the men on the battlefield.[51]

Turning to the Axis propagandists, the President ridiculed their efforts to divide the United Nations by trying "to create the idea that if we win the war, Russia, and England, and China, and the United States are going to get into a cat-and-dog fight."[52] This, said the President,

---

[48] Hans Speier takes the same view as Langer, but adds that the policy may also have served as a warning to the Russians to stop flirting with the National Committee "Free Germany" and the Union of German Officers. "War Aims in Political Warfare," *Social Research: An International Quarterly of Political and Social Science*, vol. 12, No. 2 (May 1945), pp. 157–180.

[49] Embassy of the U.S.S.R., *Information Bulletin*, No. 47, May 4, 1943, p. 1.

[50] Carroll, *op. cit.*, pp. 314–315.

[51] Rosenmann, *Public Papers*, 1943 volume, Item 16, pp. 74–77.

[52] *Ibid.*, p. 79.

. . . is their final effort to turn one Nation against another, in the vain hope that they may settle with one or two at a time—that any of us may be so gullible and so forgetful as to be duped into making "deals" at the expense of the allies.

To these panicky attempts . . . we say—all the United Nations say—that the only terms on which we shall deal with any Axis Government . . . are the terms proclaimed at Casablanca: "unconditional surrender." . . .

The Nazis must be frantic . . . if they believe that they can devise any propaganda that would turn the British and the American and the Chinese Governments and peoples against Russia—or Russia against the rest of us.[53]

Finally, the President said that the "tragedy of the war has sharpened the vision and leadership" of all the United Nations, and from this there resulted the conviction of "the utter necessity of our standing together after the war to secure a peace based on principles of permanence."[54]

It would be difficult to find a clearer example of the crucial rôle played by unconditional surrender in the President's grand strategy of the war. In the President's mind, unquestionably, preservation of American unity of opinion was an indispensable condition both of victory and of success in the peace to follow. The two major threats to this unity, as the President saw it, were: domestic indifference, arising from a failure to grasp the nature of the issues in this total war; and international resentment and hostility arising from a conflict of aims between the United States and, above all other Allies, the Soviet Union. In his address the President tried to deal with both these threats, explicitly and directly. He emphasized "our determination to fight this war through to the finish,"[55] and he stressed the preservation of unity between all the allies as the indispensable condition of victory. Of course the two objectives were intimately related. Any relaxation of effort short of victory, on the home front, would result in disunity between the Allies; and any evidence of disunity—such as might arise from putting forward conflicting post-war aims—might well produce a relaxation of effort short of victory.

In this connection it seems somewhat strange to this writer that no mention has been made—by either Sherwood, Churchill or Baldwin—of the controversial rôle played by "unconditional surrender" in World War I, and especially in the anti-Wilson speeches of Theodore Roosevelt. But the President's own memory was apparently not so short and, as Sherwood observes, the ghost of Woodrow Wilson was often at his shoulder. Indeed, in retrospect it may well be asked, what better device could be imagined to serve the President's purpose than the very slogan popularized by the "bitter-enders" in the previous war? Surely the President's political genius never burned more brightly than when he rescued this phrase from oblivion, and made it serve American purposes.[56]

Additional evidence of the President's views may be gathered from the remarks of some of the President's associates. Wallace Carroll mentions the President's well-known aversion to stating positively any war aims at all, and the fact that the President gave the war the uninspiring name, "The Survival War." According to Carroll

[53] *Ibid.*, pp. 79–80.

[54] *Ibid.*, p. 80.

[55] This was the thought which, the President said at the beginning of his speech, was "uppermost in our minds." *Ibid.*, p. 72.

[56] For an excellent study of the earlier controversy, see Earl S. Pomeroy, "Sentiment for a Strong Peace, 1917–1919," *The South Atlantic Quarterly*, vol. XLIII, No. 4 (October 1944), pp. 325–337.

the President believed that "if he attempted to give the war a social purpose, he would arouse the hostility of the same groups which had opposed his domestic policies."[57]

Similarly, Sumner Welles has written that the President

> . . . believed his primary obligation was to concentrate the attention of public opinion upon the winning of the war. He was convinced that if he spoke to the American people . . . of postwar problems, they might be distracted from the cardinal objective of victory, and controversies might develop which would jeopardize national unity.[58]

The relevance of unconditional surrender to these purposes should be evident. It was in fact the inescapable product both of the conflicting streams of American public opinion about the war, and of the divergent aims and purposes of the principal members of the Great Coalition. In both cases it served to bridge important differences and to make concerted action possible.

Brief reference may be made here to the President's unrelenting opposition to any modification of the policy. At Teheran a joint declaration to the Germans on the basis of unconditional surrender was considered by the three leaders. According to a British account, "Marshal Stalin. . .informed President Roosevelt on November 29 that he thought this [i.e., unconditional surrender] would be bad tactics toward Germany and suggested instead that the Allied Governments concerned should work out terms together and make them generally known to the German people."[59]

The President, however, was so unalterably opposed to any modification that he later denied any knowledge of the occurrence. This prompted Carroll to remark that the President may have "followed the example of Lord Nelson, who raised a telescope to his blind eye when he did not want to see, and turned a selective ear to Stalin when he chose not to hear."[60]

Russian opposition to the policy did not stop at Teheran. In December 1943, Molotov inquired of Harriman whether the policy could be modified. The President's instruction to Hull stated that the three major Powers had "agreed not to make any peace without consultation with each other," and that "each case should stand on its own merits in that way."[61] Again in February 1944, the Russians began negotiations with the Finns, but not on the basis of unconditional surrender. The British made this the occasion for a proposal to drop the formula, at least toward the satellites, and the Soviets stated their agreement with the British view. Still the President persisted, however, stating that "from time to time there will have to be exceptions not to the surrender principle but to the application of it in specific cases. That is a very different thing from changing the principle."[62]

The net result from this and further requests for modification was the final consent of the President to omit mention of the formula, for propaganda purposes only, to the satellite states alone.[63] It was never explicitly renounced, and in the case of Germany was not even implicitly qualified. According to Robert Sherwood, even

---

[57] Carroll, op. cit., p. 308.

[58] Sumner Welles, Where Are We Heading? (New York, 1946), pp. 18–19.

[59] Hull, op. cit., p. 1572.

[60] Carroll, op. cit., p. 316.

[61] Hull, op. cit., pp. 1573 et seq.

[62] Ibid., p. 1577.

[63] No mention was made of unconditional surrender in the Joint Declaration to the Four Axis Satellites, May 12, 1944. See Documents on American Foreign Relations, edited by L. M. Goodrich and M. J. Carroll (Boston, 1944), vol. V, p. 189.

at Yalta Roosevelt was "adhering to the basic formula of unconditional surrender; beyond that, he demanded only . . . 'freedom of action'."[64]

The record of Soviet opposition to the policy indicates that from their point of view it had probably served its usefulness after the United States had become irrevocably committed to opening the second front in Western Europe. It has already been suggested that one of the President's purposes in adopting the policy was to take the sting out of the Allied postponement of the promised second front. The fact that the Russians suggested modifying the policy only after the West was so committed indicates, therefore, that the President's immediate tactical purpose was well served by the policy.

Had this been his only purpose, however, no reason would have existed for retaining the policy once the United States was fully committed to the Western European invasion. Hence the President's continued opposition, after this point had been reached, must be understood as indicating his belief that there were still advantages to be gained from it, in spite of its tactical disadvantages which, incidentally, the President never denied the existence of. The question then is, what were these continuing advantages?

Sherwood's observation that the President wanted "freedom of action" probably provides the best clue to the answer. How could the President enjoy such freedom with respect to Germany (or any other post-war problem) unless he was in fact free to commit the United States fully and completely, or only partially, to whatever degree he saw fit? The President was well aware, as Sherwood makes clear, of the danger that the United States might return to a policy of isolationism after the war. He was also well aware of the vital importance attached by the Soviet government to a solution of the German problem; and of the necessity for ending the threat to the United States of recurring European wars caused by Germany. The danger of a return to isolationism could be averted, and the basis for Allied coöperation in Germany could be laid, only if the United States were fully committed not only to immediate victory but also to whatever measures of intervention in Germany were necessary after the war to keep the peace.

The President's determined adherence to the policy may therefore be taken as evidence of his determination to win the larger objectives, and of his judgment that the policy of unconditional surrender furthered these ends. Any just assessment of the policy must take these points into consideration, along with the tactical propaganda arguments so frequently mentioned.[65]

One final aspect of the policy may be mentioned here. Secretary Hull objected to the policy not only on tactical grounds but also because he felt that it "logically required the victor nations to be ready to take over every phase of the national and local Governments of the conquered countries, and to operate all governmental activities and properties. We and our Allies were in no way prepared to undertake this vast obligation."[66]

[64] Sherwood, op. cit., p. 862.

[65] James Warburg discusses these at length in Germany—Bridge or Battleground, pp. 259–265; for the German reaction see also Allen W. Dulles, Germany's Underground, pp. 132 et seq.; B. H. Liddell Hart, The German Generals Talk (New York, 1948), pp. 292 et seq.; Hans Rothfels, The German Opposition to Hitler (Hinsdale, 1948), passim; H. R. Trevor-Roper, The Last Days of Hitler (New York, 1947), pp. 237–238; and Churchill, Hinge of Fate, pp. 685 and 688–691.

[66] Hull, op. cit., p. 1570.

In simpler terms Hull's objection seems to be that unconditional surrender is an assertion of unlimited power, and therefore of an unlimited obligation. This would seem to be additional confirmation of the point that unconditional surrender preserved the President's freedom to commit the United States in Germany after the war to any degree he desired. At the same time it should be noted that the nature of the Allied commitment, lacking any other statement, had been given a specific form in the Atlantic Charter. It does seem, therefore, that although the President successfully avoided the Wilsonian error (as the President and Mr. Churchill considered it) of giving the Germans a semi-legal basis for asserting their rights, he nevertheless involved the Allies, and particularly the United States, in a moral obligation of a very far-reaching extent. This was, at any rate, the feeling of some, and was to be voiced later by some critics of the policy.[67]

In conclusion it may be stated that the unconditional surrender policy served both tactical and strategic purposes. For the short run it prevented Russian recrimination in spite of the further postponement of the promised second front. At the same time it served notice on Germans, Russians and Americans alike that there would be no compromises or deals with the Axis governments by any of the Allies. Its longer-term advantages lay in the fact that it reinforced the ban on discussion of post-war territorial issues, thus preserving a measure of international harmony necessary to the effective prosecution of the war, unified American public opinion on the need for winning the war, and laid the basis for post-war coöperation between the Allies by preserving American freedom of action with regard to post-war policy in Germany. One might note in passing that there is nothing in the record to show that Mr. Churchill proposed any feasible alternative policy which would have achieved the same objectives. On all counts, and contemporary criticisms of it notwithstanding, it was one of the most effective achievements of American statesmanship of the entire war period.

---

[67] This criticism was made, for example, by Ernest Bevin of Great Britain in the Commons, as reported in *The New York Times*, July 22, 1949.

24 / Origins of the Cold War

Arthur Schlesinger, Jr.

After two decades, historians are turning their sights on the tangled web that was and remains the Cold War. Already recognizable camps supporting orthodox and revisionist interpretations have arisen among historians who are trying to explain the genesis of the Cold War. As the United States Government and other governments relax restrictions on their presently classified documents now reposing in archives, scholars will be able to answer questions about which they may presently only hazard intelligent guesses. In the following article, Arthur Schlesinger, Jr. surveys the tensions between East and West that contributed to the Cold War after 1945. He suggests that the international dilemmas during the late 1940s ran very deep, and therefore it is not a very useful service merely to pin a tag of guilt or innocence on those American or Russian statesmen who made the difficult decisions. He concludes that even the most prudent of policies could not have averted some kind of Cold War. Future historians who contemplate Cold War scholarship may well consider this article a signal point for departure.

For further reading: Gar Alperovitz, *Atomic Diplomacy* (New York: 1965); Dean Acheson, *Present at the Creation* (New York: 1969); Denna F. Fleming, *The Cold War and its Origins, 1917–1960.* 2 vols. (Garden City: 1961); Hajo Halborn, "American Foreign Policy and European Integration," *World Politics,* VI (1953), 1–30; Walter Lippmann, *The Cold War: A Study in United States Foreign Policy* (New York: 1947); John A. Lukacs, *A History of the Cold War* (Garden City: 1961); William C. Mallalieu, "The Origin of the Marshall Plan: A Study in Policy Formation and National Leadership," *Political Science Quarterly* LXXIII (1958), 481–504; Louis Morton, "The Decision to Use the Atomic Bomb," *Foreign Affairs,* XXXV (1956), 334–353; Robert E. Osgood, *Limited War: The Challenge to American Strategy* (Chicago: 1957) and *NATO: The Entangling Alliance* (Chicago: 1962); Hugh Seton Watson, *Neither War Nor Peace* (New York: 1961).

Arthur Schlesinger, Jr. is Schweitzer Professor of History at the City University of New York. This article is reprinted with the permission of the author and of the editors of *Foreign Affairs.* From *Foreign Affairs,* XLV (October 1967). Copyright © 1967 by the Council on Foreign Relations, Inc., New York.

The Cold War in its original form was a presumably mortal antagonism, arising in the wake of the Second World War, between two rigidly hostile blocs, one led by the Soviet Union, the other by the United States. For nearly two somber and dangerous decades this antagonism dominated the fears of mankind; it may even, on occasion, have come close to blowing up the planet. In recent years, however, the once implacable struggle has lost its familiar clarity of outline. With the passing of old issues and the emergence of new conflicts and contestants, there is a natural tendency, especially on the part of the generation which grew up during the Cold War, to take a fresh look at the causes of the great contention between Russia and America.

Some exercises in reappraisal have merely elaborated the orthodoxies promulgated in Washington or Moscow during the boom years of the Cold War. But others, especially in the United States (there are no signs, alas, of this in the Soviet Union), represent what American historians call "revisionism"—that is, a readiness to challenge official explanations. No one should be surprised by this phenomenon. Every war in American history has been followed in due course by skeptical reassessments of supposedly sacred assumptions. So the War of 1812, fought at the time for the freedom of the seas, was in later years ascribed to the expansionist ambitions of Congressional war hawks; so the Mexican War became a slaveholders' conspiracy. So the Civil War has been pronounced a "needless war," and Lincoln has even been accused of manœuvring the rebel attack on Fort Sumter. So too the Spanish-American War and the First and Second World Wars have, each in its turn, undergone revisionist critiques. It is not to be supposed that the Cold War would remain exempt.

In the case of the Cold War, special factors reinforce the predictable historiographical rhythm. The outburst of polycentrism in the communist empire has made people wonder whether communism was ever so monolithic as official theories of the Cold War supposed. A generation with no vivid memories of Stalinism may see the Russia of the forties in the image of the relatively mild, seedy and irresolute Russia of the sixties. And for this same generation the American course of widening the war in Viet Nam—which even non-revisionists can easily regard as folly—has unquestionably stirred doubts about the wisdom of American foreign policy in the sixties which younger historians may have begun to read back into the forties.

It is useful to remember that, on the whole, past exercises in revisionism have failed to stick. Few historians today believe that the war hawks caused the War of 1812 or the slaveholders the Mexican War, or that the Civil War was needless, or that the House of Morgan brought America into the First World War or that Franklin Roosevelt schemed to produce the attack on Pearl Harbor. But this does not mean that one should deplore the rise of Cold War revisionism.[1] For revisionism is an essential part of the process by which history, through the posing of new problems and the investigation of new possibilities, enlarges its perspectives and enriches its insights.

More than this, in the present context, revisionism expresses a deep, legitimate and tragic apprehension. As the Cold War has begun to lose it purity of definition, as the moral absolutes of the fifties become the moralistic clichés of the sixties,-some have begun to ask whether the appalling risks which humanity ran during the Cold War were, after all, necessary and inevitable; whether more restrained and rational policies might not have guided the energies of man from the perils of conflict into the

[1] As this writer somewhat intemperately did in a letter to *The New York Review of Books*, October 20, 1966.

potentialities of collaboration. The fact that such questions are in their nature un-
answerable does not mean that it is not right and useful to raise them. Nor does it
mean that our sons and daughters are not entitled to an accounting from the generation of Russians and Americans who produced the Cold War.

II

The orthodox American view, as originally set forth by the American government
and as reaffirmed until recently by most American scholars, has been that the Cold
War was the brave and essential response of free men to communist aggression.
Some have gone back well before the Second World War to lay open the sources
of Russian expansionism. Geopoliticians traced the Cold War to imperial Russian
strategic ambitions which in the nineteenth century led to the Crimean War, to
Russian penetration of the Balkans and the Middle East and to Russian pressure
on Britain's "lifeline" to India. Ideologists traced it to the Communist Manifesto of
1848 ("the violent overthrow of the bourgeoisie lays the foundation for the sway of
the proletariat"). Thoughtful observers (a phrase meant to exclude those who speak
in Dullese about the unlimited evil of godless, atheistic, militant communism) concluded that classical Russian imperialism and Pan-Slavism, compounded after 1917
by Leninist messianism, confronted the West at the end of the Second World War
with an inexorable drive for domination.[2]

The revisionist thesis is very different.[3] In its extreme form, it is that, after the

[2] Every student of the Cold War must acknowledge his debt to W. H. McNeill's remarkable
account, "America, Britain and Russia: Their Cooperation and Conflict, 1941–1946" (New
York, 1953) and to the brilliant and indispensable series by Herbert Feis: "Churchill, Roosevelt,
Stalin: The War They Waged and the Peace They Sought" (Princeton, 1957); "Between
War and Peace: The Potsdam Conference" (Princeton, 1960); and "The Atomic Bomb and
the End of World War II" (Princeton, 1966). Useful recent analyses include André Fontaine,
"Histoire de la Guerre Froide" (2 v., Paris, 1965, 1967); N. A. Graebner, "Cold War Diplomacy,
1945–1960" (Princeton, 1962); L. J. Halle, "The Cold War as History" (London, 1967);
M. F. Herz, "Beginnings of the Cold War" (Bloomington, 1966) and W. L. Neumann, "After
Victory: Churchill, Roosevelt, Stalin and the Making of the Peace" (New York, 1967).

[3] The fullest statement of this case is to be found in D. F. Fleming's voluminous "The Cold
War and Its Origins" (New York, 1961). For a shorter version of this argument, see David
Horowitz, "The Free World Colossus" (New York, 1965); the most subtle and ingenious
statements come in W. A. Williams' "The Tragedy of American Diplomacy" (rev. ed., New
York, 1962) and in Gar Alperowitz's "Atomic Diplomacy: Hiroshima and Potsdam" (New
York, 1965) and in subsequent articles and reviews by Mr. Alperowitz in *The New York Review
of Books*. The fact that in some aspects the revisionist thesis parallels the official Soviet argument
must not, of course, prevent consideration of the case on its merits, nor raise questions about the
motives of the writers, all of whom, so far as I know, are independent-minded scholars.
I might further add that all these books, in spite of their ostentatious display of scholarly apparatus, must be used with caution. Professor Fleming, for example, relies heavily on newspaper
articles and even columnists. While Mr. Alperowitz bases his case on official documents or
authoritative reminiscences, he sometimes twists his material in a most unscholarly way. For
example, in describing Ambassador Harriman's talk with President Truman on April 20, 1945,
Mr. Alperowitz writes, "He argued that a reconsideration of Roosevelt's policy was necessary"
(p. 22, repeated on p. 24). The citation is to p. 70–72 in President Truman's "Years of Decision."
What President Truman reported Harriman as saying was the exact opposite: "Before leaving,
Harriman took me aside and said, 'Frankly, one of the reasons that made me rush back to Washington was the fear that you did not understand, as I had seen Roosevelt understand, that Stalin

death of Franklin Roosevelt and the end of the Second World War, the United States deliberately abandoned the wartime policy of collaboration and, exhilarated by the possession of the atomic bomb, undertook a course of aggression of its own designed to expel all Russian influence from Eastern Europe and to establish democratic-capitalist states on the very border of the Soviet Union. As the revisionists see it, this radically new American policy—or rather this resumption by Truman of the pre-Roosevelt policy of insensate anti-communism—left Moscow no alternative but to take measures in defense of its own borders. The result was the Cold War.

These two views, of course, could not be more starkly contrasting. It is therefore not unreasonable to look again at the half-dozen critical years between June 22, 1941, when Hitler attacked Russia, and July 2, 1947, when the Russians walked out of the Marshall Plan meeting in Paris. Several things should be borne in mind as this reexamination is made. For one thing, we have thought a great deal more in recent years, in part because of writers like Roberta Wohlstetter and T. C. Schelling, about the problems of communication in diplomacy—the signals which one nation, by word or by deed, gives, inadvertently or intentionally, to another. Any honest reappraisal of the origins of the Cold War requires the imaginative leap—which should in any case be as instinctive for the historian as it is prudent for the statesman—into the adversary's viewpoint. We must strive to see how, given Soviet perspectives, the Russians might conceivably have misread our signals, as we must reconsider how intelligently we read theirs.

For another, the historian must not overindulge the man of power in the illusion cherished by those in office that high position carries with it the easy ability to shape history. Violating the statesman's creed, Lincoln once blurted out the truth in his letter of 1864 to A. G. Hodges: "I claim not to have controlled events, but confess plainly that events have controlled me." He was not asserting Tolstoyan fatalism but rather suggesting how greatly events limit the capacity of the statesman to bend history to his will. The physical course of the Second World War—the military operations undertaken, the position of the respective armies at the war's end, the momentum generated by victory and the vacuums created by defeat—all these determined the future as much as the character of individual leaders and the substance of national ideology and purpose.

Nor can the historian forget the conditions under which decisions are made, especially in a time like the Second World War. These were tired, overworked, aging men: in 1945, Churchill was 71 years old, Stalin had governed his country for 17 exacting years, Roosevelt his for 12 years nearly as exacting. During the war, moreover, the importunities of military operations had shoved postwar questions to the margins of their minds. All—even Stalin, behind his screen of ideology—had

is breaking his agreements'." Similarly, in an appendix (p. 271) Mr. Alperowitz writes that the Hopkins and Davies missions of May 1945 "were opposed by the 'firm' advisers." Actually the Hopkins mission was proposed by Harriman and Charles E. Bohlen, who Mr. Alperowitz elsewhere suggests were the firmest of the firm—and was proposed by them precisely to impress on Stalin the continuity of American policy from Roosevelt to Truman. While the idea that Truman reversed Roosevelt's policy is tempting dramatically, it is a myth. See, for example, the testimony of Anna Rosenberg Hoffman, who lunched with Roosevelt on March 24, 1945, the last day he spent in Washington. After luncheon, Roosevelt was handed a cable. "He read it and became quite angry. He banged his fists on the arms of his wheelchair and said, 'Averell is right; we can't do business with Stalin. He has broken every one of the promises he made at Yalta'. He was very upset and continued in the same vein on the subject."

became addicts of improvisation, relying on authority and virtuosity to conceal the fact that they were constantly surprised by developments. Like Eliza, they leaped from one cake of ice to the next in the effort to reach the other side of the river. None showed great tactical consistency, or cared much about it; all employed a certain ambiguity to preserve their power to decide big issues; and it is hard to know how to interpret anything any one of them said on any specific occasion. This was partly because, like all princes, they designed their expressions to have particular effects on particular audiences; partly because the entirely genuine intellectual difficulty of the questions they faced made a degree of vacillation and mind-changing eminently reasonable. If historians cannot solve their problems in retrospect, who are they to blame Roosevelt, Stalin and Churchill for not having solved them at the time?

III

Peacemaking after the Second World War was not so much a tapestry as it was a hopelessly raveled and knotted mess of yarn. Yet, for purposes of clarity, it is essential to follow certain threads. One theme indispensable to an understanding of the Cold War is the contrast between two clashing views of world order: the "universalist" view, by which all nations shared a common interest in all the affairs of the world, and the "sphere-of-influence" view, by which each great power would be assured by the other great powers of an acknowledged predominance in its own area of special interest. The universalist view assumed that national security would be guaranteed by an international organization. The sphere-of-interest view assumed that national security would be guaranteed by the balance of power. While in practice these views have by no means been incompatible (indeed, our shaky peace has been based on a combination of the two), in the abstract they involved sharp contradictions.

The tradition of American thought in these matters was universalist—*i.e.* Wilsonian. Roosevelt had been a member of Wilson's subcabinet; in 1920, as candidate for Vice President, he had campaigned for the League of Nations. It is true that, within Roosevelt's infinitely complex mind, Wilsonianism warred with the perception of vital strategic interests he had imbibed from Mahan. Morever, his temperamental inclination to settle things with fellow princes around the conference table led him to regard the Big Three—or Four—as trustees for the rest of the world. On occasion, as this narrative will show, he was beguiled into flirtation with the sphere-of-influence heresy. But in principle he believed in joint action and remained a Wilsonian. His hope for Yalta, as he told the Congress on his return, was that it would "spell the end of the system of unilateral action, the exclusive alliances, the spheres of influence, the balances of power, and all the other expedients that have been tried for centuries—and have always failed."

Whenever Roosevelt backslid, he had at his side that Wilsonian fundamentalist, Secretary of State Cordell Hull, to recall him to the pure faith. After his visit to Moscow in 1943, Hull characteristically said that, with the Declaration of Four Nations on General Security (in which America, Russia, Britain and China pledged "united action . . . for the organization and maintenance of peace and security"), "there will no longer be need for spheres of influence, for alliances, for balance of power, or any other of the special arrangements through which, in the unhappy past, the nations strove to safeguard their security or to promote their interests."

Remembering the corruption of the Wilsonian vision by the secret treaties of the First World War, Hull was determined to prevent any sphere-of-influence nonsense after the Second World War. He therefore fought all proposals to settle border questions while the war was still on and, excluded as he largely was from wartime diplomacy, poured his not inconsiderable moral energy and frustration into the promulgation of virtuous and spacious general principles.

In adopting the universalist view, Roosevelt and Hull were not indulging personal hobbies. Sumner Welles, Adolf Berle, Averell Harriman, Charles Bohlen—all, if with a variety of nuances, opposed the sphere-of-influence approach. And here the State Department was expressing what seems clearly to have been the predominant mood of the American people, so long mistrustful of European power politics. The Republicans shared the true faith. John Foster Dulles argued that the great threat to peace after the war would lie in the revival of sphere-of-influence thinking. The United States, he said, must not permit Britain and Russia to revert to these bad old ways; it must therefore insist on American participation in all policy decisions for all territories in the world. Dulles wrote pessimistically in January 1945, "The three great powers which at Moscow agreed upon the 'closest coöperation' about European questions have shifted to a practice of separate, regional responsibility."

It is true that critics, and even friends, of the United States sometimes noted a discrepancy between the American passion for universalism when it applied to territory far from American shores and the preeminence the United States accorded its own interests nearer home. Churchill, seeking Washington's blessing for a sphere-of-influence initiative in Eastern Europe, could not forbear reminding the Americans, "We follow the lead of the United States in South America;" nor did any universalist of record propose the abolition of the Monroe Doctrine. But a convenient myopia prevented such inconsistencies from qualifying the ardency of the universalist faith.

There seem only to have been three officials in the United States Government who dissented. One was the Secretary of War, Henry L. Stimson, a classical balance-of-power man, who in 1944 opposed the creation of a vacuum in Central Europe by the pastoralization of Germany and in 1945 urged "the settlement of all territorial acquisitions in the shape of defense posts which each of these four powers may deem to be necessary for their own safety" in advance of any effort to establish a peacetime United Nations. Stimson considered the claim of Russia to a preferred position in Eastern Europe as not unreasonable: as he told President Truman, "he thought the Russians perhaps were being more realistic than we were in regard to their own security." Such a position for Russia seemed to him comparable to the preferred American position in Latin America; he even spoke of "our respective orbits." Stimson was therefore skeptical of what he regarded as the prevailing tendency "to hang on to exaggerated views of the Monroe Doctrine and at the same time butt into every question that comes up in Central Europe." Acceptance of spheres of influence seemed to him the way to avoid "a head-on collision."

A second official opponent of universalism was George Kennan, an eloquent advocate from the American Embassy in Moscow of "a prompt and clear recognition of the division of Europe into spheres of influence and of a policy based on the fact of such division." Kennan argued that nothing we could do would possibly alter the course of events in Eastern Europe; that we were deceiving ourselves by supposing that these countries had any future but Russian domination; that we should therefore relinquish Eastern Europe to the Soviet Union and avoid anything which would make things easier for the Russians by giving them economic assistance or by sharing moral responsibility for their actions.

A third voice within the government against universalism was (at least after the war) Henry A. Wallace. As Secretary of Commerce, he stated the sphere-of-influence case with trenchancy in the famous Madison Square Garden speech of September 1946 which led to his dismissal by President Truman:

> On our part, we should recognize that we have no more business in the *political* affairs of Eastern Europe than Russia has in the *political* affairs of Latin America, Western Europe, and the United States. . . . Whether we like it or not, the Russians will try to socialize their sphere of influence just as we try to democratize our sphere of influence. . . . The Russians have no more business stirring up native Communists to political activity in Western Europe, Latin America, and the United States than we have in interfering with the politics of Eastern Europe and Russia.

Stimson, Kennan and Wallace seem to have been alone in the government, however, in taking these views. They were very much minority voices. Meanwhile universalism, rooted in the American legal and moral tradition, overwhelmingly backed by contemporary opinion, received successive enshrinements in the Atlantic Charter of 1941, in the Declaration of the United Nations in 1942 and in the Moscow Declaration of 1943.

IV

The Kremlin, on the other hand, thought *only* of spheres of interest; above all, the Russians were determined to protect their frontiers, and especially their border to the west, crossed so often and so bloodily in the dark course of their history. These western frontiers lacked natural means of defense—no great oceans, rugged mountains, steaming swamps or impenetrable jungles. The history of Russia had been the history of invasion, the last of which was by now horribly killing up to twenty million of its people. The protocol of Russia therefore meant the enlargement of the area of Russian influence. Kennan himself wrote (in May 1944), "Behind Russia's stubborn expansion lies only the age-old sense of insecurity of a sedentary people reared on an exposed plain in the neighborhood of fierce nomadic peoples," and he called this "urge" a "permanent feature of Russian psychology."

In earlier times the "urge" had produced the tsarist search for buffer states and maritime outlets. In 1939 the Soviet-Nazi pact and its secret protocol had enabled Russia to begin to satisfy in the Baltic states, Karelian Finland and Poland, part of what it conceived as its security requirements in Eastern Europe. But the "urge" persisted, causing the friction between Russia and Germany in 1940 as each jostled for position in the area which separated them. Later it led to Molotov's new demands on Hitler in November 1940—a free hand in Finland, Soviet predominance in Rumania and Bulgaria, bases in the Dardanelles—the demands which convinced Hitler that he had no choice but to attack Russia. Now Stalin hoped to gain from the West what Hitler, a closer neighbor, had not dared yield him.

It is true that, so long as Russian survival appeared to require a second front to relieve the Nazi pressure, Moscow's demand for Eastern Europe was a little muffled.

Thus the Soviet government adhered to the Atlantic Charter (though with a significant if obscured reservation about adapting its principles to "the circumstances, needs, and historic peculiarities of particular countries"). Thus it also adhered to the Moscow Declaration of 1943, and Molotov then, with his easy mendacity, even denied that Russia had any desire to divide Europe into spheres of influence. But this was guff, which the Russians were perfectly willing to ladle out if it would keep the Americans, and especially Secretary Hull (who made a strong personal impression at the Moscow conference) happy. "A declaration," as Stalin once observed to Eden, "I regard as algebra, but an agreement as practical arithmetic. I do not wish to decry algebra, but I prefer practical arithmetic."

The more consistent Russian purpose was revealed when Stalin offered the British a straight sphere-of-influence deal at the end of 1941. Britain, he suggested, should recognize the Russian absorption of the Baltic states, part of Finland, eastern Poland and Bessarabia; in return, Russia would support any special British need for bases or security arrangements in Western Europe. There was nothing specifically communist about these ambitions. If Stalin achieved them, he would be fulfilling an age-old dream of the tsars. The British reaction was mixed. "Soviet policy is amoral," as Anthony Eden noted at the time; "United States policy is exaggeratedly moral, at least where non-American interests are concerned." If Roosevelt was a universalist with occasional leanings toward spheres of influence and Stalin was a sphere-of-influence man with occasional gestures toward universalism, Churchill seemed evenly poised between the familiar realism of the balance of power, which he had so long recorded as an historian and manipulated as a statesman, and the hope that there must be some better way of doing things. His 1943 proposal of a world organization divided into regional councils represented an effort to blend universalist and sphere-of-interests conceptions. His initial rejection of Stalin's proposal in December 1941 as "directly contrary to the first, second and third articles of the Atlantic Charter" thus did not spring entirely from a desire to propitiate the United States. On the other hand, he had himself already reinterpreted the Atlantic Charter as applying only to Europe (and thus not to the British Empire), and he was, above all, an empiricist who never believed in sacrificing reality on the altar of doctrine.

So in April 1942 he wrote Roosevelt that "the increasing gravity of the war" had led him to feel that the Charter "ought not to be construed so as to deny Russia the frontiers she occupied when Germany attacked her." Hull, however, remained fiercely hostile to the inclusion of territorial provisions in the Anglo-Russian treaty; the American position, Eden noted, "chilled me with Wilsonian memories." Though Stalin complained that it looked "as if the Atlantic Charter was directed against the U.S.S.R.," it was the Russian season of military adversity in the spring of 1942, and he dropped his demands.

He did not, however, change his intentions. A year later Ambassador Standley could cable Washington from Moscow: "In 1918 Western Europe attempted to set up a *cordon sanitaire* to protect it from the influence of bolshevism. Might not now the Kremlin envisage the formation of a belt of pro-Soviet states to protect it from the influences of the West?" It well might; and that purpose became increasingly clear as the war approached its end. Indeed, it derived sustenance from Western policy in the first area of liberation.

The unconditional surrender of Italy in July 1943 created the first major test of the Western devotion to universalism. America and Britain, having won the Italian war, handled the capitulation, keeping Moscow informed at a distance. Stalin complained:

> The United States and Great Britain made agreements but the Soviet Union received information about the results . . . just as a passive third observer. I have to tell you that it is impossible to tolerate the situation any longer. I propose that the [tripartite military-political commission] be established and that Sicily be assigned . . . as its place of residence.

Roosevelt, who had no intention of sharing the control of Italy with the Russians, suavely replied with the suggestion that Stalin send an officer "to General Eisenhower's headquarters in connection with the commission." Unimpressed, Stalin continued to press for a tripartite body; but his Western allies were adamant in keeping the Soviet Union off the Control Commission for Italy, and the Russians in the end had to be satisfied with a seat, along with minor Allied states, on a meaningless Inter-Allied Advisory Council. Their acquiescence in this was doubtless not unconnected with a desire to establish precedents for Eastern Europe.

Teheran in December 1943 marked the high point of three-power collaboration. Still, when Churchill asked about Russian territorial interests, Stalin replied a little ominously, "There is no need to speak at the present time about any Soviet desires, but when the time comes we will speak." In the next weeks, there were increasing indications of a Soviet determination to deal unilaterally with Eastern Europe—so much so that in early February 1944 Hull cabled Harriman in Moscow:

> Matters are rapidly approaching the point where the Soviet Government will have to choose between the development and extension of the foundation of international cooperation as the guiding principle of the postwar world as against the continuance of a unilateral and arbitrary method of dealing with its special problems even though these problems are admittedly of more direct interest to the Soviet Union than to other great powers.

As against this approach, however, Churchill, more tolerant of sphere-of-influence deviations, soon proposed that, with the impending liberation of the Balkans, Russia should run things in Rumania and Britain in Greece. Hull strongly opposed this suggestion but made the mistake of leaving Washington for a few days; and Roosevelt, momentarily free from his Wilsonian conscience, yielded to Churchill's plea for a three-months' trial. Hull resumed the fight on his return, and Churchill postponed the matter.

The Red Army continued its advance into Eastern Europe. In August the Polish Home Army, urged on by Polish-language broadcasts from Moscow, rose up against the Nazis in Warsaw. For 63 terrible days, the Poles fought valiantly on, while the Red Army halted on the banks of the Vistula a few miles away, and in Moscow Stalin for more than half this time declined to coöperate with the Western effort to drop supplies to the Warsaw Resistance. It appeared a calculated Soviet decision to let the Nazis slaughter the anti-Soviet Polish underground; and, indeed, the result was to destroy any substantial alternative to a Soviet solution in Poland. The agony of Warsaw caused the most deep and genuine moral shock in Britain and America and provoked dark forebodings about Soviet postwar purposes.

Again history enjoins the imaginative leap in order to see things for a moment from Moscow's viewpoint. The Polish question, Churchill would say at Yalta, was for Britain a question of honor. "It is not only a question of honor for Russia," Stalin replied, "but one of life and death. . . . Throughout history Poland had been the corridor for attack on Russia." A top postwar priority for any Russian régime must be to close that corridor. The Home Army was led by anti-communists. It clearly hoped by its action to forestall the Soviet occupation of Warsaw and, in Russian eyes, to prepare the way for an anti-Russian Poland. In addition, the uprising from a strictly operational viewpoint was premature. The Russians, it is evident in retrospect, had real military problems at the Vistula. The Soviet attempt in September to send Polish units from the Red Army across the river to join forces with the Home Army was a disaster. Heavy German shelling thereafter prevented the ferrying of tanks necessary for an assault on the German position. The Red Army itself did not take Warsaw for another three months. None the less, Stalin's indifference to the human tragedy, his effort to blackmail the London Poles during the ordeal, his sanctimonious opposition during five precious weeks to aerial resupply, the invariable coldness of his explanations ("the Soviet command has come to the conclusion that it must dissociate itself from the Warsaw adventure") and the obvious political benefit to the Soviet Union from the destruction of the Home Army—all these had the effect of suddenly dropping the mask of wartime comradeship and displaying to the West the hard face of Soviet policy. In now pursuing what he grimly regarded as the minimal requirements for the postwar security of his country, Stalin was inadvertently showing the irreconcilability of both his means and his ends with the Anglo-American conception of the peace.

Meanwhile Eastern Europe presented the Alliance with still another crisis that same September. Bulgaria, which was not at war with Russia, decided to surrender to the Western Allies while it still could; and the English and Americans at Cairo began to discuss armistice terms with Bulgarian envoys. Moscow, challenged by what it plainly saw as a Western intrusion into its own zone of vital interest, promptly declared war on Bulgaria, took over the surrender negotiations and, invoking the Italian precedent, denied its Western Allies any role in the Bulgarian Control Commission. In a long and thoughtful cable, Ambassador Harriman meditated on the problems of communication with the Soviet Union. "Words," he reflected, "have a different connotation to the Soviets than they have to us. When they speak of insisting on 'friendly governments' in their neighboring countries, they have in mind something quite different from what we would mean." The Russians, he surmised, really believed that Washington accepted "their position that although they would keep us informed they had the right to settle their problems with their western neighbors unilaterally." But the Soviet position was still in flux: "the Soviet Government is not one mind." The problem, as Harriman had earlier told Harry Hopkins, was "to strengthen the hands of those around Stalin who want to play the game along our lines." The way to do this, he now told Hull, was to

> be understanding of their sensitivity, meet them much more than half way, encourage them and support them wherever we can, and yet oppose them promptly with the greatest of firmness where we see them going wrong. . . . The only way we can eventually come to an understanding with the Soviet Union on the question of non-interference in the internal affairs of other countries is for us to take a definite interest in the solution of the problems of each individual country as they arise.

As against Harriman's sophisticated universalist strategy, however, Churchill, increasingly fearful of the consequences of unrestrained competition in Eastern Europe, decided in early October to carry his sphere-of-influence proposal directly to Moscow. Roosevelt was at first content to have Churchill speak for him too and even prepared a cable to that effect. But Hopkins, a more rigorous universalist, took it upon himself to stop the cable and warn Roosevelt of its possible implications. Eventually Roosevelt sent a message to Harriman in Moscow emphasizing that he expected to "retain complete freedom of action after this conference is over." It was now that Churchill quickly proposed—and Stalin as quickly accepted—the celebrated division of southeastern Europe: ending (after further haggling between Eden and Molotov) with 90 percent Soviet predominance in Rumania, 80 percent in Bulgaria and Hungary, fifty-fifty in Jugoslavia, 90 percent British predominance in Greece.

Churchill in discussing this with Harriman used the phrase "spheres of influence." But he insisted that these were only "immediate wartime arrangements" and received a highly general blessing from Roosevelt. Yet, whatever Churchill intended, there is reason to believe that Stalin construed the percentages as an agreement, not a declaration; as practical arithmetic, not algebra. For Stalin, it should be understood, the sphere-of-influence idea did not mean that he would abandon all efforts to spread communism in some other nation's sphere; it did mean that, if he tried this and the other side cracked down, he could not feel he had serious cause for complaint. As Kennan wrote to Harriman at the end of 1944:

> As far as border states are concerned the Soviet government has never ceased to think in terms of spheres of interest. They expect us to support them in whatever action they wish to take in those regions, regardless of whether that action seems to us or to the rest of the world to be right or wrong. . . . I have no doubt that this position is honestly maintained on their part, and that they would be equally prepared to reserve moral judgment on any actions which we might wish to carry out, i.e., in the Caribbean area.

In any case, the matter was already under test a good deal closer to Moscow than the Caribbean. The communist-dominated resistance movement in Greece was in open revolt against the effort of the Papandreou government to disarm and disband the guerrillas (the same Papandreou whom the Greek colonels have recently arrested on the claim that he is a tool of the communists). Churchill now called in British Army units to crush the insurrection. This action produced a storm of criticism in his own country and in the United States; the American Government even publicly dissociated itself from the intervention, thereby emphasizing its detachment from the sphere-of-influence deal. But Stalin, Churchill later claimed, "adhered strictly and faithfully to our agreement of October, and during all the long weeks of fighting the Communists in the streets of Athens not one word of reproach came from *Pravda* or *Izvestia*," though there is no evidence that he tried to call off the Greek communists. Still, when the communist rebellion later broke out again in Greece, Stalin told Kardelj and Djilas of Jugoslavia in 1948, "The uprising in Greece must be stopped, and as quickly as possible."

No one, of course, can know what really was in the minds of the Russian leaders. The Kremlin archives are locked; of the primary actors, only Molotov survives, and he has not yet indicated any desire to collaborate with the Columbia Oral History Project. We do know that Stalin did not wholly surrender to sentimental illusion about his new friends. In June 1944, on the night before the landings in Normandy, he told Djilas that the English "find nothing sweeter than to trick their allies. . . . And Churchill? Churchill is the kind who, if you don't watch him, will slip a kopeck out of your pocket. Yes, a kopeck out of your pocket! . . . Roosevelt is not like that. He dips in his hand only for bigger coins." But whatever his views of his colleagues it is not unreasonable to suppose that Stalin would have been satisfied at the end of the war to secure what Kennan has called "a protective glacis along Russia's western border," and that, in exchange for a free hand in Eastern Europe, he was prepared to give the British and Americans equally free hands in their zones of vital interest, including in nations as close to Russia as Greece (for the British) and, very probably—or at least so the Jugoslavs believe—China (for the United States). In other words, his initial objectives were very probably not world conquest but Russian security.

V

It is now pertinent to inquire why the United States rejected the idea of stabilizing the world by division into spheres of influence and insisted on an East European strategy. One should warn against rushing to the conclusion that it was all a row between hard-nosed, balance-of-power realists and starry-eyed Wilsonians. Roosevelt, Hopkins, Welles, Harriman, Bohlen, Berle, Dulles and other universalists were tough and serious men. Why then did they rebuff the sphere-of-influence solution?

The first reason is that they regarded this solution as containing within itself the seeds of a third world war. The balance-of-power idea seemed inherently unstable. It had always broken down in the past. It held out to each power the permanent temptation to try to alter the balance in its own favor, and it built this temptation into the international order. It would turn the great powers of 1945 away from the objective of concerting common policies toward competition for postwar advantage. As Hopkins told Molotov at Teheran, "The President feels it essential to world peace that Russia, Great Britain and the United States work out this control question in a manner which will not start each of the three powers arming against the others." "The greatest likelihood of eventual conflict," said the Joint Chiefs of Staff in 1944 (the only conflict which the J.C.S., in its wisdom, could then glimpse "in the foreseeable future" was between Britain and Russia), ". . . would seem to grow out of either nation initiating attempts to build up its strength, by seeking to attach to herself parts of Europe to the disadvantage and possible danger of her potential adversary." The Americans were perfectly ready to acknowledge that Russia was entitled to convincing assurance of her national security—but not this way. "I could sympathize fully with Stalin's desire to protect his western borders from future attack," as Hull put it. "But I felt that this security could best be obtained through a strong postwar peace organization."

Hull's remark suggests the second objection: that the sphere-of-influence approach would, in the words of the State Department in 1945, "militate against the establishment and effective functioning of a broader system of general security in which all countries will have their part." The United Nations, in short, was seen as the alternative to the balance of power. Nor did the universalists see any necessary incompatibility between the Russian desire for "friendly governments" on its frontier and the

American desire for self-determination in Eastern Europe. Before Yalta the State Department judged the general mood of Europe as "to the left and strongly in favor of far-reaching economic and social reforms, but not, however, in favor of a left-wing totalitarian regime to achieve these reforms." Governments in Eastern Europe could be sufficiently to the left "to allay Soviet suspicions" but sufficiently representative "of the center and *petit bourgeois* elements" not to seem a prelude to communist dictatorship. The American criteria were therefore that the government "should be dedicated to the preservation of civil liberties" and "should favor social and economic reforms." A string of New Deal states—of Finlands and Czechoslovakias—seemed a reasonable compromise solution.

Third, the universalists feared that the sphere-of-interest approach would be what Hull termed "a haven for the isolationists," who would advocate America's participation in Western Hemisphere affairs on condition that it did not participate in European or Asian affairs. Hull also feared that spheres of interest would lead to "closed trade areas or discriminatory systems" and thus defeat his cherished dream of a low-tariff, freely trading world.

Fourth, the sphere-of-interest solution meant the betrayal of the principles for which the Second World War was being fought—the Atlantic Charter, the Four Freedoms, the Declaration of the United Nations. Poland summed up the problem. Britain, having gone to war to defend the independence of Poland from the Germans, could not easily conclude the war by surrendering the independence of Poland to the Russians. Thus, as Hopkins told Stalin after Roosevelt's death in 1945, Poland had "become the symbol of our ability to work out problems with the Soviet Union." Nor could American liberals in general watch with equanimity while the police state spread into countries which, if they had mostly not been real democracies, had mostly not been tyrannies either. The execution in 1943 of Ehrlich and Alter, the Polish socialist trade union leaders, excited deep concern. "I have particularly in mind," Harriman cabled in 1944, "objection to the institution of secret police who may become involved in the persecution of persons of truly democratic convictions who may not be willing to conform to Soviet methods."

Fifth, the sphere-of-influence solution would create difficult domestic problems in American politics. Roosevelt was aware of the six million or more Polish votes in the 1944 election; even more acutely, he was aware of the broader and deeper attack which would follow if, after going to war to stop the Nazi conquest of Europe, he permitted the war to end with the communist conquest of Eastern Europe. As Archibald MacLeish, then Assistant Secretary of State for Public Affairs, warned in January 1945, "The wave of disillusionment which has distressed us in the last several weeks will be increased if the impression is permitted to get abroad that potentially totalitarian provisional governments are to be set up without adequate safeguards as to the holding of free elections and the realization of the principles of the Atlantic Charter." Roosevelt believed that no administration could survive which did not try everything short of war to save Eastern Europe, and he was the supreme American politician of the century.

Sixth, if the Russians were allowed to overrun Eastern Europe without argument, would that satisfy them? Even Kennan, in a dispatch of May 1944, admitted that the "urge" had dreadful potentialities: "If initially successful, will it know where to stop? Will it not be inexorably carried forward, by its very nature, in a struggle to reach the whole—to attain complete mastery of the shores of the Atlantic and the

Pacific?" His own answer was that there were inherent limits to the Russian capacity to expand—"that Russia will not have an easy time in maintaining the power which it has seized over other people in Eastern and Central Europe unless it receives both moral and material assistance from the West." Subsequent developments have vindicated Kennan's argument. By the late forties, Jugoslavia and Albania, the two East European states farthest from the Soviet Union and the two in which communism was imposed from within rather than from without, had declared their independence of Moscow. But, given Russia's success in maintaining centralized control over the international communist movement for a quarter of a century, who in 1944 could have had much confidence in the idea of communist revolts against Moscow?

Most of those involved therefore rejected Kennan's answer and stayed with his question. If the West turned its back on Eastern Europe, the higher probability, in their view, was that the Russians would use their security zone, not just for defensive purposes, but as a springboard from which to mount an attack on Western Europe, now shattered by war, a vacuum of power awaiting its master. "If the policy is accepted that the Soviet Union has a right to penetrate her immediate neighbors for security," Harriman said in 1944, "penetration of the next immediate neighbors becomes at a certain time equally logical." If a row with Russia were inevitable, every consideration of prudence dictated that it should take place in Eastern rather than Western Europe.

Thus idealism and realism joined in opposition to the sphere-of-influence solution. The consequence was a determination to assert an American interest in the postwar destiny of all nations, including those of Eastern Europe. In the message which Roosevelt and Hopkins drafted after Hopkins had stopped Roosevelt's initial cable authorizing Churchill to speak for the United States at the Moscow meeting of October 1944, Roosevelt now said, "There is in this global war literally no question, either military or political, in which the United States is not interested." After Roosevelt's death Hopkins repeated the point to Stalin: "The cardinal basis of President Roosevelt's policy which the American people had fully supported had been the concept that the interests of the U.S. were worldwide and not confined to North and South America and the Pacific Ocean."

VI

For better or worse, this was the American position. It is now necessary to attempt the imaginative leap and consider the impact of this position on the leaders of the Soviet Union who, also for better or for worse, had reached the bitter conclusion that the survival of their country depended on their unchallenged control of the corridors through which enemies had so often invaded their homeland. They could claim to have been keeping their own side of the sphere-of-influence bargain. Of course, they were working to capture the resistance movements of Western Europe; indeed, with the appointment of Oumansky as Ambassador to Mexico they were even beginning to enlarge underground operations in the Western Hemisphere. But, from their viewpoint, if the West permitted this, the more fools they; and, if the West stopped it, it was within their right to do so. In overt political matters the Russians were scrupulously playing the game. They had watched in silence while the British shot down communists in Greece. In Jugoslavia Stalin was urging Tito (as Djilas later revealed) to keep King Peter. They had not only acknowledged Western preeminence in Italy but had recognized the Badoglio régime; the Italian Communists had even voted (against the Socialists and the Liberals) for the renewal of the Lateran Pacts.

They would not regard anti-communist action in a Western zone as a *casus belli*; and they expected reciprocal license to assert their own authority in the East. But the principle of self-determination was carrying the United States into a deeper entanglement in Eastern Europe than the Soviet Union claimed as a right (whatever it was doing underground) in the affairs of Italy, Greece or China. When the Russians now exercised in Eastern Europe the same brutal control they were prepared to have Washington exercise in the American sphere of influence, the American protests, given the paranoia produced alike by Russian history and Leninist ideology, no doubt seemed not only an act of hypocrisy but a threat to security. To the Russians, a stroll into the neighborhood easily became a plot to burn down the house: when, for example, damaged American planes made emergency landings in Poland and Hungary, Moscow took this as attempts to organize the local resistance. It is not unusual to suspect one's adversary of doing what one is already doing oneself. At the same time, the cruelty with which the Russians executed their idea of spheres of influence—in a sense, perhaps, an unwitting cruelty, since Stalin treated the East Europeans no worse than he had treated the Russians in the thirties—discouraged the West from accepting the equation (for example, Italy = Rumania) which seemed so self-evident to the Kremlin.

So Moscow very probably, and not unnaturally, perceived the emphasis on self-determination as a systematic and deliberate pressure on Russia's western frontiers. Moreover, the restoration of capitalism to countries freed at frightful cost by the Red Army no doubt struck the Russians as the betrayal of the principles for which *they* were fighting. "That they, the victors," Isaac Deutscher had suggested, "should now preserve an order from which they had experienced nothing but hostility, and could expect nothing but hostility . . . would have been the most miserable anticlimax to their great 'war of liberation'." By 1944 Poland was the critical issue; Harriman later said that "under instructions from President Roosevelt, I talked about Poland with Stalin more frequently than any other subject." While the West saw the point of Stalin's demand for a "friendly government" in Warsaw, the American insistence on the sovereign virtues of free elections (ironically in the spirit of the 1917 Bolshevik decree of peace, which affirmed "the right" of a nation "to decide the forms of its state existence by a free vote, taken after the complete evacuation of the incorporating or, generally, of the stronger nation") created an insoluble problem in those countries, like Poland (and Rumania) where free elections would almost certainly produce anti-Soviet governments.

The Russians thus may well have estimated the Western pressures as calculated to encourage their enemies in Eastern Europe and to defeat their own minimum objective of a protective glacis. Everything still hung, however, on the course of military operations. The wartime collaboration had been created by one thing, and one thing alone: the threat of Nazi victory. So long as this threat was real, so was the collaboration. In late December 1944, von Rundstedt launched his counter-offensive in the Ardennes. A few weeks later, when Roosevelt, Churchill and Stalin gathered in the Crimea, it was in the shadow of this last considerable explosion of German power. The meeting at Yalta was still dominated by the mood of war.

Yalta remains something of an historical perplexity—less, from the perspective of

1967, because of a mythical American deference to the sphere-of-influence thesis than because of the documentable Russian deference to the universalist thesis. Why should Stalin in 1945 have accepted the Declaration on Liberated Europe and an agreement on Poland pledging that "the three governments will jointly" act to assure "free elections of governments responsive to the will of the people"? There are several probable answers: that the war was not over and the Russians still wanted the Americans to intensify their military effort in the West; that one clause in the Declaration premised action on "the opinion of the three governments" and thus implied a Soviet veto, though the Polish agreement was more definite; most of all that the universalist algebra of the Declaration was plainly in Stalin's mind to be construed in terms of the practical arithmetic of his sphere-of-influence agreement with Churchill the previous October. Stalin's assurance to Churchill at Yalta that a proposed Russian amendment to the Declaration would not apply to Greece makes it clear that Roosevelt's pieties did not, in Stalin's mind, nullify Churchill's percentages. He could well have been strengthened in this supposition by the fact that *after* Yalta, Churchill himself repeatedly reasserted the terms of the October agreement as if he regarded it, despite Yalta, as controlling.

Harriman still had the feeling before Yalta that the Kremlin had "two approaches to their postwar policies" and that Stalin himself was "of two minds." One approach emphasized the internal reconstruction and development of Russia; the other its external expansion. But in the meantime the fact which dominated all political decisions—that is, the war against Germany—was moving into its final phase. In the weeks after Yalta, the military situation changed with great rapidity. As the Nazi threat declined, so too did the need for coöperation. The Soviet Union, feeling itself menaced by the American idea of self-determination and the borderlands diplomacy to which it was leading, skeptical whether the United Nations would protect its frontiers as reliably as its own domination in Eastern Europe, began to fulfill its security requirements unilaterally.

In March Stalin expressed his evaluation of the United Nations by rejecting Roosevelt's plea that Molotov come to the San Francisco conference, if only for the opening sessions. In the next weeks the Russians emphatically and crudely worked their will in Eastern Europe, above all in the test country of Poland. They were ignoring the Declaration on Liberated Europe, ignoring the Atlantic Charter, self-determination, human freedom and everything else the Americans considered essential for a stable peace. "We must clearly recognize," Harriman wired Washington a few days before Roosevelt's death, "that the Soviet program is the establishment of totalitarianism, ending personal liberty and democracy as we know and respect it."

. At the same time, the Russians also began to mobilize communist resources in the United States itself to block American universalism. In April 1945, Jacques Duclos, who had been the Comintern official responsible for the Western communist parties, launched in *Cahiers du Communisme* an uncompromising attack on the policy of the American Communist Party. Duclos sharply condemned the revisionism of Earl Browder, the American Communist leader, as "expressed in the concept of a long-term class peace in the United States, of the possibility of the suppression of the class struggle in the postwar period and of establishment of harmony between labor and capital." Browder was specifically rebuked for favoring the "self-determination" of Europe "west of the Soviet Union" on a bourgeois-democratic basis. The excommunication of Browderism was plainly the Politburo's considered reaction to the impending defeat of Germany; it was a signal to the communist parties of the West that they should recover their identity; it was Moscow's alert to communists everywhere that they should prepare for new policies in the postwar world.

The Duclos piece obviously could not have been planned and written much later than the Yalta conference—that is, well before a number of events which revisionists now cite in order to demonstrate American responsibility for the Cold War: before Allen Dulles, for example, began to negotiate the surrender of the German armies in Italy (the episode which provoked Stalin to charge Roosevelt with seeking a separate peace and provoked Roosevelt to denounce the "vile misrepresentations" of Stalin's informants); well before Roosevelt died; many months before the testing of the atomic bomb; even more months before Truman ordered that the bomb be dropped on Japan. William Z. Foster, who soon replaced Browder as the leader of the American Communist Party and embodied the new Moscow line, later boasted of having said in January 1944, "A post-war Roosevelt administration would continue to be, as it is now, an imperialist government." With ancient suspicions revived by the American insistence on universalism, this was no doubt the conclusion which the Russians were reaching at the same time. The Soviet canonization of Roosevelt (like their present-day canonization of Kennedy) took place after the American President's death.

The atmosphere of mutual suspicion was beginning to rise. In January 1945 Molotov formally proposed that the United States grant Russia a $6 billion credit for postwar reconstruction. With characteristic tact he explained that he was doing this as a favor to save America from a postwar depression. The proposal seems to have been diffidently made and diffidently received. Roosevelt requested that the matter "not be pressed further" on the American side until he had a chance to talk with Stalin; but the Russians did not follow it up either at Yalta in February (save for a single glancing reference) or during the Stalin-Hopkins talks in May or at Postdam. Finally the proposal was renewed in the very different political atmosphere of August. This time Washington inexplicably mislaid the request during the transfer of the records of the Foreign Economic Administration to the State Department. It did not turn up again until March 1946. Of course this was impossible for the Russians to believe; it is hard enough even for those acquainted with the capacity of the American government for incompetence to believe; and it only strengthened Soviet suspicions of American purposes.

The American credit was one conceivable form of Western contribution to Russian reconstruction. Another was lend-lease, and the possibility of reconstruction aid under the lend-lease protocol had already been discussed in 1944. But in May 1945 Russia, like Britain, suffered from Truman's abrupt termination of lend-lease shipments— "unfortunate and even brutal," Stalin told Hopkins, adding that, if it was "designed as pressure on the Russians in order to soften them up, then it was a fundamental mistake." A third form was German reparations. Here Stalin in demanding $10 billion in reparations for the Soviet Union made his strongest fight at Yalta. Roosevelt, while agreeing essentially with Churchill's opposition, tried to postpone the matter by accepting the Soviet figure as a "basis for discussion"—a formula which led to future misunderstanding. In short, the Russian hope for major Western assistance in postwar reconstruction foundered on three events which the Kremlin could well have interpreted respectively as deliberate sabotage (the loan request), blackmail (lend-lease cancellation) and pro-Germanism (reparations).

Actually the American attempt to settle the fourth lend-lease protocol was generous and the Russians for their own reasons declined to come to an agreement. It is not clear, though, that satisfying Moscow on any of these financial scores would have made much essential difference. It might have persuaded some doves in the Kremlin that the U.S. government was genuinely friendly; it might have persuaded some hawks that the American anxiety for Soviet friendship was such that Moscow could do as it wished without inviting challenge from the United States. It would, in short, merely have reinforced both sides of the Kremlin debate; it would hardly have reversed deeper tendencies toward the deterioration of political relationships. Economic deals were surely subordinate to the quality of mutual political confidence; and here, in the months after Yalta, the decay was steady.

The Cold War had now begun. It was the product not of a decision but of a dilemma. Each side felt compelled to adopt policies which the other could not but regard as a threat to the principles of the peace. Each then felt compelled to undertake defensive measures. Thus the Russians saw no choice but to consolidate their security in Eastern Europe. The Americans, regarding Eastern Europe as the first step toward Western Europe, responded by asserting their interest in the zone the Russians deemed vital to their security. The Russians concluded that the West was resuming its old course of capitalist encirclement; that it was purposefully laying the foundation for anti-Soviet régimes in the area defined by the blood of centuries as crucial to Russian survival. Each side believed with passion that future international stability depended on the success of its own conception of world order. Each side, in pursuing its own clearly indicated and deeply cherished principles, was only confirming the fear of the other that it was bent on aggression.

Very soon the process began to acquire a cumulative momentum. The impending collapse of Germany thus provoked new troubles: the Russians, for example, sincerely feared that the West was planning a separate surrender of the German armies in Italy in a way which would release troops for Hitler's eastern front, as they subsequently feared that the Nazis might succeed in surrendering Berlin to the West. This was the context in which the atomic bomb now appeared. Though the revisionist argument that Truman dropped the bomb less to defeat Japan than to intimidate Russia is not convincing, this thought unquestionably appealed to some in Washington as at least an advantageous side-effect of Hiroshima.

So the machinery of suspicion and counter-suspicion, action and counter-action, was set in motion. But, given relations among traditional national states, there was still no reason, even with all the postwar jostling, why this should not have remained a manageable situation. What made it unmanageable, what caused the rapid escalation of the Cold War and in another two years completed the division of Europe, was a set of considerations which this account has thus far excluded.

VII

Up to this point, the discussion has considered the schism within the wartime coalition as if it were entirely the result of disagreements among national states. Assuming this framework, there was unquestionably a failure of communication between America and Russia, a misperception of signals and, as time went on, a mounting tendency to ascribe ominous motives to the other side. It seems hard, for example, to deny that American postwar policy created genuine difficulties for the

Russians and even assumed a threatening aspect for them. All this the revisionists have rightly and usefully emphasized.

But the great omission of the revisionists—and also the fundamental explanation of the speed with which the Cold War escalated—lies precisely in the fact that the Soviet Union was *not* a traditional national state.[4] This is where the "mirror image," invoked by some psychologists, falls down. For the Soviet Union was a phenomenon very different from America or Britain: it was a totalitarian state, endowed with an all-explanatory, all-consuming ideology, committed to the infallibility of government and party, still in a somewhat messianic mood, equating dissent with treason, and ruled by a dictator who, for all his quite extraordinary abilities, had his paranoid moments.

Marxism-Leninism gave the Russian leaders a view of the world according to which all societies were inexorably destined to proceed along appointed roads by appointed stages until they achieved the classless nirvana. Moreover, given the resistance of the capitalists to this development, the existence of any noncommunist state was *by definition* a threat to the Soviet Union. "As long as capitalism and socialism exist," Lenin wrote, "we cannot live in peace: in the end, one or the other will triumph—a funeral dirge will be sung either over the Soviet Republic or over world capitalism."

Stalin and his associates, whatever Roosevelt or Truman did or failed to do, were bound to regard the United States as the enemy, not because of this deed or that, but because of the primordial fact that America was the leading capitalist power and thus, by Leninist syllogism, unappeasably hostile, driven by the logic of its system to oppose, encircle and destroy Soviet Russia. Nothing the United States could have done in 1944–45 would have abolished this mistrust, required and sanctified as it was by Marxist gospel—nothing short of the conversion of the United States into a Stalinist despotism; and even this would not have sufficed, as the experience of Jugoslavia and China soon showed, unless it were accompanied by total subservience to Moscow. So long as the United States remained a capitalist democracy, no American policy, given Moscow's theology, could hope to win basic Soviet confidence, and every American action was poisoned from the source. So long as the Soviet Union remained a messianic state, ideology compelled a steady expansion of communist power.

It is easy, of course, to exaggerate the capacity of ideology to control events. The tension of acting according to revolutionary abstractions is too much for most nations to sustain over a long period: that is why Mao Tse-tung has launched his Cultural Revolution, hoping thereby to create a permanent revolutionary mood and save Chinese communism from the degeneration which, in his view, has overtaken Russian communism. Still, as any revolution grows older, normal human and social motives will increasingly reassert themselves. In due course, we can be sure, Leninism will be about as effective in governing the daily lives of Russians as Christianity is in

4 This is the classical revisionist fallacy—the assumption of the rationality, or at least of the traditionalism, of states where ideology and social organization have created a different range of motives. So the Second World War revisionists omit the totalitarian dynamism of Nazism and the fanaticism of Hitler, as the Civil War revisionists omit the fact that the slavery system was producing a doctrinaire closed society in the American South. For a consideration of some of these issues, see "The Causes of the Civil War: A Note on Historical Sentimentalism" in my "The Politics of Hope" (Boston, 1963).

governing the daily lives of Americans. Like the Ten Commandments and the Sermon on the Mount, the Leninist verities will increasingly become platitudes for ritual observance, not guides to secular decision. There can be no worse fallacy (even if respectable people practiced it diligently for a season in the United States) than that of drawing from a nation's ideology permanent conclusions about its behavior.

A temporary recession of ideology was already taking place during the Second World War when Stalin, to rally his people against the invader, had to replace the appeal of Marxism by that of nationalism ("We are under no illusions that they are fighting for us," Stalin once said to Harriman. "They are fighting for Mother Russia.") But this was still taking place within the strictest limitations. The Soviet Union remained as much a police state as ever; the régime was as infallible as ever; foreigners and their ideas were as suspect as ever. "Never, except possibly during my later experience as ambassador in Moscow," Kennan has written, "did the insistence of the Soviet authorities on isolation of the diplomatic corps weigh more heavily on me . . . than in these first weeks following my return to Russia in the final months of the war. . . . [We were] treated as though we were the bearers of some species of the plague"—which, of course, from the Soviet viewpoint, they were: the plague of skepticism.

Paradoxically, of the forces capable of bringing about a modification of ideology, the most practical and effective was the Soviet dictatorship itself. If Stalin was an ideologist, he was also a pragmatist. If he saw everything through the lenses of Marxism-Leninism, he also, as the infallible expositor of the faith, could reinterpret Marxism-Leninism to justify anything he wanted to do at any given moment. No doubt Roosevelt's ignorance of Marxism-Leninism was inexcusable and led to grievous miscalculations. But Roosevelt's efforts to work on and through Stalin were not so hopelessly naïve as it used to be fashionable to think. With the extraordinary instinct of a great political leader, Roosevelt intuitively understood that Stalin was the *only* lever available to the West against the Leninist ideology and the Soviet system. If Stalin could be reached, then alone was there a chance of getting the Russians to act contrary to the prescriptions of their faith. The best evidence is that Roosevelt retained a certain capacity to influence Stalin to the end; the nominal Soviet acquiescence in American universalism as late as Yalta was perhaps an indication of that. It is in this way that the death of Roosevelt was crucial—not in the vulgar sense that his policy was then reversed by his successor, which did not happen, but in the sense that no other American could hope to have the restraining impact on Stalin which Roosevelt might for a while have had.

Stalin alone could have made any difference. Yet Stalin, in spite of the impression of sobriety and realism he made on Westerners who saw him during the Second World War, was plainly a man of deep and morbid obsessions and compulsions. When he was still a young man, Lenin had criticized his rude and arbitrary ways. A reasonably authoritative observer (N. S. Khrushchev) later commented, "These negative characteristics of his developed steadily and during the last years acquired an absolutely insufferable character." His paranoia, probably set off by the suicide of his wife in 1932, led to the terrible purges of the mid-thirties and the wanton murder of thousands of his Bolshevik comrades. "Everywhere and in everything," Khrushchev says of this period, "he saw 'enemies', 'double-dealers' and 'spies'." The crisis of war evidently steadied him in some way, though Khrushchev speaks of his "nervousness and hysteria . . . even after the war began." The madness, so rigidly controlled for a time, burst out with new and shocking intensity in the postwar years. "After the war," Khrushchev testifies,

> the situation became even more complicated. Stalin became even more capricious, irritable and brutal; in particular, his suspicion grew. His persecution mania reached unbelievable dimensions. . . . He decided everything, without any consideration for anyone or anything.
>
> Stalin's wilfulness showed itself . . . also in the international relations of the Soviet Union. . . . He had completely lost a sense of reality; he demonstrated his suspicion and haughtiness not only in relation to individuals in the USSR, but in relation to whole parties and nations.

A revisionist fallacy has been to treat Stalin as just another Realpolitik statesman, as Second World War revisionists see Hitler as just another Stresemann or Bismarck. But the record makes it clear that in the end nothing could satisfy Stalin's paranoia. His own associates failed. Why does anyone suppose that any conceivable American policy would have succeeded?

An analysis of the origins of the Cold War which leaves out these factors—the intransigence of Leninist ideology, the sinister dynamics of a totalitarian society and the madness of Stalin—is obviously incomplete. It was these factors which made it hard for the West to accept the thesis that Russia was moved only by a desire to protect its security and would be satisfied by the control of Eastern Europe; it was these factors which charged the debate between universalism and spheres of influence with apocalyptic potentiality.

Leninism and totalitarianism created a structure of thought and behavior which made postwar collaboration between Russia and America—in any normal sense of civilized intercourse between national states—inherently impossible. The Soviet dictatorship of 1945 simply could not have survived such a collaboration. Indeed, nearly a quarter-century later, the Soviet régime, though it has meanwhile moved a good distance, could still hardly survive it without risking the release inside Russia of energies profoundly opposed to communist despotism. As for Stalin, he may have represented the only force in 1945 capable of overcoming Stalinism, but the very traits which enabled him to win absolute power expressed terrifying instabilities of mind and temperament and hardly offered a solid foundation for a peaceful world.

VIII

The difference between America and Russia in 1945 was that some Americans fundamentally believed that, over a long run, a modus vivendi with Russia was possible; while the Russians, so far as one can tell, believed in no more than a short-run modus vivendi with the United States.

Harriman and Kennan, this narrative has made clear, took the lead in warning Washington about the difficulties of short-run dealings with the Soviet Union. But both argued that, if the United States developed a rational policy and stuck to it, there would be, after long and rough passages, the prospect of eventual clearing. "I am, as you know," Harriman cabled Washington in early April, "a most earnest advocate of the closest possible understanding with the Soviet Union so that what I am saying relates only to how best to attain such understanding." Kennan has similarly made it clear that the function of his containment policy was "to tide us over a difficult time and bring us to the point where we could discuss effectively with the Russians the dangers and drawbacks this status quo involved, and to arrange with them for its peaceful replacement by a better and sounder one." The subsequent careers of both men attest to the honesty of these statements.

There is no corresponding evidence on the Russian side that anyone seriously sought a modus vivendi in these terms. Stalin's choice was whether his long-term ideological and national interests would be better served by a short-run truce with the West or by an immediate resumption of pressure. In October 1945 Stalin indicated to Harriman at Sochi that he planned to adopt the second course—that the Soviet Union was going isolationist. No doubt the succession of problems with the United States contributed to this decision, but the basic causes most probably lay elsewhere: in the developing situations in Eastern Europe, in Western Europe and in the United States.

In Eastern Europe, Stalin was still for a moment experimenting with techniques of control. But he must by now have begun to conclude that he had underestimated the hostility of the people to Russian dominion. The Hungarian elections in November would finally convince him that the Yalta formula was a road to anti-Soviet governments. At the same time, he was feeling more strongly than ever a sense of his opportunities in Western Europe. The other half of the Continent lay unexpectedly before him politically demoralized, economically prostrate, militarily defenseless. The hunting would be better and safer than he had anticipated. As for the United States, the alacrity of postwar demobilization must have recalled Roosevelt's offhand remark at Yalta that "two years would be the limit" for keeping American troops in Europe. And, despite Dr. Eugene Varga's doubts about the imminence of American economic breakdown, Marxist theology assured Stalin that the United States was heading into a bitter postwar depression and would be consumed with its own problems. If the condition of Eastern Europe made unilateral action seem essential in the interests of Russian security, the condition of Western Europe and the United States offered new temptations for communist expansion. The Cold War was now in full swing.

It still had its year of modulations and accommodations. Secretary Byrnes conducted his long and fruitless campaign to persuade the Russians that America only sought governments in Eastern Europe "both friendly to the Soviet Union and representative of all the democratic elements of the country." Crises were surmounted in Trieste and Iran. Secretary Marshall evidently did not give up hope of a modus vivendi until the Moscow conference of foreign secretaries of March 1947. Even then, the Soviet Union was invited to participate in the Marshall Plan.

The point of no return came on July 2, 1947, when Molotov, after bringing 89 technical specialists with him to Paris and evincing initial interest in the project for European reconstruction, received the hot flash from the Kremlin, denounced the whole idea and walked out of the conference. For the next fifteen years the Cold War raged unabated, passing out of historical ambiguity into the realm of good versus evil and breeding on both sides simplifications, sterotypes and self-serving absolutes, often couched in interchangeable phrases. Under the pressure even America, for a deplorable decade, forsook its pragmatic and pluralist traditions, posed as God's appointed messenger to ignorant and sinful man and followed the Soviet example in looking to a world remade in its own image.

In retrospect, if it is impossible to see the Cold War as a case of American aggression and Russian response, it is also hard to see it as a pure case of Russian aggression and American response. "In what is truly tragic," wrote Hegel, "there must be valid moral powers on both the sides which come into collision. . . . Both suffer loss and yet both are mutually justified." In this sense, the Cold War had its tragic elements. The question remains whether it was an instance of Greek tragedy— as Auden has called it, "the tragedy of necessity," where the feeling aroused in the spectator is "What a pity it had to be this way"—or of Christian tragedy, "the tragedy of possibility," where the feeling aroused is "What a pity it was this way when it might have been otherwise."

Once something has happened, the historian is tempted to assume that it had to happen; but this may often be a highly unphilosophical assumption. The Cold War could have been avoided only if the Soviet Union had not been possessed by convictions both of the infallibility of the communist word and of the inevitability of a communist world. These convictions transformed an impasse between national states into a religious war, a tragedy of possibility into one of necessity. One might wish that America had preserved the poise and proportion of the first years of the Cold War and had not in time succumbed to its own forms of self-righteousness. But the most rational of American policies could hardly have averted the Cold War. Only today, as Russia begins to recede from its messianic mission and to accept, in practice if not yet in principle, the permanence of the world of diversity, only now can the hope flicker that this long, dreary, costly contest may at last be taking on forms less dramatic, less obsessive and less dangerous to the future of mankind.

25 / Cuba and Pearl Harbor: Hindsight and Foresight

Roberta Wohlstetter

National decision-making in time of crisis is difficult, maybe impossible, for the historian at some later time to recreate from available documentation. In the following article, Roberta Wohlstetter makes a comparison between salient ingredients in the approaching confrontation between the United States and Japan in 1941, and the Russian-American confrontation over missile bases in Cuba in 1962. From her survey based on intelligence records, she draws conclusions that should prove useful to an understanding of just why Uncle Sam seemed to be caught with his pants down. The well-known results were that the United States in the first instance became the target for Japanese aggression and in the second it moved precipitously close to a head-on collision with Soviet power in the Caribbean. The confrontation of 1962 probably posed the greatest risk of war between Soviet Russia and the United States of any crisis since the end of World War II. Comparative studies of international crises can be extremely valuable for the student interested in political processes.

For further reading: Robert J. Alexander, *Communism in Latin America* (New Brunswick: 1957); Lionel M. Gelber, *America in Britain's Place* (New York: 1961); Henry A. Kissinger, *Nuclear Weapons and Foreign Policy* (New York: 1957); Frank E. Manuel, *The Realities of American-Palestine Relations* (New York: 1949); Robert E. Osgood, *Limited War: The Challenge to American Strategy* (Chicago: 1957); Frederick Pike, "Guatemala, the United States and Communism in the Americas," *Review of Politics*, XVII (April, 1955), 232–261; Roberta Wohlstetter, *Pearl Harbor: Warning and Decision* (Stanford: 1962).

Roberta Wohlstetter is a member of the Social Science Division of the Rand Corporation. This article is reprinted with the permission of the editors of *Foreign Affairs*. From *Foreign Affairs*, XLIII (1965). Copyright © 1965 by the Council on Foreign Relations, Inc., New York.

I

To recall the atmosphere of September and October 1962 now seems almost as difficult as to recreate the weeks, more than two decades earlier, before the attack on Pearl Harbor. But if we are to understand the onset of the Cuban missile crisis, it is worth the effort. Indeed we may learn something about the problems of foreseeing and forestalling or, at any rate, diminishing the severity of such crises by examining side by side the preludes to both these major turning points in American history. In juxtaposing these temporally separate events, our interest is in understanding rather than in drama. We would like to know not only how we felt, but what we did and what we might have done, and in particular what we knew or what we could have known before each crisis.

Afterthoughts come naturally following the first wave of relief and jubilation at having weathered the missile crisis and forced the withdrawal of the missiles. But it is good to keep in mind the obvious contrast with Pearl Harbor. At the least, Pearl Harbor was a catastrophe, a great failure of warning and decision. At the very worst, the missile crisis was a narrow escape. Taken as a whole, however, its outcome must be counted as a success both for the intelligence community and the decision-makers. But a comparison of the failure at Pearl Harbor and the Cuban success reveals a good deal about the basic uncertainties affecting the success and failure of intelligence.

It is true for both Pearl Harbor and Cuba that we had lots of information about the approaching crisis. In discussing this information it will perhaps be useful to distinguish again between signals and noise. By the "signal" of an action is meant a sign, a clue, a piece of evidence that points to the action or to an adversary's intention to undertake it, and by "noise" is meant the background of irrelevant or inconsistent signals, signs pointing in the wrong directions, that tend always to obscure the signs pointing the right way. Pearl Harbor, looked at closely and objectively, shows how hard it is to hear a signal against the prevailing noise, in particular when you are listening for the wrong signal, and even when you have a wealth of information. (Or perhaps especially then. There are clearly cases when riches can be embarrassing.)

After the event, of course, we know: like the detective-story reader who turns to the last page first, we find it easy to pick out the clues. And a close look at the historiography of Pearl Harbor suggests that in most accounts, memories of the noise and background confusion have faded quickly, leaving the actual signals of the crisis standing out in bold relief, stark and preternaturally clear.

After the crisis, memories fade and recriminations take their place. For a time the Cuban missile crisis figured as an outstanding triumph for the United States—in the swift discovery of "hard evidence," in the retention of American initiative, in the strict security maintained and in the taut control of power by the Executive Committee. Today, some of these aspects of the Cuban crisis have been thrown into doubt, and in particular, critics talk of a significant intelligence failure in anticipating the crisis. In both Pearl Harbor and Cuba the notion of a conspiracy of silence has been raised, the suggestion that we knew all along and failed to act, that Kennedy, like Roosevelt, had some special information which he withheld, or that information was so obvious that even a layman could have interpreted it correctly.

New York's Senator Keating, for example, was explicit and articulate in insisting that he believed long-range or medium-range missiles and Soviet combat troops were in Cuba as early as August. On August 31 he said in the Senate that he had reliable information on landings between August 3 and August 15 at the Cuban port of Mariel of 1200 troops wearing Soviet fatigue uniforms. He also reported that "other observers" had noted "Soviet motor convoys moving on Cuban roads in military formation," the presence of landing craft, and of suspicious cylindrical objects that had to be transported on two flatcars, and so on. He claimed that his statements had been verified by official sources within the U.S. Government. Between August 31 and October 12 he made ten Senate speeches warning of the Soviet military build-up.

After the crisis, Congressmen naturally wondered why we had not listened to Senator Keating, why it was possible to have had these warnings and many others and still be surprised on October 15. But failures to foresee and to forestall catastrophes are by no means abnormal. Military men and statesmen have no monopoly on being taken by surprise. The example of the Dallas police department springs to mind, and the murder of Oswald which gave rise, like Pearl Harbor, to rumors of conspiracy in high places and in local governments. Nor are American businessmen and financiers immune. Witness the $150 million De Angelis vegetable-oil scandal, where normally cautious bankers suddenly found they were holding empty storage tanks as security for their loans.

Conspiracy with the culprit, however, is hardly a universal line of explanation, as is suggested by a recent natural catastrophe—the earthquake in and near Alaska that sent a tidal wave to shatter the northern shore of California and caught some towns unprepared in spite of timely warnings. For the warnings sounded just like many others in the past that had not been followed by tidal waves. These are all American examples, but Singapore, "Barbarossa" (the German attack on Russia) and many others suggest that we are not dealing with a purely national susceptibility to surprise.

II

Defense departments and intelligence agencies, of course, continually estimate what an opponent can do, may do, intends to do. They try to gauge the technical limits within which he is operating, to determine his usual ways of behavior, under what conditions he will probe, push or withdraw. They try to measure what risks he will take, and how he might estimate the risks to us of countering him. Much of this work by American analysts is sound, thorough, intelligent, frequently ingenious and sometimes brilliant—but not infallible. Unhappily, any of these estimates may be partly, but critically, wrong. A wealth of information is never enough.

To get a rapid idea of the mass of data available for predicting the Cuban crisis and the Pearl Harbor attack, let us run through the main intelligence sources. In the case of Cuba, there was first of all magnificent photographic coverage as well as visual reconnaissance. The Navy ran air reconnaissance of all ships going in and out of Cuba, especially ships originating in Soviet or satellite ports during the summer of 1962, and intensified this sort of coverage during September. High-level photographic reconnaissance by U-2s over the island of Cuba was taking place at the rate of one flight every two weeks until the month of September, when it increased to once a week.[1] Low-level photographic reconnaissance began only after the President's speech of October 22—the first being on October 23. In addition to photography,

---

[1] Flights over the island took place on September 5, 17, 26, 29, October 5, 7 and 14. The irregularity is attributed to bad weather.

we had voluminous accounts from Cuban refugees who were leaving the island in a steady stream. We had agents stationed on the island who were reporting, and we were listening to radio broadcasts from Cuba. The Cuban press, while carefully controlled, was making some announcements which are interesting in retrospect. A number of European correspondents stationed on the island were reporting to their newspapers, although the American press was not welcome.

Finally, but by no means least, we had Castro's pronouncements. His casual interviews with reporters, debates with students, interrogation of prisoners, and nearly interminable television speeches offer a rich fount of information. If you wait long enough, it seems, Castro will tell you everything. The only problem in a crisis is that you may not be able to wait that long. Castro is noted for his slyness, and he is perhaps better able than most Cubans to keep a secret. But sometimes he cannot resist hints that may reveal a trap before his victim falls into it. And often in real rather than calculated anger he will show his hand.

For predicting the Pearl Harbor attack, the United States Government had an equally impressive array of intelligence sources. Though aerial surveillance of the Japanese fleet was limited, the Navy had developed a system of pinpointing the location of ships and deducing their types by radio-traffic analysis. This was accomplished by analyzing the call signs of various ships, even though we could not read the content of the messages. Any change in call signs was in itself a cause for alarm, and it took usually several weeks of close listening to an enormous amount of traffic to re-identify the call signs. Call signs were changed on November 1, 1941, and again on December 1. We had not identified the new ones by December 7.

While we had not broken any military codes, we did have one superlative source that is perhaps comparable to the evidence provided by U-2 photography. That was the breaking of the top-priority Japanese diplomatic code, known as MAGIC, as well as some less complicated codes used by Japaneses consular observers. We were listening in on diplomatic messages on all the major Tokyo circuits—to Rome, Berlin, London, Washington and so on. Colonel Friedman, an Army cryptographer, had devised a machine for rapidly decoding these messages, so that, in general, we knew what a message said before its intended Japanese recipients. Our ground observers, stationed in key ports along the coast of China and Southeast Asia, were reporting in by radio.

Ambassador Grew and his Embassy staff in Tokyo were experienced observers of local economic and political activities. Grew himself had a very sound estimate of Japanese character and diplomacy, but as Japanese censorship closed in during the last few weeks before the attack, Grew had to warn Washington that he was unable to report accurately on any military preparations then under way. American newspaper correspondents in Japan were also quite well informed and shrewd in their reporting. In addition to our own sources, we exchanged information with British intelligence. At that date, our own intelligence officers did not trust British intelligence fully. They expressed a certain amount of unease over British methods of picking up information, which they regarded as sophisticated but underhanded. As General Sherman Miles put it, U.S. intelligence preferred to be "above board." However, the British provided us with some good leads and lots of corroborative information. And there was, of course, the Japanese press, which proclaimed Japan's undying hostility to the American presence in Asia, and announced with increasing violence the Japanese intention to expand to the south.

In sum, for each of the two crises there was plenty of information suggesting its advent. Even though Cuba is a closed society, and even though Japan, in the last weeks, was under heavy censorship and tight security, the data provided by U.S. intelligence agencies were excellent. Once more, then, we come to the question, what went wrong? With all these data, why didn't we know that Japan would attack Pearl Harbor on December 7? Why, when it seems so clear in retrospect, didn't we anticipate that Khrushchev might put medium-range missiles into Cuba? Why didn't we seize the first indications that such installations were on the way? Weren't these early signs clear enough?

Unfortunately, they were not, and almost never are. Even with hindsight, we are not able to reconstruct the exact sequence of events that led to the Cuban missile crisis. Most of our sources are alive, and some of them are talking. But what can we say with certainty about Cuban and Soviet motives? Castro, for example, has spoken on many occasions about why missiles were put into Cuba. But he swings between the view that he requested them and the view that Khrushchev suggested the idea and that he, Castro, felt so indebted economically he had to accept. He has mentioned two motives—one, defense against an American invasion that he believed was imminent, and the other, the need to advance the international cause of socialism, which implied that the missiles were for offense as well as defense. Khrushchev's story is more consistent, but also more "official": he cites only the need to help Cuba prepare against an American invasion. But of course for active Cuban defense, long-range missiles are not necessary. Speculation on Soviet and Cuban motives still continues.

With hindsight, we can look back now and see that during the crisis there were naturally many confusions embedded in the mass of intelligence reports. A report of a "missile" might refer to a surface-to-air missile which is approximately 30 feet long, to the nose cone of a surface-to-surface missile which is about 14 feet long, to its body which is almost 60 feet long, or to a fuel storage tank. Or perhaps it might just represent the imagination of an excited Cuban refugee. Most of these objects were seen at night through closed shutters and in motion. Visual observation, except by a highly trained observer, was not likely to be accurate even as to the length of the object. And Senator Keating did not act altogether responsibly in perpetuating this confusion centering around the word "missile." He was right when he described the total build-up as alarming, but he was proceeding beyond the evidence in suggesting, as he did, that he had positive proof of the presence of medium-range missiles,[2] and of the capability for rapid transformation of surface-to-air missiles into medium-range surface-to-surface missiles.

Or take the presence of Soviet combat troops. President Kennedy's critics noted after the crisis that in his October 22 speech he made no mention of combat troops in Cuba, although the American public was later informed of their presence. Actually, Soviet troops, organized into four regimental units, totaled approximately 5,000 men. They were located at four different spots, two near Havana, one in Central Cuba and one in Eastern Cuba. They were equipped with modern Soviet ground-force fighting equipment, including battlefield rocket launchers similar to the American "Honest John." This equipment, along with the accompanying barracks and tent installations, was not identifiable, or at least was not identified, until we started photographing at low level. For this reason, President Kennedy made no demand

[2] See testimony, September 17, 1962: United States Senate, Committee on Foreign Relations and Committee on Armed Services, *Situation in Cuba*, 87th Cong., 2d Sess., 1962, p. 7, 12; *U. S. News and World Report*, November 19, 1962 (distributed week of November 12), p. 87; and speech to the Senate, October 12, 1962.

about removal of troops on October 22, but kept to the colorless term, "Soviet technicians." While U-2 photography is almost as magical as the MAGIC code at the time of Pearl Harbor, like the code, it is limited; it cannot reveal all.

III

For the layman, the feeling persists that there must be some marvelous source that will provide a single signal, a clear tip-off that will alert the American forces and tell them exactly what to do. Unfortunately, there is no instance where such a tip-off arrived in time, except perhaps in the Philippines in 1941, when General MacArthur had a minimum of nine hours' warning between his knowledge of the Pearl Harbor attack and the initial Japanese assault on his own forces. The news of the attack on Pearl Harbor clearly did not tell him what alert posture to take, since his planes were found by the Japanese attackers in formation, wing-tip to wing-tip on their bases.

Instead we must wait for a number of signals to converge in the formation of a single hypothesis about the intentions and actions of an opponent. This is a necessary but slow process. In 1962, for example, General Carroll, head of the Defense Intelligence Agency, became suspicious of Soviet activities on the basis of several pieces of data from different sources. According to Secretary McNamara's testimony,

> . . . [Carroll] had had thousands of reports like this. What gradually formed in his mind was a hypothesis based on the integration of three or four pieces of evidence, one of which was not a report at all, one of which was a recognition through photographic analysis that a SAM (surface-to-air missile) site appeared to be in a rather unusual place. . . . Gradually over a period of time—I do not know over what period of time—but sometime between the 18th of September and the 14th of October, there was formulated in his mind a hypothesis specifically that there was the possibility of a Soviet ballistic missile installation in a particular area, a hypothesis that had been formulated previously and had been tested previously and found to be in error with respect to other locations.
>
> His only action here—I think quite properly his only action here—was to test that hypothesis, to submit it to the targeting group that targets the reconnaissance missions, and place that target on the track for the next reconnaissance mission, which was the October 14 mission.[3]

This period of time from September 18 to October 14 is not long for the crystallization of a hypothesis.[4] It is long only in relation to the speed of the missile installation. This sort of time difference is a perpetually agonizing aspect of intelligence interpretation. Collection, checking of sources and interpreting all take time. There is always delay between the intelligence source and the evaluation center, and between the center and the final report to the decision-maker. Even then, the decision-maker may merely request more information before taking action. In the meantime, the opponent moves forward.

[3] U. S. Congress, House of Representatives, Subcommittee on Department of Defense Appropriations, *Department of Defense Appropriations for 1964*, 88th Cong., 1st Sess., 1963, p. 45–46. These hearings contain most of the intelligence data cited in this article.

[4] According to Roger Hilsman, the request for a U-2 flight covering the western end of the island was made on October 4—ten days before the flight was actually made. "The Cuban Crisis: How Close We Were to War," *Look*, August 25, 1964, p. 18.

In the Cuban missile crisis, for example, there were delays in the identification of surface-to-air missiles. From July 29 to August 5, Cuban refugees reported that "an unusual number of ships" unloaded cargo and passengers at the ports of Havana and Mariel. All Cubans were excluded from the dock. By August 14 these reports reached U. S. intelligence agencies, which the next day requested U-2 photo coverage of the suspect areas. On August 29 the flight was made. From the first visual observation on July 29 to the over-flight on August 29 a full month passed.

This August 29 flight turned up the first hard evidence of surface-to-air missiles in Cuba. During September, surveillance flights seem to have been stepped up: the U-2 flew on September 5, 17, 26, 29, and on October 5, 7 and 14. On the September 5 flight, which took in the San Cristobal area a hundred miles east of Havana, the photographs showed no evidence of medium-range missiles. A flight scheduled for September 10 was canceled, perhaps because a U-2 had been shot down over Red China the previous day. According to the American press, all U-2 flights stopped while the United States waited for the world reaction.

Secretary McNamara testified that available evidence indicated the first landing of mobile M.R.B.M.s occurred on September 8, and that construction of the sites did not begin before September 15 to 20. It is possible that September 10 photography might have shown some activity at the San Cristobal site. The September 17 flight was of little use because cloud cover obscured the areas photographed. However, between September 18 and 21 further Cuban reports came to U. S. intelligence, and these were evaluated on September 27. They eventually led to the flight on October 14, again over San Cristobal. This flight produced the first reliable evidence of medium-range missiles on the island.

In spite of the frequency of the U-2 flights, there is a lag of 33 days from the first visual observation made by a Cuban exile on September 8, and reported on September 9, to October 14, the day that hard evidence was obtained. There is a lag of 39 days between September 5 and October 14, during which no flights covered the San Cristobal area. This gap in coverage was not apparent until some inquiring Congressmen pressed their cross-examination. When William Minshall of Ohio asserted that the U-2 flights had been covering the wrong end of the island, General Carroll pointed out that it was necessary to cover the eastern and central portions also. Secretary McNamara supported him by pointing out that the September 5 flight over San Cristobal "showed absolutely no activity whatsoever." He also recalled that this was the hurricane season, "and the weather in that part of the Caribbean is very bad. We had a number of flights canceled during that period." Mr. Minshall then produced the official weather report showing clear days in the vicinity of Havana, and said that "the weather from September 25 to October 2, at least at 7:00 in the morning, was generally clear." No one pointed out at that time that weather forecasts, not actual weather, determined the schedule of U-2 flights.

Photographic coverage, then, was apparently being scheduled on the assumption that any Soviet construction would proceed at a pace which might be considered rapid according to our own experience in installing similar equipment. Secretary McNamara repeated several times that there was no missile construction activity in the Havana area on September 5, as if this, coupled with the pressing need to get clear pictures of other parts of the island, were sufficient reason for not covering the area again until October 14. This judgment, with hindsight, may have been correct, but in the absence of the full intelligence picture the layman can only wonder why it was not possible to cover more than one section of the island on a single U-2 sortie, or why it was not possible to make several simultaneous sorties when good weather prevailed. Perhaps Secretary McNamara's statement, made under pressure of Mr. Minshall's criticism, to the effect that "we were facing surface-to-air missile systems that might be coming into operation," indicates that the flight schedule was sensitive to the political atmosphere. The fact is that there *were* increasing dangers to our pilots as the SAM sites became operational. With the Republicans now in opposition, it was easy for some of them to forget the extreme embarrassment of the Eisenhower régime at the shooting down of the U-2 over the Soviet Union in 1960 and the collapse of the Paris summit that followed. Certainly after the publicity given to the U-2 shot down over Red China on September 9, the United States would not want to lose such a plane over Cuba. U-2 planes are never armed; and the August 29 flight had showed surface-to-air missile installations in western Cuba.

Naval photography shows a somewhat similar gap. Photographs of the crates containing IL-28 bombers were taken on September 28 but not evaluated until October 9, and not disseminated until October 10. This identification of bombers capable of carrying a nuclear or non-nuclear payload of 6,000 pounds and with a combat radius of about 700 nautical miles[5] came together with a report of October 15 evaluating the U-2 photographs of M.R.B.M.s.

This sort of delay can easily be paralleled in the Pearl Harbor intelligence picture. In the handling of the coded messages, there was inevitably a delay—from interception of the message at the intercept station through transmission to the decoding center in Washington, determination of priority in handling, assignment for full decoding, assignment for translation and the actual translation, to final delivery to the approved list of recipients. The longest delay recorded in the Congressional hearings is 54 days between interception and translation. Part of the delay is a function of the time necessary for transmission. Part of the delay comes from checking the accuracy of the reports, which is necessary for responsible decision. But these delays in response must all be seen against the forward march of events.

In Cuba, the rapidity of the Russians' installation was in effect a logistical surprise comparable to the technological surprise at the time of Pearl Harbor. Before September 1962 we were scheduling U-2 flights approximately two weeks apart, because we couldn't believe that capabilities could change significantly within a shorter period. But Secretary McNamara testified in his first background briefing (October 22) that the medium-range mobile missiles were planned to have a capability to be de-activated, moved, reactivated on a new site and ready for operation within a period of about six days. The Stennis Report, which reviewed the entire intelligence operation, refers to "a matter of hours."[6] In one instance, between two sets of photographs separated by less than 24 hours, there was an increase of 50 percent in the amount of equipment visible. On the date of withdrawal, October 28, the medium-range missiles were fully operational. Intelligence estimates set December 15 as the outside date for the non-mobile I.R.B.M.s to be operational.

[5] According to W. W. Kaufmann, *The McNamara Strategy*, Harper & Row, 1964, p. 270. According to John Hughes, Special Assistant to General Carroll, "about 600 nautical miles," *Hearings*, p. 15.

[6] U. S. Congress, Committee on Armed Services, Preparedness Investigating Subcommittee, *Investigations of the Preparedness Program, Interim Report on Cuban Military Build-Up*, 88th Cong., 1st Sess., 1963, p. 3.

This kind of technological or logistical surprise may be either a secret so carefully guarded that it doesn't reach our intelligence agencies until after the event; or it may happen too swiftly, too near the outbreak of the crisis, to be transmitted and evaluated in time. In the case of Pearl Harbor, there were two technological changes that failed to reach either the intelligence agencies or the commanding officers who needed the information: (1) that the Japanese had fitted fins to their torpedoes which would permit bombing in the shallow waters of Pearl Harbor; and (2) that the combat radius of the Zero fighter plane had been stretched to 500 statute miles, making possible aerial attack on the Philippines from Formosa. Both of these developments came to fruition only a few weeks before Pearl Harbor.

IV

Besides technological surprise and the inevitable physical delays involved in transmission and checking, there are more subtle obstacles to accurate perception of signals. First, there is the "cry-wolf" phenomenon. Admiral Stark actually used this phrase in deciding not to send Admiral Kimmel any further warnings about the Japanese. An excess of warnings which turn out to be false alarms always induces a kind of fatigue, a lessening of sensitivity. Admiral Kimmel and his staff were tired of checking out Japanese submarine reports in the vicinity of Pearl Harbor. In the week preceding the attack they had checked out seven, all of which were false.

General Carroll had the same problem with missiles in Cuba. Refugee reports of missiles had been coming in for a year and a half and the first San Cristobal report of September 9 describing that suspect area, later confirmed as harboring medium-range missiles, was "comparable to many other reports . . . similarly received and checked out," and found to reveal not surface-to-surface missiles, but surface-to-air or nothing at all. This history of mistaken observations by the refugees tended to reinforce the feelings of fatigue and disbelief. There was also a justifiable reaction to the fact that refugee exaggerations of anti-Castro ferment in Cuba had not been properly discounted at the time of the Bay of Pigs, and that their self-interest in wanting to return to Cuba had not been properly weighed. This background increased the reluctance of the intelligence agencies to credit their reports without careful verification. Besides the refugees, members of the Congresssional opposition were also using exaggeration and pressure, because they had an interest in overstating provocation in order to indicate laxness on the Administration's part. Senator Keating claimed to have hard evidence at a time when, it seems, such evidence did not exist. Opposition pressure tended to evoke a natural counter-pressure from the Administration, which responded by charging irresponsibility in its critics, and which insisted on caution and the necessity for special evidence before entering on such serious action. In this way the opposition served in some respects as rein rather than simply as spur.

Another obstacle to objective evaluation is the human tendency to see what we want to see or expect to see. The Administration did not want open conflict with the Soviet Union. It was working on a program of trying to relax tensions, of which a test-ban agreement was one important though distant goal. It most definitely did not want an offensive Soviet base in Cuba, in the same way that Zermatt, the famous Swiss ski resort, did not want typhoid fever and refused to acknowledge its existence until epidemic proportions had been reached. Just as President Roosevelt wanted no war in the Far East—no war on two fronts—and didn't want to believe that it could happen, so we didn't want to believe that the Soviets were doing what they were doing.

When this is the background of expectation, it is only natural to ignore small clues that might, in a review of the whole or on a simple count, add up to something significant. For example, the large ships that turned out to be the villains in the Cuban case had especially large covered hatches. They were unloaded at night by Soviet personnel, and all Cubans were excluded from the docks. The contents, whatever they were, were moved at night. The decks were loaded with 2½- and 5-ton trucks and cars. But these ships, in transit, had been noted to be riding high in the water. If intelligence analysts in the American community had been more ready to suspect the introduction of strategic missiles, would this information have led them to surmise, before as well as after October 14, that these ships carried "space-consuming [*i.e.* large volume, low density] cargo such as an M.R.B.M.'"[7] rather than a bulk cargo? Roger Hilsman points out that these vessels had been specially designed for carrying lumber, and "our shipping intelligence experts presumably deduced that lumbering ships could be more easily spared than others." "We knew," Hilsman writes, "that the Soviets had had some trouble finding the ships they needed to send their aid to Cuba."[8] This is a good illustration of the way we can adjust (without doing violence to the facts) a disturbing or unusual observation to "save" a theory—in this case that the Soviets would not send strategic missiles to Cuba.

Our estimate of Soviet behavior included, of course, some expectation of how the Russians would react to what we were telling them, to our warnings in words and acts. However, we overestimated the clarity of our signals. General Maxwell Taylor had visited Florida bases on August 25 with a great deal of publicity. Naval reconnaissance of ships approaching Cuba had been stepped up to the point where U. S. planes were shot at by nervous Cubans on September 2. Castro reacted with great restraint in commenting on this incident—a fact which might in itself have been thought suspicious. But above all, on September 4, President Kennedy announced the installation of surface-to-air missiles in Cuba which had been confirmed by the photographs of August 29. He said with the greatest care that we would not tolerate an offensive base or the installation of missiles capable of reaching U. S. territory. He made the distinction between offensive and defensive weapons, and he did this publicly in a way that put him on the spot. To anyone familiar with the workings of the American political system, this should have indicated that we were "contracting-in." The President was deliberately engaging his own prestige and that of the country. He was reacting to the Republicans as well as to Castro. He was justifying not acting up to a certain point, but making it more likely that he would act beyond that point. In other words, he was drawing a line, and he was making it extremely unlikely that we would back down if that line were crossed. Again on September 13, the President called attention to the firmness of his commitment.

To the official Administration statements, we must add the formal announcements by the opposition party. Senator Everett Dirksen of Illinois and Charles Halleck

---

[7] "Department of Defense, Special Cuba Briefing by the Honorable Robert S. McNamara, Secretary of Defense, State Department Auditorium, 5:00 p.m., February 6, 1963." A verbatim transcript of a presentation actually made by General Carroll's assistant, John Hughes.

[8] *Op. cit.*, p. 18.

of Indiana, the Republican Congressional leaders, both issued statements on Cuba on September 7. Halleck warned that the increases in armaments and numbers of military technicians supplied by the Soviet Union to Cuba made the situation there "worse from the point of view of our own vital interests and the security of this country." Senator Dirksen invoked the Monroe Doctrine and defined current Soviet military aid to Cuba as a violation of that doctrine. He pointed out that, in view of our treaty commitments, either the Organization of American States should immediately agree on a course of action or, quoting President Kennedy's speech of April 20, 1961, the United States should act on its own, "if the nations of this hemisphere should fail to meet their commitments against outside Communist penetration."

American elections and their accompanying distractions have been the subject of world-wide speculation and concern. Yet they are not always easy for an outsider to understand. These protests from the opposition were taking place in a setting of pre-election debate, and Khrushchev may have hoped to exploit that fact. He may not have been aware that the alarm expressed by the Republicans was something President Kennedy could not ignore. In addition to explicit proposals and resolutions about the Monroe Doctrine, there was the President's request for Congressional authorization to call up 150,000 reserves. This action too should have been a warning signal; it did trigger a Soviet reassurance that Moscow had no need for an offensive base in Cuba. However, the Soviets did not find these warnings weighty enough to reverse their plans for installation.

V

Another major barrier to an objective U. S. evaluation of the data was our own estimate of Soviet behavior. The Stennis Report isolated as one "substantial" error in evaluation "the predisposition of the intelligence community to the philosophical conviction that it would be incompatible with Soviet policy to introduce strategic missiles into Cuba."[9] Khrushchev had never put medium- or long-range missiles in any satellite country and therefore, it was reasoned, he certainly would not put them on an island 9,000 miles away from the Soviet Union, and only 90 miles away from the United States, when this was bound to provoke a sharp American reaction.

In considering this estimate of Soviet behavior, let us remember that the intelligence community was not alone. It had plenty of support from Soviet experts, inside and outside the Government. At any rate, no articulate expert now claims the role of Cassandra. Once a predisposition about the opponent's behavior becomes settled, it is very hard to shake. In this case, it was reinforced not only by expert authority but also by the knowledge both conscious and unconscious that the White House had set down a policy for relaxation of tension with the East. This policy background was much more subtle in its influence than documents or diplomatic experience. For when an official policy or hypothesis is laid down, it tends to obscure alternative hypotheses, and to lead to overemphasis of the data that support it, particularly in a situation of increasing tension, when it is important not to "rock the boat."

In the case of Pearl Harbor, there was a concentration on Atlantic and European affairs, which led to a kind of neglect of, or tendency to ignore, Far Eastern signals, and to a policy of staving off the outbreak of a Pacific war as long as possible. In

---

[9] *Op. cit.*, p. 3.

the last months especially, this tendency was combined with a desire to avoid incidents. The wording of the final warning messages to the Army and Navy reflected this concern:

> If hostilities cannot repeat not be avoided the United States desires that Japan commit the first overt act. This policy should not repeat not be construed as restricting you to a course of action that might jeopardize your defense. Prior to hostile Japanese action you are directed to undertake such reconnaissance and other measures as you deem necessary but these measures should be carried out so as not repeat not to alarm civil population or disclose intent. . . . Undertake no offensive action until Japan has committed an overt act.[10]

These directives have been frequently characterized as "do-don't."

Another attempt to avoid incidents was the Navy order of October 17 to re-route all trans-Pacific shipping to and from the Far East through the Torres Straits (between New Guinea and Australia), thus clearing the sea lanes to the north and northwest of the Hawaiian Islands. This order followed a warning of possible hostile action by Japan against U.S. merchant shipping. We avoided any incidents in these sea lanes, and at the same time we cut off the possibility of visual observation of the Japanese task force bound for Pearl Harbor.

In the autumn of 1962, pursuing a policy of reducing tension, the Kennedy Administration made very little allowance for deception in Soviet statements, for false reassurances that would quiet justifiable American fears. On September 2, TASS published a joint communiqué on Soviet military aid to Cuba, referring to the August 27 visit to Moscow of Che Guevara and Emilio Aragones. The Soviet Government announced assistance in metallurgical work and the sending of technical specialists in agriculture to Cuba. They added that

> views were also exchanged in connection with threats of aggressive imperialist quarters with regard to Cuba. In view of these threats the government of the Cuban Republic addressed the Soviet government with a request for help by delivering armaments and sending technical specialists for training Cuban servicemen.
>
> The Soviet government tentatively considered this request of the government of Cuba. An agreement was reached on this question. As long as the above-mentioned quarters continue threatening Cuba, the Cuban Republic has every justification for taking necessary measures to insure its security and safeguard its sovereignty and independence, while all Cuba's true friends have every right to respond to this legitimate request.[11]

This was reassuring in a negative understated way: it limited military aid to vague "armaments" and "technical specialists." On September 11, in response to the President's request to call up reserves, a higher-keyed, if not hysterical, pronouncement was issued by TASS. This started with an attack on "bellicose-minded reactionary elements" and "the provocations the United States Government is now staging, provocations which might plunge the world into disaster of a universal world war with the use of thermonuclear weapons." In the U.S. Congress and in the American press, the Soviet Government claimed, an unbridled propaganda campaign was

---

[10] U. S. Congress, Joint Committee on the Investigation of the Pearl Harbor Attack, *Pearl Harbor Attack*, 79th Cong., 2d Sess., 1946, Part 14, p. 1407.

[11] *The New York Times,* September 3, 1962.

calling for an attack on Cuba and on Soviet ships "carrying the necessary commodities and food to the Cuban people." "Little heroic Cuba" was pictured as at the mercy of American imperialists, who were alarmed by the failure of their economic blockade and calling for measures to strangle her. Particularly serious was the President's action in asking Congress' permission to call up 150,000 reservists. The statement then embarked on a series of jeers at the ridiculous fears of the American imperialists. The peace-loving Soviet Union was sending agronomists, machine-operators, tractor-drivers and livestock experts to Cuba to share their experience and knowledge and to help the Cubans master Soviet farm machinery.

> What could have alarmed the American leaders? What is the reason for this Devil's Sabbath? . . . Gentlemen, you are evidently so frightened you're afraid of your own shadow. . . . It seems to you some hordes are moving to Cuba when potatoes or oil, tractors, harvesters, combines, and other farming industrial machinery are carried to Cuba to maintain the Cuban economy. We can say to these people that these are our ships and that what we carry in them is no business of theirs. . . . We can say, quoting a popular saying: "Don't butt your noses where you oughtn't." But we do not hide from the world public that we really are supplying Cuba with industrial equipment and goods which are helping to strengthen her economy.[12]

A bit farther on, having had its fun, TASS recalled that "a certain amount of armaments is also being shipped from the Soviet Union to Cuba" and that Soviet military specialists had also been requested by the Government of Cuba. However, the number of Soviet military specialists sent to Cuba "can in no way be compared to the number of workers in agriculture and industry sent there. The armaments and military equipment sent to Cuba are designed exclusively for defensive purposes and the President of the United States and the American military just [like] the military of any country know what means of defense are." The statement went on to imply that any threat to the United States was a figment of the American imagination. The major reassurance then followed:

> The Government of the Soviet Union also authorized TASS to state that there is no need for the Soviet Union to shift its weapons for the repulsion of aggression, for a retaliatory blow, to any other country, for instance Cuba. Our nuclear weapons are so powerful in their explosive force and the Soviet Union has so powerful rockets to carry these nuclear warheads, that there is no need to search for sites for them beyond the boundaries of the Soviet Union. We have said and we do repeat that if war is unleashed, if the aggressor makes an attack on one state or another and this state asks for assistance, the Soviet Union has the possibility from its own territory to render assistance to any peace-loving state and not only to Cuba. And let no one doubt that the Soviet Union will render such assistance just as it was ready in 1956 to render military assistance to Egypt at the time of the Anglo-French-Israeli aggression in the Suez Canal region.

This sort of reassurance had also been privately delivered to the President, and the misuse of the private channel apparently shocked President Kennedy as much as the creation of the strategic base in Cuba.

President Kennedy and his staff had believed the Soviet reassurances. Their reaction to what they regarded as deception was one of genuine outrage, for one of the

[12] Text of Soviet statement, *The New York Times*, September 12, 1962.

President's basic tenets had been that a state of mutual trust between the great powers was an important part of the problem of relaxing tension. And there is a considerable body of literature which goes farther and isolates the attitude of mutual suspicion itself as the central danger today in international relations.

It is a permanent problem of diplomacy to know where to draw the line in extending trust to unfriendly states. A certain amount of healthy suspicion of the opponent's public statements is in order. The President deliberately tested the willingness of Gromyko to lie, after the President knew the truth, but before the Russians knew that he knew. The trap set by the President aroused the indignation of some of those very Americans who urge mutual trust. But the President of the United States would be simple indeed if he did not build his trust cautiously on the basis of many such probings. The Russian performance in the fall and winter of 1962 made it perfectly clear that we cannot take at face value Russian statements—even those made only to the top American leadership in privacy and without those constraints that might be imposed by having the Chinese or other Communist powers or the non-aligned or our own allies listening.

In periods of high tension it is commonly accepted that deception will be an enemy tactic. Before the Pearl Harbor attack Japanese deception was very refined and ingenious. It involved, among other things, giving shore leave to large numbers of Japanese sailors, reinforcing garrisons on the northern border of Manchuria to give an impression of a thrust to the north, issuing false war plans to Japanese commanders and substituting true ones only days before the attack, and on the diplomatic side continuing the appearance of negotiation. For deception is not confined to statements, but must also be translated into actions.

It is important for the enemy's security that he keep his signals quiet. On the Soviet side this meant that all movement on the island of Cuba must take place at night. The Cubans were excluded from the docks and from many of the missile construction areas. Troops were kept below decks, and unloaded equipment was camouflaged or hidden under the trees. On our own side, in the period before October 22, tight security was important to preserve the initiative. And this tight security was maintained through the next few weeks. The members of the group close to the President, known as the Executive Committee or EXCOM, were directly supervising decisions normally left to lower command levels and were doing paper work normally handled by their staffs. This sort of procedure is fine for a couple of weeks, but it means the neglect of other areas of government and, in particular, other areas of foreign policy.[13] Richard Neustadt, a keen observer, reminds us that the Sino-Indian conflict was in progress at the same time, and offers a "lay impression" that "at least one side effect of Cuba" was to tighten the time and narrow the frame of reference of the decision—then in the making—on Skybolt.[14] Under conditions of tight security, there is also a danger that we may keep signals not only from the enemy but also from ourselves. There are a good many who feel that careful study by a wider range of experts might have been useful at the time and would be useful

[13] According to Secretary Rusk, "Senior officers did their own typing; some of my own basic papers were done in my own handwriting, in order to limit the possibility of further spread. . . ." *C.B.S. Reports,* televised interview of Secretary Rusk by David Schoenbrun, November 28, 1962.

[14] U. S. Congress, Senate Subcommittee on National Security Staffing and Operations of the Committee on Government Operations, *Administration of National Security,* 88th Congress, 1st Session, 1963, Part 1, p. 97, testimony of March 25, 1963.

now, particularly with regard to the Kennedy-Khrushchev communications. These, like MAGIC, were very closely held during the crisis and had to be read and interpreted swiftly at the time.

Another set of signs we may have misread or missed were those appearing in official Cuban statements. Castro is so verbose and temperamental that we tend not to listen carefully to his speeches. And his controlled press is so dull that we are equally careless about that. In addition, the policy of embargo and explicit isolation of the island tends to carry over in a curious way to ignoring the voice of Cuban officialdom.

It is interesting now to review the Cuban press of 1962 for clues we might have picked up. After Raul Castro's July visit to Moscow, the warmth of the references to the Soviet Union increased noticeably. Thanks and praise became the order of the day. On September 11, the day of the falsely reassuring TASS statement, the Cuban newspaper *Revolución* underlined the threat of thermonuclear war invoked by TASS. The front page was printed with a single white headline on a black background, and it said: "Rockets Over the United States if Cuba is Invaded." Forcing the Soviet Union's hand in this way had been Cuban policy for some time, so that it was natural for our experts to take this as another instance of Cuban wishful thinking.

Finally, in intelligence work the role of chance, accident and bad luck is always with us. It was bad luck that September–October is the hurricane season in the Caribbean, so that some reconnaissance photography was unclear and certain flights were canceled. It was bad luck that the Red Chinese shot down a U-2 on September 9. In 1941 it was bad luck that we had cut all traffic on the Northwest Passage to Russia, and thereby made visual observation of the Pearl Harbor task force impossible. It was bad luck that there was a radio blackout in the Hawaiian Islands on the morning of December 7, and that Colonel French of the Communications Room then decided to use commercial wire instead of recommending the scrambler telephone for the last alert message.

VI

To sum up then, in both the Pearl Harbor and Cuban crises there was lots of information. But in both cases, regardless of what the Monday morning quarterbacks have to say, the data were ambiguous and incomplete. There was never a single, definitive signal that said, "Get ready, get set, go!" but rather a number of signals which, when put together, tended to crystallize suspicion. The true signals were always embedded in the noise or irrelevance of false ones. Some of this noise was created deliberately by our adversaries, some by chance and some we made ourselves. In addition, our adversary was interested in suppressing the signs of his intent and did what he could to keep his movements quiet. In both cases the element of time also played against us. There were delays between the time information came in, was checked for accuracy, evaluated for its meaning, and made the basis for appropriate action. Many of these delays were only prudent, given the ambiguities and risks of response.

The interpretation of data depends on a lot of things, including our estimate of the adversary and of his willingness to take risks. To make our lives more complicated, this depends on what he thinks the risks are, which in turn depends on his interpretation of us. We underestimated the risks that the Japanese were willing to take in 1941, and the risks that Khrushchev was willing to take in the summer and fall of 1962. Both the Japanese and the Russians, in turn, underestimated our ultimate willingness to respond.

It is important to understand that the difficulties described are intrinsic. By focusing on misestimated capabilities, dispositions and intentions, we obscure the fact that, without a very large and complex body of assumptions and estimates, the data collected would not speak to us at all. If there were no technological constraints whatsoever— if, for example, a large missile installation could be put in place in an instant—no reconnaissance, no matter how frequent, could provide assurance that we would not at any moment face a massive new adversary. The complex inferences involved in the act of interpreting photographs are made possible only by a large body of assumptions of varying degrees of uncertainty, ranging from principles of optics and Euclidean geometry through technological, economic and political judgments. The inferences from the interpretations themselves in turn are based on an even wider range of uncertain beliefs. But just because a very large body of partially confirmed beliefs and guesses is involved in interpreting a reconnaissance photograph or the observations of a Cuban refugee or intelligence agent, it is possible to interpret the photograph or observations in many differing ways. Our beliefs, as Willard Van Orman Quine has put it, are "underdetermined" by our experience, and they do not face experience separately, statement by statement, but always in mass, as a collection. We have a good deal of freedom as to what statements to adjust in the light of any new and seemingly disturbing report.

An observation or its report does not seize us, then, and force any specific interpretation. This relatively free situation of hypotheses in intelligence is no different in kind from that of hypotheses in the more exact sciences such as physics. A more naïve empiricism once suggested that statements in physics could be refuted definitively by observation, by the result of a crucial experiment. But a great many physicists and students of the logic of science, at least since Pierre Duhem, have shown that even the interpretation of the simplest experiment depends implicitly on comprehensive theories about the measuring instruments and a great deal else. It is always possible therefore to "save" a theory or hypothesis by altering some other one of the large set of our beliefs that connects it with any given observation.

If this is true in the more exact sciences it is most obviously true for the role of observations and their interpretation in such spheres of practical activity as the operation of an intelligence agency, and the inferences and decisions of an executive. Here the assumptions that shape interpretation are likely to be more multifarious and also less explicit and therefore often less tentatively held. This puts it mildly. Some of the relevant assumptions may be held passionately. They are likely to include wishful or self-flattering beliefs, items of national pride or claims at issue in partisan debate. In the case of Japan, some of the critical assumptions concerned technology—the range, speed and manœuvrability of the Zero plane, the supposed inability of the Japanese to do any better than the Americans in launching torpedoes in shallow water. In the case of Cuba again some critical assumptions were technological; for example, the minimum time required to put into place and make operational a medium-range ballistic missile. Others concerned the politics and character of the Soviet, Cuban and American leadership and their estimates of each other's willingness to take a chance. Our expectations and prior hypotheses guide our observations and affect their interpretation. It is this prior frame of mind, now changed, that we forget most easily in retrospect. And it is this above all that makes every past surprise nearly unintelligible —and inexplicable except perhaps as criminal folly or conspiracy.

The genuine analogies between Pearl Harbor and Cuba should not obscure the important differences. A study of the Pearl Harbor case makes clear that the problem of getting warning of an impending nuclear raid today is much harder than the problem of detecting the Japanese attack some 20 years ago. It is against this increased difficulty that we must balance improvements in intelligence techniques and organization. But the missile crisis illustrates something else, namely that there are other acts very much short of nuclear war of which we want to be apprised, and here our improved techniques and organization can put us ahead of the game. Action *was* taken during the missile crisis and taken in time to forestall Soviet plans. For while we can never ensure the complete elimination of ambiguity in the signals that come our way, we can energetically take action to reduce their ambiguity, by acquiring information as we did with the U-2. And we can tailor our response to the uncertainties and dangers that remain.

In the Cuban missile crisis action could be taken on ambiguous warning because the action was sliced very thin. After reconnaissance reduced the ambiguity, the response chosen kept to a minimum the actual contact with Russian forces, but a minimum compatible with assuring Khrushchev that we meant business: quarantine, the threat of boarding, the actual boarding of one Lebanese vessel chartered to the Soviet Union. Further, it was a response planned in great detail as the first in a sequence of graded actions that ranged from a build-up of U.S. Army, Marine and Tactical Air Forces in Florida and our southeastern bases to a world-wide alert of the Strategic Air Command. We had been partially prepared for such sequences of action short of nuclear war by the Berlin contingency planning, and this put us in a position to use the warning we had accumulated. If we had had to choose only among much more drastic actions, our hesitation would have been greater.

The problem of warning, then, is inseparable from the problem of decision. We cannot guarantee foresight. But we can improve the chance of acting on signals in time to avert or moderate a distaster. We can do this by a more thorough and sophisticated analysis of observers' reports, by making more explicit and tentative the framework of assumptions into which we must fit any new observations, and by refining, subdividing and making more selective the range of responses we prepare, so that our response may fit the ambiguities of our information and minimize the risks both of error and of inaction. Since the future doubtless holds many more shocks and attempts at surprise, it is comforting to know that we do learn from one crisis to the next.

26 / The Stakes in Viet Nam

Franz Michael

Given the depth of public feeling about the war in Vietnam, it is no simple matter to choose a single article that will do justice to the enormous complexities at issue. For a volume having the broad scope of treating the totality of the history of American foreign relations, it seemed wise to choose an article which seeks to explain, even to the point of defending, American involvement rather than to choose one of many possible critiques. Students of American foreign relations, regardless of their personal views, should have some appreciation of at least the American Government's rationale for its military intervention in Indo-China. Lacking this understanding, which is too often absent from the contemporary dialogue over Vietnam, the criticisms may prove ineffectual. Franz Michael's article which follows does not present an official American governmental interpretation; it represents one mature scholar's discussion of how he perceives the fundamental issues at stake in that conflict.

For further reading: A. Doak Barnett, *Communist China and Asia: Challenge to American Policy* (New York: 1960); George McT. Kahin and John W. Lewis, *The United States in Vietnam* (New York: 1967); David Kraslow and Stuart H. Loory, *The Secret Search for Peace in Vietnam* (New York: 1968); Arnold Wolfers, "Collective Security and the War in Korea," *Yale Review*, XLIII (1954), 481–496; Quincy Wright, "The Chinese Recognition Problem," *American Journal of International Law*, XLIX (July, 1955), 320–338.

Franz Michael is Professor of Politics at the Sino-Soviet Institute, George Washington University. This article is reprinted with the permission of the Editors of *Orbis*. From *Orbis*, XII (Spring 1968). Copyright © 1968 *Orbis*, published by the Foreign Policy Research Institute.

One of the most common and fallacious assumptions about the war in Viet Nam is that neither side can win it. From this assumption the conclusion is drawn that the only possible way to end the war is a compromise which can be obtained solely by negotiating with our opponent, who is believed to share this assumption. Negotiations to end the fighting may succeed; they are obviously a better way of concluding the war than a fight to the bitter end. But, with or without such negotiations, there are only two possible outcomes to the war. One is that the communist attempt to take over South Viet Nam is defeated; the other, that it eventually will succeed. One is our victory—whether gained in battle or by negotiations; the other is theirs—obtained by our military defeat or our political surrender. No negotiations, no talk about honorable peace, can affect these alternatives.

The reason why this basic issue is so little understood is the confusion about two fundamental concepts relating to the war in Viet Nam. We have been confused regarding the concept of "victory" in this kind of modern war, and we have little understanding of the strategy of so-called wars of national liberation with which we are confronted in Viet Nam and which affects the world balance between communism and the Free World. The two misconceptions are interrelated.

I

As to "victory," let us remember Korea. There the communists attempted to invade and conquer the South and were repulsed. This was our "victory," a victory not only of South Korea and the United Nations, but of all Free World nations.

The issue in Korea became confused because, at one time, we went beyond our original purpose by moving on to the Yalu River in an attempt to unify Korea under a noncommunist government. We were defeated in the sense that we finally abandoned the idea of unification and limited our aim to the original goal of defending the South. This goal we achieved. Communist propaganda claiming that Korea was a communist triumph has never been adequately countered, even in our own thinking. Whether the larger prize of Korean reunification could have been won is another question. As it was, the defeat of the communist attack against South Korea was a clear victory for the Free World.

Today, the communist goal in Viet Nam is the same as it was in Korea: to conquer the South. The defeat of the communist purpose will be our victory; their success will be our defeat, whatever formula is found to resolve the issue or save someone's face. There is no middle ground between communist takeover and communist defeat, *since communism, by creed, will not share power except as a temporary device for subversion and conquest.* It is for this reason that no true negotiations for a lasting compromise are feasible. We should know by now that "coalition" government is impossible with a dishonest partner.

The Western concept of coalition government assumes that the parties brought together have accepted the system and the rules of democratic procedure and compromise. From all of our practical experience and knowledge of communism, we must know that this is not the communist purpose. Past experiences with communism in Eastern Europe and elsewhere should have taught us that lesson. The failure of a "coalition" government in China after World War II should not be forgotten. For communists, a coalition government is but a means to move into the decisive positions of power which shortly enable them to take over. If it is necessary to demonstrate the application of this communist tactic in Viet Nam, one need only examine those communist documents and directives that have fallen into Allied hands. From a captured notebook taken from a member of a Viet Cong unit we learn: "What is important is that we must have tight control over the government, the workers and the peasants . . . to all appearances it will be a coalition government, but the real power will be in our hands and we will follow the Front's political program, the revolutionary line." To impose such a system on South Viet Nam would mark the end of the U.S. effort to build a viable noncommunist national state there.

This is clearly understood by our South Vietnamese allies. If we attempt to force them to accept a solution imposed by us and the communists, we will destroy the very structure we have helped to establish, even before the coalition is created. We can perhaps maintain a facade of compromise, but we will bring disaster to a large majority of the population which has resisted communism for more than two decades. As a people who have not lived under totalitarian rule, Americans find it difficult to grasp the full impact of terror which is a major weapon of communist "wars of national liberation." At a rate which proportionately in the United States would amount to 70,000 people killed yearly by *assassination,* the toll of local leadership, teachers, village elders, magistrates, monks and other social leaders has been shocking—yet it goes virtually unnoticed in the Free World, including the United States. The miracle is that there have been no important defections of units or leaders to the communist side and no breakdown of government despite years of terror and the latest onslaughts, the TET offensive and the indiscriminate rocket attacks on Saigon. The very fact that they continue to fight speaks for the Vietnamese determination to resist communist control. The suggestion by some American politicians and scholars that, to ease our consciences, we should help selected South Vietnamese leaders to escape in the event of a communist takeover demonstrates a failure to understand the attitude of most of the population and the size of the catastrophe that awaits the Vietnamese if the communists come to power. The very discussion by U.S. political leaders about a coalition with the Viet Cong is bound to undermine South Vietnamese morale and weaken our position. Any proposal for coalition government is at best a face-saving formula under which we deliver our allies to the enemy.

If we surrender South Viet Nam, we must also have no illusions about the effect of our weakness on the whole of Asia and eventually the rest of the world. A communist victory in this decisive test will not remove the communist danger; it will greatly increase it. It will be a communist victory—a victory for the strategy of wars of national liberation—and the impact will reach far beyond Viet Nam. We have to understand this strategy and find a way to combat it.

II

The strategy of national liberation movements is not new. Its architects were Lenin and Stalin. Its doctrinal basis was Lenin's theory of imperialism according to which the fight against the "imperialist powers" in the colonial and quasi-colonial agrarian countries was an attack against that "monopoly capitalism" which the "proletarian" revolutionaries fought from within. The twin strategies of "proletarian revolutions" and "wars of national liberation" had, then, the same target, monopoly capitalism, and the same goal, communist world revolution.

It was after World War I and the failure of the "proletarian revolution" to materialize in Central Europe that Lenin, and later Stalin, turned East to promote and organize in China and the Asian world this second communist strategy of "wars of national liberation." The phrase "the way to Paris leads via Peking," which has been ascribed to Lenin, popularized this shift to a strategy under which the conquest of the Afro-Asian agrarian countries would undermine the industrial countries of the West. The strategy of "wars of national liberation" has ever since formed the second half of the overall communist campaign for world revolution. Its primary role has only recently been reasserted by such communist leaders as the late Aidit of Indonesia and Lin Piao of China. It is this strategy that we face in Viet Nam.

To apply this strategy, Lenin and Stalin and their Soviet and Asian successors sought to exploit two revolutionary elements in the countries concerned. Since there was no proletariat to speak of, the communists pressed into the service of the world revolution the forces of peasant discontent and nationalism, doctrinally described as "anti-feudal" and "anti-imperialist" movements.

To the West, the nonproletarian aspects of the communist strategy have been confusing. It took time to recognize that Mao Tse-tung was not a "peasant leader." Even today, it is not always understood that the agrarian strategy in China came from Stalin and was not Mao's invention. For many who are unfamiliar with communist history and the recent planning and actions of Moscow, it is still harder to realize that Ho Chi-minh, one of the oldest Bolsheviks, a past Comintern figure and coworker with Borodin, is no more a nationalist than Mao was an agrarian reformer. This misjudgment of the war in Viet Nam by well-meaning Western writers today is as serious as was the misjudgment of communism in China after World War II.

One widespread myth holds that "wars of national liberation" are Peking's *specialité de la maison*. Their Soviet origin is no longer remembered; nor is the importance attached by Moscow today to this part of communist strategy fully understood. Yet it is for good reason that the main support of the war in Viet Nam comes from Moscow, not from Peking. As Lenin once turned East when the revolution in Germany did not come off, so today the activation of "wars of national liberation" (in the East) is a logical counterpart to the shift of communist strategy toward "peaceful coexistence" in the area of "proletarian revolution" (i.e., the West).

"Peaceful coexistence" as a communist strategy has, of course, been employed before. When Stalin was threatened by Nazi Germany and the German-Japanese-Italian pact, the world of the "imperialist powers" abruptly became the world of the "Western democracies": Stalin's "peaceful coexistence" and united front policy of the 1930's created hope in many Western minds that communism was disappearing from the Soviet Union. Hope that communism has changed drastically and no longer menaces the West has been engendered in the 1960's by a similar Soviet "peaceful coexistence" strategy.

Today's "peaceful coexistence" has a broader scope than it had in the 1930's. The advent of nuclear weapons forced the communists to abandon their concept of the "fatalistic inevitability" of world wars if they hoped to retain any doctrinal appeal. This in turn has enabled the communists to pose as the "camp of peace." Not only have they abjured the dictum of Marx and Lenin that wars in the capitalistic world were inevitable and advantageous to communism, but they have now also usurped the role of guardian of world peace against the imperialist "warmongers" of the industrial West. In assuming this new role, the communists have not abandoned the goal of world revolution or the use of violence in reaching it. Peaceful coexistence is strictly reserved to the problem of nuclear war—but it does not mean "peace," as we understand the term. Not only does political and ideological warfare continue, but war, except at the nuclear level, is not banned as a means of communist strategy. Revolutionary wars—that is, civil wars and, most of all, "wars of national liberation"—remain a legitimate instrument of communist strategy. They are, in the words of Khrushchev and his successors, "just wars," wars that deserve all possible support. On this there is no argument between Moscow and Peking; both have given full backing to Hanoi.

III

It is often contended today that since communism is no longer monolithic it is no longer a real threat. This is a *non sequitur*. A complex and multifaceted movement can be much more dangerous than a simple "monolithic" one, since the basic system, the main tenets of the doctrine, the final goals and the strategies remain the same.

This is not to say that there is no ferment within the communist world: the Hungarian rebellion, current restlessness in Eastern Europe, and the crisis in China, are signs of the communist dilemma that may yet break the doctrine and its system. But the decentralization of strategy has eased the strain. Perhaps communism was never as monolithic as we often assumed. Even in Stalin's time the degree of centralization depended on the twists and turns of strategy. Unified direction was, of course, assured by the fact that there was only one "fatherland" of communism and that the security of the home base was a major communist objective. When the growing alignment between Nazi Germany and Japan threatened that base, the policy of united fronts and "peaceful coexistence" with the West required a lessening of emphasis on the Comintern and a greater autonomy for what were claimed to be national communist parties. In 1943 the Comintern was rather unceremoniously dissolved. In 1947, with the emergence of eleven fatherlands of communism and the Cold War, a new centralized communist organization, The Comintern, was created—albeit in a different form. This, in turn, was dissolved when in 1956 Khrushchev inaugurated a new "peaceful coexistence" policy.

The Soviet leadership has insisted that there is no longer a need for a center of the movement, that all communist parties are equal and independent, and that "proletarian internationalism" will be accomplished through a sort of osmosis—assisted where necessary by a little Soviet pressure. The Chinese communists, who are seeking to discredit Moscow's alleged revisionism and are stressing revolutionary violence, have claimed that Mao Tse-tung is the leader of the world communist movement.

If the conflict between Moscow and Peking has affected communist policy, the central issue has been the interrelationship of the two strategies. The Maoist group in China fully supports "national wars of liberation" and has denounced the strategy of peaceful coexistence as applied to the area of "proletarian revolution." In the words of Lin Piao, Mao's closest comrade-in-arms and heir apparent: "Since World War II, the proletarian revolutionary movement has for various reasons been temporarily held back in the North American and West European countries, while the peoples' revolutionary movement in Asia, Africa and Latin America has been growing vigorously." All support must be given to a relentless pursuit of "national liberation wars" that alone can bring down the capitalist world.

The Soviets have not been so provincial in outlook as the Maoists, who ignore the grand strategy of Lenin and the present Soviet leaders, in which "wars of national liberation" remain related to an overall plan. For Moscow, the pressure exerted against the United States to abandon resistance to communist aggression in Viet Nam for the sake of promoting "peaceful coexistence" and détente has been designed to undermine our will to counter strategy number two. The tie-in between the military-political warfare of national liberation, as in Viet Nam, and the peaceful coexistence strategy of breaking down our will to resist has not been fully appreciated by the United States and its Western allies. Indeed Viet Nam threatens rapidly to become the classic example of successful communist psychological warfare—not within that country but throughout the rest of the world.

If Western public opinion and many Western intellectual leaders, uneducated in the ways of communism, have not grasped this relationship, neither has the Maoist wing of the Chinese Communist Party. It has proved to be impatient and possibly unwilling or unable to understand the Soviet design. It has been contemptuous of the strategy of "peaceful coexistence," has ridiculed the Soviet assertion of support for Viet Nam, and has accused the Soviets of cooperation with imperialist America in selling out national liberation movements and world revolution in favor of accepting merely a share in world power.

Not all Chinese communist leaders have seen it this way. In 1965, when last-minute U.S. military intervention in South Viet Nam prevented a communist victory, the Soviets found it necessary to appeal for communist unity to revive the communist chance in Viet Nam. This appeal was not entirely ignored in communist China. Some of the Chinese party leaders, now purged or in disgrace, inclined toward reconciliation with Moscow. Sympathy for cooperation with Moscow also reappeared in the Chinese Army. The second in command, Lo Jui-ch'ing, Chief of Staff and head of the Chinese communist secret police, echoed the Soviet call for unity on several occasions. He seemed to have a broader understanding of the interrelationship of the strategies of Moscow and Peking and of "peaceful coexistence" and "wars of national liberation" than had been demonstrated by the Maoist group. For Lo, the Sino-Soviet conflict—which he called a "debate"—had served its purpose in confusing the West and advancing the communist cause on the broadest front. In Lo's words:

> One aspect of the historic significance of the *debate* of the last few years between the two lines in the international Communist movement is that it has enabled Marxism-Leninism *to spread on an unprecedented scale* and has promoted the integration of the universal truth of Marxism-Leninism with the concrete practice of the peoples' revolution *in every country.* (Emphasis added.)

No other communist has so clearly pointed to the overall advantage of directing two different but mutually helpful communist strategies from two different headquarters. Mao, of course, could not yield to the Soviet strategic outlook without relinquishing his claim to be the only true leader on the road to the communist future, a road which he asserted the Soviets had abandoned in their revisionist return to capitalism. Lo became a political zero after his flirtation with Moscow. Sometime in

November 1965, two months after he made this last public statement, he disappeared and was not heard of again until he was publicly attacked and humiliated by Mao's Red Guards.

Even though the official Sino-Soviet exchange of accusation continued, a partial understanding must have been reached between Moscow and Peking around March 1966. Soviet arms to Viet Nam were again permitted to roll on the trains through China; the Soviet tanks that overran the outpost near Khesanh in February 1968 had been observed in transit through China.

IV

The United States faces in Viet Nam not just a local fight in another Southeast Asian country, but a confrontation with a world communist strategy in the larger battle between communist revolution and our concept of a free world. Every communist statement, whether it emanates from Moscow, Peking or Budapest, is directed against "imperialist" America as the main target. In communist strategic thinking, the war in Viet Nam is an integral part of the war against the industrial world of capitalism of which America is, in communist eyes, the leader. At stake, ultimately, is our national security and the freedom of the noncommunist world.

The fact of U.S. resistance in Viet Nam has hampered communist strategy and in many ways strengthened the Free World. The defeat of the communist putsch in Indonesia; the collapse of Sukarno's campaign against Malaysia; the strengthening of a free Asian community of countries through cooperation in the Asian and Pacific Council (ASPAC) and other recent intercountry agreements; the firm Indian stand vis-à-vis China and the outcome of recent major battles at the Tibetan border; Burma's willingness to stand up against Communist China; the continuing Laotian resistance; Prince Sihanouk's defiance of Peking; and even the recent defeats of communist efforts in Africa and South America—none of these developments can be fully understood in isolation from the U.S. stand in Viet Nam.

It has been said that U.S. forces are over-extended, but it should be clear from the map that a communist breakthrough in Viet Nam would greatly extend the frontier of defense for the Free World. Should the Vietnamese dike give way, the flood will threaten neighboring countries where the communists are already preparing the ground, as in Thailand, Cambodia, Malaya, or for that matter, in the Philippines, for more "wars of national liberation." The communists would be emboldened to step up operations in the whole Afro-Asian world. Most of all, the Indians, who by now realize how much Viet Nam has been their line of defense, will be threatened by a communist breakthrough in Southeast Asia that could easily be correlated with the communist advance in the Islamic world.

The 18th parallel is still the most narrow frontier that we can hope to defend unless we want to withdraw to fortress America, or, as Walter Lippmann suggests, draw the line at the white man's world of Australia and New Zealand—a peculiarly antiquated attitude in today's world.

Our opponents have a larger design into which the Viet Nam conflict fits. It can scarcely be accidental that the areas of Soviet-supported communist advance form two large pincer movements, each with its own central objective. One objective is India and the Middle East; the other, mainland China. The threat to India is similar to the one posed by the Axis powers in World War II, when Hitler's thrust toward the Suez and the Japanese campaign through Southeast Asia seemed to presage a linkup of the Axis powers in India. The threats to Burma and the tribal frontier area of India and the attack at the Himalayan frontier are, in actuality if not in design, a counterpoint to the new Soviet presence in the Arab and Islamic worlds.

Of more immediate concern is the connection between recent communist aggressiveness in Korea and the war in Viet Nam. There has been extensive speculation as to the timing and meaning of the new attacks against South Korea, e.g., (the Pueblo crisis, the assassination attempt against President Park, infiltration of terrorists) and their relationship to the intensified efforts of the Vietnamese communists. At the very least, the new North Korean aggressiveness is designed to aggravate the U.S. dilemma of having to spread its military strength to cover widely separated fronts in Asia.

But one can also relate this move in Korea to the crucial developments in Communist China itself. The crisis in China today, provoked by Mao's attempt to reassert his leadership in China as well as in the communist world, has been directly affected by the successes and failures of communist strategy abroad. The U.S. stand in Viet Nam and the setbacks administered to communist revolutionary movements in Southeast Asia, South Asia and Africa have exacerbated Mao's difficulties at home. The military takeover in China has swept that crisis to its moment of truth. Whether Maoism and its Hitlerian *Führerkult* will prevail or whether Mao will fail in his attempt to rebuild the communist structure in his image will be decided in the near future. The real issue, however, seems not to be that of a Maoist survival, which in the long run is highly doubtful, but the course to be taken by whatever military-political leadership eventually takes over. A communist victory in Viet Nam, backed by the Soviet Union, will leave little leeway for China's future leaders to assert their independence doctrinally or institutionally from the Moscow club. The recent North Korean actions have compounded the problem for the Chinese military, and their response has been surprisingly unenthusiastic. Looking at the two fronts in the Asian war in purely geographical terms, one can see the two arms of the second Kremlin pincer movement directed not only against the U.S. position in East Asia from north to south but also encircling with a bear hug the group of Chinese communist brothers quarreling among themselves. If the communists win in Viet Nam, those men who come out on top in China will have no place to go except back to the fold.

V

The outcome of the war in Viet Nam will thus have a decisive impact not only on the balance of power in Asia but on the course of our confrontation with the communist world. It will affect the issues of unity or division within communist ranks, the future role of "national liberation wars," and the credibility of longstanding U.S. pledges to help defend free peoples. It could lead to greater regional cooperation and strength in East Asia or to disarray and a feeling of hopelessness.

It is unfortunate that the emotional climate in the United States almost precludes a rational discussion of the stakes of the war. The label of "immoral war" has been used assertively by political leaders, columnists, newspaper editors and civic and social leaders without serious challenge and with no attempt even to analyze the moral issues involved—as if war itself, with its inevitable killing of the innocent, could ever be moral. And yet the central issue, properly understood, is the same as that of the fight for civil rights in this country. Anyone acquainted with totalitarianism should know that freedom remains indivisible. It is impossible to withdraw from world responsibility into neo-isolationism and hope to maintain at home the principles for which we are fighting both here and abroad.

Appendix

FOREIGN TRADE—VALUE OF MERCHANDISE EXPORTS AND IMPORTS, 1821–1957 (IN MILLIONS OF DOLLARS)

Year	Exports	Imports	Excess of exports (+) or imports (−)
1821	55	55	[less than $500,000]
1822	61	80	− 19
1823	68	72	− 4
1824	69	72	− 3
1825	91	90	+ 1
1826	73	78	− 5
1827	74	71	+ 3
1828	64	81	− 17
1829	67	67	[less than $500,000]
1830	72	63	+ 9
1831	72	96	− 24
1832	82	95	− 13
1833	88	101	− 13
1834	102	109	− 7
1835	115	137	− 22
1836	124	177	− 53
1837	111	130	− 19
1838	105	96	+ 9
1839	112	156	− 44
1840	124	98	+ 26
1841	112	123	− 11
1842	100	96	+ 4
1843	83	42	+ 41
1844	106	103	+ 3
1845	106	113	− 7
1846	110	118	− 8
1847	157	122	+ 35
1848	138	149	− 11
1849	140	141	− 1
1850	144	174	− 30
1851	189	211	− 22
1852	167	207	− 40
1853	203	264	− 61
1854	237	298	− 61
1855	219	258	− 39
1856	281	310	− 29
1857	294	348	− 54
1858	272	263	+ 9
1859	293	331	− 38
1860	334	354	− 20

Year	Exports	Imports	Excess of exports (+) or imports (−)
1861	220	289	− 69
1862	191	189	+ 2
1863	204	243	− 39
1864	159	316	−157
1865	166	239	− 73
1866	349	435	− 86
1867	295	396	−101
1868	282	357	− 75
1869	286	418	−132
1870	394	436	− 42
1871	443	520	− 77
1872	444	627	−183
1873	522	642	−120
1874	586	567	+ 19
1875	513	533	− 20
1876	540	461	+ 79
1877	602	451	+151
1878	695	437	+258
1879	710	446	+264
1880	836	668	+168
1881	902	643	+259
1882	751	725	+ 26
1883	824	723	+101
1884	741	668	+ 73
1885	742	578	+164
1886	680	635	+ 45
1887	716	692	+ 24
1888	696	724	− 28
1889	742	745	− 3
1890	858	789	+ 69
1891	884	845	+ 39
1892	1,030	827	+203
1893	848	866	− 18
1894	892	655	+237
1895	808	732	+ 76
1896	883	780	+103
1897	1,051	765	+286
1898	1,231	616	+615
1899	1,227	697	+530
1900	1,394	850	+544
1901	1,488	823	+665
1902	1,382	903	+479
1903	1,420	1,026	+394
1904	1,461	991	+470
1905	1,519	1,118	+401

Year	Exports	Imports	Excess of exports (+) or imports (−)
1906	1,744	1,227	+ 517
1907	1,881	1,434	+ 447
1908	1,861	1,194	+ 667
1909	1,663	1,312	+ 351
1910	1,745	1,557	+ 188
1911	2,049	1,527	+ 522
1912	2,204	1,653	+ 551
1913	2,466	1,813	+ 653
1914	2,365	1,894	+ 471
1915	2,769	1,674	+ 1,095
1916	5,483	2,392	+ 3,091
1917	6,234	2,952	+ 3,282
1918	6,149	3,031	+ 3,118
1919	7,920	3,904	+ 4,016
1920	8,228	5,278	+ 2,950
1921	4,485	2,509	+ 1,976
1922	3,832	3,113	+ 719
1923	4,167	3,792	+ 375
1924	4,591	3,610	+ 981
1925	4,910	4,227	+ 683
1926	4,809	4,431	+ 378
1927	4,865	4,185	+ 680
1928	5,128	4,091	+ 1,037
1929	5,241	4,399	+ 842
1930	3,843	3,061	+ 782
1931	2,424	2,091	+ 333
1932	1,611	1,323	+ 288
1933	1,675	1,450	+ 225
1934	2,133	1,655	+ 478
1935	2,283	2,047	+ 236
1936	2,456	2,423	+ 33
1937	3,349	3,084	+ 265
1938	3,094	1,960	+ 1,134
1939	3,177	2,318	+ 859
1940	4,021	2,625	+ 1,396
1941	5,147	3,345	+ 1,802
1942	8,079	2,756	+ 5,323
1943	12,965	3,381	+ 9,584
1944	14,259	3,929	+10,330
1945	9,806	4,159	+ 5,647
1946	9,738	4,942	+ 4,796
1947	14,430	5,756	+ 8,674
1948	12,653	7,124	+ 5,529
1949	12,051	6,622	+ 5,429
1950	10,275	8,852	+ 1,423

Year	Exports	Imports	Excess of exports (+) or imports (−)
1951	15,032	10,967	+ 4,065
1952	15,201	10,717	+ 4,484
1953	15,774	10,873	+ 4,901
1954	15,110	10,215	+ 4,895
1955	15,547	11,384	+ 4,163
1956	19,090	12,615	+ 6,475
1957	20,810	12,978	+ 7,832

Historical Statistics of the United States: Colonial Times to 1957 (Washington: Government Printing Office, 1960), pp. 550–553.

558